The Indian Mutiny

1857

SAUL DAVID

VIKING
an imprint of
PENGUIN BOOKS

VIKING

Published by the Penguin Group
Penguin Books Ltd, 80 Strand, London WC2R 0RL, England
Penguin Putnam Inc., 375 Hudson Street, New York, New York 10014, USA
Penguin Books Australia Ltd, 250 Camberwell Road, Camberwell, Victoria 3124, Australia
Penguin Books Canada Ltd, 10 Alcorn Avenue, Toronto, Ontario, Canada M4V 3B2
Penguin Books India (P) Ltd, 11 Community Centre,
Panchsheel Park, New Delhi – 110 017, India
Penguin Books (NZ) Ltd, Cnr Rosedale and Airborne Roads,
Albany, Auckland, New Zealand
Penguin Books (South Africa) (Pty) Ltd, 24 Sturdee Avenue,
Rosebank 2196, South Africa

Penguin Books Ltd, Registered Offices: 80 Strand, London WC2R 0RL, England

www.penguin.com

First published 2002
1

Set in 11/13.75pt Monotype Bembo
Typeset by Rowland Phototypesetting Ltd, Bury St Edmunds, Suffolk
Printed in Great Britain by Clays Ltd, St Ives plc

A CIP catalogue record for this book is available from the British Library

ISBN 0-670-91137-2

For Yarah

Contents

Acknowledgements

During the four years it took to research and write this book, I was assisted by a number of people. My greatest debt of gratitude is to Hew Strachan, the newly appointed Chichele Professor of The History of War at Oxford University, who encouraged me from the start.

I am also beholden to the trustees of the General Palit Military Studies Trust – in particular Major-General D. K. Palit himself, John Miller and T. K. Mukherjee – for awarding me a Fellowship and supporting my research in India. Other advice, assistance and companionship during my trip to India and Pakistan in 2000 was provided by my sister Catherine, Dr Kaushik Roy, Dr Ganeswar Nayak of the National Archives of India, Nigel Bryan, Khurshid Sohail, Lieutenant-Colonel Hameed Ullah Afridi and the officers of the Khyber Rifles. Thank you.

The following people were especially helpful during my research in Britain and I am grateful: Professor Sam Cohn, Professor Evan Mawdsley, Dr Simon Ball, Dr David Omissi, Alison Peden, Chris Fildes, Pamela Strachan, Dr Stewart and Noreen Harper, Paul Strathern, Lieutenant-Colonel John Inglis (the direct descendant of Brigadier John Inglis of Lucknow fame), the Revd Giles Goddard (ditto), Mary Jane Gibbons (a descendant of the Gough brothers) and Dr Margaret Bruce (a descendant of John Nicholson).

As ever, I must acknowledge the invaluable help given to me by the staffs of various institutions: the British Library, London Library, University of Glasgow Library, Monmouth Library, National Army Museum, National Archives of India, National Archives of Scotland and National Library of Scotland.

Finally, I would like to thank my new editor Andrew Kidd (for sticking with me through some very protracted negotiations), my agent Julian Alexander (for conducting those negotiations) and, last but not least, my wife Louise.

The spelling of place names is generally the one in current usage. The exceptions are those places which are far better known to a British readership by their 'colonial' spelling: Benares (Varanasi), Cawnpore (Kanpur), Oudh (Awadh), Madras (Chennai) and Bombay (Mumbai), among others. When Indian personal names are shortened, the first name is used.

List of Illustrations

Picture credits:

By kind permission of the British Library: 1, 5, 6, 7, 11, 12, 13, 14, 16, 17, 18, 19, 21, 22, 24, 26, 30, 31, 32; National Army Museum: 2, 25, 27, 28, 29; By courtesy of the National Portrait Gallery, London: 3, 9, 10; Hulton Archive – Getty Images: 4, 8, 15, 20, 23.

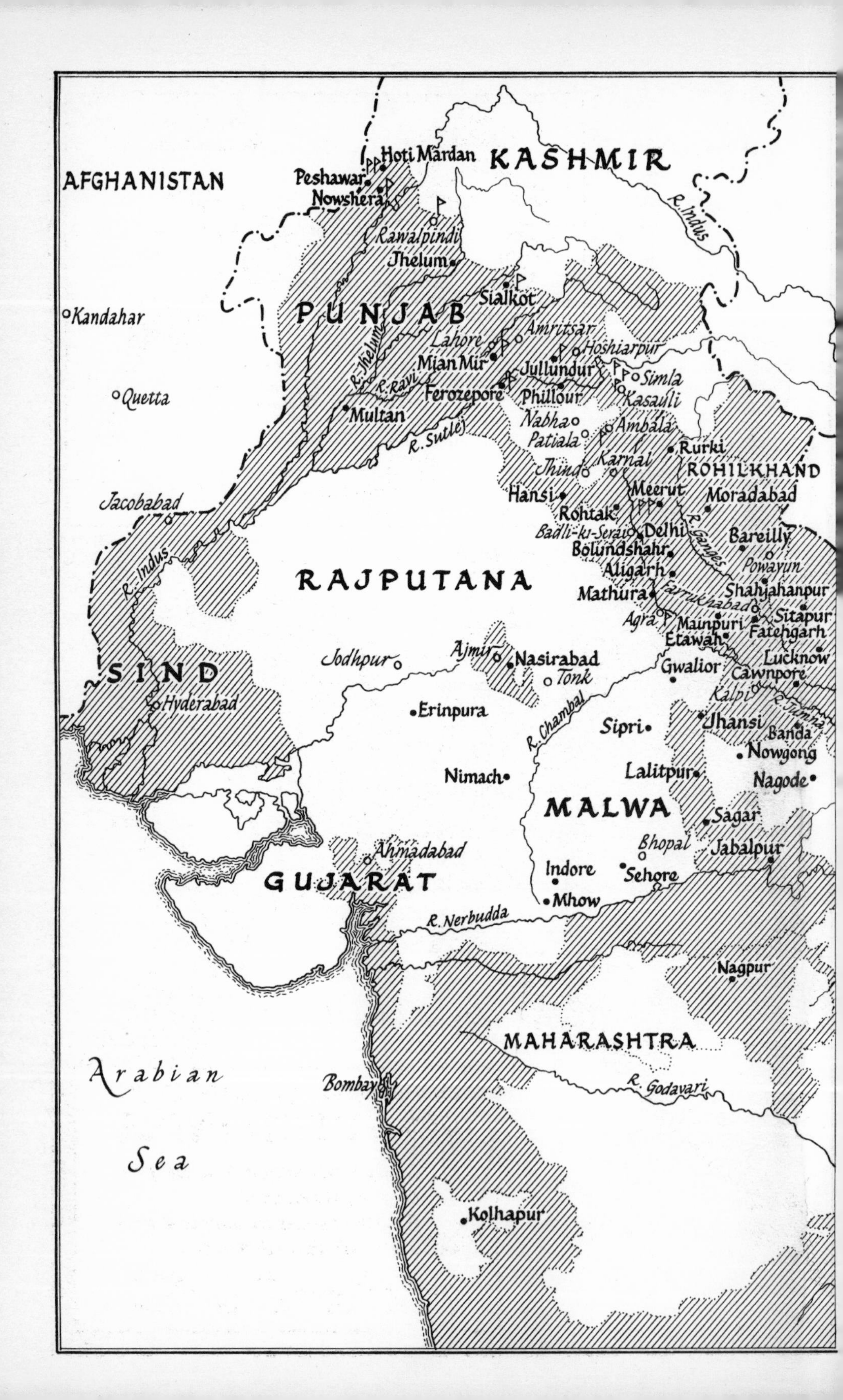

AFGHANISTAN
KASHMIR
Hoti Mardan
Peshawar
Nowshera
Rawalpindi
Jhelum
Sialkot
PUNJAB
Kandahar
Amritsar
Lahore
Hoshiarpur
Mian Mir
Jullundur
Simla
R. Jhelum
R. Ravi
Ferozepore
Phillour
Kasauli
Quetta
Multan
Nabha
Ambala
Patiala
R. Sutlej
Rurki
Jhind
Karnal
ROHILKHAND
Meerut
Moradabad
Hansi
Rohtak
Jacobabad
Badli-ki-Serai
Delhi
Bareilly
Bolundshahr
R. Ganges
Powayun
R. Indus
Aligarh
RAJPUTANA
Mathura
Shahjahanpur
Farrukhabad
Sitapur
Agra
Mainpuri
Fatehgarh
Etawah
Lucknow
Ajmir
Nasirabad
Jodhpur
Gwalior
Cawnpore
SIND
Tonk
Hyderabad
Kalpi
R. Jumna
Erinpura
R. Chambal
Sipri
Jhansi
Banda
Nowgong
Lalitpur
Nimach
Nagode
MALWA
Sagar
Bhopal
Jabalpur
Ahmadabad
Indore
Sehore
GUJARAT
Mhow
R. Nerbudda
Nagpur
MAHARASHTRA
Arabian
Bombay
R. Godavari
Sea
Kolhapur

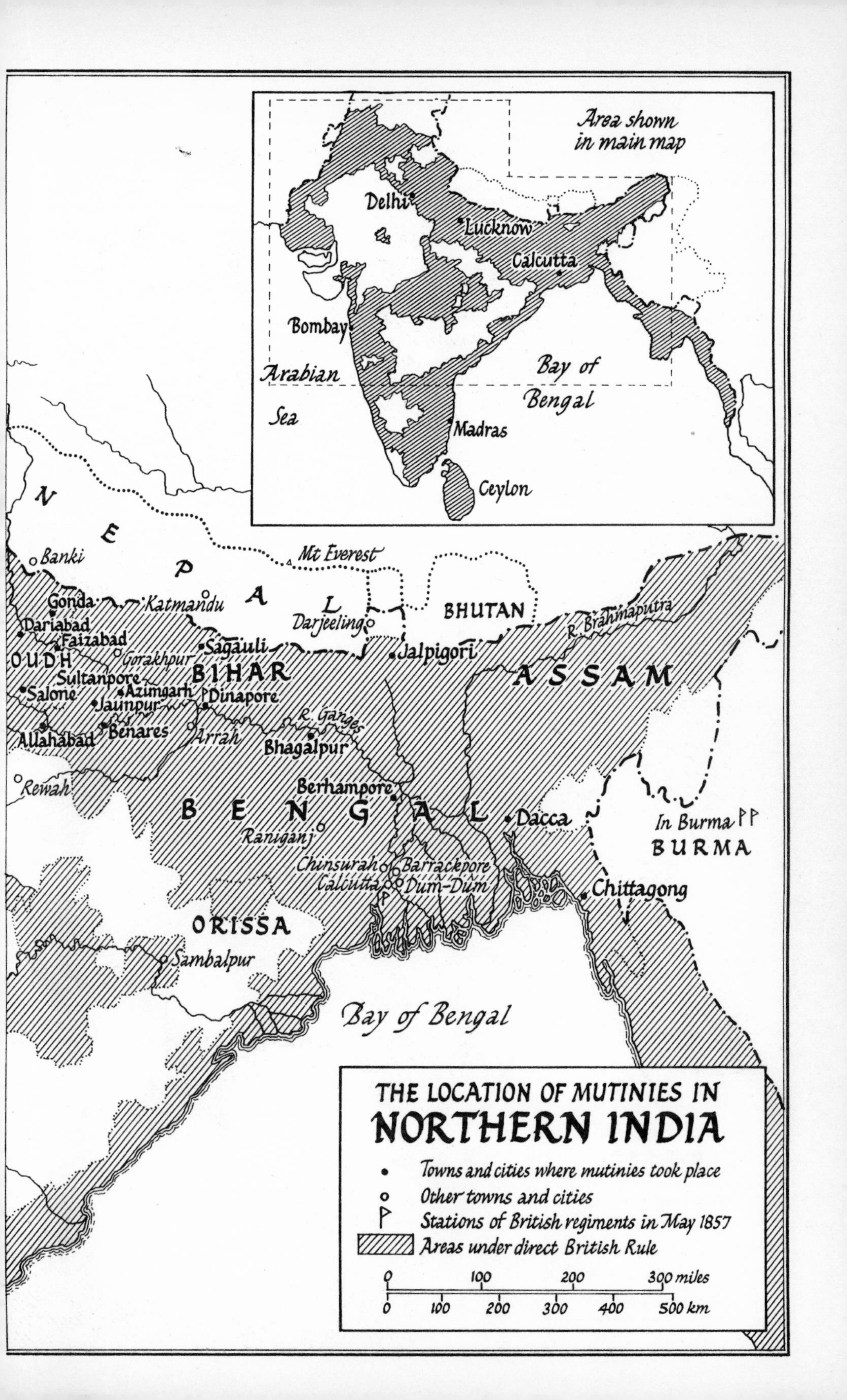
THE LOCATION OF MUTINIES IN NORTHERN INDIA
Towns and cities where mutinies took place
Other towns and cities
Stations of British regiments in May 1857
Areas under direct British Rule
0
100
200
300 miles
0
100
200
300
400
500 km
Area shown in main map
Delhi
Lucknow
Calcutta
Bombay
Arabian Sea
Bay of Bengal
Madras
Ceylon
NEPAL
Banki
Mt Everest
Gonda
Katmandu
Darjeeling
BHUTAN
Dariabad
Faizabad
Sagauli
Jalpigori
R. Brahmaputra
OUDH
Gorakhpur
BIHAR
ASSAM
Sultanpore
Salone
Azimgarh
Dinapore
Jaunpur
R. Ganges
Allahabad
Benares
Arrah
Bhagalpur
Rewah
Berhampore
BENGAL
Dacca
Raniganj
In Burma
BURMA
Chinsurah
Barrackpore
Calcutta
Dum-Dum
Chittagong
ORISSA
Sambalpur
Bay of Bengal

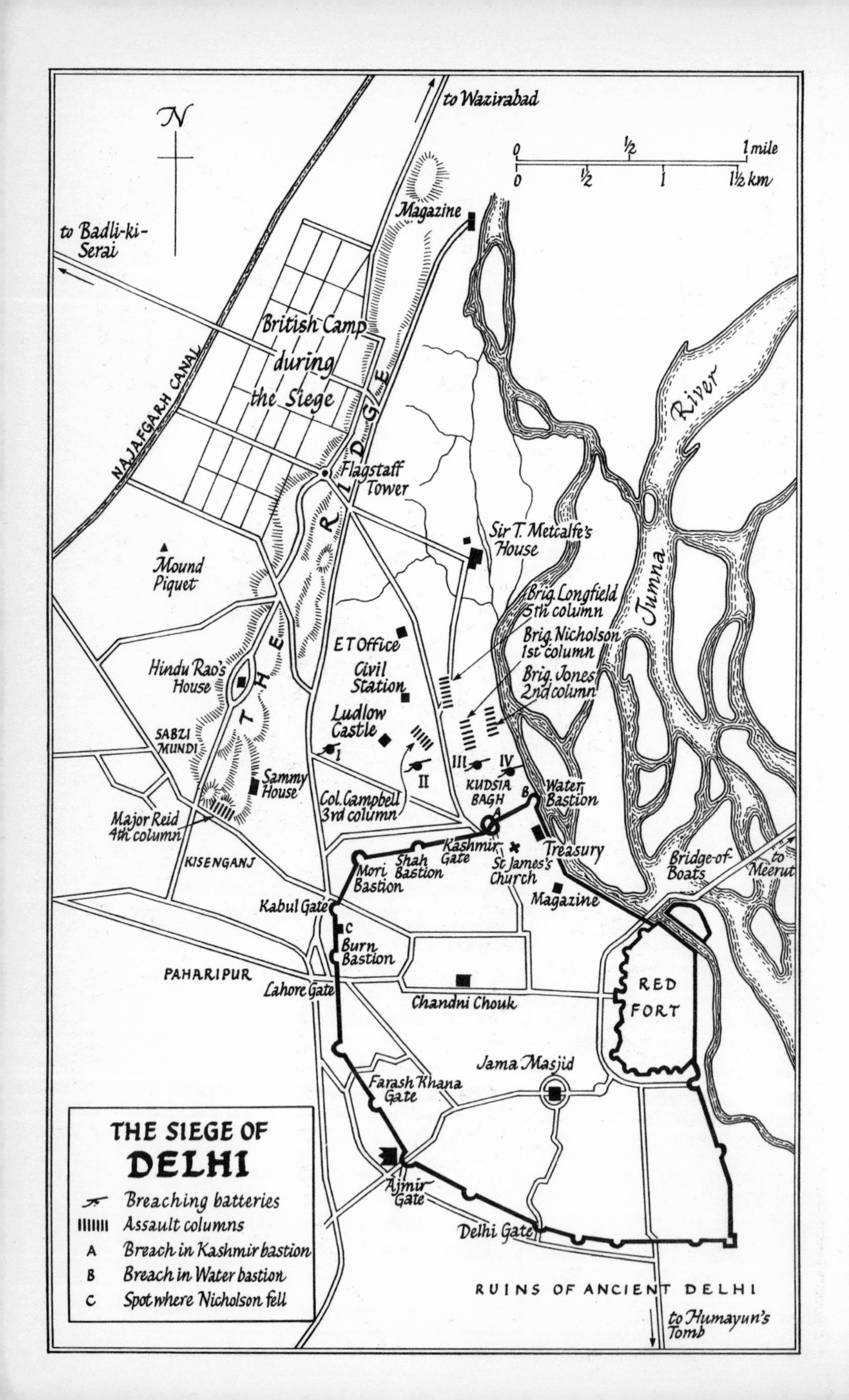
THE SIEGE OF
DELHI
Breaching batteries
Assault columns
A Breach in Kashmir bastion
B Breach in Water bastion
C Spot where Nicholson fell
N
to Wazirabad
0 1/2 1 mile
0 1/2 1 1 1/2 km
Magazine
to Badli-ki-Serai
British Camp during the Siege
NAJAFGARH CANAL
THE RIDGE
Flagstaff Tower
Sir T. Metcalfe's House
River Jumna
Mound Piquet
Brig. Longfield 5th column
Brig. Nicholson 1st column
Brig. Jones 2nd column
E T Office
Civil Station
Hindu Rao's House
Ludlow Castle
SABZI MUNDI
I
II
III
IV
KUDSIA BAGH
Sammy House
Col. Campbell 3rd column
Water Bastion
Major Reid 4th column
Kashmir Gate
Treasury
KISENGANJ
Shah Bastion
Mori Bastion
St James's Church
Bridge-of-Boats
to Meerut
Magazine
Kabul Gate
Burn Bastion
PAHARIPUR
Lahore Gate
Chandni Chouk
RED FORT
Jama Masjid
Farash Khana Gate
Ajmir Gate
Delhi Gate
RUINS OF ANCIENT DELHI
to Humayun's Tomb

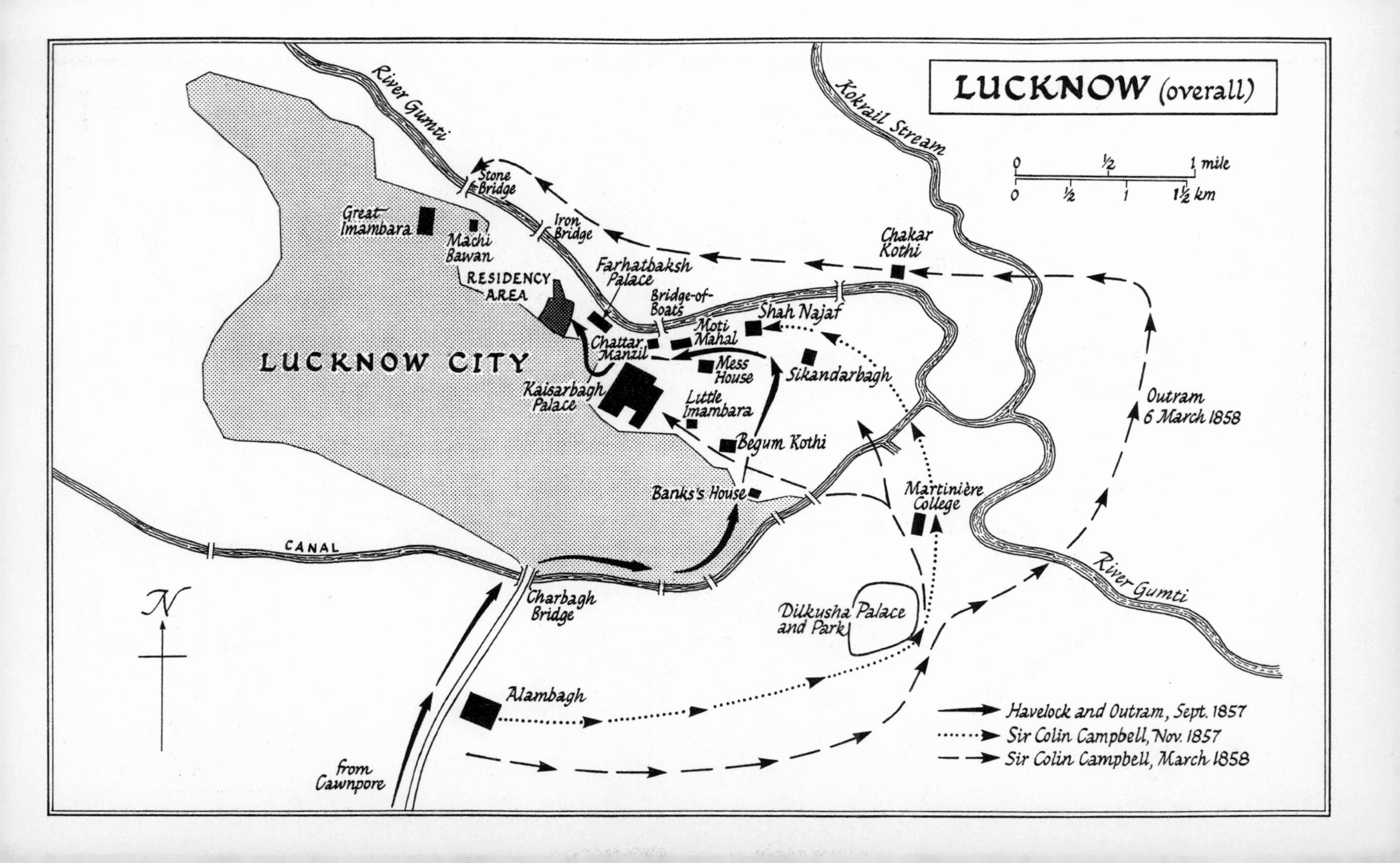
LUCKNOW (overall)
0 1/2 1 mile
0 1/2 1 1 1/2 km
River Gumti
Kokrail Stream
Stone Bridge
Iron Bridge
Great Imambara
Machi Bawan
RESIDENCY AREA
Farhatbaksh Palace
Bridge-of-Boats
Chakar Kothi
Shah Najaf
Moti Mahal
Chattar Manzil
Mess House
Sikandarbagh
LUCKNOW CITY
Kaisarbagh Palace
Little Imambara
Outram 6 March 1858
Begum Kothi
Banks's House
Martinière College
CANAL
N
Charbagh Bridge
Dilkusha Palace and Park
River Gumti
Alambagh
Havelock and Outram, Sept. 1857
Sir Colin Campbell, Nov. 1857
Sir Colin Campbell, March 1858
from Cawnpore

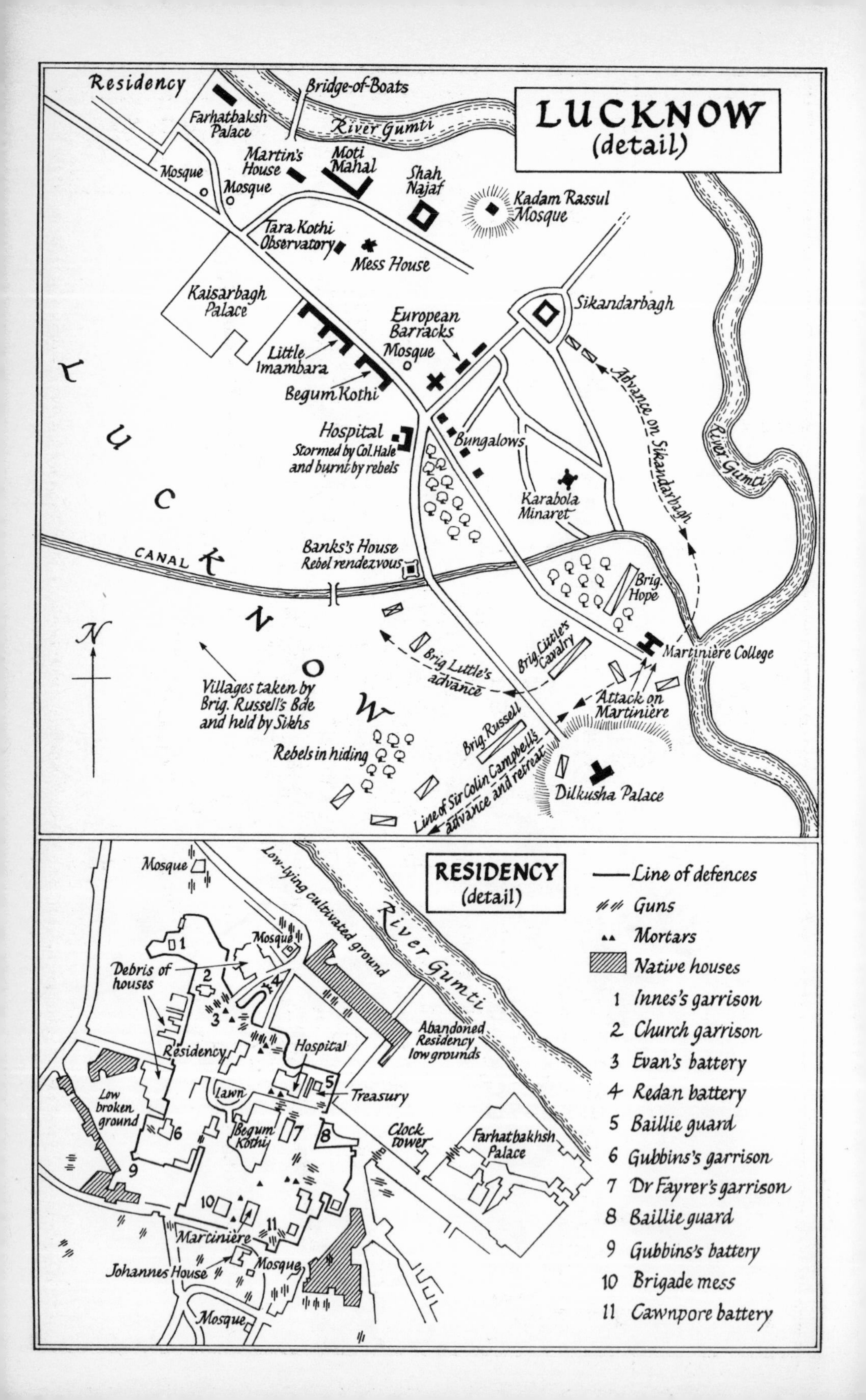

LUCKNOW
(detail)
Residency
Bridge-of-Boats
Farhatbaksh Palace
River Gumti
Martin's House
Moti Mahal
Shah Najaf
Mosque
Mosque
Kadam Rassul Mosque
Tara Kothi Observatory
Mess House
Kaisarbagh Palace
Sikandarbagh
European Barracks
Mosque
Little Imambara
Begum Kothi
Advance on Sikandarbagh
River Gumti
Hospital
Stormed by Col. Hale and burnt by rebels
Bungalows
Karabola Minaret
LUCKNOW
CANAL
Banks's House
Rebel rendezvous
Brig. Hope
N
Martinière College
Brig. Little's advance
Brig. Little's Cavalry
Villages taken by Brig. Russell's Bde and held by Sikhs
Attack on Martinière
Brig. Russell
Rebels in hiding
Line of Sir Colin Campbell's advance and retreat
Dilkusha Palace
RESIDENCY
(detail)
Mosque
Low-lying cultivated ground
River Gumti
Mosque
Debris of houses
Abandoned Residency low grounds
Residency
Hospital
Lawn
Treasury
Low broken ground
Begum Kothi
Clock tower
Farhatbakhsh Palace
Martinière
Johannes House
Mosque
Mosque
Line of defences
Guns
Mortars
Native houses
1 Innes's garrison
2 Church garrison
3 Evan's battery
4 Redan battery
5 Baillie guard
6 Gubbins's garrison
7 Dr Fayrer's garrison
8 Baillie guard
9 Gubbins's battery
10 Brigade mess
11 Cawnpore battery

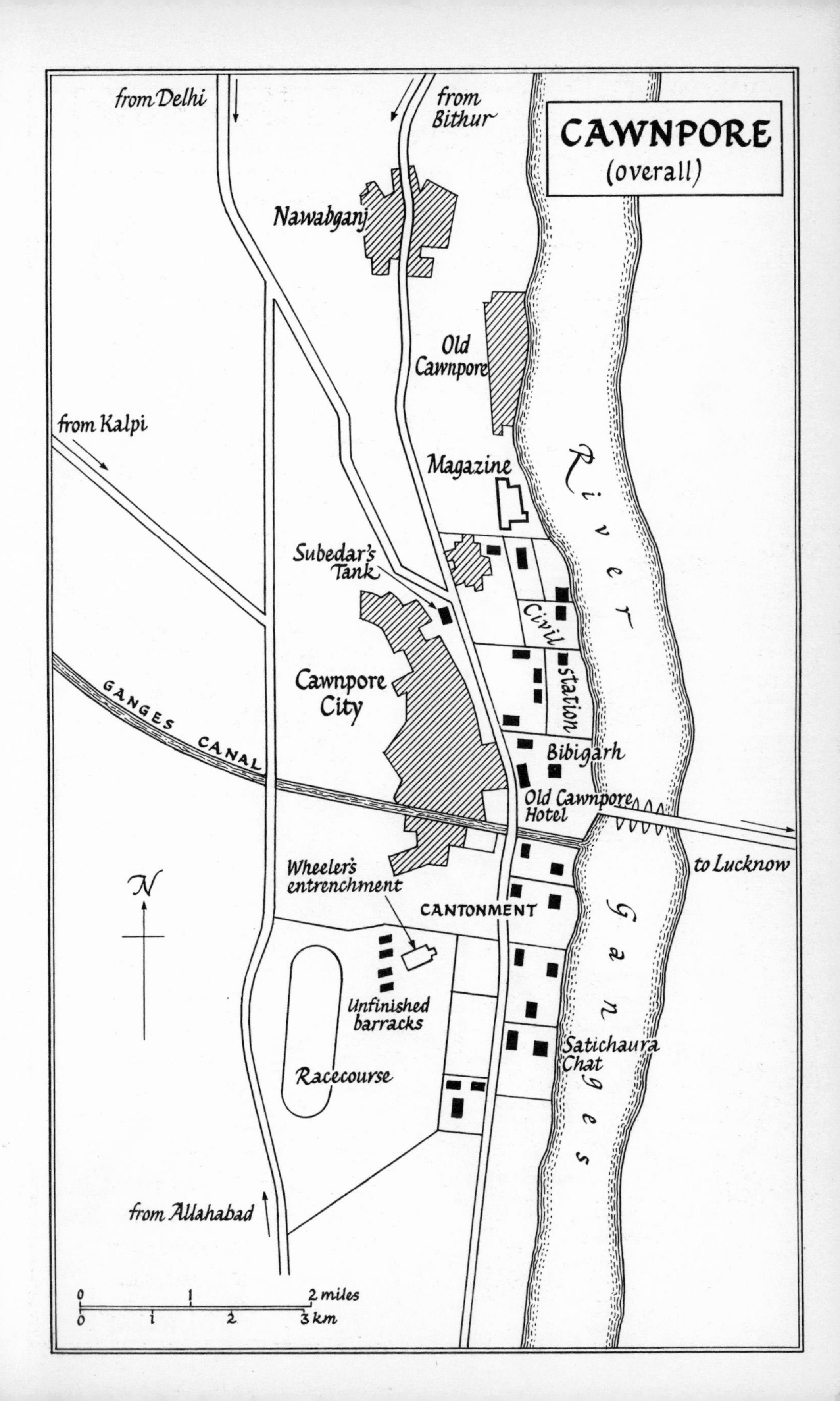
CAWNPORE
(overall)
from Delhi
from Bithur
Nawabganj
Old Cawnpore
from Kalpi
Magazine
River Ganges
Subedar's Tank
Civil station
Cawnpore City
GANGES CANAL
Bibigarh
Old Cawnpore Hotel
to Lucknow
Wheeler's entrenchment
N
CANTONMENT
Unfinished barracks
Satichaura Ghat
Racecourse
from Allahabad
0
1
2 miles
0
1
2
3 km

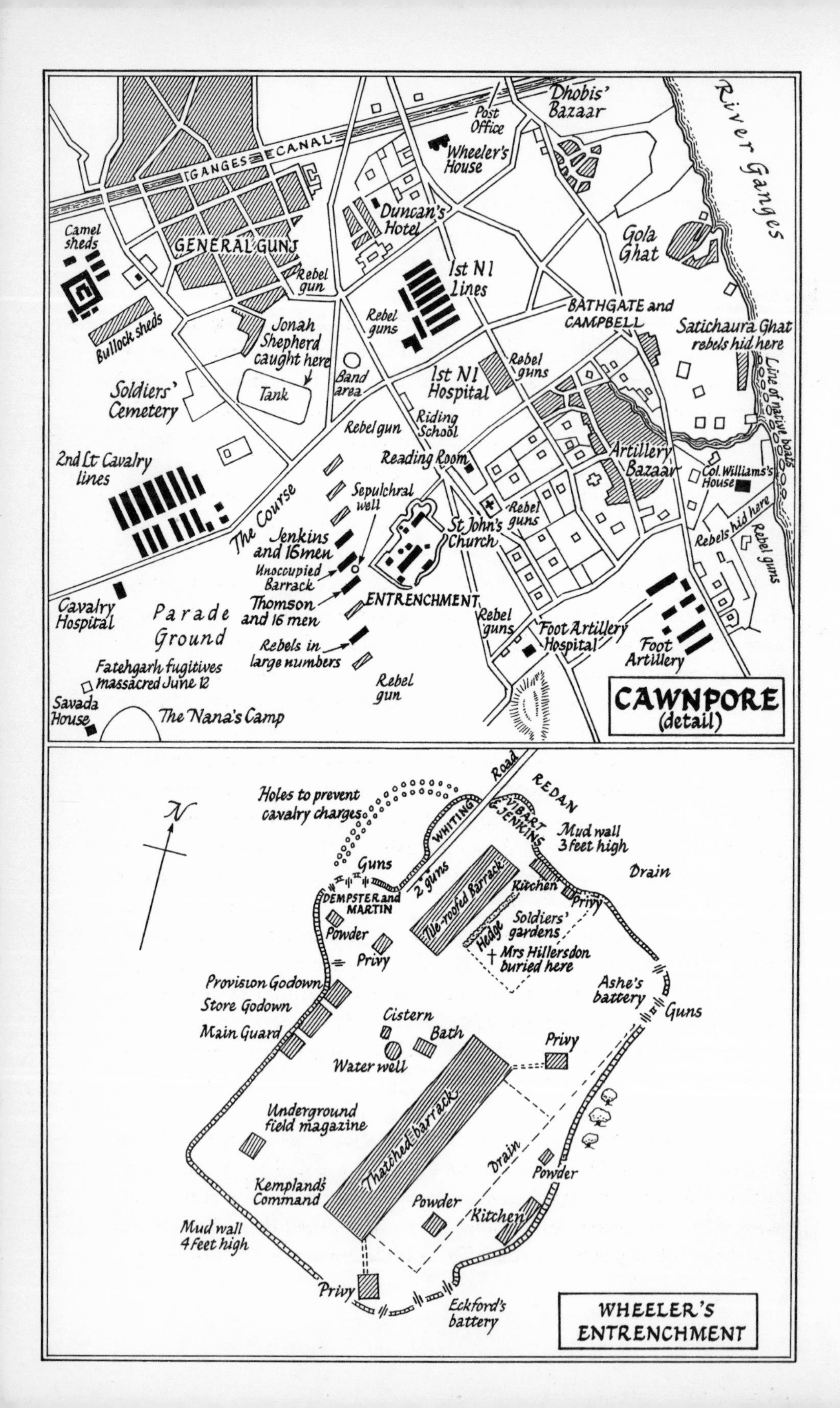

CAWNPORE (detail)
River Ganges
Dhobis' Bazaar
Post Office
Wheeler's House
GANGES CANAL
Duncan's Hotel
Camel sheds
GENERAL GUNJ
Rebel gun
Gola Ghat
1st NI Lines
Rebel guns
BATHGATE and CAMPBELL
Satichaura Ghat rebels hid here
Bullock sheds
Jonah Shepherd caught here
Band area
1st NI Hospital
Line of native boats
Soldiers' Cemetery
Tank
Riding School
Rebel gun
Artillery Bazaar
Col. Williams's House
2nd Lt Cavalry lines
Reading Room
The Course
Sepulchral well
Rebels hid here
Rebel guns
St John's Church
Jenkins and 16 men
Unoccupied Barrack
Thomson and 16 men
ENTRENCHMENT
Cavalry Hospital
Parade Ground
Rebels in large numbers
Foot Artillery Hospital
Foot Artillery
Fatehgarh fugitives massacred June 12
Savada House
The Nana's Camp
WHEELER'S ENTRENCHMENT
N
Road
REDAN
Holes to prevent cavalry charges
WHITING
VIBART & JENKINS
Mud wall 3 feet high
Drain
Guns
2 guns
Tile-roofed Barrack
Kitchen
Privy
DEMPSTER and MARTIN
Soldiers' gardens
Hedge
Powder
Privy
Mrs Hillersdon buried here
Provision Godown
Ashe's battery
Store Godown
Guns
Cistern
Main Guard
Bath
Privy
Water well
Underground field magazine
Thatched barrack
Drain
Powder
Kempland's Command
Powder
Kitchen
Mud wall 4 feet high
Privy
Eckford's battery

Prologue: 'The Electric Telegraph has saved us'

Sunday, 10 May 1857, was typical of the north Indian summer: heat, dust and wind combining to produce a suffocating, furnace-like atmosphere. At Delhi, the former Mogul capital, the mercury had risen above a hundred degrees by eight in the morning. It was the start of the hot season, and the only way a European could gain respite from the heat and flies was by having a cold bath or lying motionless in a room whose outer doors and windows had been sealed with 'tatties', grass-shutters kept constantly wet by Indian water-bearers so that the 'hot wind, after passing through them, became quite cool'.

In the telegraph office, about halfway along the two-mile stretch of road that separated the city walls from the military cantonment, the staff had been at work since daybreak. But as telegraph offices closed on the sabbath between nine and four, Charles Todd, the assistant in charge, and his two young Eurasian signallers, Brendish and Pilkington, were about to return to their bungalows to rest.

As Brendish rose from his desk, the telegraph needle began to move. It was an unofficial message from the office at Meerut, a large military station about 30 miles to the north-east, and referred to 'the excitement that prevailed there on account of the sentence that had been passed on the men of the 3rd Light Cavalry for refusing to use the new cartridges'. It stated that eighty men had been imprisoned and were to be blown away from guns. In fact, eighty-five Indian cavalrymen had been given sentences ranging from five to ten years for refusing to accept the same carbine cartridges they had always been issued with. But the ill-advised decision by the Meerut authorities to have the prisoners shackled in irons at a morning parade on 9 May had caused considerable discontent among their fellow soldiers. Despite this potential for trouble, the telegraph offices at both stations were closed at the usual hour.

On reopening the office at four, Todd discovered that the line to Meerut had been severed. He therefore sent Brendish and Pilkington across the bridge-of-boats to the north-east of the city to check the line at the point where the underwater cable emerged from the River Jumna. They found that they could signal back to the office at Delhi but not on towards Meerut, which confirmed that the break was beyond the river. With the sun setting at six-thirty, they decided it was too late to do anything further that evening and returned to the office.

At eight the following morning Todd set off in a *gharry* drawn by two ponies to locate and repair the break in the line. He was never seen again. At first Brendish and Pilkington tried to reassure Todd's wife and child that he would soon return. But, as the hours ticked by, the two young signallers picked up fragments of alarming news from Indian messengers attached to the telegraph office. They learnt that mutineers from Meerut had crossed the bridge-of-boats and entered the city; and later that a regiment of native infantry from the Delhi garrison, which they had seen march past the telegraph office in the direction of the Kashmir Gate, had disobeyed orders and allowed their officers to be shot down by the mutinous cavalry. Around midday, with no sign of Todd and no official news, Brendish went outside and met a wounded officer making his way along the road to the cantonment. 'For God's sake,' implored the officer, 'get inside and close your doors.' The warning was repeated by Indian fugitives from the city who said that the mutineers were murdering shopkeepers and that white men had little chance of survival. Fearful of their isolated position, Brendish and Pilkington proposed heading towards the Flagstaff Tower on the Ridge, where the officers and European refugees were congregating. But Mrs Todd was reluctant to leave without her husband, and it was around two when she finally agreed. Before departing, Brendish sent the following message to Ambala, 120 miles to the north: 'We must leave office, all the bungalows are on fire, burning down by the sepoys of Meerut. They came in this morning. We are off. Mr C. Todd is dead, I think. He went out this morning and has not yet returned. We learned that nine Europeans are killed.'

When the occupants of the telegraph office reached the Flagstaff Tower, at around three in the afternoon, they found it full to overflowing. The main circular room, about 18 feet in diameter, was crammed with European refugees and their Indian servants, and so hot and airless that one observer likened it to a 'Black Hole in miniature, with all but the last horrible features of that dreadful prison'. Despite his withered leg – which required a special boot – Pilkington was almost relieved when an officer asked him if he would return to the telegraph office with an escort of loyal sepoys to send another telegram to Ambala. He agreed, and the message was duly dispatched. It read:

Cantonment in a state of siege. Mutineers from Meerut – 3rd Light Cavalry – numbers not known, said to be one hundred and fifty men, cut off communication with Meerut; taken possession of the bridge of boats. 54th Native Infantry sent against them refused to act. Several officers killed and wounded. City in a state of considerable excitement. Troops sent down, but nothing known yet. Information will be forwarded.

It was the last transmission from Delhi. Later that afternoon the signaller at Ambala noticed the telegraph needle moving as if someone were trying to send a message. But as the sender refused to identify himself, the signaller assumed that it was somebody unfamiliar with the apparatus and that all the Delhi staff had been murdered.

From Ambala the news of the Delhi outbreak was flashed north to Lahore, the capital of the Punjab, and on to the other stations of that vital province that had been part of British India only since 1849. A rider was also sent to inform General Anson, the Commander-in-Chief of India, who was at Simla in the hills. The tidings from Delhi reached the civil station of Anarkali, on the outskirts of Lahore, during the morning of 12 May. With Sir John Lawrence, the Chief Commissioner of the Punjab, on his way to join his family in the Murree Hills, the senior civil authority in Lahore was Robert Montgomery, the judicial commissioner. An Ulster Protestant imbued with a godly sense of self-discipline and duty, Montgomery was at the same time a man of impulse, devoid of caution and circumspection.* It was just as well. Shortly after reading the telegram from Ambala, Montgomery received word from a Brahman spy that the four native regiments at Lahore were on the verge of mutiny. After a hastily organized meeting with his senior officials, he drove over to the military cantonment at Mian Mir to ask the military authorities to confiscate the sepoys' ammunition.

By a happy coincidence, the commander of the Lahore garrison, Brigadier Stuart Corbett, was also a man of resolve. Though fifty-five years old – about average for a Bengal brigadier – he had 'none of that incapacity to grasp strange incidents and new situations, none of that timid shrinking from responsibility, which is so often evinced by feeble minds, trammelled by the associations of long years of convention and routine'. He was, in short, not your typical time-serving Indian officer.

When Montgomery arrived at Mian Mir with the news from Delhi and the intelligence about the Lahore sepoys, Corbett was quick to appreciate the danger. The 4,000 or so Indian soldiers at Mian Mir outnumbered the

* The complete opposite of his celebrated grandson, Field-Marshal Montgomery of El Alamein.

Europeans by more than three to one. If they rose and took possession of Lahore Fort – which was garrisoned by half a regiment of native infantry and just one company of Europeans – there was every likelihood that they would be joined by the city population of nearly 100,000, most of them Sikhs and Muslims who had little love for the British (though, as it turned out, even less for the high-caste Hindus who dominated the Bengal Army). Corbett therefore agreed to Montgomery's suggestion that he confiscate the sepoys' ammunition, though he knew most of his officers would be outraged. He decided to 'go the whole hog' and disarm the Indian troops altogether after receiving further intelligence from the cantonment magistrate's spies that the four Indian regiments intended to mutiny and seize the fort on 15 May, when the monthly relief took place and 1,100 armed sepoys would have been present. There was also an intimation that simultaneous risings would occur at other Punjab stations.

To disarm the sepoys, a general parade was ordered for the following morning. So as not to excite the suspicions of the sepoys, however, a ball hosted by the officers of the 81st Foot went ahead as planned. 'The evening has passed very pleasantly,' noted one young officer in his journal, 'a perfect sham of smiles over tears. Half the ladies were not present and those who were there could barely disguise their anxiety, while we gentlemen had to give the brightest picture of the case possible, tho' they must often have heard pieces of subdued conversations anything but hopeful.'

Shortly after daybreak on 13 May the four Indian regiments were drawn up in columns on the grand parade at Mian Mir. Facing them, at a distance of 350 yards, were the ten 6-pounders and two 12-pound howitzers of the European horse artillery, primed with canister and ready to fire. Behind the cannon were six companies of the 81st Foot with loaded muskets. Corbett and his staff rode to within a few yards of the European officers at the head of two central Indian columns. 'The Brigadier soft-sawdered them,' recalled a member of his staff, 'saying what splendid regiments they were, how he loved them, how he longed to win their further honour and to keep their name unsullied, and so he was going to order them to show their loyalty in laying down their arms.'

Then came the critical moment. 'Order the 16th to pile arms!' commanded Brigadier Corbett. All European eyes were on the tall, black-faced ranks of the 16th Grenadiers – one of the 'beautiful' regiments that had fought under Nott at Kandahar – resplendent in white trousers, tight red coatees*

* Swallow-tail coat.

with white cross-belts and black shako headdresses that resembled inverted coal scuttles. 'Grenadiers,' shouted their commanding officer, 'shoulder arms!' They did so. 'Ground arms!' It was done. 'Pile arms!' A few complied, most hesitated. But a quick glance at the black artillery muzzles must have proved decisive. All muskets, bayonets and swords were placed on the ground. 'Stand away from your arms . . . Right about face . . . Quick march!' And away they went unarmed. The 26th, which had been made a Light Infantry corps for sterling service under Pollock in the First Afghan War, followed suit, as did the 49th. Lastly the French-grey coated sowars of the 8th Light Cavalry, many of them veterans of the Gwalior and Sikh wars of the 1840s, were ordered to drop their sabres, pistols and carbines. They obeyed, before backing up their horses and riding off the parade-ground. A simultaneous disarmament of the Indian garrison of Lahore Fort was carried out by the remaining four companies of the 81st Foot.

The importance of Montgomery and Corbett's decisive action was illustrated the following day when it was discovered that the disarmed regiments were planning to march that night and seize the magazine at Ferozepore, 45 miles to the south. A couple of hundred sepoys did manage to desert, but most were picked up by the civil authorities, both on the road and at Ferozepore itself. The previous evening an Indian regiment had mutinied at Ferozepore on seeing its comrades replaced as the magazine guard by a company of European troops. But the uprising failed to secure the magazine, and the mutineers fled.

By enabling the authorities at Lahore, in the words of one senior official, to 'disarm the native troops before they had received one word' of the uprisings at Meerut and Delhi, the telegraph messages played a key role in the preservation of British India. 'The Electric Telegraph has saved us,' wrote Donald MacLeod, the Financial Commissioner of the Punjab. He was right. If Lahore had fallen to the rebels, the rest of the Punjab would probably have followed suit. And if the Punjab – where the majority of European troops were stationed – had been lost, British India might not have endured. As it was, its survival was in the balance for many months to come.

1. The East India Company

On the last day of the sixteenth century the London trading house known as the Honourable East India Company was granted its charter by Queen Elizabeth I. It was not the first European company to do business with the subcontinent – the Portuguese had been conducting commerce there since 1510 – but it would rapidly become the most successful.

The paramount power in India at the time was the Mogul Empire of Akbar the Great (1556–1605). Akbar's grandfather, Babur – a descendant of both Genghis Khan and Timur the Great – had established the Timurid dynasty in Delhi in 1527 after his armies had swept all before them during an epic march south from Samarkand, via Kabul and the Hindu Kush. But Akbar, with his unique combination of military talent, political acumen and cultural learning, was the greatest of the six Mogul Emperors who were to dominate Indian politics for almost two centuries. He hugely expanded Mogul rule – a confusing patchwork of imperial provinces, subordinate states and semi-independent towns and villages – and by his death his domains covered much of central and northern India. In 1613 Akbar's successor, Jahangir Khan, allowed the East India Company to locate a trading post at Surat on the coast north of Bombay. Further permanent stations were established at Madras, Bombay and Calcutta in 1639, 1664 and 1696 respectively.

By 1700 the East India Company's only serious competitors for Indian trade were the French companies based at Pondicherry on the south-east coast and Chandarnagar on the Hooghly River. The Portuguese still retained the enclave of Goa, south of Bombay, but were spent as a commercial force. The Dutch and the Danes also had trading posts, but their share of the market was falling. The East India Company, on the other hand, was going from strength to strength. Its success was based upon the seemingly insatiable demand in Europe for cheap calico, chintz, silks, fine china and tea. During the first half of the eighteenth century its annual dividends never fell below 6 per cent. Its yearly sales of £2 million made up a fifth of Britain's total annual imports, and so profitable did it become that, in 1744, it was able to lend the British government £1 million. Pre-eminent on the London stock market, it occupied a position in the City comparable only to that of the Bank of England.

The Company's gradual metamorphosis from mercantile to political power was prompted by the death of Aurangzeb, the last of the great Mogul Emperors, in 1707. His wars of consolidation and expansion, which had continued on and off for the previous twenty years, had exhausted the imperial coffers. But there was no respite as his numerous male offspring fought a lengthy war of succession and his Muslim empire – more than two thirds of whose inhabitants were unbelievers, mainly Hindus – began to disintegrate. Between 1739 and 1761 there were five successful invasions of northern India: the first by Nadir Shah of Persia, who sacked Delhi and removed the Mogul's Peacock Throne to Tehran; the next four by the Afghan ruler Ahmad Shah Abdali. Meanwhile, former Mogul governors, vassal princes and soldiers of fortune were carving out their own independent states. By the mid eighteenth century the Mogul empire had been superseded by a host of powerful polities, including Bengal, Hyderabad, Mysore, Oudh and the Maratha Confederacy of Deccan principalities. Meanwhile a number of looser political entities had been formed by the Rohilla nobles of Rohilkhand, the Rajput princes of Rajputana and the Sikh rulers of the Punjab.

To protect its valuable trade during this time of political flux, the East India Company stepped up its recruitment of Indian troops. The Company had been enlisting modest numbers of Indian soldiers (or sepoys, from the Persian for 'soldier') since 1684, but it was not until the wars with the French in the 1740s that the need for a permanent regular army became evident. Even before the outbreak of global war between Britain and France in 1744, the underfunded French Compagnie des Indes had begun to cultivate the native rulers of southern India in an attempt to acquire territory and revenue. The East India Company retaliated by supporting rival princes. But the inadequacy of the Company's forces was revealed in 1747 when Madras would have fallen to the French had it not been for the timely arrival of the Royal Navy. The Company's response was to authorize Major Stringer Lawrence, who had arrived with the British fleet, to recruit and organize Indian troops on the European model. Led by Lawrence and his deputy, Robert Clive, these troops inflicted a string of defeats upon the French and their allies in the early 1750s, as the British consolidated their economic and military presence in southern India.

But the events that were to establish the East India Company as a powerful political force in the subcontinent took place in Bengal. The Company had been granted extensive commercial privileges in that province, the richest and most populous in India, by the Emperor Farrukhsiyar in 1717. By the 1750s, however, Bengal had become the personal fiefdom of the descendants of the former imperial governor, or nawab, Murshid Quli Khan. They regarded the Company's favoured position, in particular its permanent trading station at Calcutta and its exemption from transit levies, as both an affront to their sovereignty and harmful to their finances. So in 1756, shortly after becoming the Nawab of Bengal at the age of twenty-one, Siraj ud-Daula ordered his troops to occupy the Company's bases at Kasimbazar and Calcutta. During the night of 20 June scores of European prisoners died at the Calcutta base after being crammed into a small and airless room. The so-called 'Black Hole of Calcutta' was an atrocity akin to the Cawnpore massacres a century later – and was to reap a similar revenge.

The Madras Council gave Robert Clive the task of reoccupying Calcutta and restoring the Company's trading concessions. Born in 1725, the eldest son of a struggling Shropshire squire who supplemented his meagre rent-roll by practising as a lawyer, Clive had joined the East India Company's civil service as a junior tally clerk in the hope of reviving his family's fortunes. But it was his success as an ad hoc military commander in southern India – particularly the courage and dash he displayed during the epic defence of Arcot in 1751 – that had brought him to prominence. Accompanied by six hundred European soldiers and nine hundred sepoys, Clive accomplished the first part of his mission with minimal bloodshed on New Year's Day, 1757. The subsequent fighting was indecisive, however, and Siraj agreed to terms in February. But Clive was determined to replace the nawab and used the hiatus to strengthen his position. In March 1757, two months after raising the first battalion of Bengal sepoys at Calcutta, Clive captured the French base at Chandarnagar. He then negotiated a secret alliance with a group of Calcutta's leading merchants and bankers, who were anxious to keep in with the British, and also with Mir Jafar, one of Siraj's senior commanders, who promised huge sums in return for the throne. With his preparations complete, Clive gave battle at the village of Plassey, 80 miles north of Calcutta, on 23 June 1757: his force numbered just 3,000 soldiers and sailors (two thirds of them Indian); Siraj had more than 50,000 troops, albeit many who were unpaid and disgruntled. The action was decided by the superiority of the British artillery fire – as so many future battles in India would be – which panicked the Bengalis' elephants and bullocks, and caused chaos in their lines. Even before Mir Jafar could defect, the nawab's army had melted away.

Siraj was later captured and murdered. Having replaced him as nawab, Mir Jafar rewarded senior Company officials and the business community at Calcutta with huge cash payments (members of the Bengal Council, for example, received a share of £275,000, or £16.5 million today). He also ceded tax districts to the Company and dismantled the state control of inland trade. Such concessions were to prove fatal for the Bengal state. When Mir Jafar objected to the economic exploitation, in 1760, the Company replaced him with his more pliant son-in-law, Mir Kasim, and received the districts of Burdwan, Chittagong and Midnapur into the bargain. Eventually Kasim too tried to reassert Bengal's independence, but his army was roundly defeated by Company forces at Buxar on 23 October 1764. So began a long period of commercial and territorial expansion throughout India as obdurate states were annexed and the more amenable became allies.

In 1773, alarmed by the growth of this private 'empire within an empire', not to mention the venality of Company officials (many of whom, including Clive, had returned home with enormous fortunes), Parliament passed the Judicature and Regulating Acts: the former paid lip service to the legal rights of Indians by establishing a Supreme Court in Calcutta from which appeals could be made to the Privy Council in London; the latter established the principle by which the British government could interfere in the affairs of India, as well as creating the framework for the Company's rule. Henceforth the Governor-General of Bengal, the largest and richest of the Company's three presidencies, would have supervisory control over the other two, Madras and Bombay. He would be advised by a Supreme Council, some of whose members were appointed by the Crown. Yet little was done to reform the local administration of India, beyond the stipulation that Company officials and officers were not to receive gifts or rewards from Indian princes.

Nine years later the issue of corrupt Company servants was again raised in the Commons when Whig MPs called for the dismissal of the Governor-General of Bengal, Warren Hastings. So began the Whigs' two-year struggle for new regulations that ended with William Pitt the Younger, the new 24-year-old Tory Prime Minister, stealing their thunder by passing the India Act of 1784. Its chief provision was to give executive control of Indian affairs to the newly created Board of Control in London, whose President was a Cabinet minister and therefore answerable to Parliament. But the Court of Directors retained their monopoly of patronage, and officials in India still enjoyed considerable freedom of action. At the end of the eighteenth century it took up to six months for instructions from London to reach Calcutta by sea; by 1857, using early steamships and the express route across the Suez isthmus, the journey time to Bombay, the nearest of the three presidencies, was still a month.

Hard fought victories by Sir Gerard (later Viscount) Lake and Sir Arthur Wellesley (the future Duke of Wellington) in the Second Maratha War of 1803–4 brought to a close a remarkable four-year period of military conquest and territorial acquisition. In 1799, after the defeat of the Muslim ruler Tipu Sultan, the powerful southern kingdom of Mysore was partitioned between the Company, its ally the Nizam of Hyderabad and the former Hindu rulers. That same year saw the annexation of the Hindu principality of Tanjore, the most fertile tract in southern India; and in 1801 the nominal ruler of the Carnatic formally renounced his mortgaged kingdom in return for a Company pension and the titular rank of nawab. In a few months the Madras Presidency had been transformed 'from a few scattered districts' into a British province covering most of southern India.

The Bengal Presidency was also considerably enlarged during this period. In 1798 it was made up of just Bengal, Bihar and Benares (the last two provinces acquired in 1775 and 1781 respectively). But in 1801 the Nawab of Oudh was pressurized into ceding the lion's share of his territory in return for kingly status. The acquisitions included the districts of Allahabad, Fatehpur and Cawnpore in the lower part of the Gangetic Doab, and most of the province of Rohilkhand to the north-west. Bengal was now bounded to the west by the states of the Maratha Confederacy, which stretched from Malabar (south of Bombay) to the Himalayas. The most powerful Maratha prince, Maharaja Scindia of Gwalior, had been in possession of Delhi and the Mogul Emperor, the blind and enfeebled Shah Alam, great-grandson of Aurangzeb, since 1784. After Delhi fell to the British in 1803, Shah Alam regained some of his dignity but little of his power. He was given a Company allowance in excess of £100,000 a year, the title of King of Delhi and the revenue from a handful of districts. Yet his temporal authority was confined to the Red Fort and its immediate environs.

The Second Maratha War was fought because Lord Wellesley, the Governor-General (1798–1805), was determined to nullify the threat posed by the European-trained armies of the Maratha Confederacy. Scindia's defeat by Lake at the battles of Aligarh, Delhi and Laswari cost him Gujarat in west India, which became part of the Bombay Presidency, and all his lands north of the Jumna River, including Agra, Delhi and Meerut. These last territories were amalgamated with Benares and the districts recently relinquished by the King of Oudh into the Bengal administrative unit known as the North-Western Provinces.

The Bombay Presidency was the chief beneficiary of the Third Maratha War of 1817–18. The chief protagonists were Peshwa Baji Rao II, the head of the Maratha Confederacy, and Appa Sahib, the Maharaja of Nagpur. Their respective forces were defeated by Company armies totalling more than 115,000 men, the most ever devoted to one campaign, in battles at Kurki, Nagpur and Mahidpur. The Peshwa was exiled to Bithur on the Ganges with an annual pension of 800,000 rupees, while all his territory in western India was swallowed by the Bombay Presidency. Appa Sahib was replaced by a kinsman, the last Maharaja of Nagpur, who agreed to cede a large tract of country in central India that became known as the Sagar and Nerbudda Territories.

The Company had become the undisputed master of India. Henceforth it conducted the odd campaign against unruly Indian principalities and rebellious subjects. But its major wars were fought against powerful neighbouring states.* The chief acquisitions of these closely contested, but ultimately successful, conflicts were Assam, Arracan and Tenasserim in 1824, Sind in 1843, the Punjab in 1849 and Pegu in 1853. Sind went to the Bombay Presidency, the rest to Bengal.

There were, however, a number of bloodless additions to Company territory. In 1848, for example, Lord Dalhousie, the new Governor-General, annexed the state of Satara in western India – the original Maratha principality founded in the seventeenth century – after its raja had died without a natural heir. Because sons are necessary to perform Hindu funeral rites, thereby preventing their deceased fathers from descending to hell after death, Hindu law acknowledges adopted sons and enables them to inherit personal wealth and to succeed their royal fathers. But Dalhousie refused to recognize the Raja of Satara's young heir, a relation adopted on his deathbed, on the principle 'that, on all occasions, where heirs natural shall fail, the territory should be made to lapse, and adoption should not be permitted', unless there were strong political reasons for making an exception. He added: 'I cannot conceive it possible for any one to dispute the policy of taking advantage of every just opportunity which presents itself for consolidating the territories that already belong to us, by taking possession of States that may lapse in the midst of them.' This so-called 'Doctrine of Lapse' – a pseudo-legalistic triumph of expediency over tradition – was also used to justify the annexation of Sambhalpur in 1849, and Jhansi and Nagpur in 1854. Dalhousie revealed the cynical thinking behind such appropriations when he told a family friend that the huge state of Nagpur, with its annual revenue of £400,000 a year, was 'too good a "plum" not to pick out of the "Christmas pie"'.

* Wars were fought against Burma in 1824–6 and 1852–3, Afghanistan in 1838–42, Sind in 1843, the Sikh Kingdom of the Punjab in 1845–6 and 1848–9, and Persia in 1856–7.

Not all Indian officials agreed with the new policy. Colonel William Sleeman, the British Resident in Oudh who had made his name suppressing the murderous cult of Thagi,* wrote a number of letters of protest that were eerily prescient. In September 1848, for example, he warned Dalhousie that 'the system of annexing and absorbing Native States – so popular with our Indian Services, and so much advocated by a certain class of writers in public journals – might some day render us too visibly dependent upon our Native Army; that they might see it, and that accidents might occur to unite them, or too great a portion of them, in some desperate act'.

Another critic of annexation was Colonel John Low, a member of the Supreme Council, who had spent most of his career as a political officer. In February 1854 he wrote two minutes protesting against the impolicy and injustice of the annexation of Nagpur. (The raja had died without adopting a son, which made it even easier for Dalhousie to apply the Doctrine of Lapse.) The confiscation of Satara had, he said, already shaken the confidence of ordinary people in the justice and good faith of the Indian government. Many Indians had asked him, with regard to Satara: 'What crime did the late Rajah commit that his country should be seized by the Company?' They understood 'acquisition by conquest', particularly when Indian rulers had brought it upon themselves (as in the case of the Punjab), but they could not accept the extinction of a loyal Indian state simply because the ruler had failed to provide a natural heir. Low also pointed out that while the British system of administration might be better than the Indian system, the people did not necessarily want it. They, like all indigenous peoples, preferred 'their own habits and customs' to 'those of foreigners'. In any case, said Low, there was no legal justification for the annexation of Nagpur because the treaty between the late raja and the Indian government did not limit the succession to heirs of the body.

Nagpur was not the last of the Governor-General's peacetime acquisitions. British Residents at the Court of Oudh had long complained of the corruption and maladministration of its rulers. But it was not until 1847 that the Indian government acted. The new King, Wajid Ali Shah, was given two years to reform the administration. He did nothing. 'Sunk in the

* 'Thugs' were worshippers of Kali, the Hindu goddess of destruction, who carried out ritual killings by befriending fellow travellers and then strangling them with a piece of sacred cloth. During his time as Superintendent of the Thagi and Dakaiti Department in the late 1830s Sleeman recruited hundreds of informers whose intelligence enabled the authorities to intercept parties of thugs and excavate their burial grounds.

uttermost abysses of enfeebling debauchery,' wrote Sir John Kaye, 'the King pushed aside the business which he felt himself incapable of transacting, and went in search of new pleasures . . . [He] turned to the . . . delights of dancing, and drumming, and drawing, and manufacturing small rhymes.'

The pressure for intervention was building. In the early 1850s the Resident, Colonel Sleeman, repeatedly urged the Company to assume the administration of Oudh but not to appropriate its revenues. Sleeman retired in poor health towards the end of 1854, but his successor, Colonel James Outram, was equally determined that the Indian government should step in. So was John Low, the opponent of annexation by lapse, who noted in a minute of March 1855 that the 'shameful oppressions committed on the people by Government officers in Oudh have of late years been constant and extreme'. It was by now generally agreed that the government of Oudh would have to be transferred to European administrators. The outstanding question was what to do with the surplus revenue after the expenses of government had been paid. Lord Dalhousie's answer – in his notorious minute of 18 June 1855 – was to appropriate the revenue but to stop short of outright annexation. The King of Oudh, while retaining the sovereignty of his dominion, would 'vest all power, jurisdiction, rights and claims thereto belonging in the hands of the East India Company'. Quite what this 'sovereignty' would entail, without territorial rights or revenues, was not explained. Sir John Kaye made the obvious point that when the Nawab of the Carnatic and the Raja of Tanjore were 'deprived of their rights and revenues, they were held to be not territorial, but titular sovereigns'. The settlement of Oudh was no different. By arranging for the balance of its finances to be paid to the Indian government, Dalhousie was ensuring that Oudh 'became a component part of the empire'. The distinction between the King of Oudh and the titular sovereigns was purely one of semantics.

Rubber-stamped by the Court of Directors and the Board of Control, Dalhousie's thinly disguised annexation of Oudh was instigated in January 1856. But the King was not taken in, and, on 4 February, he refused to sign the proposed treaty. Whereupon Outram, in line with his instructions, issued a proclamation declaring Oudh to be henceforth part of British India. The annexation of Oudh was to set in chain a series of events that would culminate in the great mutiny of 1857. It was not the only cause of mutiny, but it was a vital ingredient, not least because a significant proportion of the Bengal Army – as many as three quarters of all sepoys, according to one authority – were recruited from Oudh.

The contradiction between the Company's dual role as ruler and trader had been finally removed in 1833 by the Act of Parliament that renewed its charter: in return for an annuity of £630,000, taken from the territorial revenues of British India, it was ordered to cease all commercial transactions. The same Act renamed the Governor-General of Bengal as the Governor-General of India and increased the powers of his Supreme Council. It also created a distinct Governor of Bengal on the same footing as the Governors of Madras and Bombay.*

By 1857 the East India Company was directly ruling about two thirds of the subcontinent as the agent of the British government. It had, moreover, long been recognized as the paramount power by the Indian princes who controlled the remaining third: all were advised by political representatives of the Company; many had armies that had been raised, and were still commanded, by Company officers. To police its own territories and to guard the frontiers of British India, the Company had three separate armies, one for each presidency. They contained troops raised and paid for by the Company – European and Native – and regiments of the British Army stationed in India. In 1857 the total strength of the three presidency armies was 45,000 European and 232,000 Indian troops, a ratio of 1:5. The Bengal Army – by far the largest, with 24,000 Europeans and 135,000 Indians – had a slightly worse ratio. But if all Indian troops commanded by European officers are taken into account – including regulars, irregulars, local corps, military police and the contingents of Indian princes – then the ratio falls back to 1:6 for India generally and more than 1:7 for Bengal.

It has often been stated that a gradual reduction in the relative number of European troops was partly responsible for the mutiny. In fact the ratio in India was the same in 1857 as it had been twenty-two years earlier – 1:6 – though the total number of rank and file in 1835 was much smaller: 18,000 Europeans to 112,000 Indians. Lord William Bentinck, the then Governor-General, had recommended reducing the ratio to 1:4 on the grounds that the Company's Indian troops represented British India's sole 'internal danger' in 1835. His target of an extra 10,000 European troops had been easily surpassed by 1857; but the expansion of Company territory had ensured that the Indian Army grew proportionately. Nevertheless, the ratio

* Two years later, a separate piece of legislation created the lieutenant-governorship of the North-Western Provinces. Further constitutional and administrative reform was introduced in 1853 by the Act of Parliament that gave the Company another twenty-year lease of life. It included the downgrading of the post of Governor of Bengal to that of Lieutenant-Governor and the establishment of a Legislative Council.

of European to Indian troops would have been slightly better in 1857 if two of the three Queen's regiments removed during the Crimean War had not been retained by the British government. Lord Dalhousie had told his superiors that he regarded the removal of '*any* European infantry in 1854 *as being absolutely unsafe to the maintenance* of our power in India'. A year later, with the Sonthal rebellion in full swing, he reflected upon 'the danger of withdrawing for any purpose too many troops from a country which, though tranquil and unwarlike in itself, is yet liable to such volcanic outbursts of popular violence as this now before us'.

2. 'Carlo' Canning

The man upon whose shoulders the survival of British India would depend during the dark days of 1857 was Dalhousie's successor, Lord Canning. Born in 1812, the third son of George Canning whose sudden death as Prime Minister in 1827 prompted King George IV to raise his widow to the rank of viscountess, Charles ('Carlo') Canning was still at Eton when his last surviving brother was drowned and he became heir to his mother's title and sizeable fortune in 1828. He continued his education at Christ Church, Oxford, where he was part of a brilliant set that included William Gladstone, Sidney Herbert, Robert Vernon Smith and the future Lords Dalhousie, Elgin, Cardwell and Granville, and from which he graduated in 1833 with a first in Classics and a second in Mathematics. Two years later he married Charlotte Stuart, the eighteen-year-old daughter of Lord Stuart de Rothesay, but the union would remain childless.

In 1836 Canning followed in his father's footsteps by entering the House of Commons as a Tory MP. Within a year his mother's death had elevated him to the upper chamber and relieved him of the expensive and time-consuming business of re-election. He served as a diligent junior minister in the governments of Sir Robert Peel, Lord Aberdeen and Lord Palmerston. But his consistent failure to achieve senior Cabinet status was probably the main reason why he accepted Palmerston's offer to succeed Lord Dalhousie as Governor-General of India in 1855. There was also the financial incentive: the Governor-General received a salary of £25,000 a year (£1.25 million today), out of which he had to pay for his personal servants; the Company provided for the upkeep of his two official residences at Calcutta and Barrackpore, paid the salaries of most of his household staff and defrayed the cost of the annual ball to celebrate the Queen's birthday. Lord Ellenborough believed a prudent Governor-General could save £1,000 a month. Dalhousie considered such a figure to be optimistic, but during his eight-year tenure he still managed to accumulate enough money to pay off a 'large debt', buy a cotton mill and leave himself with 'about £7000 of savings in hand'.

Canning was under no illusions as to the potential for trouble in India. 'I wish for a peaceful term of office,' he told the Court of Directors at a farewell banquet, 'but . . . we must not forget that in the sky of India, serene as it is, a small cloud may arise, at first no bigger than a man's hand, but which, growing larger and larger, may at last threaten to burst and overwhelm us with ruin.'

Canning's closest friend was Lord Granville, the Lord President of the Council,* whom he had known since childhood. The two agreed to correspond and Granville was given permission by both the Prime Minister, Lord Palmerston, and the Queen to include Cabinet secrets in his letters to India. He later wrote this revealing sketch of Canning:

He was handsome, with singularly fine eyes . . . He had extraordinary powers of continuous work for months and years, when the occasion arose, together with a facility for being perfectly idle for long periods, hardly looking at a newspaper . . . He was of temperate habits, but on one solitary occasion, he rather exceeded at a dinner at The Angel, and I found him in his rooms kneeling before his candle, praying it to light itself . . . He inherited from his father a strong sense of the ridiculous; but his fun, bubbling over at the moment, was never ill-natured . . . His departure [for India] and that of the beautiful and clever Lady Canning created a great void in a very intimate society.

Canning, his wife and her two maids left London for Paris on 26 November 1855. After an audience with Napoleon III, they travelled by train through France and endured a stormy passage across the Mediterranean in the steamship *Caradoc*. At Alexandria they were lavishly entertained by the corrupt Egyptian government of Said Pasha; leisurely expeditions were arranged to Luxor, the Valley of the Kings and the great rock temple of Medinet Hebu. Early in the New Year the Cannings re-embarked at Suez on the Indian ship *Feroze* and finally reached Calcutta – via Bombay, Ceylon and Madras – in late February 1856.

The city of Calcutta was situated on a mud ridge beside the Hooghly River, the westernmost channel of the Ganges Delta. It had been chosen as the site of a British trading post in 1690 because, at 80 miles from the sea, it was the furthest point that ocean-going ships could reach. A young British lieutenant described his river-borne approach to the city in 1857:

More cocoa and palm trees on the banks; more tangled jungle; more mud villages; more sly creeks; more white spectral forms; more naked children; till the ever-twisting river discloses to our view scenery of a somewhat more civilized description: a house! . . . then a bit more jungle, then another house! – two! – three! opening upon us in quick succession as we enter 'Garden Reach,' till the banks present one long vista of

* The Cabinet Minister with the responsibility for presiding at meetings of the Privy Council.

pretty villas, with their green verandahs, looking bright and pleasant in the warm sun . . . English faces peep from the windows, ayahs (native nurses) carrying English children stroll about the beautiful gardens which stretch down to the water's edge, and so rapid has been the transition from barbarous wilds to civilized scenes, that one can hardly credit that the eye . . . was but five minutes since gazing on rude mud villages, surrounded by nought save the dense and savage jungle.

Gazing through a tangle of shipping – from 'long, low river steamers' to 'gun-boats, fishing boats, beautiful clipper ships, huge merchantmen, still larger transports, noble Peninsular and Oriental steamers, and stately men-of-war' – the lieutenant's eye was 'forcibly arrested by the vast parapets' of Fort William, the citadel built to defend the original settlement, with its 'noble outline, its scientifically traced ditches, and its long white row of barracks, but half visible above the green fortifications'. He also noted, stretching away from the fort along the banks of the river, 'the "Chowringee," or immense Maidan, which forms the Hyde Park, the Rotten-row of Calcutta'. He was struck by the bustle and grandeur of the city, and by the contrast between its European and Indian quarters. He wrote:

First, by its position, beauty, and size, stands the noble structure of Government House, while around it, as though paying it homage, gather those hundreds of smaller buildings – the clubs, the residences of the rich merchants, the public offices, the palatial hotels, the magnificent shops, the extensive warehouses, the churches and the temples, which have earned for Calcutta the hackneyed, but well merited title 'The City of Palaces'. Far away does this prospect of architectural beauties extend – far away, till it dwindles imperceptibly into the dirty native town, where the tapering minarets and the curved domes of temples rise high above the confined and squalid streets . . . Along the crowded banks of the river are the various *ghauts* (or landing-places), the scenes of a busy trade; at some, passengers are landing; at others, merchant's ships are disgorging their freights into the greedy jaws of huge warehouses, receiving in return a rich cargo of silks or indigo.

Lord and Lady Canning disembarked at Garden Reach on 29 February 1856. They were met by city officials and a guard of honour before being conducted, in separate carriages, to Government House, where Canning was received on the front steps by Frederick Halliday, Lieutenant-Governor of Bengal, and the members of the Supreme Council. 'Dalhousie was on the top of the steps,' noted Canning in his diary, 'and after welcoming me very prettily, led me towards the Council Chamber and then went back to the private apartments to Lady C.

The ceremony of hearing appointments read and swearing in took about 20 minutes; the room was full of official spectators, besides the Members of the Council, and as soon as I had sworn, Fort William fired its salute.'

Government House had been designed by a captain in the Bengal Engineers, a nephew of the celebrated architect James Wyatt, who had based his plans on Robert Adam's drawings for Kedleston Hall in Derbyshire. It was a classical, white, three-storeyed structure with two enormous wings, one of which contained the Governor-General's private apartments. Most of the rest of the building was turned over to government offices. Canning admired its fine proportions, but not the fact that it was 'miserably furnished' with 'private apartments incapable of ever being made really comfortable'. He particularly regretted the absence of a single WC, 'there being no fall for drainage' in Calcutta.

Canning, however, had little time to dwell on such matters as he devoted all his considerable energy to mastering the detail of Indian business: by day he was surrounded by dispatch boxes; at night he met councillors and officials. In a letter to Lord Granville, he described a new Governor-General as 'little better than a galley slave'. He added: 'Quite apart from writing, composing, commenting, and minuting, excess of which is the vice of the Indian Government, there are such innumerable matters crowding up each day for his decision (be it ever so curtly given), and matters upon which, as long as there is a Governor-General, nobody but him ought to decide, that the shortest perusal of each case leaves little leisure for going deeply into any.' Fortunately the five secretaries, or heads of the various government departments – Foreign, Home, Financial, Military and Public Works – were all 'first-rate men'. If they had not been 'as willing as they were good', said Canning, the work would have been 'impracticable'.

As if the weight of official business was not enough, Canning also had to contend with the oppressive climate. He recorded:

> Any attempt to go out, even in a carriage, makes one gasp and dissolve immediately, and an open window or door lets in a flood as though one were passing through the mouth of a foundry. At 5 p.m. windows and Venetians and doors are thrown open, and in comes the strong wind, blowing one's papers off the table (which is performed by the punkah at other times) and making the chandeliers swing, and their glass drops jingle, all night long. But even at night (if one gets out of the draught, which we never do . . .) one becomes what Shelburne would call natando in sudor in an instant.

Canning's nephew Lord Dunkellin, who arrived in the summer of 1856 to take up his duties as Military Secretary, resented the lack of fresh air 'as all day one lives shut up in a room with the blinds down close to the windows to prevent the glare and heat of the sun from coming in'. The summer rains brought further irritants: giant cockroaches on the floor, bats in the bedrooms, lizards on the walls and red ants everywhere; so numerous did the last become that saucers of water were placed beneath the legs of tables and chairs. To combat the swarms of flying insects, wine glasses were protected by silver covers and the Governor-General and his wife each had a pair of servants behind their chairs armed with horse-tail swats. Then there was the all-pervading damp: writing paper became unusable, books mouldy, shoes furry and Canning's dispatch-box 'assumed the appearance of a bottle of curious old port – white and fungus-y'.

All the inhabitants of Government House found the legions of servants strangely obtrusive. Lord Dunkellin wrote:

> The free and easy way which the natives have of coming into one's rooms at all times is rather a bore; the more so as they glide in so noiselessly that one never really knows whether there is really one hovering about or not, and I have more than once been startled on looking up from my book to find a meek black clad in white waiting with his hands before his breast in an attitude of submission for me to acknowledge his presence, and he may have been there any time. In fact as Uncle C. observes, one never knows how one may have committed oneself before being aware of the arrival.

This lack of privacy caused Lady Canning, in a letter home, to reminisce about 'creaking footmen'. But she found obtrusive servants more bearable than her social obligations. 'The plan here is for everyone to come very early, long before they are asked, and no one to go till the greatest lady gets up to take leave,' she recorded. 'These dinners are very wearisome. Neither C. nor I can get at all the people. Not a man has ever voluntarily spoken to me since I came to India . . . and the ladies look terribly afraid of me . . . The Indian families – I don't mean half-caste or Indian blood, but people who are of the families always connected with India and who have only been sent home to be educated . . . – are more insipid and dull than words can express, and generally very underbred.'

To outward appearances, however, the first lady of India was coping well with her responsibilities. 'Aunt C. is in rude health and wonderful looks to the detriment of the very few ladies with any pretension to beauty here,' Lord Dunkellin told his mother. 'She does the honors very well and as far as I can make out is immensely liked. I am inclined to believe it, as her manner to everybody is charming and she is always cheery and in good humour.' Canning, on the other hand, was looking thin and 'rather pasty'. He told his nephew that he had been ill. Dunkellin thought he worked too hard and advised him to set aside at least two hours for himself each day. He also tried to encourage his uncle to drink wine, 'but he won't and if pressed complains rather indignantly that he always takes a glass of sherry at lunch'. Mostly he drank soda water with his meals.

Canning's careworn appearance was caused partly by the ongoing problem of Oudh. Its first chief commissioner, Sir James Outram, had returned to Britain on sick leave in April 1856. Canning replaced him with Coverly Jackson, whom Kaye described as 'a civilian from the North-West Provinces, an expert revenue officer, held in high esteem as a man of ability, but more than suspected of some infirmity of temper'. The consequence was that Jackson quarrelled with his financial commissioner, Martin Gubbins, the possessor of an equally contentious nature, while Canning tried to keep the peace. But the real losers during this early stage of British administration were the inhabitants of Oudh.

Shortly after the annexation in February 1856 King Wajid Ali, his senior advisers and family had left Oudh for Calcutta. His intention was to travel on to Britain to petition the Queen for the return of his kingdom. But the journey wearied the obese King, and he decided to remain in the riverside villa the Indian government had provided for him at Garden Reach (the former house of the Chief Justice), while his mother, brother and eldest son led the deputation to London. It was not a success: the first two died en route and were buried in France; the son, having failed in his mission, was forced to borrow half a lakh of rupees from the Company to pay for his return. The Oudh people, meanwhile, were genuinely distressed by the plight of their King:

> Noble and peasant all wept together
> And all the world wept and wailed
> Alas! The chief has bidden adieu to
> His country and gone abroad.

Those most affected by British rule in Oudh were the *taluqdars*, the feudal lords who had never entirely submitted to royal authority. The more powerful rajas among them – men such as Man Singh and Beni Madho – possessed substantial mud forts. No sooner had the British taken control of Oudh than these forts were earmarked for destruction. But the greatest cause of discontent – even worse than the loss of their homes – was the revenue settlement.

As most Indian revenue was derived from the land, the British needed to assess who was responsible for its payment, and in what quantity. The principle they applied was that the settlement was to be made 'with the actual occupants of the soil', in other words with village *zemindars*, or joint owners. But by equating the taxpayer with the proprietor of the land, the British upset the status quo of Oudh's quasi-feudal agrarian society. Many *taluqdars* were dispossessed: Man Singh, the biggest revenue payer in the Faizabad district, lost all but three of his villages; Lal Madho Singh of Amethi was left with three hundred of his eight hundred villages; Hanwant Singh and Beni Madho, who both became leading rebels, forfeited 55 and 44 per cent of their villages respectively.

On top of all this, ex-King Wajid Ali charged British officers with quartering dogs and horses in his Lucknow palaces, breaking into his treasure houses, selling his private property and threatening to stop the allowances paid to his descendants. Jackson was asked by Canning to investigate these charges so that they could be refuted, but he was too preoccupied with fighting his subordinates and failed to do so. Furious, Canning replaced him with the highly experienced Sir Henry Lawrence. It was an inspired choice.

Born in Ceylon in 1806, the fourth son of a British officer from Ulster who had served with Wellesley at Seringapatam, Lawrence was educated at Foyle College in Londonderry, 'a tough, no-nonsense, God-fearing institution that produced boys ideally matched to the East India's needs'. Like two of his elder brothers before him, he was nominated for a cadetship at the East India Company's military academy at Addiscombe by John Huddleston, a director of the Company, who had married his mother's first cousin. There he acquired a reputation for hard work and integrity that would remain with him for the rest of his life. 'When anything mean or shabby roused his ire,' noted a fellow cadet, 'the curl of his lip and the look of scorn he could put was most bitter and intense.' He was a deeply religious young man and cared little for frivolous pleasures. 'What a wretched unprofitable evening!' he once remarked after returning from a ball. 'Not a Christian to speak to. All the women decked out with flowers on their heads, and their bodies half naked.' In 1823 he arrived in India as a second-lieutenant in the Bengal Artillery and quickly came under the influence of the chaplain at the artillery depot at Dum-Dum. He had been there less than a year when war was declared on Burma and he sailed with his battery to Chittagong. He excelled during the successful attack on the fortified heights of Arracan, but the rigours of a long march through a malarious country eventually told on his constitution and he was forced to return to Ulster for two and a half years to recuperate.

He was back in India in 1830 and within two years had passed his examination in Persian, Urdu and Hindi. So impressed were his examiners that they took the unusual step of recommending him to the Commander-in-Chief. His potential was duly noted, and a year later he was appointed an assistant in the Revenue Survey Department. All his subsequent service was away from his regiment – the preferred career option for an ambitious army officer – with either the Revenue Survey or the Political Department. Yet he never forgot his military training and, in the 1840s and early 1850s, wrote a series of anonymous and prescient articles for the *Calcutta Review* that warned of the threat an unreformed Bengal Army posed to British India.

Lawrence's chief achievements, however, were in the Punjab. He was appointed Resident at Lahore in 1846 and knighted on a visit to England two years later. In 1849, following the annexation of the Punjab, he became the senior member of its three-man Board of Administration. Thereafter he did much to restore order and prosperity in the province by drawing up a simple legal code, imposing 'a summary and equitable settlement of the land revenue' and instituting an ambitious public works programme. In direct contrast to the policy practised in Oudh, he avoided alienating the feudal chiefs by upholding their proprietary rights. This stand caused Lawrence to quarrel with his younger brother John, a co-member of the Board of Administration, and ultimately cost him his job. Henry was demoted to the post of Governor-General's Agent in Rajputana, while John became Chief Commissioner of the Punjab. But the chiefs repaid Henry's support when they sided with the British in 1857, thereby enabling John Lawrence to release troops for the reconquest of Delhi.

Much of Lawrence's early reserve had been softened by his marriage in 1837 to his striking, intelligent and down-to-earth cousin Honoria, the daughter of the Revd George Marshall. They had two boys and two girls, the last born in 1850. Four years later Honoria died of rheumatic fever, depriving the children of a mother and Lawrence of a much needed emotional crutch. A contemporary described him: 'Above the middle height, of a spare, gaunt frame, and a worn face bearing upon it the traces of mental toil and bodily suffering, he impressed you, at first sight, rather with a sense of masculine energy and resolution than of any milder and more endearing qualities. But when you came to know him, you saw at once that beneath that rugged exterior there was a heart as gentle as a woman's, and you recognised in his words and in his manner the kindliness of nature, which won the affection of all who came within its reach.' Unfortunately for the British, this remarkable man did not take up his appointment in Oudh until March 1857 when it was too late to make a difference.

3. Professional Grievances

'*Na Iran ne kiaya, na Shah Russ ne, Angrez ko tabah kiya kartoosh ne* ["The mighty English who boast of having vanquished Russia and Persia, have been overthrown in Hindustan by a single cartridge"],' wrote the octogenarian King of Delhi at the height of the mutiny.

Historians have tended to agree. Generations of British schoolchildren have been taught that the mutiny came about because the Indian troops of the Bengal Army refused to bite cartridges greased with cow and pig fat: the former unacceptable to Hindu soldiers and the latter abhorrent to Muslims. But were the prime motives for mutiny really the preservation of caste and religion, or were grievances particular to the Bengal Army more to blame? Did the sepoys act of their own volition, or was there an element of manipulation both inside and outside the military?

In 1857 the biggest single element of the Bengal Army was its seventy-four regiments of regular native infantry.* This branch was also the most homogeneous in terms of its recruits' ethnic and provincial origin, and therefore the most liable to general mutiny. So it proved in 1857 when fifty-four of the seventy-four regiments mutinied or partially mutinied. Most of the rest were either disarmed or disbanded. Just three regiments were considered loyal enough to retain their arms (and one of those was composed of Gurkhas). The Bombay Army, by contrast, experienced partial mutinies in only three out of twenty-nine native infantry regiments; the Madras Army had no mutinies, though elements of one of its fifty-two regiments of native infantry – the 36th – refused to volunteer for service in Bengal in August 1857.

One of the reasons why mutiny was largely confined to the Bengal Army was because of its unique pattern of recruitment. The first companies of sepoys under British command were raised in the Madras Presidency by Major Stringer Lawrence in 1748. But Bengal saw the formation of the first Indian battalion – the famous Lal Paltan, or 'Red Regiment', from the colour of the sepoys' coats – by Robert Clive at Calcutta in January 1757. Its recruits were chosen from the agricultural classes of India because

* The Bengal Native Infantry had an establishment strength of just under 86,000 men.

Company officials had already decided that, as in Britain, they would make the best soldiers.

After Clive's victory at Plassey had established British supremacy in the province, the Company began to recruit from the rural areas of Bengal, particularly around Burhanpur and Dinapore. But not enough recruits of the requisite size were available, causing the recruitment base to be extended westward to the wheat-growing areas of north India. These new infantrymen were clothed by the Company, armed with firelocks rather than matchlocks, commanded by European officers and 'drilled and disciplined according to the methods first tried out in the South in the decades preceding Plassey'. They came to be known by the old name of *purbia* and were simply 'new incarnations of the same old soldiering tradition of Hindustan' in which Rajputs and pseudo-Rajputs from Purab – a term that describes the Oudh, Bihar and Benares region – had travelled far and wide to find employers. Most of these new recruits from outside Bengal were high-caste Hindu peasants: Rajputs, the traditional warrior caste of northern India; or Bhumimars, the military wing of the priestly caste of Brahmans; or Brahmans themselves. This reliance on high-caste recruits was partly because they were the most physically imposing, partly because the Company assumed that these 'traditional high-caste warriors' would prove to be the most loyal, and partly because Warren Hastings, the first Governor-General (1774–85), believed that the high-caste overtones of the army 'provided the requisite legitimacy to Company rule'.

According to the sacred Shastras, Hindu society is divided into four pre-ordained and mutually exclusive *varna* or classes: Brahman (priest), Kshatriya (warrior), Vaishya (farmer and merchant) and Shudra (serf). To marry, take food from or mix with a person from a lower *varna* is to become ritually polluted. The Mleccha (Untouchables) are outside the system and traditionally performed degrading tasks like sweeping and working with leather. Christians and Muslims, by the same token, are also ritually unclean. The caste system developed gradually as Brahmans sought to divide the invading Aryans and the indigenous population into a large number of distinctive groups, or *jati*, based loosely on region and occupation, and each internally bound by rules concerning diet and marriage. Castes were regulated by local committees of senior members who could formulate rules and judge those who infringed them. The ultimate sanction was expulson: a person who was ritually polluted would lose his place both in the cosmic order (his *varna*) and in society (his caste). Castes, however, were not immutable: new castes appeared, rules changed and membership was not necessarily exclusive. One British commentator, writing in the early nineteenth century, observed that Bhumimars (or military Brahmans), like Rajputs, were 'not scrupulous in admitting into their number whatever tribes adopted their manners'. This was mainly because Indian civil society did not begin to take caste distinctions seriously until the nineteenth century. 'The boundaries between individual orders or classes was still open and ambiguous in the early decades of British expansion; the language of caste or castelike relationships still allowed for the great man who could reshape or disregard conventional marriage rules or dietary codes.' As the nineteenth century progressed, caste distinctions became increasingly important to those well-born Indians who were fighting to preserve their economic and social status – in particular, to the self-same impoverished gentry that Stokes identified as the dominant force in the Bengal Army. Enhanced caste status was a means of compensating for their increasingly humble standard of living. But because this Rajput and Brahman preoccupation with caste was a relatively recent phenomenon, caste rules were never as rigid as they might have appeared.

The same could be said about caste consciousness in the Bengal Army. According to the Shastras, the role of warrior was confined to the Kshatriya class. From the earliest times, however, the Hindu armies of India were composed of men from different *varna*. The Rajputs of western India, whose name was later synonymous with Kshatriya, were descendants of non-Aryan invaders. Brahmans turned to soldiering because there was not enough employment for priests. At no time in Indian history was there a caste barrier to men serving as soldiers. All this was to change in the late eighteenth century, as Warren Hastings and his successors strove towards the creation of a high-caste monopoly in the Bengal Army.

As Seema Alavi, a scholar of the Indian military labour market, has noted, 'by providing a forum for sorting out the social tensions hinging around the ritual purity of the rural high caste, the army formalized these tensions and made them more obvious and rigid'. But for the Bengal Army's recruitment policy, she added, 'the evolution of high-caste status in rural north India would have progressed differently'. Part of the process of achieving this high-caste monopoly was the promotion of the sepoys' religious, dietary and travel preferences. In 1779, during the First Maratha War, Hastings sent reinforcements from Bengal to Bombay by the slower overland route because he knew that a sea crossing would offend the religious feelings of the high-caste sepoys (who would, in theory, lose their caste if they travelled over the 'black water'). By the early nineteenth century a complex set of rules governed the Bengal sepoys' diet, manner of preparation and mode of eating. According to Alavi, the sepoys began to eat food 'which had previously been associated exclusively with high caste and ritual purity'. They were therefore able 'to mark out their high-caste status much more effectively than would have been possible in their own villages'. In a sense, the Company was promoting the 'sanskritization of the military'.

The initial method of recruitment was for the commanding officer of a battalion to enlist from the area in which his regiment was stationed. Occasionally recruiting parties were sent out to neighbouring areas when sufficient recruits were not available. But by the beginning of the nineteenth century the preferred method was to encourage sepoys on furlough to bring recruits from their own villages. This was because the serving sepoy 'acted as the guarantor of the respectable antecedents and future loyalty' of the new recruit. One such recruit was Sitaram Pandy, a high-caste Brahman from the Rai Bareilly district of southern Oudh. The son of a small landholder, he was persuaded to join up in 1812 by his maternal uncle who was a jemadar on leave from his battalion of Bengal infantry. Sitaram recalled:

> My uncle was a very handsome man, and of great personal strength. He used of an evening to sit on the seat before our house, and relate the wonders of the world he had seen, and the prosperity of the great Company *Bahadur* he served . . . Nothing else could I think of, day or night. The rank of *Jemadar* I looked on as quite equal to that of Ghazidin Hydar, the King of Oudh himself . . . He had such a splendid necklace of gold beads,* and a curious bright red coat, covered with gold buttons; and, above all, he appeared to have an unlimited supply of gold *mohurs* . . . My uncle had observed how attentive I was to all his stories . . . he repeatedly told me privately that if I wished to be a soldier, he would take me back with him on his return to the regiment.

In 1815, so tight was the stranglehold that high-caste Hindus enjoyed over recruitment to the Bengal infantry that they made up almost four fifths of one newly raised battalion. Yet by 1842, the high-caste proportion of the Bengal Native Infantry as a whole had fallen to around two thirds. This reduction was largely the result of the 'General Order', issued by Lord William Bentinck in 1834, which removed all official objection to the recruitment of 'men belonging to the respectable classes of the native

* Native officers wore one strand of gold beads; sepoys three strands of white beads.

community' (including both *ashraf* Muslims and 'middling' Hindu castes such as Ahirs, Bhats, Kaits and Kumbis). Bentinck and his advisers had come to the conclusion that the tendency of Brahmans and Rajputs to put caste issues before duty was a serious threat to military discipline. The General Order was issued to widen the recruitment base.

Further inroads were made into the high-caste monopoly as a result of the two Sikh wars of the 1840s. After the successful conclusion of the first war, two local regiments of Sikh infantry – the Ferozepore and Ludhiana – were raised to protect the new frontier with the Punjab. The famous Corps of Guides was also formed in 1846 to assist the Sikh rulers of the Punjab in policing the turbulent North-West Frontier with Afghanistan. Following the Second Sikh War (1848–9) and the annexation of the Punjab, five regiments of irregular infantry and five of cavalry were enlisted in the province to pacify and protect the frontier. They were composed of roughly equal proportions of Pathans, Punjabi Muslims, Sikhs and Hindus.

The necessity for an alternative instrument of authority was made clear in 1849 when a number of Bengal infantry regiments reacted angrily to the withdrawal of foreign service batta* in the Punjab. Sir Charles Napier, the Commander-in-Chief, believed that as many as twenty-four regiments (a third of the total) were tainted with a 'mutinous spirit'. His response was to enhance the status of the three irregular Gurkha battalions – the Nasiri, Sirmur and Kemaon that had been raised in the wake of the First Nepal War of 1814–15 – by paying and equipping them as regulars. He also disbanded the most mutinous regiment of native infantry – the 66th – and replaced it with the Nasiri Battalion, henceforth known as the 66th (Gurkha) Native Infantry. 'I resolved to show these *Brahmins* that they cannot control our enlistment,' he informed Lord Dalhousie on 27 February 1850. There was one other significant change in the Bengal Army's recruitment policy before Napier's departure in December 1850: Sikhs and Punjabi Muslims were made eligible for service in regular infantry regiments, though their total number in any one regiment was 'never to exceed 200, nor are more than 100 of them to be Seikhs'.

The high-caste monopoly was to receive a further blow in the summer of 1856 when the new Governor-General, Lord Canning, ordered that all enlistment to the armies of the East India Company would henceforth be for general service. Hitherto it had been the practice in Bengal to ask for

* A monetary allowance for troops serving outside British India, ranging from 2 to 3½ rupees a month.

volunteers when troops were needed for service beyond the sea, in deference to its Brahman and Rajput sepoys. As a result, only the Bengal Artillery and six of the seventy-four regiments of Bengal Native Infantry had been recruited for general service. Now all new recruits would be taken on that basis.

The 'General Service Enlistment Order' has often been cited as a major cause of mutiny. But Lord Canning did not believe that the new regulation was in any way responsible for the disaffection shown by certain Bengal regiments in early 1857. 'Not a murmur has been heard against it anywhere,' he informed Robert Vernon Smith, the President of the Board of Control, 'and the two regiments who have shown the worst spirit, the 2nd and 34th, have enrolled as many recruits monthly under the new system as the old & without any signs of difference between the old sepoys & their new comrades.' Sir Henry Lawrence was of a different opinion. 'The General Service Enlistment Oath is most distasteful,' he told Canning on 1 May 1857, 'keeps many out of the service, and frightens the old [sepoys], who imagine that the oaths of the young recruits affect the whole regiment.'

If the General Service regulation is seen in the context of the previous twenty years, when successive governments had sought to broaden the recruitment base of the Bengal Army, then it is possible to understand why, in Kaye's words, it caused 'the old race of [sepoys]' to leap to the conclusion 'that the English had done with the old Bengal Army, and were about to substitute for it another that would go anywhere and do anything, like coolies and pariahs'. Canning may have insisted that the new legislation had not affected the recruitment pattern of the 34th Native Infantry, but the writing was clearly on the wall. On 21 April 1857, shortly before its disbandment for mutinous conduct, the proportion of high-caste sepoys in the 34th Regiment was just 52.6 per cent. There are no figures available for the Bengal Native Infantry as a whole in 1857; but of those 22,000 or so Bengal sepoys who had not mutinied, deserted or been disbanded by April 1858, around 57 per cent were high caste.

A typical early-nineteenth-century Bengal sepoy has been described as follows: 'He was a Hindu of high caste, a resident of Bihar and Oudh regions and had Hindustani as his mother tongue. He was a person of good physique and . . . hailed from the peasantry and a station which possessed a social heritage. In fact, as like as not, he was of the landed gentry and did not seek escape in the ranks; rather by enlistment he gained status in his society to which he continued to retain his allegiance.' Yet by the outbreak of mutiny, these 'representative' high-caste sepoys were barely in a majority. In 1858 a senior officer testified that the Bengal Native Infantry 'was composed of Mahommedans, Brahmins . . . [Rajputs], Gwallahs, Kaits, Aheers, Jats, and that some few low caste men . . . had crept into corps'. They hailed, he said, from Oudh, North and South Bihar, the Doab of the Ganges and Jumna, Rohilkhand, 'a few' from Bundelkhand and 'a proportion' from the Punjab. Some historians have suggested that mutiny was a means of reversing this trend.

Once in the army, these peasant soldiers were relatively insulated from civilian life. They sent and received letters and went on leave once a year. For the rest of the time they 'lived in cantonments, mostly situated at some distance from the towns and usually alongside the civil lines where the British officers lived'. Lord Elphinstone, the Governor of Bombay (1853–60), was convinced that the mutiny came about because the Bengal sepoys were more influenced by their intra-regimental brotherhood than by their family ties. The 'influence of the family and the village', he wrote, was 'wholly wanting' in the regiment of a high-caste Bengal sepoy. On the other hand, 'any attack real or fancied upon the susceptibilities of one regiment was thus felt by the whole, and when one mutinied, the rest followed'.

As far as the other arms of the Bengal Army were concerned, the Company's recruitment policy was much less provocative. By 1857 the ten regiments of Bengal Light Cavalry were also dominated by high-caste Hindus. If anything, their proportion seems to have increased in the decades prior to the mutiny. But despite being more secure as a group, they would naturally have sympathized with their high-caste kinsmen in the infantry. This might explain why the majority of Bengal cavalry regiments were so willing to follow the lead taken by mutinous sepoys in 1857.

The members of the eighteen regiments of Bengal Irregular Cavalry, however, were overwhelmingly Muslims from the Delhi region and Rohilkhand (and always had been). This lack of kinship with the Bengal sepoys is probably one of the reasons why only ten irregular cavalry regiments mutinied or partially mutinied in 1857 (the lowest proportion of the three native arms of Bengal infantry and cavalry), why three regiments retained their weapons and fought on the side of the British, and why eight regiments were later considered loyal enough to be incorporated into the post-mutiny Bengal Army.

Muslims were also the largest single ethnic group in the Bengal Artillery, but they were not in an absolute majority. Their proportion was just over two fifths, with Hindus of inferior caste and high-caste Hindus sharing the remaining 57 per cent. With such a mixed level of recruitment, it is perhaps logical that artillerymen rarely took the initiative in the mutinies of 1857. Of the nine out of eighteen companies of foot artillery and two out of five troops of horse artillery that mutinied or deserted, only one unit – the 6/8th Foot Artillery – actually took an active part in the plotting. Most of the others were coerced to join the rebels by mutinous sepoys. None is credited with having murdered its European officers, and many actually helped them to escape.

The Madras Army – the next biggest with 51,000 Indian troops – had few ethnic ties to its Bengal counterpart. The Bombay Army – the smallest with 45,000 troops – was a mixture of the two in that a significant proportion of its men was recruited from the same classes and areas that supplied the Bengal Army. Yet only six of its twenty-nine native infantry regiments gave any cause for anxiety during the mutiny. This was chiefly because the Bombay Army was more disciplined, more meritocratic and less inclined to pander to caste than its Bengal counterpart.

All armies have grievances relating to conditions of service, particularly pay, promotion and relations with officers. What sets a colonial force like the Bengal Army apart is that it was a volunteer mercenary force officered by men of a different race and religion. Its loyalty to its paymasters, therefore, was entirely dependent upon the incentives for service outweighing the disincentives. By 1857 this was no longer the case: mainly because the number and seriousness of the sepoys' grievances were increasing, while the Bengal Army's control over its soldiers was weakening.

Of particular irritation to sepoys in all three presidency armies were their European-style uniforms and equipment. In place of his baggy native dress, a sepoy had to wear a tight red coatee and close-fitting dark blue trousers (white in summer). On his head he wore a shako dress cap that weighed from two and a half to three pounds with its brass rim, scales and badge, 'a heavy unwieldy *thing*, more like an inverted fire-bucket'. Sitaram Pandy, who joined a Bengal regiment in 1812, recalled: 'At first I found it very disagreeable wearing the red coat; although this was open in front, it was very tight under the arms. The Shako was very heavy and hurt my head, but of course it was very smart. I grew accustomed to this after a time, but I always found it a great relief when I could wear my own loose dress.' Describing other elements of a sepoy's equipment, one Madras officer wrote:

On his back is slung a great knapsack, fastened to his body by means of leather-straps going round his shoulders and his chest, tight enough to cut him in two . . . Across his chest he has two broad belts, held together by a brass plate passing on either side of him. To one of these is fastened his bayonet, and to the other his pouch or [cartridge-box], large enough to contain some sixty rounds of ball ammunition, the whole sufficent to break a poor man's back. Round his waist passes another belt, intended to keep the others together, but tight enough to cut his very intestines out of him.

Upon his feet the sepoy wore 'a pair of clumsy things called sandals', while constricting his neck was a stiff black leather stock. But most irksome of all was his unwieldy musket known as the 'Brown Bess', weighing more than ten pounds and with an effective range of 300 yards, though only accurate up to 100. Sitaram found his musket 'very heavy, and for a long time my shoulder ached when carrying it'. The Madras officer noted that it was 'heavy enough for a roast-beef-fed Englishman to carry, but too much for the delicately-formed light body and slender limbs of the sepoy lad'. Though Bengal sepoys were generally bigger than their southern counterparts, they still struggled to carry and fire this large weapon.*

There were many calls for the reform of the Indian soldiers' dress and equipment in the years prior to the mutiny. Ironically, though, the only pre-1857 reform of dress or equipment was the replacement of the sepoys' smooth-bore muskets with the lighter Enfield rifle (8 lb 14 oz) whose greased cartridge was the ostensible cause of mutiny.

Indian troops, particularly Bengal sepoys, also griped about the nature of their peacetime duties: these included a morning parade for cleaning arms and accoutrements, an evening parade for orders, guard duties, a brigade exercise once a week and regimental exercises four times a week. The situation became particularly acute during the first half of the nineteenth century because 'campaigns were waged at less and less frequent intervals

* The dress and accoutrements of the light cavalry were also styled on the British Army, though their quilted tunics – short-waisted and extremely tight – were French grey rather than the dark blue or scarlet of the British light cavalry. They too wore the awkward shako (made even more top-heavy by its horse-hair plume), choking leather stock, clumpy jackboots and close-fitting leather or cloth breeches. But the most unsuitable pieces of their equipment were the heavy, slightly curved light dragoon sword and the tall, European-style saddle. The former was a clumsy weapon that could neither cut nor thrust to any real effect; the latter pushed the rider so high above the horse that he was forced to ride by balance alone. The irregular cavalry, by contrast, wore turbans, long loose *alkalahs*, and baggy *pyjamas* with either puttees or long boots. They were armed with the lightly curved and extremely sharp Indian sword known as the *tulwar* and seated on low, local pattern saddles.

and the native soldiery was restricted to duties which it considered to be monotonous and tiring'. For while annexations reduced the chances of active service, they increased the need for policing new areas. Such duties – which included escorting treasure and guarding prisoners – were increasingly undertaken by sepoys.

Poor housing was another cause of soldier dissatisfaction. When a Bengal sepoy arrived at a new station, he had to buy or build for himself a hut on a plot of land 30 feet by 10 feet. Each infantry regiment contained ten lines of such huts, one per company, with a street between each. The huts belonging to sepoys and NCOs were about 10 feet long, 8 feet wide and 7 feet high, with mud walls, thatched roofs and a small enclosed front yard; native officers had two or three huts around a tiny courtyard, fenced in by a low mud wall. Unlike their comrades in the Madras and Bombay Armies, who had their families with them, the Bengal sepoys lived alone with minimal possessions: usually a *charpoy*, *dhurrie* and a few cooking pots.

There was much criticism of this system of housing. *The Times* described the huts as 'relics of barbarism', adding that they were crowded, leaked in the rainy season (July to September) and were sited on land that was often swampy because of the lack of subsoil drainage. Florence Nightingale, while criticizing the poor state of European barracks in India, commented: 'But all these conditions paled before what was endured by native troops. The native troops had no barracks, no lavatories, no baths, no kitchens, no sanitary supervision of any kind. They used the ground round them as privies without hindrance and left cleansing to the rains. The squalor of their huts was indescribable, bodies of animals and of human beings were left unburied for days; the water they drank was stinking. Consequently, though temperate, the Bengal native soldiers were decimated by disease.'

An even more serious grievance was low pay. There was a strong financial incentive to serve the East India Company in the late eighteenth and early nineteenth centuries because it offered regular pay, pensions and other economic benefits like foreign service batta – perks largely unheard of in the armies of Indian states. Yet the basic pay for ordinary sepoys – 7 rupees, or 14 shillings, a month – was the same in 1857 as it had been at the turn of the century (and would remain so until it was raised to 9 rupees in 1895). Given that the cost of living in the form of grain prices 'nearly doubled between 1796 and 1852' – with the wages of civilian workers such as ploughmen and agricultural labourers rising proportionately – the sepoy's pay fell in real terms by almost 50 per cent during the first half of the nineteenth century.

By contrast, the domestic servants of European officers could earn between 4 and 20 rupees a month, field labourers between 2 and 6 rupees, carpenters between 5 and 10 rupees and blacksmiths between 5 and 20 rupees. A private in one of the East India Company's European regiments, meanwhile, received a basic 10 rupees, 3 annas and 2 pice a month (with supplements for long service and duty beyond a certain distance from the presidency capital), while a private in the British Army was paid a shilling a day – or roughly 15 rupees a month – with an extra penny a day for every five years of good conduct.

The relative decline of pay for Indian troops was partially offset by the introduction, in 1837, of long-service pay, which increased a sepoy's monthly wage by 1 rupee after sixteen years' service and 2 rupees after twenty. It was, however, dependent upon good service and would be forfeited by those who had been convicted by a court martial 'of some serious offence' or whose names had been twice entered in the regimental defaulter book during the two years prior to qualification. Furthermore it was a flat rate that took no account of rank.

New pension regulations were also introduced in 1837. They reduced the number of years that a sepoy had to serve to qualify for a pension from twenty to fifteen, and increased the basic rate from 3 rupees a month to 4. The minimum higher rate of 7 rupees a month – which applied to those sepoys who had served forty years, those disabled by wounds and the families of those killed in action – was unaltered. Both lower and higher rates of pension were on a sliding scale depending on rank: a subedar or subedar-major, for example, still received 25 rupees after fifteen years' service and 40 rupees a month after forty years. To qualify for either rate of pension, moreover, an Indian soldier had to be pronounced unfit for duty by a board of surgeons – which was easier said than done. 'There is,' wrote the Judge Advocate-General of the Bengal Army in 1857, 'no chance whatever' of a Bengal soldier 'being granted a pension as long as he can put one foot before another.'

In short, Bengal sepoys found it hard to make ends meet. They were charged for a number of items of dress and equipment, including three undress tunics, three pairs of white linen trousers, one pair of coloured trousers, one set of beads, one knapsack and one greatcoat. As of 1828, they were given a jacket and a pair of woollen pantaloons every two years free of charge, while deductions for the other items were not to exceed 5 rupees per annum. But they often did. And there were other expenses, such as paying for the services of a washerman, barber and sweeper, and defraying the cost of transporting their baggage when on the march (a sum that generally came to more than the marching batta of 1½ rupees a month).

Above all, sepoys had to pay for their own food. The diet of high-caste Hindu soldiers was strictly vegetarian: *atta*, rice, dal, ghee, salt, sugar and some vegetables. They were not supposed to consume fish, meat, pulao, curry or alcohol. Tubular vegetables like potatoes, aubergines, radishes, leeks and onions were also avoided. To maintain their ritual purity the high-caste sepoys cooked their own food, ate alone and even spread cow-dung on their place of repast – as laid down in the Shastras. The type of food available at the permanent station bazaars and temporary camp bazaars mirrored these preferences, as did the rations provided by government for overseas expeditions. The problem was not availability but cost: it has been estimated that Bengal sepoys spent between 3 and 5 rupees a month on food alone. Those who sent the most money back to their families – often as much as three quarters of their total pay – were forced to live on less. As a result, even lower-caste Hindu and Muslim sepoys could rarely afford to eat anything other than chapattis and cooked dal. If they ate curry, it was usually made from the cheapest vegetable. Was it any wonder, asked one authority, that the Bengal sepoy 'found himself in straitened circumstances, lived on the cheapest kind of food, and at times even starved so as to fulfil his various social obligations'.

Of the other regular Bengal troops, only the cavalry and the horse artillery received more pay than the infantry, with a trooper receiving a basic 9 rupees a month. Irregular cavalrymen were paid 20 rupees a month, but they had to pay for and maintain their own horses and equipment. In an essay published in 1844, Henry Lawrence pointed out that Bengal irregulars were mostly well-born Muslims with 'expensive habits'. He added:

> Every man . . . had not only to purchase his horse and equipments, but to pay one hundred and fifty rupees or thereabouts to the estate or family of the man whose decease or invaliding caused the vacancy. Such donation of course throws the recruit at once into the moneylender's hands, and often leaves him for life a debtor. If the man . . . has not the cash to purchase a horse, he rides one belonging to a Native officer or to some privileged person, and becomes what is called a bargeer – the soldier receiving only seven or eight rupees a month, and the owner of the horse the balance of the twenty.

Lawrence suggested redeeming all debts and only admitting those recruits who could bring their own horse. Other experienced officers – like John

Jacob, Sir Charles Napier and Lord Gough, Commander-in-Chief of India from 1843 to 1849 – recommended a pay increase of at least 5 rupees a month. Yet nothing was done, and the irregular regiments continued to accumulate debts. The 10th Irregular Cavalry, for example, 'owed nearly £10,000' to its regimental banker by 1857. The irregular sowars, therefore, had a very strong financial incentive to mutiny that, in certain instances in 1857, may have overriden the fact that only a small proportion of them had ethnic links to the mutinous native infantry.

The reduction in the real value of pay suffered by all Indian troops in the decades prior to the mutiny was partially offset by successful military campaigns and the accumulation of war booty. Plunder had long been a welcome supplement to the ordinary pay of Indian mercenaries; the East India Company had even legitimized the practice in the form of prize money. But by the 1850s the internal conquest of India was complete and the occasional action against the tribes of the Sonthal and North-West Frontier did not provide the same opportunity to loot as a conventional campaign. Henceforth the only way for native troops to augment their diminishing pay was to serve in wars outside India. Under the circumstances, an uprising against their colonial masters – and a return to the traditional cycle of war – would have appealed to many.

But money was not the only advantage to be gained from a successful rebellion. Power and prestige were also on offer: incentives that were virtually non-existent for the East India Company's Indian troops. Even the most senior Indian officer was subordinate to a junior European officer, nor could he give orders to a European NCO. Writing in the *Calcutta Review* in 1844, Henry Lawrence pointed out the danger of this situation 'in a land . . . that above all others, has been accustomed to see military merits rewarded, and to witness the successive rise of families from the lowest conditions'. The army of the East India Company, he added, 'offered no inducement to superior intellects, or more stirring spirits' who left in disgust. There were, as a result, many men like General Dhokul Singh, who had been a drill naik in the Bengal Army before transferring to the Sikh Army. While nine out of ten were no doubt satisfied with the possibility of reaching the rank of subedar-major by the age of sixty, noted Lawrence, it was for the tenth – 'the bold and daring spirit that disdains to live for ever in subordinate place' – that a greater stimulus was necessary. Lawrence recommended that Indian soldiers be given command of irregular regiments, grants of land and pensions to the second and third generations. Sir Charles Napier agreed. To allow a veteran subedar to 'be commanded by a fair-faced beardless Ensign, just arrived from England', he wrote, was the 'imposition of conquerors' and 'one which the Native gentlemen feel deeply and silently resent'. Equality between natives and Europeans was being ceded in the civil service, he added, 'so it must be for the military'.

Yet no reforms had been instituted by the time Lawrence wrote to Canning on 2 May 1857, warning him that 'until we treat Natives, and especially Native soldiers, as having much the same feelings, the same ambition, the same perception of ability and imbecility as ourselves, we shall never be safe'. The accuracy of Lawrence's prediction was proved during the coming months: in the majority of mutinous regiments, the Indian officers were either behind the plot to rise or they quickly assumed control once their European counterparts had been driven off or killed. Some commanded rebel brigades and even armies. For a short time, at least, the frustrated ambitions of these experienced soldiers were realized.*

The inadequacy of career prospects for Indian soldiers was particularly acute in the Bengal Army because its system of promotion was based upon length of service rather than merit. In Bombay and Madras the opposite was true: recruits to the two smaller presidency armies could become junior officers (jemadars) in under fifteen years, whereas Bengal troops took twice as long to attain that rank. Few Bengal jemadars were under fifty, while most subedars were over sixty. Sitaram Pandy, for example, served forty-eight years of 'hard wear and tear' in the Bengal Native Infantry before being promoted to subedar. 'I was an old man of sixty-five years of age,' he recalled, 'and had attained the highest rank to be gained in the Native Army, but I would have been much better fitted for this position thirty years earlier.' The subedar-major of the 7th Bengal Light Cavalry, which partially mutinied at Lucknow on 31 May 1857, was seventy years old. Three years earlier John Jacob had warned that the unavoidable outcome of promotion by seniority was the 'ultimate ruin of the army' because it failed to reward 'talent, skill, energy, high principle, and soldierlike pride'.

The seniority system of promotion had three potentially disastrous consequences: it deprived the commanding officer of an important power to reward, thereby reducing his authority over his men; it frustrated ambitious and talented sepoys who had to wait in line for promotion; and it produced old, inefficient and often bitter Indian officers who had no worthwhile occupation. These last two groups may hold the key to the mutiny. Lawrence believed that, on average, three out of every hundred sepoys were 'danger-

* See Appendix Three.

ously discontented' in 1856 because they felt 'they have that in them which elsewhere would raise them to distinction.' It is highly probable that such men were the instigators of the mutinies in 1857, and that they used the religious and caste implications of the cartridge question to persuade the rank and file to join them in rebellion.

Yet the vast majority of rebel regiments were led by their old Indian officers. The implications are twofold: first, that the mutinous regiments retained their cohesiveness and former command structure, and that they did so because their rebellion was simply an attempt to find an employer who could offer them more attractive incentives to serve; second, that a significant number of Indian officers were so alienated by service under the British that they were prepared to put both their lives and their future pensions at risk. Twelve years before the mutiny Sir Henry Hardinge applauded the Bengal policy of 'preferring inefficiency & seniority, to activity and selection' because aged and inactive Indian officers were less likely to lead an armed insurrection than their younger and more zealous counterparts. He could not have been more wrong.

4. 'Go to hell – don't bother me!'

The popular image of an East India Company army officer is of a gentleman, the younger son of a small country squire or vicar who could not afford to set him up at home. Often as not he had Scots or Irish blood and was 'well-educated, hardy and ambitious'. He tended to be a man of firm religious convictions, and went out to India not only to make his fame and fortune but because he believed it to be his Christian duty.

There were men like this: John Nicholson, of well-born Ulster Protestant stock, who made his name as a political officer on the North-West Frontier before becoming, at thirty-four, the youngest brigadier-general in the Bengal Army; William Hodson, the Cambridge-educated younger son of the Archdeacon of Stafford, who developed into a first-rate intelligence officer and commanded the finest irregular cavalry in India; and 'Joe' Lumsden, the scion of a Scottish artillery officer, who pacified the unruly Hazara region with Sikh troops at the age of twenty-five, shortly before founding the Corps of Guides. But these men were exceptional. By the mid nineteenth century the typical Indian Army officer was of modest social origins, ill-educated and only interested in India as a means of bettering himself. 'People do not come here to live, to enjoy life,' commented one French traveller in 1830. 'They come – and this is true of all classes of society – in order to earn the wherewithal to enjoy themselves elsewhere.'

It is a common misconception that the East India Company's white officers were drawn from the same social élite – the aristocracy, gentry and rich upper middle classes – that dominated the British Army's officer corps. In truth they came 'from the "pseudo gentry", from the genteel poor and from the sons of East India Company servants who were effectively barred, by their lack of connexions and lack of cash, from access to the traditional areas of gentlemanly employment – government service, the established church, medicine, the armed forces of the Crown and the English bar'. These impecunious middle-class parents could not have afforded the high purchase price of a commission in the British Army; cadetships in the East India Company's army, on the other hand, were in the gift of the Court of Directors, who were only too happy to assist their less prosperous colleagues.

Given that most cadets were relatively poor, it follows that their chief motive for entering the Company's service was because it was well paid and 'offered an accessible avenue to social status and financial security'. A newly commissioned Company ensign, for example, received a minimum of 182 rupees (£18) a month; this was more than double the amount paid to his British Army counterpart, who was expected to supplement it with a private income. Extra-regimental appointments were even better paid: an officer serving as an adjutant in a Bengal Irregular Cavalry regiment, for instance, was given an allowance of 170 rupees on top of his normal pay. As a result, most officers could hardly wait to abandon regular regimental duty for these lucrative detached posts. 'Financial considerations produced a distaste for the ordinary round of sepoy management and training,' wrote one commentator, 'and conspired to create a positive dislike of the sepoy and of all things Indian, a development pregnant with danger.'

It did not help that the standard of training and education that Company officers received before joining their regiments was generally poor. In 1809 a military seminary was established at Addiscombe, near Croydon; but even Addiscombe officers were inadequately taught. The curriculum was dominated by mathematics. Of the other subjects, civil and military drawing were 'trifles of more use in the salon than on the battlefield', fortification based on Marshal Vauban, the celebrated seventeenth-century engineer, 'was largely obsolete and irrelevant to Indian conditions', chemistry and classics were too narrow in their focus, and the study of Hindustani was 'perfunctory'. Addiscombe produced many high achievers; but they seem to have succeeded in spite of, rather than because of, the seminary. 'My education consisted in kicks,' recalled Sir Henry Lawrence. 'I was never taught anything – no, not even at Addiscombe.'

Direct-entry cadets, who accounted for two thirds of all new officers, were more poorly educated still. Until 1851 – when the Company introduced exams for non-Addiscombe cadets – there was no academic bar to becoming an officer. The vast majority of these cadets were educated at cheap proprietory schools, well known for their 'slavish devotion to the classics and frequent recourse to the birch'. They had, as a result, received only 'a bare minimum of education' by the time they reached India.

Company officers were characterized by inadequate learning and an unseemly desire to abandon their regiments for better-paid detached appointments. This was a particular problem in the Bengal Presidency because the large expansion of its territory in the first half of the nineteenth century meant an increasing demand for civil administrators, political officers, staff officers, surveyors, engineers and commandants of local and irregular corps. In 1835 the total number of East India Company officers on detached employ was five hundred and thirty-two; by 1852 the figure had almost doubled with the Bengal Army supplying an average of six officers per regiment, the Bombay Army five, and the Madras Army three and a half. At the outset of the mutiny the total figure had climbed to 1,237 with the Bengal Army still the worst affected. If officers on sick leave and furlough are also taken into account, most Bengal infantry regiments had fewer than half their twenty-four officers present in May 1857. Even more alarming was the fact that the majority of absentees were field officers (majors and above) and captains. 'Deduct commanding officer, adjutant and quartermaster, and all ensigns under two years' service,' noted Lieutenant-General Sir Patrick Grant, the temporary Commander-in-Chief of India, 'and there remains 5¾ officers per regiment for company duty.' In a regiment of ten companies, this meant just over one qualified officer for every two companies.

Such high levels of absenteeism were bound to have a detrimental effect on regimental morale and discipline, particularly in the Bengal Army. Referring to the period before the mutiny, Sitaram Pandy recalled that 'any clever officer was always taken away from his regiment for some appointment' and that when he returned many years later 'he knew very little about the men'. One of the reasons that Sir Charles Napier gave for first tendering his resignation in April 1850 was because officers were withdrawn for detached duty 'by the civil authorities, without any distinct recommendation through the military authorities'. Officers, as a result, 'looked at their regiments merely as stepping stones to lucrative civil appointments' that were not dependent upon 'professional character'. He added: 'Thus the mainspring of the Army was relaxed. The officers saw that the posts of emolument were not granted for military duties, and military duty became a painful task.'

Napier's fears were confirmed by Montagu Hall who, in 1852, did duty as an ensign with a 'distinguished' Bengal Native Infantry regiment. 'I was awfully disappointed with what I saw of native Regiments,' recalled Hall, 'the whole thing seemed to be a sham and a delusion . . . The senior officers were all either absent on Staff employ, leave, or married. We went most mornings to be drilled under the European Sergeant-Major, but parades of the regiment, there seemed none. The Adjutant did all the work and the chief idea of the officers seemed how to get away from regimental duty.' Major John Jacob was even more dismissive. 'The "REFUSE" only remain,' he wrote in 1854. 'All proper feeling is thus totally destroyed between the native soldier and his European superior.' This was not because there were too few officers, but rather because too many of those left were mediocre and uninterested in their duty or their men. Jacob believed that 'one active, energetic, right-feeling, and right-thinking English gentleman can, even when alone, infuse an excellent spirit into thousands of these Eastern soldiers'. His solution, therefore, was to appoint only three European officers, 'carefully selected and entrusted with full powers', to each regiment.

But nothing had changed by the outbreak of the mutiny. In a memorandum to Lord Canning of 29 June 1857 General Sir Patrick Grant identified a 'want of officers in whom the sepoy could confide' as one of the key factors that had given rise to a feeling of 'dissatisfaction and distrust' among the Bengal troops long before their religious fears were played upon by conspirators. This, in turn, was caused by the fact that so few officers were present with their regiments. 'Further, these officers are discontented,' wrote Grant, 'only looking forward to leaving their regiments for some more pleasant employment, so that they perform, and unwillingly, the bare outline of their duty, and never, as a general rule, mix or converse with their men; but, on the contrary, too often refuse to listen to their complaints, at the best telling them to go to the adjutant, and not unfrequently, "Go to hell – don't bother me!"'

Part of the problem was boredom. A regimental officer in a medium-sized station in upper India had very few duties and even fewer distractions, particularly during the hot season. Most were unmarried and lived in rows of detached brick bungalows in the European section of the military cantonment, itself a mile or two from the main civil settlement. Even the junior officers were looked after by a host of servants who generally lived with their families in whitewashed huts at the back of their employer's large compound. They could number anything up to fifteen, including a bearer, cook, *syce*, sweeper, *bhisti*, laundryman, tailor, gardener, several *punkah-wallahs* and a *khidmatgar*, or butler, who, in the case of an officer stationed at Dum-Dum, 'did credit to [his master's] selection, arranging for ice, fresh fish and other luxuries to be brought in daily by a coolie from Calcutta'.

A typical day for a regimental officer began with an early ride before the short morning parade. He then bathed, read the papers and had breakfast, a substantial meal that included anything from eggs to beef chops, fried fish to curried fowl. The rest of the morning was taken up with reading and writing. From noon to two, calls were made on local society, both military and civil, followed by tiffin (light lunch) and a siesta. Some spent the afternoon reading or playing billiards. In the larger stations an officer would go for an early evening walk or ride in the company of the garrison's ladies.

He then had dinner, the main meal of the day, in his own bungalow, the regimental mess or as the guest of a European family. 'Smoking, drinking, and singing are kept up till a very late hour,' wrote one officer who regularly dined with his brother officers, 'when the whole adjourn to a hot supper, composed of devilled bones, mulligatawny, and hot stews, beer and other drinks being matters of course.'

Apart from the occasional stint on guard duty and the odd parade, a regimental officer had very little to do. He therefore spent most of his time with his fellow officers. But an educated young subaltern like William Hodson found the limitations of garrison life extremely dull. From Subathu, in the foothills of the Himalayas, he wrote:

> Ladies' society there is none: there are a few who call themselves such, but with very little reason, save that they are not *men*. There is much in India to interest one, much worthy of all one's efforts, many most important duties and influences, but nothing to call forth one's affections or any of the softer and more delightful feelings of youth and life. In fact, one's life is a harsh reality; nothing is left to the imagination; no amenities; no poetry; no music; nothing elegant; nothing refined. There is nothing left but to be *up and doing* . . .

Most regimental officers had neither Hodson's culture nor his positive frame of mind. Ensign Allen Johnson of the 5th Bengal Native Infantry was typical. 'My disgraceful laziness is appalling,' reads his diary entry for 18 July 1850. 'I have hardly opened a book or written a line for the last ten days. In fact have done absolutely nothing but lounge and saunter about, now taking up a book and gazing at it with lack luster [*sic*] eye or kicking about restlessly on my bed. My only fixed idea having been yearnings for home and a detestation of natives and native things.'

The relationship between officers and Indian soldiers had not always been so lacking in mutual respect. Recalling his early years in a sepoy regiment, Sitaram Pandy wrote: 'The *sahibs* often used to give *nautches* [entertainment by erotic dancers] for the regiment, and they attended all the men's games. They also took us with them when they went out hunting, or at least those of us who wanted to go. Nowadays they seldom attend *nautches* because the Padre *sahibs* have told them it is wrong.' Sitaram also had fond memories of his company commander – nicknamed the 'Wrestler' because he used to join the men in the wrestling arena – entertaining a constant stream of men at his house. Some went to further their chances of promotion, but most 'because we liked the *sahib* who always treated us as if we were his children'.

It helped that many of the officers had Indian mistresses (*bibis*) and even wives, which naturally facilitated their grasp of Hindustani and the ease with which they could communicate with their men. But the practice began to die out in the 1820s and 1830s as more European wives and female relatives of civil and military officers came to live in India, and it became socially unacceptable to keep a *bibi* or marry a Eurasian. 'The root of the problem,' wrote the author of a book on British women in India, 'was that women represented home.' She added:

They were sent out as portable little packets of morality, to comfort their men, keep the blood-line clean, and remind them of their mothers. Those fitted to the part sought security in an extremely strange land in creating for themselves a hidebound home from home involving all the parochial strictures of English provincial life. Pianos and plush-draped dining tables and dismal prints of *The Monarch of the Glen* would be shipped over to furnish their parlours; there would be amateur theatricals, musical soirées, and elaborate great dinners to be endured . . . There was snobbery and scandal: life might almost have been bearable, in fact, were it not for the stupid heat and natives.

With Europeans increasingly keeping their own society, contact between officers and men was reduced to a minimum. 'I have lived to see great changes in the *sahibs*' attitude towards us,' wrote Sitaram. 'I know that many officers nowadays only speak to their men when obliged to do so, and they show that the business is irksome and try to get rid of the *sepoys* as quickly as possible. One *sahib* told us that he never knew what to say to us. The *sahibs* always knew what to say, and how to say it, when I was a young soldier.' It is surely no coincidence that the only two traditionally recruited Bengal Native Infantry regiments to remain loyal and keep their weapons in 1857 were commanded by men with Indian family ties: Major Henry Milne of the 21st Native Infantry was married to the Eurasian granddaughter of Colonel James Skinner; Major William Hampton of the 31st Native Infantry had two daughters by an Indian mistress.

In 1844, in an attempt to improve relations between officers and men, the Indian government ordered that no subaltern could command a troop or company until he had passed a colloquial examination in the Hindustani language. For officers who had joined since 1837, the appointments of adjutant and interpreter were already dependent upon possession of the basic qualification in written and spoken Hindustani. Yet, according to one correspondent to the *United Service Magazine*, the number of Indian Army officers who were qualified as interpreters in two languages – Hindustani and Persian – was becoming 'small by degrees and beautifully less'. The writer put this down to the fact that young officers had begun to realize that, as far as their career prospects were concerned, patronage was far more important than a knowledge of native languages: 'the cadet comes out, studies hard, and then finds that without interest all his efforts and money have been thrown away. His brother cadets seeing this, are warned in time, and consequently resolve to pitch Hindustani books and moonshees [native language teachers] to the devil.'

Sir Charles Napier, during his time as Commander-in-Chief, dealt with a number of cases in which sepoys were court-martialled for insolence when they were simply trying to make their officer understand what they were saying. The root of the problem, according to Napier, was that officers were 'now more numerous than formerly, and associate apart'. He added: 'All old officers of name in the Company's service . . . have complained that the younger race of Europeans keep aloof from Native officers; showing thereby want of foresight, and casting away, as of no value, the strong attachment these natives are so susceptible of forming for them. How different this from the spirit which actuated old men of Indian renown!' Other commentators believed intimacy had been replaced by contempt. 'The sepoy is esteemed an inferior creature,' wrote a contemporary. 'He is sworn at. He is treated roughly. He is spoken of as a "nigger". He is addressed as a "suar" or pig, an epithet most opprobrious to a respectable native, especially a Mussalman . . . The old men are less guilty as they sober down. But the younger men seem to regard it as an excellent joke.'

Relations between Bengal officers and troops continued to deteriorate in the years leading up to the mutiny. In 1856 Sir Henry Lawrence recommended the abolition of Indian officers on the grounds that it would force European officers to look into the 'interior economy' of their regiments of companies. 'Seldom is anything of the kind done at present,' he wrote. 'So long as all is smooth and quiet on the surface, few inquiries are made. All may be rotten below; the jog-trot is followed – a mine may be ready to be sprung, for all that nine-tenths of the officers would know.'

Two other factors that contributed to the worsening relations between officers and men were the generally poor quality of regimental commanding officers and the fact that many of them were unfamiliar to their men. Both were the result of the same system of promotion by seniority that applied to the sepoys. All officers became colonels if they served for long enough, regardless of ability. But promotion was so slow, particularly in the Bengal

Army, that officers did not reach the upper ranks until a relatively late age. In 1857 the average age of Bengal divisional, brigade and regimental commanders was sixty-six, fifty-five and fifty years respectively. The exceptions in Bengal were commandants of irregular cavalry regiments: they were more sprightly than their regular counterparts – the average was a little under forty years old – because they had been appointed on the basis of selection rather than seniority.

As well as being old and inefficient, many colonels were virtual strangers to their men. This was because all officers, on reaching the rank of lieutenant-colonel, were removed from their regimental lists to a branch list for the whole army. Once on that general list, an officer would only be appointed to command his original regiment if the major were either absent or the most junior in the branch. Otherwise he would take command of the regiment with the most junior commander; which is why so many regiments were commanded by men who had spent the majority of their service elsewhere. Sitaram Pandy stressed the importance of continuity when he noted that new commanding officers were never welcome. 'Among us there is a great dislike for new ways,' he added. 'One *sahib* upsets what the other has done, and we do not know what to do because what we have been taught one day is wrong the next.'

An even more important reason for the breakdown of officer–sepoy relations was the gradual weakening of the regimental commanding officer's power to punish as more authority was concentrated at army headquarters in the decades prior to the mutiny. This move towards a more centralized military system was part of a wider process of government reform in India that was being driven by the political philosophy of Utilitarianism: a belief that human legislators were required to 'assist men to avoid harmful acts by artificially weighting such acts with the pain of punishment'. Utilitarianism retained, therefore, an immense faith in the power of law and government to shape conduct and transform character. With regard to India, its chief proponents were men like James Mill, his son John Stuart Mill and Edward Strachey, all senior officials at the London headquarters of the East India Company in Leadenhall Street, and Lord William Bentinck, Governor-General of India from 1827 to 1835. At a farewell dinner in London, attended by a number of leading Utilitarians including Jeremy Bentham, Bentinck is said to have remarked to James Mill: 'I am going to British India, but . . . it is you that will be Governor-General.'

The Utilitarian passion for uniformity, mechanistic administration and legislative regulation resulted in, among other things, an erosion of the commanding officer's power to impose summary punishments. For most of the first three decades of the nineteenth century Bengal commanding officers were able to impose a wide range of punishments without recourse to a court martial – including dismissal, corporal punishment with a rattan cane, reduction of NCOs to the ranks, refusing furlough and awarding extra drill and duty. But these powers were gradually reduced by the introduction of official regulations. By 1845, when the first Articles of War were enacted for all three presidency armies, summary punishments were restricted to fifteen days' extra drill, seven days' confinement in the quarter-guard, removal from staff situations or acting appointments, piling shot and cleaning accoutrements. The effect this reduction of power could have on the discipline of a regiment is illustrated by Lieutenant-Colonel Drought who, after three years' furlough, resumed command of the 60th Bengal Native Infantry in January 1857. He wrote:

I saw very great laxity in the ranks, worse even than when I got command of the regiment in 1849. The authority of the commanding officer had become less than mine was as a subaltern, as regards punishment drill to non-commissioned officers, owing to army standing orders being set aside by circulars, and by station orders issued by officers perfectly ignorant of the proper method of keeping sepoys in subjection, and thereby interfering with the commanding officer's authority, and rendering him a mere cipher in the eyes of his men . . .

As well as the curtailment of their powers of summary punishment, Bengal colonels also experienced considerable interference with their authority to convene and confirm courts martial. At the same time the range of sentences these courts martial could impose was reduced. In 1835, for example, Lord William Bentinck abolished corporal punishment throughout the native army. Bentinck's rationale was that flogging deterred 'young men of respectable connections' from joining up and produced 'a baneful influence upon the pride, the manly feeling and the character of the whole service'. Its abolition was therefore a practical manifestation of the Utilitarian theory that human character could be transformed by enlightened legislation.

Most of the Indian military regarded the abolition as a mistake, particularly those British Army officers who occupied the senior commands. Their colleagues were in the process of seeing off a sustained campaign by Radical MPs to abolish flogging in the British Army, though the maximum number of lashes was limited to fifty in 1846. No supporter of corporal punishment was more strident than the Duke of Wellington. He believed, as did many in India, that army discipline depended upon a regimental commanding officer having the ultimate sanction of flogging to back up his power to impose summary punishments. Without it, he informed the adjutant-general, 'We might as well pretend to extinguish the lights in our houses or theatres by extinguishers made of paper as to maintain the discipline of the army.'

After much lobbying, corporal punishment was reintroduced by the Governor-General, Lord Hardinge (himself a British Army officer), in 1845. But a separate resolution confined its application to serious military crimes like mutiny, insubordination and drunkenness on duty; it could not be used to punish 'disgraceful' offences such as stealing, embezzlement and the self-infliction of wounds. Moreover, officers were advised to 'inflict corporal punishment as seldom as possible, commuting it for other punishment in all cases where it can be done with safety to the discipline of the army'. As a result of these restrictions, flogging was used sparingly in all three presidencies, particularly Bengal. So sparingly, in fact, that sepoys did not regard it as a deterrent. One Bengal colonel was frequently told by his native officers: 'As long as [the lash] was hanging over that bad man's head he was all right, but now they do not care for the commanding officer or anyone else.'

Having effectively lost the sanction of corporal punishment, Bengal commanding officers were further undermined by the frequency with which sepoys attempted to overturn the sentences of courts martial by petitioning the commander-in-chief. In theory, no Indian soldier could petition his commander-in-chief except through the medium of his commanding officer. Yet in the Bengal Army petitions were regularly sent from sepoys directly to the commander-in-chief without censure; and, to add insult to injury, these appeals were often upheld. According to Brigadier Coke, many Bengal commanding officers had had men who had been dismissed as unfit, or by sentence of court martial, returned to their regiments after they had presented petitions at headquarters. The general feeling engendered among sepoys by these and other similar acts (such as the lack of 'discretion to promote, save by seniority') was, said Coke, 'that their commanding officer was helpless to punish or reward'. This gradual erosion of a commanding officer's power was, in his opinion, 'one of the principal causes of bringing about the mutiny'.

By 1857 the indiscipline of the Bengal Army was notorious. In February of that year, before the first news of the cartridge question had reached Britain, the *United Service Gazette* described the Bengal sepoy as a 'lackadaisical, discontented idler, prompt to seize excuses for refusing to do his duty, and absolutely rendering the presence of Europeans necessary . . . to keep him to his allegiance'. On 31 May, with the mutiny in full swing, the Magistrate of Benares blamed the 'fake and hollow' system of military government. He added: 'The system of centralization has proved to be the ruin of the native army. All power is centred in the highest authority. Regimental officers have no authority, they are mere puppets, and the sepoys cannot look up to such weak and powerless men with respect. In days of yore the commanding officer was the [lord] of every sepoy, he could punish neglect & reward [diligence]. He was therefore respected and beloved. *Now* he cannot promote a sepoy to be a naik without the sanction of proper authority.'

There was also a belief that the laxity of discipline in the Bengal Army had inflated the sepoys' sense of importance, and that confrontation had been inevitable. 'The [Bengal sepoys] are confident of their power to dictate terms to their masters,' declared the English-language *Friend of India* on 7 May 1857. Giving evidence to the post-mutiny Peel Commission, one Bengal general remarked upon the 'leniency with which various acts of misconduct, all more or less bordering on mutiny, were on several occasions dealt with', in consequence of which the Bengal sepoys, 'who under their own system would have been ruled with a rod of iron, lost the awe necessary to the preservation of discipline in a large army'.

The mutiny has been characterized as a sepoy backlash against the excessive brutality of white officers. The truth could not have been more different. Bengal sepoys had many professional grievances, not least their poor relations with their European officers who were both neglectful and often appallingly disrespectful towards them. But harsh discipline was not one of them. The officers lacked the power to be brutal and, if anything, were too lenient. Discipline suffered and the sepoys interpreted this as a sign of weakness. 'The principal cause of the rebellion,' recorded Sitaram Pandy, 'was the feeling of power that the *sepoys* had, and the little control the *sahibs* were allowed to exert over them. Naturally, they assumed from this the *Sirkar* must be afraid of them, whereas it only trusted them too well.'

5. The Conspiracy

By 1857 the Bengal Army was ripe for mutiny. Its infantry regiments, in particular, contained a significant proportion of malcontents who were seeking an end to British rule. They were, by definition, ambitious men drawn from a complete cross-section of army ranks. Their aim was to replace their British employers with a native government that would, at the very least, provide greater career opportunities and increased pay.

A similar network of conspirators had, according to Sir Charles Napier, coordinated the Punjab mutinies of 1849/50. He explained:

> In all mutinies, some men more daring than others are allowed to take the lead while the more wary prepare to profit when the time suits; a few men in a few corps, a few corps in an army begin; if successful they are joined by their more calculating, and by their more timid comrades . . . To what extent [the conspiracy] was secretly carried is unknown; but the four sepoys condemned [at Wazirabad] went from company to company administering unlawful oaths to insist on higher pay from a Government of a different religion, and a different race! Many regiments were of the same mind, and it may be assumed that each had, at least, four agitators similarly employed.

Similar cabals were present in most Bengal native regiments in 1857. During his twelve years as adjutant of the 17th Native Infantry, Major Frederick Burroughs had established a 'thorough system of espionage' that enabled him to know exactly what was going on in the regiment. But when he tried to resurrect the system on returning to the 17th as commanding officer in early 1857, he found 'no one willing or possessing sufficient courage' to give him any information. This, and other circumstances, caused him to conclude that 'the plot for revolt was not recent, although probably known to a select few only in each Regiment'.

It was not just disgruntled sepoys who were plotting to topple the British. Indian civilians were also involved, particularly members of princely families who had lost out during Dalhousie's time as Governor-General: men like Nana Govind Dhondu Pant, better known as Nana Sahib,* the adopted son

* 'Nana' being a term of endearment meaning 'few in years', for he was his parents' second and reputedly favourite son.

of Baji Rao II, the last Peshwa of the Maratha Confederacy. Exiled from Poona after his defeat in the Third Maratha War, Baji Rao had arrived at Bithur on the Ganges in February 1819, accompanied by thousands of bedraggled retainers. He provided for them out of his Company pension and the residue of a vast fortune that had once topped 50 million rupees. He also used the money to build a sprawling palace known as Saturday House on the banks of the Ganges, filled with carpets, tapestries, European chandeliers and 'twenty-five chiming clocks'. But despite his eleven wives and countless dancing girls, Baji Rao managed to produce only two sons and both died in infancy. So in 1827, to ensure a smooth passage to the afterlife, he adopted two infant brothers with impeccable Maratha pedigrees: Nana Sahib, two, and his brother, Bala Rao, one. Their father, Mahadev Rao, a learned Deccani Brahman who had travelled the 700 miles from his home in the Western Ghats to join the former Peshwa's court at Bithur, had the same caste name as his royal master; their mother was a sister of one of Baji Rao's wives.

Baji Rao died, at the age of seventy-six, in 1851. According to the terms of his will, the Nana was left 'the throne of the Peshwa', his 'Dominions, Wealth . . . family possessions, Treasure' and all his 'real and personal property'. Yet Baji Rao had long since lost his kingdom, and the British had made it clear that his huge annual pension would not be extended to his heir – adopted or not. After his death the British commissioner at Bithur informed the Nana that he would also forfeit Baji Rao's seal, his honorific title of maharaja and even his annual allocation of blank cartridges. That left just his Bithur estate and a huge personal fortune, including an annual income of 80,000 rupees from public securities.

The Nana made repeated efforts to recover Baji Rao's titles and pension. He petitioned the Governor-General, the Court of Directors and the Board of Control – all to no avail. He even enlisted a British barrister, John Lang, to plead his case. Lang had made his reputation by successfully suing the East India Company on behalf of Joti Prasad, an Agra banker who had lent the British almost half a million pounds to fight wars in Afghanistan and Gwalior. Not content with reneging on its debt, the Company had charged Prasad with criminal behaviour. Lang secured both his acquittal and the return of his money – an unlikely feat that was acknowledged when a large Indian crowd carried the tubby lawyer shoulder high from the Agra courthouse. He was still basking in the success of this case when he was invited to Bithur to discuss the Nana's suit.

Lang's recollection of their meeting gives a fascinating glimpse of the Nana's eccentric court. On arriving at Saturday House, Lang was conducted to a suite of guest rooms where he was offered 'every kind of European drink' and even a beef dinner. But mindful of the Nana's brahmanical sensibilities, he opted for rice and vegetables and ate alone at the former mess table of a British cavalry regiment. The soup was served from a trifle dish, the pudding in a soup-plate and the claret in a 'richly cut champagne glass'. A bedroom towel served as a napkin. After the meal, Lang was taken through a maze of dark passages to the royal apartment, where he found the Nana reclining on a Turkish carpet, surrounded by a sword, a hookah and a nosegay. Lang recalled a portly, sallow, expressionless thirty-year-old of medium height with an aquiline nose and large eyes. As a youth he had affected a small upturned moustache, but now his face and head were clean-shaven but for a small area covered by his skullcap. One Cawnpore surgeon, who treated the Nana for an infected toe, described him as 'an excessively uninteresting person' who might have passed for a bazaar trader had it not been for his tight *kimkhob* (gold-embroidered) blouse, necklace of large pearls and small, jewel-encrusted Maratha turban.

The Nana began by complimenting Lang on winning the Prasad case ('The whole world is ringing with the praise of your illustrious name'). He then offered the barrister a puff of his hookah before getting down to business. A *munshi* was summoned to read aloud the detailed petition that had been sent to Lord Dalhousie. Lang, fighting off sleep, expressed astonishment that 'so much injustice can possibly exist'. Eventually he was escorted back to his room and massaged to sleep by four burly attendants. The following morning, during a carriage trip to Cawnpore, the Nana repeated his gripe with the government and Lang promised to take it up with Dalhousie in person; if that did not succeed, he would, on returning to England, seek an audience with Queen Victoria herself. Lang, of course, knew that the Nana's case was hopeless and had no intention of approaching the Queen. He later described the Nana as 'not a man of ability, nor a fool', a man not dissimilar to most Indian princes. 'During my rambles in India,' he wrote, 'I have been the guest of some scores of rajahs, great and small, and I never knew one who had not a grievance.'

At Saturday House, Lang also came across Tatya Tope, or 'Bennie' as he was called then, the son of Baji Rao's dispenser of charities. Lang wrote: 'He was not a servant exactly – at all events not a menial servant – but one of those numerous "hangers-on" of Nana Sahib who repaid by flattery the favours they received in the shape of board, lodging and presents.' Lang added:

He was a man of about the middle height – say five feet eight – rather slightly made, but very erect. He was far from good-looking. The forehead was low, the nose rather broad at the nostrils, and his teeth irregular and discoloured. His eyes were expressive and full of cunning, like those of most Asiatics; but he did not strike me as a man of eminent ability. There were a few men amongst Nana Sahib's flatterers who were really clever men, but they were not Mahrattas; and my impression is that Bennie was not a Mahratta, but a member of some obscure family in the Upper Provinces of India, under British rule. Like the rest of the tribe of flatterers who surrounded Nana Sahib, Bennie was obsequious and cringing to every European who visited Bithoor. This demeanour, of course, was not the offspring of respect, but prompted rather by the impression that it might tend to some advantage.

The most noteworthy non-Maratha member of the Nana's court was a handsome and intelligent young Muslim of Pathan descent named Azimullah Khan. He and his mother had arrived in Cawnpore as starving refugees during the famine of 1837 and were fortunate enough to be employed as household servants by Revd Carshore, founder of the Cawnpore mission of the Society for the Propagation of the Gospel (SPG), and later by Revd Perkins, Carshore's successor. Perkins encouraged the quick-witted Azimullah to attend the Free School, where he became fluent in both English and French. But Azimullah would not submit to his mentor's crude attempts to convert him to Christianity, and it was during this period, wrote one historian, that his 'gratitude toward his British benefactors degenerated into what would later manifest itself as a genocidal loathing'. The same writer has suggested that the 'pretty' young Muslim may have been the victim of an unwelcome sexual advance from a 'tortured' Englishman. If so, it did not prevent him from working for Europeans – first as a *khidmatgar*, then as a *munshi* – until he was sacked by Brigadier Ashburnham in 1850 'under an accusation of bribery and corruption'. Fortunately he was well acquainted with the former Peshwa's adopted sons, having taught them English at the SPG's academy at Bithur in the 1840s, and after Baji Rao's death he became one of the Nana's most trusted advisers.

As such he was sent to London with another Muslim, Mahomed Ali Khan, to plead the Nana's case. The mission failed, but Azimullah made a lasting impression on English society with his Western clothes, impeccable manners and formidable intellect. At East India House, the Company's neo-classical headquarters in Leadenhall Street, he met the great Utilitarian philosopher John Stuart Mill, then the Company's liaison officer with the Indian princely states, and through him Lady Duff Gordon, the 33-year-old wife of the Prime Minister's cousin. A beautiful eccentric who smoked cheroots and whose dress was memorably described as 'half-way between [that of] a German student and an English waterman', Duff Gordon was also a brilliant linguist and translator whose salon was patronized by the great writers and thinkers of her day. It was there that Azimullah was introduced to, among others, Dickens, Tennyson, Thackeray, Carlyle and Macaulay. His interest in Duff Gordon, however, was not purely intellectual and many suspected them of being lovers. He certainly cut a swathe through a number of other ladies' bedrooms, including that of a 'Miss A' of Brighton who addressed him as 'Mon cher Goody' and promised never to reveal the secrets of their passionate liaison. He later tried – in his role as royal studmaster – to lure Lady Duff Gordon, Miss A and others to Bithur to meet Nana Sahib. But without success – or regret. Privately he had little respect for Western women: unless they were restrained as they were in the East, he commented, it was inevitable that 'like moths in the candlelight, they will fly and get burned'.

During his stay in England, Azimullah spent tens of thousands of the Nana's pounds hiring lawyers, bribing clerks and entertaining officials. But the Court of Directors would not budge in their determination to withhold all of Baji Rao's pension and titles from his adopted son. Azimullah and Mahomed Ali finally accepted defeat and set off for India in the summer of 1855. En route they learnt of a British setback in the Crimea and decided to see for themselves. At Constantinople, Azimullah came across William Howard Russell of *The Times*, who was on the first assignment of a long and illustrious career as a war correspondent. Russell remembered the Muslim envoy as a 'handsome, slim young man, of dark-olive complexion, dressed in an Oriental costume', who told him that he was anxious to see Sebastopol and 'those great Roostums, the Russians, who have beaten French and English together'. But it was Azimullah's boasting of his success in London society, and the tone of his remarks, that caused Russell to 'regard him with suspicion, mingled, I confess, with dislike'.

They met again a few weeks later in the Crimea where, according to Russell, Azimullah discovered a British Army in a depressed state and formed 'a very unfavourable opinion of its *morale* and *physique* in comparison with that of the French'. In India, the bazaars of the great military stations were soon buzzing with the news that Britain had suffered a catastrophic reverse in the Crimea. '[The] news was always fabricated to show that the *Sirkar* was usually defeated, and that the Russians had destroyed all the English soldiers and sunk all their warships,' recalled Sitaram Pandy. 'This idea was fostered by interested parties with the result that when the Mutiny broke out, most Indians believed that the *Sirkar* had no other troops than those which were already in India.' The sepoys' belief in British invincibility had already been shaken by the ignominious retreat from Kabul in 1842. The reverses of the Sikh and Crimean Wars were seen as further proof that British military power was in irreversible decline.

Mahomed Ali later claimed that, having returned to Constantinople, Azimullah was approached by 'certain real or pretended Russian agents' who promised substantial material support if Azimullah could stir up a rebellion in India. 'It was then,' he recalled, 'that I and Azimullah formed the resolution of attempting to overthrow the Company's Government.' Once back in India, Azimullah appears to have convinced his royal master that the British would never provide redress for his grievances; a successful uprising, on the other hand, would give him the opportunity to re-establish the Peshwa's rule. In pursuit of this aim, wrote Russell, the Nana and Azimullah spent much time in Lucknow and subsequently the 'worthy couple, on the pretence of a pilgrimage to the hills – a Hindoo and a Mussulman joined in a holy excursion – visited the Military stations all along the main trunk road, and went as far as [Ambala]'.

Corroboration of the Nana's scheming is provided by an Indian emissary called Sitaram Bawa. In a statement given to the Judicial Commissioner of Mysore in January 1858, Sitaram claimed that the Nana was sounding out a host of Indian princes – including the rulers and former rulers of Gwalior, Assam, Jaipur, Jodhpur, Jammu, Baroda, Hyderabad, Kolapur, Satara and Indore – as early as the autumn of 1855. At first nobody replied to his letters; but after the annexation of Oudh the 'answers began to pour in' from both Hindus and Muslims. Among the Nana's first adherents, said Sitaram, was Raja Man Singh, the Oudh *taluqdar* who had lost all but three of his villages in the revenue settlement of 1856. Other dispossessed *taluqdars* then joined the conspiracy, as did the leading citizens of Lucknow and Golab Singh, the Maharaja of Jammu and Kashmir. An agreement was also made with the King of Delhi. The financial assistance provided by many of these influential plotters was used to seduce serving sepoys and disbanded members of the King of Oudh's army alike. 'The military classes were enticed by a promise of restoring the old times of licence,' commented Sitaram Bawa, 'and they all prefer that to a regular form of Government.'

Kaye, for one, was convinced by this and other evidence. 'There is nothing in my mind more clearly substantiated,' he wrote, 'than the complicity of the Nana Sahib in wide-spread intrigues before the outbreak of the mutiny. The concurrent testimony of witnesses examined in parts of the country widely distant from each other takes this story altogether out of the regions of the conjectural.' Kaye particularly referred to machinations between the Nana and the family of the late Raja of Satara, whose south Maratha state had 'lapsed' to the Bombay Presidency in 1848. He also links the Nana's plot to the attempt by adherents of the King of Oudh to tamper with the troops in the Presidency Division in early 1857.

Russell's claim that Nana Sahib and Azimullah both visited military stations as far as Ambala is not quite accurate. Kaye believed that the Nana, who rarely ventured beyond the limits of Bithur, made three journeys in the early months of 1857: to Kalpi, Delhi and finally to Lucknow. Other evidence proves that Azimullah travelled further. On 30 December 1856 Nana Sahib wrote from Bithur to Azimullah, who was en route to Delhi. He began by requesting the addresses of Lady Gordon and a Mrs Massy, so that he could write to them through the medium of Mrs Todd, the wife of his English tutor. He then asked Azimullah how long he proposed 'remaining at Delhi and on what day it is your intention to start hence on your further progress towards the north'? The answer was soon, because in January 1857 Lieutenant Edward Martineau bumped into Azimullah at the *dâk*-bungalow in Ambala, shortly after taking up his appointment as instructor of the musketry depot. Martineau had first made Azimullah's acquaintance the previous October on the overland journey from Suez to Aden, and had been struck by the bitterness with which he spoke of Lord Dalhousie's recent annexation of Nagpur. On meeting him again at Ambala, Martineau gained the impression that he was on a 'tour of inspection to feel the temper of the Mahratta, Rajpoot, & Seik Chiefs on his route from Bombay to enable him to report progress to his master'. A 'skilful agent' such as Azimullah, wrote Martineau, 'was doubtless feeling his way, & was able from his reports to work on the mind of the Nana, already incensed by the stoppage of the stipend accorded to the Peishwa, & to induce him shortly after his return to visit Lucknow, there doubtless to confer with Alli Nuckee Khan [the former Prime Minister of Oudh] & other servants of the Ex King'.

But for the conspiracy to break out into open rebellion, the disgruntled elements of the Bengal Army needed an issue controversial enough to win over their fellow sepoys and so tip their general feelings of discontent – over British arrogance, over pay, over poor career prospects – into a readiness to take up arms. It arrived in the form of a new rifle cartridge.

6. The Greased Cartridges

Where the British Army led, its Indian counterpart followed. So in 1840, a year after British troops had switched from flintlock to percussion small-arms, the soldiers of the East India Company did the same.* Over the next decade or so nearly 460,000 percussion muskets, carbines and pistols were dispatched to India. The procurement of these smooth-bore guns ceased in 1851, however, when the British government decided to replace its percussion musket with the revolutionary Minié rifle.

Rifles had been used by British and Company troops for skirmishing and sniping since the turn of the century. But their accuracy had been more than offset by a slow rate of fire, a seemingly inevitable consequence of the need for the ball or bullet to have a loose fit during loading and a tight fit in the rifling grooves when fired. This conundrum was solved in the 1840s by two French officers – Delvigne and Minié – who developed an elongated bullet with a hollow base that expanded on ignition. As it was Minié who had perfected the design, it became known by his name alone. Yet the Minié rifle was never generally issued to the British Army because its ·702 bore was considered too large; the Enfield rifle, modelled along similar lines but with a ·577 bore, was selected instead.

In 1854 the East India Company was promised 30,000 new Enfields by the British government. But supply problems and the outbreak of the Crimean War prevented the first batch of 1,500 rifles from reaching the Bengal Presidency until the spring of 1856. Earmarked for Bengal troops, they were eventually assigned to a British regiment, the 60th Rifles, on the grounds that their existing weapons were 'unserviceable and should be replaced immediately'. A total of 12,000 Enfields had arrived in Bengal by the outbreak of mutiny in May 1857. But only one regiment, the 60th, had been issued with them; the rest were in magazines and musketry depots.

It was not the rifles themselves but their bullets that were to prove so controversial. Cartridges for most muzzle-loading firearms of the period took the form of a tube of paper that contained a ball and enough powder

* The muzzle-loading muskets retained the same 'Brown Bess' design that had been in use since the eighteenth century, but with their flints replaced by percussion caps.

for a single shot. The approved method of loading was to bite the top off the cartridge and then pour the powder down the barrel. The rest of the cartridge, including the ball, was then forced down the barrel with a ramrod. This type of ammunition was used by both the existing percussion musket and the Enfield rifle. The crucial difference between the two was that the Enfield's grooved bore required the bottom two thirds of its cartridge to be greased to facilitate loading.

In 1853, when the first Enfield cartridges were sent to India to test their reaction to the climate, General Sir William Gomm, the Commander-in-Chief of India (1850–56), had warned that 'unless it be known that the grease employed in these cartridges is not of a nature to offend or interfere with the prejudices of caste, it will be expedient not to issue them for test to Native corps'. But the Military Board chose to ignore Gomm's counsel, and the ammunition was tested over a period of some months by being carried in the pouches of sepoy guards at various garrisons. No objection to these cartridges was raised by either the sepoys themselves or the committees of European officers set up to report on them. The tests confirmed that the grease could stand up to the Indian climate, and the consignment was returned to England in 1855. A year later, following hard on the heels of the first batch of Enfield rifles, was a shipment of greased cartridges and bullet moulds. Thereafter the Bengal Army's Ordnance Department began to manufacture its own cartridges at its Fort William, Meerut and Dum-Dum arsenals. The grease used for the rifle patch – a mixture of wax and oil – was discounted because its lubricating properties disappeared when cartridges were bundled. Instead the same combination preferred by the Royal Woolwich Arsenal – five parts tallow, five parts stearine (purified fatty acids) and one part wax – was used. But the department made the fatal, and unforgivable, error of not specifying what type of tallow was to be used.

In early January 1857 Bengal Native Infantry regiments were ordered to send detachments to one of three musketry depots – Dum-Dum near Calcutta, Ambala in the Cis-Sutlej and Sialkot in the Punjab – for instruction in the care and handling of the new weapon. Not a cartridge had been issued or a practice shot fired by the time a rumour began to circulate among the sepoys at the Dum-Dum depot that the grease was offensive to both Hindus and Muslims, and that this was part of a systematic plot by government to convert all Indians to Christianity. The origin of the rumour was a conversation on 22 January between a Brahman sepoy and a low-caste *khalasi* who worked in the Dum-Dum magazine. The *khalasi* is said to have asked the sepoy if he could have a drink from his *lota*. The sepoy refused: 'I have scoured my *lota*, you will defile it by your touch.' 'You think much of your caste,' replied the *khalasi*, 'but wait a little, the *Sahib-logue* will make you bite cartridges soaked in cow and pork fat, and then where will your caste be?'

A report of the incident was submitted to the station commander on 23 January. It included details of a parade held the evening before at which two thirds of the Indian troops at the depot, including all the Indian officers, had stated their objection to the grease and requested wax and oil to be used instead. Both documents were then forwarded to Major-General John Hearsey, commanding the Presidency Division, whose headquarters were at Barrackpore, 16 miles north of Calcutta. 'There could hardly, in such a crisis, have been a better man in command,' wrote Kaye. Hearsey was very much an old-style Indian officer: he had two Eurasian sons by his first wife, Harriet – the daughter of his own Eurasian half-brother and a native lady – and spoke fluent Hindustani; he also had a well-deserved reputation for gallantry and tact, having quelled, almost single-handedly, a mutinous regiment at Wazirabad in 1849. Despite his age, sixty-four, he was still remarkably active and saw at once the potential consequences of the grease rumour. The *khalasi*'s claim was 'no doubt totally groundless', he told his superiors, but so 'suspiciously disposed' were the sepoys that the only remedy was to allow them to grease the cartridges themselves with materials from the bazaar.

The Indian government, ever sensitive to issues of religion and caste, was swift to concur: on 27 January Colonel Richard Birch, the Military Secretary, ordered that all cartridges at the depots of instruction were to be issued free from grease and that the sepoys were to be allowed 'to apply, with their own hands, whatever mixture for the purpose they may prefer'. At the same time Colonel Augustus Abbott, the Inspector-General of Ordnance, made inquiries as to the exact composition of the cartridge grease. On 29 January he reported to Birch that, in line with the instructions received from the Court of Directors, 'a mixture of tallow and bees' wax' had been used and that 'no extraordinary precaution' appeared to have been taken to ensure 'the absence of any objectionable fat'. In a separate letter that day Abbott informed Birch that strict orders would be given for the exclusive use of sheep or goat fat if it was decided that some form of tallow was necessary.

While it has never been confirmed that the cartridge grease contained beef or pork fat, the circumstantial evidence is compelling. In a letter of 7 February Canning himself stated that the grease grievance had 'turned out to be well founded'. In March the officer in charge of the Fort William arsenal testified that no one had bothered to check what type of animal fat was used. At the same tribunal Abbott admitted that the tallow may well 'have contained the fat of cows or other animals'. At this stage, therefore, the Dum-Dum sepoys appear to have had a genuine grievance – though not one of them had been, or ever would be, issued with a greased cartridge. Moreover, no greased cartridges were ever made at the Dum-Dum magazine – its operatives were still learning the complicated process of manufacture when the rumour began – nor were any greased cartridges ever sent from Fort William to the Dum-Dum depot. Which raises the question: how did the Dum-Dum *khalasi* discover the 'truth' about the cartridge grease in the first place?

The government, meanwhile, had moved swiftly to correct its earlier error. But no sooner had it authorized its troops to apply their own grease than sepoys at Barrackpore were voicing fears that the cartridge paper contained objectionable fat. These suspicions first arose when ungreased Enfield cartridges and the paper used for making them were shown to a parade of the 2nd Native Infantry at Barrackpore on 4 February. At a subsequent court of inquiry, four days later, witness after witness stated his belief that the cartridge paper was offensive. This objection to the paper was groundless: it contained no grease and certainly no tallow. Suspicions had arisen partly because the English manufactured paper was slightly thicker than that used to make musket cartridges. But the lack of a genuine grievance prompts the speculation that some guiding hand – within or without the regiments – was trying to keep the cartridge controversy alive by switching attention from the grease (which was no longer an issue) to the paper. Canning suspected such a conspiracy and told Vernon Smith that there was a mutinous spirit in the 2nd Native Infantry, or at least in part of it, that had 'not been roused by the cartridges alone if at all'.

The first definite signs of a conspiracy were revealed on 26 January 1857 when senior Indian officers of the 34th Native Infantry made an abortive attempt to capture key installations in Calcutta with the assistance of troops en route to Chittagong. All four infantry regiments at Barrackpore – the 2nd, 34th, 47th and 70th – were later implicated in the plot, as were elements of the Calcutta Native Militia and senior advisers to Wajid Ali, the ex-King of Oudh, who was still living at the villa in Garden Reach. The conspirators had attempted to rally support by citing the 'objectionable cartridges' and offering a pay increase of 3 rupees a month. But the plan came unstuck when a jemadar of the 34th, commanding the Treasury Guard, refused to cooperate.

The conspiracy was not confined to the Calcutta area. On 28 January General Hearsey reported to government the simultaneous burning of European property at Barrackpore and the railhead of Raniganj, where separate wings of the 2nd Native Infantry were stationed. It was later alleged by Mainodin Hassan Khan, one of the leading rebels at Delhi, that the burning of the Raniganj telegraph office was a preconcerted signal for mutiny, and that those in the know would respond with similar acts. Mainodin also claimed that the central cause of the mutiny was the annexation of Oudh in 1856, and that it was no coincidence that two of the three regiments in Lucknow at that time – the 19th and 34th – were at the centre of the conspiracy. Mainodin explained:

> Both these regiments were full of bitterness . . . and from them letters were written to other Purbeah regiments. The 34th took the lead. These letters reminded every regiment of the ancient dynasties of Hindustan; pointed out that the annexation of Oude had been followed by the disbandment of the Oude army, for the second time since the connection of the English with Oude; and showed that their place was being filled by the enlistment of Punjabis and Sikhs, and the formation of a Punjab army. The very bread had been torn out of the mouths of men who knew no other profession than that of the sword. The letters went on to say that further annexations might be expected, with little or no use for the native army. Thus was it pressed upon the Sepoys that they must rebel to reseat the ancient kings on their thrones, and drive the trespassers away. The welfare of the soldier caste required this; the honour of their chiefs was at stake.

A large proportion of Bengal sepoys came from Oudh. The annexation was not only a blow to their national pride, it also brought an end to the privilege enjoyed by all Company soldiers from Oudh of being able to prosecute their legal cases and petitions through the British Resident. So abused had this privilege become – with some sepoys receiving up to ten months' leave for the sole purpose of prosecuting their claims – that in 1853 the maximum period of leave was set at that which 'would enable the applicant to travel to Lucknow, remain there for 10 days, and then return (unless the Resident certified that the man's continued presence was necessary)'. Yet the privilege remained until annexation, and there is no doubt that its loss was keenly felt. In a letter to Canning of 1 May 1857 Sir Henry Lawrence mentioned that he had received a number of letters attributing the 'present bad feeling *not* to the cartridge or any specific question, but to a pretty general dissatisfaction at many recent acts of Government which have been skilfully played upon by incendiaries'. Lawrence gave the example of an Oudh sowar in the Bombay cavalry who was asked if he liked annexation. 'No,' the sowar replied. 'I used to be a great man when I went home; the best in the village rose as I approached; now the lowest puff their pipes in my face.'

Sitaram Pandy later admitted that the 'seizing of Oudh filled the minds of the *sepoys* with distrust and led them to plot against the Government'. He added: 'Agents of the Nawab [King] of Oudh and also of the King of Delhi were sent all over India to discover the temper of the army. They worked upon the feelings of the *sepoys*, telling them how treacherously the foreigners had behaved towards their king. They invented ten thousand lies and promises to persuade the soldiers to mutiny and turn against their masters.' The involvement in this plot of Wajid Ali, the ex-King of Oudh, or at least members of his entourage, is highly likely. The commanding officer of the 17th Native Infantry later claimed that it, the 19th and 34th regiments all offered their services to the King of Oudh at the time of annexation in early 1856.

From the start senior figures in the Bengal Presidency suspected outside interference. In a letter of 28 January Major-General Hearsey blamed 'Brahmins or agents of the religious Hindu party in Calcutta (I believe it is called the *Dhurma Subha*)' for the rumour that the cartridges were part of a government plot to convert natives to Christianity. Canning himself was not entirely convinced. 'I cannot say that [Hearsey's] evidence is very conclusive,' he told Vernon Smith on 22 February, 'but if there has been any attempt to seduce them with a view to embarrassing the Government it is much more likely to have come from the Oude courtiers than the Brahmins as was first suspected.' Within a month Canning's belief in an external conspiracy had hardened. He informed Vernon Smith that while many sepoys, even the majority, were sincere in their alarm for their religion, these fears had been put into their heads by civilians, though once such feelings had taken root they were 'disseminated from one corps to another without aid from without'. He was convinced that the prime movers had no ostensible connection with the army, though whether they were political malcontents such as the King of Oudh's followers or religious alarmists he could not say. But despite the emphasis on religion, he added, the 'moving purpose may be purely political' and there were some small incidents to point the finger at the 'Oude herd'. Hearsey, who prided himself on his close relations with Indian troops, was of a similar opinion. 'Rajah Maun Sing and other [senior advisers] of the ex-King of Oude,' he informed the government on 5 April, 'have been bribing some evil-minded & traiterous

Hindoos of the 19th and 34th N.I. to seize the first opportunity to incite disturbance. This cartridge business came opportunely for them & they seized it even before the cartridges were made for distribution . . . In short, the sepoys have never even seen a *greased cartridge*.'

In a letter to the government of 11 February Hearsey likened the disaffection at Barrackpore to a 'mine ready for explosion'. The minds of the sepoys, he added, had 'been misled by some designing scoundrels who have managed to make them believe *that their religious prejudices, their caste*, is to be interfered with by Government'. That some of the scoundrels were probably soldiers themselves does not seem to have occurred to Hearsey at this juncture. These ringleaders were almost certainly behind the move to spread the net of disaffection. On 12 February an Indian doctor overheard a sepoy of the 2nd Native Infantry telling a comrade that a *cossid* had been sent to the 19th Native Infantry at Berhampore and to the three infantry regiments at Dinapore, 'informing them that ten or twelve of us have raised a disturbance, and we want you to support us'.

The small cantonment town of Berhampore was situated on the left bank of the Hooghly River, 120 miles upstream from Calcutta. In February 1857 Berhampore was garrisoned by elements of two Indian regiments: the 19th Native Infantry and a wing of the 11th Irregular Cavalry. The 19th contained an unusually high proportion of Brahmans – around 40 per cent – who had been especially disaffected since the annexation of Oudh. This bad feeling was not helped by the presence of an unfamiliar commanding officer, Lieutenant-Colonel William Mitchell, forty-nine, who had been with the regiment for less than eighteen months.

Matters came to a head in late February. On the 25th, an escort party of the 34th Native Infantry arrived at Berhampore and camped beside the 19th's lines. The following day the sepoys of the 19th refused to accept copper caps for a blank firing exercise because they had been led to believe that the cartridge paper contained objectionable grease. Mitchell reminded them that not only were the blank cartridges the same ones they had been using for years, but that they had been made up in the regimental magazine by sepoys of another regiment. Any sepoy who refused to accept the cartridges at the parade the following morning, he warned, would be court-martialled. The sepoys' response, shortly before midnight, was to break into their bells-of-arms and seize their muskets. Roused from his bed, Mitchell ordered a detachment of the 11th irregulars and two post-guns to cover the mutinous sepoys while he and his officers went to speak to them.

He found the men 'in undress formed in line and shouting'. Some were calling out: 'Do not come on, the men will fire.' At which point he ordered the guns to load with grape and called in his Indian officers. When they had assembled, he asked them the meaning of the disturbance:

The native officers made all kinds of excuses, begging that I would not be violent with the men. I then addressed the men and asked them what they had to complain of. I told them that I had explained to the native officers some days ago that if grease was required to be used for the new cartridges I would apply to the [General] to allow the pay-havildars of companies to make up what was required . . . the men said they were never told so by the native officer.

Mitchell then told the Indian officers to order their men to lay down their arms. They replied that the men would not do so in the presence of guns and cavalry. Finally, at three in the morning, Mitchell lost his nerve and withdrew the covering force. Only then did the men lodge their weapons and return to their lines.

During the subsequent court of inquiry, the 19th's Indian officers, NCOs and sepoys sent a petition to General Hearsey to explain their behaviour. They stated that the rumour about the new cartridges containing objectionable fat had been in circulation for 'two months and more', and that they were very much afraid for their religion. Their minds had been temporarily put at ease by Lieutenant-Colonel Mitchell's announcement that grease for the new cartridges would be made up in front of the sepoys by the company pay-havildars. But their fears returned when they inspected the blank cartridges at their bells-of-arms on the afternoon of 26 February. 'We perceived them to be of two kinds,' they wrote, 'and one sort appeared to be different from that formerly served out. Hence we doubted whether these might not be the cartridges which had arrived from Calcutta, as we had made none ourselves, and were convinced that they were greased.' It was for this reason, they claimed, that they refused to accept the firing caps. Mitchell had angrily responded by threatening to take the regiment to Burma, where they would all die of hardship, if they did not accept the cartridges. This outburst had convinced them that the cartridges were greased. They had seized their arms in fear of their lives amid shouts that they were about to be attacked by Europeans, the cavalry and the guns.

The sepoys' objections, it seems, had switched from the grease on the Enfield cartridge to the paper used for the Enfield cartridge, and finally to the paper on the old musket cartridge. The reference to two different kinds of blank cartridge is explained by the fact that, since the mid 1850s, some of the paper used for musket ammunition had been produced by the Serampore mills near Barrackpore. Its paper was of a slightly darker shade than the familiar English product of John Dickinson & Co. Yet it contained no grease, nor was grease ever applied to cartridges for smooth-bore muskets. There is, therefore, no proper rational explanation for the behaviour of the 19th regiment on the night of 26 February beyond a complete breakdown of trust between the sepoys and their European officers. Lieutenant-Colonel Mitchell had assured them that the cartridges were of the old type and contained no grease, and yet they preferred to believe the wild rumour that the Indian government was planning their forcible conversion to Christianity. It is highly probable that certain members of the regiment were playing upon the fears of their comrades to incite mutiny.

On 11 March Canning told Vernon Smith that there was much evidence to show that the 19th regiment had been 'seduced from without', particularly by the sending of emissaries from Barrackpore and the arrival of the guard of the 34th. But the clincher came after the regiment had been disbanded on 31 March. In two petitions to Major-General Hearsey, the 'faithful' officers and men of the 19th claimed that the regiment had been led astray by the 'advice of some wicked men'. The names of the instigators, they added, were known only to their enemies who were young sepoys and therefore 'independent of the Honourable Company's service'. Those thought to be faithful had not been let in on the plot. They were prepared to say, however, that the guard of the 34th was the cause of the mutiny.

Given that the disbanded men of the 19th were trying to secure a reversal of the government's punishment, there is every reason not to accept these two petitions at face value. It is extremely unlikely that the 'loyal' officers and sepoys would not have known the identity of at least some of the ringleaders. Their decision not to hand them over is probably an indication that a sizeable proportion of the regiment was disaffected. Certainly there is evidence that, having dispersed, the disbanded men of the 19th incited other regiments to mutiny. In May, for example, the commanding officer of the 17th Native Infantry prohibited the admittance of strangers into the regimental lines in an attempt to prevent fraternization between his sepoys and those former members of the 19th who lived in the vicinity (the two regiments had forged close links during their time at Lucknow). But contact was made, none the less, and the 17th mutinied soon after. So who were the ringleaders? One clue was provided by a conversation between the regiment's British doctor and a group of disbanded Muslim sepoys. Asked the real reason behind the mutiny, the Muslims replied that the Hindus in the regiment 'had threatened them with instant death' if they told the authorities, yet they promised to disclose the 'true cause' of the supposed cartridge outbreak after the Hindus had dispersed to their homes. They never did – but high-caste Hindus are the obvious suspects.

By mid March the disaffection had spread to the musketry depot at Ambala, where detachments from forty-one infantry regiments were being instructed in the use of the new rifle. Ambala was the headquarters of the Sirhind Division of the Bengal Army and was situated in an open plain three miles east of the River Chaghar, and 120 miles north-east of Delhi. As well as the musketry depot, its large military garrison housed two native infantry regiments, the 5th and 60th, one light cavalry regiment, the 4th, one British cavalry regiment, the 9th Lancers, and two troops of European horse artillery.

On the morning of 16 March, as all the Indian detachments at the musketry depot were being paraded for drill, the instructor Lieutenant Martineau called the Indian officers to one side and expressed his surprise that the men were still discussing whether to use the Enfield cartridges despite his assurance that they could apply their own grease. To which a subedar of the 71st regiment replied that the men were against using any of the new cartridges until they had ascertained that their doing so was 'not unacceptable to their comrades in their respective corps'. This provoked an immediate response from a jemadar of the 36th regiment, who said that the previous speaker knew 'perfectly well that many of the detachments here entertain no such feelings'. The jemadar added:

> I will fire when I am told, & I know many others will do the same. I have sufficient confidence in Government & my officers to know that no improper order will be given to us, & to demur using cartridges merely because they are of a different form, or made of different paper, is absurd, in fact there is no question of caste in the matter, & he who refuses to obey proper orders, or who cavels about doing so on the pretext of religion, is guilty of mutinous and insubordinate conduct.

According to Martineau, the jemadar's sentiments were backed up throughout by the Indian officers of the 10th and 22nd regiments. Clearly not all Indian soldiers were sufficiently disillusioned with either their European officers or the government to believe, or even claim to believe, that the cartridge question was still a legitimate issue. Those who continued to do so were, in this Indian officer's opinion, using religion as a pretext.

On 19 March the Commander-in-Chief of India, General the Hon. George Anson, arrived in Ambala on a tour of inspection with his escorting regiment, the 36th Native Infantry. Aged fifty-nine, the second son of the first Viscount Anson and the brother of the first Earl of Lichfield, he had served with the Scots Guards at Waterloo but had seen no active service since. He had spent much of the intervening period as MP for South Staffordshire and aide-de-camp to Prince Albert. His favourite pursuits were the Turf and cards: he won the 1842 Derby with a horse bought for £120 and was described by Disraeli as the 'finest whist player in Europe'. He and his wife Isabella, the daughter of Lord Forester, were a handsome and popular couple, and it was a great surprise to London society when Anson accepted the offer of a Bengal division in 1853. Within a year he was given command of the Madras Army, and in January 1856, after less than three years in India, he became Commander-in-Chief. This meteoric rise owed much to his court and aristocratic connections, but was also testament to his affable yet discerning nature. Lord Elphinstone admired his 'good sense and tact'; one of his officers described him as 'an able, intelligent man, an excellent judge of character'. Since his arrival in India, however, Anson had aroused a good deal of resentment by his open prejudice against Company troops. Canning found him a disappointment and described as 'injudicious' his habit of appointing all his aides-de-camp from British regiments, favouring the Queen's troops 'to the disadvantage of the sepoys' and never seeing an Indian sentry 'without turning away in disgust'. Yet on a personal level Canning and Anson got on well. 'His temper is charming,' wrote the Governor-General, 'and I know no one whom I should not be sorry to see substituted for him.'

No sooner had Anson's infantry escort pitched their tents at Ambala than they were visited by two of their comrades, a havildar and a naik, who were being instructed at the musketry depot. But instead of the usual salutations, the pair were refused entry to their colleagues' tents, and one subedar taunted them with having become Christians by handling the new rifle. Martineau conducted an inquiry among all the depot's detachments and discovered the existence of a rumour that the Enfield rifle was 'nothing more or less than a Government missionary to convert the whole Army to Christianity'. That 'so absurd a rumour should meet with ready credence' was proof, he told Anson, that the feeling of native troops was anything but sound.

On 23 March General Anson addressed a parade of Indian officers at the depot. Through the medium of an interpreter, he told them that the rumoured intention of the government to interfere with their caste and religion was 'utterly groundless and false' and that he looked to them to satisfy those under their authority on this point. Their response, via Lieutenant Martineau, was that *they* knew the rumour to be false, but it was 'universally credited, not only in their regiments, but in their villages & their homes'. They would not disobey an order to fire, they said, but they wanted the Commander-in-Chief to understand the social consequences to themselves – namely loss of caste. Martineau himself regarded the greased cartridge 'more as the medium than the original cause of this wide spread feeling of distrust that is spreading dissatisfaction to our Rule'. Part of his reason for believing this, he later testified, was that only Hindu sepoys were genuinely concerned by the cartridge question; Muslim sepoys, on the other hand, simply 'laughed at it'.

Anson was of a similar opinion. 'The "Cartridge" question is more a pretext, than reality,' he informed the Governor of Bombay on 29 March, adding: 'The sepoys have been pampered & given way to, & have . . . grown insolent beyond bearing.' Yet he accepted that the Indian officers at Ambala genuinely feared social ostracism, and so ordered the deferment of actual target practice at the three musketry depots until the government had voiced its opinion.

Meanwhile, on 27 March, Canning had ordered the disbandment of the 19th Native Infantry for 'open and defiant mutiny'.* In the same general order he assured the native army that it had ever been 'the unvarying rule of the Government of India to treat the religious feelings of all its servants, of every creed, with careful respect', and that had the sepoys of the 19th 'confided in their Government, and believed their commanding officer, instead of crediting the idle stories with which false and evil-minded men have deceived them, their religious scruples would still have remained inviolate'.

One of the means by which ill-feeling spread through the Bengal Army was the fraternization of detachments at the musketry depots. In mid March Lieutenant Martineau was told by sepoys at the Ambala depot that all Bengal regiments contained cabals determined to brand those who used the new cartridges as outcastes. These secret committees had one aim: to convince their comrades that the cartridge question was part of a wider government conspiracy to deprive them of their religion and caste. In case they were doubted, a number of other rumours were spread to reinforce this belief.

* The 19th was duly disbanded at Barrackpore on 31 March, in the presence of the garrison's four regiments of native infantry, the Governor-General's Bodyguard and five companies of the 84th Foot that had been sent up from Calcutta and Chinsurah respectively.

In early March a sepoy at Ambala had shown Martineau a letter from his brother in the 1st Native Infantry at Cawnpore that referred to contaminated flour. It was being claimed that flour from government depots had been deliberately mixed with the ground bones of cows and pigs. 'I was excessively startled,' recalled Martineau, 'and saw at once that some brain of more than ordinary cunning had succeeded in combining for the time being the parties of both Hindus and Mahomedans against us.' According to W. H. Carey, resident in India at the time, the rumour originated on 8 March when a merchant, hoping to clear his stock before other supplies arrived, sold a large quantity of flour at an unusually low price in the market at Cawnpore. Carey identified a sepoy who bought some of the flour as the man responsible for spreading the 'evil report' that it had been mixed with bullock and pig bone at the Canal Department's mills at Cawnpore. The fact that the mills were run by Indian contractors with whom the owners of the grain made their own arrangements was either not known or deliberately concealed. The cartridge question had been so skilfully handled by the conspirators that many of their fellow soldiers were willing to believe the government was capable of just about anything. In the coming months more than one officer would hear his men repeat the contaminated flour rumour as if it were fact. It was taken so seriously by the sepoys of the 10th Oudh Irregulars that, in early June, they insisted on emptying into the river carts of flour that had been procured for them by the Indian mayor. They and other troops at Sitapur mutinied the following day.

More sinister than the bone-dust rumour, however, was the mysterious spread of chapatties across central and northern India. One of the earliest sightings was in late January 1857 in the vicinity of Mathura, a large city on the Jumna River, 34 miles from Agra. The magistrate, Mark Thornhill, had just returned to his *cutcherry* when he noticed four chapatties lying on the table, 'dirty little cakes of the coarsest flour, about the size and thickness of a biscuit'. On questioning his staff, Thornhill discovered that an unidentified man had arrived at a nearby village and given a single chapatti to the watchman, 'with injunctions to bake four like it, to distribute them to the watchmen of the adjacent villages, and to desire them to do the same'. The watchman obeyed but also informed the police, who sent the cakes on to the magistrate. Thornhill recalled:

The following day came similar reports from other parts of the district, and we next learnt from the newspapers that these cakes were being distributed in the same manner over all Upper India. The occurrence was so singular that it attracted the attention of the Government, who directed inquiries; but notwithstanding all the efforts that were made, it could not be ascertained either by whom the distribution had been contrived, where it commenced, or what it signified. After being a nine days' wonder the matter ceased to be talked about, and was presently for the time forgotten . . .

The chapatties are said to have originated in the Maratha principality of Indore in central India. From there they moved up through the Indian state of Gwalior and the Company's Sagar and Nerbudda Territories to the North-West Provinces, eventually reaching Rohilkhand to the north, Oudh to the east and Allahabad to the south-east. One official estimated their rate of travel at up to 200 miles a night. The origin and purpose of the chapatties has never been established, though contemporary speculation was rife. Sir Syed Ahmed Khan pointed out that, with cholera prevalent at the time, some people regarded the chapatties as a talisman to ward off the disease. Most interpretations were not so benign. The Indian newspapers at Delhi thought their appearance was 'an invitation to the whole country to unite for some secret object afterwards to be disclosed'. Mainodin Hassan Khan, then *thanadar* of a police station outside Delhi, told the local magistrate that he regarded the chapatties as 'significant of some greater disturbance, that would follow immediately'. Before the downfall of Maratha power, Mainodin explained, a sprig of millet and a morsel of bread had been passed from village to village to signify a forthcoming upheaval. The British spy Jat Mall, a resident of Delhi, claimed that some people regarded the chapatties as a warning of an impending calamity, others that their purpose was to warn against the government's plot to force Christianity upon the people, and still others that they were being circulated by government to intimate to the people of Hindustan that they would all be compelled to eat the same food as Christians: one food and one faith. This last view, according to Martineau, was prevalent among 'the sepoys of every regiment that furnished a detachment to the depot at Ambala'. Lady Canning concurred. 'They all think it is an order from Government,' she wrote on 8 April, 'and no one can discover any meaning in it.'

At the time the British did not attach particular importance to the chapatties. 'Is it treason or jest?' asked the *Friend of India* on 5 March. 'Is there to be an "explosion of feeling" or only of laughter?' An officer at Cawnpore noted that 'various speculations were made by Europeans as to the import of this extreme activity', but it was invariably dismissed as Indian superstition. The exceptions, according to Thornhill, were those 'few who remembered that a similar distribution of cakes had been made in Madras towards the end of the last century, and had been followed by the mutiny of Vellore'. Mrs Sneyd, the mother of a Bengal officer, was among those who at once expressed a 'firm conviction that it was . . . some deep laid plot & treachery on the part of the natives' and that 'something *terrible was at hand*'. But only in retrospect were the chapatties generally regarded as the harbingers of mutiny. A lieutenant in the 3rd Light Cavalry later described them as 'in some way a signal, understood by the sepoys, of warning to be in readiness for coming events'. In his report of the outbreak at Agra, the commissioner said he had reason to believe the appearance of the chapatties 'had some bearing upon the Hindoo prophecy limiting British rule to a centenary of years' and that sepoys of the 34th Native Infantry were involved in some way. This reference to the 34th is the only tenuous link between the military conspirators and the chapatties. Yet the appearance of the cakes in January 1857, at the outset of the cartridge question, suggests a connection. If the intention was to unsettle the minds of sepoys and civilians alike, and make them more receptive to wild rumour, then it certainly succeeded.

7. Mungul Pandy

Eliza Sneyd was passing through Cawnpore in late March 1857 when she first noticed a change in the demeanour of Indian troops. Born Eliza Halhed, the daughter of a London underwriter, she had arrived in India in 1819 to stay with her older brother Robert who was serving with a Bengal regiment. There she met Edward Sneyd, a Commissariat officer, and within a year they were married. But Captain Sneyd was tragically drowned off Burma in 1826, and his widow returned to England with her four young children: Anna, Alice, Louisa and Henry.

Henry returned to India in 1840 as a fifteen-year-old Bengal ensign. His mother and sisters joined him in 1853. But Mrs Sneyd's joy at seeing Anna marry her brother's best friend, Corney Lysaght, quickly turned to despair when Alice, 'the most blooming and strongest' of her girls, died of a 'feverish attack'. After retiring to the hills to recover, she and her youngest daughter rejoined Henry's regiment at Shahjahanpur in Rohilkhand in May 1856. There the family moved into a substantial house, 'very prettily situated in a beautiful large compound filled with fine forest trees from various countries which blossomed in succession'. Louisa's residence did not last long: in September 1856 she married Dr Robert Hutchinson and moved to Fatehpur in the Doab where her husband was the civil surgeon.

In the spring of 1857 Louisa fell ill and Mrs Sneyd travelled down from Shahjahanpur to nurse her. On stopping to rest at the Old Cawnpore Hotel – the only one suitable for European ladies – she was informed that all the best rooms had been booked by a party of 'native princes & chiefs' whose unruly 'host of retainers & armed men' were milling around the courtyard. (These 'native princes' may well have been Nana Sahib and his adviser Azimullah Khan, who passed through Cawnpore on their way to Lucknow at around this time.) She was given two little veranda rooms that were usually occupied by the head clerk, 'in a most dirty and comfortless state'. But it was the behaviour of the 'motley group' in the courtyard that most alarmed her. She recalled:

I saw a number of sepoys just in front of my apartment, whose conduct struck me as very strange & uncourteous, unlike what I had ever before observed or experienced from any of our native soldiers, who, when not on duty with their regiments & officers, used invariably, on meeting any ladies or gentlemen, to salute them in the sepoy fashion, by just putting their hand to the side of the hat or cap, whereas these men did nothing but point & laugh at me amongst themselves, while talking a great deal together in an undertone, keeping seated on the ground the whole time. My mind misgave me – it appeared very ominous of evil.

It was nearly six in the evening before Mrs Sneyd was given any food, and then 'only a small quantity of the stale remnants of the natives' dinner', which she could not bring herself to eat. Disgusted by her treatment, she ordered her *gharry* to be brought round so that she could continue her journey to Fatehpur. It took another twenty-four hours of exhausting travel, over rutted roads and in stifling heat, before she finally reached her destination.

Another who was acutely aware of Indian hostility at this time was Amy Horne, the seventeen-year-old daughter of a Eurasian woman and a captain in the Royal Navy. Her father had died while she was still a baby, leaving her mother to remarry an agent named John Cook with whom she had five more children. In February 1857 Cook was hired to look after the dwindling Lucknow business interests of John Brandon, the unscrupulous proprietor of the North-Western Dak Company who had used his contacts at the King of Oudh's court to undercut competitors. The Cooks moved into a small house near the iron bridge over the River Gumti, a thoroughfare so busy, recalled Amy, that 'night after night, without exception, was one of merrymaking and rejoicing, and little sleep could we obtain'. She added:

They carried vice and depravity to such an extent that the very walls of some houses and even palaces, bore paintings such as no gentleman of refinement could even look at without a feeling of disgust; it was however amusing to see this corrupt set arrayed in all the splendour imaginary [*sic*], their dress generally of the richest satins, and spangled over with silver and gold, dazzled the eye, and left an impression on the beholder of the wealth of the city; but this was shabby finery, for they are filthy beyond description, the streets are never swept, and flies abound in such numbers that sometimes the shops can only be opened at night.

Amy detested Lucknow, regarding its people as 'the most indecent, abusive set in the wide universe'. Two months after the Cooks' arrival, she was out for an evening stroll when a gang of rowdy youths threw a garland of flowers round her neck. For her stepfather it was the final straw. In April 1857, seeing in 'the insolence of the natives' the 'shadow of coming events', he moved his family to Cawnpore.

By the time of Amy Horne's flight to Cawnpore, the first substantial outbreak of mutinous violence had already taken place at Barrackpore. In the late afternoon of Sunday, 29 March, Sergeant-Major James Hewson of the 34th Native Infantry was resting in his bungalow when a naik burst in and reported that a sepoy, under the influence of *bhang*, had 'armed himself with his loaded musket, and was walking about in front of the quarter-guard'. Hewson told the naik to warn the adjutant. Then he put on his tunic, grabbed his sword and hurried towards the parade-ground.

As Hewson reached the light company's bell-of-arms, he was confronted by a sepoy in 'regimental dress', wearing a dhoti rather than trousers, and armed with a sword and a musket. He recognized him as Mungul Pandy of No. 5 Company. Seeing Hewson, the sepoy raised his musket, took deliberate aim and fired. The ball missed and Hewson ran behind the bell-of-arms, shouting for the guard to fall in. On reaching the quarter-guard, he asked the jemadar, Issuree Pandy, why he had not arrested the sepoy. 'What can I do?' replied the jemadar. 'My naik is gone to the adjutant, the havildar is gone to the field officer? Am I to take him myself?'

Hewson ordered him to fall in his guard and tell them to load. He complied, but so loud was the grumbling that he did not repeat the order. Hewson gave up and went outside, where he found the jemadar and colour-havildar from No. 5 Company trying to persuade Mungul Pandy to give up his weapons. A minute or so later the drumming of horses' hoofs heralded the arrival of the adjutant, Lieutenant Henry Baugh.

'Where is he? Where is he?' shouted Baugh.

'To your left!' Hewson cried. 'Sir, ride to your right for your life, the sepoy will fire at you!'

The warning came too late: a shot rang out and Baugh's horse collapsed under him. Having extricated himself, the adjutant drew one of his two pistols from its saddle holster and ran towards Mungul Pandy, who was in the act of reloading. This caused Mungul to abandon his musket and retire. At a distance of about 20 yards, Baugh fired his pistol but missed. He then drew his sword and rushed forward. 'I had proceeded about half way,' recalled Baugh, 'when the prisoner drew a *tulwar*. I looked back to see where my horse was, intending to get my other pistol, but saw that he was gone; so continued my advance and engaged the prisoner.'

He was assisted by Sergeant-Major Hewson, sword in hand, who had ordered the quarter-guard to follow him. Hewson remembered:

> Mungul Pandy made a cut with a *tulwar* at me, but did not strike me. He struck the adjutant. The next cut I received myself. . . At the same time I was knocked down from behind by one or two blows from a sepoy's musket. I could not recognize the features of the man who struck me; he was regimentally dressed. On rising I advanced again towards [Pandy], and caught him by the collar of the coat with the left hand. I struck him several times with my sword, and received another cut from his *tulwar*. I was again knocked down from behind.

Baugh, meanwhile, had received three wounds: a sword cut that had entirely disabled his left hand, another deep cut on his neck and a gash on the back of his head – the last from a musket butt. He and Hewson were saved from certain death by the intervention of a Muslim sepoy, Shaik Pultoo, who, though injured, managed to grab Mungul Pandy round the waist and hold him until the Europeans had made their escape. Shaik Pultoo only released Mungul when members of the quarter-guard threatened to shoot him if he did not.

Colonel Steven Wheler, fifty-five, the commanding officer of the 34th, now arrived on the parade-ground. A God-fearing man with a reputation for proselytizing, Wheler had been in temporary command when the original 34th was disbanded in 1844, and had only returned to the new regiment in 1856 after an absence of seven years. For all three reasons he was not popular with his men. Making straight for the quarter-guard, Wheler ordered the jemadar to take his men and arrest the sepoy. 'The men won't go,' murmured the jemadar. Wheler had to repeat the order twice more before the jemadar instructed his men to advance. But after about a few paces they stopped and refused to go on. 'I felt it was useless going any further in the matter,' Wheler told the subsequent court of inquiry. 'Someone, a native in undress, mentioned to me that the sepoy in front [was] a Brahmin, and that no one would hurt him. I considered it . . . a useless sacrifice of life to order an European officer, with the guard, to sieze him, as he would no doubt have picked off the European officers, without receiving any assistance from the guard itself. I then left the guard, and reported the matter to the Brigadier.'

By now word of the commotion had reached Major-General Hearsey. Fearing a general outbreak, he dashed off two quick notes to the officers commanding the European troops at Chinsurah and Dum-Dum, asking them to march at once for Barrackpore. His intention was to hold the

Governor-General's residence with any troops who remained loyal until help arrived. But he decided not to send the letters until he had gauged the seriousness of the outbreak for himself. Accompanied by his two sons, Hearsey galloped towards the 34th's parade-ground, which was crowded with 'sepoys in their undress and unarmed'. There he found a group of European officers – some mounted, some on foot – including Brigadier Charles Grant and the station commander, Major Ross. Colonel Wheler was nowhere to be seen. The officers told Hearsey that the sepoy had cut down the adjutant and sergeant-major of the 34th, and was now pacing up and down in front of the quarter-guard, 'calling out to the men of the brigade to join him to defend and die for their religion and their caste'.

As Hearsey turned his horse in the direction of the quarter-guard, one of the officers called out, 'His musket is loaded!'

'Damn his musket!' replied the general.

At the quarter-guard he found the jemadar and a dozen men. 'Follow me!' ordered Hearsey.

'He is loaded!' responded the jemadar, 'and he will shoot us.'

Pointing his revolver at the jemadar, Hearsey repeated the order.

'The men of the guard are putting caps on the nipples,' came the jemadar's hasty reply.

'Be quick and follow me!' said Hearsey gruffly. He then headed towards Mungul Pandy, followed by the guard, his two sons covering the jemadar with their pistols. As they approached the mutineer and quickened their pace, Hearsey's eldest son called out: 'Father, he is taking aim at you, look out sharp!'

'If I fall, John,' said Hearsey, 'rush upon him, and put him to death.' At which point a shot rang out, causing all but three of the guard to duck in self-defence. Hearsey wrote:

> It appeared the mutineer had suddenly altered his mind, I suppose, seeing there was no chance of escape . . . He turned his musket muzzle towards his own breast hurriedly, touching the trigger with his toe. The muzzle must have swerved, for the bullet made a deep graze, ripping up the muscles of the chest, shoulder and neck, and he fell prostrate; we were on him at once. The guard calling out – 'He has shot himself'. A Sikh sepoy of the guard took his bloody *tulwar* from under him, for in falling he partly covered his sword with his body. His regimental jacket and clothes were on fire and smoking. I bid the jemadar and the sepoy to put the fire out, which they did . . . Dr Hutchinson being present, it was soon ascertained that the wound, though severe, was superficial, and the man was conveyed to the hospital . . .

Mungul Pandy's intention had been to incite the whole regiment to mutiny. 'Come out, you *bhainchutes*, the Europeans are here,' he is said to have shouted on emerging from his hut. 'From biting these cartridges we shall become infidels. Get ready, turn out all of you.' A separate statement by the same witness has Mungul warning the men that the 'guns and Europeans had arrived for the purpose of slaughtering them'. He was presumably referring to the arrival that day of fifty men of the 53rd Foot from Calcutta. Hewson recalled him saying: '*Nikul ao, pultun; nikul ao hamara sath* ["Come out, men; come out and join me – You sent me out here, why don't you follow me"].' Mungul himself admitted that he had recently been taking *bhang* and opium, and was not aware of what he was doing at the time of the attack.

It seems likely, therefore, that an intoxicated Mungul acted before his co-conspirators were ready. Certainly his false references to the murderous intentions of Europeans and the loss of religion were repeated in many other mutinies, and they had clearly been decided upon as the best way to win over waverers. But in the case of the 34th Native Infantry, there had been no specific dispute over the issue of cartridges – though the men had expressed their suspicions about the paper for the new Enfield cartridge – and the time was not yet ripe for mutiny. Nor had enough members of the other Barrackpore regiments, particularly the 43rd and 70th, been won over to the cause of mutiny, and even the 34th was not of one opinion. Like the 19th Native Infantry, its pro-mutiny faction was dominated by high-caste Hindus. This explains why, during the drama of 29 March, one sepoy told Colonel Wheler that no one would use force against Mungul Pandy because he was a Brahman. Captain Drury confirmed this impression when he told the court of inquiry that the quarter-guard would have refused any order to shoot Mungul on account of their fear of the bad 'opinion of their comrades in the lines as it was impossible to say, there being a large proportion of Brahmins in the regiment, who approved of what he was doing and who did not'.

Many believed that Colonel Wheler's proselytizing was to blame for his regiment's disaffection. Wheler himself admitted that he had been in the habit of speaking to 'natives of all classes, sepoys and others' on the subject of Christianity 'in the highways, cities, bazaars and villages', though 'not in the lines and regimental bazaars'. He had, he said, often addressed sepoys of his own and other regiments with the aim of converting them to Christianity. Such an officer was, in Canning's opinion, 'not fit to command a regiment'.

Other opinion was divided. An anonymous correspondent to the *Friend of India* asked 'by what law a man who lives as a Christian, and peaceably endeavours to induce others to be Christians like him, is made an offender'. The *Bengal Hurkaru* responded with the comment that the 'least likely way of making Christians of the Natives in this country, is to get turned out of it ourselves'. As far as most sepoys were concerned, however, proselytizing was not an issue. Lieutenant Martineau later testified that he had never heard any sepoys at Ambala speak complainingly of the efforts of Wheler and missionaries in general to convert natives to Christianity and did not think 'they cared one bit about it'. Anson did not believe the disaffection of the Bengal Army could be 'traced to the preaching of Commanding officers' because Wheler was an isolated case. The *Bengal Hurkaru* also had 'no reason to suppose that the prevalence of disaffection and insubordination in the Bengal Army had been caused by the proceedings of proselytizing officers'. Yet, it added, what was 'more likely to cause general disaffection in an army of illiterate natives than the suspicion of a design against their national faith', what 'more likely to excite such a suspicion than the spectacle of a military Commander . . . teaching and preaching a foreign religion'. In other words, the actions of Wheler and men like him were grist to the mill of those who wished 'to win away the allegiance of the sepoys from Government'.

In civil society as a whole, many Indians had become increasingly wary of the government's policy of Anglicization. In 1813, to ensure the twenty-year renewal of its charter, the East India Company agreed to spend £10,000 a year on educating Indians and to remove the long-standing ban on Christian missionaries. As a result of the first initiative, Anglicizers and Orientalists began a fierce debate as to what kind of education – English or classical Indian – should be funded. The question was finally settled in 1835 when Thomas Babington Macaulay, law member to the new Legislative Council of India, penned his notorious 'Minute on Education' that recommended raising up an English-educated middle class 'who may be interpreters between us and the millions whom we govern – a class of persons Indian in colour and blood, but English in tastes, in opinions, in morals, and in intellect'.

Already a new Anglicized élite in Calcutta had begun 'to create institutions to serve its own interests'. Founded in the 1810s and 1820s, these were largely educational establishments that taught English language, literature and Western sciences, and included the Hindu College, the Calcutta School Society, the Sanskrit College and the Oriental Seminary. They were supplemented by missionary schools that generally taught Indians of all religions and castes free, notably Dr Duff's Free Church Mission in Calcutta. But even the Calcutta élites who accepted the necessity of learning English were split between conservatives who wanted to limit the incorporation of foreign culture within Hindu society (including members of the Hindu Dharma Sabha) and 'cultural radicals who rejected Hindu social norms in favour of English culture and secular rationalism imported from Europe' (led by the brilliant young Eurasian Henry Derozio, who supported the abolition of suttee in 1829, just two years before his untimely death at the age of twenty-two). Yet these cultural developments hardly registered in rural communities and military cantonments. The abolition of suttee (self-immolation by high-caste widows), for example, caused barely a ripple among the Company's Indian troops.

The upshot of the 34th Native Infantry's aborted rising was that Mungul Pandy and Issuree Pandy, the jemadar of the quarter-guard, were found guilty of mutiny by separate native courts martial and hanged on 8 and 21 April respectively. The jemadar's fate was sealed when three Sikh members of his guard testified that he had 'positively ordered them not to' arrest Mungul Pandy. Both executions took place on the parade-ground at Barrackpore in the presence of the four Indian regiments and a strong contingent of Europeans. But the behaviour of the two condemned men could not have been more different: Mungul Pandy, still suffering from his self-inflicted wound, met his end with quiet dignity; Issuree Pandy, defiant and remorseful in turn, was loud in his pleas for deliverance. Of the latter's execution, General Hearsey wrote:

> The Prisoner shouted out lustily on his coming on Parade in a cart & when his hands were being pinioned. He addressed himself to the sepoys & men of the Regiment, then shouted to the officers & to the Honourable Company for mercy. I let him have his full say, and he ended with 'Seeta Ram' 'Seeta Ram' just before he was turned off. I sincerely hope this will be the last of hanging on the Parade at Barrackpore, for I shall get the 'sobriquet' of *General Executioner*. The quarter distance columns were brought up to about 50 paces of the gallows where the Jemadar was suspended 'Dead', & I addressed them in these few words in Hindoostanee. 'Men, Sepoys, witness the punishment for mutiny.'

The executions were not the end of the matter. Canning and his councillors decided that all seven of the 34th's companies present on 29 March were guilty of passive mutiny and they were disbanded on 6 May.

The reaction of the *Hindoo Patriot* to the violence at Barrackpore was to indicate a cause far deeper than the cartridge question. '*Months before* a single cartridge was greased with beef-suet or hogslard,' it commented on 2 April, 'we endeavoured to draw public attention to the unsatisfactory state of feeling in the sepoy army . . . There is no want of distinctness or prominence in the symptoms which have already appeared to warn us against the existence of a powder mine in the ranks of the native soldiery that wants but the slightest spark to set in motion gigantic elements of destruction.'

The Indian government was well aware that agitators were manipulating the cartridge question for their own sinister ends. So in early April, to remove any remaining objection to the new cartridges, it altered the firing drill for both rifles and muskets. Instead of tearing the top of the cartridge with their teeth, sepoys would now do so with their left hand. With this concession in place, Canning authorized the musketry depots to commence firing practice. Any further postponement, he observed on 3 April, would be viewed by the sepoys as a victory; the government would be seen to have 'admitted the justice of the objection or at least as having doubts upon it, and the prejudice would take deeper root than ever'.

Canning was now quietly confident that the worst of the cartridge crisis was past. On 9 April he wrote to Granville:

> I have had a very mauvais quart d'heure since my last letter . . . in the matter of the Mutiny; but it is well over, so far as danger goes; although troubles enough will spring out of it. It has been a much more anxious matter than Persia, ten times over; for a false step might have set the Indian army in a blaze. As it is, I am rather pleased with the way in which it has been dealt with. Do not whisper it, but, to say the truth, I have been rather glad to have the Commander-in-Chief up in the far North-West. He has plenty of pluck and plenty of coolness; but I doubt his judgement as to when and what to yield.

In a separate letter that day to Vernon Smith, the President of the Board of Control, Canning said that he was not particularly bothered about the postponement of regiments leaving Britain for India as long as they embarked by steamship 'not later than June'. Two weeks later he rejected Vernon Smith's offer of extra British regiments instead of more Company Europeans. 'I am opposed to putting into the hands of the Government at home an increased power to diminish our main strength here for the sake of meeting exigencies elsewhere,' he wrote on 22 April. Canning preferred to reduce each regiment of native infantry from one thousand to eight hundred sepoys, thereby saving enough money to raise four new European regiments of Company infantry. But these plans were rapidly overtaken by events.

The first live firing of Enfield rifles, using cartridges greased by the sepoys with a composition of ghee and beeswax, took place at the Ambala musketry depot on 17 April. The Indian troops at the depot had warned Lieutenant Martineau that it would lead to an outbreak in the station, and the increased frequency of arson attacks seemed to confirm this. As early as 26 March an attempt had been made to burn down the hut of the first Indian officer to declare his willingness to fire the new cartridges. The fires resumed on 13 April, when the authorities at Ambala first received orders to commence firing practice, and continued on into May. That no one would identify the incendiaries despite the offer of a large reward was, Martineau was told, 'a certain sign of general dissatisfaction and some impending outbreak'.

Live Enfield cartridges were also fired – without incident – at the Sialkot and Dum-Dum depots in late April. After a visit to Sialkot in early May, Sir John Lawrence informed Canning that the sepoys were 'highly pleased with the new musket, and quite ready to adopt it', not least because they realized the advantage it would give them in mountain warfare on the North-West Frontier. At Dum-Dum one of the first soldiers to fire an Enfield cartridge was Subedar Bholah Upadhya, a Brahman from the 17th Native Infantry. His loyalty was rewarded when his commanding officer, Major Burroughs, recommended him for the vacant subedar-majorship, though he was second in seniority. The subedar who was passed over, a member of the Ahir caste named Bhondu Singh, would later lead the regiment in mutiny at Azimgarh on 3 June. In the preceding weeks the men of the 17th frequently voiced their suspicions about the new cartridges. Unable to understand their objections in the light of the government's concessions over greasing and loading, Burroughs sought an answer from his shrewdest and most intelligent havildar, Juggernath Tewarry. While refusing to enter into specifics, Juggernath pointed out that it was the object of all smart sepoys to get into their regiment's rifle company (if it had one), and once there to use patches greased in the government magazines.

'We do not know what that grease is made of,' added Juggernath, 'but did you ever hear any sepoy objecting to it?'

'Then why,' asked Burroughs, 'is an objection made now?'

'From villainy,' replied Juggernath, but would say no more.

As commander of the Ambala musketry depot, Lieutenant Martineau was in an ideal position to assess the temper of the army. Yet even he was in the dark. On 5 May 1857 he revealed his fears to Captain Septimus Becher, assistant adjutant-general with Army Headquarters at Simla in the hills:

Feeling . . . is as bad as can be and matters have gone so far that I can hardly devise a suitable remedy. We make a grand mistake in supposing that because we dress, arm and drill Hindustani soldiers as Europeans, they become one bit European in their feelings and ideas. I see them on parade for say two hours daily, but what do I know of them for the other 22? What do they talk about in their lines, what do they plot? For all I can tell I might as well be in Siberia. I know that at present an unusual agitation is pervading the ranks of the entire native army, but what it will result in, I am afraid to say. I can detect the near approach of the storm, I can hear the moaning of the hurricane, but I can't say how, when, or where it will break forth.

8. The Storm Bursts

The British station at Meerut in the upper Doab, midway between the Jumna and Ganges Rivers, was one of the most salubrious in India. Established in 1804 on four miles of plain to the north of the city, it was well known for its pretty bungalows, flower-filled gardens and healthy climate. One British cavalryman, garrisoned there in the 1830s, regretted being transferred to the dusty cantonment at Cawnpore because it was not as 'pleasant' as Meerut.

The station was roughly divided into two halves, north and south, by the Abu Nullah watercourse. At the top of the northern sector were the north-facing European lines. They extended for two and a half miles and included, from west to east, the barracks, officers' bungalows and parade-grounds of the cavalry, infantry and artillery. Further east still was the enclosed Artillery School of Instruction known as the Damdammah; St John's, the largest and finest church in northern India, was on the periphery of the infantry parade-ground. Forming the southern perimeter of the European lines was the Mall, a wide tree-lined road along which the British residents took their evening promenade.

The Indian lines were to the west of the southern sector. They consisted of a main block running north–south and facing west over a large parade-ground. To the rear of the main block were the European officers' bungalows and messes, and beyond them the Sudder Bazaar, the biggest in the cantonment, serving the Indian lines as a whole. Further east were the courts, offices and scattered bungalows of the British civil station. South of the civil station was the city of Meerut. No longer walled, it still retained a number of its original gates.

As the headquarters of both the Bengal Artillery and a division of the Bengal Army, Meerut was a key military station. Moreover, it had, in May 1857, the highest proportion of European to Indian troops of any station in India: 1:1¼. The European garrison included two British regiments: the 6th Dragoon Guards (the Carabiniers), which had recently arrived from England and contained a majority of raw recruits on part-broken horses; and the 60th Rifles, which had been in India for two years and was the only corps equipped with Enfields. The remaining European troops were gunners.

The Indian contingent was made up of three regiments: the 11th and

20th Native Infantry, and the 3rd Light Cavalry. The 11th had only been in Meerut since the beginning of May. Prior to that it had been split into two wings, one at Allahabad and the other at Mirzapur. Its commanding officer, Colonel John Finnis, had been in command for less than a year and was completely unknown to the left wing. The 20th Native Infantry had arrived in Meerut from Peshawar in January 1856. Its regular commander, Lieutenant-Colonel John Craigie-Halkett, was on leave and the regiment in the care of 37-year-old Captain John Taylor. Though Taylor had served with the regiment for eighteen years, seeing action in the First Afghan War and against the Afridi tribesmen in 1853, he may not have commanded the same respect as a more senior officer. The 3rd Light Cavalry, the senior Indian regiment at Meerut, was one of the most celebrated in the Bengal Army. Formed in 1796, it had served with distinction in numerous campaigns. For its efforts at the Battle of Delhi in 1803 the regiment had been awarded an extra jemadar and an honorary standard inscribed with the words 'Lake and Victory'. It had been at Meerut since 1854 under the command of Colonel George Carmichael-Smyth.

Descended from the Earls of Hyndford and an heiress named Smyth, the colonel had been born in London in 1803, the eighth and youngest son of a Scottish doctor. Five of his brothers had served in India as officers and administrators before he joined the 3rd Light Cavalry as a cornet in 1820. But his career had never taken off: apart from a brief stint on the staff in 1825, he had remained a regimental officer, seeing action in a number of battles, notably Aliwal during the First Sikh War when the regiment famously charged with the 16th Lancers. Such a long-serving regimental commander was usually respected by both officers and men; not Carmichael-Smyth. 'He was not wanting in intelligence or in zeal,' wrote a contemporary, 'but he lacked temper and discretion, and the unquestionable honesty of his nature was of that querulous, irritable cast which makes a man often uncharitable and always unpopular.' In late March 1857 Carmichael-Smyth travelled from Meerut to the holy town of Haridwar in the Himalayan foothills to buy remounts at the triennial Kumbh Mela festival. When the Mela ended early because of cholera, he took a short leave in the hills. There an acquaintance told him about a recent conversation he had had with an old Indian soldier. 'I have been 36 years in the service and am a havildar,' said the soldier, 'but I still would join in a mutiny and what is more I can tell you the whole army will mutiny.' Carmichael-Smyth was much affected by this story.

At Meerut, meanwhile, the Europeans were more concerned with the onset of the burning winds than soldier unrest. In a letter of 8 April to his father, one artillery subaltern wrote:

The weather seems the great topic of conversation at present, against which I and all others are fortifying ourselves by blockading the windows with [tatties] and having punkas placed up in the rooms. We have certainly a very pleasant prospect before us for the next six months, not getting out of doors in the middle of the day, dinner at 8 o'clock in the evening (just fancy what an hour to dine at . . .). But it is impossible to do otherwise here, for the only time you can take any exercise is after the sun goes down, and the sun does not set now until ¼ or half past six. We rise at gun fire every morning which is now at quarter to 5, so you see we are very early.

But it was the cartridge question rather than the weather that was very much on the minds of the Indian troops. The first outbreaks of arson took place in the native lines on 13 April. Ten days later Carmichael-Smyth arrived back in Meerut and was shown a copy of the new firing drill by which cartridges were to be torn with the hand rather than the teeth. Determined to put the drill into practice, he gave orders for the regiment's ninety skirmishers to attend a firing parade the following morning. Whether he conferred with his superiors before issuing such a contentious order is doubtful. It was the start of the hot weather, the season of reduced duties, and many officers were on leave.

Among the absentees was the station commander, Brigadier Archdale Wilson, who was recuperating from smallpox in the hills. A clever, affable and undemonstrative man, the fifth son of a well-born Norfolk clergyman and the nephew of the first Lord Berners, Wilson had done well enough at Addiscombe to gain a commission in the Bengal Artillery at the age of fifteen. Since arriving in India in September 1819, his active service had been confined to the siege of Bharatpur and some minor engagements in the Jullundur Doab during the Second Sikh War. He had spent much of his time in detached posts and on the staff: including posts as adjutant-general of the artillery and superintendent of the artillery's main foundry at Cossipore. In 1855, thoroughly acquainted with the details of his profession, he was promoted to brigadier and given command of both the Bengal Artillery and the Meerut station. His high rank was matched by his distinctive appearance. 'He is a tall man,' wrote one contemporary, 'with very large contemplative eyes, a high forehead, grizzled [grey] hair, no whiskers, but a moustache and a goat's beard.' In 1857 he was still only fifty-three, with a 'spare and wiry frame' and 'active athletic habits', and looked to have a successful career ahead of him. But having served for almost forty years, he wanted nothing more than to retire with his 'dear old woman' to the 'heaven' of a small cottage in Norfolk.

The other senior officers absent were Colonel Jones of the Carabiniers and Craigie-Halkett of the 20th Native Infantry. That just left Major-General William Hewitt, sixty-six, the kindly but corpulent commander of the Meerut Division, whose 'Bloody Bill' nickname was a relic of the 1820s. Hewitt does not appear to have been consulted about the firing parade. But Carmichael-Smyth did write to Colonel Curzon, Anson's military secretary, on the same day to pass on the havildar's warning that the whole native army was about to mutiny. In the light of this letter, the firing-parade order appears more reckless still.

The ninety skirmishers of the 3rd Light Cavalry were 'more or less picked men, and quite the elite of the regiment'. Among their senior ranks were two Muslim naiks, Pir Ali and Kudrat Ali, who were almost certainly conspirators; for no sooner had Carmichael-Smyth's order been posted than they told their fellow skirmishers that the practice cartridges had been deliberately prepared with beef and pork fat. Seemingly convinced, the whole group swore not to use the cartridges until the entire Bengal Army had accepted them. That evening five of the six troop commanders were warned that the skirmishers would not fire the cartridges for fear of getting a bad name. One of these officers informed the acting adjutant, 22-year-old Lieutenant Melville Clarke, that the men had said 'if they fire any kind of cartridge at present they lay themselves open to the imputation from their comrades and other regiments of having fired the objectionable ones'. In other words they did not care whether the cartridges they were being asked to fire were contaminated or not; their concern was to escape social ostracization.

During the firing parade the following morning eighty-five of the ninety skirmishers refused to accept the three blank cartridges they were offered, despite Carmichael-Smyth's assurance that they were not greased and were the same as they had been using all season. According to the colonel, none of those who refused gave any reason for doing so 'beyond that they would get a bad name; not one of them urged any scruple of religion; they all said they would take these cartridges if the others did'. They numbered forty-eight Muslims and thirty-seven Hindus. Of the five non-commissioned officers who took the cartridges, three were Muslims and two Hindus.

Carmichael-Smyth's action was severely criticized by one of his youngest officers, eighteen-year-old Cornet John MacNabb, who wrote:

Our Colonel Smyth most injudiciously ordered a parade of the skirmishers of the regiment to show them the new way of tearing the cartridges. I say injudiciously because there was no necessity to have the parade at all or to make any fuss of the sort just now, no other Colonel of Cavalry thought of doing such a thing, as they knew at this unsettled time their men would refuse to be the first to fire these cartridges, but that by not asking they would not give their men the chance of refusing, and that next parade season when the row had blown over they would begin to fire as a matter of course . . .

[They] refused to fire them as they did not want to be the first regiment who had fired . . . But the real case is that they hate Smyth, and, if almost any other officer had gone down they would have fired them off . . . The men of course had *no* real excuse for not doing what they were ordered, and they knew what these cartridges were made of, as they had fired them off privately in riding school since the 19th N.I. were disbanded, and they would have continued to do so if they had been left alone, instead of being paraded, and addressed, and all that humbug.

At the subsequent court of inquiry both the Indian quartermaster-havildar and his predecessor testified that the blank cartridges involved had been manufactured in the regimental magazine the previous year. They also confirmed that the paper was the same as that in use for many years, and that there was nothing in the material of the cartridges or the manner in which they had been made up that would be objectionable to either a Hindu or a Muslim. The former quartermaster-havildar, one of the five men to accept the cartridges, had even supervised their production. And yet, there was a general rumour or suspicion that there was something wrong with them. The court, made up of seven Indian officers, concluded that there was 'no adequate cause' for the disobedience the previous day beyond a vague rumour that the cartridges contained a suspicious material.

As a result of the court of inquiry's findings, the eighty-five skirmishers were tried for collective disobedience by a general court martial of fifteen Indian officers. The trial began on 6 May and ended two days later. By a majority verdict of fourteen to one, all eighty-five defendants were found guilty and sentenced to ten years' imprisonment with hard labour. The court recommended favourable consideration on the grounds of good character and the fact that the men had been misled by rumours. But the reviewing officer, General Hewitt, thought that the latter circumstance aggravated rather than mitigated the crime. He therefore confirmed the majority of the sentences, while halving those of the eleven men who had served less than five years on the basis that they had been led astray by their more experienced comrades. 'They could not have hit upon a more severe punishment,' wrote Cornet MacNabb to his mother, 'as it is much worse to them than death. It is in fact 10 years of living death. They will never see their wives and families, they are degraded, and one poor old man who has been 40 years in the regiment, and would have got his pension, is now thrown back the *whole* of his service.'

The sentence was carried out in the early morning of Saturday, 9 May. MacNabb recorded: 'We were paraded at 4 o'clock on foot, and marched up to the [European] Parade ground where all the troops in the station were assembled. The prisoners were escorted by a company of Rifles, and some of the 6th Dn. Guards. It is lucky that this had happened in Meerut where there are so many European troops, for if it had been at a small station I would not have given much for the officers' lives.' Another officer of the 3rd Cavalry, Lieutenant Alfred Mackenzie, recalled:

In sullen silence, the two native infantry corps, the 11th and 20th, and my own regiment, which was dismounted on that occasion, witnessed the degrading punishment. It would have been madness for them then to have attempted a rescue; for they would have been swept off the face of the earth by the guns of the artillery and the rifles of Her Majesty's 60th Foot, not to speak of the swords of the 6th Dragoon Guards [the Carabiniers], all of whom were provided with service ammunition, and were so placed as to have the native regiments at their mercy.

For more than an hour the troops stood motionless, their nerves at the highest tension, while the felon shackles were being methodically and of necessity slowly hammered on the ankles of the wretched criminals, each in turn loudly calling on his comrades for help, and abusing, in fierce language, now their colonel, now the officers who composed the court-martial, now the Government.

It took two hours for the sentence to be read and the shackling completed. If the morning had not been overcast, noted Cornet MacNabb, 'we would have been grilled'. He added: 'The men in the ranks behaved very well, with the exception of a few who wept for their brothers and fathers among the mutineers. When the irons were put on they were marched past the whole parade and when they passed us of course they began to cry, and curse the Colonel, and threw away their boots, almost at him, but they blessed [Captain] Craigie, and called out that "they hoped he would be a Prince and a Lord".'

The prisoners were then escorted by a company of the 60th Rifles across the two miles that separated the parade-ground from the New Gaol, a large rectangular building on the east side of the native city. There they were handed over to the civil authorities. Inexplicably, given the volatile state of the Indian troops, additional security was provided not by the 60th Rifles but by two dozen sepoys of the 20th Native Infantry. Later that day some of the officers went down to the gaol to see the prisoners and pay them their wages. 'They say it was heart-rending to see them,' wrote MacNabb, 'yet they accused no one, but thanked them for coming to see them . . . When they were being paid, one man said, "Oh give it to my Wife", another, "Oh give it to my Brother; what good is it to me; I am a dead man now." '

In the evening, some of the prisoners' comrades sought consolation in the brothels of the Sudder Bazaar. But they were given short shrift by the prostitutes, among them a European woman called Dolly, the widow of a British sergeant, who had been cast out of cantonment society for stealing: ' "We have no kisses for cowards!" was the cry. Were they really men, they were asked, to allow their comrades to be fitted with anklets of iron and led off to prison? And for what? Because they would not swerve from their creed! Go and rescue them, they were told, before coming to us for kisses.' Dolly and her fellow prostitutes could not know it, but preparations for a rising were already in hand. Soon after dark an Indian officer appeared at the bungalow of his troop commander, Lieutenant Hugh Gough, and warned him that the Indian garrison would mutiny the following day: the infantry would rise first, followed by the cavalry, who planned to release their comrades from gaol. Gough at once reported the conversation to Carmichael-Smyth, who treated the matter with 'contempt', reproving him 'for listening to such idle words'. Later that evening Gough repeated the story to Brigadier Wilson, who had returned from sick leave on 2 May. Again it was given short shrift. Wilson did not even see fit to replace the Indian guard at the gaol with European troops.

Unrest was not confined to the Indian soldiers. During dinner with Colonel Custance of the Carabiniers, Mrs Elisa Greathed, the wife of the civil Commissioner of Meerut, mentioned a report that placards had been raised in the city 'calling upon all true Mussulmans to rise and slaughter the English'. It was not taken seriously.

Sunday, 10 May 1857, was stiflingly hot. The clouds of 9 May had burst in the evening and by eight the following morning the temperature was almost unbearable. Thankfully for churchgoers, the morning service at St John's began at seven. Lieutenant Gough remembered driving to the service 'with young MacNabb, a very fine fellow who had lately joined us, full of bright youth and vigour'. They were wearing their summer undress uniform of white overalls and light frock-coats, and Gough, noticing that MacNabb had the wrong type of braid on his alpaca coat, advised him to alter it 'or the colonel would find fault'. In church they sat next to Hervey Greathed, the commissioner, and his wife Elisa. Another European gentleman, already seated, recalled seeing 'the tall, commanding presence of poor Colonel Finnis, bible in hand, marching down the aisle, and take his seat also'. After the service Mrs Greathed spoke a few words to MacNabb. Little did she know that he, Finnis and many other members of the congregation would be dead by sunset.

For most of the day, the British community sheltered from the sun's burning rays by staying indoors: Gough played with his pet bear, Lieutenant Mackenzie read and MacNabb visited a friend in the artillery lines. The gentleman who had noticed Finnis in church, however, got little peace as his servants gave him repeated warnings 'of what was about to take place'. He recorded: 'The bazaars and city and roads of Meerut were full of anger. My servants rushed in and out, like people distraught, bringing me news of the impending mutinies, urging me to fly at once, saying every European would be killed at night.' But he took no notice: 'A fatal temerity seemed to have possessed us all, and no preparations were made of defence.'

Just after five in the afternoon a cry was raised in the Sudder Bazaar that the Europeans were coming to deprive the Indian regiments of their arms. It seems to have been started by men of the 20th Native Infantry, though sepoys from both the 11th and 20th ran back to their lines to warn their comrades. Captain Taylor, the temporary commander of the 20th, was sitting in his bungalow with a group of officers when he was told about the disturbance. He and his officers made straight for the regimental lines where they found a large crowd of sepoys outside their huts in a state of high excitement. They tried to reassure them, but at the regimental magazine they discovered a group of *badmashes* blocking the road to the Sudder Bazaar. Taylor ordered his élite grenadiers – none shorter than five foot nine – to disperse the unruly crowd; but they refused. The task was eventually accomplished by Christian drummers armed with staves.

Shortly before six, ignoring the pleas of their officers, members of the quarter-guard began to steal away with loaded muskets. The point of no return was reached when a sowar of the 3rd Light Cavalry galloped into the 20th's lines and shouted that the Europeans were on their way and that if the sepoys intended to do something, they should do it at once. Their response was to break open the bells-of-arms, assisted by the rabble from the bazaar.

In the adjacent lines of the 11th Native Infantry, meanwhile, Colonel Finnis and his officers were trying to quell a similar disturbance. Ensign Everard Phillipps recorded:

We were suddenly called to the Parade ground by our colonel whom we found speaking to our men who were violently excited. We were ordered to search our lines for any arms there might be hid. While doing so we heard a great loud shouting from the 20th parade and, on going to see what was the matter, found the 20th had seized their arms and were advancing loaded upon us. We [officers] at once went towards the arms, to prevent our men getting hold of theirs, and succeeded in doing so for nearly half an hour when the fire of the 20th became too thick and near for us to remain. Some of our men entreated Colonel Finnis to let them have their arms, saying they would stand by us and drive off the 20th. The Colonel would not trust them, upon which several sepoys forced us from the parade and thus saved our lives.

As we were mounting our horses, the Colonel fell by my side, shot through the heart. The 20th afterwards put 15 bullets into him. As I mounted my horse, my servant, who was holding him, was knocked over, bullets falling as thick as peas. Had not the brutes been infernally bad shots we would all have perished.

Phillipps and the rest of the 11th's officers managed to reach the safety of the European lines. Others were not so fortunate. Killed at the same time as Finnis were Captain Macdonald of the 20th and Mr Tregear, the inspector of education, who was visiting a friend in the lines. The sepoys responsible were mainly from the 20th's right wing. The left wing was generally less disaffected and some of its sepoys persuaded the rest of their officers to leave. Lieutenant Humphrey had his horse shot under him but managed to hide all night in an outhouse of the hospital. Ensign Lewis was wounded and chased, but a passing carriage saved him.

Six officers left together on foot: Captain Taylor, Lieutenants Henderson, Shuldham, Pattle and Tytler, and Assistant-Surgeon Adley. After a couple of close shaves with the mob, they took refuge in a latrine in the compound of Carmichael-Smyth's bungalow, which was to the north of the 11th's lines. Three stayed put and were eventually rescued. But Taylor, Henderson and Pattle made the mistake of returning to their lines. Henderson was shot by a sepoy and died in the hospital. Taylor and Pattle were also wounded – the former by a butcher from the bazaar – and helped to Taylor's bungalow by a friendly havildar. They were later joined by Captain Earle, another of the 20th's officers, who had been hiding in the lines. Taylor gave Earle his buggy and told him to make for the bungalow of Captain Whish, the brigade-major, which was also in the native lines. But the route was blocked, so Earle headed north. Attacked several times, he got across the nullah and met European troops on the Mall. Taylor followed on foot but was killed by civilians on the road leading to the Dragoon Bridge.

Colonel Carmichael-Smyth had just finished dining with Surgeon Robert Christie and Veterinary Surgeon John Philips when Major Harriott, the judge advocate, arrived at his bungalow with news of the disturbances. Shots could be heard in the distance, so Carmichael-Smyth advised Harriott to take his buggy and head for the European lines. Christie and Philips left together in a separate buggy. As Carmichael-Smyth was preparing to leave, Captain Fairlie and Adjutant Clarke galloped up. Carmichael-Smyth told them to go to the regimental lines and order the men to stand by their horses. He did not accompany them because, as field officer of the week, his duty was to report to his superiors. Instead he mounted his horse and, accompanied by two native orderlies, rode hard for Mr Greathed's bungalow in the civil station, close to the northern edge of the city.

Mr and Mrs Greathed had been on the verge of setting off for the evening church service when shots and smoke from the direction of the Indian lines altered their plans. As the sound of rioting got ever nearer, they acceded to their servants' pleas and hid themselves on the rooftop terrace. When Carmichael-Smyth arrived, considerably shaken by a narrow escape from the mob, he was told nobody was at home. He next went to General Hewitt's house, which was also in the civil station. But Hewitt had already left for the European lines, so Carmichael-Smyth headed north towards Brigadier Wilson's bungalow. It was also empty. Wilson had been about to set off for an evening drive at six thirty when Whish, the brigade-major, arrived with the news that 'both Native Regiments and the third Cavalry were in a state of open mutiny and were murdering every European they could meet'. Wilson had made straight for the parade-ground of the 60th Rifles, 'having first sent orders to the Artillery and Carabiniers to harness, mount, and join me on the rifle parade as soon as possible'. Carmichael-Smyth did likewise.

Among the civilians fleeing towards the safety of the European lines was the unidentified gentleman who had noticed Finnis in church. He had been woken from an afternoon sleep by the sound of a 'strange, rolling sea-like noise'. Wishing to show his servants a bravado he did not feel, he sat down for dinner. But shouts brought him out into the garden. 'Frightened people were running to and fro,' he remembered, 'and sounds of firing distinctly heard in the direction of the Sudder Bazaar and sepoy lines. Englishmen and Ladies drove past for life, lashing their horses with fury, and I was called to by several to escape at once, as no assistance could be afforded me.' He continued:

My stubbornness at last yielded to the earnest entreaties of my servants. I heard the yells of the murderers nearing my gate, and darting inside I tore off my clothes and put on a native dress, dashed ink into my face and hands and went out accompanied by a Seikh. Reaching a backroad, I turned about, like Lot's wife, to gaze on the horrid scene. Burning bungalows sent their horrid brightness far up. Cattle sheds and Godown's Commissariat were blazing away . . . and I fancied I could hear the crackling of the casks within . . . Cattle were flying wildly about – torches, held by demon hands, lighted up the work of destruction and swords reeking with the blood of Europeans were flourished aloft by fiends and shouts, never before heard out of hell, rent the air. 'Allah-I-Allah! Mare Feringhee! [''By the help of Mohamed, let us kill the Christians!'']' I turned from the spectacle sick at heart and made my way to the European barracks.

At a quarter to six, before any European officers had reached their lines, about fifty sowars of the 3rd Cavalry mounted their horses and headed towards the New Gaol. Most went round the north of the city; a few rode through it, via the Kamboh and Shahrah Gates, calling on the people as they passed to join them in a religious war. On arriving at the gaol they fraternized with the sepoy guard before freeing their comrades.

Meanwhile, Fairlie and Clarke had reached the regiment's lines and sounded the assembly. The men refused to respond. A party of sowars – possibly en route to the prison – had already attempted to murder Lieutenant Mackenzie in the road outside his bungalow, but he was saved by the timely arrival of Captain Henry Craigie, who lived in the same street. They were both anxious about loved ones: Mackenzie's sister and Craigie's wife had already left for church together in Craigie's carriage; there was no knowing they had arrived safely. None the less, the two officers agreed that their first duty was to their regiment, and they rode hard for the parade-ground. Mackenzie recalled:

Most of the men were already mounted, and were careering wildly about, shouting and brandishing their swords, firing carbines and pistols into the air, or forming themselves into excited groups. Others were hurriedly saddling their horses, and joining their comrades in hot haste.

Nearly every British officer of the regiment came to the ground, and used every effort of entreaty, and even menace, to restore order, but utterly without effect. To their credit be it said the men did not attack us, but warned us to be off, shouting that the Company's Raj was over for ever. Some even seemed to hesitate about joining the noisiest mutineers; and Craigie, observing this, was led to hope that they might be won over to our side. He was an excellent linguist, and had great influence among them, and he eventually managed to get some forty or fifty troopers to listen to him and kept apart in a group. Suddenly a rumour reached us that the jail was being attacked and the prisoners released. Calling to . . . Lieutenant Melville Clarke and myself to come with him, Craigie persuaded the group which he had assembled to follow him, and away we went towards the jail.

The party was cheered by excited civilians who, in the gathering dusk, were unable to distinguish the three British officers who led it. It was also too dark for Mackenzie to see the severed telegraph wire that then caught him in the chest and unhorsed him. He later wrote:

Fortunately I was not hurt, and regaining my horse I remounted, and soon nearly overtook Craigie and Clarke, when I was horror-struck to see a palanquin-gharry – a sort of box-shaped venetian-sided carriage – being dragged slowly onwards by its riderless horse, while beside it rode a trooper of the 3rd Cavalry, plunging his sword into the body of its already dead occupant, an unfortunate European woman [probably Mrs Courtenay, the wife of the hotel-keeper, who was on her way to church]. But Nemesis was upon the murderer. In a moment Craigie had dealt him a swinging cut across the back of the neck, and Clarke had run him through the body. The wretch fell dead . . . All this passed in a second, and it was out of the power of our men to prevent it; but the fate of their comrade greatly excited and angered them. Shouts of 'Maro! Maro' ('Kill! Kill!') began to be heard among them, and we all thought the end was approaching. However, none of the men attacked us, and in a few minutes we reached the jail. The prisoners were already swarming out of it; their shackles were being knocked off by blacksmiths before our eyes; and the jail guard of native infantry, on our riding up to it, answered our questions by firing at us, fortunately without hitting any of us. There was nothing to be done but ride back to the cantonment.

On the way, Mackenzie obtained Craigie's permission to search for his sister and Mrs Craigie. A dozen sowars volunteered to go with him. 'Every house we passed was in flames, mine included, and my heart sank within me,' he recalled. 'Craigie's house alone was not burning when we reached it – a large double-storeyed building, in very extensive grounds, surrounded, as was then usual, by a mud wall. Here I found Mrs Craigie and my sister.' They had not made it to church. Advised to turn back by Indian servants at the regimental mess, they were driving down the road that fringed the Sudder Bazaar when a British dragoon 'rushed out of a bye-lane, pursued by a yelling crowd'. With great courage the ladies ordered their carriage driver to stop so that the terrified Briton could clamber aboard. They set off again just in time to escape the mob, but not before the carriage hood was penetrated several times by slashing *tulwars*. Having returned to Craigie's house, the ladies struggled to load his three double-barrelled shotguns; the young dragoon was in a 'state of nervous collapse' and could offer them no assistance. They were understandably relieved when Mackenzie and his sowars arrived. But the danger was far from over.

Mackenzie's first act was to entrust the sowars with the ladies' lives. 'Like madmen they threw themselves off their horses and prostrated themselves before the ladies,' he recorded, 'seizing their feet, and placing them on their heads, as they vowed with tears and sobs to protect their lives with their own. Greatly reassured by this burst of evidently genuine emotion, I now ordered the men to mount and patrol the grounds, while I took the ladies upstairs, and then loaded all the guns with ball.'

Craigie, meanwhile, had returned to the parade-ground, where he and the other officers made vain efforts to return the regiment to its duty. Eventually, with the men becoming more and more uncontrollable, they retired over the Dragoon Bridge to the European lines, taking the now disgraced colours with them. But when Craigie discovered that his wife and Mackenzie's sister were not there, he recrossed the nullah at great personal risk, still accompanied by a handful of loyal sowars. At his house, as yet unburnt, he was reunited with Mackenzie and the ladies. Mackenzie told him that the mob was becoming bolder and that their only hope was to retire to a small Hindu shrine in the grounds. Craigie agreed. With the men carrying the guns and ammunition and the ladies concealed in dark blankets, they dashed across to their new refuge.

The mob threatening Craigie's house had been looting, burning and murdering in the bungalow area to the east of the Indian lines since the first shots were fired by sepoys of the 20th. The culprits were mainly *badmashes* from the bazaars, though some Indian troops were also involved. Among their victims was pretty Charlotte Chambers, twenty-three, the heavily pregnant wife of the 11th's adjutant who had fled with his brother officers to the European lines. Unlike Craigie, whose house was opposite his, Chambers did not return to look for his wife. Lieutenant Möller of the 11th volunteered instead, and was in sight of the Chambers bungalow when he was compelled to beat a hasty retreat by a party of mutinous sowars. The stables were torched first, then the house. Mrs Craigie could hear the horses shrieking as they were burnt alive, followed by the still more awful screams of Mrs Chambers herself. She sent her servants across to see if they could save her neighbour. But she was already dead: her throat cut and her unborn child cut out and laid mockingly across her chest by a Muslim butcher whom she had recently castigated for bringing her bad meat. Three days later he was arrested in the bazaar by Lieutenant Möller and soon hanged.

Another to perish at the hands of the mob was Mrs Macdonald, the wife of the captain of the 20th who was shot by his own men. Three of her servants tried to save her and her children by dressing them in native clothes. But she was unmasked by civilians at the rear of the bungalow area and hacked to death with swords. The servants got away with the orphaned children and delivered them safely to the Damdammah the following morning. No such escape was possible for Veterinary Surgeon Dawson and his wife, who were killed, in Mackenzie's words, 'under circumstances of ghastly horror'. They were both in bed with smallpox when the sound of the mob roused them. Still dressed in his nightclothes, Dawson appeared on the veranda and fired his shot-gun into the crowd to keep it at bay. The mob returned fire and Dawson was riddled with bullets. 'His wife met with a worse fate,' noted Mackenzie. 'The cowardly demons, afraid to touch her because of the danger of infection, threw lighted brands at her. Her dress caught fire; and she perished thus miserably.' Also murdered, by a sword stroke that cut her skull in two, was the seven-year-old daughter of the 3rd Cavalry's riding-master. Her parents survived.

The soldiers who died included a number of riflemen, dragoons and gunners who happened to be in the Sudder Bazaar when the outbreak occurred. A favourite venue was a stall near the *kotwali* known as 'the pop shop' where the British soldiers quenched their thirst on bottles of ginger beer and lemonade. It was here that some were set upon with swords, sticks and stones. But not all of them perished: one dragoon was saved by Mrs Craigie and Miss Mackenzie; others escaped over a wooden bridge near the Roman Catholic church.

Of the officers killed, none was more regretted than Cornet MacNabb, who had spent the day visiting friends in the artillery lines. On hearing of the disturbances, he had borrowed a horse and galloped off to his regiment.

But he was waylaid by the mob and hacked to pieces. His face was so badly mutilated that Lieutenant Gough, who discovered his body in a ditch, could identify him only by his height and the non-regulation braid on his coat. Another fatality was Veterinary Surgeon Philips of the 3rd Light Cavalry. He and Surgeon Christie were attacked in their buggy near to Brigadier Wilson's house by sowars from their own regiment. Philips was shot to death; Christie badly wounded. This was one of the few instances when mutineers penetrated the European lines to the north of the nullah. The only other murders in this area were of Sergeant Law and two of his daughters by villagers from the surrounding countryside, many of them Gujar tribesmen, who arrived to join in the mayhem at around ten in the evening. These same villagers later released the civilian prisoners from the New Gaol. Mutinous sepoys had already broken open the Old Gaol between the Sudder Bazaar and the city.

Though news of the disturbances reached the European lines shortly after six, no troops moved off for more than an hour. The cavalry were delayed because Colonel Custance felt it necessary to take a roll call and then find a staff officer who knew the ground. The infantry had to change from their white drill uniforms to service dress, be issued with extra ammunition and await the arrival of the horse artillery. It had gone seven when the column of British infantry and artillery set off for the Indian lines under the direction of Brigadier Wilson. Hewitt was also present and, as the senior officer, in nominal command; but so shaken was he by the events of the evening that he was happy to defer to Wilson.

Proceeding at a snail's pace, the column crossed the nullah by the Dragoon Bridge and finally reached the north-west corner of the Indian parade-ground at around eight fifteen. There it was joined by the cavalry column, which had taken a more circuitous route. But there was no sign of the main body of mutineers. 'The whole had made off and it being dark we could not follow them,' wrote Wilson to his wife in the hills. 'We only saw a few of the 3rd Cavalry who on our approach rode off to warn the others. We then retired and took up a position on the Mall protecting the Europeans' Barracks and lines.' In his official report Hewitt also cited darkness as the reason for his and Wilson's circumspection. The only offensive action by the European troops was to fire a handful of artillery rounds into a nearby tope that was thought to contain mutineers. No bodies were found. On the way back to the Mall, however, the column picked up a number of European and Eurasian fugitives, including the three officers of the 20th Native Infantry who had remained hidden in Carmichael-Smyth's compound. Others survived by their own initiative. It was midnight before Captain Craigie and his party considered it safe enough to leave their sanctuary and set off for the European lines in a buggy. Even then they had to scatter a knot of mutinous sowars before reaching the safety of the European picket on the Dragoon Bridge. The Greatheds hid until morning, and owed their lives to a faithful servant who drew off the mob from their burning house while they moved from the roof terrace to the back garden.

Wilson's column came across many European corpses, including Cornet MacNabb, but they were not recovered until the following morning. The exact number of Christians murdered at Meerut on 10 May 1857 may never be known. The official body count was forty-one Europeans: eight officers, one invalid surgeon, twelve soldiers, four male civilians, eight women and eight children. A later estimate put the total, including Eurasians, nearer to fifty.

The bulk of mutineers left Meerut during the dark hours between sunset and moonrise: from seven to nine in the evening. They moved in small groups of twenty to thirty, some in uniform, others in undress. Three miles along the Delhi road they gathered at the village of Rethanee to agree on a course of action. Most wanted to head for their homes in Rohilkhand to the east and Agra to the south. But the conspirators convinced the majority that a march to either destination without artillery would be fatal. Delhi was a much more attractive proposition, they argued, because it was void of European troops and would be easy to capture. It also contained a large magazine and, more importantly, was home to the King of Delhi, who could serve as a rallying point. After a long and noisy debate, Delhi was the destination agreed upon.

The senior commanders at Meerut were harshly criticized for their failure to pursue the mutineers. Captain Rosser of the Carabiniers is said to have volunteered to set off with a force of cavalry and horse artillery, though both Archdale Wilson and Colonel Custance denied any such offer was made. Wilson excused his inactivity on the grounds that the safety of Europeans at Meerut was his first priority and he had no way of knowing the mutineers' destination. What he failed to mention was that both he and General Hewitt were told that Lieutenant Möller had overheard a sepoy shouting, 'Quick, brother, quick! Delhi! Delhi!' Wilson and Hewitt even refused to allow Möller to ride to Delhi with a warning.

Hewitt tried to evade responsibility by pointing out that Wilson was the station commander and he had let him get on with it. But the government believed Wilson's assertion that Hewitt had asked for his advice and then acted upon it. Hewitt was relieved of his command on 2 June, though the initial order went astray and he was not actually replaced by Major-General Penny until early July. Many considered his punishment far too lenient. Sir John Lawrence told Brigadier-General Chamberlain that Hewitt had done 'more harm than 5000 Pandees' and, if he had been Governor-General, he would have had him arrested. Robert Vernon Smith expected a court of inquiry at the very least for such 'pusillanimous behavour'.

Could more resolute commanders have saved Delhi and nipped the mutiny in the bud? Not according to the official inquiry that took place the following year at Hewitt's request. In a memorandum of 20 August 1858 the chief-of-staff wrote: '[Wilson's] recommendation to Major-General Hewitt to attend to the defence of the station was a wise one. To have hazarded the small amount of cavalry at his disposal in an aimless pursuit without means to support, and without a plan for the future employment of the troops, would have been rashness rather than prudent boldness.'

If Hewitt and Wilson deserved any criticism, added Mansfield, it was for their 'treatment of the 3rd Light Cavalry' and their 'want of care & forethought when the signs of impending danger were visible', such as the obvious need to place a European guard on the gaol, 'and not for pusillanimity or want of action after it had become a reality'.

But others thought differently. Lieutenant Mackenzie of the 3rd Cavalry wrote:

> The European troops, 1500 strong, were paralysed by the irresolution of their chief. Had the gallant Hearsey or Sidney Cotton [commanding at Peshawar] occupied Hewitt's place at Meerut, it is safe to say that, in spite of the wings which fear lent to the mutineers on their flight to Delhi, few of them would have reached that haven of their hopes. The shrapnel of the artillery and the swords of the carabineers would have annihilated them . . . But General Hewitt . . . acted on the ill-starred advice of the Brigadier to withdraw the whole force to the European lines. No greater mistake from any point of view was committed.

A similar view was expressed by Lieutenant-General Sir Patrick Grant, the acting Commander-in-Chief, when he confirmed Hewitt's removal on 6 July: 'The Major-General's own account of his proceedings . . . on the 10th of May fully proves that he is quite unequal to dealing with an emergency where decision, promptitude, and action are of the greatest consequence.

Had a wing of the 60th Rifles, supported by a squadron of the 6th Dragoons and some guns, been sent in immediate pursuit of the mutineers on that occasion, Sir Patrick Grant feels persuaded that the insurrection would have been nipped in the bud.' Mackenzie and Grant may well be right.

One question remains: was the Meerut mutiny planned in advance? Not according to India's official historian. His version of events is that the mutiny began after a cook's boy from the 60th Rifles started a rumour in the Sudder Bazaar that European troops were coming to disarm the natives. The rumour was believed, said General Hewitt, because the 60th Rifles were parading for evening church service. But this account can be rejected on the grounds that the story of the cook's boy was hearsay and the church parade was not due to take place until six thirty, a full hour and a half after the rumour began. The most likely origin of the rumour was a sepoy, or sepoys, of the 20th Native Infantry: certainly the rising began in the 20th's lines before spreading to the other regiments. The 20th's leading role may also be connected to the appearance of a mysterious Hindu fakir at Meerut a month before the mutiny. According to a havildar, he arrived on an elephant with ten followers and stayed a number of days in the 20th's lines before being ordered out of the station by the magistrate. During his subsequent investigation of the outbreak, Major G. W. Williams discovered that, prior to arriving at Meerut, the fakir had been seen at the musketry depot at Ambala, but despite these 'suspicious facts' nothing of a seditious nature was ever proved against him.

Two other events suggest that the outbreak was premeditated: the warning given to Lieutenant Gough during the evening of 9 May that the Indian troops would mutiny the following day; and the cutting of the telegraph line between Meerut and Delhi before four o'clock on 10 May. There is also evidence that, at two in the afternoon, a Kashmiri prostitute named Sophie was told by a sepoy in the Sudder Bazaar that a mutiny would occur that day. The conclusion drawn by Major Harriott, the prosecutor at the trial of the King of Delhi, was that the outbreak at Meerut did not occur on 9 May, the day the skirmishers were put in irons, because the conspirators needed time to warn the Delhi regiments. Even the hour of mutiny – five o'clock – was evidence of 'cunning and craft' in that the Indian lines were two miles from their European equivalent. The conspirators would have calculated on the lapse of at least one and a half hours before the Europeans could have made an appearance. By that time it would have been dark, said Harriott, and the mutineers long gone – which is exactly what happened.

The mutineers' debate as to their eventual destination is sometimes cited as proof that the rising at Meerut was not premeditated. Yet this event is entirely consistent with the theory that only a small number of sepoys and sowars were part of the conspiracy. The pro-Delhi speakers have never been identified, but it is safe to assume that they were the self-same conspirators who had already been in contact with the Delhi troops. 'It is very possible, indeed probable,' wrote Sir John Lawrence, 'that the native soldiers [at] Delhi were so far in the scheme that they had engaged to stand by their comrades at Meerut. Such, indeed, was the case all over the Bengal Presidency.'

9. Delhi

Bahadur Shah II, grandson of the last Mogul Emperor Shah Alam, was already sixty-two when he succeeded to the honorific title of King of Delhi in 1837. Two decades on he was a short, frail man with a white beard and a crooked nose. In his physical prime he had been famed for his athletic prowess, his horsemanship and his ability to shoot birds from the back of an elephant. In later years he preferred the more sedate pursuits of poetry writing, manuscript illustration and miniature painting. He also enjoyed cooking and is said to have invented a pepper-flavoured sweetmeat. He did not drink alcohol but may have been addicted to opium, which would explain his eccentric belief that he could transform himself into a fly or gnat and 'in this guise convey himself to other countries and learn what was going on there'. His most redeeming quality was his religious toleration. The product of a Muslim–Hindu marriage – his Sufi father, Akbar Shah, had married a Rajput princess – he always displayed a marked respect for his mother's faith. He would not eat beef, appointed several Hindus to high positions in his court, and always wore a caste mark on his forehead and the brahmanic thread round his throat when visiting Hindu temples. He even employed a Christian convert in his household, silencing the man's critics with the words, 'There is no cause for shame in what he has done.'

He lived in the Lal Qila, or Red Fort, the magnificent palace built by Shah Jahan during the height of Mogul rule in the mid seventeenth century. A thousand yards long and six hundred wide, it stood on the west bank of the Jumna in the heart of the walled city. Its centrepiece was the beautiful Diwan-i-Am, or Hall of Public Audience, where the Emperor would sit in a marble-panelled alcove, inset with precious stones, to hear the complaints of his subjects. But more lavish still was the Diwan-i-Khas, or Hall of Private Audience, 'built of white marble, beautifully ornamented, the roofs supported on colonnades of marble pillars'. It was here, seated on the peerless Peacock Throne, that the Moguls used to hold their private meetings. Wrought of solid gold, the throne was ascended by steps and covered by a canopy surmounted with four peacock figures, their beautiful colours replicated by countless inlaid jewels. By Bahadur Shah's time only its marble pedestal remained; the throne itself had been looted by Nadir Shah of Persia in 1739. But the Diwan-i-Khas still justified the famous inscription on its exterior: 'If there be a paradise on earth, it is this, it is this, it is this!'

On one side of the Diwan-i-Khas were the Royal Baths and the small enclosed Pearl Mosque; to the other the Khas Mahal, the King's private apartments, and the Rang Mahal, which housed his favourite wife, Zinat Mahal. All were set upon a solid masonry wall of red sandstone, 20 yards high, which looked down upon the sands of the river. The wall extended for about a mile and a half and on the city side rose to a height of 35 yards. There were two main points of entry, both from within the city: the Delhi Gate to the south and the bigger Lahore Gate to the west, the latter containing the apartments of Captain Douglas, the British commander of the King's Bodyguard. But not all the dwellings within the fort were of palatial standard. 'Inside . . . was a maze of houses,' wrote Charles Metcalfe, son of the former Resident, 'some of masonry, some of mats, some of mud. The larger houses contained underground rooms, intricate passages, enclosed courtyards . . . Dirt and filth were everywhere, inside and outside. Rich carpets and dirty mats were side by side on the floors; ivory and silver chairs were covered with filthy rags.' Metcalfe added:

Men and women skilled in the preparation of poisons, of drugs to cause unconsciousness, so as to facilitate robbery and incest, throve within the palace walls. Wrestlers, jesters, dancing-girls, who danced naked to inflame the passions of old age, musicians, forgers, swindlers, thieves, receivers of stolen property, distillers of spirits, compounders of sweetmeats and opium, all formed a part of the palace community . . . Wives intrigued against wives, mothers against sons; men and women scoured the country far and wide for beautiful girls to sell as slaves within the palace. In such a hotbed of villany [*sic*], any conspiracy was possible.

Bahadur Shah ruled over this inflammable mass of competing interests – but not much else. Like his father and grandfather before him, he was a Company pensioner whose temporal power did not extend beyond the walls of the Red Fort. Moreover, his relations with the British had been strained since his accession: first Calcutta refused to increase his already generous stipend of a lakh of rupees a month; then Lord Ellenborough did away with the tradition of presenting him *nazirs* three times a year. The final insult was Dalhousie's refusal to recognize as heir the King's youngest and favourite son, eleven-year-old Mirza Jawan Bakht, after the death of the heir-apparent in 1849. Instead the government nominated Bahadur

Shah's eldest surviving son, Mirza Fakir-ud-din, on condition that he vacated the Red Fort on becoming King. Fakir-ud-din's compliance probably cost him his life. He died in agony in July 1856, after eating a dish of curry, and was almost certainly poisoned. Once again Bahadur Shah proposed Jawan Bakht as his heir; and once again the British chose his next eldest son, Mirza Korash, but as Shahzadah rather than King and with a reduced pension of 15,000 rupees a month.

It was all too much for the octogenarian monarch. Egged on by Queen Zinat Mahal, Jawan Bakht's ambitious mother, Bahadur Shah began to plot against the British. According to his personal physician and close adviser, Ahsanullah Khan, the King's intrigues actually began in 1855 when he sent his nephew with a letter to the Shah of Persia, requesting money and troops to fight the British. Despite subsequent letters, Ahsanullah was not aware of any reply, though during the Persian War of 1856–7 the King told him that he had 'strong hopes' of receiving financial and military assistance from the Shah. An itinerant mendicant, with good contacts in the palace, claimed that these hopes were fostered by Hasan Askari, an influential Muslim priest, who told the King that he had had a divine revelation that the dominion of Persia would extend over the whole of Hindustan and 'that the splendour of the sovereignty of Delhi will again revive'. Delhi Muslims in particular were excited by the possibility that Persian troops might invade India to eject the British. The anticipation was heightened by the anti-British sentiment of the leading Indian journal, *Sadik-ul-Akhbar* (*Authentic News*), copies of which were delivered to the Red Fort. Ahsanullah claimed that the royal princes attached great importance to the journal's false reports that the British were being defeated by the Persians, and may have communicated its contents to the King.

So was Bahadur Shah party to the army's conspiracy to mutiny? It is difficult to say. Ahsanullah was not aware that the King had been in contact with Bengal troops during the cartridge question, though his master undoubtedly 'believed that his own prosperity would go hand in hand with the ruin of British power'. According to the King's secretary, however, the Red Fort received intelligence that the troops would mutiny at Meerut a full twenty days before they actually did. Three days before the outbreak, he added, the King's personal attendants were predicting that the army would soon revolt and 'come to the palace, when the government of the King would be re-established'.

There seems little doubt, therefore, that the rising at Meerut was anticipated by some soldiers and civilians at Delhi. The key evidence linking the outbreaks at Meerut and Delhi was provided by Jat Mall,* a British spy who was a regular visitor to the Red Fort. He claimed to have been told by sepoys on duty at the fort, a few days before the outbreak, that 'it had been arranged in case greased cartridges were pressed upon them, that the Meerut troops were to come here, where they would be joined by the Delhi troops'. An officer of the 38th Native Infantry later testified that a carriage containing sepoys from Meerut arrived in his regiment's lines during the afternoon of 10 May. His wife concluded that they were 'emissaries sent over from Meerut to warn the soldiers to be prepared for the next day's proceedings'. Jat Mall confirmed the arrival of letters at the palace that day 'bringing intelligence that 82 [*sic*] soldiers had been imprisoned, and that a serious disturbance was to take place in consequence'. As a result of this, the sepoys guarding the palace made no secret of their belief that, after mutinying, the troops at Meerut would come to Delhi. The King may not have been personally aware of the plans for a joint rising, but members of his household certainly were.

The first mutineers to reach Delhi were twenty sowars of the 3rd Cavalry. At seven in the morning of 11 May, they rode up to the toll-house at the eastern end of the bridge-of-boats and cut down the toll-keeper. As they were setting fire to the toll-house, a European civilian† drove up in a *gharry*. He was shot and his body thrown in the Jumna. The sowars then crossed the bridge, one man continuing on through the city's Calcutta Gate, the rest turning left on to the tract of ground beneath the eastern wall of the Red Fort known as the Zer Jharokha ('below the balcony').

The lone rider made straight for the Lahore Gate of the fort, but was refused entry by a guard of the 38th Native Infantry. His presence was at once reported to Captain Douglas, the Commandant of the Palace Guard, whose quarters were above the gate's long vaulted entrance. Douglas came

* Ahsanullah Khan went even further than Jat Mall by revealing that men of the 38th Native Infantry had told him that 'they had leagued with the troops at Meerut' before the mutiny, and that the latter had 'corresponded with the troops in all other places, so that from every cantonment troops would arrive at Delhi'. Even after the outbreak, said Ahsanullah, 'letters were received at Delhi from which it was evident that [sepoys all over India] had beforehand made common cause among themselves'. Later the mutinous officers at Delhi wrote – and got the King to write – to many more regiments, inviting them to join the rebellion. (See additional evidence of Ahsanullah Khan, PP, HC, 1859, XVIII, 268.)

† He may well have been Charles Todd, the assistant in charge of the Delhi telegraph office. Yet Todd is not supposed to have left the office to check the line across the Jumna until 8 a.m. See Prologue.

down and asked the sowar what he wanted. His bold reply was that he had just arrived in Delhi, having mutinied at Meerut, and had come to the guard for a drink of water and a pipe. On hearing this, Douglas ordered his arrest, but he galloped off before the guard could act.

Meanwhile, in the royal quarters at the opposite end of the fort, Ahsanullah Khan overheard a disaffected sepoy of the 38th telling the door-keepers of the Diwan-i-Khas that the Meerut garrison had mutinied and was about to enter Delhi, and that he and the rest of them 'would no longer serve the Company, but would fight for their faith'. Before he could intervene, he was summoned to his master's private sitting room. 'Look!' said Bahadur Shah, pointing out of the window, 'the cavalry are coming in by the road of the Zer Jharokha!'

Ahsanullah advised shutting the gate below, and the King gave the necessary orders. But no sooner had this been done than five or six sowars reached the closed gate and began to call out: '*Dohai Badshah!* ["Help, O King!"] We pray for assistance in the fight for the faith.' Afraid to reply, Bahadur Shah sent Ghulam Abbas, his *vakil*, to fetch Captain Douglas.

When Douglas arrived, he asked for the gate below the sitting room to be opened so that he could speak to the mutineers. The King refused, saying the men were murderers. Eventually Ahsanullah persuaded Douglas to speak to the soldiers from the relative safety of the stone-lattice railing that ran between the King's apartments and the Diwan-i-Khas. Ghulam accompanied him and could see thirty to forty troopers gathered below. 'Some had their swords drawn,' recalled Ghulam, 'others had pistols and carbines in their hands; more were coming from the direction of the bridge, accompanied by men on foot, apparently grooms, with bundles on their heads.'

Douglas leant over the balcony and said loudly: 'Don't come here! These are the private apartments of the ladies of the palace. Your standing opposite them is a disrespect to the King.' On hearing this, the troopers moved off, one by one, in the direction of the Rajghat Gate, which gave access to the south-east quarter of the city. When they had gone, the King instructed Douglas to close all the gates of the palace and city 'lest these men should get in'.

Douglas went first to the city's Calcutta Gate, the closest to the bridge-of-boats, where he found the commissioner, Simon Fraser,* the magistrate,

* Late on 10 May a mounted policeman is said to have arrived at Fraser's residence with a letter from the civil authorities at Meerut warning him of the outbreak. But Fraser was tired and put it into his pocket without reading it. It was still there when the mutineers arrived the following morning. (See *Two Native Narratives*, 42.)

John Hutchinson, and Fraser's head clerk, Mr Nixon. Fraser had already closed the Calcutta Gate and was telling the *kotwal* to see to the others when a report arrived that the mutineers had entered the city by the Rajghat Gate and were plundering the adjacent European quarter of Dariagunge. As if in confirmation, five sowars appeared at the gallop from the direction of Dariagunge and fired a volley at the huddle of Europeans, hitting Hutchinson in the arm and causing the others to scatter. Fraser took cover in a sentry-box, where he found an abandoned musket and used it to shoot dead one of the sowars; the other mutineers fled down a side-street. Fraser then mounted his buggy and drove off in the direction of the fort.

Douglas and the others followed on foot, but were attacked by sowars en route. Nixon was killed and, to save themselves, Douglas and the wounded Hutchinson leapt into the ditch that surrounded the fort. Unfortunately Douglas fell awkwardly and landed on some rocks, badly injuring his feet and back. When the sowars had departed, Douglas's servants carried him and Hutchinson up to his apartments in the Lahore Gate. There the casualties were received with some consternation by Douglas's house guests: the Delhi chaplain, Revd Jennings, his beautiful and recently engaged daughter Miss Jennings and her friend Miss Clifford. Fraser was also present.

Anxious to save the two young ladies, Douglas sent for Ahsanullah Khan and Ghulam Abbas. When they arrived, he told them to ask the King for two palanquins so that the ladies could be taken to Queen Zinat Mahal and placed under her protection. Fraser made an additional request for the King to send two of his cannon and a detachment of infantry to defend Douglas's quarters. Ahsanullah and Ghulam hurried back to Bahadur Shah, who gave orders for the immediate dispatch of the palanquins and the guns. But it was too late.

Fraser, armed only with a sword, had accompanied the King's advisers as far as the covered walkway that linked the Lahore Gate to the royal palace. There he encountered a large crowd of men and boys, clapping their hands in mock congratulation. Jat Mall, who was present, recalled:

Mr Fraser, seeing such marked feelings of hostility, began to return to Captain Douglas' quarters, and as he reached the foot of the stairs, Haji, lapidary [seal-engraver], raised his sword to make a cut at him. Mr Fraser, who had a sheathed sword in his hand, turned sharply around, and thrust at him, with the sword in its sheath, saying to the havildar of the gate guard, 'What kind of behaviour is this?' Upon which the havildar made a show of driving off the crowd; but no sooner was

Mr Fraser's back turned, than the havildar nodded with his head to the lapidary, to signify to him that now he should renew his attack. The lapidary, thus encouraged, rushed upon Mr Fraser, and inflicted a deep and mortal wound on the right side of his neck. Mr Fraser at once fell, when three other men . . . who had been concealed in an out-house adjoining, rushed out and cut him with their swords over the head, face and chest till he was quite dead.

One of the three men who joined in the attack was an armed retainer of the King; the other two were in the service of the King's chief minister, Mahbub Ali Khan.

The crowd then rushed up the stairs to Douglas's apartments but found its way barred. Jhokun, Douglas's mace-bearer, had locked the door and was in the process of securing the others when some of the mob burst in a different entrance and gave admission to Fraser's murderers. They rushed into the inner apartments and began to attack the inhabitants with *tulwars*. Jhokun fled, but was caught at the bottom of the stairs by Mamdoh, one of the King's bearers, and asked where he had hidden Captain Douglas. 'He forced me upstairs with him,' remembered Jhokun.

I said, 'You have yourselves killed all the gentlemen already;' but on reaching the room where Captain Douglas was, I saw that he was not quite dead. Mamdoh perceiving this also, hit him with a bludgeon on the forehead, and killed him immediately. I saw the other bodies, including those of the two ladies.* Mr Hutchinson was lying in one room, and the bodies of Captain Douglas, Mr Jennings, and the two young ladies in another, on the floor, with the exception of that of Captain Douglas, which was on a bed.

When Bahadur Shah learnt of the murders, shortly after ten, he gave orders for all the gates of the fort to be closed. But the two companies of 38th Native Infantry on guard at the palace refused to obey. Soon after,

* It was later reported in British newspapers that Miss Jennings and Miss Clifford, among other European ladies and girls, were raped 'before death put an end to their sufferings'. But after conducting an extensive inquiry, the officiating Commissioner of Delhi concluded: 'There is no ground whatever for the supposition that they were in any way ill-treated before death. Every account which I have received confirms the fact that they were at once killed by the Palace rabble and others . . . There may have been rare and exceptional cases in which ladies at other stations have been ill-treated, and possibly some half-caste women may yet be alive who have been obliged to sacrifice their honour, but I doubt much if there have been many such.' (C. B. Saunders to W. Muir, 17 December 1857, *Freedom Struggle*, V, 23–4.)

recalled Ghulam, these sepoys and about fifty sowars marched into the courtyard of the Diwan-i-Khas 'and commenced firing their muskets, carbines, and pistols in the air, at the same time making a great clamour'. Ghulam added:

> The King hearing the noise, came out, and standing in the door of the hall . . . told his immediate attendants to direct the troops to discontinue the noise . . . On this the noise was quelled and the officers of the cavalry came forward, mounted as they were, and explained that they had been required to bite cartridges, the use of which deprived both Hindus and Mahomedans of their religion, as the cartridges were greased with beef and pork fat, that they accordingly killed the Europeans at Meerut, and had come to claim his protection. The King replied, 'I did not call for you; you have acted very wickedly.' On this about one or two hundred of the mutinous infantry, the infantry from Meerut having also arrived by this time, ascended the steps, and came into the hall, saying, 'that unless you, the King, join us, we are all dead men, and we must in that case just do what we can for ourselves'. The King then seated himself in a chair, and the soldiery, officers and all, came forward one by one, bowed their heads before him, asking him to place his hand on them. The King did so, and each withdrew . . . The tumult and noise was very great, all speaking loudly together.

Captain Robert Tytler of the 38th Native Infantry had been up since dawn. A tall, thick-set officer in his late thirties, he lived with his second wife in the military cantonment north-west of the city, beyond the rocky spine known as the Ridge. Tytler had lost his first wife Isabella to a fatal illness, leaving him to care for two infant boys. A replacement was essential, and in 1848 he had married nineteen-year-old Harriet Earle, ten years his junior. The daughter of a Bengal officer, Harriet was a plain but hardy soul who had spent her early years in India. At the age of eleven she went to live with an aunt in England and never saw her father again: he died shortly before her return in 1846; her mother left India soon after. Harriet's need for emotional and financial security, therefore, was as great as Tytler's need for a surrogate mother. But they grew to love each other and, by May 1857, had two boys and a girl of their own, making five children in all. The three eldest were at school in England, leaving Harriet with two infants and another one on the way. Amiable, motherly and eight months pregnant, she was known as the 'angel of the regiment' and the subalterns used to beg her 'to ask their young women to lunch . . . to give them a better opportunity of carrying on their little flirtations'.

That morning, 11 May, the whole Delhi Brigade* had paraded to hear the general order announcing the execution of Jemadar Issuree Pandy of the 34th. Tytler, fluent in Hindustani, stood in for the sick regimental interpreter. As he read out the order, the men began to hiss and shuffle their feet, 'showing by their actions their sympathy with the executed sepoy'. Tytler was still fuming when he returned home, telling his wife that he would give his men 'drill to their heart's content'. Harriet Tytler added:

The early morning passed as usual, every door being . . . hermetically sealed to keep out the raging hot wind. Tattees were fixed to the outer doors and watered. We had all had our baths and Marie [her French nanny] and the children had had their breakfast, when my husband and myself sat down to ours. This was about eight o'clock . . . Just as we were getting through our last course (melons), the door flew open and the tailor rushed in with his hands clasped and in a most excited manner said, 'Sahib, Sahib, the fanj [army] has come.'

Tytler buckled on his sword and made straight for the adjutant's house, where he found his commanding officer, Lieutenant-Colonel Knyvett, Captain Gardner and the brigade-major. He was told that mutineers were marching from Meerut to Delhi and given orders to take his company, along with Captain Gardner's, to the White House at the northernmost point of the Ridge, overlooking the new powder magazine, to ensure that no mutineers crossed over from the other side of the Jumna. But the earlier signs of disaffection were repeated as men in both companies seized more cartridges than they were entitled to and marched off with excited cries that their officers were unable to silence.

Lieutenant Edward Vibart of the 54th Native Infantry – 'Butcher' to his family – was also in his bungalow when he received word that his regiment had been ordered to march down to the city to deal with some sowars from Meerut who were 'creating disturbances'. Still just nineteen, the eldest son of a well-regarded cavalry officer,† Vibart was already a company commander on account of the high number of officers absent from his regiment. When he reached the parade-ground he found Colonel Ripley, who had

* The Delhi Brigade was made up entirely of Indian troops: the 38th, 54th and 74th regiments of Native Infantry and a battery of bullock-drawn artillery.

† Major Edward Vibart, commanding the 2nd Light Cavalry, had been present at the storming of Ghazni in 1839 and, four years later, won a bronze star at the Battle of Punniar.

been with the regiment for barely a year, excitedly giving orders to the assembled officers. Vibart's company and the Grenadiers, under the command of Major Paterson, were sent to the artillery lines to escort two guns to the city, while the rest of the regiment made straight for the Kashmir Gate, the closest of the nine main gates in the city's outer wall that extended for seven miles and contained up to 160,000 people.

Within the Kashmir Gate was a small fortified enclosure known as the Main Guard that was always garrisoned by a European officer and fifty sepoys: on duty this week was Lieutenant Proctor of the 38th Native Infantry. As the 54th, with its band playing and Ripley at its head, passed through the inner gates of the Main Guard into the open ground in front of St James's Church, it was confronted by a body of mutinous sowars. 'Our quarrel is not with you but with your officers,' they exclaimed, before opening fire on Ripley and the others. Ripley ordered his men to load and return fire, but most shot in the air or at their own officers. In desperation Captain Wallace of the 74th, the field-officer of the day who had taken command of the Main Guard, ordered the 38th to engage the mutineers but they would not, saying that the time had come to avenge themselves on those who had tried 'to subvert their caste and religion'. After shooting two of the rebels, Colonel Ripley was chased and cut down with swords before the horrified eyes of Wallace and Proctor in the Main Guard. He was then bayoneted by his own men. Four of his officers and the regimental surgeon were also slain, though a further three officers managed to escape.

The two guns and the remaining two companies of the 54th were still some distance off when they heard the distinctive sound of musketry. They quickened their pace and were nearing the Kashmir Gate when they met Captain Wallace galloping in the opposite direction. He implored Paterson and Vibart to hurry, as their fellow officers were being murdered beyond the Main Guard. 'At this moment,' recalled Vibart, 'the body of our unfortunate colonel was carried out, literally hacked to pieces. Such a fearful sight I never beheld. The poor man was still alive, and, though scarcely able to articulate, I distinctly gathered from the few words he gasped out, that we had no chance against the cavalry troopers, as our own men had turned against us.' Ripley was placed in a carriage and driven back to the cantonment. Vibart wrote:

I now entered the Main Guard, and found everything in confusion. On looking out into the open space in front of the church, a few cavalry troopers in their

French-grey uniforms were seen galloping back in the direction of the palace. Lieutenant Wilson [of the Bengal Artillery] brought a gun round to bear on them, but they were out of sight before he had time to fire. As for the men of my own regiment . . . they had all vanished . . . At length it was determined to hold the Main Guard, and for this purpose the two guns were placed in position at the gate, which commanded the approach from the palace and swept the open ground in front; some of our sepoys were drawn up in support, whilst others were sent to man the ramparts and bastion, and keep a sharp look-out on every side.

With the men in position, Vibart and some others went through the inner gates to look for survivors. They recovered the corpses of four officers. 'I shall never forget my feelings that day as I saw our poor fellows being brought in,' wrote Vibart, 'their faces distorted with all the agonies of a violent death, and hacked about in every conceivable way. Only a couple of hours previously we had been laughing and chatting together, utterly unconscious to the danger which threatened us.' But Vibart had little time for such melancholy thoughts because reports now reached the Main Guard that two regiments of native infantry, the 11th and 20th, had also arrived from Meerut and were on their way to attack them.

Vibart later marvelled at the fact that the two companies of the 54th 'did not, there and then, in combination with the detachment of the 38th . . . on duty at the Main Guard, openly join in the outbreak, and murder every European in the enclosure'. He attributed their hesitation to commit themselves to the fact that they expected European troops to arrive from Meerut at any moment. Certainly Vibart and the others had no reason to doubt that 'sooner or later assistance would be forthcoming, could we only hold out long enough'. The European officers' spirits were soon raised by successive reinforcements. The first to appear were the three officers who had escaped, though Captain Butler was covered in blood and 'faint from a blow he had received on his head from a large brickbat'. Then, at about one o'clock, Major Herbert Abbott arrived with one hundred and fifty volunteers from the 74th Native Infantry and two guns. Lastly, and most surprisingly, nearly two hundred men of the 54th returned with their regimental colours, claiming they had been 'seized with panic in the confusion' but had since reformed. It was obvious to Vibart, however, that these 'loyal' sepoys could not be trusted.

Back at the cantonment, news of the 54th's treachery had prompted Brigadier Harry Graves, the 53-year-old station commander, to call out his remaining

Indian troops. Detachments of the 38th and 74th regiments were sent to occupy the principal roads leading from the city, while the brigadier himself, with a strong detachment and four guns, took up a central position at the Flagstaff Tower on top of the Ridge. All European civilians were told to congregate at the tower because, though small and far from impregnable, Graves thought it offered the best defensive option until help arrived from Meerut.

Among the civilians who gathered at the tower were Mrs Peile and her young son, the family of Lieutenant Peile of the 38th who was sick and due to set off for England on 15 May. On hearing that Colonel Ripley was 'lying at the bells of arms, dreadfully wounded', Mrs Peile and another lady went to see if they could help.

We found him lying on a bed of very rough manufacture [recalled Mrs Peile], and a sergeant's wife brought us a nice soft *rezaie* [quilt], which we folded once or twice double, and laid him upon it. This appeared to comfort his wounds, and after we had applied some lavender-water to his temples he seemed much better, and talked to us. He was, of course, in great agony, and begged of his native doctor to give him a dose of opium to deaden his sufferings, and, after some persuasion, the doctor did so. The colonel was then so much better, that he pointed to one frightful wound in his left shoulder, and told us that the men of his own regiment had bayoneted him.

Mrs Peile returned to the Flagstaff Tower at two o'clock, followed by her husband and a doolie containing the stricken colonel. Mrs Peile wrote:

By this time the people at the Flagstaff were in a great state of alarm, having heard that the King of Delhi, instead of aiding us, was sending ladders for the sepoys to scale the walls of the Magazine, and numbers of gentlemen and merchants from the city, assisted by several ladies, were bringing in boxes upon boxes of powder, caps and bullets, which were all being lodged at the top of the Tower. Our alarm was further intensified when a cart drawn by bullocks shortly after arrived at the Flagstaff, which it was whispered contained the bodies of the unfortunate officers, who had been so brutally killed in the city. The cart was covered over with one or two ladies' dresses, to screen the dead from view; but one of their arms . . . was hanging over the side of the cart. Some now advised leaving for Kurnaul, a distance of about seventy miles from Delhi; but several ladies present declaimed against going, as their husbands had been absent since the morning.

One of these ladies was Harriet Tytler, who, after much toing and froing, had finally reached the Flagstaff Tower with her French nanny and two young children in the carriage of Mrs de Tessier, the wife of the artillery commander. At one point her four-year-old son, Frank, having overheard the native servants talking, came to her in tears and asked, 'Mamma, will these naughty sepoys kill my papa and will they kill me too?' She recalled: 'He was a very blue-eyed, fair child. I gazed at his little white throat and said to myself, "My poor child, that little throat will be cut ere long, without any power on my part to save you." It was a dreadful moment, but I pulled myself together and said, "No darling, don't be frightened. No one will harm you. Stay close to your mother."'

An even more tortured soul on the Ridge at this time was Lieutenant Charles Thomason of the Bengal Engineers, still recovering from illness. The 23-year-old son of a former Lieutenant-Governor of the North-Western Provinces, Thomason had recently become engaged to the chaplain's vivacious daughter, Miss Jennings. When he heard that the rebels were murdering civilians, he made up his mind to ride to the fort to rescue his fiancée. But his brother officers would not let him go, saying: 'You can never save her. She must have been killed long ago.' They were right.

As the day wore on, a number of European civilians sought refuge in the Main Guard, including Mr de Gruyther, the deputy collector, and Mrs Forrest and her three daughters, the family of the assistant commissary of ordnance. But there were no means of sending them up to the cantonment and they were 'forced to remain in the densely crowded enclosure of the Main Guard throughout the scorching heat of the day, without food or sustenance of any kind'. Such an ordeal was infinitely preferable to the fate of many other Europeans. When the Delhi Bank was attacked and plundered around noon, Mr Beresford, the manager, retreated to the roof of one of its outbuildings with his wife and children. Armed only with a sword and a spear, the couple managed to prevent the mob from climbing the staircase. But others scaled the wall and soon put an end to their desperate resistance, though not before the plucky Mrs Beresford had impaled one man on her spear.

The officers at the Main Guard could see 'dense pillars of smoke' from the direction of the city and knew that a 'great destruction of property was going on'. But they were powerless to intervene. The church was plundered before their eyes by an excited mob who smashed the monuments and cut down the bells before departing with the plate, the stools and even the cushions. The adjacent government treasury was also sacked. Most galling of all for Vibart and his fellow officers was their inability to respond to repeated requests for assistance from Lieutenant George Willoughby, commissary of ordnance, who was in charge of the Delhi magazine, the biggest in upper India with a vast store of muskets, field guns, ammunition and powder. Willoughby, a shy, undistinguished man – short and fat with a penchant for side-partings and twin-moustaches – had barricaded the gates of the magazine with the intention of holding out until evening when 'the European troops would be certain to arrive from Meerut'. His tiny garrison consisted of two veteran officers, Lieutenants Forrest and Raynor – fifty-seven and sixty-one years old respectively – and six other British employees of the Ordnance Department. Together they had placed two 6-pounder guns loaded with double charges of grape inside each gate, in case they were forced, and a further four guns near to the central office. They had also issued muskets to their reluctant Indian assistants, who were already showing signs of insubordination, and laid a powder-train between the main store and a tree in the centre of the yard so that, *in extremis*, the magazine could be blown up.

At about ten thirty a detachment of palace guards arrived and demanded possession of the magazine in the name of the King. Willoughby ignored them. An hour later, recalled Forrest,

> the subadar of the guard on duty at the magazine informed Lieutenant Willoughby and me that the King of Delhi had sent down word to the mutineers that he would without delay send scaling ladders from the palace for the purpose of scaling the walls; and which shortly after arrived. On the ladders being erected against the wall, the whole of our Native establishment deserted us by climbing up the sloped sheds on the inside of the magazine and descending the ladders on the outside. After which the enemy appeared in great numbers on the top of the walls, and on whom we kept up an incessant fire of grape, every round of which told well, as long as a single round remained.

The one-sided battle raged for some time. During a lull in the fighting, Willoughby and Forrest went to the main gate to ask who was commanding the attack. The response was that 'a son and grandson of the King's were present, organizing the attack on us; but the men who ascended the scaling ladders and entered the magazine were all sepoys of the 11th and 20th regiments'. Conductor Buckley, assisted only by Lieutenant Forrest, was loading and firing the four guns near the magazine office. Together they fired at least four rounds from each gun, though 'the enemy were then some hundreds in number, and kept up a continuous fire of musketry on us from within forty or fifty yards'. But these guns were put out of action shortly after three o'clock when, in quick succession, Buckley was hit by a musket ball in the right arm and Forrest by one in the left hand.

> It was at this critical moment that Lieutenant Willoughby gave the signal for firing the Magazine. Conductor Scully, who had from the first evinced gallantry by volunteering for this dangerous duty, now coolly and calmly, without hesitation, and yet without confusion, set fire to the several trains. In an instant and with an explosion that shook the city and was heard distinctly in Meerut, the Magazine blew up. The wall was thrown flat upon the ground, and it is said that some hundreds of the enemy were buried under the ruins or blown into the air.

One rebel source estimated that twenty-five sepoys and up to four hundred onlookers were killed by the massive explosion, with many of their bodies 'blown far into the city'. The European fatalities included Scully and the pair who had been manning the guns covering the gates, Sergeant Edwards and Sub-Conductor Crow. But the rest of the tiny garrison somehow survived and, singed and bloody, reached the Main Guard, where they were given a joyous reception by their fellow Europeans.*

About this time, Major Abbott's detachment was recalled by Brigadier Graves. Convinced that the Main Guard was lost without the sepoys of the 74th, Major Paterson sent Mr de Gruyther to remonstrate with the brigadier. But the guns set off, nevertheless, and were seized en route by a mutinous picket of the 38th which returned them to the Kashmir Gate. 'On seeing them re-enter the Main Guard without an officer we were all greatly astonished,' remembered Lieutenant Vibart, 'and on Major Abbott asking the drivers why they had returned, they gave some evasive reply. Meanwhile several of the 38th Sepoys kept entering the enclosure in parties of threes and fours, and we could observe our men getting very restless and uneasy.' Abbott, determined to wait no longer, ordered his men to set off for the Ridge with the two guns. The civilians were to accompany them on one of the gun wagons. But less than half of Abbott's command had passed through

* Vibart wrote later that the heroic defence of the magazine had 'scarcely a parallel in history'. But, as Forrest himself acknowledged, it could not prevent 'large quantities of stores from falling into the hands of the enemy', primarily from the new powder magazine outside the city that fell to the rebels intact. (Vibart, 40 and 44.)

the Kashmir Gate when some of the 38th Sepoys closed it and began to fire at the remaining Europeans.* Vibart recorded:

> Almost at the first discharge I saw Captain Gordon [of the 74th] fall from his horse; a musket-ball had pierced his body, and he fell without a groan within a few feet of where I was standing. The next moment I saw Miss Forrest hastily dismount from the gun wagon on which she was seated and jump across his prostrate body . . . Scarcely knowing what I was doing, I made for the ramp which leads from the courtyard to the bastion above. Everyone appeared to be doing the same. Twice I was knocked over as we all frantically rushed up the slope, the bullets whistling past us like hail . . . Poor Smith and Reveley, both of the 74th, were killed close beside me . . . Osborn, of my own corps, was shot through the thigh.

The first officers to reach the bastion immediately jumped the 25 feet that separated its embrasures from the ditch below and scrambled up the counterscarp.† The rest were about to follow when, hearing the 'despairing cries' of women sheltering in the nearby officers' quarters, they turned back and found a group of them 'in a state bordering on distraction', notably the Misses Forrest and their mother, who had been shot through the shoulder. Leading the terrified ladies to the parapet, the officers tried to make a rope by tying their sword-belts together; but it broke when tested. So some of the officers dropped first so that they could break the fall of those who followed. One by one the ladies jumped. But the last, a fat old lady by the name of Mrs Forster, was too terrified to leap and had to be pushed 'headlong into the ditch beneath'. For a time the fugitives huddled close to the recessed wall to avoid the bullets from above. Eventually all the mutineers left to loot the treasury and they were free to attempt the steep counterscarp. 'Again

* Abbott recalled: 'I then ordered the men with me, about a hundred, to return to their assistance. The men said, "Sir, it is useless; they are all killed by this time. We have saved you and we are happy; we will not allow you to go back and be murdered." The men formed around me and hurried me along the road on foot, back to cantonments, to our quarter-guard.' Abbott later escaped to Meerut with five officers and a farrier-sergeant. (Major Abbott to Major Waterfield, 13 May 1857, *State Papers*, I, 265.)

† Among them were Captain Butler, Lieutenant Osborn and Ensign Angelo, the three officers of the 54th who had survived the massacre in front of the church, and Lieutenant Willoughby, who had commanded the gallant defence of the magazine. All four made good their escape from Delhi on foot but Osborn could not keep up because of his thigh wound. He was eventually carried into Meerut on a *charpoy* by well-meaning villagers; the other three were murdered as they tried to resist being robbed.

and again,' noted Vibart, 'did the ladies almost reach the top, when the earth, crumbling away beneath their feet, sent them rolling back into the ditch. Despair, however, gave us superhuman energy, till at length we all succeeded in gaining the summit.'

Vibart's group – the last to leave the Main Guard – was composed of five officers, six women and one Indian servant.* As they struggled through a belt of thorny bushes and thick undergrowth in the direction of Metcalfe House, to the north of the city, Mrs Forster was unable to keep up. A combination of her fall into the ditch, a slight bullet wound on her temple and the intense heat had sapped all her energy and, for a time, she was carried by two officers. But her enormous weight made such a task impossible and, having fallen unconscious, she was left on the ground and never seen again. The rest of the group, their clothes in tatters and parched with thirst, eventually reached Metcalfe House where they were hidden in the cellar by Sir Theophilus's *khidmatgar* and refreshed with food and beer.

Captains Tytler and Gardner had spent most of the day on picket duty at the White House. On the pretext of sheltering their men from the sun, but really to prevent them from witnessing the disorder in the city, they had ordered the majority to pile arms and rest in the house. But one by one the sepoys had slipped outside to watch the fires and listen to the gunfire. Tytler recalled:

> When I went into one of the rooms, I [saw] a native, from his appearance a soldier, haranguing the men of the companies and saying that every power or Government existed its allotted time, and that it was nothing extraordinary that that of the English had come to an end, according to what had been predicted in their native books. Before I could make a prisoner of him the magazine in the city exploded, and then the men of the two companies with a tremendous shout took up their arms and ran off to the city exclaiming, '*Prithiviraj ki jai!*' or 'Victory to the Sovereign of the World!'

The two officers ran after them and managed to round up about thirty men from each company, mainly old soldiers who had served with them in

* The members of the group were: Lieutenant Vibart of the 54th; Lieutenant Proctor of the 38th; Lieutenant Wilson of the Bengal Artillery; Lieutenant Salkeld of the Bengal Engineers; Lieutenant Forrest of the Ordnance Department; Forrest's wife and three daughters, the youngest of whom was nine; Mrs Fraser; Mrs Forster; and a native servant of Salkeld's.

Afghanistan. They then marched them up to the Flagstaff Tower, collecting any stray troops along the way. 'The Brigadier, European officers and civilians were congregated in front of the door facing the road leading to the Cashmere Gate of the city,' recalled Tytler, 'from whence they expected momentarily an attack to be made on them by the mutineers in the city; in front of this body of officers, were the only two remaining guns of the Delhi brigade in position, and to their left was a cart containing the mangled remains of the officers murdered in front of the church in the city . . . The remnants of the native infantry regiments were to the right of the tower, sitting and standing in groups in a most sulky mood, whilst in rear of the tower stood some of the carriages and horses of the officers.' Inside the tower Tytler found that the women and children 'had been sent into the narrow confined stair-case leading to the top, which added to their misery and discomfort, from the suffocating heat of the day'. Convinced their position was hopeless, Tytler urged Brigadier Graves to order an immediate retreat to Meerut by a ford on the right of the cantonment. The brigadier was unconvinced, saying they would all be shot down as soon as they left the safety of the tower. 'My men will never shoot us,' replied Tytler.

On hearing this a number of the officers present shouted their dissent. 'For God's sake don't listen to Tytler,' said one. 'He has been talked over by his men.'

'Look here gentlemen,' responded Tytler, 'it is not for you to say listen or don't listen to Tytler. We cannot hold our post, therefore it is our duty to form a retreat.' Tytler then told the brigadier that the remaining men of the 38th were the best in the regiment and would almost certainly cover the retreat.

'Go and ask your men,' said the brigadier in a resigned tone, overwhelmed as he was with anxiety, fatigue and the heavy responsibility of protecting the European community.

So Tytler approached the remaining two hundred men of the 38th and asked them whether they would protect the retreat. Most said that they would, but only if he commanded and arranged for the two guns to accompany them. Tytler agreed and went to tell the brigadier, who was swayed, ultimately, by the arrival of Major Paterson and the survivors from the Main Guard. The order to retreat was given and there was an unseemly rush for the carriages. Tytler had had the presence of mind to order up his *gharry* and into it tumbled his wife and two children, their French maid Marie, and Mrs Gardner and her young son. Like Harriet Tytler, Mrs Gardner was also eight months pregnant. Harriet recalled:

It was a terrible crush, for a carriage only meant for two persons inside to have six. How we all got in I don't know. Marie and myself sat with our backs to the horses with little Edith on my lap and Frank crouching with terror at my feet, hiding himself in our petticoats, while Mrs Gardner and her boy sat opposite . . .

Poor Colonel Ripley, on hearing we were all taking refuge, ordered his doolie (litter) bearers to carry him in his bed to where we were . . . I can never forget his poor death-stricken face, and could realize his feelings of despair at coming to be with his comrades and then being left by them to his sad fate. It was nobody's fault. There were not enough conveyances as it was to save the lives of all those in the Flag Staff Tower. Those who could get away on horseback or in carriages had a chance of escape. Those who had not almost to a man met their deaths on the way.

The carriages with the women and children went first, followed by the guns and lastly the officers with the remnants of the 38th and 74th regiments. But as the troops, headed by Captain Tytler, reached the cantonment at the bottom of the Ridge they were met by two sepoys of the 38th who had been 'scorched in a frightful manner'. They were, they said, the sole survivors of the guard from the magazine that had been deliberately blown up by the English. Hearing this, some of the 'loyal' sepoys moved off towards their lines; others asked Tytler why he had broken his promise by letting the guns go ahead. Tytler offered to ride to the front of the column and bring back the guns, but the sepoys would not have it. 'Sir, we cannot follow you,' explained one of the veterans. 'The Europeans and natives are two, we fight for you, we spill our blood for you, and you treat us in return by blowing up our brothers with gunpowder. Go, Sir, go, you have been our father and mother, always kind to us, with *bahana* (subterfuge) we will prevent the cavalry from following you; but we cannot come ourselves.'

In a final attempt to win over the sepoys, Tytler borrowed another officer's horse and galloped after the guns that had gone down the Karnal road. But when he caught up with them, two miles from the Flagstaff Tower, their drivers ignored his entreaty to halt. 'Oh no, no halting now,' one sneered, 'when we do halt, it shall be in the city of Delhi.'

As a disconsolate Tytler rode back down the crowded road, he came across his wife's carriage, which, like most of the column, had followed the fast-moving guns instead of crossing the ford towards Meerut. Harriet implored him to stay with them, and for a time he was torn between family and duty. But Mrs Gardner's pleas for him to find her husband settled the issue. Telling Harriet to hurry on to Karnal, a further 60 miles up the Grand Trunk Road, he headed back to the cantonment. The road now looked like the aftermath of a large fair, 'carriages, horses, men running and screeching to each other in sad and awful confusion'. At the bridge over the canal that marked the western boundary of the cantonment, Tytler met Captain Gardner, 'running and walking, quite faint and exhausted'. Tytler could see 'dense crowds of natives' pouring into the cantonment from the south and, realizing there was no time to lose, shouted to Gardner to jump up behind him. Together they galloped after the motley procession of Europeans, passing their sickly quartermaster, Lieutenant Holland, whose horse was lame. Holland was later overtaken by mutinous sowars, badly wounded in the back and left for dead.* The European death toll would have been much higher if most of the mutinous sowars had not preferred to loot the houses between the city and the cantonments.

The fugitives faced other hazards, notably Gujar tribesmen and hostile Hindu villagers. Tytler and Gardner had to beat off two attacks by lathi-wielding Gujars before catching up with the carriage containing their families. Transferring the *syce* to his horse, Tytler drove the *gharry* while Gardner stood behind it. Another attack by Gujars resulted in the loss of the horse, however, and the *syce* was put on the roof. But the combined weight proved too much for the tiny carriage and, a mile or two further on, one of its wheels splintered. They continued on foot, the men carrying the bigger children and Marie the youngest, and eventually requisitioned a bullock-drawn government cart at the point of a gun. The cart took them as far as Panipat, where another cart, this time horse-drawn, and a separate carriage were procured.

> The two coachmen were suspiciously dressed [remembered Captain Tytler], each armed with a double-barrel gun, swords and pistols, and amused us the whole way with news about [Ambala] having fallen, that the European Artillery guns had been seized by the native troops, and various other fabrications, advising us strongly to leave the road and strike off to the right; when they found this would not answer, they tried to separate our two carriages . . . by one driving rapidly, and the other very slow; this, however, we soon put a stop to.

They finally reached the post office at Karnal, after an exhausting and nerve-racking journey of more than sixteen hours, at ten in the morning of 12 May. There they met up with a number of other fugitives and, the following day, continued on to Ambala, passing a detachment of the 4th

* Incredibly Lieutenant Holland survived his wounds, thanks to the kindness of villagers, and eventually reached Meerut and safety on 28 May.

Light Cavalry, who told their cart-men, 'Drive on, let them go, they have only three days to live.'

The last Europeans to leave the Delhi cantonment were Colonel Knyvett of the 38th and his adjutant, Lieutenant Gambier. They had followed their sepoys back to their lines in an attempt to bring them to order. When this failed, they decided to spend the night at the quarter-guard but were woken at nine by the sound of gunshots: the mutineers were coming in from the city. They left immediately, Gambier pulling his exhausted colonel by the wrist. The following morning, on an island in the Jumna, they met up with the survivors from the Main Guard, one of whom was Gambier's great friend Lieutenant Proctor. This group had left Metcalfe House with a bag of provisions at dusk on the 11th, narrowly avoiding a band of sepoys on the plain beyond the Najafgarh Canal.

The fugitives now numbered eight men and five women and considered themselves a 'match' for any 'straggling party of mutineers'. But they did not reckon with hostile civilians. After fording the main stream of the Jumna, they were captured and stripped by a howling mob of Gujars, and only the intervention of a yellow-robed fakir, his face covered with paint and ashes, saved them. During their stay with the fakir they managed to bribe a villager to carry a letter in French to Meerut. They were also joined by two sergeant's wives who had escaped from Delhi with their babies. On Sunday, 17 May, having left the fakir's house the day before, they were taken to the house of an elderly German-born Jew named Francis Cohen who had been rewarded for some previous service to the government with the *zemindaree* of several villages, and was 'native now in all but religion and kindness of heart'. He put the upper storey of his house at the fugitives' disposal, and produced 'skirts and petticoats' for the women and 'all kinds of native attire' for the men.

That afternoon, recalled Vibart, having eaten a 'plentiful repast' washed down with beer and cognac, 'we were all sitting round the table, quietly talking over our recent adventures and hairbreadth escapes, and looking forward with light hearts to setting out next day on our journey to Meerut, when all of a sudden a tremendous shout was raised without'. The noise gradually grew louder and more distinct until the fugitives realized with horror what was being shouted, '*Badsháh ká fouj! Badsháh Delhi ká fouj aya!* ("The King's troops! The King of Delhi's troops have come!")'

And there [wrote Vibart], sure enough, on looking out, we saw some forty troopers, dressed in the French-grey uniform of the mutinous 3rd Cavalry, drawn up in line just outside the walls and demanding admittance. The first thing we called for was to be supplied with arms; the next thing we did was to throw off the clean clothes we had on and jump into our former old ones . . . In the space of a very few seconds we were once more clad in the filthy garments of the previous day, and stood ready to meet the worst. In the midst of all of this excitement two European officers were observed riding up the street, and as they were followed very quietly a few paces in rear by the troopers themselves we came to the conclusion that they were friends not enemies . . . I was not long in recognizing both officers to be old friends – Gough and Mackenzie, of the 3rd Cavalry.

Mackenzie later told Vibart that General Hewitt had at first discounted their letter because 'it was considered hopeless to send a party to succour fugitives who were in such close proximity to Delhi'. But Mackenzie had insisted on making an attempt to save the women and children, and Gough had volunteered to go with him. 'Amongst the many praiseworthy deeds recorded during the Mutiny,' wrote Vibart, 'perhaps few are deserving of more commendation than the self-sacrificing devotion of these two officers.'

The seventeen fugitives finally reached Meerut the following morning and were taken to the Damdammah, where their arrival caused a 'considerable sensation'. Gambier wrote: 'There was something affecting in seeing ladies suffering such hardships. Mrs Forrest, with her painful wound, and others of them unable to walk, with scorched arms, and faces peeling from the sun, torn clothes and shoeless feet, presented a sufficiently pitiable spectacle. All around us looked so dazzlingly clean, that we hung our heads like convicts.' But none was more downcast than Mrs Fraser, who had just been informed of the death of her husband.*

Lieutenant Forrest, on the other hand, had reached safety with all his family. He and the other two survivors from the Delhi magazine, Lieutenant Raynor and Conductor Buckley, became the first Indian mutiny recipients of the recently instituted Victoria Cross.† Promoted captain, Forrest was killed in action at Dehra Dun in 1859.

* Captain Edward Fraser, the Commandant of the Sappers and Miners, was killed when four of his companies mutinied at Meerut on Friday, 16 May 1857.

† Willoughby and the other dead defenders of the magazine did not qualify because the Victoria Cross could not be awarded posthumously until 1902. Raynor, at sixty-one, is still the oldest winner of the award.

The Indians in the greatest peril in Delhi on 11 May were Christian converts and government officials. Among those murdered on sight was Kalla Saheb, the deputy collector, whose body was seen with his son's in front of the Treasury. Others fled, including the *kotwal* and his deputy, while the more resourceful switched allegiance. Mainodin Hassan Khan, *thanadar* of Pahargunge, was on official business at Hutchinson's *cutcherry* when the mutineers reached Delhi. For a time his conduct was exemplary: he located the *kotwal* and gave him Hutchinson's order to close all the city gates; he then returned to his police station outside the city, where he met Sir Theophilus Metcalfe, Hutchinson's deputy, and helped him to escape.

Realizing that British authority in Delhi was at an end, Mainodin changed from his uniform into Indian dress and headed for the Red Fort, in his words, to 'ask for an interview with the King, in hopes that I might get some appointment to give me influence to stop the butchery of Europeans, and ensure the protection of my own family'. En route he noticed that the *kotwali* had been sacked and that all the shops were closed. 'On every side the scum of the population was hurrying to and fro,' he wrote, 'laden with the plunder of European houses.' The Lahore Gate of the fort was guarded by a line of 38th Sepoys 'ready for action'. But they ignored him, and he entered the fort on foot, finding it deserted. He eventually located a senior royal official and gained admittance to the King's apartments.

Prostrating himself before Bahadur Shah, Mainodin stated that his object in seeking an audience was to put an end to the plunder and butchery, particularly that of European and Christian women and children. 'I am helpless,' responded the King, 'all my attendants have lost their heads or fled. I remain here alone. I have no forces to obey my orders: what can I do?'

Mainodin replied that if he was appointed *kotwal* in the King's name, he would do his best to restore order.

'My son,' said the King, 'this duty I will expect from you; you have come to me in a moment of difficulty and danger; do whatever seemeth good to you: I command you.'

Mainodin then asked if he could have the services of two of the King's *chobdars* to give him more authority to stop the slaughter. He also suggested sending one of the royal princes through the city to order the shops to open. The King seemed to approve, but wanted to check with his *hakim*. So Ahsanullah Khan was sent for and Mainodin repeated his proposal. 'What necessity is there for *chobdars* to accompany you?' asked Ahsanullah, 'the *bagheelog* (mutineers) will never abandon the slaughter of Christians. If they are interfered with, yet worse things may happen. When satiated with the blood of Christians, they will direct their attention to us and to our property. Let us take care of ourselves.'

Mainodin replied: '*Hakimjee*, your judgement is not good. The massacre of innocent women and children is not a good work in the eyes of the Most High God. When this insurrection is suppressed, and the English power re-established, the saving of these lives will stand you in good stead. Even if you incline to the opinion that the English power is gone, these lives you have saved will redound to your glory and honour.' Mainodin added that in his opinion the insurrection would continue 'only a short while'.

Ahsanullah did not respond and seemed lost in thought. But the King had been swayed by Mainodin's argument and ordered his *chobdars* to go with him.

Mainodin made straight for the Dariagunge district and was horrified to find rebels still burning bungalows and killing women and children. 'I and the *chobdars* loudly proclaimed the orders of the King,' he recalled. 'Our interference was so far effectual, that the lives of some dozen persons were spared. They were sent to the Palace, and confined in the *chota kasa* apartments, and orders were given to feed them.' Mainodin claimed to have saved another nineteen Christian converts by confining them in the *kotwali* and sending them out of the city when it was dark.

By the morning of 12 May, thanks to the intervention of Mainodin and others, almost fifty Europeans and Eurasians, mainly women and children,* had been saved from certain death and were confined in a single dark room in the bowels of the fort. 'We were very much crowded together,' recorded Mrs Aldwell, the Eurasian wife of a government pensioner, 'and in consequence of the sepoys, and every one who took a fancy to do so, coming and frightening the children, we were obliged frequently to close the one door that we had, which then left us without light and air.'

Most of the sources seem to agree that Bahadur Shah was neither aware of the plot to mutiny nor particularly enthusiastic when presented with the *fait accompli*. He gives the impression of a frightened man, overwhelmed by events and trying desperately to keep in with both the rebels and the British. One of the most reliable Indian accounts of what went on in the city and

* Among the prisoners were Mrs Scully and her three children, the family of Conductor Scully who had been killed at the magazine.

palace after the rising was compiled by Munshi Jiwan Lal,* the administrator of the King's Company pensions and a trusted conduit between him and Simon Fraser. Late on 11 May, according to Jiwan Lal, two subedars 'formally tendered' the services of the rebel soldiery to the King, who directed them 'to take their orders from Hakim Ahsanullah Khan'. Jiwan continued:

Ahsanullah looked much perplexed what reply to give. He looked upon the outbreak as a passing thunder-cloud too black to last long. His reply was: 'You have been long accustomed under the English rule to regular pay. The King has no treasury. How can he pay you?' The officers replied: 'We will bring the revenue of the whole Empire to your treasury.' Hakim Ahsanullah then called for a return of the troops who had mutinied . . . [Later] Ahsanullah sought a private audience of the King, and on his advice a camel sowar was sent off with a letter to the Lieutenant-Governor [of the North-Western Provinces] at Agra. From time to time more troops arrived. The Court of the Palace became a scene of the wildest confusion, quarreling, and disputes. With a view to introduce discipline among the troops orders were issued by Ahsanullah Khan directing the different Princes to assume command of the several regiments.

Ahsanullah's version of events is that it was the King who initiated the letter to John Colvin, the Lieutenant-Governor of the North-Western Provinces, informing him of the arrival of the mutineers, his 'inability to take any measures against them, and begging for help in the shape of European troops'.

The following day, wrote Jiwan Lal, the mutinous officers increased the pressure on the King by presenting him with *nazirs* and describing themselves as 'faithful soldiers awaiting his orders'. This prompted Ahsanullah to warn the King 'that no dependence could be placed on them' and that as 'soon as a sufficient number had been gathered together there would be a general plunder of the city'. That afternoon the palace 'was thronged by a turbulent mob of soldiers, calling out that all the grain-shops were closed and the King's loyal servants were starving'. Yielding to their demands 'to personally allay the fears of the citizens' by appearing in public, the King passed through the streets on an elephant and ordered the shops to be reopened. But

* Jiwan Lal was an educated native gentleman, closely associated with the court life of the King of Delhi. His father, Girdhari, was a lineal descendant of Raja Ragonath, Aurangzeb's chief minister, and had been *munshi*, or writer, to Sir David Ochterlony and Sir Charles Metcalfe during their stints as British Resident in Delhi.

most shopkeepers ignored this directive and the complaints continued. 'Throughout this eventful day,' noted Jiwan, '[the King] was distraught, perplexed and cowed at finding himself in a position which made him the mere puppet of those who had formerly been only too glad humbly to obey his orders, but who now, taking advantage of the spirit of insubordination which was rife in all classes of the city . . . were not ashamed to mock and humiliate him.'

The rebel officers were the real power in Delhi. They had already forced the King to write letters to the Rajas of Patiala, Jajjar, Bulbugarh, Bahadurgarh and Ellore, requesting them 'to march at once upon Delhi with all their forces to join the King's army, and to repel any attack on the city by the English'. Now, according to Mainodin Khan, they persuaded him to send *perwanahs* to other regiments of the Company army, 'promising monthly salaries of thirty rupees to infantry soldiers and fifty to cavalry, if they would join the king's army'. Mainodin is probably guilty of exaggeration because the famous 'Delhi Proclamation', issued by the rebels at this time, offered the more realistic sum of 10 rupees a month to a foot soldier and 30 to a sowar.

A chilling example of Bahadur Shah's powerlessness was given on 16 May when the rebel soldiers accused the King and his advisers of 'saving the lives of European ladies and gentlemen and concealing them in the Fort, and through them communicating with the Europeans at Meerut'. They had seized an incriminating letter that, they claimed, had been signed by both Ahsanullah Khan and Mahbub Ali Khan. Both vehemently denied involvement, but the mutineers would be satisfied only by the immediate execution of the European and Eurasian prisoners. According to Mainodin, who had been given command of the 38th Native Infantry,* the prisoners were 'treacherously' handed over by Ahsanullah Khan, who feared for his own life. Bahadur Shah tried to intervene by asking the rebel soldiers 'to consult their religious advisors to see if there were any authority for the slaughter of helpless men, women, and children'. He was ignored. At nine in the morning a party of sepoys and some of the King's servants arrived at the makeshift prison to collect the Christians. Only the five 'Muslim' prisoners – an old Indian woman who had been arrested for giving food and water to some Christians, and Mrs Aldwell and her three children who had managed to persuade the guards that they were Muslims from Kashmir – were allowed to remain. Mrs Aldwell recalled what happened next:

* Mirza Mogul, the King's eldest son, was colonel-in-chief and Mainodin's nominal superior.

> The women and children began crying, saying they knew they were going to be murdered; but the Mahomedans swore on the Koran and the Hindus on the Jumna, that such was not the case; that they wanted to give them a better residence . . . On this they went out, and were counted . . . a rope was thrown round to encircle the whole group, the same as prisoners are usually kept together when on the move; and in this manner they were taken out of my sight, and, as I heard, brought under the pipal tree by the small reservoir in the courtyard, and there murdered with swords by the King's private servants. None of the sepoys took part in killing them.

Mainodin's version is slightly different. 'A sowar first fired a carbine,' he recalled, 'then all were mercilessly massacred, to the horror of the whole city. In other parts of the city, fugitives were found and [killed] at the order of native officers in command of detached parties.'

As news of the Meerut and Delhi atrocities spread to other areas of British India, it caused panic and consternation – nowhere more so than at Agra, the capital of the North-Western Provinces.

10. 'The worst of the storm is past'

Charles Raikes, judge of the Sudder Court at Agra, was working in his library on the morning of 11 May when a servant handed him a copy of the *Mofussilite Extra*. It contained the gist of a telegram sent the previous evening by the sister of the Meerut postmaster to a relative in Agra, warning of a large-scale rising by Indian troops.*

For Raikes, a former Commissioner of Lahore, the outbreak was not wholly unexpected. 'It was,' he wrote later, 'the bursting of the thunder-cloud I had been long and anxiously watching ... The fabric of the Bengal army was tottering to ruin.' At midday Raikes and his fellow judges assembled at the Sudder Court as usual. 'Cases were tried, pleadings heard, and decrees passed,' he recalled. 'But the mind of the European functionaries was, more or less, absent.'

Raikes was a senior member of the government of the North-Western Provinces, the huge British territory that stretched from the foothills of the Himalayas to Jabalpur in central India. Its seat of government was the imperial city of Agra, but it also encompassed Delhi, the great Hindu city of Benares, the strategically vital fortress of Allahabad, and the flourishing commercial centres of Mirzapur and Cawnpore. For administrative purposes the territory was divided into eight civil divisions, or commissionerships,† each containing five or six districts, with a total surface area of 72,000 square miles and a population of 30 million. At the apex of the British administration was the fifty-year-old lieutenant-governor, John Colvin. A conscientious and capable administrator who oversaw the conduct of his subordinates with 'untiring vigilance', Colvin lacked 'that iron firmness – that rare self-confidence – which enables a man to impress his will upon others'.

Colvin's first act on learning of the outbreak was to inform Calcutta. But his ability to respond to the crisis was limited. The whole North-Western

* The telegram stated: 'The cavalry have risen, setting fire to their own houses and several officers' houses besides having killed and wounded all European officers and soldiers they could find near their lines: if aunt intends starting tomorrow evening, please detain her from doing so as the van has been prevented from leaving the station.' It was the only warning of the Meerut outbreak to reach Agra before the rebels cut the wire. (Maclagan, 78–9.)

† Agra, Allahabad, Benares, Delhi, Jabalpur, Jhansi, Meerut and Rohilkhand.

Provinces contained just three European regiments: two at Meerut, which could not be contacted, and one at Agra, the 3rd Bengal Europeans.* This last corps and a battery of European artillery were counterbalanced at Agra by two regiments of native infantry: the 44th and 67th. Most of the British officials and merchants at Agra lived in the civil station to the north of the city. A full five miles separated them from the military cantonment to the south-west, but only three from the imposing red sandstone fort on the west bank of the Jumna. Its massive walls, over 25 yards high and a mile and a half in circumference, had been built by Emperor Akbar in 1565.† The maze of buildings within – from marble halls, apartments, courtyards and pavilions to simple barracks, storehouses, cells and hovels – were largely the work of his grandson, Shah Jahan, who was also responsible for the spectacular domes and minarets of the nearby Taj Mahal, built as a memorial to his beloved second wife, Mumtaz Mahal, who died in childbirth in 1631.

The rambling fort was an obvious place of refuge for Europeans. But Colvin was anxious to prevent panic and refused to issue the necessary orders. On 13 May, having received intelligence that the mutineers were marching on Agra, he held a council of war in Government House, a large single-storey building set in parkland dotted with thorny trees. Ominously, Colvin was either unwilling or unable to control the noisy assembly. 'One officer rushed in to suggest we should all retire to the fort,' recalled Raikes, 'another to ask what was to be done at the jail, a third to speak about provisions, a fourth about the sepoy regiments in cantonments.' Colvin had come round to the idea of abandoning the station and taking up residence in the fort. But he was strongly opposed by most of his subordinates who felt that Agra could be saved only by showing a bold front. It was eventually decided to secure the fort with a detachment of Europeans and to raise volunteer corps in the district.

The following morning, by which time it had become clear that Agra was not about to be attacked, Colvin held a parade of his troops. Addressing the Europeans first, he urged them not to distrust their Indian comrades, whom they should consider as brothers-in-arms. But the effect was rather spoilt when Colvin added that 'the rascals at Delhi have killed a clergyman's daughter and if you should meet them in the field you will not forget this'. Turning to the sepoys, Colvin said that 'he fully trusted them, asked them

* The East India Company had nine regiments of European infantry – three in each presidency army – recruited mostly in Britain.

† Agra was the capital of the Mogul Empire until Aurangzeb moved it to Delhi in 1648.

to come forward if they had any complaints to make, and offered to discharge on the spot any man who wished to leave his colours'. None took up his offer. Instead, prompted by their officers to cheer, the sepoys 'set up a yell' while regarding the assembled Europeans with a 'devilish scowl'.

Colvin was convinced that the Mogul dynasty was behind the mutinies at Delhi and Meerut. To oppose the rejuvenated Moguls, therefore, he appealed to their old enemies among the nearby princely states: in particular to Gwalior and Bharatpur. Though his country had been defeated by the British as recently as 1843, when he was still a minor, the reaction of Maharaja Scindia of Gwalior was favourable: on 13 May, the 1st Gwalior Cavalry and a battery of artillery left Gwalior for Agra, 100 miles to the north. At around the same time the Bharatpur Legion* – under the command of the assistant agent, Captain Nixon – was sent to protect the city of Mathura to the north of Agra.

Colvin's confidence was returning. 'I am doing everything possible here to keep together and prevent the Native troops from giving trouble,' he cabled to Canning on the 15th, 'and trust to succeed.' A day later, having received details from Meerut of General Anson's preparations to retake Delhi, he added: 'The worst of the storm is past, and the aspect of affairs is fast brightening.'

News of the Meerut rising had reached Government House at Calcutta on 12 May. Further cables from Agra on the 13th and 14th completed the picture: Delhi was in the hands of the mutineers, Bahadur Shah had been proclaimed Emperor, and many Europeans had been killed. Canning was aghast. A month earlier he had informed Granville that the cartridge question was over. Now a key area of northern India was in rebellion and others would surely follow. Almost 1,000 miles of the Grand Trunk Road separated Calcutta from Delhi. Strung out along it were large Indian garrisons at Barrackpore, Dinapore, Benares, Allahabad, Cawnpore, Bareilly and throughout the province of Oudh. Holding them in check were just five British regiments: the 53rd and 84th Foot near Calcutta, the 10th Foot at Dinapore, the 32nd Foot at Lucknow and the 3rd Bengal Europeans at Agra.

Fortunately for Canning, the Persian War had just been brought to a successful conclusion,† and part of Sir James Outram's force was on its way back to India. On 14 May the Governor-General cabled Lord Elphinstone

* A mixed force of cavalry, infantry and artillery, officered by Indians.

† The peace treaty had been ratified by the Persians on 2 May.

in Bombay with a request to send on to Calcutta at least two British regiments and some artillery as soon as they arrived from Persia. He also sent a telegraph message to Lord Harris, the Governor of Madras, to prepare the 43rd Foot and the 1st Madras European Fusiliers for immediate embarkation, and dispatched a steamer to collect the 35th Foot from Pegu. Two days later he sent instructions to General Anson and Sir John Lawrence via Agra and Meerut: the former was to make every exertion to retake Delhi with troops from Meerut and the hills; the latter to support Anson by sending down to Delhi every man he could spare from the Punjab. Canning had already asked Elphinstone to assist Lawrence by shipping the 2nd Bombay European Fusiliers up the Indus River towards Ferozepore.

Also on 16 May Canning issued a proclamation denying that the Indian government wanted to 'interfere' with its subjects' religion or caste. The Governor-General 'knows', it stated, 'that endeavours are [being] made to persuade Hindoos and Mussulmans, soldiers and civil subjects, that their religion is threatened secretly, as well as openly, by the acts of Government, and that the Government is seeking in various ways to entrap them into a loss of caste for purposes of its own'. Some had already been 'deceived' by such 'tales'. And yet the government had 'invariably treated the religious feelings of all its subjects with careful respect' and would 'never cease to do so'. The proclamation ended with a plea for all persons of 'habitual loyalty and orderly conduct' not to 'listen to false guides and traitors, who would lead them into danger and disgrace'. Canning regretted not issuing the proclamation sooner, as some had urged. Whether it would have made any difference is doubtful. The mere fact that the government was prepared to respond to the rumours at all was proof enough for some Indian soldiers that they were not without foundation. That was certainly the line peddled by the army conspirators. If General Hearsey, one of the most respected officers in the Bengal Army, had not been believed when he gave similar assurances at Barrackpore in February, what hope was there for the Governor-General?

A more tangible initiative, but one that underlined earlier failings, was the passing on 16 May of an Act that gave civil and military officers increased powers of punishment and reward: on the one hand, courts martial were made easier to convene and their sentences could be carried out without confirmation from higher authority; on the other, both magistrates and commanding officers were given the summary power to promote Indian soldiers and to confer upon them the Order of Merit. But it was too little, too late.

Canning knew the only way to stamp out rebellion was by force, and he left no stone unturned in his search for reinforcements. When the monthly mail packet left Calcutta on 19 May, it carried a request for Sir Henry Ward, Governor of Ceylon, to send as many European troops as he could spare. 'I have asked for at least 500 Europeans,' Canning told Vernon Smith, 'but will accept Malays in place or besides them.' The same ship also carried letters to Lord Elgin and General Ashburnham, the leaders of a punitive expedition to China,* who were expected to call in at Ceylon en route. Canning, on his own initiative, wanted them to divert their regiments to India. To Elgin, he wrote:

> Our hold of Bengal – and the Upper Provinces – depends upon the turn of a word – a look. An indiscreet or irritating phrase from a foolish Commanding Officer at the head of a mutinous or disaffected company, may, whilst the present condition of things at Delhi lasts, lead to a general rising of the Native Troops in the Lower Provinces, where we have no European strength – and where an army in rebellion would have everything its own way for weeks and months to come . . . I do not want aid to put down the Meerut and Delhi rebels – that will be done easily as soon as the European troops can converge upon Delhi – but not sooner. Meanwhile every hour of delay – unavoidable delay – is an encouragement to the disaffected troops in other parts; and if any one of the many unwatched regiments on this side of Agra should take heart, and give the word, there is not a fort, or cantonment, or station in the plain of the Ganges that would not be in their hands in a fortnight. It would be exactly the same in Oude.

In the event the mail packet missed the China expedition. Fortunately Canning had sent another steamer with the same messages to Singapore, and it caught up with the British force as it was passing through the Sunda Strait between Sumatra and Java. Elgin at once gave orders for the whole force to divert to India while he continued on to Hong Kong in the expectation that his regiments would soon rejoin him. When it became clear that this would not happen for some time, he sailed for Calcutta to await fresh troops from England.

The mail continued on to England with letters for Robert Vernon Smith, the President of the Board of Control, and Ross Mangles, the Chairman of

* A diplomatic row had broken out between Britain and China at the beginning of 1857 following the Chinese seizure of a British-registered but locally-owned boat, *Arrow*, on suspicion of smuggling opium. A British force with Elgin as Plenipotentiary and Ashburnham as Commander-in-Chief had been dispatched to resolve the dispute by force.

the Court of Directors. 'Delhi is in the hands of the five insurgent regiments & has been so since the 11th,' Canning informed Vernon Smith. 'Meerut is quiet & safe in possession of European troops of the station. On all sides of Delhi, but especially from the hill stations on the north . . . European troops & irregulars are collecting & when the Europeans are in sufficient strength they will close upon the town & crush the rebels.' He then detailed the steps he had taken to procure troops and closed the letter with a request for yet more: 'From England what I ask is that you immediately send out the regiments which are due to the full complement of Queen's corps in India without making us wait for the issue of events in China, & that you will give support for the demand of 3 European regiments to be added to the Company's army in place of the 6 [mutinous regiments] which have now erased themselves from the Army List.' A similar appeal was directed to Mangles.

There was little more that Canning could do. The nearest reinforcements at Madras and Pegu would take at least two weeks to arrive; those from the Persian and Chinese expeditions a good deal longer. He could only wait and hope that Anson was able to retake Delhi with the troops at hand. In the meantime he was determined to put on an outward show of 'business as usual'. He refused to alter the routine at Government House or replace its Indian guard with Europeans. The State Ball to celebrate the Queen's Birthday went ahead as planned on 25 May, and Lady Canning continued to take her evening drives around the city. Yet many of the Europeans at Calcutta were unable to display the same *sang froid*. One English lady, who refused to attend the ball because she thought she would be murdered by the sepoy guard, hired two sailors to protect her for the night 'but they got tipsy, and frightened her more than imaginary enemies'. The men were not much better: many placed their families on ships in the river and went around with loaded revolvers. A mortified Canning wrote:

I never came across such a set of old women – some of them with swords by their sides – as those who fetch & carry the news of this town amongst the clubs & gossiping 'tiffin' rooms of their acquaintance. Men, soldiers, whose authority on matters relating to the Army & the Sepoys is readily credited, & whose words are caught up by Newspaper caterers, are spreading not reports only – in those they themselves be deceived – but opinions as to the state of things present & future, which make me ashamed for Englishmen. And it is not the shame only, there is mischief in it. The example will be catching. Hitherto the merchants (even the native merchants, greatly as they hate the Sepoys) & the non-official community have (most of them) shown sense & calmness. But how long this will last if our officers & officials crawl about with their tails between their legs, frightening themselves and everybody else, I cannot say.

Canning's disgust at the panic in Calcutta may have contributed to his decision not to accept an offer from the Masonic Lodges, Trades Association, and French, Armenian and Christian communities to form a volunteer corps for the defence of the city. Such a body would, he believed, have simply alarmed the Indian community without being militarily effective. He did, however, accept the volunteers as Special Constables. This refusal, coupled with Canning's natural reserve and outward display of unconcern, led many to conclude that he did not appreciate the seriousness of the crisis. But a private letter to Lord Granville proves that he was only too aware of the peril they were in:

If this disaffection should spread and burst out into such violence as has been exhibited at Meerut and Delhi, you may imagine the plunder, slaughter, consternation, and ruin which would ensue. The flame would spread without a check straight on end for 700 or 800 miles, over the richest tracts of India . . . Whether the infection will spread or not, no mortal man can say. None are more surprised at what has happened at Meerut than those who know the sepoys best; and I have lost *entirely* all confidence in the commanding officers of regiments, who with scarcely an exception swear to the fidelity of their men, and when a scoundrel is caught in the act have nothing to say but 'Who'd have thought it?'

General Anson and his headquarters staff were relaxing at Simla, the picturesque hot season retreat in the foothills of the Himalayas, when an exhausted rider arrived from Ambala on the morning of 12 May. It was Captain Barnard, the son and aide-de-camp of Major-General Sir Henry Barnard, the local divisional commander. He had ridden through the night with news of a telegraph message from Delhi stating that 'regiments there had mutinied, joined with others from Meerut, seized the bridge-of-boats, and that several officers had been killed'. A fuller account of the Meerut rising, written by one of General Hewitt's staff officers, was brought the same day by the Ambala postmaster.

At first Anson was not unduly concerned. 'He appears to rather pooh-pooh the thing,' noted Colonel Keith Young, his judge advocate-general, on 13 May. Young's wife was amazed by Anson's decision to remain at Simla until the 14th. 'When he first received the bad news on Tuesday morning,' she wrote, 'he ought to have started off at once. Colonel Becher,

Quartermaster-General, did his utmost to persuade him not to lose any time: but he said *no*; he would wait for the dâk. What is the use of the electric telegraph if the news it brings is not at once to be attended to?'

Anson had not been entirely idle. Aware that the vast quantity of military stores at Delhi had been lost to the rebels, he at once issued orders for European troops to secure most of the great arsenals of the Punjab. 'I have sent express,' he wrote to Canning on the 13th, 'to desire that the fort of Firuzpur [Ferozepore] may be secured by the 61st Foot, and the Fort at Govindgarh by the 81st. Two companies of the 8th from Jalandhar [Jullundur] to Philur [Phillour].' He also sent an artillery officer to arrange for the dispatch of a siege-train from Phillour.

Closer at hand, in the hills near Simla, were three European infantry regiments: the 75th Foot at Kasauli, and the 1st and 2nd Bengal European Fusiliers lower down at Dagshai and Subathu respectively. On 12 May the 75th Foot were ordered down to Ambala. Over the next two days, as the seriousness of the outbreak became more apparent, the other two European regiments were given similar instructions. At the same time the Sirmur Battalion of Gurkhas at Dehra Dun and the Sappers and Miners at Rurki were directed to Meerut. The three European regiments arrived at Ambala between 14 and 16 May and linked up with the 9th Lancers and two European batteries of Bengal Horse Artillery. The Indian portion of the Ambala garrison, however, was by now deeply mistrusted. In a curious echo of events at Meerut, the 60th Native Infantry and, to a lesser extent, the 5th had behaved mutinously on 10 May and again three days later. 'They are still doing their usual duties and will be retained as part of this force,' recorded Anson after reaching Ambala on 15 May. 'But it is impossible to conceal from oneself that there is some hazard in employing them on this service. The conduct of the Native Army has destroyed all confidence in any regiment, notwithstanding they may still profess to be faithful and loyal.'

The uncertain loyalty of all Indian troops at this time was underlined by the case of the Nasiri Battalion of Gurkhas. Stationed at Jutogh near Simla, the battalion was ordered on 14 May to set off the following morning to rendezvous with the siege-train at Phillour. But that afternoon reports reached Simla that the Gurkhas had 'refused to go' and 'would attack Simla and loot it instead'. The deputy commissioner, Lord William Hay, tried to reassure the undefended civilians at Simla that the report was false and the regiment was 'staunch'. But Mrs Young was unconvinced. 'Some of the Goorkhas were seen in the bazaar laughing and talking about the Delhi business,' she informed her sister, 'and when an Englishman passed he was hissed at.' Yet another report was that they 'intended to go down as ordered, but would join either Europeans or Natives, whichever was strongest'. The Europeans at Simla were understandably alarmed and held a meeting at which it was decided to place pickets of volunteers on the roads. That night, fearful that Simla would be attacked by the Gurkhas, more than seventy civilians slept in Dr Peskett's house. It looked like a 'crowded steamer' with every floor covered with bodies. 'None of us could close our eyes all night,' recalled Mrs Young, 'we were all listening for the guns. But morning came quite quietly.' During the evening of 15 May, after yet more scares, most of the European community fled Simla and spent the next five days under the protection of a friendly hill raja. The Youngs were among them. 'I haven't the least fear for myself,' wrote Colonel Young on 17 May, 'but the late dreadful excesses at Meerut and Delhi have made everybody over-anxious, and had we remained at Simla, F. [his wife] would have been about the only lady there; and as all the rest of the Head-Quarter officers had left the day before yesterday, there was no use of my staying on in an official point of view.'

Young's explanation of his behaviour is not entirely convincing and he was later criticized by the *Lahore Chronicle* for not setting a better example. But the general overreaction at Simla to events at Jutogh, where the Gurkhas had simply demanded the redress of professional grievances, was perhaps understandable in the uncertain days that followed the outbreak at Meerut.

By now Anson had other – logistical – problems to contend with. On 16 May, at a meeting of senior officers at Sir Henry Barnard's house,* he discovered that the Commissariat and Medical Departments, in particular, were 'totally unprepared to provide for the wants of a force in the field'. He noted:

> The regiments from the hills having been brought down so quickly, they had nothing with them. Tents and camp equipage were all at Kalka [in the hills]. No conveyance could be procured for it. No dhoolies for the sick, supplies difficult to collect, bazaars partially deserted, and a scarcity of contractors. The Deputy Commissary-General and Superintending Surgeon both of opinion that it would not be possible to move under from fifteen to twenty days. Ammunition for small arms and artillery also deficient. Already sent for from Phillour, and expected to arrive in two or three days.

* All five senior officers at this conference were dead within seven weeks: General Anson, Brigadier Halifax, commanding the Ambala station, and Colonel Mowatt, commanding the artillery, died within ten days; Colonel Chester, adjutant-general of the army, was killed at Badli-ki-Serai on 8 June; and Sir Henry Barnard died at Delhi on 5 July.

The main problem was a lack of transport: three years earlier, in a cost-cutting exercise, the Company had done away with the army's permanent establishment of draught animals. Now it was reaping the whirlwind.

Despite exhortations from Lord Canning and Sir John Lawrence to retake Delhi as quickly as possible, Anson was inclined to wait for physical and material reinforcements. 'It becomes now a matter for your consideration,' he wrote to Lawrence on 17 May, 'whether it would be prudent to risk the small European force we have here in an enterprise on Delhi. I think not. It is wholly, in my opinion, insufficient for the purpose.' When Anson added that Barnard and his senior staff officers were united in their belief that no advance could take place for at least sixteen to twenty days, Lawrence was aghast. 'I am persuaded that all you can require to take with you must be procurable in two or three,' he replied on the 21st. 'We have had an extraordinarily good harvest, and supplies must be abundant between Ambalah and [Meerut]. The greater portion of the country is well cultivated. We are sending our troops in every direction without difficulty, through tracts which are comparatively desert . . . I would spare no expense to carry every European soldier – at any rate, to carry every other one. By alternately marching and riding, their strengths and spirits will be maintained.'

Stung by Lawrence's reproaches and Canning's urgings, Anson was ready to leave Ambala on 23 May. 'I venture to say that not an hour has been lost,' he wrote to the Governor-General, 'and that the movement of the troops from Ambalah will have been accomplished in a space of time which was not considered possible on my arrival here.' His force consisted of the 9th Lancers, the 75th Foot, the 1st and 2nd Bengal Europeans, two troops of Bengal Horse Artillery, the 60th Native Infantry and a squadron of the 4th Light Cavalry.* On 17 May he had received a letter from Robert Montgomery at Lahore, urging him to disarm the 5th and 60th regiments. But, having consulted both commanding officers, he did not consider this action 'advisable or immediately necessary'. The 5th was broken up into detachments and sent into the surrounding countryside; the 60th accompanied Anson's force because he did not know what else to do with it.†

* Four companies of the 1st Europeans, a squadron of the 9th Lancers and two guns had already been moved to Karnal, arriving on 20 May.

† Elements of both regiments later mutinied: the whole of the 60th at Rohtak on 10 June; two companies of the 5th at Jagadhri on 12 July. The rest of the 5th was disbanded at Ambala on 29 and 30 May.

Rid of its potentially mutinous sepoys, the Ambala station was relatively secure. Most of the women and children had been sent to Kasauli. The remaining non-combatants took refuge at night in the large entrenchment that had been constructed around the church compound. It was defended by a garrison of five hundred sick and invalid European soldiers, supported by some Patiala troops. As early as 13 May Sir John Lawrence had urged Anson to trust the three great Sikh chiefs of the Cis-Sutlej States: the Maharaja of Patiala and the Rajas of Jhind and Nabha. 'They had survived the ruin of the old Sikh Empire,' wrote Kaye, 'and were grateful to us for the protection which we had afforded and the independence which we had preserved.' Their allegiance was vital because their lands dominated the routes north to the Punjab. Yet it could not be guaranteed. Soon after receiving word of the outbreak at Delhi, Douglas Forsyth, the Deputy Commissioner of Ambala, went to sound out the ruler of Patiala. During their conversation Forsyth asked if it were true that emissaries from the King of Delhi had come to Patiala. 'There they are,' replied the maharaja, pointing to some men seated a short distance away. So Forsyth requested a word in private.

As soon as they were alone, he said: 'Maharaja sahib, answer me one question: Are you for us, or against us?'

'As long as I live I am yours,' replied the maharaja, 'but you know I have enemies in my own country; some of my relations are against me – my brother for one. What do you want done?'

Forsyth then asked him to send some of his troops to Karnal to keep the Grand Trunk Road open. The maharaja agreed on the understanding that European soldiers would soon be sent to support them. He knew that his own troops could not be trusted unless they were convinced the British would prevail.

While most European eyes were on General Anson and his efforts to retake Delhi, the events that would determine the immediate survival of British India were taking place in the Punjab. A recently conquered province that included the turbulent North-West Frontier with Afghanistan, the Punjab was considered the greatest security risk in the subcontinent. For that reason it contained a higher proportion of European to Indian troops than any other province: 13,335 Europeans to 50,214 natives, or more than one in four. But it also contained the warlike tribes of the North-West Frontier and, like Oudh, many thousands of demobilized soldiers. The fear among British officials, when news of the Delhi outbreak reached the Punjab on

12 May, was that the tribesmen and former members of the Sikh Army might form an unholy alliance with mutinous Bengal sepoys to oust their colonial rulers. So their priority was to nullify the threat from the Bengal troops: either by disarming them or relieving them of the responsibility of guarding key installations like forts and magazines.

Robert Montgomery and Brigadier Corbett at Lahore were the first to act. On 12 May they dispatched a company of the 81st Foot in native wagons to secure the fortress of Govindgarh near Amritsar, the holy city of the Sikhs, 30 miles to the east.* Early the next day, acting on intelligence that the Bengal sepoys intended to seize Lahore Fort on the 15th, they disarmed the Indian garrison at Mian Mir and thereby prevented an outbreak that could have had disastrous consequences for the British. The seriousness of the threat at Lahore was underlined the following day when spies reported that 'all the four disarmed corps intended to desert to Ferozepore (45 miles off) that night, and seize the magazine, and thus resupply themselves with arms'. Shortly before noon, as arrangements were being made to intercept the deserters, Corbett was informed that the sepoys had jumped the gun and 'were making off as fast as possible'. He sent six horse artillery guns in pursuit and they had the desired effect as all but a couple of hundred deserters 'slunk back to their lines'. The others were arrested by the civil authorities on the road and at Ferozepore itself.

The existence of a plot for combined action between the native troops at Lahore and Ferozepore, the largest arsenal in upper India, is borne out by the behaviour of the sepoy regiments at the latter station. The brigadier at Ferozepore was Peter Innes, an experienced and well-respected sepoy officer, who had only arrived at the station on 11 May. A day later he received word from Lahore of the outbreaks at Meerut and Delhi, and of Corbett's determination to disarm all the troops in the Punjab capital. Innes was in a comparatively strong position with one British regiment, the 61st Foot, and a battery of European artillery to deal with three Indian regiments. Instead of following Corbett's example, however, he held a morning parade on 13 May to gauge the temper of his native troops. It was inconclusive and a subsequent council of war, attended by civil and military officers, agreed only to divide the two regiments with a view to disarming them a day later.

That evening, as a company of the 61st Foot was in the process of relieving the Indian guard in the entrenched magazine, the two native infantry

* That night a detachment of the 8th Foot at Jullundur marched 24 miles to secure the magazine at Phillour on the right bank of the Sutlej.

regiments were given orders to march to separate camping grounds outside the cantonment. They started off quietly enough. But as the 45th drew level with the magazine and saw the Europeans marching in, the majority broke away, loaded their weapons, 'and made a sudden rush on to the ramparts'. They were assisted by the men of the 57th still inside the magazine, who provided ladders that must have been prepared beforehand. However, the European troops stood firm and managed to drive off their attackers. Thereafter Innes seems to have been stricken with the same paralysis that afflicted the military authorities at Meerut. By withdrawing most of the European troops into a defensive position, he allowed the three hundred or so mutineers to sack the cantonment with impunity. The church was burnt, as were most of the officers' bungalows and the mess house of the 61st. But not all the European inhabitants were intimidated. 'Such cowards as the mutineers I never saw,' wrote the Revd Maltby. 'I saved my own house by remaining in it. They were afraid to come near, and took 3 shots at me, and had I only 50 Europeans I could have cleared the place.' Early next morning, the mutineers fled the station with their colours, heading south-east towards Delhi. For 12 miles they were 'vigorously pursued and cut up' by the sowars of the 10th Light Cavalry, who, at this stage, were still loyal. Some were brought back as prisoners; others were seized and imprisoned by the Maharaja of Patiala. But the mutineers were bolstered by a number of deserters from the 57th Native Infantry and three hundred members of both regiments made it through to Delhi by late June.

Officials as far afield as Lahore and Karachi were unimpressed by Innes's performance. 'Our military rulers are generally infatuated,' wrote Montgomery on 18 May. 'They deal with mankind only on parade, and do not know human nature. A severe example of one regiment would have saved much bloodshed and a campaign. By a severe example, I mean destroying them.' Bartle Frere, the Commissioner of Sind, was even more severe in a letter to Brigadier John Jacob. 'Even you, who foresaw all this,' he wrote on 3 June,

> can have no idea of the utter incapacity of the Bengal officers to meet the crisis. One of their best men, Innes, was at Ferozepore . . . After [the mutiny on 13 May] the Brigadier allows the Colonels of the Regiments to go and reason with the men! to bring them back!! & to persuade him of their penitence!!! He finds he has the wolf by the ears. The C-in-C orders him to dismiss the men. The Brigadier delays compliance and refers again, hoping to save the honor of the regiments!!!! – & these things occur every where, & men up there [in Bengal] bother their heads to find in

new cartridges, or a preaching fool of a Colonel, provocation sufficient to account for the simultaneous outbreak.

Only in Peshawar, wrote Frere two days later, had the Bengal military 'acted with much vigour'.

The city of Peshawar was the most northerly outpost of British India. It lay at the head of a large fertile valley, almost entirely surrounded by mountains, and was less than ten miles from the entrance to the legendary Khyber Pass into Afghanistan. On both sides of the frontier lived fierce Pathan tribesmen. To police them and to prevent foreign incursion, particularly from Afghanistan, the Company had stationed a vast number of regular and irregular troops in the region. Peshawar alone had ten regiments – two of British infantry, five of native infantry, one of light cavalry and two of irregular cavalry – and four batteries of European artillery. Much of the Punjab Irregular Force was also in the vicinity.

The leading civil authorities at Peshawar were, by necessity, men of resource and determination – not least the commissioner, Herbert Edwardes. Born in Shropshire in 1819, the second son of a clergyman, he was an atypical Company officer in that he graduated from King's College, London, before joining the 1st Bengal Europeans at the relatively late age of twenty-one. His aptitude for languages soon marked him out as an outstanding officer, and in 1846, after the Company's victory in the Second Sikh War, he and a handful of other talented young officers were selected as political assistants to Henry Lawrence, the Resident and effective ruler of the Punjab. Known as Lawrence's 'Young Men', they were given the seemingly impossible task of stabilizing the war-torn districts of a foreign country. It helped that they, like Lawrence, were all God-fearing Christians of varying degrees of fervency. Edwardes, then a 26-year-old lieutenant, was more zealous than most and saw his role of pacifier of the lawless frontier province of Bannu as that of a militant missionary: 'officially a soldier, practically a bishop'. The risks he and the other 'politicals' were prepared to take were prodigious. During one cavalry charge into the camp of a refractory chieftain, he was horrified to discover that all but twelve of his Sikh escort had abandoned him. He pressed on, nevertheless, and only survived because a jezail pressed to his midriff misfired.

Edwardes's deputy at Peshawar, John Nicholson, was even more famous. Born in Ulster in 1822, the descendant of Scottish Plantation stock, he too had served in the native infantry before becoming one of Lawrence's acolytes. By 1848, at the age of twenty-five, he was in charge of a frontier province the size of Wales. A tall, powerful man of few words but mighty deeds, his courage and physical strength were legendary. He once rode alone into a robber village and decapitated its chief in full view of his men. On another occasion he is said to have disorientated a tiger by galloping around it in ever-decreasing circles, eventually killing it with his sabre. Some of his Sikh subordinates were so impressed they formed a religious sect called the 'Nikal Seynis'. Their idol's response was to have them flogged. Nicholson's appearance was awe-inspiring. 'He was a man cast in a giant mould,' recorded a contemporary, 'with massive chest and powerful limbs, and an expression ardent and commanding, with a dash of roughness; features of stern beauty, a long black beard, and deep sonorous voice. There was something of immense strength, talent, and resolution in his whole frame and manner, and a power of ruling men on high occasions which no one could escape noticing.'

One of the most promising young staff officers in Peshawar at this time was Second-Lieutenant Frederick Sleigh Roberts of the Bengal Artillery. Born in Cawnpore in September 1832, the son of a former commander of the Peshawar Division,* Roberts had served in India for less than four years when he was appointed acting deputy assistant quartermaster-general at Peshawar in early 1856. He was aware of John Nicholson's reputation but did not meet him until he went on a surveying expedition in the hills outside Peshawar in April 1857. Returning to his camp one evening, he found a tent pitched alongside his own: it was Nicholson's. The two shared a meal together and Roberts wrote later:

> Nicholson impressed me more profoundly than any man I had ever met before, or have ever met since. I have never seen anyone like him. He was the beau-ideal of a soldier and a gentleman. His appearance was distinguished and commanding, with a sense of power about him which to my mind was the result of his having passed so much of his life among the wild and lawless tribesmen, with whom his authority was supreme. Intercourse with this man amongst men made me more eager than ever to remain on the frontier, and I was seized with ambition to follow in his footsteps.

Nicholson was dining at Edwardes's bungalow on the evening of 11 May 1857 when an officer burst in with the news from Delhi. The following day, having received a similar message from Meerut, Edwardes ordered the

* Later Lieutenant-General Sir Abraham Roberts, KCB.

seizure of all Indian correspondence at the post office. 'The number of seditious papers seized was alarmingly great,' wrote Roberts. 'They were for the most part couched in figurative and enigmatical language, but it was quite sufficiently clear from them that every Native regiment in the garrison was more or less implicated and prepared to join the rebel movement.'

Fearing outbreaks throughout the Punjab, Edwardes and Nicholson came up with the idea of forming a 'strong moveable column' of European and irregular troops. It 'should take the field in the Punjab at once,' wrote Edwardes to Sir John Lawrence on 12 May, 'perhaps at Lahore would be best, so as to get between the stations which *have* mutinied and those that have *not*, and move on the first station that stirs next . . . This disaffection will never be talked down now. It must be put down – and the sooner blood be let the less of it will suffice.' Edwardes also dispatched a rider to Kohat to fetch Brigadier Neville Chamberlain, the 37-year-old commander of the Punjab Irregular Force and yet another of Lawrence's 'Young Men'. 'He was in the prime of his life, and the fulness of his active manhood,' wrote a contemporary. 'Of a fair stature, of a light but sinewy frame, he had every physical qualification that could make a dashing leader of Irregular Horse.'

The following morning, soon after Chamberlain's arrival, a council of war was held in the bungalow of Major-General Thomas Reed, the local divisional commander. The principals were Reed, Edwardes, Nicholson, Chamberlain and Brigadier Sydney Cotton, the sixty-four-year-old station commander who, despite his age, was a man of 'unusual energy and activity, a fine rider, a pattern drill, and a thorough soldier all round'. Reed, though three years younger and more experienced in war, had not aged as well as Cotton and was happy to defer to the two 'soldier civilians'. Edwardes had, in any case, just received Lawrence's approval of his plan for a Movable Column, and the meeting was something of a rubber-stamping exercise. Roberts, who took the minutes, was 'greatly impressed with the calm and comprehensive view of the situation taken by Edwardes and Nicholson'. The latter told the council that he had long expected a mutiny in the Bengal Army. 'Neither greased cartridges, the annexation of Oude, nor the paucity of European officers were the causes,' he said. 'For years I have watched the army and felt sure they only wanted the opportunity to try their strength with us. Mutiny is like a smallpox. It spreads quickly and must be crushed as quickly as possible.'

Their chief problem, said Nicholson, was how best to secure the Punjab with such a small number of European troops. In all stations there was a majority of Indian troops, and in some there were no European soldiers at all. 'Edwardes and Nicholson gave it as their opinion,' recalled Roberts, 'that the only chance of keeping the Punjab and the frontier quiet lay in trusting the Chiefs and people, and in endeavouring to induce them to side with us against the Hindustanis. They undertook to communicate, regarding the raising of levies and fresh troops, with their friends and acquaintances along the border, who had proved such staunch allies in 1848–49, when we were fighting the Sikhs.' They also recommended that General Reed, 'as the senior officer in the Punjab, should join the Chief Commissioner at Rawal Pindi, leaving Brigadier Cotton in command at Peshawar'; that a Movable Column of 'reliable troops' should be formed at Jhelum, prepared to move 'in any direction where its services might be required'; that regular Bengal regiments should be scattered 'as much as possible, in order to prevent dangerous combinations'; that a detachment of Punjab irregulars from Kohat should replace the Bengal sepoys in the fort of Attock, which contained a magazine and covered the Indus crossing; and that a small guard of Pathan levies should be placed in charge of the Attock Ferry.

All these proposals were meekly agreed to by Reed and his subordinates. 'The old General,' read one account, 'in his sleeping drawers and slippers, looked puzzled and almost before he knew what had taken place, the proceedings were on paper; orders out for the movement and collection of troops at various dispositions . . . Even at the last, the old General looked bewildered and puzzled . . . presiding in silence while these efforts to save India were manfully and nobly made.' He may not have been the most vigorous general in the subcontinent, but at least he knew when to take a back seat. 'Old Reed I don't think much of,' wrote Second-Lieutenant Roberts. 'He has one good quality, namely: listening to reason, which is better than being obstinate, when ability is not combined.' All that remained was to appoint a commander of the Movable Column. 'It was a position for which Cotton and Nicholson would have given much,' noted Roberts, 'and for which they were well qualified, but there was important work for them to do at Peshawar.' So Brigadier Chamberlain was selected by general consensus. He, in turn, appointed Roberts as his quartermaster-general.*

Reed set off by *dâk* to join Sir John Lawrence at Rawalpindi during the evening of 14 May. Roberts went with him, intending to link up with the northernmost elements of the Movable Column. 'I took with me only just enough kit for a hot-weather march,' noted Roberts, 'and left everything

* A staff position analogous to a chief-of-staff, with responsibility for operations and intelligence.

standing in my house just as it was, little thinking that I should never return to it or be quartered in Peshawar again.' They reached Attock Ferry on the Indus the following morning and met up with Chamberlain, who had brought his 2nd Punjab Cavalry from Kohat. Also there was Captain Henry Daly, commanding the Corps of Guides, who had arrived with five hundred men the day before. Daly was struck by the contrast between the two senior officers. Reed he found to be 'a poor, weak, old gentleman in HMS, of a very different temper and style; frivolous in all points; petty, with no grasp, no knowledge; writing little notes to subordinates with much care and little grammar,' whereas Chamberlain was 'neither punctilious nor pedantic; a resolute, thoughtful *soldier*, neither brilliant nor cultivated, but sensible, grave, and solid'. His unruffled demeanour, which so impressed Daly, was largely the result of his Christian faith. Writing to his mother with news of his appointment, he begged her not to worry about the mutiny, 'for we are in the hands of the true and only God . . . and the convulsion now going on around us must be intended in the end to advance His glory, and therefore as Christians and soldiers our duty is to meet the storm with calm fortitude'.

Reed, Chamberlain and Roberts arrived at Rawalpindi during the evening of 16 May. Two days later Chamberlain was joined at Sir John Lawrence's residence by Daly and Edwardes: the former had just marched in with his Guides; the latter had been summoned from Peshawar because Lawrence was uneasy about his plan to raise more Pathan levies. Daly's diary entry for 18 May reads: 'Started at 1 a.m. Overtaken within 4 or 5 miles of Pindi by Edwardes, travelling down in a buggy to consult Sir John. I jumped into the buggy and went with him to Sir John's – reached at 5 a.m. Chamberlain in bed at the door. Sir John in bed within, called us and began conversing on affairs with his old frankness and cordiality. Affairs are bad.'

During the subsequent discussions it was agreed that, in line with Canning's request, the capture of Delhi was to have priority over the Punjab. This, in effect, meant sending most of the regiments earmarked for the Movable Column down to Ambala to join Anson. The Punjab would, as a result, be dangerously denuded of trustworthy troops and the only solution was to raise more irregulars. With the survival of British India at stake, it was considered to be a risk worth taking. As at Peshawar, the civilian officials were the chief decision-makers, and General Reed, the senior officer in the Punjab, was not even present during the key debates. Daly, who was, recorded:

In the sort of Council of Discussion at Sir John's, the line of operations was fixed on, papers actually written by Edwardes, and then the remark – 'Now let us send for the Dictator' [Edwardes's ironic nickname for Reed]. Thus, cut-and-dried affairs are put affirmatively to the General . . . Sir John, full of pluck, fearing no responsibility; without communication or means of communication with the Governor-General, he has raised and is raising large bodies of troops, passing all the best corps of the Punjab Irregular Force towards India.

The first to move were Daly's Guides, who set off from Rawalpindi in the late evening of 19 May.

Edwardes returned to Peshawar on 21 May to find Nicholson 'immersed in cares and anxieties': the Bengal regiments were on the verge of mutiny, and the Pathans, convinced the British Raj was finished, were refusing to enlist. As a result of the council of war of 13 May, the regiment considered to be the most disaffected at Peshawar, the 64th Native Infantry, had been broken up and sent to join detachments of the more reliable Kelat-i-Ghilzie irregulars at various stations in the Khyber Pass. On 18 May conspirators in the 51st Native Infantry at Peshawar sent a letter to the headquarters of both regiments at Fort Shubkudr. It claimed to have been written on behalf of the whole Peshawar cantonment and warned that cartridges would have to be bitten on 22 May. 'O brother!' it continued. 'The religion of Hindoos and Mahommedans is all one. Therefore all you soldiers should know this. Here all the sepoys are at the bidding of the Jemadar, Subadoor, Buhadoor, and Havildar-Major. All are discontented with this business, whether small or great. What more need be written? Do as you think best.' A postscript in a different hand urged the regiments to march into Peshawar on the 21st.

The bearer of the letter, a Brahman priest, gave it to a sepoy of the 64th. He or one of his comrades turned it over to the commanding officer, Lieutenant-Colonel Garrett. Edwardes was particularly surprised by this act of loyalty because the earlier seizure of mutinous correspondence between Muslim 'bigots' at Patna and sepoys of the 64th had convinced him that the regiment was ripe for mutiny. The letters had also alluded to a lengthy correspondence between the same native soldiers and 'Hindoostanee fanatics in [nearby] Swat and Sitana'. The letter from the 51st was given up, Edwardes concluded, because the 64th knew the Kelat-i-Ghilzie regiment would not rise with them. The other possibility is that the letter was handed to a member of the regiment who was neither part of the conspiracy nor sufficiently disaffected to keep it secret. To Edwardes the letter proved 'beyond a doubt that whatever moved the Mahommedans, the Hindoos were moved by the cartridges'. He is right in the sense that the majority were being manipulated by the minority. For the conspirators at Peshawar knew only too well that cartridges were no longer 'bitten'; for the rising to succeed, however, a religious cause that embraced both faiths was essential.

That night Edwardes and Nicholson went to bed fully dressed and with weapons to hand. They were woken at midnight with the news that a detachment of the 55th Native Infantry at Nowshera, 22 miles down the Peshawar Valley, had mutinied, and the 10th Irregular Cavalry had refused to act against it. They at once roused Brigadier Cotton and told him that it was imperative to disarm the five regular Bengal regiments at Peshawar – the 21st, 24th 27th, 51st Native Infantry and 5th Light Cavalry – before the mutiny could spread. He agreed, but exempted the senior regiment of native infantry, the 21st, on the basis that it had not been implicated in the mutinous correspondence. The commanding officers of all nine regiments still at Peshawar, two of them British, were then summoned to Cotton's quarters to hear the news. 'A most painful scene ensued,' wrote Edwardes. 'The commandants of those regiments which were to be disarmed unanimously and violently declared their implicit confidence in their men. One advised conciliation, and another threatened us that his men would resist and take the guns.' This, for Edwardes, was the clincher, and he interrupted the heated discussion with the observation that 'the matter rested entirely with Brigadier Cotton'. To which Cotton responded: 'Then the troops as originally determined will be disarmed. No more discussion, gentlemen! These are my orders and I must have them obeyed.'

It was now six in the morning and within an hour the two wings of the cantonment had formed up on separate parade-grounds. Each wing was covered by a British infantry regiment and half the artillery, their muskets loaded and cannon primed. Edwardes and Cotton dealt with the right wing, Nicholson the left, both parties accompanied by a troop of irregular cavalry and a line of empty ammunition wagons. As each earmarked regiment was approached, the order was given to pile arms. The sepoys and sowars responded without hesitation. 'It was a painful and affecting thing to see them putting their own firelocks into the artillery wagons,' wrote Edwardes to his wife, 'weapons which they had used honourably for years. The officers of a cavalry regiment [the 5th Light Cavalry], a very fine set of fellows, threw in their own swords with those of their men, and even tore off their spurs. It was impossible not to feel for and with them; but duty must be done, and I know that we shall never regret the counsel that we gave.' The beneficial effect of this decisive action was immediate. 'As we rode down to the disarming,' recalled Edwardes, 'a very few chiefs and yeomen of the country attended us, and I remember, judging by their faces, that they came to see which way the tide would turn. As we rode back friends were as thick as summer flies, and levies began from that moment to come in.'

Cotton's thoughts now turned to the 55th Native Infantry. After its minor mutiny on the 21st, the detachment at Nowshera had been brought back under the control of its officers and that night was ordered to rejoin the main body of the regiment at Hoti Mardan. But Cotton suspected that the whole regiment was disaffected, and, the following evening, he dispatched a small force to disarm it. Commanded by Colonel Chute of the 70th Foot, the force comprised three hundred British soldiers, eight guns and four hundred irregular horsemen. Nicholson went along as political officer. Resting up by day, the force began its final march to Hoti Mardan during the night of 24 May. But news of its approach was not welcomed by the colonel of the 55th, Henry Spottiswoode,* who had earlier begged Cotton not to act against men in whom he had 'implicit confidence'. When his Indian officers now came to ask him why British troops were approaching, he was unable to satisfy them and the regiment passed beyond his control. In despair he blew his brains out.

At daybreak, as the head of Chute's column came in sight of the 'rude' star-shaped fort at Hoti Mardan, the men of the 55th hastily left, but in good order and with colours flying, each man laden with as much ammunition and treasure as he could carry. Chute ordered a halt: his infantry were done up after the long march and in no condition for a pursuit in the heat of the day. But Nicholson was determined not to let the mutineers get away and, with Chute's permission, gave chase with the cavalry.

On observing the pursuing column of horsemen, headed by Nicholson's distinctive grey charger, the 55th's Indian officers ordered their men to halt and prepare to receive cavalry. They did so in parade-ground fashion but were still in the act of loading when the cavalry's flashing sabres swept in amongst them. The line began to disintegrate, and the sepoys fled in panic into the broken countryside, hotly pursued by Nicholson and his riders. 'They were hunted out of villages,' wrote Edwardes in his official report, 'and grappled with in ravines, and hunted over the ridges all that day from Fort Mardan to the borders of Swat, and found respite only in the failing light.'

By the time an exhausted Nicholson returned to Hoti Mardan, he had been in the saddle for twenty hours and had covered more than 70 miles.

* The irony of Spottiswoode's implicit faith in his men is that he had only been in command of the 55th for two years.

'The 55th fought determinedly,' he wrote to Edwardes on 26 May, 'as men, who have no chance of escape but by their own exertions, always do.' One hundred and twenty mutineers had been killed and a similar number captured with the regimental colours and two hundred muskets. Most of the damage had been done by Nicholson and his mounted police; the sowars of the 10th Irregulars, by contrast, had only 'pretended to act'. The surviving mutineers fled to the Lund Khur Hills in Swat, but were expelled within a month by the local chiefs. They made for Kashmir because they believed its Hindu ruler, Maharaja Golab Singh, was sympathetic to their cause. But their route was blocked by Hazara tribesmen, and those not taken prisoner and executed were forced north into the mountains and defiles of Kohistan. Some died of starvation and exposure, others were drowned in mountain torrents. Only a few survived capture by agreeing to convert to Islam, thereby forfeiting the religion and caste they had allegedly rebelled to protect.

At first, as a warning to others, all one hundred and twenty sepoys captured by Nicholson were sentenced to be blown away from guns. But petitions for partial clemency were submitted by both Nicholson and Sir John Lawrence. 'The officers [of the 55th] all concur in stating that the Sikhs were on their side to the last,' wrote Nicholson to Edwardes. 'I would, therefore, temper stern justice with mercy, and spare the Sikhs and young recruits. Blow away all the rest by all means, but spare boys scarcely out of their childhood, and men who were really loyal and respectful up to the moment when they allowed themselves to be carried away in a panic by the mass.'

Edwardes and the military authorities concurred and forty were selected for execution. They were not the first Indian troops to be put to death at Peshawar. A few days after the general disarmament, when it became clear that their treasonable correspondence had been intercepted, the subedar-major and two hundred and fifty men of the 51st Native Infantry had fled into the mountains. Many were returned by Pathan tribesmen, including the subedar-major, who was hanged on 29 May. Five days later four NCOs and eight sepoys suffered the same punishment.

The execution of the forty mutineers of the 55th took place a week later on the parade-ground of the 87th Foot. The whole Peshawar garrison had been formed into three sides of an open square. The fourth was made up of forty cannon. Watching eagerly from the edge of the parade-ground were thousands of civilian spectators. Once the sentence had been read, the guns were primed with powder but no shot, and the prisoners were led forward. Each one was tied by the wrists to the upper part of the gun's wheels so that the muzzle pressed into the pit of his stomach. The artillery officer then gave the word and the guns were fired simultaneously. At first the smoke obscured all view. As it cleared, the only visible remnants of the prisoners were their arms, still attached to the guns. Then here and there, having been shot hundreds of feet into the air, fell a number of slightly blackened but otherwise intact heads. Apart from that there was nothing. The bystanders reacted with a collective gasp; the Indian troops were dumbstruck.

Many commentators have vilified the British for blowing mutineers from guns. But the practice needs to be seen in context: it was a punishment first used in India not by the British but by the Moguls; it was regarded by Indian troops as an instantaneous and honourable 'soldier's death' and infinitely preferable to the degradation of death by hanging; and, as Lawrence makes clear, it was used not as an act of vengeance but of deterrence, *pour encourager les autres*. Moreover, such ruthless acts were generally popular with the apprehensive European community in India at this time. 'I fancy you will ere long hear of some sharp and decisive punishments amongst the mutinous prisoners at Lahore, Ferozepore and Peshawur,' wrote the superintending surgeon at Sialkot to a nephew. 'Mercy to them is out of the question; firmness and decision, and the fate of our empire all require the last penalty, and die they must. Maudlin humanity and over-indulgent sentimental feelings have placed us in our present position. Had we been rigid, stern and unhesitating in our rule our present difficulties would never have shown themselves.'

11. The Mutiny Spreads

Even as the authorities prevented a wide-scale rising in the Punjab, the vulnerable North-Western Provinces were being rocked by fresh outbreaks of mutiny. The earliest, at Muzaffarnagar, a town 25 miles north of Meerut, was the direct result of a collective lack of nerve on the part of the European community. The chief offender was the magistrate, Mr Burford. On receiving news on 11 May of the outbreak at Meerut, along with false reports of the imminent arrival of the mutineers and a large band of dacoits, Burford panicked and ordered all government offices to close for three days. They never reopened. '[The order] could only tend to unsettle men's minds, to produce doubt, confusion and suspicion,' wrote Burford's successor. And so it proved. The treasury guard rose on the 14th, and was quickly joined in an orgy of destruction by civilians from the town and outlying villages. Order was not fully restored to the district until long after the arrival of R. M. Edwards, Burford's replacement, with a detachment of Nasiri Gurkhas on 2 July 1857.

At Meerut itself four companies of Bengal Sappers and Miners mutinied on 16 May despite the presence of the powerful European garrison. Lieutenant Chapman, a sapper officer, and a handful of European gunners were the first on the scene. He recalled:

> We ran straight into a few figures we saw in front of the tents, which proved to be, Captain Fraser, mortally wounded, the Havildar Major dead, and 2 or three faithful sepoys attending their dying Commanding Officer. At the same time Lieutenant Mannsen, Dr Turnbull and [Quartermaster-Sergeant] Stuart came out of the bells-of-arms, the doors of which they had actually been holding against the mutineers . . . It was universally believed in the regiment that an Afghan shot Captain Fraser from behind, but I never heard the name of the supposed murderer of the Havildar Major. The latter I remember was lying with a pencil and paper in his hand and with a frightful gunshot wound that had carried away both eyes.

Retribution was swift. No sooner had the alarm been raised than a squadron of the Carabiniers and two horse artillery guns, led by Brigadier Wilson himself, were off in pursuit. 'We were at first led astray and lost time and ground by having to make a detour,' wrote Wilson to his wife, 'but after a six mile ride we came up with a party of 50, posted in a small Tope. It took us some time and no little trouble as the Dragoons could not get at them but by dismounting . . . We at last destroyed every one of them. They had shot their Commanding Officer in a deliberately cold-blooded manner and I therefore neither offered nor gave any quarter . . . Yesterday morning I would have trusted the Sappers as I would a European Regiment: to-day I can trust no Native Regiment, not even the Ghoorkhas.'

More serious were mutinies by detachments of the 9th Native Infantry in the Agra area. At first it had seemed as if this much vaunted regiment would remain loyal. During the night of 16 May some sepoys of the 9th at Etawah killed four and arrested two mutineers from the 3rd Cavalry who were returning to their homes. Three days later a group of sepoys from the headquarters detachment at Aligarh were attending a wedding at a nearby village when they overheard a local Brahman *zemindar* claim responsibility for a recent arson attack in the cantonment. On the basis of this evidence, he was arrested, found guilty of plotting rebellion and sentenced to death by hanging. The execution took place during the evening of 20 May in the presence of the entire garrison. As the parade was about to be dismissed, a lone sepoy stepped out of the ranks, pointed to the gallows and shouted, 'Behold, a martyr to our faith.' The detachment at once dissolved into noisy rebellion.

As word of the Aligarh rising spread through the Agra region, the other detachments of the 9th at Mainpuri, Bolundshahr and Etawah rose in sympathy. The plan in each case was to loot the treasury before marching off to Delhi. Only in Etawah did the mutineers fail to secure the money thanks to the bravery of the civil and military officers, the loyalty of a handful of sepoys and policemen, and the support of Rao Bowani Singh, the cousin of the Raja of Mainpuri. News of the mutinies caused panic in Agra. 'Mr V.[ansittart] called on [Colvin] today,' noted the wife of the cantonment magistrate on 22 May, 'and actually found them talking of flight to Calcutta or Gwalior, the latter recommended by Mr Colvin. Cowardly policy. Mr V. advised them to remain here.'

General Anson and his staff finally left Ambala for Karnal on 24 May. That same day the vanguard of Anson's force,* which had been at Karnal since

* Four companies of the 1st Bengal Fusiliers, a squadron of the 9th Lancers, and two horse artillery guns.

20 May, was sent 20 miles up the Delhi road to Panipat. Anson's plan was to advance from Karnal with the bulk of his force on 1 June and reach a point close to the bridge across the Jumna at Baghpat on the 5th. There he would link up with the Meerut Brigade and the siege-train from Phillour, and continue his march towards Delhi. Sir John Lawrence had urged the Commander-in-Chief to join the two forces at Meerut, but Anson preferred the direct route to Delhi because it avoided a detour across the Jumna and would save the Ambala troops at least four marches. He also believed that Hewitt had 'sufficient force for his own protection and to punish the inhabitants of the bazaars' if necessary.

The most active member of Anson's staff at this time was Lieutenant William Hodson of the 1st Bengal Fusiliers. Hodson had much in common with Herbert Edwardes at Peshawar: both were sons of clergymen who had graduated from university before joining a regiment of Bengal sepoys at a relatively late age (twenty-four in Hodson's case); both became protégés of Henry Lawrence. But there the similarities end. Hodson, a year younger at thirty-six, was better educated, having attended Dr Arnold's Rugby and Trinity College, Cambridge. He might even have become an academic had not 'a constitutional tendency to headache very much stood in the way of any close application to books'. His temperament was, in any case, unsuited to such a sedentary pursuit. If Edwardes was self-controlled and calculating, a born diplomat, Hodson had more of the dash and impulse of a natural soldier. He was described by one of his teachers at Rugby as 'arrogant, brash and domineering', with the qualification that his 'impulsive nature won him much affection'. He may even have been the inspiration for the fictional Harry Flashman of *Tom Brown's Schooldays*, set at Arnold's Rugby. Hodson, however, displayed little of Flashman's carnal appetite. He only ever loved one woman, Susan Henry, the daughter of a naval captain whom he had met as a young man in Guernsey. After he left for India she married a man twice her age, later accompanying him to Calcutta, where he died in 1851. On hearing the news, Hodson hurried down from the Punjab and married her himself. The following year they had a daughter, Olivia, and wrote daily when apart.

Hodson's military career could not have begun more promisingly. In December 1845, just two months after reaching India, he led a company of sepoys into action at the hard-fought battle of Ferozshah in the First Sikh War. He enjoyed the experience, even if the poor performance of his men left something to be desired. 'It was a fearful crisis,' wrote Hodson, 'but the bravery of the English regiments saved us. The Colonel, the greater part of my brother officers, and myself, were left with the colours and about thirty men immediately in front of the batteries!' So mistrustful of Indian troops did Hodson become after this experience that he requested, and was granted, a transfer to the 1st Bengal Fusiliers, 'the finest regiment in India, with white faces too'.

He was not with them long. In 1847, after a short spell as Sir Henry Lawrence's assistant in Lahore, Hodson was given the plum appointment of adjutant to the recently formed Corps of Guides. In this role he oversaw the drilling of the men, the construction of their headquarters fort at Hoti Mardan and the introduction of the Guides' distinctive uniform: influenced by Lawrence, who argued that a native soldier should be 'loosely, comfortably and suitably clad', Hodson rejected the tight, scarlet uniform of the regulars in favour of baggy smocks and pyjama trousers. And to make the Guides 'invisible in a land of dust', the smocks and pyjamas were treated with a dye from a local dwarf palm to produce a drab yellow-green colour, known in Hindustani as *khaki*, or 'dust-coloured'. (By the time the Guides stopped dyeing their uniforms in 1904, khaki was the standard service dress throughout the Indian and British Armies.) Hodson also arranged for three hundred rifled carbines and a quantity of 'Prussian-style' helmets to be sent out from England. The latter were not a success and were soon replaced by turbans, indigo for the cavalry and khaki for the infantry.

Hodson did excellent service with a detachment of Guides during the Second Sikh War and got his reward in the spring of 1852 when he replaced Harry Lumsden, who was returning to England on leave, as Commandant of the Corps and acting Deputy Commissioner of Yusufzai. He was, he wrote, 'quite the most fortunate man in the service'. But his luck was about to run out and the blow, when it came, was largely self-inflicted. In 1853, reeling from the recent death of his infant daughter, Hodson began to crack down on what he saw as lax discipline in the corps. His abrasive approach made him immensely unpopular with both his European and Indian officers. 'I don't know exactly why this is,' John Lawrence told the Governor-General. 'He is gallant, zealous and intelligent, and yet few men like him.' A year later, on the strength of claims made by his adjutant, Ensign Turner, and Najaf Ali, the regimental *munshi*, Hodson was relieved of his command and charged with improper use of regimental funds. The subsequent court of inquiry found him guilty of both gross negligence and persistent falsification. But his excellent record of service saved him from being cashiered, and Lord Dalhousie, much to his regret, sent him back to the 1st Bengal Fusiliers.

In 1855 John Lawrence asked Reynell Taylor, the temporary Commandant of the Guides, to undertake a thorough review of the charges against Hodson relating to financial wrongdoing. The subsequent report, presented in March 1856, exonerated the former commandant. Taylor had gone through the accounts with a fine-tooth comb and considered them to be 'an honest and correct record from beginning to end'. He had examined every claim of alleged irregularity and had found 'Lieutenant Hodson's statements borne out by the facts of the case'. Though the accounts had been 'irregularly kept', Hodson had inherited a highly unorthodox system from his predecessor. In a covering letter Taylor recommended a second court of inquiry to consider his own findings. John Lawrence's response was that neither the Commander-in-Chief nor the new Governor-General, Lord Canning, saw the need for a new inquiry. They were, however, prepared to grant Hodson a 'full acquittance' on matters relating to the Corps' accounts and thereby hoped to put an end to 'this harassing and painful business'.

Hodson saw his 'full acquittance' for what it was – an attempt to sweep the matter under the carpet – and continued to demand a public inquiry. In April 1857 he travelled to Simla to lobby Anson in person and received a sympathetic hearing. 'He would write himself to Lord Canning and try to get justice done me,' wrote a delighted Hodson to his brother. 'I do trust the light is breaking through the darkness and that before long I may have good news to send you.' Anson never did write to Canning. News of the mutinies at Meerut and Delhi reached Simla a few days after his meeting with Hodson and thereafter he had more urgent business to attend to. But he had been impressed by the forthright subaltern and, after reaching Ambala, appointed him assistant quartermaster-general with special responsibility for intelligence. Hodson's first task was to re-establish contact with Meerut, from which place only 'very imperfect' information had been received. He set off on 21 May, paused for a time at Karnal, where he was joined by an escort of the Raja of Jhind's cavalry, and finally reached Meerut at daybreak on the 22nd. 'He had left Karnal (76 miles off) at nine the night before,' wrote an officer at Meerut, 'with one led horse and an escort of Sikh cavalry and, as I had anticipated, here he was with despatches for Wilson! . . . Hodson rode straight to Wilson, had his interview, a bath, breakfast, and two hours' sleep, and then rode back the seventy-six miles, and had to fight his way back for about thirty miles of the distance.' He rested for a few more hours at Karnal and then continued on to Ambala, arriving in the early hours of 23 May. He had covered more than 250 miles in two days.

Anson was impressed and at once commissioned him to raise and command a corps of irregular cavalry. So came into being Hodson's Horse, mainly Sikhs from the Amritsar, Jhind and Lahore districts of the Punjab. They too wore khaki tunics and could be distinguished from the Guides Cavalry by their scarlet turbans and shoulder sashes. Their commandant was even more distinctive. 'A tallish man,' wrote a contemporary, 'with yellow hair, a pale, smooth face, heavy moustache, and large, restless, rather unforgiving eyes.' He still suffered from migraines and wore tinted spectacles to protect his bright blue eyes from the fierce Indian sun. Yet as one of his British officers observed: 'As a cavalry soldier he was perfection, a strong seat on horseback (though an ugly rider), a perfect swordsman, nerves like iron, and a quick, intelligent eye, indefatigable and zealous, and with great tact.'

Anson arrived at Karnal on 25 May. He was billeted in relative comfort with General Palmer, a retired sepoy general; his staff had to make do with the *dâk*-bungalow where they were crammed in six to a room. Nevertheless it was Anson who fell ill with cholera on the morning of 26 May and was dead within twenty-four hours. He lived long enough to appoint Sir Henry Barnard, just arrived in camp, as his successor. 'Barnard,' he said faintly, 'I leave you the command. You will say how anxious I have been to do my duty. I cannot recover. May success attend you. God bless you. Good-bye.' 'Poor General Anson!' wrote Colonel Keith Young in his diary. '[Colonel] Chester returned about three in the morning to say he was dead, poor man. Chester tells me that he must have felt himself quite unequal to the present emergency; and anxiety of mind has had much to do with his fatal illness. He seems to be popular with very few; and the Native troops have apparently a great hatred for him, honestly thinking that he was commissioned to convert them. Quite a private funeral in the burial-ground in the evening, Chester reading the service.'

Both before and after his death, Anson was widely criticized for his plodding response to the outbreak. 'He ought to have been before Delhi days ago,' wrote a doctor at Nowgong in central India on 29 May. 'The natives even ask what he is doing. Such delay is unpardonable, particularly as so much depends upon the celerity of his movements.' Even Canning, while recognizing that Anson had faced many problems, was convinced that he had delayed unnecessarily.

With Anson dead, Barnard took charge of the force at Karnal and the dithering General Reed succeeded by right to the command of the Bengal Army. Only the Queen, acting on advice from the British government, could appoint Anson's permanent successor as Commander-in-Chief of

India. Yet a temporary replacement was essential, and Canning and his advisers plumped for 53-year-old Lieutenant-General Sir Patrick Grant, Commander-in-Chief of Madras and a former Adjutant-General of the Bengal Army. It was a brave decision because no Company officer had ever held the Supreme Command. But in the unique circumstances that then prevailed, it was thought right to appoint a vigorous officer who had an intimate knowledge of Indian troops. Grant did not reach Calcutta to take up his temporary appointment until 17 June. Until then, Reed was supreme in Bengal, and on 28 May, defying instructions from Calcutta to leave Barnard to his own devices, he left Rawalpindi to take charge of the force advancing upon Delhi. His already frail health deteriorated en route, however, and Barnard remained in command.

Born in Oxfordshire in 1799, the son of a parson, Barnard had been educated at Westminster and Sandhurst before joining the Grenadier Guards in 1814. Since then he had spent most of his career in staff appointments, including a stint as chief-of-staff to General Simpson, Lord Raglan's successor in the Crimea. But he had also commanded a brigade and a division in the recent war against the Russians, and, though he had only been in India for a matter of months, Canning considered him the best man for the critical task of retaking Delhi. Described by a member of the headquarters staff as a 'very good, gentlemanly little man' who did not 'want for pluck', his early zeal seemed to confirm Canning's judgement. 'So long as I exercise any power,' he wrote to Sir John Lawrence on 28 May, 'you may rest assured that every energy shall be devoted to the objects I have now in view, viz., concentrating all the force I can collect at Delhi, securing the bridge at Baghpat, and securing our communication with Meerut.'

For a time Barnard was as good as his word. The bulk of his force set off from Karnal in the evening of 30 May and five days later was at Alipore, 11 miles north of Delhi. It left in its wake a trail of death and destruction. 'We burnt every village,' wrote Lieutenant Kendal Coghill of the 2nd Bengal Fusiliers, 'and hanged all the villagers who had treated our fugitives badly until every tree was covered with scoundrels hanging from every branch.' Some positively enjoyed this gruesome task. 'There were eleven more villagers hung yesterday, to the great delight of Fawcett, Blair, and Evans, who nearly forfeited their dinner for the butchery,' wrote an officer of the 9th Lancers to his wife on 4 June. 'Hope [Grant, the CO] had to approve of their sentence, and gave directions about a strong enough rope just before he sat down. All this is very horrid work, preceding as it does the blood-stained horrors of the battle-field.' Trials were little more than drumhead courts martial with officers and men vowing to kill prisoners whether they were found guilty or not. A private in the 9th Lancers wrote on 1 June:

> News was gained today that it was here that some of the Europeans making their escape from Delhi were ill used and a Doctor, his wife and child, killed. Mr Hodson went to the village where the guilty parties were and some eleven prisoners were brought in. One among them, a young man who violated the lady and then killed her and also the infant child. They were all lodged in the Provost Guard and the Provost had hard work from keeping [the members of the guard] from taking the law in their own hands. As it was their heads were shaved and pork fat rubbed all over them and then spat in their mouths; according to their beliefs this sent their soul to hell and made them unclean. About 4 o'clock in the afternoon these men were all tried and sentenced to be hung at sunset. During the time their trial was going on a number of men assembled near to the tent armed with sticks and swore by all that was good if this man, the murderer, was not sentenced to be hanged they would beat his brains out on the spot. But when the Provost came out and announced their fate and pointing to a large tree at the same time, all were satisfied . . . At last they made their appearance under a strong guard. On reaching the tree the villains called upon their countrymen to avenge their blood, but not one dared to move. They were hung and buried under the tree . . . All these men confessed their guilt before death.

Sometimes trials were dispensed with entirely. Tales of atrocities against women and children, many of them exaggerated, had infuriated the British soldiers and almost any Indian male was considered fair game. Harriet Tytler, whose husband had been appointed paymaster to the Delhi force, was shocked to see the body of a harmless Muslim baker dangling from the branch of an acacia tree. 'From what we could gather,' she wrote, 'this poor man had been late for several days with his bread for the men's breakfast, so Tommie Atkins threatened to hang him if this happened again and so they did. I can't understand how such a cruel deed was allowed, for they in turn should have been hanged, but I suppose a single soldier could not have been spared, even in the cause of justice.'

Meanwhile Brigadier Wilson's force had finally left Meerut on 27 May. It was made up of six companies of the 60th Rifles, two squadrons of the 6th Dragoon Guards, a troop of horse artillery, a battery of foot artillery and a small number of Sappers and Miners: a total of one thousand men and fourteen guns, two of them 18-pounders. To avoid the worst of the sun the force marched at night and rested by day. The effect was debilitating none the less. 'I hope Barnard's force will move down soon,' wrote Wilson from his camp at Ghazi-ud-din-Nagar on the left bank of the Hindan River, nine miles from Delhi, on 30 May, 'for I am quite sure no European can long withstand the exposure we are now undergoing. The heat and dust are dreadful and we are all, particularly the officers, marching in the greatest discomfort, from the [Commissariat] not being able to supply us with carriage. I sit or lie all day with a wet towel round my head.' He had, moreover, been sleeping in his boots, 'ready to turn out at a moment's notice,' since the outbreak at Meerut. Second-Lieutenant Hugh Chichester of the Bengal Artillery found the dust a particular torment. 'It is nothing but perpetual sand storms in the day,' he informed his mother. 'Your tent and everything one has gets covered, you swallow oceans, it is something abominable.'

At four in the afternoon of 30 May Wilson's camp on the Hindan was fired upon by a mixed force of mutineers that had marched out of Delhi under the nominal command of Bahadur Shah's grandson, Mirza Abu Bakr. The main rebel position was in a village on rising ground across the river. They had, in addition, placed two guns and a strong force of infantry to cover the 600-yard causeway across the Hindan. Ensign Everard Phillipps of the 11th Native Infantry was with two companies of riflemen ordered to take the bridge:

On reaching the bridge the two companies extended, two more came in support and the long range of the rifles forced the enemy to abandon the guns. The Colonel sent me down to order the two leading companies to reform on the causeway and take the guns at the point of the bayonets. One of the 11th's colours was with the guns – the sepoys carried it off on our taking the guns. One sepoy, Dars Singh of the 11th, fired his musket into a cart full of ammunition. Captain Andrews, Wilton and myself and about nine men were around a tumbril when it blew up. Andrews was blown to pieces and four men killed. Wilton's head was bruised – God only knows how I escaped. I'm merely bruised, just a little blood drawn from about five places . . . When the smoke cleared up the enemy had retired to a village strongly walled, on rising ground about 200 yards off. We fired a few shots and cleared it at the point of the bayonet. The sepoys fought like fiends – in one place we left about 35 dead all in a heap, killed altogether 50 and lost five men of rifles.

The rebels' cause had not been helped by the antics of their inexperienced royal commander, who watched the early stages of the battle from the roof of a house near to the bridge. 'From time to time,' wrote Mainodin Hassan Khan, 'he sent messages to his Artillery to tell them of the havoc their fire was creating in the English ranks . . . Presently a shell burst near the battery [at the bridge], covering the gunner with dust. The Commander-in-Chief, experiencing for the first time in his life the effects of a bursting shell, hastily descended from the roof of the house, mounted his horse, and galloped off with his escort of sowars into the rear of the position, not heeding the cries of his troops. A general stampede then took place.' The British captured five guns, four of them heavy calibre.

That evening Wilson set up camp on the Delhi side of the river. The bridge was not considered strong enough to bear the weight of the guns so, with some difficulty, they were dragged through the quicksand of a nearby ford by teams of elephants and bullocks. The following day, shortly after noon, the rebels attacked again in even greater strength. 'They had taken up nearly the same position as the previous day,' wrote Second-Lieutenant Chichester, 'only a little more to the right and a higher position. We could only see the muzzle of the guns peeping over the hill and they had a most capital protection from our firing. Having no end of heavy guns in position they made some excellent long and straight shooting. The grape rattled in amongst the troop of Horse Artillery like a hail storm, and the Artillery having only two heavy guns, the rest being 6- and 9-pounders, we found great difficulty in reaching them.' Eventually the two 18-pounders were brought forward to support the horse artillery, causing the rebel fire to slacken. At this point Wilson ordered a general advance, and the enemy withdrew under the cover of a light field battery, so preventing the loss of any heavy guns. The British troops 'were so knocked up by the sun and want of water' that they were unable to pursue for long. Of the forty or so British casualties during the two-day battle, several died from the effects of the sun.

On 1 June Wilson's small force was considerably strengthened by the arrival of six hundred Gurkhas of the Sirmur Battalion. With no news from Barnard it remained on the Hindan for two further days. Finally, during the evening of 3 June, the long-awaited order arrived: Wilson was to make for the bridge-of-boats at Baghpat and a rendezvous with the main force on the 7th. Both Hewitt and Hervey Greathed, who was accompanying Wilson as his political adviser, were against such a move because they thought it would expose Meerut and the Doab to rebel attack. Barnard and his staff considered such a threat to be negligible. 'Our object is Delhi,' recorded Colonel Young, 'and everything must be sacrificed to this . . . as to Meerut itself, they have fortified the school of instruction and can hold their own against any number.' Wilson was in agreement: 'While we are before Delhi they will not dare to detach any large force from thence.' Hewitt's objections he put down to fear. 'Old Hewitt is furious with me,' he informed his wife on 3 June, 'and says I shew him great disrespect because I pay no attention to his orders, quite forgetting that I am commanding a Field Force under the orders of Gen. Barnard and therefore independent of him. He is a dreadful old fool, and thinks of nothing but preserving his old carcase from harm.' Wilson began his march on the night of 4 June and reached the bridge at Baghpat two days later. On the 7th he linked up with Barnard at Alipore. 'I can't tell you how well they all looked,' Keith Young informed his wife, 'the Brigadier himself in high health . . . [Captain] Edwin Johnson [Bengal Artillery] the picture of health; and Colonel Jones of the Rifles, as fat and rosy as ever.'

As the siege-train from Phillour had arrived a day earlier, there was nothing to prevent Barnard from continuing his march towards Delhi. He now had under his command the best part of four regiments of European infantry, two of European cavalry, three troops of horse artillery, two companies of foot artillery and a detachment of artillery recruits. The 60th Native Infantry and a squadron of the 4th Light Cavalry had been sent to Rohtak and Saharunpur respectively, and the only native troops now with Barnard were the Sirmur Battalion of Gurkhas, fifty sowars of the 4th Irregular Cavalry and a small quantity of sappers and miners. The total strength of the so-called Delhi Field Force was now around 3,200 men, most of them Europeans, with twenty-two field guns and twenty-four siege guns.

Barnard knew, thanks to William Hodson and his scouts, that his advance was barred by a strong rebel force in well-constructed positions at the village of Badli-ki-Serai, halfway down the Grand Trunk Road between Alipore and Delhi. It numbered about 9,000 men and thirty guns, and was commanded by Mirza Kizr Sultan, the uncle of the disgraced Abu Bakr. Barnard's plan was to attack the rebels from three directions: the two infantry brigades would advance on either side of the road, while the cavalry, under Brigadier Grant, crossed the canal to the west of the village 'with a view to taking the enemy in the flank'. The plan could have been disrupted by the arrival in camp of General Reed in the early hours of 8 June. Fortunately Reed was suffering from 'severe sickness and fatigue' and did not interfere with Barnard's arrangements.

The British force left Alipore in darkness and appeared before the enemy positions at Badli-ki-Serai at dawn. As the assault brigades deployed in the plain, the artillery advanced to engage the rebel guns. But the latter were mostly heavy pieces and got the better of the early exchanges. 'I have never seen such splendid artillery practice as theirs was,' noted Lieutenant Kendal Coghill. 'They had the range to a yard and every shot told.' One staff officer told his son that he 'was never under a hotter fire, even at Chilianwalla'. Hugh Chichester, who was with four heavy British guns – two 18-pounders and two 8-inch mortars – recalled: 'We had marched about 5 miles when all of a sudden a bomb was heard, and the shots went right over our heads killing several, amongst them one or two officers.' The most grievous loss was Colonel Charles Chester, the adjutant-general, who was hit in the side by a roundshot that also killed his white horse, 'Sir Walter'. Keith Young was on the opposite side of the road when Chester fell and was shocked when he came upon his body. 'It seems he lived for a minute or two after he was struck down,' wrote Young, 'and young Barnard, the Aide-de-Camp, jumped off his horse and went to his assistance, holding his head until he died. He was quite sensible at first, and spoke to Barnard, asking him to raise his head that he might look at his wound; and seeing . . . that he couldn't live, he wanted Barnard to leave him, which he would not do, but gave him some water to drink, on which he said, "What's the use of giving me water?" But it seemed to revive him a little, and he died without apparent pain.'

Finding that his light field pieces were unable to silence the rebel guns, and that he was 'losing men fast', Sir Henry Barnard ordered the 1st Brigade to charge the left of the rebel defences. Lieutenant Kendal Coghill recalled:

> When [the 1st Brigade were] within 300 yards [the rebels] poured awful volleys of round shot, shell and grape into the line, but a hearty good English cheer and a charge at the double brought the 75th Foot and 1st Fusiliers on their guns and the bayonets did the rest. About 3000 of the enemy's infantry, some cavalry and horse artillery bolted across towards our lines on the left and met the 60th Rifles and 2nd Fusiliers who gave them a few well directed volleys and then ceased firing for close in their rear a wing of our 9th Lancers charged across, cut up a lot and captured 2 guns! It was then our turn for the sport, so the left Brigade (ours) brought its left round, went through a large jungle or forest, killed all we found, went through a large village, rooted them out and potted them and then fired it. We then turned their guns on them, gave them a few rounds of grape into the retiring mass and by half nine that position was ours . . .

As at Ghazi-ud-din-Nagar, the rebel commander was the first to flee. Intercepted by Mahbub Ali Khan, the King's chief minister, Mirza Kizr

Sultan explained that he was 'hurrying back to the city for more artillery and ammunition' and, 'in spite of all remonstrances, galloped away'.

The victorious British troops were hot, thirsty and exhausted. But Barnard was determined to push on to the Ridge and allowed just half an hour's rest before ordering an advance. A short way beyond Badli-ki-Serai, at a fork in the road, Barnard split his troops into two columns. Brigadier Wilson led one to the right down the continuation of the Grand Trunk Road towards the picturesque suburb of Sabzi Mundi at the bottom of the Ridge. Barnard took the other to the left through the destroyed British cantonments. 'I soon found,' reported Barnard, 'that the enemy had posted himself strongly on the ridge over the cantonments, with guns in position, and under the range of which we soon found ourselves; upon which I determined on a rapid flank movement to the left, in the hope of gaining the ridge under cover of the cantonments, and taking the position in flank.' Lieutenant Coghill, whose 2nd Bengal Fusiliers were at the point of the attack, recalled:

> At the foot of the hill we extended in skirmishing order about 8 or 900 of us and when we got within 100 yards of the top the word to charge was given and with a yell like so many demons we rushed up and in ten minutes the battery was ours – we spiked the guns and rushed after them down the opposite side of the hill until we were fairly done and then we came up and finished off some lurkers and some wounded men who shammed dead and potted at us. We killed two blackguard Englishmen who begged for mercy swearing they had been compelled to fight but had aimed over our heads, but as they had served the guns and every shot had come into our columns and they were recognised as great blackguards by their own men, the artillery, no mercy was shown and they were killed on the spot.

These two English rebels were deserters who had converted to Islam. One British officer attributed the accuracy of the rebel fire to their expertise as former artillerymen. Their summary execution was inevitable.

At Hindu Rao's House, the deserted former home of a Maratha nobleman on the southern end of the Ridge, Barnard 'had the satisfaction of meeting Brigadier Wilson', whose column had had to fight the rebels the whole way into Delhi 'through the strongest ground, gardens and villages that could be imagined'. There many of Barnard's officers urged him to continue on into the city. But he refused, saying, 'No, no, we will fight them in the open.' It was, according to Mainodin Hassan Khan, a mistake. 'If they had instantly marched on the city, the place would have fallen easily into their power . . . The hesitation on the part of the English inspired the Sepoys with confidence and, arming the city walls with guns, they soon began to fire shots in the direction of the cantonments.'

Barnard responded by placing pickets and gun batteries at four strong-points along the Ridge: (from north to south) the Flagstaff Tower, a ruined mosque, an ancient observatory and Hindu Rao's House. The Sirmur Battalion of Gurkhas reached this last building, just 1,200 yards from the city walls, at around one in the afternoon. 'Had just made ourselves comfortable,' wrote Major Reid, 'when the alarm was sounded. In ten minutes the mutineers were seen coming up towards Hindu Rao's house in force. I went out with my own regiment and two companies of Rifles, and drove them back into the city. This, however, was not accomplished till five p.m., so that we were under arms for sixteen hours. Heat fearful. My little fellows behaved splendidly, and were cheered by every European regiment . . . They had (because it was a Native regiment) doubts about us; but I think they are now satisfied.'

Barnard may have missed a golden opportunity to retake Delhi. But he had won a great victory, nevertheless, thanks largely to the unflinching courage of his European infantry. Thirteen rebel guns had been captured, two of them 24-pounders, at a cost of 51 killed, 132 wounded and 2 missing. The rebel deaths alone were estimated at 400. As the fighting died down, Barnard ordered a tented camp to be set up on the old parade-ground, beyond the reach of the rebel guns on the city walls. The cantonments themselves were a scene of devastation, 'only the walls standing, and things lying about the roads in every direction – broken dinner-sets, music-books, etc.' But this was nothing compared to the carnage of the battlefield. Harriet Tytler, who accompanied her husband over the ground in the afternoon, remembered seeing scores of dead British soldiers lying neatly in a row. The rebels, including members of her husband's regiment, were left where they fell. 'I saw some of our fine, tall, handsome men,' she wrote, 'lying somewhat swollen by the heat of those four hours and stark naked, for every camp follower robbed them of their gold and silver jewels, and the last comers of the clothes on their bodies, leaving the poor fellows just as God had made them. Such handsome, splendid specimens of high caste Hindus. One man had a hole as large as a billiard ball through his forehead, a perfect giant in death. I could not help saying, "Serve you right for killing our poor women and children who had never injured you."'

The following morning Henry Daly's Corps of Guides marched into the British camp. One of the first officers to greet them was William Hodson, their former commandant. 'It would have done your heart good to see the welcome they gave me,' he wrote to his wife at Simla, 'cheering and shouting and crowding round me like frantic creatures. They seized my bridle, dress, hands, and feet, and literally threw themselves down before the horse with the tears streaming down their faces. Many officers who were present hardly knew what to make of it, and thought the creatures were mobbing me; and so they were, but for joy, not for mischief.' Everything about the new arrivals excited wonder in their onlookers. 'The Guides Corps is a sight to see,' noted a cavalry officer. 'Their dress is highly peculiar and the men are chiefly of two sorts, viz., the tall, powerful, swarthy Afghan, and the short, muscular, olive-skinned Gurkha. They are the admiration of the camp, having marched 580 miles in twenty-two days – a feat unparalleled in the records of Indian marching.' The epic trek was all the more incredible for having been accomplished during the feast of Ramadan and in the hottest time of the year.

The Guides had only been in the camp a matter of hours when they were given a further opportunity to impress. Shortly after two in the afternoon, the rebels launched a strong attack on the pickets at the southern end of the Ridge. Daly and his cavalry helped to drive them back to the walls of the city – but not without cost. 'The men hotly engaged,' recorded Daly, 'Battye mortally wounded – noble Battye ever in front; Khan Singh Rosa hard hit; Hawes clipt across the face with a sword and many good men down. Men behaved heroically, *impetuously*.' Lieutenant Quintin Battye, the popular commander of the Guides Cavalry, had been shot in the groin and died that evening. His last muttered words are typical of the patriotic sentiments expressed by many British officers at this time: '*Dulce et decorum est pro patria mori*.'

The British position on the Ridge was, in the words of one staff officer, 'not only a coign of vantage for attack, but a rampart of defence'. The conundrum now facing Sir Henry Barnard was what to do next: dig in and await reinforcements or risk a surprise attack. Most of the officers on the Ridge, particularly the young ones, were for the bolder course. Any delay, they argued, would be to the advantage of the rebels, whose strength was increasing daily with the arrival of fresh mutineers. British numbers, on the other hand, could only decline in the short term. At first Barnard too seemed to favour the aggressive option. On 11 June he asked William Hodson and three young Engineer officers – Greathed, Chesney and Maunsell – to assess the feasibility of a sudden assault. That same day they reported that the Kabul and Lahore Gates had not yet been bricked up, that their bridges were still intact, and that troops could approach within 400 and 900 yards of them respectively under cover. They recommended blowing up both gates simultaneously, followed by a dawn assault by two columns.

Barnard approved the scheme and gave orders for it to be carried out during the morning of 13 June. The assaulting troops, including almost all the fit Europeans, were ordered to assemble at one in the morning. But at the appointed hour three hundred members of the 1st Bengal Fusiliers were missing. The duty officer, Brigadier Graves, was to blame. A couple of hours earlier he had received a verbal order from Barnard that all European troops on picket duty were to be withdrawn for special duty. This order included a 'vague hint that a night-assault was in contemplation'. When Graves reached the Flagstaff picket, however, and realized that it was about to be left in the sole charge of Indian troops, he instructed the Europeans to stand fast while he galloped down to the general's tent to seek confirmation of the original order. Barnard told him that every British infantryman was needed for an immediate assault. But he was evidently having second thoughts because he then asked Graves, who knew Delhi well, the assault's chances of success. 'You may certainly take the city by surprise,' replied the brigadier, 'but whether you are strong enough to hold it is another matter.' This response is said to have shaken Barnard's faltering resolve still further. It was, in any case, too late to carry out the original order, because, as one senior officer commented, 'it would have been broad daylight before we could all get down to the Gates'. The operation had to be cancelled.

The majority of Barnard's staff officers were secretly relieved. 'Most fortunate, I think, that we did not attack,' noted Keith Young in his diary, 'for failure would have been death – and success was not quite certain; and we are not reduced to such a desperate state yet as to risk all. My own idea is – wait till the Sikh corps comes.' There were, wrote Captain Norman, the acting adjutant-general, 'few who did not feel that the accident which hindered this attempt was one of those happy interpositions in our behalf of which we had such numbers to be thankful for'.

But Barnard was still under intense pressure from Calcutta and the Punjab to capture Delhi. The plan for an assault, therefore, had been delayed rather than abandoned. 'I have nothing left,' Barnard informed Canning on 13 June, 'but to place all on the hazard of a die and attempt a *coup-de-main*, which I purpose to do. If successful, all will be well. But reverse will be fatal, for I can have no reserve on which to retire. But, assuredly, you all greatly under-estimated the difficulties of Delhi. They have twenty-four-pounders on every gate and flank bastion; and their practice is excellent – beats ours *five* to *one*. We have got six heavy guns in position, but do not silence theirs, and I really see nothing for it but a determined rush, and this, please God, you will hear of as successful.'

The new assault was scheduled for the morning of 16 June. Twenty-four hours before it was due to take place, however, Barnard received word that 4,000 reinforcements were on their way from the Punjab. A council of war duly met in the afternoon of 15 June to decide whether the attack should go ahead. In attendance were Barnard, a fit-again General Reed, Brigadier Wilson, Hervey Greathed and the senior Engineer officers. Hervey Greathed was opposed to a further postponement on the political grounds that it would 'disappoint expectations, protract the disorders with which the country is afflicted, increase the disaffection which is known to exist amongst the Muhammadan population in the Bombay Presidency, and cause distrust on the part of the Native allies'. Wilberforce Greathed, the young Engineer, was even more forceful in his advocacy of an immediate attack, 'but his talk was too fiery and wild for any one to listen to'. Most of the senior officers present, on the other hand, were for delaying the assault until at least some reinforcements had arrived. Even Wilson, who had been urging an immediate assault, was now of the opinion that the Delhi Field Force was 'perfectly safe' on the Ridge and 'with fresh troops' would be able 'to take Delhi with but little loss and with a certainty of destroying the mutineers'. But with so much at stake, a final decision was postponed until the following day.

At the reconvened council of war on 16 June, the balance was tipped in favour of delay by Archdale Wilson's written assessment, which concluded: 'It would be impossible, with the small force we now have, to leave a sufficient force for the protection of Delhi, and at the same time to send out such brigades as will be required. It appears to me a question of time only.' Later that day Wilson informed his wife: 'It has been decided principally at my recommendation to delay the assault till we are joined by the moveable column from Lahore.' No one was more tormented by the decision than Sir Henry Barnard. 'I confess,' he wrote to Sir John Lawrence on 18 June, 'that, urged on by the political adviser acting with me, I had consented to a *coup-de-main* . . . accident alone prevented it; it may be the interposition of Providence. From what I can hear, and from the opinion of others whom it became my duty to consult, I am convinced that success would have been as fatal as failure . . . Be sure that I have been guided by military rule, and that it required moral courage to face the cry that will be raised against our inactivity before Delhi; I can but act for the best, and wait any favourable opportunity for striking the blow.'

Was it a mistake to delay? Probably. General Rose would demonstrate during the Bundelkhand campaign of 1858 what a bold commander could achieve with limited resources. Every day that Barnard remained on the defensive at Delhi, his position became relatively weaker. By 21 June nearly half the native corps in the regular Bengal Army had mutinied, partially mutinied or been disbanded. They had been joined in rebellion by three local corps, the whole of the Oudh Irregular Force, the Malwa Contingent, the Bharatpur Legion and most of the Gwalior Contingent. A further thirteen regiments of native infantry, six of cavalry, seven companies of foot artillery and two troops of horse artillery had also been disarmed by this time. In the majority of cases – as if in confirmation of Ahsanullah Khan's claim that it was agreed by the conspirators beforehand – the mutinous corps headed for Delhi. But only a relatively small number of trained Bengal troops, perhaps a couple of thousand in all, had reached the Mogul capital by the time the first council of war was held on 15 June. Over the next ten days, however, the rebels at Delhi were augmented by mutinous elements of a further ten regiments of infantry, two of cavalry and one artillery battery from stations as far afield as Nasirabad in Rajputana, Bareilly in Rohilkhand and Jullundur in the Punjab: roughly 7,000 troops in all. During the same period the British at Delhi received fewer than a thousand reinforcements. The possibility of a successful assault was becoming ever more distant; and while Delhi remained in the hands of the mutineers, the rebellion would continue to spread.

12. Oudh

The British official in the least enviable position by late May 1857 was Sir Henry Lawrence, the Chief Commissioner of Oudh. The province of Oudh as a whole contained almost 20,000 Indian troops, some of them former soldiers of the ex-King, and many times that number of civilians who were clamouring for an end to Company rule. To deter them from rising, Lawrence had less than a thousand European troops in the form of a weak regiment of British infantry and a single battery of Bengal foot artillery. These Europeans were all concentrated in Lucknow, the capital, alongside 7,000 native soldiers.

Lawrence lived in the Residency, a large three-storey building that had been enlarged by successive Residents in a variety of styles since its original construction in 1780. Its main entrance was from the east, through a superb portico, while the western front included a wide colonnaded veranda. As well as a number of spacious apartments on the ground and two upper floors, it had several lofty underground rooms on the south side, built to shelter the Residents from the extreme heat of the Oudh sun. Surrounding the Residency was the official district, which covered an area in excess of 60 acres. It contained a variety of detached buildings – including a banqueting hall, treasury, hospital, church, storerooms and houses for Lawrence's subordinates – and was entered through a brick archway known as the Baillie Guard Gate. The whole Residency compound was situated on rising ground close to the River Gumti, with the sprawling city of 600,000 souls spread out beneath it. A quarter of a mile to its north-west lay the iron bridge across the River Gumti and beyond that, on a natural eminence and surrounded by a high, buttressed wall, stood a ramshackle stronghold known as the Machi Bawan, which commanded a stone bridge across the river.

To the south and east, on both sides of the city walls, were the principal palaces, walled gardens and tombs of the former Kings of Oudh, including the Kaisarbagh, the Chattar Manzil, the Moti Mahal, the Shah Najaf and the Sikandarbagh. Three miles to the south-east, beyond the canal that encircled that part of the city, was the Martinière College for European and Eurasian boys, and to the south of that the Dilkusha (or Heart's Delight), a royal hunting lodge set in an enclosed park of deer and antelope. Observing the city from the roof of the Dilkusha, William Howard Russell described it as a 'vision of palaces, minars, domes azure and golden, cupolas, colonnade, long façades of fair perspective in pillar and column, terraced roofs – all rising up amid a calm still ocean of the brightest verdure'. He added: 'There is a city more vast than Paris, as it seems, and more brilliant.'

The location of the troops at Lucknow was, Lawrence believed, 'as bad as bad can be – all scattered over several miles – the Infantry in one direction, the Cavalry another, the Artillery in a third, the magazine in a fourth and almost unprotected'. The main cantonments were at Muriaon, three miles from the Residency, on the Sitapur road. They contained three regiments of native infantry – the 13th, 48th and 71st – three batteries of native artillery (two of them irregular) and one of European artillery. A mile and a half further on towards Sitapur were the lines of the 7th Light Cavalry at Mudkipur. Quartered south of the river were two regiments of Oudh Irregular Infantry: the 4th and 7th. The sole British regiment, the 32nd Foot,* was in barracks two miles to the east of the Residency. In the same locality, but on the other side of the river, was the 2nd Oudh Irregular Cavalry, while detachments of military police, both horse and foot, were scattered all over the city.

No sooner had news of the Meerut rising reached Lucknow than Lawrence bowed to pressure from Martin Gubbins, his financial commissioner, and began to prepare for a possible outbreak. But this could be done only with the cooperation of the military, and it was not immediately forthcoming because the senior officer, Brigadier Isaac Handscomb, the 51-year-old son of a lace merchant, could not bring himself to believe that his sepoys would mutiny. On 16 May, therefore, Lawrence asked for and was granted 'plenary military power in Oudh' by Lord Canning. Three days later he was promoted to the rank of brigadier-general, thereby outranking Handscomb. Armed with this new authority, he ordered the removal of the magazine and other supplies to the dilapidated but still formidable Machi Bawan; he also sent three companies of the 32nd Foot with six guns to keep an eye on the main body of Indian troops at Muriaon cantonments; and he constructed entrenchments in the form of an irregular pentagon around the Residency compound. Another precaution, on 25 May, was the removal of all European women and children into houses within the Residency compound. Maria Germon, the wife of a captain in the 13th Native Infantry, was given just two hours' warning to leave her bungalow at Muriaon. She noted in her journal:

* Later the Duke of Cornwall's Light Infantry.

When we drove up to the Residency everything looked so warlike – guns pointed in all directions, barricades and European troops everywhere – such a scene of bustle and confusion . . . Mr Harris went over to see if Dr Fayrer could take us in – he came back saying yes, and away we went, thankful to get into such good quarters – two ladies were there already and five came after us with three children, so that every room was full. This house as well as Mr Gubbins' and Mr Ommaney's (both also full) are within the Residency compound and are barricaded all round.

Cramped as conditions were in Dr Fayrer's house, they were nothing compared to the crush in the Residency. 'I never witnessed such a scene – a perfect barrack – every room filled with six or eight ladies, beds all round and perhaps a dining-table laid for dinner in the centre, servants thick in all the verandahs,' wrote Maria Germon on 26 May. 'Lots of the 32nd soldiers and their officers, and underneath all the women and children of the 32nd barracks . . . It is an upper storied house – the upper storey not nearly so large as the under one and yet in that, including servants and children, there are 96 people living.'

To deprive an attacking force of cover, Lawrence had even considered razing buildings – including temples and mosques – in the proximity of the Residency perimeter; but he decided not to for fear of inciting the volatile citizenry. Some Europeans at Lucknow, particularly Handscomb and his sepoy officers, regarded Lawrence's precautions as premature and provocative. But most were impressed by his energy and attention to detail. L. E. Routz Rees, a Swiss-born wholesale merchant, recalled:

Sir Henry Lawrence was indefatigable, and seemed almost never to sleep. Often he would sally out in disguise, and visit the most frequented parts of the native town, to make personal observations, and see how his orders were carried out. He several times had a thin bedding spread out near the guns at the Bailey-guard Gate, and retired there among the artillerists, not to sleep, but to plan and to meditate undisturbed. He appeared to be ubiquitous, and to be seen everywhere. All loved and respected the old gentleman, and indeed everyone had cause, for none was too lowly for his notice, and no details were too uninteresting for him . . . The uncovenanted, particularly, had a kind friend in him, and with the common soldier he was equally if not even more popular.

Lawrence was often described as 'old' at this time. He was in fact just fifty, though he looked much older. 'His face bore the traces of many years' toil beneath an Indian sun and the still deeper marks of a never-ending conflict with self,' wrote a contemporary. 'His eyes, overhung by massive, craggy brows, looked out with an expression in which melancholy was strangely blended with humour: his thin wasted cheeks were scored down their whole length by deep lines; and a long ragged beard added to his look of age.'

Despite the weakness of his position at Lucknow, Lawrence was mindful of those in even greater danger. At the important military station of Cawnpore on the Ganges, 48 miles from Lucknow, a handful of European soldiers were heavily outnumbered by around 3,000 native troops. So on 21 May, in response to a request from Major-General Sir Hugh Wheeler, the local divisional commander, Lawrence sent fifty of his precious British infantrymen and two squadrons of the 2nd Oudh Irregular Cavalry, regarded as more trustworthy than the regulars, to support the authorities at Cawnpore. Two days later he urged Canning by cable to reinforce Cawnpore 'with all speed'. Canning's reply, the following day, was that it would be 'impossible to place a wing of Europeans at Cawnpore in less time than 25 days'. The railway from Calcutta only extended up-country as far as Raniganj, a distance of 120 miles. Beyond Raniganj the only means of transport were horse *dâk*, bullock-cart or river steamer; it was far too hot for European troops to march any significant distance, even by night. Canning explained:

> The Government dâk and the dâk companies are fully engaged in carrying a company of the 84th [from Raniganj] to Benares at the rate of eighteen men a day. A wing of the [1st] Madras Fusiliers arrived yesterday and starts today; part by bullock train, part by steamer. The bullock train can take 100 men a day, at the rate of thirty miles a day. The entire regiment of the Fusiliers, about 900 strong, cannot be collected at Benares in less than nineteen or twenty days. One hundred and fifty men, who go by steam, will scarcely be there so soon. I expect that from this time forward troops will be pushed up at the rate of 100 men a day from Calcutta, each batch taking ten days to reach Benares. From Benares they will be distributed as required. The regiments from Pegu, Bombay, and Ceylon will be sent up in this way . . . This is the best I can do for you.

Lawrence feared that such a tiny trickle of troops would not be enough to prevent more mutinies. On 27 May he 'strongly' advised Canning to hire as many private *dâks* as possible to transport European troops to Cawnpore. He ended the short telegram: 'Spare no expense.' His own precautions at Lucknow, he told Canning in a separate cable, were now complete, with both the Residency and the Machi Bawan 'safe against all probable comers'. The likelihood of a general revolt in Oudh was increasing by the day. 'All

1. Government House (*centre*), Calcutta, with the Maidan in the foreground

2. Sepoys preparing for firing practice

3. Sir Henry Lawrence

4. Major-General Sir Archdale Wilson

5. Mutineers destroy a bungalow at Meerut during the outbreak of 10 May 1857

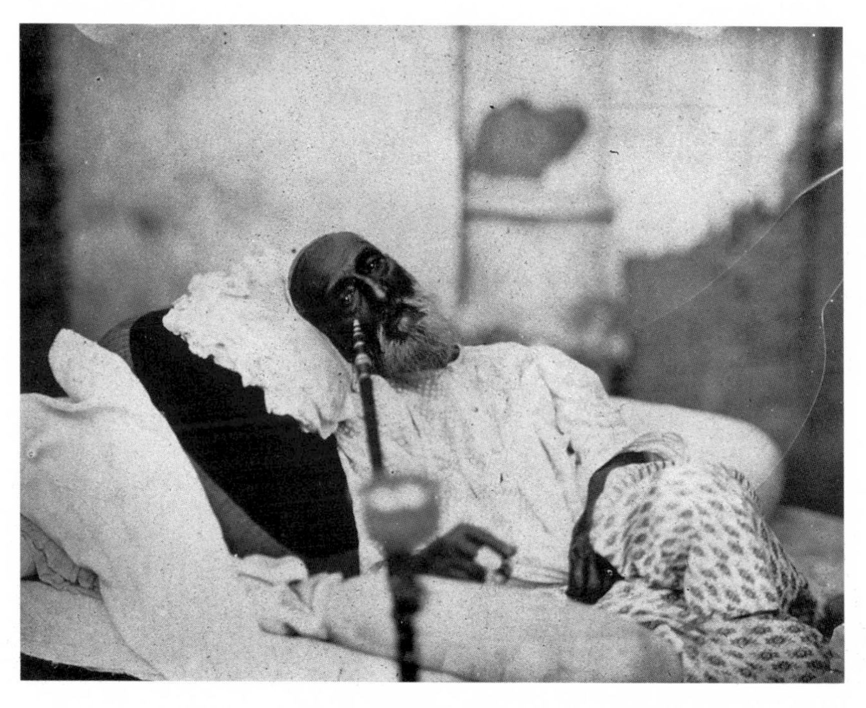

6. Bahadur Shah II, the last Mogul King of Delhi

7. The Lahore Gate of the Red Fort at Delhi, containing the apartments of Captain Douglas, the commander of the King's Guard. Douglas, the Revd Jennings, his daughter and her friend were murdered there on 11 May 1857

8. Mutinous sowars of the 3rd Light Cavalry attacking Europeans at Delhi on 11 May 1857

9. Herbert Edwardes

10. John Nicholson

11. Mutinous sepoys being blown from guns

12. The larger of the two barracks in Wheeler's entrenchment. A former dragoon hospital, measuring 60 by 350 feet, its thatched roof was set on fire by an incendiary shell on 12 June 1857

13. Satichaura Ghat, Cawnpore, from the Oudh bank of the Ganges. In the centre is the small boatman's temple from where the rebel leaders directed the massacre of 27 June 1857

14. General Sir Mowbray Thomson, one of only four men to survive the massacre at Satichaura Ghat

15. Brigadier-General James Neill

16. Sir Henry Havelock

quiet, but great uneasiness in Lucknow,' Lawrence informed Calcutta on 29 May. 'Tranquillity cannot be much longer maintained, unless Delhi be speedily captured.'

Everywhere in the city there were signs of growing unrest. 'Seditious placards were found stuck up in all the principal streets,' wrote one of Lawrence's assistants, 'calling upon all good Mussulmen and Hindoos to rise and kill the Christians.' Dolls were dressed up as European children and, 'much to the amusement of the mob', their heads cut off with swords. The servants of the European community began to complain that the grain merchants and shopkeepers would no longer give them credit, while 'Government paper was selling as low as thirty-seven rupees for the hundred, and even less!' An obvious precaution would have been to disarm the Indian troops at Lucknow, a solution repeatedly urged by Martin Gubbins. But Lawrence refused on the grounds that the regiments in the outlying districts might mutiny in protest.

During the early evening of Saturday, 30 May, a sepoy of the 13th Native Infantry, who had earlier been rewarded by the chief commissioner for assisting in the capture of a spy, went to the bungalow of a staff officer, Captain T. F. Wilson, and told him that a mutiny of the native troops at Muriaon had been arranged for nine that night. It would, he claimed, begin in the lines of the 71st Native Infantry, the most disaffected of the three regiments at Muriaon. But Lawrence refused to act. He had taken to sleeping in the Resident's bungalow at Muriaon to demonstrate his trust in the Indian troops, and was dining with his staff there when the firing of the nine o'clock gun came and went. 'Wilson,' he remarked drily, 'your friends are not punctual!' The words were hardly out of his mouth when the rattle of musketry filled the air. Lawrence ordered his horse and, as he waited for it on his front step, the Indian officer of the guard strode forward and asked Captain Wilson, 'Am I to load?' Wilson repeated the question to Lawrence who replied, 'Yes, let him load.'

The order was at once given [recalled Wilson] and the ramrod fell with that peculiar dull sound on the leaden bullets. I believe that Sir Henry was the only man of all that group whose heart did not beat the quicker for it. But he, as the men brought up their muskets with the tubes levelled directly against us, cried out – 'I am going to drive those scoundrels out of cantonment: take care while I am away that you remain at your posts, and allow no one to do any damage here, or to enter my house, else when I return I will hang you.' Whether through the effect of the speech, and Sir Henry's bearing, I know not, but the guard remained steadily at its post, and with the bungalows blazing and shots firing all round, they allowed no one to enter the house.

Lawrence and his staff rode to the European lines, where they found the detachment of the 32nd Foot and six cannon drawn up ready for action. To prevent the mutineers from marching on Lucknow, Lawrence took a company of the 32nd and two guns to the road leading from the cantonment to the city. The rest of the European infantry and artillery was led by the commanding officer of the 32nd, Lieutenant-Colonel John Inglis, to a position on the right of the lines of the 71st Native Infantry. For a time they were engaged by sepoys of the 71st firing muskets from these lines. But when the guns replied with grape, the mutineers withdrew to the cantonment. On the way they murdered Lieutenant Grant of the 71st, who was commanding the main picket in the centre of the Indian lines. 'His men remained with him till the mutineers were close upon him,' wrote a fellow officer. 'They then broke; but the subadar of the guard, and some men of the 13th and 48th Regiments, composing the guard, tried to save him, by placing him under a bed. A man of the 71st Native Infantry, who was on guard with him, however, discovered the place of his concealment to the mutineers, and he was brutally murdered – receiving no less than fifteen bayonet wounds, besides some musket balls.' The highest-ranking fatality was Brigadier Handscomb, shot in the chest as he tried to remonstrate with the mutineers.

Of the Indian troops at Muriaon who did not mutiny, the largest proportion was from the 13th Native Infantry. When the firing broke out in the lines of the 71st, more than half the six hundred or so members of the 13th obeyed the orders of their officers and fell in on their parade-ground. They were then marched over to support the main body of British troops, complete with colours and treasure chest, and took up a position to the right of the 32nd Foot. Soon after they were joined by a small number of 71st sepoys. Nothing was heard of the 48th until the following day, when most of the Indian officers and about three hundred sepoys returned to duty. Meanwhile all but thirty of the headquarters wing of the 7th Light Cavalry at Mudkipur had remained loyal. These troopers spent much of that night patrolling the grounds of the Residency and the Machi Bawan, but by morning had linked up with the main British force at Muriaon.

Shortly after daybreak on 31 May, having received word that the mutineers had occupied the nearby cavalry lines at Mudkipur, Lawrence advanced to attack. The rebels, about a thousand strong, were drawn up on the plain in front of the cavalry lines. As soon as the 7th's 'loyal' troopers came into view, in the van of Lawrence's force, a single horseman rode out of the rebel ranks and waved his sword. This prearranged signal caused about two thirds of the cavalrymen to desert to the enemy with loud yells. Lawrence responded by halting the infantry and ordering the guns to open fire. Just a few shots were enough to cause the rebels to withdraw down the Sitapur road. They were pursued for about seven miles by the remnants of the cavalry and a number of mounted officers and civilians, including Lawrence and Martin Gubbins, who managed to capture sixty mutineers between them.

In total, about seven hundred sepoys remained loyal during the events of 30 and 31 May. The majority were from the 13th and 48th Regiments, though all but ninety of the latter were sent on indefinite leave after news reached Lucknow that two companies of the 48th sent into the Khyrabad Division had, along with the two troops of 7th Light Cavalry, mutinied and murdered their officers on 7 June. The loyalty of the greater part of the 13th was probably due to Major Charles Bruère, their much loved commanding officer, who had served with the regiment for more than two decades. Lieutenant-Colonel Henry Palmer of the 48th was also a familiar figure to his men, having joined the regiment as an ensign in 1826. Colonel William Halford, on the other hand, had been with the 71st – the most disaffected regiment – for only eighteen months. Aged sixty, he was the second-eldest regimental commander in the Bengal Army; Bruère, by contrast, was forty-four and Palmer forty-nine.

The mutiny at Lucknow was followed by city riots on 31 May when green flags, the standard of the prophet Muhammad, were raised and one European clerk was murdered. Though the riots were easily suppressed by the city police, evidence soon came to light of an 'extensive conspiracy in the city and in the cantonments'. A former *tahsildar* pointed the finger at Shurruf-ud Daula, a senior figure in the court of the ex-King, Wajid Ali Shah, and Prime Minister to two of Wajid's predecessors. He and two of his relations were imprisoned on Lawrence's orders, as were Mustapha Ali Khan, the ex-King's elder brother, the Raja of Tulsipur and two members of the Delhi royal family who lived in Lucknow. Far harsher was the treatment of twenty-two alleged conspirators, said to have been sent from Benares and elsewhere to corrupt the troops, who were shot after a drumhead court martial. The captured mutineers were hanged in batches of eight or nine on the open ground in front of the Machi Bawan.

*

The upheavals of 30 and 31 May were not necessarily a bad thing for the British: their enemies were now out in the open and they could concentrate on defending their posts without fear of betrayal. 'We are in a much better position at Lucknow,' wrote Lawrence to Canning on 1 June, 'but I fear the effects of the *émeute* in the districts.' He had good reason to. On 2 June came the news that some troops sent to Cawnpore a fortnight earlier had mutinied and murdered their officers. The original detachment had consisted of half a company of the 32nd Foot under Captain Lowe and a squadron of the 2nd Oudh Irregular Cavalry under Lieutenant Barbor. In overall command was Captain Fletcher Hayes, military secretary to the chief commissioner, who went 'to confer with [General] Wheeler and report back on the state of affairs to Sir Henry Lawrence'. Hayes was not your typical Bengal officer. An erudite Oxford graduate, he had amassed during his relatively short time in India a 'splendid library . . . of priceless Oriental manuscripts; the standard literary and scientific works of every nation of Europe; dictionaries of every language spoken on earth' (all of which he had generously sacrificed for the barricades around the Residency compound). He had also gained a reputation as a skilful diplomatist during his time as Assistant Resident at the Court of Oudh in the period prior to annexation. Few officers knew the province and its inhabitants better than Hayes.

The detachment had set out from Lucknow at dawn on 21 May. One officer wrote: 'Owing to the intense heat, the Europeans were conveyed in dâk gharries, buggies and any other conveyance that came to hand. The party reached Cawnpore the same evening, having covered the distance – forty-eight miles – in something less than twelve hours.' They found the cantonment and city quiet. After a few days kicking his heels, Hayes asked Sir Hugh Wheeler for permission to take the cavalry up the Grand Trunk Road as far as Aligarh. He was convinced, he wrote in his last letter, 'that a bold front and daring would best assist the cause of order'. Wheeler acquiesced, and Hayes and Barbor left with the cavalry on 27 May. They were accompanied by two volunteers: Robert Fayrer, the doctor's nephew, and Captain Thomas Carey of the 17th Native Infantry. During the evening of 31 May the column reached the village of Bhongaon, 100 miles from Cawnpore. Hearing reports that a local raja had risen against British rule, Hayes told Barbor and Fayrer to stay with the men while he and Carey rode to the nearby station of Mainpuri to consult the magistrate. The pair stayed the night at Mainpuri and rejoined the column the following morning. Carey recorded:

They were on one road, we on another. I said, 'Let us cross the plain and meet them.' As we approached they faced towards us and halted, and when we had cantered up to within about fifty yards of them, one of two of the native officers rode out to meet us, and said in a low voice, 'Fly, Sahibs, fly.' Upon this poor Hayes said to me as we wheeled round our horse – 'Well, we must fly now for our lives,' and away we went with the two troops after us like demons, yelling and sending the bullets from their carbines all around us. Thank God, neither I nor my horse was hit. Hayes was riding on the side nearest the troopers, and before we had gone many yards, I saw a native officer go up alongside of him, and with one blow cut him down from his saddle . . . On they all came shouting after me and every now and then 'ping' came a ball near me. Indeed, I thought my moments were numbered, but as I neared the road at the end of the maidan, a ditch presented itself. It was but a moment I thought, dug my spurs hard in, and the mare flew over it, though she nearly fell on the other side; fortunately, I recovered her, and in another moment I was leaving all behind but two sowars, who followed me and poor Hayes' horse tearing on after me . . . I eased the mare as much as I could, keeping those fiends about 100 yards in rear; and they, I suppose, seeing I was taking it easy, and not urging my horse, but merely turning round every now and then to watch them, pulled up, after chasing me two good miles.

Carey eventually made it back to Mainpuri and safety. The fate of Barbor and Fayrer was later revealed by a Sikh native officer, Shere Singh, who stood aloof from the mutiny and made his way to Mainpuri with a handful of loyal troopers. According to Singh, it was very hot and the column had stopped to refresh itself beside a well. Fayrer was cut down as he drank water from a leather cup. 'The poor lad, he was only 23, fell dead on the spot: his spine was cut through. The old Native officer . . . who came back and told us of it said he muttered "Mother" as he fell.' On Fayrer being struck, a loyal sowar rushed forward to help him, shouting to the others to arrest the murderer. But as he lifted Fayrer's head he was shot by his comrades. Barbor was killed trying to escape.

The news, when it reached Lucknow, was all the more distressing for the fact that both Hayes and Barbor were married, the latter only recently. Hayes, moreover, had seven children.

The military cantonment at Sitapur, 41 miles north of Lucknow, was the second biggest in Oudh. It contained four regiments – the 41st Native Infantry, the 9th and 10th Oudh Irregular Infantry and the 2nd Oudh Military Police – and was situated to the east of the town in a bend of the

Esan River. Next to the cantonment was the civil station and, at its eastern extremity, the bungalow of the commissioner, George Christian, which was bounded on three sides by water. Near by were the bungalows of the deputy commissioner, Mr Thornhill, and his two assistants, Lieutenant Lester and Sir Mountstuart Jackson, Bt.

Sir Mountstuart was the nephew of Coverly Jackson, Lawrence's predecessor as Chief Commissioner of Oudh. His father, an officer in the 4th Dragoon Guards, had died in Germany when Mountstuart was still a boy, bequeathing him a baronetcy but no money. His mother had also died when he was a child, leaving him and his three sisters to be brought up by their grandmother in a modest cottage at Walmer in Kent. In 1852, at the age of sixteen, Jackson used his uncle's connections to secure a writership in the Bengal Civil Service and he arrived in India four years later. He was now twenty-one and had been at Sitapur, his first posting, for just four months. Living with him were his two eldest sisters: Georgina, nineteen, and Madeline, seventeen. They had arrived in India from their Paris school at the turn of the year. Madeline described their house as 'a nice little bungalow, with a big garden, and our pets which Uncle C. had mostly given us – our Arab, two spotted deer (one we had brought up with milk), two gazelles, two spotted Barbary goats, and an Argus pheasant . . . We had two white bullocks to irrigate the garden, and my brother had a buggy and horse and his Arab.' This carefree existence was shattered by the news from Meerut.

On 1 June, having received word the night before that mutineers from Lucknow were heading towards Sitapur, Colonel Birch left the station with a wing of the 41st Native Infantry to intercept them. According to one officer, the men 'went off in good spirits, loudly proclaiming their loyalty, and boasting of the deeds they would do when they met the mutineers'. Fortunately their professions of loyalty were not put to the test because, having covered a fair distance towards Lucknow, Birch was informed by villagers that the mutineers had left the Sitapur road for Maliabad, with Delhi as their ultimate destination. He and his column arrived back at Sitapur in the evening of 2 June.

Commissioner Christian, meanwhile, was labouring under the delusion that the local troops could be trusted. On 1 June he had written to Lawrence: 'If [the 41st] go over we know the worst. Even then I believe the 9th and 10th Oudh Irregular Infantry and the Military Police will stand firm . . . I have placed all the ladies and children and women, except some four who will not leave the lines of the 41st . . . in my house, and have made all secure . . . I now only wait for the attitude of the 41st.' In theory Christian's defensive position around his bungalow was a good one. The local troops were well sited to meet a frontal attack, while the river – wide, deep and fordable in only a couple of places – covered the rear and flanks. But all Christian's calculations depended upon the fidelity of the Oudh troops: if they turned against their officers, the river would prevent the Europeans from escaping and the position would become a death-trap.

At around ten in the morning of 3 June word reached Colonel Birch that the 10th Irregulars were about to plunder the treasury that was being guarded by a company of the 41st. He at once set off to foil the attack at the head of four companies. But when he reached the treasury, situated to the north of the station about a mile from the lines of the 41st, Birch found no sign of a disturbance and so decided to return. The order, 'Threes, left shoulders forward', had hardly left his lips when a sepoy of the treasury guard stepped forward and shot him in the chest, causing him to topple from his horse. Lieutenant Smalley and the sergeant-major were also killed by a volley from the ranks, but the adjutant, Lieutenant Graves, the only other European present, managed to gallop off with a slight bullet wound to his head. He returned to his lines in time to warn his brother officers before the rest of the regiment rose. They quickly gathered together their families and, with an escort of twenty loyal sepoys and the Christian drummers, set off in carriages and on horseback towards Lucknow.

The rest of the station was not so fortunate. On hearing the firing from the treasury, the irregular regiments turned on their officers. Captain Gowan, Lieutenant Green, Dr Hillaud and the sergeant-major of the 9th were all killed on their parade-ground, as were Lieutenants Dorin and Snell of the 10th. Snell's wife and child were murdered near their bungalow. The only European survivors from the two irregular regiments were Lieutenant Barnes and Quartermaster-Sergeant Morton of the 10th, and Quartermaster-Sergeant Abbott of the 9th, all of whom fled to the commissioner's house. Abbott arrived out of breath and with a severe flesh wound on his left arm. 'He [had been] shot by a sepoy of his own regiment,' recalled a British clerk who had reached the house minutes earlier, 'and was considerably excited, stating that he feared his family had perished. I succeeded in pacifying him and bound up his arm. He soon after left the premises with some others . . . These crossed the river which was about 200 yards from the Commissioner's house and, under cover of a *Dhak* Jungle on the opposite bank, extending for some miles, sought protection from the villagers.' The clerk added:

> The firing was increased and the Military Police displayed no inclination to co-operate with us. I besought the Commissioner to escape with his family, but he

declined, and went forward, armed with his rifle towards the position occupied by the Military Police. I followed reiterating my conviction of the urgent necessity of escape but that gentleman unfortunately could not divest himself of his firm, yet as the event showed, mistaken confidence in the loyalty of the Military Police, declaring that he feared no danger, and could never think of abandoning his post.

By now the military policemen and government *chaprassis* had also risen, though the commandant of the former, Captain Hearsey, was protected by a group of his men and allowed to escape. Madeline Jackson was cowering in the house when Christian and the other European men rushed in shouting that the 'police and soldiers had all turned against us'. She recalled:

The confusion was dreadful; people could not find their husbands. Mrs Christian was crying, my dear sister trying to comfort her. They all came in and our brother had not come. I asked Mr Christian where he was? Poor man, he could not answer. At last Mountstuart came – the last in. The house was barricaded, and they fired through holes, but the natives were breaking in, and we all got out at the jungle side. Everyone had been told to try and get to the [Raja of Mithauli's] palace . . . Well, only half of a French window could be got open, and everyone was forcing their way through, regardless of anyone else.

Directly we were out we ran across an open plain towards the jungle . . . Then I noticed an extraordinary whistling sound round us and stopped. I had never been out in the middle of the day before, and thought it had something to do with the sun! – and said, 'What's that?' My brother quietly answered, 'The bullets.' Then I got frightened, said, 'Oh, we must not stop here,' and pulled him on with me, but after a second stopped, noticing Georgie [her sister] was not with us. Looking back we saw her with Mrs Christian's English nurse trying to quiet the baby, and cover it from the sun . . . It was the last time I saw her, my dear sister. We went towards her, but a lot of sepoys came between us and we could not get to her and had to cross the bridge.

The 'bridge' in question, a temporary walkway, was soon filled with sepoys who began to fire at the fleeing Europeans. Madeline and her brother kept running until they came across the deputy commissioner, Mr Thornhill, his wife and little girl. He cheered the Jacksons by telling them that he had seen Georgina cross the river. But half a dozen sepoys were approaching and there was no time to talk. 'We ran on,' wrote Madeline, 'and thought we had got away from our pursuers when we saw them on the other side of the ravine. We got down it to hide from their shots, and the last we saw of the poor Thornhills was him hiding his wife and child in a cleft of the rocks and standing in front to cover them.' Madeline lost her shoes wading across this second river, and her hat soon after. She took off her muslin skirt during one halt because it kept getting caught in thorn bushes. Eventually, too exhausted to go any further, she and Mountstuart collapsed behind some undergrowth. She remembered: 'We sat there a long time. Then some men came, not sepoys – parsees, with bows and arrows. They used to be watchmen I think. They saw my dress, and were evidently pitying the poor murdered people. We kept still and asked them to help us. They said they would take us to a better place, which they did . . . Later on they came back and took us further into the jungle.' In the early hours of the morning, however, the Parsis announced they would go no further. Mountstuart had already bartered his pistol for some food and handed over his sword as a goodwill gesture. His boots he had given to his barefoot sister, tying leaves around his feet with strips of handkerchief as a substitute, while she had been tricked into handing over their last weapon, a rifle. With nothing more to acquire, the Parsis wanted to return home. When Mountstuart objected, the tallest Parsi stepped forward and drew back his bow. Madeline intervened by placing her arms around her brother who eventually conceded that they would have to continue alone.

At noon the next day, having just escaped the clutches of some sword-wielding villagers, one of whom wanted to make Madeline his 'wife', they were met by a group of 'very poor looking men' who said there were other Europeans in the next village. A short time later they were united with Lieutenant Barnes, Quartermaster-Sergeant Morton and two-year-old Sophie Christian, who knew Madeline well and cried when she saw her. Barnes related their dramatic escape. He was the last to leave the commissioner's house and had soon caught up with the Christians, who were burdened by their two infant children. On hearing Mrs Christian, who was struggling to carry Sophie, cry, 'Oh save my child, who will save my child!', Barnes had picked her up. At the river he came across Morton, who was mounted, and handed him the girl. But the horse was shot by a sepoy in midstream, pitching rider and child into the water. Barnes went to their rescue and they escaped together. Meanwhile Sophie's family had barely made it across the river when George Christian, carrying his six-month-old son, was shot and killed. As the mutineers approached, Mrs Christian was sobbing by her husband's corpse, the baby in her arms. Without pity they beheaded her with a sword and impaled the baby on a spear before throwing it into the river.

Led by the poor but friendly peasants, the enlarged party set off for Mithauli in the heat of the day. Sophie wanted Madeline to carry her but she was too heavy – 'almost three, and big' – and the men took turns instead. They tried to cover her fair skin with a sheet, but she insisted on holding on to Madeline's hand and her arm was soon blistered from the sun. At one point Madeline collapsed from heat exhaustion and a small pony had to be found before she could continue, with Sophie mounted ahead of her. Finally, during the morning of 5 June, the five fugitives reached the outskirts of Mithauli.

They were taken in by the raja, Loni Singh, and then a couple of days later were moved to the mud fort at Kutchiani, where they received daily parcels of food from a mysterious benefactor. He turned out to be Captain Patrick Orr, the Assistant Commissioner of nearby Muhamdi, who was hiding in the jungle with his wife and child.* Eventually the Orrs were allowed to join them in the fort and there they remained until early August, when Loni Singh sent them back into the jungle because, he said, the mutineers were searching all his residences. During their time in the fort they sent and received letters via the Orrs' servants, who hid the messages in quills or in the soles of their shoes. One brought the Jacksons the joyful news that their sister Georgina had survived the massacre at Sitapur. Soon a letter arrived from Georgina herself. Letters were also received from Captain Hearsey, who wrote to say that Georgina's courage and kindness were a 'great comfort to them all', and from Sir Henry Lawrence, with an enclosure for Loni Singh, promising the raja a huge reward if the fugitives were delivered safely to Lucknow.

Their chief torments at this time were the heat and boredom. Madeline spent much of her time fanning Sophie in an effort to keep her cool; she even did it in her sleep and developed a lump on her hand as a consequence. Sophie, in return, kept her occupied and amused. 'The children were a great comfort,' remembered Madeline. 'Little Sophie called me Mama, and was a very clever little girl, imitated the natives most amusingly and was a great pet. She had grown quite strong too from being always in the open air. There were no doors or windows except the gateway which was always shut, the servants going through the small one . . . The poor men used to

* Orr, a Eurasian who had previously commanded a regiment of the King of Oudh's infantry, was the sole survivor of the infamous massacre of thirty European fugitives at Aurungabad on 5 June 1857. He had previously sent his wife and daughter to seek refuge with Loni Singh, the Raja of Mithauli, and was reunited with them on the evening of the 5th.

walk up and down for exercise like tigers in a den.' Then in late August, by which time they were living in makeshift tents in the jungle, came a final letter from Georgina saying she feared her party had been betrayed. They later heard that Georgina and the others had fled to the jungle. Then nothing.

The survivors from Sitapur reached the Residency compound at Lucknow during the evening of 4 June, escorted the last five miles by Captain Forbes and a party of mounted volunteers. Almost every subsequent day brought news of a fresh outbreak in Oudh and the surrounding localities. During the evening of 3 June the 17th Native Infantry mutinied at Azimgarh, a small town just beyond Oudh's southern border. Five days later, as the mutinous sepoys of the 17th approached, the Indian garrison at Faizabad in Oudh rose. The officers and their dependants were unharmed and, next morning, were allowed to depart in boats down the River Gogra. But, unbeknown to the officers, their former soldiers had alerted the sepoys of the 17th, who were lying in wait on the river bank. Only six of the twenty-two fugitives survived both the ambush and subsequent attacks by rebel villagers.*

Within three days of the Faizabad rising the rest of Oudh's garrisons followed suit: Dariabad, Secrora, Salone and Sultanpur on 9 June; Pershadipur and Gonda on 10 and 11 June respectively. In less than a fortnight the British administration in Oudh had virtually ceased to exist. Only Lawrence's tenuous foothold in Lucknow remained – and he was beginning to feel the strain of his onerous responsibility. 'If anything happens to me, during present disturbances,' he cabled to Canning on 4 June, 'I earnestly recommend that Major [John] Banks succeed me as Chief Commissioner and Colonel [John] Inglis in command of the troops, until better times arrive. This is no time for punctilio – as regards seniority. They are the right men, in fact the only men for the places.' This was typical of Lawrence's meritocratic principles. Banks, the 46-year-old Commissioner of the Lucknow Division, was the youngest and least experienced of Lawrence's four deputies. He was, on the other hand, an expert linguist with a quiet air of authority and had greatly impressed the chief commissioner during their short acquaintance. Inglis had risen to the command of his regiment, the 32nd Foot, in the comparatively short time of seventeen years. He had

* Five – all officers – were in one boat. They finally reached Dinapore and safety on 17 June. 'They were in a terrible state, not a thing to their name, all lost,' commented Ensign Stansfeld of the 10th Foot. (Stansfeld Letters, NAM, 7603–43.)

fought with the 32nd in the Canadian insurrection of 1837 and in both Sikh wars of the 1840s, receiving a lieutenant-colonelcy for his services in the latter campaign. Though outranked at Lucknow by Brigadier Gray, the commander of the Oudh Irregular Force, Inglis was in the 'prime of his life, an excellent soldier, active, energetic, and quick-sighted', and Lawrence was convinced that he would make the best military successor.

Before Canning's affirmative reply could reach Lucknow, however, the Indian troops rose at Cawnpore and cut the telegraph link to Calcutta. Four days later, as more bad news arrived from the outlying stations in Oudh, Lawrence collapsed with nervous and physical exhaustion and Dr Fayrer prescribed a complete rest from official business. Lawrence reluctantly agreed and a provisional council* was appointed to govern in his stead. The council's rapid demise was due to the unilateral decision of its hot-headed President, Martin Gubbins, to dismiss the remaining Indian troops and rely on the military police alone. Lawrence's furious response, on 12 June, was to rise from his sickbed, dissolve the council and reassume power. 'Not that he was well,' commented Dr Fayrer, 'for his frame was worn and wasted, but he was sufficiently rested to *under the circumstances* return to work.' His first act was to recall the disbanded sepoys 'who returned to their posts with tokens of delight, the honesty of which was verified by their loyalty during the siege'. Lawrence was convinced that Lucknow could only be held with their assistance and that trusting them was a risk worth taking. So, in addition to the regular sepoys, he enlisted one hundred and seventy pensioners from the five hundred or so who had answered his call to arms, increasing his Indian garrison to almost eight hundred.

He also began to prepare for a last stand at the Residency by ordering his engineer officers to supervise the construction of artillery-proof defences. Two powerful batteries, the Redan on the north side and the Cawnpore on the south, were constructed. The intervening perimeter was protected by an elaborate system of embraced garden walls, ditches, parapets and palisades. Breastworks were built on the roofs of houses, windows and doors barricaded, and walls loopholed. Ammunition was brought down from the Machi Bawan and stored in cellars that had been excavated and strengthened. Two hundred artillery pieces without gun carriages were found in the old arsenal in the city, carried into the compound and placed near to the Redan Battery. 'Fancy if the enemy had got them,' commented Captain Fulton,

* Its five members were Martin Gubbins, the financial commissioner, Mr Ommaney, the judicial commissioner, Colonel Inglis, Major Banks and the chief engineer, Major Anderson.

the engineer responsible. A decision was also taken to ignore local sensibilities and use Indian labourers to demolish many of the high buildings overlooking the compound. But because it was assumed that the chief threat during a siege would be from 'comparatively distant artillery and musketry fire', a compromise was reached whereby the upper storeys of the nearest structures were knocked down so that the lower floors could act as bulwarks to the enemy's fire. Only where the British defences were weakest were the houses earmarked for complete destruction. It was, wrote Captain Fulton, 'a stupendous undertaking. Wall after wall went down. Nawabs' palaces and coolie huts alike, but alas not a third of the work was done [in time].'

Such precautions seemed doubly necessary on 14 June, when spies confirmed that mutinous regiments were converging on Lucknow from the north, east and south. 'An attack may be expected on the 18th or 19th June,' Lawrence's private secretary informed the authorities at Allahabad. 'We . . . are anxiously waiting for news. All communication has been cut off since the 6th instant. All the outposts are fallen.' On 16 June Lawrence reluctantly turned down a request from General Wheeler to send two hundred Europeans to the assistance of the beleaguered garrison at Cawnpore. 'I would risk the absence of so large a portion of our small force,' he wrote to the Commissioner of Benares,

> could I see the smallest prospect of its being able to succour him, but no individual here cognizant of the facts, except Mr Gubbins, thinks that we could carry a single man across the [Ganges] river, as the enemy holds all the boats, and completely commands the river. May God Almighty defend Cawnpore, for no help can we afford; our own positions are daily strengthening, and our supplies increasing, but all the outposts are gone, and the rebels and mutineers are said to be closing in on us.

13. Cawnpore

Major-General Sir Hugh Massy Wheeler, commanding the Cawnpore Division, was the last of a dying breed. Born in Ireland in June 1789, the son of an East India Company officer who had married the daughter of the first Lord Massy, he joined a sepoy regiment at the age of sixteen and had been in India virtually ever since. In that time he had acquired a formidable reputation as a fighting soldier; his one regret was that he had never served as a staff officer, a circumstance he put down to the fact that he 'had no Friends and . . . had nothing from Govt. that it could withhold from me'.

A more likely explanation was the scandal caused by his long-term relationship with the Eurasian wife of a fellow officer. Born Frances Marsden, the daughter of an Irish major and his Muslim *bibi*, she was just fifteen and more than eight months pregnant when she married Thomas Oliver, a Bengal officer of mixed descent, in 1810. Within four years she had had an illegitimate child by Wheeler and they had produced another six by the time Oliver's death in Afghanistan, in late 1841, enabled them to marry. This time the bride, now forty-seven, was only six months pregnant. Yet a marriage certificate did not confer respectability – Eurasians were seen by the Anglo-Indian community as 'promiscuous, uncultivated and a little ludicrous with their English lady-like affectations' – and Mrs (later Lady) Wheeler was never a welcome guest in cantonment society. So apart did she keep herself that people assumed she was a full-blooded Indian.*

Wheeler's military career had flourished, none the less, thanks to his reputation as a cool and courageous officer. For distinguished conduct in the three major campaigns of the 1840s he was appointed, successively, a CB, an aide-de-camp to the Queen and a knight. 'My service has been extraordinary,' he would say. 'With the exception of my two years in Europe – when unemployed – I have had but three months' General leave and was never absent on medical certificate.' This two-year furlough in Europe followed his promotion to unattached major-general in 1854. On returning to India in the

* Eurasians were invariably Christian and therefore tended to side with the British during the mutiny. Many were killed by the rebels, though there were instances of Eurasian drummers joining the mutineers.

spring of 1856, he was appointed to the command of first the Presidency Division and then, three months later, the Cawnpore Division. Now sixty-seven, he was 'short, of a spare habit, very grey, with a quick and intelligent eye; not imposing in appearance except by virtue of a thoroughly military gait'. Like Hearsey, his successor at Barrackpore, he was an old-style Company officer: the father of half-caste children, fluent in the vernacular, loved by his men, proven in battle – the ideal man to prevent Cawnpore from falling into the hands of the rebels. 'Cawnpore is now the most anxious position,' noted Lady Canning in her diary, 'but every one speaks alike of Sir Hugh Wheeler and his brave spirit. There is not a better soldier, and all say, if any one can hold it, he will.' He had, in the opinion of a subordinate, just one flaw: he placed 'too much reliance upon the Easterns'.

News of the outbreak further north reached Wheeler on 14 May. He was in a particularly precarious position because his tiny European garrison – seventy invalids from the 32nd Foot and sixty-one artillerymen with six guns – was heavily outnumbered by its large native counterpart, all of whom were regulars. The latter comprised the 1st, 53rd and 56th Native Infantry, the 2nd Light Cavalry and two companies of Golandaze, giving an overall ratio of more than seventeen Indian soldiers to each European.* At first Wheeler was unperturbed, telling Canning on 16 May that the troops were 'well disposed'. But he was not taking any chances.

The British station at Cawnpore, one of the largest in India, extended for six miles along the right bank of the Ganges and covered an area of ten square miles. It lay in a rough semicircle between the city and the river, with the military cantonment forming its southern arm. On 20 May, in response to a telegram from Calcutta to begin immediate and obvious preparations for the 'accommodation of a European force', he selected two large barracks in an open space at the centre of the cantonment. They were both brick-built, with walls at least 18 inches thick, and consisted of a central row of rooms flanked on both sides by inner and outer verandas; only the inner rooms had doors and window screens. The larger of the two barracks, a former dragoon hospital, was thatched and measured about 60 feet by 350 feet; the smaller one, housing the families and invalids of the 32nd Foot, was tiled and no more than 50 feet by 190 feet.

To prevent a sudden attack, Wheeler ordered the construction of a rectangular trench around the barracks, with the earth thrown up on the

* The breakdown of troops at Cawnpore on 14 May 1857 was roughly 3,000 natives to 170 Europeans (including officers). Golondaze were Indian artillery men.

outside so as to form a parapet. When completed this mud wall was barely three feet high, in places, and far from bullet-proof. It enclosed an area of about nine acres and contained, apart from the two barracks, a kitchen, four privies, a well, a large masonry godown, a soldiers' garden, various huts and four underground powder magazines. The perimeter of the entrenchment was ultimately defended by just ten cannon, mostly 9-pounders, sited in three batteries:* one to cover the lines of the 53rd and 56th regiments to the south; one to cover the open plain that extended north-west to the lines of the 1st and the city beyond; and one to cover the artillery lines even further to the east, between the barracks and the Ganges River. Not far from the south-west corner of the entrenchment was another well and a row of nine half-finished barracks. The general's intention was to use these barracks as a first line of defence, and they were left as they were; all the other buildings in the immediate vicinity were flattened.

Wheeler was later criticized for not choosing the fortified magazine, six miles to the north, as his place of refuge. He 'ought to have gone there', wrote Brigadier Neill with the benefit of hindsight. But at the time Wheeler assumed that any mutinous troops would repeat the pattern of Meerut and quickly abandon the station for Delhi. The entrenchment was therefore designed to provide a temporary bastion for European residents in the event of an outbreak; not to withstand a siege. A withdrawal to the magazine, he reasoned, would deprive the sepoys of the calming influence of their officers and make a mutiny more likely, as would the removal of the Indian guard at the magazine.

Yet it was becoming increasingly obvious to Wheeler that nothing could prevent a rising. During the evening of 20 May a fire in the lines of the 1st Infantry was interpreted by Europeans as the 'probable signal for revolt', but the presence of the 1st's officers and the arrival of the European artillery deterred an outbreak. That same night the 2nd Cavalry also showed signs of disaffection, excited by a message from a sepoy of the 56th that the Europeans were on their way to destroy them. It also came to nothing. The following day Wheeler ordered all women and children to move into the entrenchment, though some would return to their cooler bungalows by day; many officers preferred to sleep in their regimental quarter-guards to show the men that they had 'confidence in them'. Wheeler had already asked Sir

* When first constructed the entrenchment was defended by just seven guns: six 9-pounders and a small 3-pounder that had been rifled by Lieutenant Fosbury a year or two earlier. They were augmented in late May by Lieutenant Ashe's half-battery from Lucknow: two 9-pounders and one 24-pounder howitzer.

Henry Lawrence to send as many European troops as he could spare and was mightily relieved when Captain Lowe and fifty-five dusty men of the 32nd Foot arrived in carriages from Lucknow later that evening. Less welcome were the two hundred and forty sullen troopers of the 2nd Oudh Irregular Cavalry who accompanied them. But Captain Hayes, the doomed commander of the column, was more concerned with the 'confusion, fright and bad arrangement' he found in the entrenchment. He wrote:

People of all kinds, of every colour, sect, and profession, were crowding into the barracks. Whilst I was there, buggies, palki-gharrees, vehicles of all sorts, drove up and discharged cargoes of writers, tradesmen, and a miscellaneous mob of every complexion, from white to tawny – all in terror of the imaginary foe; ladies sitting down at the rough mess-tables in the barracks, women suckling infants, ayahs and children in all directions, and – officers too! . . . I saw quite enough to convince me that if any insurrection took or takes place, we shall have no one to thank but ourselves, because we have now shown to the Natives how very easily we can be frightened, and when frightened utterly helpless.

Under the circumstances, it is easy to see why General Wheeler was willing to disregard Lawrence's advice and trust the most influential Indian in the district: Nana Sahib. A month earlier, with Azimullah Khan back from his nefarious tour of military stations, the Nana and his confidential agent had visited Lucknow. There they almost certainly conferred with leading figures of the *ancien régime*, including Begum Hazrat Mahal, the beautiful and fiercely ambitious junior wife of Wajid Ali Shah, who had advised the ex-King to reject Dalhousie's ultimatum in the name of their nine-year-old son, Birjis Qadr.* The Nana was also 'kindly' received by Lawrence, who 'ordered the authorities of the city to show him every attention'. But Martin Gubbins found the Maratha prince 'arrogant and presuming' and became suspicious when he departed suddenly for Cawnpore on 'urgent business'. Gubbins wrote: 'The Chief Commissioner concurred in my suspicions, and by his authority I addressed Sir Hugh Wheeler, cautioning him against the Nana, and stating Sir Henry's belief that he was not to be depended on.' Unfortunately there were many Europeans at Cawnpore, Wheeler among them, who had a high regard for the Maratha prince. None more so than Charles Hillersdon, the 35-year-old collector, who had been a regular guest at Saturday House and who regarded the Nana

* Though rumour had it that Birjis was really the illegitimate son of her lover.

as a 'great friend'. On first hearing of the rebellion at Delhi, the Nana had driven into Cawnpore to discuss the implications with Hillersdon, telling an officer en route that he 'lamented the outbreak' and thought it 'most shameful'. To Hillersdon himself he offered Saturday House as a refuge for his young pregnant wife, Lydia, and their two small children. The collector gratefully accepted and, two days later, even asked the Nana if he would 'forward his wife and children to England'. The Nana agreed but the opportunity never arose.

On 20 May Hillersdon moved his family into the Ewarts' bungalow in the cantonment and sent an opium contractor with elephants to transport the government treasure to the entrenchment. But the sepoys guarding the treasury would allow only an eighth of the 800,000 rupees to be taken, insisting that they were 'perfectly loyal and would guard the treasure to the last'. The collector consulted Wheeler, who wisely decided not to force the issue. Instead he agreed to Hillersdon's proposal to ask Nana Sahib to bring a small force from Bithur to watch the treasury. Having received Wheeler's assurance that Agra would pay his men, the Nana left Saturday House in the care of his nephew Rao Sahib and set off for Cawnpore during the morning of 21 May. Following his lead elephant were two brass guns and three hundred troops under the command of Jwala Prasad, a tall, thin Brahman with a whining, nasal voice and a pockmarked face. His men were no more impressive: elderly horsemen atop thin, bony mounts, clutching lances and rusty sabres; foot soldiers in a variety of uniforms, armed with pikes, lathis and ancient muskets. But Wheeler was glad to see them. 'Their being Mahrattas,' he told Canning on 22 May, 'they are not likely to coalesce with others.'

The general would have been less optimistic if he had known about the secret contact that Jwala Prasad had already established with disgruntled members of the 2nd Cavalry, particularly Subedar Teeka Singh, an Oudh Rajput, whose hut was used for regular meetings. In true Maratha fashion the Nana was preparing for all eventualities: if the troops remained loyal – or even if they mutinied and fled the station – he hoped to be rewarded by the restoration of his father's pension and titles; but if the mutineers remained and beat the British he might well be restored to the Peshwa's throne.

On 1 June six of the 2nd Cavalry's ringleaders – Subedar Teeka Singh, Havildar-Major Gopal Singh and four sowars – had a secret two-hour meeting on a Ganges riverboat with Nana Sahib and his younger brother, Bala Rao. Bala was now thirty, a tall, dark man with a broken nose, bad skin and no front teeth; physical defects that can only have exacerbated his lisping fits of rage when he did not get his way. With the formal greetings out of the way, Teeka

Singh told the Nana: 'You have come to take charge of the Magazine and Treasury of the English. We all, Hindus and Mahomedans, have united for our religions, and the whole Bengal Army have become one in purpose. What do you say to it?' 'I also am at the disposal of the army,' replied the Nana. The meeting ended with the soldiers convinced that the 'Raja of Bithur' would join them when the time was right.

Hillersdon heard about the rendezvous from one of his clerks. He confronted the Nana, who explained that he had been trying to ensure that the troops remained 'firm and loyal'. This appeared to satisfy Hillersdon, who told his subordinates that the Nana had merely been 'remonstrating' with the sowars 'on the part of the government'.

At the entrenchment, meanwhile, news of the rising at Lucknow and the slow progress of the Delhi Field Force had dashed hopes that an outbreak could be avoided. 'Our weak position here with a mere handful of Europeans places us in very great danger, and daily and hourly we are looking for disasters,' wrote Emma Ewart, the wife of Colonel Ewart of the 1st Infantry, on 1 June. 'It is supposed that the Commandants here have shown wonderful tact and that their measure of baldly facing the danger by going out to sleep amongst their men has had a wonderful effect in restraining them. But every body knows that this cannot last. Any accidental spark may set the whole of the three regiments of infantry and one of cavalry in a blaze of mutiny.'

Wheeler, however, had been cheered by a steady trickle of British troops from Calcutta. On 30 May, by which time seventy members of the 84th Foot had reached Cawnpore, he returned the half company of 32nd Foot to Lucknow. Four days later, with his garrison augmented by another thirty-four Europeans, he felt secure enough to send Lawrence another two officers and fifty men of the 84th. 'This leaves me weak,' he informed the Governor-General, 'but I trust to holding my own until more Europeans arrive.' On 4 June, in a letter to Sir Henry Lawrence, he admitted that the 2nd Cavalry was in 'an almost acknowledgeable state of Mutiny and ready to start at any moment for Delhi'. The 1st Infantry, he added, was 'sworn to join' and they spoke of leaving that night or the next, 'doing all the mischief in their power first, this to include an attack on our position'. Yet, wrote Wheeler, 'I fear them not altho' our means are very small' and 'the other two Native Infantry Corps may be carried off by the excitement to join the others'. He spent the rest of the letter criticizing Calcutta's decision to appoint Sir Patrick Grant instead of him as Anson's temporary successor. Grant was 'long, very long my junior', he complained, and it was his connection to Lord Gough, his father-in-law, that had 'carried him over me on every occasion'. He would, he added, continue to serve to the best of his ability. But once 'tranquillity' had been 'restored' he would take the only course acceptable to his 'professional Character and soldierly feelings' – in other words resign.

Worn out by his heavy responsibility and constant exertions, his confidence in his Indian troops at an end, Wheeler now ordered all his officers to sleep in the packed entrenchment. But the colonels of the 53rd and 56th objected, and, as he considered their regiments to be the least disaffected, he let them and their officers remain.

At one thirty in the morning of 5 June three cracks of a pistol signalled the start of the long-awaited mutiny in the lines of the 2nd Cavalry. In the absence of Major Vibart and his officers, the sole obstacle to the rising was provided by Subedar-Major Bhowani Singh, a grizzled veteran of the Sikh wars and the only sowar to be readmitted into the regiment after its disbandment for cowardice in Afghanistan in 1840. On duty at the quarter-guard, he drew his sword and refused to hand over the colours and the regimental treasure-chest to the mutineers, saying he 'would only obey and serve Government'. They eventually lost patience and knocked him out with the flat of a blade. Then, having gathered up the colours and the chest, they galloped off to a prearranged rendezvous at Nawabganj, north of the Ganges Canal, firing their pistols as they went.

On the way a delegation rode into the lines of the 1st Infantry and, speaking in the name of the subedar-major whom they had just left senseless in the quarter-guard, asked why the regiment had not yet joined them. The sepoys' response was to buckle on their cross-belts and grab their muskets. At this point Colonel John Ewart appeared on his charger, having ridden alone from the entrenchment, shouting, 'My children! This is not your way! Don't do this!' He had promised Wheeler that his men would mutiny over his dead body. Instead they ran round him, leaving him humiliated but alive. Ewart galloped back to the entrenchment and urged Wheeler to send Lieutenant's Ashe's half-battery of Oudh Irregulars, the only mobile guns, in pursuit. Wheeler agreed, but Ashe had hardly started when the general received word that the 53rd and 56th might break out at any moment and attack the entrenchment en route to Nawabganj. So Ashe was recalled.

Meanwhile the 53rd and 56th regiments had been turned out by their officers and were on parade, under arms, near their respective quarter-guards with orders to shoot any mutineers who approached. There they remained until about six in the morning, when the two regiments were dismissed and told to have breakfast. Jemadar Khoda Bux, the senior Indian officer present with the 56th, had removed his uniform and was smoking a hookah in his hut when a havildar burst in and announced, 'Jemadar, the regiment is turning out.'

Khoda asked by whose order and why, but the havildar did not know. So Khoda went outside and 'saw that the havildar was dreadfully frightened, and was buttoning his coat'. Together they ran over to the company tent, where some men were 'packing up their clothes, and others throwing them away'.

'The 53rd is getting ready,' they explained, 'and so are we.'

'Your regiment is the 56th,' replied the jemadar, 'what have you to do with the 53rd? It would be better for you first to shoot me and then do what you like afterwards.'

'You are our senior officer,' one said. 'We will not kill you, come with us.'

Khoda agreed and said he would go and 'get ready'. But, having left the tent, he headed straight for the entrenchment, 'very slowly for about 100 yards' and then as fast as he could run. There he sought out Colonel Williams and gave him the bad news. Williams wanted Khoda to accompany him and his adjutant back to the regimental lines so they could see for themselves. Khoda was horrified. 'Oh! gentlemen,' he exclaimed. 'All the regiment has mutinied, and are your enemies. It is not right for you to go to them.'

Williams ignored him and, with his adjutant in tow, rode off towards the lines. With 300 yards to go, however, the officers were greeted with three musket shots that prompted them to execute a rapid about-turn and return to the entrenchment.

A little earlier the Indian officers of the 53rd had been summoned to the entrenchment by their commanding officer, Major Hillersdon, and asked whether the regiment was staunch. Jemadar Shaikh Salamat Ali recalled: 'We told him it could not be depended on. Just then an officer of the 56th drove up with his family in a carriage and reported that the 53rd and 56th also had broken into mutiny and were plundering the regimental treasure chests . . . Hillersdon then ordered us inside the entrenchments.' No sooner had the Indian officers departed than a party of mutinous sowars appeared in the 53rd's lines and informed the sepoys, many of whom were tending to their breakfast fires, that their comrades guarding the treasury would open the gates only to their own regiment. Minutes later a havildar and a sepoy entered the quarter-guard, overwhelmed the subedar on duty and seized the treasure-chest and the colours. They then fled in the direction of Nawabganj, followed by a number of their comrades. But most of the 53rd's sepoys had not yet mutinied.

As Wheeler scanned the activity in the 53rd's line through his binoculars, Hillersdon tried to convince him that his men were staunch or they would have run off already. But other officers urged Wheeler to fire on the 'mutineers' before it was too late, and the clincher was provided by Lieutenant Ashe, who told the general that the only way to commit his artillerymen to the defence of the entrenchment was by ordering them to fire on their comrades. Finally, reluctantly, Wheeler gave his permission and Ashe's three guns burst into life. 'On this the regiment fled,' recalled a sepoy who remained loyal, 'with the exception of a few men who concealed themselves in the lines and in an adjacent nullah.' Numbering about forty non-commissioned officers and men, they were eventually rounded up by two subalterns and brought into the entrenchment. But it quickly became clear that there was no room for these extra bodies – the two barracks were overflowing with Europeans and Eurasians, while their Indian servants were occupying every other inch of shade – and Wheeler was, in any case, not entirely disposed to trust them. So he mounted his horse and led most of the remnants of the 53rd and 56th regiments* to the empty artillery hospital, about 500 yards to the east of the entrenchment. When they complained that the position was a death-trap because it was exposed to artillery fire from all sides, Wheeler told them there was nothing to fear and asked them to 'look after the rear of the building'. He then abandoned them to their fate. A short while later the subedar in command of the treasury guard arrived at the entrenchment with the startling news that the 'Nana had plundered the treasury'. This was the first confirmation that Wheeler's trust in the Maratha prince had been misplaced.

That morning, Nana Sahib had been visited in his temporary residence in Nawabganj by representatives of the mutineers – a sowar of the 2nd Cavalry and a subedar from the 1st Native Infantry – and given the option of a kingdom if he joined with them or death if he sided with the British. He is said to have replied: 'What have I to do with the British? I am with you.' Having sworn to be their chief, he instructed the mutineers to carry the government treasure to the nearby village of Kalyanpur, where he would join them for the march to Delhi. He then consulted his advisers. Azimullah Khan is said to have 'pointed out the folly of proceeding to Delhi, where their individual power and influence would necessarily cease'. He wanted

* A handful of loyal troops – Subedar-Major Bhowani Singh, two havildars, three sowars and a native doctor of the 2nd Cavalry; and Jemadar Khoda Bux, a naik, two sepoys, a musician and the native doctor of the 56th – were given special permission by General Wheeler to remain in the entrenchment.

the Nana to recall the mutineers, take possession of Cawnpore and extend his authority as far as he could to the eastward. He was, he added, 'thoroughly acquainted with the resources of the British' and knew that the 'number of Europeans in India was scarce one-fourth that of the Native army'.

The Nana could see the sense of this argument and before long had set off in pursuit of the mutineers on his state elephant. It was almost midnight when he found them camped in their thousands around the *dâk*-bungalow at Kalyanpur, 11 miles north of Cawnpore. As he stepped down from his kneeling elephant, Teeka Singh and his fellow officers appeared from the *dâk*-bungalow to welcome him. He told them he understood their reasons for proceeding to Delhi but asked them to think for a moment what they were leaving behind: most of the treasure, the magazine, the quantities of powder and ammunition moored at various ghats,* and a small but growing British garrison. Why not overwhelm the British at Cawnpore before they became too strong? Then they could march to Delhi in triumph.

At first the rebel officers rejected the plan. But the Nana's agents swung the balance by spreading reports through the camp that their master would double the mutineers' pay and provide them with free food if they agreed to return to Cawnpore. As an added inducement they were each promised a gold bracelet worth 100 rupees for destroying Wheeler's entrenchment. Sensing the men were in favour, Teeka Singh hailed Nana Sahib as the new Peshwa and was rewarded with the appointment of subedar-major of the army. The camp was immediately dismantled and, with the Nana's elephant at their head, the four mutinous regiments headed back to Cawnpore.

No sooner had they arrived at the camping ground between Nawabganj and the Ganges Canal, with horns blaring and kettle-drums thumping, than the Nana commandeered a house next to the theatre and began to issue a string of orders and edicts. He appointed Jwala Prasad as brigadier of the army, Azimullah Khan as collector and his elder brother Baba Bhutt as judge. Baba was about fifty-five years old, tall and heavily built, with a high forehead, a long nose and big eyes behind heavy spectacles. He was believed to have been suffering from the early stages of leprosy, though the red patches on his face may well have been a birth-mark.

* Thomson wrote: 'Thirty boat-loads of shot and shell that were lying in the canal fell into their hands, and the profusion of the material of war which they obtained from the cantonments (where one magazine alone contained 200,000 lbs of gunpowder, besides innumerable cartridges and percussion caps) furnished them with supplies amply sufficient for a campaign.' (Thomson, *The Story of Cawnpore*, 42.)

In addition the Nana ordered a body of his Maratha troops under Tatya Tope to raise a flag at the old Residency in Nawabganj to mark the start of his rule, sent groups of sowars into the city to plunder and murder all Christians who had not yet taken refuge in the entrenchment, and ordered the immediate execution of any Indian found harbouring Christians. A Rajput resident of Cawnpore recorded the consequences: 'Some Christians, who had taken refuge in the shops in the City, were shot by the troopers, who set on fire the shops they had taken shelter in. Two or three Christians were also massacred opposite the abkaree godowns. A lady and gentleman, with a child, who had hid themselves in a bungalow . . . were found and taken by the sowars and sepoys to the Nana, by whose orders they were shot on the plain.'

The Nana's chief priority was to destroy Wheeler's entrenchment, which was now packed with about nine hundred souls, most of them European.* Having ordered the guns in the magazine to be sited within range of the entrenchment, he sent General Wheeler a formal letter notifying him that an attack would commence at ten that morning, 6 June. Wheeler was shocked, having thought the mutineers well on their way to Delhi, and at once ordered all his officers to report to the entrenchment. 'With such expedition was the summons obeyed,' recorded Lieutenant Thomson of the 53rd, 'that we were compelled to leave all our goods and chattels to fall a prey to the ravages of the sepoys; and after they had appropriated all movables they set fire to the bungalows.'

With the perimeter secured, Lieutenant Ashe and thirty volunteers† went out with the three horse-drawn guns to reconnoitre. Five hundred yards from the entrenchment 'they caught sight of the enemy, in possession of one of the canal bridges, close by the lines of the 1st Native Infantry'. Heavily outnumbered, Ashe ordered an immediate withdrawal to the entrenchment. They arrived back at the trot, but without one officer, Lieutenant Ashburner of the artillery, whose horse had bolted into the sepoy ranks. He was killed instantly. Lieutenant Thomson recalled:

* A rough breakdown is as follows: 210 European soldiers (61 artillerymen, 70 invalids and sick of the 32nd Foot, 50 men of the 84th Foot, 15 men of the 1st Madras Fusiliers); 70 European officers; 100 European civilians (mainly merchants and civil servants); 160 women and children of soldiers; 120 women and children of writers, merchants and drummers; 50 women and children of officers; 100 native servants; 40 Christian drummers; 20 loyal and sick native officers and sepoys. (Mr Shepherd's narrative, *State Papers*, II, intro., 125.)

† During the afternoon of 5 June, all of Ashe's native gunners had left the entrenchment and joined the mutineers after Wheeler had told them they were at 'liberty to depart' if they 'did not wish to serve the Government any longer'.

Shortly after the return of Lieutenant Ashe, the first shot fired by the mutineers came from a nine-pounder, on the north-west; it struck the crest of the mud-wall and glided over into the puckah roofed barrack. This was about 10 o'clock A.M.; a large party of ladies and children were outside the barrack; the consternation caused amongst them was indescribable; the bugle-call sent every man of us instantly to his post, many of us carrying in our ears, for the first time, the peculiar whizzing of round shot, with which we were to become so familiar. As the day advanced, the enemy's fire grew hotter and more dangerous, in consequence of their getting their guns into position. The first casualty occurred at the west battery; McGuire, a gunner, being killed by a round shot . . . Several of us saw the ball bounding toward us, and he evidently saw it, but, like many others whom I saw fall at different times, he seemed fascinated to the spot.

The uproar at the start of the bombardment had been mainly caused by senior military wives like Mrs Ewart, who had chosen to avoid the cramped conditions of the barracks by living in canvas tents. As the first cannonballs fell, they grabbed their screaming children and dashed for the relative safety of the tile-roofed barrack, which was already full to bursting point. Stepping over the Eurasians who were crammed along the outer verandas, they made for the relative safety of the inner rooms, where they were generously received by their European friends and acquaintances. Those with less influence, however, were forced to scurry from room to room in a vain search for space. Even in moments of crisis the strict seniority of Anglo-Indian society had to be upheld.

Among the least privileged inhabitants of the two barracks was Amy Horne, the pretty Eurasian girl who had left Lucknow with her family the previous March. She wrote later:

The site of our entrenchment was surrounded by large and substantial buildings, from three to eight hundred yards distance, occupied by the rebels, and from roof and window, all day, a shower of bullets poured down upon us in our exposed position. Shell likewise kept falling all over the entrenchment, and every shot that struck the barracks was followed by the heart-rending shrieks of the women and children, who were either killed outright by the projectiles, or crushed to death by the falling beams, masonry, and splinters. One shell killed seven women as it fell hissing into the trenches and burst. Windows and doors were soon shot off their sockets, and the shot and shell began to play freely through the denuded buildings.

By the afternoon of the first day the rebels had set up five batteries – fourteen guns in all, most of them heavy* – to the north and west of the entrenchment. At first the British tried to give as good as they got, one shell from their single howitzer killing two sowars, five sepoys and a dozen bazaar-wallahs who had come to watch the fun. But the garrison had to conserve its limited supply of ammunition and, in any case, the rebels' heavy batteries were beyond the reach of all but one of its guns. Emboldened by the cover of darkness, the mutineers would creep to within 50 yards of the mud walls and pepper them with musket fire. Particularly vulnerable was the detachment of sixteen railwaymen holding the fourth of the nine unfinished barracks beyond the entrenchment perimeter. 'Creeping up by hundreds under the cover of these walls,' wrote Lieutenant Thomson, 'the sepoys pressed so heavily upon the occupants of barrack No. 4, that the general soon found it necessary to strengthen them with a military command. Accordingly Captain Jenkins, of the 2nd Cavalry, headed this fine volunteer force . . . Foiled in all their efforts to surprise this party, the sepoys in a few days occupied barrack No. 1, and thereupon Lieutenant Glanville, of the 2nd Bengal Fusiliers, was posted with a detachment of sixteen men in barrack No. 2, which, as it was only 200 yards from the intrenchment, became the key of the position.' When Glanville was wounded, he was replaced first by a Captain Elmes and then by Thomson himself, who recalled:

It was most harassing work to stand hour after hour, watching for the approach of the rebels. By daylight we did manage to get a little rest, as one or two were sufficient then to keep the look out; and as well as the sun with its intense heat would permit, we used to squeeze down between the sharp edges of brickbats and get a nap, sweeter than that often obtained in beds of down, though I am sure that in a whole fortnight I did not get two hours of consecutive sleep . . . Our greatest apprehensions were always excited when they ceased to fire, as this was invariably the prelude to a coming attack. Then, we seventeen men had to hold that barrack No. 2 against a black swarm compassing about us like bees, and had it not been for their most surprising cowardice in attack, we could not have held the place for four and twenty hours.

* The standard British artillery pieces of the period – 6- and 9-pounders – were smooth-bore and fired either roundshot (solid iron balls) or grape (a larger quantity of smaller balls); the more destructive 12- and 24-pounder howitzers were rifled and fired the exploding shell (hollow projectiles packed with gunpowder and bullets) developed by Colonel Henry Shrapnel in 1803. For sieges the British used 18-pounders (also firing solid balls) and two types of mortar: 5½-inch and 8-inch. Most of this heavy ordnance – particularly 8-inch mortars, 18-pounders and 24-pounder howitzers – was available to the rebels at Cawnpore.

The one saving grace of this out-picket duty was that it removed the participants from the 'sickening spectacles' occurring daily in the entrenchment. At one point two young girls, aged about eight or nine years, were left by their parents in an inner room of the thatched barrack because it was considered to be relatively safe. The 'agony' of the parents, wrote Amy Horne, 'when they returned and found that a shell had come through the roof and torn their dear ones to pieces', was almost unbearable. 'Bones, brains and flesh were strewed all over, and not a step could you take without treading on some portion of their remains.' Almost as appalling was the early demise of Charles Hillersdon, the collector, who had so misjudged his 'good friend' Nana Sahib. Sometime during the second day of the siege, Hillersdon left his post in the main guard to speak to his pregnant wife Lydia. To gain some privacy he led her out of the inner room she shared with Mrs Ewart in the tile-roofed barrack to the southern veranda, away from the rebel guns. This final miscalculation cost him his life because the rebels had just set up a new battery in the lines of the 56th. As he stood talking with his wife, a roundshot came arcing from this direction and caught him full in the stomach, spattering his horrified wife with blood and entrails. Her own demise was not long delayed: during the night of 9 June a heavy roundshot hit the inner veranda off her room and buried her in a pile of rubble. She was dragged out, but her skull had been crushed and she and her unborn baby died within a couple of hours. Their resting place was a cooking pit that had been dug in the soldiers' garden next to the barrack. Most of the other early casualties, including her husband, were buried in sections of trench and covered with chunks of rock-hard earth from the parapet. But there was not enough time or room to bury all the corpses this way, and it was eventually decided to dump them at night into the reserve well near the unfinished barracks. By the end of the siege, according to one who was present, the well was choked with more than two hundred and fifty bodies.

For Emma Larkins, the wife of an artillery major, death seemed inevitable. In a note to her sister of 9 June – one of the few letters written during the siege to survive* – she began:

I write this, dearest Henrietta, in the belief that our time of departure is come – the whole of the troops rose here and we took refuge in a barrack. We are so hemmed

* The letter was entrusted to her faithful ayah, who made it safely through the rebel lines and, after many hardships, all the way to Calcutta. There her tale was not believed and, in tears, she handed the letter to a servant and was never heard of again. The letter finally reached Mrs Larkins's sister in England twenty-one months after it was written.

in by overpowering numbers that there seems no hope of escape, only about forty European soldiers are left of one hundred and twenty men, a sad, sad number to hold out against such an awful enemy . . . Jessie, Emily and Georgie cling to us. Dearest George has been well up till today but he is, I grieve to say, obliged to abandon his post. This is to me a grief. Many brave men have fallen today, the siege has lasted four days!

Major Larkins was just one of many senior officers who were suffering from the fierce heat, lack of sleep and over-exertion. Wheeler was relying increasingly on his son and aide-de-camp, Godfrey, an officer in the 1st Infantry, and spent much of the time slumped on a mattress in the small room he shared with his Eurasian wife and two teenage daughters. His handsome 51-year-old deputy, Brigadier Jack, a celebrated artist and veteran of both Sikh wars, had already succumbed to the remorseless sun and incessant cannonade, as had Sir George Parker, the cantonment magistrate, and Colonel Williams of the 56th. Williams had been wounded by a piece of shell, but it was the heat that finished him off during the night of Sunday, 8 June. Left in the ruins of the outer veranda during the hours of daylight, much to the horror of his wife and daughters, his body was finally buried the following night in a section of trench. Lieutenant-Colonel Edwin Wiggins, the deputy judge advocate-general, remained healthy enough, but that was because he 'never showed himself outside the walls of the barrack, nor took even the slightest part in the military operations'. Of the senior officers only Majors Vibart and William Hillersdon (younger brother of Charles, the collector) continued to take an active part in the defence of the entrenchment.

But the officer who came to embody the defiant spirit of the garrison, its leader in all but name, was Captain John Moore of the 32nd. A tall, fair Irishman with pale blue eyes, he had been left at Cawnpore with the regiment's invalids, a sure sign that his colonel had less than complete confidence in him. If so it was Lucknow's loss and Cawnpore's gain because Moore had all the qualities required of a leader in such a predicament: courage, vigour, sensitivity and determination. He was officially in charge of the outlying pickets in the unfinished barracks, but he came to oversee all aspects of the garrison's defence, making visits at least once a day to all the pickets, batteries and even to the terrified families in the barracks. 'His never-say-die disposition nerved many a sinking heart to the conflict,' recalled Lieutenant Thomson, 'and his affable, tender sympathy imparted fresh patience to the suffering women.' His wife was of a similar stamp, and often came across with him to the unfinished barracks where Thomson and his men 'fitted up a little hut for her, made of bamboo, and covered over with canvas', where 'she would sit for hours, bravely bearing the absence of her husband, while he was gone upon some perilous enterprise'.

Despite suffering from a broken collarbone, the result of a fall from his horse before the siege began, he never shirked his responsibilities and could invariably be seen, his arm in a sling and a revolver in his belt, leading and directing his men from the front. He placed scouts on top of one of the barracks to watch the movements of the enemy, and whenever they gave the signal that the rebels were trying to advance nearer, he would 'go out with about a dozen Europeans in the midst of the most brisk firing' and expel them 'from their covert'. But his boldest foray was a midnight raid to spike the two 24-pounder howitzers that made up the rebels' most destructive battery. He and twenty volunteers, wearing dark clothes and with their faces blacked, crept on all fours along the unfinished barracks, across a drainage ditch and over the open ground that led to the battery. At a distance of a couple of hundred yards they opened fire, killing a dozen rebel gunners and causing the remainder to flee. Then they closed on the guns and drove spikes through their torch holes. The suspense felt by the remainder of the garrison, as they awaited the outcome of the raid, was almost unbearable. 'We knew that the number of sick and wounded was large,' wrote Amy Horne, 'and the idea of seeing the small number of our defenders reduced by 20, including a first rate officer, threw us into agonies of fear, every sound was hushed in no time, the stillness of death seemed to be upon us, and the very infant to understand its danger. Captain Moore came back sooner than we expected, he was about only an hour, but Oh! That hour was an eternity to us.'

Nana Sahib, who had set up his headquarters at Duncan's Hotel, just a few hundred yards beyond the wrecked battery, was furious that the sleeping gunners had failed to prevent the attack and immediately sacked the battery commander, Nizam-ud-Daula, the brother of Nunne Nawab,* the leading Muslim noble at Cawnpore. He also decided to move his camp to the open ground in front of Savada House, a large decrepit mansion standing on a promontory a mile to the south of the entrenchment. Here he set up a two-gun battery, manned by Ashe's irregulars, and pitched his opulent tents in a grove of mango trees a short way off. Teeka Singh's sowars and a

* Since his initial arrest by Nana Sahib, the nawab had embraced the rebellion enthusiastically and was in command of over a thousand Muslim soldiers and the rebel battery situated near to St John's Church, 800 yards to the north-west of the entrenchment.

regiment of sepoys were camped behind him along the road, guarding against the approach of British reinforcements from Allahabad.

Though Nana Sahib was the nominal head of the rebels at Cawnpore, in reality he had to defer to rebel officers like Teeka Singh of the 2nd Cavalry, Radhay Singh of the 1st Native Infantry and Gungadeen Missur of the 56th Native Infantry who had taken command of their respective regiments. This sharing of power between military officers and traditional elites was repeated in every centre of rebel authority – Delhi, Lucknow, Bareilly, Jhansi, Kalpi and Cawnpore – and was the main reason the rebels failed to capitalize on their initial superiority of numbers. For without unity of command it is very difficult to conduct successful military operations. At Cawnpore a determined assault by the whole rebel force would have quickly overwhelmed the tiny garrison. But it was never made because the rebel commanders lacked the conviction, or the courage, to order it. In the opinion of Jonah Shepherd, the Eurasian head clerk of the Commissariat office at Cawnpore, the mutineers were 'a most cowardly set of men, particularly the Cavalry, for very often attempts were made to charge upon us, and notwithstanding the very large number of people collected on the enemy's side . . . they seldom dared courageously to come out, for whenever they advanced, a few charges of canister would soon disperse [them]'.

The loyal band of Indian troops at the artillery hospital held out until the afternoon of 9 June, when a rebel roundshot wrapped in a flaming rag set fire to the building's thatched roof. As flames ripped through the compound, Pay-Havildar Ram Buksh and a couple of sepoys from the 53rd ran across the 500 yards of plain to seek refuge within the European garrison. Ram Buksh recalled: 'The Major then told us he could do nothing for us, there being an order of General Wheeler prohibiting any native from entering the entrenchment. He therefore recommended us to provide for our own safety, and made over a certificate to me, in which the names of all the men of the 53rd, who were in the barracks, are mentioned.'

Prevented from joining their officers, their position untenable, the sepoys abandoned the hospital compound and spent the night in a nearby ravine. 'Next morning,' remembered Sepoy Bhola Khan of the 53rd, 'we went to a village named Poorwa, about a mile east of the barracks. The zemindar of the village not allowing us to enter, we went into a mango grove, close by. After this, our party broke up in different directions. I went in the direction of Jajmow alone; some distance further on, my musket was taken from me by villagers.' Bhola Khan eventually joined up with the British relief force at Fatehpur, via Benares and Allahabad. Some, like Ram Buksh, made it in safely to their villages; others were captured by mutineers, 'brought back to Cawnpore and after being beaten & plundered were let go'.

In the early hours of 10 June, the day after the loyal troops had departed, a lone horseman appeared at the gallop from the direction of the mutineers' camp. As he got closer, the sentries on the northern wall of the entrenchment opened fire, wounding his horse. But still he kept coming until, almost at point-blank range, a voice shouted out, 'Cease fire!', allowing the stricken horse to clear the parapet with a single leap. Its rider, 'in a most distressed and exhausted condition', was no sowar but Lieutenant Augustus Boulton of the 7th Cavalry, 'to whom', wrote Thomson, 'even our desperate fortunes presented an asylum'. He was the sole European survivor of the mutiny at Chobeypur in which four of his fellow officers had perished, but in effecting his escape he had been shot through the cheek by a pistol ball which had gone on to shatter a number of teeth. 'He joined the outpicket under Captain Jenkins,' recorded Thomson, 'and although a great sufferer from the wound in his cheek, he proved a valuable addition to our strength.'

Boulton had leapt from the frying pan into the fire, but at the time he considered himself fortunate. He was among friends and had a chance, however small, of survival – which was more than could be said for those Christians unfortunate enough to fall into the hands of the Cawnpore rebels. Of the many hundreds brought before the Nana and his advisers during this period, only a handful of Eurasians were spared.* The rest were simply led away and shot or hacked to death. By far the worst atrocity involved about a hundred and twenty civilian fugitives† from the British station at Fatehgarh, most of them women and children, who had been intercepted at Bithur by sowars of the 2nd Cavalry as they tried to escape down the Ganges in boats. With their hands tied behind their backs and linked by a long rope, they finally reached the Subedar's Tank at Cawnpore during the evening of 11 June. 'It took us a long time to get there,' recalled Hingun, the deputy collector's ayah, 'for the ladies and children were without shoes and stockings, and their feet were bleeding.' Allowed only a handful of water each, the fugitives refused to go any further and were allowed to spend the night

* Notably the Greenways, the leading mercantile family of Cawnpore, headed by the formidable matriarch Rose Greenway. She, her son, daughter-in-law and four grandchildren were kept alive in Savada House on condition that they paid a huge ransom. Mrs Jacobi, the wife of a Swiss watchmaker, and her two children were also incarcerated in Savada House after she had shamed Nana Sahib into sparing them on the ground that they were not British.

† Civil officers, missionaries, planters, merchants and their families.

in the open near the tank. Next morning a fleet of bullock hackeries arrived to take them the remaining three miles to the Nana's camp.

On reaching Savada House they were herded into the large central room and, though starving, thirsty and exhausted, were relieved to be out of the blistering June sun. Meanwhile a conference was held in the Nana's tent to decide what to do with them. According to witnesses, the Nana was against murdering the fugitives and wanted to keep them as hostages. But Bala Rao was equally adamant that they should die, and he was backed by Azimullah and Teeka Singh, the commander of the cavalry, who warned that if the Nana did not give the order to kill them, he would. Finally the Nana gave way and a triumphant Bala emerged from his brother's tent to make the necessary arrangements.

It was mid afternoon when the fugitives were led out on to the plain in front of the house and told to sit in a large trench in two lines, the men at the back and the women and children in front. Their few remaining native servants, including Hingun the ayah, were pulled away and made to watch proceedings. Both sides of the trench were lined with about three hundred soldiers from the 2nd Cavalry and 1st Native Infantry, with a vast crowd of low-caste *jullads* and bazaar riff-raff jostling at their rear. Bala Rao, Azimullah and a number of other senior rebels had assembled on a nearby platform. When all was ready, Bala 'called out aloud, saying it was the Nana's orders that the Europeans should all be massacred'. In desperation, a European gentlemen 'asked him not to kill them, but keep them in confinement, and said that there would be no good derived from murdering them, and that England would never be emptied of Europeans'. But Bala would not be swayed and, on his order, the soldiers opened fire with carbines and muskets. After a succession of volleys, the troops withdrew and allowed the *jullads* into the trench to finish off the wounded.

14. Satichaura Ghat

Even if General Wheeler had known about the massacre of the Fatehgarh fugitives, he was in no position to intervene. Sunday, 13 June, saw an intensification of the rebel bombardment that, at its height, sent one round-shot or shell into the battered entrenchment every eight seconds. By now all the doors, windows and frames of the tile-roofed barrack, the strongest of the two, had been entirely shot away. 'Not a few of its occupants were killed by splinters,' wrote Thomson, 'and a still greater number by the balls and bullets which flew continually through the open spaces . . . Others died from falling bricks, and pieces of timber dislodged by shot.' An 'imperfect attempt' had been made to cover the other barrack's thatched roof with tiles and bricks, but these could not prevent 'a carcase or shell filled with burning materials' from setting it on fire during the evening of 12 June.

The barrack was both a shelter for about two hundred women and children and a makeshift hospital for a large number of wounded. 'The women and children were panic-stricken,' recalled Amy Horne; 'confronted on one side by the burning building, and on the other by the shot and shell from the enemy's guns, which fell like hail on every side, they knew not where to run for protection.' The operation to rescue the casualties in the hospital was hampered by the fact that all able-bodied men had strict orders not to abandon their posts for any reason. But some still rushed from the perimeter to help. 'The entreaties of the wounded to be helped out of the flames, and from the falling building, was more than one could bear,' wrote Amy, 'and their cries and dying groans heart-rending. They were obliged to be dragged out without any regard being paid to their excruciating pains, occasioned from wounds that perhaps would in a few days have terminated their dreadful sufferings.' Amy and her mother were struck on the head by debris from the collapsing roof; her sister, 'a little girl of five, had her leg fractured by a falling block of masonry', and their ayah 'had half of one foot torn off'. All the while the rebels were peppering the burning barrack with musket-balls, 'without regard to sex or age, or the painful and protracted toil of getting out the sufferers'. Then at around midnight on 12 June, assuming the defenders would be preoccupied with the fire, the rebels attempted their first serious assault. Thomson remembered:

They advanced by hundreds under the shelter of darkness, and without a sound from that side, with the intention of storming Ashe's battery, and they were allowed to come within sixty or eighty yards of the guns, before a piece was fired or a movement made to indicate that they were observed. Just when it must have appeared to them that their success was certain, our nine-pounders opened upon them with a most destructive charge of grape; the men shouldered successive guns which they had by their sides ready loaded; every available piece was discharged right into their midst, and in half-an-hour they left a hundred corpses in the open.

The garrison had survived, but the loss of the thatched barrack was grievous. 'Every drop of medicine in the hospital was destroyed,' recorded Amy Horne, 'and the consequences felt almost immediately and bitterly too, for putting recovery out of the question, no relief whatever could be afforded to the sick and wounded. The only accommodation now left to us were the trenches about 18 inches deep, and in a most pitiable plight we were, having no shelter at all from the burning rays of a June sun.'

As the siege wore on and the rebels tightened their noose around the entrenchment, the garrison began to run out of food. Before long the daily ration had been reduced to 'a handful of split peas and a handful of flour, certainly not more than half a pint together'. For the fortunate few, this meagre fare was occasionally supplemented with horse meat. Thomson recalled the time an old cavalry horse strayed into the range of the out-pickets: 'He was down by a shot like lightning, brought into the barrack, and hewn up. We did not wait to skin the prey, nor waste any time and consultation upon its anatomical arrangements . . . Lump, thump, wack went nondescript pieces of flesh into the fire . . . The two picquets, thirty-four in number, disposed of the horse in two meals. The head, and some mysteries of the body, we stewed into soup, and liberally sent to fair friends in the entrenchment, without designating its nature, or without being required to satisfy any scruples on that head.'

An even greater torment was the lack of water. There was only one well inside the entrenchment and the rebels were quick to fire grape at anyone brave enough to use it, even at night when the creaking of its tackle gave the game away. First the framework of wood and brick that surrounded the well was shot away, then the machinery itself so that the bucket had to be hauled up a distance of 60 feet by hand. To encourage them to undertake this prolonged and perilous labour, private soldiers were paid as much as 10 shillings a bucket. But one by one they perished, until John McKillop of the civil service became the 'self-constituted captain of the well'. Thomson recalled: 'He jocosely said that he was no fighting man, but would make himself useful where he could, and accordingly he took this post; drawing for the supply of the women and the children as often as he could.' After almost a week of this selfless work, having already survived numerous near misses, he was badly wounded in the groin by a piece of grape. Even then he thought of others, asking his stretcher-bearers to send somebody to 'draw water for a lady to whom he had promised it'. Such was the scarcity of water that Amy Horne had no compunction about drinking some 'mixed with human blood, which had fallen into our vessel from the wounds of an ayah who was close by it when the bursting of a shell carried away both her legs'. So desperate for water did some children become that they took to 'sucking the pieces of old water-bags, putting scraps of canvas and leather straps into the mouth to try and get a single drop of moisture upon their parched lips'. The men could 'scarcely endure the cries for drink which were almost perpetual from the poor little babes'.

During the evening of Sunday, 14 June, Wheeler made his first appeal to Lucknow for help. 'We have been besieged since the sixth by the Nana Sahib,' he wrote to Martin Gubbins, 'joined by the whole of the native troops, who broke out on the morning of the fourth.' The rebels had two 24-pounders and many other guns, while he only had eight 9-pounders still functioning. 'Our defence has been noble and wonderful, our loss heavy and cruel. We want aid, aid, aid!' The postscript read: 'If we had 200 men, we could punish the scoundrels and aid you.'

Carried at considerable risk by one of Wheeler's servants for a fee said to have been 5,000 rupees, the letter reached Gubbins at Lucknow on 16 June and was answered by Sir Henry Lawrence. 'I am very sorry indeed to hear of your condition,' he wrote, 'and grieve that I cannot help you. I have consulted with the chief officers about me, and, except Gubbins,* they are unanimous in thinking that with the enemy's command of the river, we could not possibly get a single man into your intrenchment . . . Pray do not think me selfish. I would run much risk could I see a commensurate prospect of success. In the present scheme I see none . . . God grant you his protection.'

At Wheeler's request, Captain Moore replied to Lawrence's letter,

* At the time Gubbins was furious with Lawrence for not even attempting to assist Cawnpore. Later he acknowledged that Lawrence had 'acted wisely' in refusing Wheeler's appeal. (Gubbins, *The Mutinies in Oudh*, 173.)

expressing his commander's regret that two hundred men could not be spared as 'he believed with their assistance we could drive the insurgents from Cawnpore and capture the guns'. Moore added: 'Our troops, officers and volunteers have acted most nobly and on several occasions a handful of men have driven hundreds before them. Our loss has been chiefly from the sun and their heavy guns. Our rations will last a fortnight and we are still well supplied with ammunition. Our guns are serviceable. Reports say that troops are advancing from Allahabad; and any assistance might save our garrison. We of course are prepared to hold out to the last.' The true situation at Cawnpore, of course, was much more desperate. So why was Moore's letter so hopeful? Probably because Moore was by nature an optimist, and possibly because he knew in his heart of hearts that, with the bridge-of-boats at Cawnpore destroyed, any help from Lucknow would not get through and would simply weaken Lawrence's position. It was designed, in this sense, to let the chief commissioner off the hook. Had Wheeler himself told Lawrence that without immediate aid he was doomed, the chief commissioner would surely have responded.

Moore had provided a temporary lift for the garrison during the night of 14 June when he led a second successful sortie to spike the enemy's guns: this time the batteries in the ruins of St John's Church and the nearby 56th officers' mess were put out of action, including one particularly destructive 24-pounder. But the rebels simply dragged more guns into position and Wheeler forbade any further raids on the ground that similar casualties, one killed and four wounded, could not be afforded. On 16 June the rebels were reinforced by two regiments of Oudh infantry, the 4th and 5th, who crossed the Ganges in boats and boldly announced that they would take the entrenchment within two days. Nana Sahib was impressed with this rare declaration of martial intent and gave orders for the new arrivals to be 'feasted with sweetmeats' and 'treated with distinction'. But their subsequent assault on 18 June, the forty-second anniversary of Waterloo, was not properly supported by the other rebels and was eventually beaten off.

The rebels' unity of purpose was not helped when Nana Sahib's criminal court, headed by his fanatical brother Baba Bhutt, sentenced two Muslim butchers to have their hands amputated for slaughtering cows in the city bazaar. This caused a large crowd of Muslims, including many members of the 2nd Cavalry, to march on Savada House and warn the Nana that they would 'displace him if he did not do as they desired'. He begged their forgiveness and assured them that they could kill as many cows as they liked, as long as it was out of sight of their Hindu neighbours. But the mutual distrust remained.

Late on 21 June, after a particularly destructive bombardment, Wheeler asked Major Vibart to write once more to Lawrence. 'This evening for three hours,' wrote Vibart, 'upwards of thirty shells [mortars] were thrown into the intrenchment. This has occurred daily for the last eight days: *an idea may be formed of our casualties*, and how little protection the barracks affords to the women. Any aid, to be effective, must be immediate. In the event of rain falling, our position would be untenable.' But the urgency of the major's plea was diminished when he added that a thousand troops from down-country were daily expected and that the rebels appeared 'not to have more than 400 or 500 infantry'.

Nana Sahib too was anxiously eyeing the Grand Trunk Road from Allahabad. Despite Azimullah's insistence that his troops could defeat anything the British might send against them, he was desperate to subdue Wheeler's garrison before any relief force could arrive. The deadline, according to his guru Dabeedeen, was 23 June, the one hundredth anniversary of the Battle of Plassey, when it had long been predicted that British rule would come to an end. So auspicious was this date that even the rebel officers were convinced and, at a conference at the Assembly Rooms on 22 June, they agreed to mark the anniversary with a general assault on the entrenchment. Plassey had a particular resonance for Subedar-Major Radhay Singh of the 1st Native Infantry because his regiment had contributed to the British success in that famous battle. Now that he and his men had a chance to right the wrongs of their predecessors, he swore on the Ganges that they would take the entrenchment or die in the attempt. Teeka Singh gave him the dubious honour of leading the assault.

By dawn on the 23rd 4,000 rebels were poised to attack. Waiting to receive them were fewer than two hundred and fifty able-bodied men, including Jonah Shepherd, on duty at the north-east corner of the entrenchment, who was struck by the diversity of the mutineers' dress. 'Some few had on their jackets and caps,' he wrote, 'others were without the former, and nearly the whole dressed like recruits [with dhotis rather than trousers].' The first move was made from the rubble of the riding-school, north of the entrenchment, by the sowars of the 2nd Cavalry and Oudh irregulars. As the Nana's batteries burst into life, a bugle sounded and the horsemen began to advance across the plain, a huge cloud of dust rising behind them. Once over the drainage ditch they tore directly towards their old commander's battery, waving their *tulwars* and carbines, and shouting, '*Deen! Deen!* ["For the faith! For the faith!"]' But they made the mistake of charging 'all the way at a hand-gallop, so that when they neared the intrenchment their horses were winded.' General Wheeler, who had left his wounded son in the care of his mother and sisters in the tiled barrack, waited until the labouring horsemen were within 100 yards of the entrenchment before he gave Vibart permission to fire his three 9-pounders. One volley of grapeshot was enough, bringing down so many horses and riders that the rest were thrown into 'hopeless confusion, and all who were not biting the dust wheeled round and retired'.

But Vibart and his gunners had hardly enough time to congratulate themselves before another attack developed from the church compound to the north-west. At first all that could be seen were large white blobs advancing across the field. They turned out to be bales of cotton, pushed by about a hundred sepoys of the 1st who 'kept up a brisk fire with their muskets'. When they had approached to within 150 yards of the parapet, they stopped and gave covering fire for the main attack. 'The insurgents in the rear gave a fearful shout,' recalled Shepherd, 'and springing up on the walls made a charge, led on by the subadar-major [Radhay Singh], who was a powerful-looking man, but the first shots from our musketry caught him, he took a bound and fell down dead; a few rounds of canister then properly directed amongst them did good execution, causing a general dispersion.'

Simultaneously Mowbray Thomson's post in the second unfinished barrack was attacked by about five hundred sepoys from the direction of the first barrack. Approaching right up to Thomson's barricaded door, the mutineers were met by a determined fire from inside. 'Mainwaring's revolver despatched two or three,' recalled Thomson. 'Stirling, with an Enfield rifle, shot one and bayonetted another; both charges of my doublebarrelled gun were emptied, and not in vain. We were seventeen of us inside that barrack, and they left eighteen corpses lying outside the doorway.' But Thomson's tiny garrison would surely have been overwhelmed had it not been for the timely arrival of Captain Moore with twenty-five volunteers.

By midday the rebels had called off the attack. Radhay Singh had been as good as his word, but few of his fellow officers had pressed the attack with any real vigour. Meanwhile General Wheeler, having spent more than three hours in the trenches, encouraging the men, returned to his room to discover that his 'favourite, darling son' had been decapitated by a 9-pounder roundshot, leaving his hair and brains smeared on the wall. For Wheeler, who had aged considerably as the siege wore on, this personal tragedy was the final straw. The following day, more in resignation than hope, he wrote a final letter to Lawrence:

British spirit alone remains, but it cannot last for ever . . . We have no instruments, no medicine, provisions for a few days at furthest, and no possibility of getting any, as all communication with the town is cut off. We have been cruelly deserted, and left to our fate: we had not 220 soldiers of all arms, at first. The casualties have been numerous. Railway gents and merchants have swollen our ranks to what they are. Small as that is, they have done excellent service, but neither they, nor I, can last for ever. We have all lost everything belonging to us, and I have not even a change of linen. Surely we are not to die like rats in a cage.

Lawrence's reply, on 27 June, was a mixture of hope and caution. Brigadier Havelock, he wrote, was due to leave Allahabad immediately with a mixed force of seven hundred infantry, guns and cavalry, 'and *must* be at Cawnpore within two days, and will be closely followed by other detachments'. Lawrence added: 'I hope, therefore, you will husband your resources, and not accept any terms from the enemy, as I much fear treachery: you cannot rely on the Nana's promises. *Il a tué beaucoup de prisonniers.*' Lawrence had learnt about the mass murder of European fugitives at Cawnpore from Gubbins's Indian spies. Wheeler, without an espionage network, was still in the dark, and Lawrence's warning would not reach Cawnpore until it was too late.

Despite repulsing the biggest rebel attack yet, the garrison was in a pitiful condition. More than a third of its members had been killed, many more were sick and wounded, and the rest were hardly recognizable as human beings, let alone as members of the pampered, arrogant race that had dominated India for a century. 'Tattered in clothing,' wrote Thomson, 'begrimed with dirt, emaciated in countenance, were all without exception; faces that had been beautiful were now chiselled with deep furrows; haggard despair seated itself where there had been a month before only smiles. Some were sinking into the settled vacancy of look which marked insanity.' No one had washed since the start of the siege, but the garrison's ripe odour was nothing compared to the stench 'from the dead bodies of horses and other animals that had been shot in the compound and could not be removed', or the torment of the unusually large number of flies that were attracted as a consequence.

On 24 May, desperate to save the remaining members of his family,*

* His wife, remaining daughter, brother, sister and her two children, sister's aged mother-in-law and orphaned niece. His other daughter, just two years old, had been killed by a musket-ball.

Jonah Shepherd went to see General Wheeler with a proposal. He found him sitting on a mattress in the corner of his room, looking 'very feeble and aged'. Also in the room were Lady Wheeler and their two daughters, perched balefully in another corner, and Postmaster Roche, who had been acting as Wheeler's aide-de-camp since the death of his son. Shepherd told Wheeler that he planned to slip through the enemy lines into the city where he would try to discover the condition of the rebel army. In return for this information, he wanted permission to leave the entrenchment with his family. At first Wheeler was hostile. But when Shepherd explained that, if personal survival was his only priority, he could easily have escaped already, Wheeler came round. He would gladly lay down his own life to save the women and children, he told Shepherd, but he was 'quite at a loss what to do'. Sowing dissension in the ranks of the rebels seemed the only hope and, to this end, Wheeler authorized Shepherd to offer large sums of money to Nunne Nawab and the city *mahajuns*. With the meeting almost over, Shepherd told the general how much everyone regretted the loss of his son. At which point Wheeler covered his face with his hands and burst into tears, his whole body shaking 'as if his heart were bursting'. Only when the distraught general had recovered his composure could Shepherd ask him what he should say if captured. 'Say that we are able to pull on very well for a month to come,' replied Wheeler, 'and, above all, let them know that we expect a speedy help from Allahabad.'

Disguised in a sepoy's loin-cloth, cook's coat and turban, Shepherd left the entrenchment at midday on 24 June, when most of the rebels were cooking lunch, and headed for the small tank beyond the first unfinished barrack. Accosted by a cowherd, he was eventually arrested by four sepoys and taken under guard to the Nana's camp. But his disguise held up during questioning and, believing he was a native cook, his interrogator asked him if he thought the garrison was 'anxious to leave the station' and might accept an offer of safe passage. Shepherd said he did not know, but added that the women and children were keen to get away and 'for their sakes no doubt such an offer would be accepted if made in a satisfactory manner'. Would he deliver such a letter from Nana Sahib? Shepherd said he would, but his reply must have been too eager because his interrogator looked at him suspiciously and then left. Later that day Shepherd overheard a rumour that an old Christian lady would be sent to offer the garrison safe passage down the Ganges. He was delighted and assumed his own release was imminent.

That evening, the look-out man on Mowbray Thomson's barrack spotted a solitary figure walking across the plain from the direction of Savada House.

As it got closer, he could see that it was female and shouted, 'There's a woman coming across!' A member of the picket, suspecting she was a spy, was about to shoot her when Thomson knocked his musket aside. 'She had a child at her breast,' he recalled, 'but was so imperfectly clothed as to be without shoes and stockings. I lifted her over the barricade in a fainting condition, when I recognised her as Mrs Greenway, a member of a wealthy [merchant] family.' When she had recovered, she handed Thomson a letter addressed 'To the Subjects of Her Most Gracious Majesty Queen Victoria'. He handed it to Moore, who took it to General Wheeler. The short message inside was written in English and read: 'All those who are in no way connected with the acts of Lord Dalhousie, and are willing to lay down their arms, shall receive a safe passage to Allahabad.' Wheeler's indignant response was that he would respond only to a communication that bore the Nana's signature. But soon the whole garrison was abuzz with the news that the Nana had offered terms.

The following morning, a little after nine, a second messenger arrived at the entrenchment in a covered litter. It was Mrs Jacobi, a stout Eurasian woman, who was also being held by the Nana. Would she stay with them? asked a gaggle of women, delighted 'to see a white face from over the border'. She could not, she replied, 'as the Nana had kept her children and would kill them if she did not go back'. Wheeler now appeared from the tiled barrack and Mrs Jacobi handed him a letter containing the same message as before, only this time with the Nana's signature. He at once called a conference of his remaining senior officers – including Vibart, Moore and Whiting, an engineer – to consider it. Wheeler spoke first and, 'still hopeful of relief from Calcutta, and suspicious of treachery on the part of the Nana', was determined not to surrender. But he was persuaded to change his mind by, of all people, Captain Moore who pointed out that their first duty was not to themselves but to the women and children. Their position, said Moore, was hopeless: they had just three days' rations, they had no medicine to relieve the suffering of the sick and wounded, their shell-torn defences were in danger of being washed away in the first rainstorm, and there was no immediate prospect of relief. Far better to make terms while they still could.

Whiting agreed with Moore. But many of the other officers, particularly the juniors like Thomson, were for fighting on. They did not trust the Nana and considered Moore, a Queen's officer, 'wholly inexperienced in native character'. Wheeler, however, was determined to put the women and children first, and Moore had convinced him that treating with the Nana was their only hope. He therefore 'consented to the preparation of a treaty of capitulation'. Thomson explained: 'Had there been only men there, I am sure we should have made a dash for Allahabad rather than have thought of surrender; and Captain Moore would have been the first to lead the forlorn hope. A braver soul than he never breathed.'

The meeting to discuss terms took place at one in the afternoon on the plain beyond the unfinished barracks. Nana Sahib was represented by Azimullah Khan and Brigadier Jwala Prasad, who appeared on horseback from the direction of Savada House. Wheeler's tattered envoys – Moore, Whiting and Roche – arrived on foot. Azimullah began speaking in English but switched to Hindi when Jwala, who could not understand, protested. He said that his master was prepared to provide the garrison with safe passage to Allahabad on a flotilla of covered boats. In return he wanted the garrison's guns, treasure and ammunition. Moore responded with terms of his own: the men to be allowed to retain small-arms and sixty rounds of ammunition each; carriages to be provided to transport the sick, wounded, women and children the mile or so down to the nearest ghat; all boats to be supplied with flour for the journey. Promising to provide 'sheep and goats also', Azimullah left to report to his master. An hour later a sowar returned with the Nana's reply: he would agree to all Wheeler's terms on condition that the garrison left that very evening. But the general insisted that they would not be ready to leave until the following evening at the earliest. Even when the Nana threatened to reopen hostilities he refused to budge and eventually got his way. The final draft of the treaty was delivered to the Nana by Mr Todd, his former tutor, who had joined the garrison from Bithur in late May. Todd reported back that he had been courteously received and that the Nana had signed the document without hesitation.

The garrison was in a state of euphoria, like a condemned man who has received a last-minute reprieve. 'The soldiers were singing and dancing by beating time with drum sticks on an empty cask,' remembered Amy Horne. 'But the merriest were the children. It was the first time since we had entered those fatal buildings that the little ones were allowed their liberty, and they were making up for lost time.' With the enemy's guns silent and rationing no longer necessary, the garrison was able to eat and drink to its heart's content. Double rations of chapatties and dal were served out and 'draught after draught' of cloudy water was drunk from the well. Only the occasional hushed note of warning was struck: 'Will they really let us go down to Allahabad in safety?'

Shortly after midday on 26 June, with the evacuation due to take place that evening, a delegation of three officers – Captain Turner of the 1st, and Lieutenants Delafosse of the 53rd and Goad of the 56th – were taken down to the nearby Satichaura Ghat on elephants to inspect the boats. There they found about forty large up-country boats, 'moored and apparently ready for departure, some of them roofed, and others undergoing that process'. They also 'saw the apparent victualling of some of the boats, as in their presence a show of furnishing them with supplies was made, though before the morning there was not left in any of them a sufficient meal for a rat'. The delegation returned to the entrenchment 'without the slightest molestation', though Captain Turner had been made 'very uneasy by the repetition of the word "*kuttle*" [massacre], which he overheard passing from man to man by some of the 56th Native Infantry, who were present on the river's bank'.

The garrison's forebodings increased when the Nana sent word that the departure would have to be delayed until the following morning because he had been unable to arrange enough carriage for those too weak to walk. Yet he insisted on the British keeping their side of the bargain by handing over the remnants of their treasure – about 120,000 rupees – and their 'shattered guns' to a guard of mutineers. As a sign of his good faith, he sent three hostages to spend the night in the entrenchment. One of them was the insufferable Jwala Prasad, who insisted on telling General Wheeler that it was a 'shocking thing' his men had turned against him and that he, Jwala, would see to it that no harm would come to any of them in the morning. His words seemed hollow in the middle of the night when the accidental discharge of a sepoy's musket in one of the unfinished barracks caused the rebels on the perimeter to open fire with guns and muskets. But, after a brief panic, one of the hostages went off to explain the mistake and the firing died away. Being so used to a constant bombardment, Mowbray Thomson found the silence 'painful'. Others slept soundly that night, 'made comfortable by extreme fatigue and prolonged suspense, and with a comfortable sense of having done all that [they] could'.

As dawn broke on 27 June, vultures could be seen tearing at the corpses and animal carcasses that littered the plain. Inured to such sights, the able-bodied survivors of the garrison were busy 'loading themselves with what each thought most precious'. Some dug up boxes filled with jewels and money that they secreted in what remained of their clothes, others clutched bibles and 'heirlooms which the dead had entrusted to their keeping'. Men stuffed their pockets with as many cartridges as they could carry. The appearance of these survivors was pitiful. 'There were women who had been beautiful,' wrote Thomson, 'now stripped of every personal charm, some with, some without gowns; fragments of finery were made available no longer for decoration, but decorum; officers in tarnished uniforms, rent and wretched, and with nondescript mixtures of apparel, more or less insufficient in all. There were few shoes, fewer stockings, and scarcely any shirts; these had all gone on bandages for the wounded.'

An hour or two after sun-up the transport arrived in the shape of sixteen elephants, eighty palanquins and numerous bullock-carts. On to the palanquins were loaded the majority of the two hundred or so casualties, though even the most 'cautious handling' caused them 'much agony'. This exhausting work was done by the fit Europeans; not a single sepoy came forward to offer assistance. Instead they invaded the entrenchment, eager for plunder. 'Our bundles, money and what little valuables we had were forcibly taken away,' remembered Amy Horne. Captain Kempland of the 56th was severely beaten by some of the cavalry because he tried to hold on to his musket and 'many other officers [were] served in like manner'. Others were more determined in their resistance, like the private who responded to a sepoy's demand for his musket by pointing it at him and saying, 'You shall have its contents, if you please, but not the gun.' Moore was typically defiant, telling one group of rebels that 'their triumph would be short, and that each man would dearly pay for his deeds'. They responded with abuse 'so gross' that it made Amy Horne's ears tingle.

But not all the mutineers were hostile. Some of the sowars sought out their former commander, Major Vibart, and insisted on carrying his remaining property out of the entrenchment, loading it on to a hackery and 'escorting his wife and family down to the boats, with the most profuse demonstrations of respect'. Mutineers of the 53rd expressed their astonishment to Thomson that the garrison had 'withstood them so long', and estimated their own deaths during the siege at between eight hundred and a thousand men. A few asked after their old officers and appeared 'much distressed at hearing of their death'. Recognizing one sepoy, Thomson asked: 'Are we to go to Allahabad without molestation?' The sepoy replied that 'such was his firm belief'.

Shortly after eight Wheeler ordered the unwieldy calvacade to set off. He and a handful of senior officers, including Captain Williamson and the pusillanimous Lieutenant-Colonel Wiggins, were at the head of the column on broken-down ponies. So too was the valiant Captain Moore and a vanguard of the 32nd. Lady Wheeler and her two daughters were also near the front on an elephant, as was Amy Horne and her mother. Most of the other ladies and their children were in hackeries, leaving their social inferiors to walk alongside the able-bodied men. The last officer to leave the entrenchment was Major Vibart, mounted on a pony. As he did so, a great crowd of townspeople rushed in to pick over the garrison's detritus.

The route the column took to the Satichaura Ghat was along a metalled road that ran north-east from Vibart's battery for about a mile, passing the artillery bazaar on its right. A right turn at Bathgate and Campbell's chemist shop took the column over a wooden bridge to the shallow ravine that led down to the river. To the right of the ravine was the vast riverside compound of the late Colonel Williams of the 56th; to the left the estate of Henry Christie, a Cawnpore merchant, who had died a few days earlier of heat exhaustion. At the mouth of the ravine was a small boatman's temple with a row of steps that led down to the water's edge when the river was at its height. But it was June, the rains had still not come, and the closest channel of the shrunken Ganges was at least a hundred yards further on.

By the time Vibart left the entrenchment Wheeler and the vanguard had already covered half a mile. For most of the column the march to the river was uneventful. Eliza Bradshaw, the mother of a drummer who was walking in the centre of the procession with the other Eurasian families, recalled: 'The sowars and sepoys were on our right and left. They said nothing to us; they did not abuse us. When we reached the bridge with the white railings near Colonel Williams's house, we saw a large crowd assembled, men from the city and villagers. The sowars, who were ahead, shouted out that they were to stand aside, and no one to come down to the ghat. We then descended into the dry nullah leading to the river.'

The loyal sepoys were in the greatest danger and so it proved. Jemadar Khoda Bux of the 56th was holding Lieutenant Goad's hand when he was recognized by a former comrade as he passed the 56th's mess house. He was at once surrounded by mutineers from his regiment and dragged from the column, as was his son and three other 56th sepoys. Ignoring Lieutenant Goad's pleas that Nana Sahib had given permission for the Indian troops to accompany their officers, the mutineers stripped Bux of his cartridge box, turban and uniform before leading him and the others away.* Sowar Ewuz Khan suffered a similar fate.

Towards the back of the column, Emma Ewart was walking beside the palanquin that contained her wounded husband, Colonel John Ewart of the 1st Infantry. Since the death of their infant daughter at the outset of the

* They were taken to Savada House, where Nana Sahib, wary of antagonizing their former comrades, ordered them to be confined until they could be tried.

siege, a grief-stricken Mrs Ewart had devoted all her energy to nursing her husband's mangled arm. They were passing the junction leading to St John's Church when a group of Ewart's former sepoys ordered the two bearers to put down their burden and step aside. As they did so, two sepoys, 'pretending to feel very sorry for his sufferings', lifted Ewart out of the palanquin and carried him to one side of the church. 'Is the parade well dressed up now?' they asked, mocking him with the 'angry expressions he sometimes used towards them on parade'. Then, as his helpless wife looked on, they slashed him to death with their *tulwars*. 'Go along, we won't kill you,' they told her. 'But throw down all you have.' In terror she handed them a small parcel she had been concealing in her skirts. But as she turned to leave they cut her down as well.

Unaware of the murders, Wheeler and the officers at the head of the column were still confident that the Nana would keep his word. As they reached the end of the ravine that led to the ghat, they acknowledged the nodded greetings of a knot of Indian gentlemen seated on the terrace of the fishermen's temple to their left. The onlookers were none other than the Nana's two brothers, Baba Bhutt and Bala Rao, his chief adviser Azimullah Khan and his cavalry commander Tatya Tope. Tope, in particular, kept sending meaningful glances towards Jwala Prasad and Teeka Singh, who were waiting on horseback near the river.

On reaching the river bank, the garrison struggled to embark. 'The boats were not very close in shore,' recalled Amy Horne, 'and we had to wade through the water as well as we could. It was really very painful to witness the exertions of the aged, the sick and wounded, who got on board with no little difficulty. All this time the enemy were looking on like so many fiends, exulting over our distressing situation, taunting and mocking us.' General Wheeler put his family into the lead boat. The other boats were filled according to social and professional hierarchy, with the senior Europeans in the foremost craft. But all had at least two European soldiers or subalterns to defend them and help the boatmen manoeuvre them into the current. Eliza Bradshaw and the families of the Eurasian musicians shared boats with 'Mr McMullen and twenty-two children of the Free School, a pensioned drum-major of the 56th, named Murray, with his wife . . . and European soldiers and their wives'. Amy Horne boarded one of the rear boats with her stepfather and five brothers and sisters; her mother, in the confusion, had been taken to another boat. 'Every boat was crowded to suffocation,' recalled Amy. 'I sat on the roof of one alongside my little sister with the broken leg. She was in agony of pains and it was utterly impossible to take her inside.'

By nine o'clock, as stragglers continued to arrive at the ghat, many of the boats were so full they could not get under way. 'They were flat down on the sandbanks, with about two feet of water rippling around them,' remembered Thomson, who was in one of the lead boats. 'We might and ought to have demanded an embarkation in deeper water, but in the hurry of our departure, this had been overlooked . . . Captain Moore had told us that no attempt at anything like order of progress would be made in the departure; but when all were aboard, we were to push off as quickly as possible, and make for the other side of the river, where orders would be given for our further direction.'

Major Vibart's boat was the first to move. It was of a lighter draught than the others and contained a relatively high proportion of capable officers – including Moore himself, Whiting, Ashe and Delafosse – who worked manfully to free it from the sandbank. But as it eased into the channel, a signal from Jwala Prasad caused all the boatmen, nine to a craft, to leap into the water and make for the shore. Before departing, many had placed burning embers in the thatch of the roofs and these now burst into flame. The full extent of the Nana's treachery became clear when the sixteen sowars who had escorted Major Vibart to the river opened fire on the boats with their carbines. They retreated as the Europeans fired back at them and the fleeing boatmen, but their place was soon taken by countless others. 'Now, from ambush, in which they were concealed all along the banks, it seemed that thousands of men fired upon us,' wrote Thomson. 'Besides four nine-pounders, carefully masked and pointed to the boats, every bush was filled with sepoys.' In support of the Cawnpore mutineers, the Nana had placed Bhondu Singh's recently arrived 17th Native Infantry and two guns on the Oudh bank of the river. Wheeler's virtually defenceless flotilla – men, women, children and wounded – was caught in the crossfire. Thomson recorded:

Those of us who were not disabled by wounds, now jumped out of the boats, and endeavoured to push them afloat, but, alas! Most of them were utterly immovable . . . Some of the boats presented a broadside to the guns, others were raked from stem to stern by the shot. Volumes of smoke from the thatch somewhat veiled the full extent of the horrors that morning. All who could move were speedily expelled from the boats by the heat of the flames. Alas! The wounded were burnt to death . . . Wretched multitudes of women and children crouched behind the boats, or waded out into deeper water and stood up to their chins in the river to lessen the probability of being shot . . . Meanwhile Vibart's boat . . . had got off and was drifting down the stream, her thatched roof unburnt. I threw into the Ganges my father's Ghuznee medal, and my mother's portrait, all the property I had left . . . and struck out swimming for the retreating boat. There were a dozen of us beating the water for life.

With most of the boats on fire, sowars and sepoys raced into the shallow water to finish off the survivors. General Wheeler is said to have been killed by a single sword cut to the neck. Near by, the Revd Moncrieff tried to protect his family by shouting: 'If we English take prisoners, we do not put them to death, but imprison them. Spare our lives, and put us into prison.' He, his wife and children were all ruthlessly sabred to death. Colonel Williams's youngest daughter had more success when she told a sepoy, who was about to bayonet her, 'My father was always kind to sepoys.' But as he turned away she was struck on the head and killed by a villager's club. Elsewhere a four-year-old child was bayoneted to death and another infant 'taken up by one leg, swung round and thrown into the river'. Eliza Bradshaw's two musician sons were killed in front of her, but she was allowed to escape with her two-year-old granddaughter. 'Suddenly shouts were heard that the Nana had ordered the firing to cease,' she recalled. 'The sepoys and sowars were not to kill any more women and children.'

According to one Indian witness, the decision to attack the Europeans at the ghat was taken the night before at a meeting attended by Nana Sahib and all his senior advisers. 'After the consultation,' the witness testified, 'an order was given that some sepoys and sowars, with zemindars, were to be present at the ghat, and that the artillery should also be there . . . The Nana and his comrades did not intend to be faithful to their oath, and intended massacring the Europeans.' But the Nana did not actually witness the killings. When Bala Rao, Azimullah Khan, Tatya Tope and Jwala Prasad left for the ghat, he remained behind at Savada House, pacing up and down in front of his tent. Eventually the sound of firing could be heard and a messenger arrived with the news that 'the enemy were being destroyed'. The Nana's response was that there was no need to kill the women and children, and he sent the sowar back with an order to stop the slaughter.

The shocked and bedraggled survivors – about one hundred and twenty-five in number – were rounded up and told to sit on the ground. Many of them were wounded, some barefoot and all 'wet and soiled'. As the sun was extremely hot, their guards took pity and gave them some water. After about half an hour they were led away in groups to Savada House, where they were confined on the Nana's orders.

*

Just three boats floated clear of the ghat. Vibart's was in the lead, but it soon became stuck on a sandbank on the Oudh side of the river, enabling Thomson and three other swimmers – two officers and a private named Murphy from the 84th Foot – to catch up with it and slither aboard. The remaining two boats were swiftly disabled by cannon-fire: one drifted over to the far bank, where its eighteen survivors were captured by the 17th Native Infantry and later handed over to the Nana; the other boat was near to Vibart's when it was holed below the waterline and its occupants were able to transfer across. Thomson recalled:

> Now the crowded state of our poor ark left little room for working her. Her rudder was shot away; we had no oars, for these had all been thrown overboard by the treacherous boatmen, and the only implements that could be brought into use, were a spar or two, and such pieces of wood as we could safely tear away from the sides. Grape and round shot flew about us from either bank of the river, and shells burst constantly on the sand-banks in our neighbourhood. Alternately stranding and drifting, we were often within a hundred yards of the guns on the Oude side of the river, and saw them load, prime, and fire into our midst. Shortly after midday we got out of range of their great guns; the sandy bed on the river-bank had disabled their artillery-bullocks, but they chased us the whole day, firing in volleys of musketry incessantly.

Among those tragically killed by musket fire while trying to free the boat from numerous shoals that day were the two men who had done most to ensure the garrison held out for as long as it did: Captain Moore and Lieutenant Ashe. Lieutenant Boulton's luck also gave out during the flight from the ghat, while two officers were killed by the same roundshot that 'shattered Lieutenant Fagan's leg to such an extent that from the knee downwards it was only held together by sinews'. One man's death was not regretted: that of Colonel Wiggins, whose behaviour in the boat was every bit as disgraceful as it had been during the siege. 'While our little craft was stuck upon a sandbank,' remembered Thomson, 'no expostulation could make him quit the shelter of her bulwark, though we were adopting every possible expedient to lighten her burden. It was positively a relief to us when we found that his cowardice was unavailing, and a bullet through the boat's side that despatched him caused the only death that we regarded with complacency.' Thomson himself was knocked senseless by a bullet that grazed the side of his head and was about to be thrown overboard when he regained consciousness.

The progress of the battered boat was torturously slow: by the morning of 28 June, twenty-four hours after departing, it was still only ten miles from Cawnpore. There was, however, no sign of their pursuers, and the fugitives 'began to indulge the hope that they had given up the chase'. But that afternoon, while stranded off Nuzzuffghur, they were attacked by the retainers of a powerful Oudh *zemindar* named Babu Ram Buksh. Whiting and Harrison were killed, Vibart was shot in his one good arm as he sought to push the boat off the sandbank, Captain Turner had both his legs smashed, and two other officers and a lady, Mrs Seppings, were wounded. At dusk another threat materialized in the form of a boat from Cawnpore with at least fifty sepoys on board, 'thoroughly armed, and deputed to board and destroy us'. But it also grounded on a sandbank and, wrote Thomson, 'instead of waiting for them to attack us, eighteen or twenty of us charged them, and few of their number escaped to tell the story'. The enemy boat contained plenty of ammunition, which was welcome, but no food.

That night a storm blew Vibart's boat off the sandbank and into a narrow channel of the river opposite Sheorajpur, where it stuck fast and was soon discovered by its rebel pursuers. So Vibart ordered Thomson, Delafosse, Sergeant Grady and eleven privates of the 32nd and 84th Foot to wade ashore and 'drive off the sepoys, while they attempted to ease off the boat again'. Thomson considered it a 'forlorn enterprise', yet it worked. The sepoys were dispersed, as was a group of Ram Buksh's retainers. But when Thomson's party returned to the sandbank the boat had gone.* 'Our only hope of safety now was in flight,' he recalled, 'and with a burning sun overhead, a rugged raviny ground, and no covering for the feet, it was no easy task for our half-famished party to make head.' Pursued for three miles by a large party of sepoys and armed peasants, they were forced to take refuge in a small temple. Thomson placed four men in the narrow doorway and the 'mob came on helter-skelter in such maddening haste that some of them fell or were pushed on to the bayonets, and their transfixed bodies made the barrier impassable to the rest, upon whom we, from behind our novel defence, poured shot upon shot into the crowd'. Ram Buksh's brother,

* During Thomson's absence, the boat had been attacked by a separate band of mutineers and, with casualties mounting, Vibart decided to surrender. He and Lieutenant Master died of their wounds during the 18-mile journey back to Cawnpore in bullock-carts. The other men were shot on arrival with one woman, Mrs Boyes, who refused to leave her husband's side. The remaining women and children, many of them wounded, were locked up with the rest in the Savada House.

who was leading the attack, was killed here. So too was Sergeant Grady, shot in the head. Eventually the rebels set fire to the temple and Thomson's band had no option but to run for it.

Jumping the parapet, we were in the thick of the rabble in an instant; we fired a volley, and ran a-muck with the bayonet. Seven of our number succeeded in reaching the bank of the river, and we first threw in our guns and then ourselves . . . I turned round and saw the banks of the river thronged with the black multitude, yelling, howling, and firing at us; while others of their party rifled the bodies of the six poor fellows we had left behind. Presently two more were shot in the head; and one private, Ryan, almost sinking from exhaustion, swam into a sandbank and was knocked on the head by two or three ruffians waiting to receive him.

The four survivors were Thomson, Delafosse, Private Murphy of the 84th and Private Sullivan of the 1st Madras Fusiliers. 'For two or three hours, we continued swimming,' recalled Thomson. 'Often changing our position, and the current helping our progress. At length our pursuers gave up the chase; a sowar on horseback was the last we saw of them.' The reason was that they had reached the territory of a powerful Oudh *taluqdar*, Raja Dirigibijah Singh of Bulrampur, who was still loyal to the British. Tempted out of the water by matchlockmen who insisted that they were friendly, the exhausted quartet were taken to the raja's fort at Morar Mhow, where they ate their first meal in four days. On at least three occasions, Nana Sahib sent mutineers to the fort with a demand for Dirigibijah to hand over the fugitives. But each time the old raja refused, sending back word that he was 'a tributary to the King of Oude, and knew nothing of the Nana's raj'.

In discussions with these mutineers, including men from his own regiment, Thomson discovered the extent to which they had been hoodwinked by the Nana. One sepoy told him that the British would never regain India because the Nana had 'sent a sowar on a camel to Russia for assistance'. Another of the 'Nana's fables', learnt Thomson, 'was that certain water-mills which were erected by the Company for grinding grain at a fixed charge for the villagers, were implements in the great work of forcible conversion, and that in the said mills pig-bone dust was mixed with flour'. But the mutineers' favourite topic of conversation was the annexation of Oudh. 'They grew energetic in discussing this theme,' recalled Thomson, 'and said that in consequence of that one act the Company's raj would cease.'

Thanks to the unwavering protection of their aged host, Thomson and his three companions eventually joined up with the British relief force marching up the Ganges. They were the only European men to escape the killings at Satichaura Ghat.

The only other survivors of the massacre, apart from the women and children taken to Savada House, were those females carried off by Muslim sowars. One, an unnamed European lady, was apprehended by a cavalryman named Ali Shah and hidden in his hackery. When Nana Sahib was told, he summoned Shah and forced him to hand her over. She joined the other women in Savada House. But at least two of the female prizes were not handed over. One of them was Amy Horne, who later wrote a graphic and harrowing account of her capture and subsequent ordeal:

The Cavalry surrounded us with drawn swords, and the infantry came into the boats to loot. A few trinkets that I had about me were forced away, but these not satisfying their avarice, one of the fiends had the barbarity to fetch me a blow . . . It was just then I was beckoned to by a sowar who was on his horse along side of my boat, the water up to his very saddle girths . . . He levelled his gun at me, but finding it had not the effect of frightening me, and not able to come near enough himself, ordered another rebel, who was on board at the time looting, to throw me into the water, which was done without any hesitation. The cries of my sister not to leave her yet ring in my ears, and her last look I never can forget. I was soon taken to the shore, where I found another young lady whom I recognised to be Miss Wheeler in the same pitiful position as myself. We were made to walk alongside their horses, the riders keeping a tight hold of our hands all the time. I was drenched to the skin, and was conducted barefoot and bareheaded under a hot sun to a Subadur's hut, the distance of about 3 miles from the Ghat.

That same day Amy was forcibly converted to Islam by two *maulvis* – one of whom, Liaqat Ali, had led the recent uprising at Allahabad. Thereafter she became the concubine of her captor, a sowar named Ismail Khan, and remained with him and the rebel army for nine terrifying months, never knowing whether each new day would be her last. Finally, in April 1858, after a lengthy spell in Lucknow, she persuaded her captor to release her in return for a written promise that she would do everything she could to 'obtain a pardon for all the atrocities he had committed, no matter of how black a dye'. Within days she had reached the house of her great-uncle in Allahabad. 'Ten long months of suffering, together with my native costume, had so altered my appearance,' she wrote, 'that even when I gave my name they could scarce believe that one they had numbered with the dead stood before them.' Ismail Khan was never brought to justice.

In her various accounts of her harrowing experience, Amy never specifically mentions rape. This was, no doubt, partly out of shame and partly out of deference to her prudish Victorian audience. She was, after all, an eighteen-year-old virgin when captured. Yet C. B. Saunders, the officiating Commissioner of Delhi who conducted an inquiry into the possible rape of European women, was surely referring to Amy when he noted that there may have been 'rare and exceptional cases' in which 'some half-caste women' had been 'obliged to sacrifice their honour'.

Another candidate seems to have been the young woman captured at the same time as Amy: General Wheeler's eighteen-year-old daughter, Margaret. It was widely reported at the time that, rather than succumb to her captor's amorous advances, she had killed him before taking her own life. Her brave and honourable death was the subject of countless Victorian theatricals and the most popular mutiny engravings. It was what the Victorian public *wanted* to believe because the alternatives were too awful to contemplate. Yet there is no doubt that, like Amy Horne, Miss Wheeler was forced to live as her captor's concubine. According to Ewuz Khan, he was Nizam Ali Khan of the 2nd Cavalry, a Pathan from Rampur, 'age 22 or 23 years, a fair complexion, height about five feet seven inches, long nose, dark eyes' and wore a 'beard and small moustache'. The authorities later made strenuous attempts to find out what had become of Miss Wheeler, and one Indian spy was told by a jemadar in the service of the Nawab of Rampur that he had seen Nizam Ali Khan at Rampur 'during the outbreak and that he had a young lady, daughter of a gentleman, with him'. She was 'disguised in native clothes' and, as a consequence, the jemadar avoided talking to Khan who shortly after left Rampur for the rebel camp at Tulsipur. Two other spies who gained entry to the rebel camp could find no trace of either Khan or the general's daughter.

Nothing more was heard of Miss Wheeler until 1874, when it was reported that she was 'still alive in one of the northern frontiers of India, and has no desire to change her condition in life'. Four years later an amateur historian claimed that she was living in Cawnpore as a Muslim. But definitive proof of her survival did not come to light until the 1880s, when a Mrs Emma Clarke, a contemporary of the Wheeler girls, settled in Cawnpore. She came to hear of an Englishwoman who lived in the bazaar and, after inviting her to visit, discovered that she was Margaret Wheeler. Mrs Clarke is said to have urged her to contact her surviving brothers. The woman replied that she was too ashamed and did not want to risk the life of Nizam

Ali Khan who, for whatever motive, had rescued her from certain death. He was probably dead when, half a century after the mutiny, an old lady called a Catholic priest to her deathbed in the Indian quarter of Cawnpore and revealed that she was General Wheeler's long-lost daughter.

The first intimation that Wheeler was about to capitulate reached Lucknow on 28 June. Lawrence suspected a rebel ploy and his fears were quickly confirmed. That evening, three separate messengers brought the tragic news that Wheeler 'had entered into a treaty with the insurgents and after embarking on boats many had been treacherously murdered; those who escaped the fire taken prisoners'. As horrific as the report was, it merely heightened the Lucknow garrison's determination, in Dr Fayrer's words, to 'fight to the last, and enter into no treaties'.

The following morning Lawrence saw an opportunity to strike back when scouts informed him that the advance guard of a large body of mutineers had reached the town of Chinhut, eight miles east of the Residency on the Faizabad road. No sooner had the report been confirmed by a cavalry patrol than he withdrew the force at the Muriaon cantonment into Lucknow and began to prepare for battle. As a keen student of Indian warfare he was aware that compact and disciplined forces, led by Europeans, had often won great victories against much larger Indian armies. He also knew the quality of his experienced British troops, who were itching to avenge their fellow countrymen and women, and wanted to test the fidelity of his remaining Indian soldiers in battle. 'We must try and blood them,' he declared, meaning commit them to the British cause. In retrospect, Lawrence's initiative was condemned by many as reckless. But he had good reason to expect it to succeed: he had been told the rebel force was not particularly large, while its slow advance implied that it was not eager for the fray. By making a reconnaissance in force he hoped to catch the rebels unawares, either at the edge of the city or at the bridge across the Kokrail Stream, halfway between Lucknow and Chinhut. Lawrence was not, however, an experienced military commander and should have left all strategic and tactical decisions to his subordinates.

Shortly before daybreak on 30 June the troops earmarked for the reconnaissance assembled near the iron bridge. They included three companies of British infantrymen, two of sepoys (more than half from the 13th Native Infantry), a squadron of Oudh Irregulars (mainly Sikhs), most of the volunteer horse, a battery of European artillery, a battery and a half of Indian artillery, and an 8-inch howitzer drawn by elephants and manned by

Europeans. Lawrence himself was in command, with the recently promoted Brigadier Inglis as his deputy and Lieutenant-Colonel Case of the 32nd, 'as fine an officer as ever stepped', the next senior officer. Unfortunately the column was delayed by the late arrival of the Machi Bawan contingent and the sun was well up by the time it departed. It was, recalled John Lawrence of the volunteer horse, a 'very close and suffocating' morning and the speed of march was not helped by the howitzer's elephants which 'literally crawled along the road'. After a two-hour march the force had reached the bridge over the Kokrail Stream with no sign of the enemy. There the troops were halted to rest and eat breakfast, while Sir Henry Lawrence and his staff rode a quarter of a mile ahead to reconnoitre from higher ground. In a tope of trees they came across a group of travellers who told them that they had seen no rebel troops between there and Chinhut. On the strength of this information Lawrence concluded that the mutineers were not going to advance into the open that day and sent Captain Wilson back to Kokrail with orders for the column to return to Lucknow. However, according to Lieutenant Birch, Inglis's aide-de-camp, Lawrence was persuaded to change his mind by the 'ardour of the younger members of his staff'. Birch recorded:

> Neither Brigadier Inglis, Colonel Case . . . nor Captain Wilson were present during the discussion. Sir Henry sent me back to ask the Brigadier if his men could go on. He gave the only possible answer, as I take it: 'Of course they could, if ordered.' I returned with this answer, and was immediately sent back with orders for the force to advance. [It] was a great mistake not halting the men for refreshments. The elephants were up with commissariat stores, and it would have been easy to give them their breakfast; but this useful opportunity was lost, and the force advanced with empty stomachs, under a burning sun.

Trudging slowly along a sandy causeway, the column was not far from Chinhut when its cavalry scouts were fired upon from the village of Ismailganj to the left. They withdrew and the 8-inch howitzer under Lieutenant Bonham was ordered to move forward. But before it could be brought into action the troops on the causeway were bombarded by roundshots at a distance of almost a mile, the first direct hits decapitating an Indian artillery driver and killing several doolie-bearers. These were fired from the main enemy position in thick mango groves to the front of the village of Chinhut, which was situated on the banks of an extensive *jhil*. Lawrence's troops were immediately deployed. The howitzer remained on the road while the ten field guns moved a little ahead to the right. Next to them was positioned the main body of sepoys, in front of a small hamlet, with the cavalry on the extreme right. The men of the 32nd Foot were posted in a hollow to the left of the road, not far from Ismailganj, with some of the 13th's sepoys acting as skirmishers.

The howitzer returned the mutineers' fire with good effect, 'its shells being seen to burst among them', but the 9-pounder field guns were not so effective at such long range. Nevertheless, after an artillery duel lasting an hour, the mutineers' guns fell silent and the centre of their position appeared to give way as if about to retreat. Convinced that victory was imminent, Captain Wilson galloped up to gunners and shouted in encouragement: 'That is it: there they go! Keep it up!' Far from retreating, the mutineers were limbering up their guns for a general advance. The volunteer horse had been moved further to the right in preparation for a British attack, and John Lawrence had a bird's-eye view of the plain between Chinhut and Ismailganj. 'It was one moving mass of men,' he recalled, 'regiment after regiment of the insurgents poured steadily towards us, the flanks covered with a foam of skirmishers, the light puffs of smoke from their muskets floating from every ravine and bunch of grass in our front. As to the mass of the troops, they came on in quarter-distance columns, their standards waving in their faces, and everything performed as steadily as possible. A field day on parade could not have been better.'

The rebels were advancing in two separate masses, on both sides of the road, with the intention of outflanking and encircling the British position. In desperation the 9-pounders fired grape, but they could not prevent an overwhelming force of rebel infantry from driving the loyal sepoys beyond the hamlet and into a company of the 32nd, which was in the act of redeploying on the right. To the left of the road the mutineers were steadily approaching the village of Ismailganj, which, inexplicably, Lawrence had failed to occupy. To oppose them, Lieutenant Alexander's battery of Oudh artillery was ordered to move to the other side of the road. The embankment was steep, and the guns lost their balance and overturned. Brigadier Inglis was convinced the act was deliberate. 'The Oudh Artillerymen and drivers were traitors,' he wrote. 'They overturned the guns into ditches, cut the traces of their horses, and abandoned them, regardless of the remonstrances and exertions of their own officers, and of those of Sir Henry Lawrence's staff, headed by the Brigadier-General in person, who himself drew his sword upon these rebels.'

Within minutes many of the loyal sepoys, most of the Sikh cavalry and all the Indian artillerymen had fled. The mutineers had occupied Ismailganj and were pouring a deadly fire into the exposed Europeans from two directions. As a last resort the men of the 32nd were ordered to take Ismailganj and, with a loud cheer, they bounded forward to be met by a hail of musket-balls. The recently married Colonel Case was the first to fall, followed by scores of his men. Captain Stevenson took command and tried to lead the men on but he too was hit, as were two subalterns. With more than a third of their number killed or wounded, the 32nd fell back. The guns were almost out of ammunition, the situation hopeless, when Sir Henry Lawrence gave the order to retreat. The European artillery limbered up and, with its gun-carriages covered with wounded, galloped to the rear. But the howitzer's frightened elephant would not allow itself to be linked up and, after a gallant but failed attempt by Lieutenant Bonham to procure an alternative limber, the big gun was abandoned.

Mixed up with the retreating 32nd were sepoys of the 13th, 'noble fellows, who were seen carrying wounded [Europeans] to the gun-carriages, leaving their own wounded comrades on the ground'. As the bedraggled and strung-out British column neared the Kokrail Bridge, a large host of mutineer cavalry could be seen gathering in its left rear, threatening to cut off the line of retreat. Not a man would have reached Lucknow, recorded one private, but for the 'bravery of the few cavalry and the cowardice of the enemy'. The volunteer horse were in a tope to the left of the road, covering the withdrawal, when Captain Radcliffe ordered: 'Three's right! Trot!' Upon which the half troop swept out of the trees towards the rebel cavalry, a quarter of a mile to their front. Two rebel 9-pounders opened on them and the first roundshot had just passed narrowly over their heads when Radcliffe shouted, 'Charge!' John Lawrence recalled: 'The notes of our trumpet sounded sharp above the din of the fight, and we rode straight at them: the cowards never bided the shock; they galloped like furies from the spot. Five hundred cavalry and two guns to be hunted by thirty-five sabres! . . . The guns got under the shelter of a regiment of the line, which we dared not charge, for the first volley they gave us emptied two saddles; so, sabring up the scattered skirmishers, we wheeled and galloped to the rear of our slow moving columns.'

The painfully slow retreat continued beyond the Kokrail Bridge, with many soldiers collapsing from heat-stroke, exhaustion and a lack of water or food. They were immediately killed by the pursuing rebels. One private of the 32nd, wounded in the leg, told his comrades to leave him while he blazed away at the mutineers. 'I shan't last long,' he declared, 'and I would never be able to reach Lucknow.' Another man, 'maddened by the heat and fatigue, charged single-handed into the ranks of the enemy and was soon put to rest'. Some of the Europeans and sepoys 'behaved with much steadiness, loading and firing with deliberate aim on those of the enemy who came near'. Others were hampered by muskets that 'had been kept long loaded without having been discharged, and had become foul'.

Only when the towers and minarets of Lucknow's skyline came into view did Sir Henry Lawrence and his staff abandon the column and gallop back to the Residency unescorted. The garrison had already been alerted to the disaster by the frantic arrival of Sikh horsemen and Indian artillery drivers, their horses 'covered with foam'; when asked by Martin Gubbins why they had fled, their only excuse was that 'the enemy had surrounded them'. On reaching the Residency, Lawrence at once dispatched a company of the 32nd to occupy the houses on the near side of the iron bridge. Supported by the guns of the Redan Battery, these troops checked the advance of the mutineers and enabled the battered remnants of Lawrence's column to cover the last leg of their harrowing retreat without hindrance. It was just as well because, according to Private Metcalfe, the exhausted survivors of Chinhut were in no condition to resist an immediate assault on the Machi Bawan. Balked at both the iron bridge and the stone bridge below the Machi Bawan, the mutinous artillerymen contented themselves with lobbing shells across the river. The cavalry and infantry simply crossed the Gumti lower down and, by afternoon, had occupied buildings close to the two British positions from which they opened a galling musket fire. The siege had begun.

So severe were Lawrence's losses at Chinhut – three hundred and sixty-five soldiers killed, wounded and missing* – that he no longer felt he had enough men to defend two separate positions. The day after the battle, therefore, he sent repeated orders for the Machi Bawan garrison to spike its guns, blow up the fort and retire on the Residency at midnight. When Indian messengers failed to get through, Lawrence resorted to semaphore.† That night the evacuation went almost without a hitch. Maria Germon was sleeping with twenty-three others in the underground room at Dr Fayrer's house when she was woken at half past twelve by a massive explosion that

* 172 Europeans and 193 Indian soldiers. With no quarter given, a staggering 118 European officers and men were killed at or during the retreat from Chinhut. The number of loyal sepoys killed and missing – mainly the latter – was 182.

† 'It was a primitive machine, consisting of one post, with a bar at the top from which were suspended, in one row, black stuffed bags, each having its own pulley to work with.' (*State Papers*, II, intro., 49.)

covered everyone with pieces of glass. Convinced a rebel attack was in progress, she was mightily relieved to hear Dr Fayrer at the head of the stairs call out: 'It is all right, the whole party are all in safe from the Muchee Bawun and it is blown up.'

The Residency compound was now home to 3,000 souls. Of the 1,720 combatants, 800 were British officers and men, 153 were civilian volunteers and the rest were loyal sepoys; the remaining 1,280 non-combatants were divided almost equally between Christian women and children and Indian servants. Opposing them was a far greater force of trained military soldiers, not to mention the hostile population of a turbulent city.

The British garrison's odds of survival, not high at the outset, were reduced still further on 2 July when Sir Henry Lawrence was mortally wounded in his Residency apartment by a shell splinter from the 8-inch howitzer that the rebels had captured at Chinhut. The day before, a shell from the same gun had burst in the room between him and his private secretary, causing injury to neither. His staff officers had immediately pleaded with him to move to a less exposed room. At first he had scotched the suggestion with the jocular remark that sailors always considered the safest place in a ship to be where the last shot had landed. Later on 1 July, as more shot entered the top storey of the Residency, he had agreed to move to an apartment below – but not until the following day. At about eight thirty in the morning of 2 July, Captain Wilson reminded the chief commissioner of his promise. Lawrence replied that he would rest for a couple of hours and then have his things moved. Half an hour later, Lawrence was lying on his bed, listening to Wilson read out a memorandum on the distribution of rations, when the room was filled with a storm of flame and flying metal. As a shaken but uninjured Wilson rose to his feet, his vision obscured by smoke and dust, he called out, 'Sir Henry, are you hurt?'

No answer. Again he shouted, and this time came the faint reply: 'I am killed.' A piece of shell had passed through the upper part of Lawrence's left thigh, shattering his thigh-bone and pelvis. He was carried down to a table in the drawing room and examined by Dr Fayrer, who knew at once the wound was fatal. Asked by Lawrence how long he had to live, the doctor replied: 'About forty-eight hours.'

Lawrence was now moved to Dr Fayrer's house because it was more sheltered from the rebel artillery. There he was visited by all the senior officers and officials, including Martin Gubbins, who had never witnessed such a 'scene of sorrow'. He recorded: 'While we clustered round Sir Henry's bed the enemy were pouring a heavy musketry fire upon the place, and bullets were striking the outside of the pillars of the verandah in which we were collected. Sir Henry's attenuated frame, and the severe nature of his injury, at once decided the medical men not to attempt amputation; but it was necessary to stay the bleeding by applying the tourniquet, and the agony which this caused was fearful to behold. It was impossible to avoid sobbing like a child.'

In the time left to him, Lawrence spoke often of his late wife and recited their favourite biblical texts. He also expressed his wishes with regard to his children and sent loving messages to them all. In his official capacity he appointed Major Banks as his civil and Brigadier Inglis as his military successors. To the former he dictated a fourteen-point memorandum, mainly advice on how to conduct the siege, such as sparing 'the precious health of Europeans . . . from shot and sun', turning out all natives 'who will not work', organizing 'working parties for night labour' and preserving ammunition 'as far as possible'. The last point concerned his epitaph. 'Put on my tomb,' he said, 'only this – HERE LIES HENRY LAWRENCE, WHO TRIED TO DO HIS DUTY. MAY GOD HAVE MERCY ON HIM.'

Lawrence died during the late morning of Saturday, 4 July, as Dr Fayrer had predicted he would. According to one who was present, 'his expression was so happy one could not but rejoice that his pain was over'. His last words were to his military successor. 'Dear Inglis,' he said, 'ask the poor fellows who I exposed at Chinhut to forgive me. Bid them remember Cawnpore and never surrender. God Bless you all.' Gubbins wrote later that Lawrence had expressed to him the same deathbed regret for Chinhut, saying that he had 'acted against his own judgement from the fear of man'. Yet it was Gubbins himself who had repeatedly urged Lawrence to send detachments to meet the rebels at Sitapur, Cawnpore, Chinhut and elsewhere. A member of the chief commissioner's staff wrote later: 'Sir Henry Lawrence did from time to time complain to me that the indomitable personal courage of Mr Gubbins, his excessive zeal and ardent temperament, had caused him to be over-earnest, importunate, and too public an advocate of military movements which, according to Sir Henry's personal judgment, could only have ended disastrously. He more than once deplored to me that . . . the Finance Commissioner had come to be regarded by some of the more spirited and less experienced officers of the force, as the real man for the crisis.' This surely is the explanation for Lawrence's enigmatic final remark to Gubbins: that simple pride – the fear of not measuring up to his gung-ho deputy, of losing the confidence of a portion of the garrison – had caused him to ignore his better judgement and give battle at Chinhut.

Lawrence's death 'cast a sad gloom over the whole garrison, and many a stout heart began to feel anxious as to how matters would be conducted after the demise of one in whom all had trusted'. Yet his corpse received no preferential treatment. 'He was buried with the rest at night,' recorded Maria Germon in her journal, 'but even he did not have a separate grave, each corpse was sewn up in its own bedding and those who had died during the day were put into the same grave.'

The day after Lawrence's demise, the sounds of wild celebration from the city marked the coronation of Birjis Qadr as King of Oudh. Not all the rebel officers had wanted the twelve-year-old Birjis as their ruler: the Muslim-dominated cavalry, for example, preferred the brother of the ex-King, Sulaiman Qadr. But they and the mainly Hindu infantry were persuaded to support Birjis's claim by Raja Jai Lal Singh, an influential ex-courtier, and Mammu Khan, the lover of Birjis's mother, Begum Hazrat Mahal, the real power behind the throne. In return they were given the following assurances by Jai Lal and Mammu (both members of the new rebel government): orders from the King of Delhi were to be obeyed without question; the King's *wazir* (chief minister) was to be selected by the army; officers were not to be appointed to the mutinous regiments without the consent of the army; double pay was to be issued from the date of their leaving the English service; and no one was to interfere with the 'treatment and disposal of those who were friends to the English'. As at Delhi and elsewhere, the rebel officers were demanding not just financial reward but professional autonomy *and* a say in the political process as well.

15. The Backlash

The tragedy at Cawnpore might have been averted had not reinforcements been delayed by two mutinies lower down the Grand Trunk Road: at Benares on 4 June and Allahabad two days later. Benares was one of the oldest, richest and most beautiful cities in India. Famous for its silks and shawls, embroidery and filigree, it was also a centre for banking and the trade of precious stones. But its chief draw lay in its status as one of India's seven most sacred cities, the home of Shiva the destroyer and the centre of brahmanical learning. Every year thousands of Hindus flock to Benares to bathe in the holy water of the Ganges, or 'river of life'. According to Hindu theology, the Goddess Ganges – or Ganga as she is more commonly known – is the mother goddess of the whole continent. To bathe in her waters is an experience akin to entering heaven, and to die immersed in them is to receive *moksha*, or final spiritual liberation. A visitor in the 1840s noted: 'The ground is covered with buildings even to the water's edge, and some of the ghats, which are constructed of large blocks of red-chunar stone, have a flight of thirty or forty steps leading down to the river. Here a most animated scene generally presents itself. Men and women, boys and girls, may be seen bathing early in the morning, and evening, and, during the cold season, also in the middle of the day.'

Reports of the mutinies further north had made the large 'ruffian population' of Benares, many of whom openly carried arms, even more volatile than usual. Fearing a civil uprising, the commissioner, Henry Tucker, and the temporary station commander, Colonel Patrick Gordon of the Ludhiana Regiment of Sikhs, were all for evacuating the garrison to the nearby stronghold at Chunar. But their proposal was vetoed by the judge, Frederick Gubbins, and the magistrate, Francis Lind, on the grounds that it would jeopardize the road, river and telegraph communications between Calcutta and upper India. The garrison at that stage was composed of Gordon's Sikhs, the 37th Native Infantry under Lieutenant-Colonel Arthur Spottiswoode,* a wing of the 13th Irregular Cavalry and a half-battery of European foot

* The younger brother of Lieutenant-Colonel Henry Spottiswoode, commanding officer of the 55th Native Infantry, who had committed suicide at Hoti Mardan on 25 May 1857.

artillery. Colonel Gordon was convinced his Sikhs would remain loyal but had 'misgivings' about the 37th. As for the irregular cavalry, they had let it be known that they would be passively faithful, but 'could not be trusted to charge or fire upon mutineers on the *cartridge* question'. Lind took this to mean they were at heart as mutinous as the sepoys.

Matters came to a head when news of the Azimgarh mutiny reached Benares during the afternoon of 4 June. By now the European garrison had been reinforced by one hundred and fifty men of the 10th Foot, sent up from Dinapore in Bihar, and about sixty of the 1st Madras Fusiliers, who had recently arrived from the rail terminus at Raniganj by bullock-train. The latter had been joined the day before by their commanding officer, Lieutenant-Colonel James Neill. Born in Ayrshire in 1810, the son of a British officer, Neill was educated at Ayr Academy and Glasgow University before joining the 1st Madras European Regiment (later Fusiliers) at the age of sixteen. A fiercely ambitious man, he had spent many years on the staff, most recently as adjutant-general of Madras troops serving in the Second Burma War. Forced to leave Burma owing to ill-health, he arrived in Britain in June 1854 and immediately volunteered for service in the Crimean War. He was eventually appointed second-in-command of the Anglo-Turkish contingent, but did not reach Constantinople until the summer of 1855 when the war was as good as over. Frustrated by this near miss, he was delighted to get another chance to prove himself in battle in May 1857, just six weeks after his return from Britain, when his regiment was ordered to Calcutta. Recently returned from the Persian War, it contained nine hundred healthy and battle-hardened veterans, 'fully equal to any regiment'.

A religious zealot who believed himself destined for great things, Neill could be utterly ruthless if crossed. At Calcutta railway station, for example, he prevented a train from leaving without a detachment of his men by threatening to shoot the station-master. Once up-country, away from central authority, he was in a position to carry out such threats. Yet to women he could be tender and chivalrous, while those who served under him were struck by his overriding concern for their welfare. 'He was the finest-looking man I ever saw,' wrote a member of his staff, 'great shaggy moustache and eye-brows, and he feared nobody . . . He was the sternest and, at the same time, kindest and best-hearted of men.'

Neill had arranged to leave Benares for Cawnpore with a detachment of his regiment in the afternoon of the 4th. But he was stopped by Brigadier George Ponsonby, the 67-year-old station commander, who had only been in his new post for a matter of days. Ponsonby told Neill that he needed every European he could muster to disarm the 37th Native Infantry, the most suspect regiment at Benares, the following morning. Neill agreed with the course of action, but wanted it to be immediate and Ponsonby eventually agreed. The intention was for the disarmament parade to take place at four o'clock with all the Europeans, Sikhs and irregular cavalry in attendance. But so hurried were the preparations that none of the supporting troops was in position by the time Colonel Spottiswoode began to order his men, by companies, to lodge their muskets in their bells-of-arms. He had got as far as No. 6 Company – and was convinced that the regiment contained a majority of loyal sepoys – when two or three voices called out, 'Our officers are deceiving us, they want us to give up our arms, that the Europeans who are coming up may shoot us down!' To calm the men, Spottiswoode galloped away to prevent the advancing Europeans from coming any closer. As he returned, shots rang out from the direction of No. 2 Company (fired, in the first instance, by the pay-havildar), causing the men to rush towards the bells-of-arms to rearm themselves.

Once in possession of their muskets, the mutineers opened up on the nearby European troops, who replied with rifle and artillery fire. Several Europeans were hit. They were joined on the dusty ground by Brigadier Ponsonby who, though unscathed, was suffering from the effects of the burning sun. He at once 'declared himself quite unfit for anything' and begged Colonel Neill, the next senior officer, to take command. Neill did so, ordering the European and Sikh troops to charge the 37th's line. In the confusion, sowars of the 13th Irregular Cavalry shot in the direction of the Sikhs, who faced about and returned fire. One Sikh attempted to murder Colonel Gordon, but a faithful havildar intervened, receiving the bullet in his arm. Assuming the Sikhs had mutinied, the European gunners opened fire on them, causing the whole regiment to scatter.

The mutineers at once fled the station in the direction of Oudh. But elements from all three native regiments remained loyal, including more than two hundred Sikhs – some of whom formed the treasury guard – and fourteen sepoys of the 37th who were guarding the paymaster's compound. Lieutenant Glasse, the adjutant of the Sikhs, thought that the fidelity of the treasury guard, in particular, was proof that the regiment had 'no design of joining the plans of the mutineers'. But he was also prepared to concede that 'a certain number out of such a body, comprising, as it did, several Poorbeahs in the superior ranks, must have cherished a mutinous spirit'. In a similar vein some of the loyal sepoys of the 37th told Spottiswoode that the 'majority of the men were entirely ignorant of the intentions of the turbulent characters' and that more would have remained loyal if they had not been shot at indiscriminately. As proof of this, the company on detached duty at Chunar stayed loyal even after hearing of the mutiny at Benares. The detachment of two companies of Sikhs at Jaunpur, on the other hand, rose up and murdered their European officer when they received the news.

The mutiny at Benares is yet another example of how a disgruntled minority was able to manipulate the majority by playing on their fears and credulity. The cry that Europeans were coming to do them harm was repeated in many other mutinies. It had probably been agreed by conspirators beforehand as the best way to win over waverers. But the fact that so many were convinced is yet more evidence of a breakdown of trust between the officers and their troops. The confidence of the 37th in Spottiswoode cannot have been helped by his absence for twenty of the previous twenty-two years on furlough and detached duty with the Stud Department. Canning, however, was convinced that the whole affair had been mismanaged. 'It was done hurriedly and not judiciously,' he informed Vernon Smith. 'A portion of a regiment of Sikhs was drawn into resistance who had they been properly dealt with would I fully believe have remained faithful.' Ponsonby, he continued, had 'lost his head & his nerve', while Neill was 'out of his element'.

The mutiny at Benares and the subsequent unrest in the outlying districts unleashed a terrible European backlash. Rows of gallows were erected the day after the rising and were soon filled with scores of suspected rebels. Colonel Neill has generally been blamed for this indiscriminate bloodshed. But he left for Allahabad on 9 June and was not responsible for some of the harsher sentences, including the hanging of 'some young boys, who, perhaps, in mere sport had flaunted rebel colours and gone about beating tom-toms'. The real culprits were the civilian officials who had been empowered by a recent piece of legislation, Act XIV of 6 July 1857, to execute any Indian even suspected of fomenting rebellion. The Act not only made the crime of 'exciting mutiny or sedition in the army' punishable by death; it also gave courts martial the power to try civilians and the supreme and local governments the authority to appoint special commissioners to try, 'with absolute and final power of judgement and execution', any 'crime against the state' or any offence 'attended with great personal violence'. At the same time volunteer hanging parties were roaming the Benares area with one gentleman executioner boasting of the 'artistic manner' in which he had strung up his victims in 'the form of a figure of eight'.

*

About 70 miles up-river from Benares, at the confluence of the Ganges and the Jumna, lies the city of Allahabad. It too was a popular pilgrim destination, though the city itself had little to recommend it apart from 'a few brick buildings without any kind of ornament'. Yet its 'lofty and extensive' fort, sited on the tongue of land formed by the meeting of the two great rivers, was of immense strategic and logistical importance. It not only commanded the navigation of both rivers but also the passage of the Grand Trunk Road, and contained the second largest magazine in India. It was, in effect, the gateway to the Doab.

News of the mutiny at Benares reached Allahabad on 5 June. That same day an order was received from General Wheeler at Cawnpore 'to man the fort with every available European, and make a good stand'. The authorities had already ordered all women and children into the fort, along with a hundred male volunteers. The only other Europeans in the fort were sixty artillery pensioners, sent over from Chunar, and a handful of Commissariat and magazine sergeants. The rest of the fort's garrison was made up of four hundred Sikhs of the Ferozepore Regiment, recently arrived from Mirzapur, and a company of the 6th Native Infantry. The majority of the 6th were in their lines, three miles to the north, with a battery of Indian artillery. Also in the vicinity, guarding the approaches to the station, was a squadron of the 3rd Oudh Irregular Cavalry sent down by Sir Henry Lawrence to assist the civil authorities.

When the news came in from Benares, Colonel Simpson of the 6th sent two of his companies and two guns to guard the bridge-of-boats over the Ganges in case the mutineers attempted to enter the Doab. He was not in the least bit concerned about his own men, who, only a day earlier, had been congratulated by the Governor-General for offering to serve against the Delhi rebels. When the general order containing Canning's response was read out at a parade in the early evening of 6 June, the sepoys of the 6th responded with 'European cheers' and declared their readiness to die for the '*Kampani Bahadoor*'. Three hours later they were murdering their officers.

The mutiny was started by the companies on duty at the bridge-of-boats. Shortly before nine a sepoy appeared in the regiment's lines and told his comrades 'that the Europeans were coming to disarm them'. Soon after, the detachment and the guns arrived without orders from the ghat and the regiment erupted. Five officers, including the adjutant, were shot down on the parade-ground. The fort adjutant and an engineer officer were also killed. But the most tragic murders were of seven rosy-cheeked ensigns, fresh from England, who were awaiting postings to various regiments. Four were shot down as they left the 6th's mess house; the other three made it to the quarter-guard, where they were discovered and bayoneted. However one, a sixteen-year-old named Arthur Cheek, did not die immediately. Though severely wounded he managed to drag himself to a ravine, where the only sustenance was water from a stream. Five days later, barely alive, he was found by some civilian rebels and incarcerated with a Christian convert. Tormented by a severe stomach wound, he called out continually for water; yet he still found the strength to shore up his companion's crumbling faith. 'Oh my friend,' he declared, 'whatever may come to us, do not deny Lord Jesus.' His faith seemed to have been rewarded on 16 June when the two of them were handed over to the authorities at the fort. But it was too late for Cheek, who died that evening 'from exposure and the long neglect of his wounds'.

The fort had been saved on the 6th by the presence of the invalid artillerymen and the 'cool courage' of Lieutenant Brayser, the commandant of the Sikh detachment, who managed by force of personality to prevent his wavering troops from joining the rising. With their loyalty assured, it was possible to disarm and expel the company of the 6th. Yet outside the fort the disorder spread unchecked. No sooner had the Indian troops risen than they were joined by the mainly Muslim population of the city who, roused by a handsome young *maulvi* named Liaqat Ali, indulged in an all-night orgy of death and destruction. The gaol was opened, the treasury plundered, the telegraph wires torn down, and the railway works destroyed. Those Europeans and Eurasians unfortunate enough to stumble into the path of the mob were instantly butchered. 'Foremost in the commission of these atrocities were the pensioners,' read one contemporary account. 'These men, unable from their infirmities to fight, were not thereby precluded from inflicting tortures of the most diabolical nature.'

Many of the mutinous sepoys left Allahabad the following morning: some for their homes, some to serve the King at Delhi and some to Cawnpore. This absence of a common purpose emphasizes the extent to which this and other mutinies took many sepoys by surprise. One Eurasian drummer, who was forced to accompany a jemadar and two hundred sepoys to Cawnpore, wrote later: 'I saw one or two native officers crying, and heard them say that three or four budmashes [*badmashes*] had ruined the regiment. I heard that many of the sepoys were sorry, and some of them went direct to their homes. The havildar-major was at first sorry, but said it could not be helped, and therefore persuaded the men to go to Delhi.'

Even with the bulk of the mutineers gone, the British remained shut up in the fort, allowing Maulvi Liaqat Ali to rule the city in the name of the King of Delhi. According to one Indian witness, he 'began to make appointments of *Kotwal*, *Tahsildar*, *Thanadar* and officers of the army', while the green flag of Islam was raised over the *kotwali*. Yet the Muslim gentry of the city refused to join the Maulvi's jihad: the Shias because, according to their religion, a jihad had to be led by a 'Prophet and Imam'; whereas the Sunnis were kept back 'on the ground that it was a political rebellion and not a *Jihad* or a religious war'.

The Maulvi's brief rule was brought to an end shortly after the arrival of Colonel Neill with fifty-four of his Madras Fusiliers on 11 June. Neill had sent Lieutenant Arnold and fifty men on ahead and they reached Allahabad during the evening of 7 June. But the bridge-of-boats was in rebel hands and Arnold was forced to wait two days for a river-steamer before he could cross the river and enter the fort. Even then the situation was desperate, with the garrison short of food and most of the Sikh troops permanently drunk on plundered liquor. Neill's appearance, after an exhausting two-day journey in burning heat, could not have been more welcome. 'Thank God, sir,' said the sentry on the gate, 'You'll save us yet.'

And so he would – but first he had to regain his strength. 'I was quite done up by my dash from Benares, and getting into the Fort in that noonday heat,' he informed his wife. 'I was so exhausted for days, that I was obliged to lie down constantly . . . For several days I drank champagne and water to keep me.' Yet his incapacity did not prevent him from directing the bombardment and recapture of the rebel-held suburb of Darya Ganj and the nearby bridge-of-boats on 12 June. A day later he drove the rebels out of a village on the left bank. On the 14th, however, he could do 'little or nothing' as 'all the soldiers, Europeans and Sikhs, were drinking to excess'. His solution was to get Lieutenant Brayser to convince his Sikhs that there would be more opportunity for plunder if they camped outside the fort; he also arranged for the Commissariat to buy up the excess liquor. A day later, with the women and children packed off to Calcutta in a steamer, he was able to resume his attacks on the rebel villages.

On 16 June, deserted by most of his followers, the Maulvi left the city with a small escort for Cawnpore. The following day, the magistrate proceeded to the *kotwali* and resumed his old authority. The British were back in control, and their retribution was, if anything, even more brutal than it had been at Benares. Hundreds of suspected rebels were hanged and 'some on slight proofs of criminality'. 'God grant I may have acted with justice,' wrote Neill on 17 June. 'I know I have with severity, but under all the circumstances I trust for forgiveness. I have done all for the good of my country, to re-establish its prestige and power, and to put down this most barbarous, inhuman insurrection.' The civil authorities were every bit as brutal. On 20 June the Commissioner of Allahabad authorized a subordinate to 'arrest all suspected and suspicious persons, and in case of their offering resistance to slay them'. The inevitable result of devolving too much power was its abuse. A private letter, written from Allahabad on 6 July, stated that an unnamed civil officer 'has adopted a policy of burning villages, which is, in my opinion, the most suicidal and mischievous that can be devised; it prevents the possibility of order being restored; the aged, women and children are sacrificed, as well as those guilty of rebellion'. The letter continued: 'Cultivation is impossible; a famine is consequently almost certain. The sternest measures are doubtless necessary, and every possible endeavour should be made to apprehend and punish those actually engaged in plunder or rebellion, but here there seems to be no discrimination.'

Part of the problem, according to the same anonymous correspondent, was the number of 'lawless and reckless Europeans' at Allahabad. He added: 'One of them cocked his pistol at Captain Brasyer in the fort: the ruffian was as likely as not to have pulled the trigger, and in that case, as Captain Brasyer himself observed to me, his Sikhs would have slain every European in the fort. This was before Colonel Neill took the command: if it had happened in his time, the probability is that the offender would have been tried and hanged.'

When Canning learnt of the indiscriminate spirit of revenge that was abroad in upper India, he issued his infamous 'Resolution' of 31 July. It was, in effect, a series of guidelines on how the civil authorities were to adminster Act XIV. Its main aim was to distinguish between sepoys from regiments that had mutinied and committed bloodshed, and those who were apprehended unarmed and whose regiments were innocent of atrocities. Canning wanted deserters or mutineers in these last categories to be tried by formal military tribunals. He also wanted provision to be made for those who could prove they were not present when a particular murder or outrage took place. The Resolution was never intended for public consumption. But inevitably a copy found its way into the Calcutta and English newspapers. It was savaged in both countries. The editor of one English-language Indian paper wrote: 'Lenity towards any portion of the conspirators is misplaced, impolitic and iniquitous, and is calculated to excite contempt and invite attack on every side, by showing to the world the Government of India . . . allows the blood of English and Christian subjects of Her Majesty to flow in torrents, and their wives, sisters and daughters to be outraged and dishonoured without adequate retribution.' *The Times* in London was less hysterical but censorious all the same. 'It really is a most amiable and beautiful document,' stated its facetious leader. 'We presume it must be called the "Clemency of CANNING", though it is our own private belief that the suggestion, as well as the composition, is due rather to the other members of the Government. It is a series of resolutions of the most humane and considerate character, taken in Council, and proclaimed to the whole world, in the form of a letter to the Civil Authorities of the North-West Provinces of Bengal. The humanity and consideration are for the sole benefit of the mutineers.' Thus was coined the unfair epithet, 'Clemency Canning', which would distort the posthumous reputation of a first-rate Governor-General. Yet the newspapers were simply reflecting the dominant mood of public opinion in England which, outraged by the sufferings of friends and relations, was demanding a ruthless policy of vengeance and reprisal. Canning, on the other hand, was all too aware of the danger of alienating ordinary Indians at a time when the outcome of the rebellion was still in the balance. 'As long as I have breath in my body,' he told Lord Granville, 'I will pursue no other policy than that which I have been following – not only for the reason of expediency . . . but because it is just. I will not govern in anger.'

He was preaching to the converted. Of the 'Clemency' Resolution, Granville wrote: 'I never liked any document so much. I would have gone to India and back, and considered that I had done my duty gloriously by the simple penning of and issuing it.' In response to hostile press reports, Granville used the opportunity of a dinner at the Mansion House to make a speech in Canning's favour. But his fellow Cabinet members were not so quick to defend the Governor-General. Canning complained to Granville: 'From nobody but yourself, Vernon Smith and [the Duke of] Argyll, have I had a helping hand since troubles began . . . Palmerston has never uttered a word of defence or approval. I am inclined to think he did not approve, at the time, of what was done about the China force, but if so he ought to have told me.'

If the home government as a whole was less than supportive, Queen Victoria was the opposite. In response to a long letter from Canning explaining his policy of moderation, she replied:

> Lord Canning will easily believe how entirely the Queen shares *his* feelings of sorrow & indignation at the unchristian spirit shown – alas! also to a great extent here

– by the public towards Indians in general & towards *Sepoys without discrimination.* It is however not likely to last and comes from the *horror produced* by the *unspeakable* atrocities perpetrated against the innocent women & children which really makes one's blood run cold. For the perpetrators of these awful horrors *no* punishment can be severe enough &, sad as it is, stern justice must be dealt out to all the guilty ones.

But to the native at large, to the peaceable inhabitants, to the many kind & friendly ones who have assisted us, sheltered the fugitives & been faithful and true – these should be shown the greatest kindness. They should know there is no hatred of brown skin.

Colonel Neill, meanwhile, was devoting only part of his energies at Allahabad to rooting out rebels. Of more concern to him was the plight of the Cawnpore garrison, and he did everything in his power to speed up its relief. He was frustrated by the Commissariat Department's inability to replace the supplies and transport that had been plundered or driven off during the brief period of rebel rule at Allahabad. On 23 June he informed Calcutta that it would be at least another four days before he was ready to depart for Cawnpore with a lightly equipped force of four hundred European infantry, three hundred Sikhs, a hundred cavalry and two guns. But a sudden attack of cholera in the fort deprived Neill of no less than seventy men and it was not until 30 June that the column, under the command of Major Renaud of the Madras Fusiliers, finally departed. Captain Spurgin with a hundred infantrymen and two 6-pounders left on 1 July aboard a steamer with instructions to rescue as many sick, wounded, women and children from Wheeler's entrenchment as possible. If Cawnpore had already fallen – which of course it had – Spurgin was to link up with Renaud. Neill later exonerated the Commissariat for the delayed departure of the relief force, noting that the officer in command had done all he could to solve the supply problem. Yet the lack of camp-followers and doolie-bearers, so necessary for the movement of any European army in India, was caused by the ferocious British response to the rising for which Neill himself was partly responsible. 'Everywhere,' wrote Kaye, 'the terror-stricken Natives stood aloof from the chastising Englishmen.'

Neill had perhaps learnt from his mistakes because his instructions to Renaud were remarkably restrained. 'Attack and destroy all places en route close to the road occupied by the enemy,' he wrote, 'but touch no others; encourage the inhabitants to return, and instil confidence into all of the restoration of British authority.' Only those suspected of being rebels –

particularly sepoys from mutinous regiments who were not able to give a good account of themselves – were to be executed. But mistakes were inevitable. One officer who followed in Renaud's wake recalled:

In the first two days of our march towards Cawnpore we passed several dead bodies hanging from trees by the road-side. These had been executed by Renaud's men, presumably for complicity in the mutiny; but I am afraid some innocent men suffered; a comrade who ought to know said that 'Renaud was rather inclined to hang *all black creation*'. In every case, where the feet were near the ground, pigs (either wild or belonging to the villagers) had eaten the lower parts of the bodies; the stench from the latter, in the moist still air, was intolerable.

By now Neill, much to his fury, had been superseded as commander of the Cawnpore relief force by the man destined to become the greatest British hero of the mutiny: Brigadier-General Henry Havelock. Born in Sunderland, the son of a rich shipowner who later fell on hard times, Havelock had planned to become a lawyer and, after leaving Charterhouse, trained for a time in a special pleader's office. But when his father cut off his allowance, he asked his elder brother, who had done well at Waterloo, to arrange a commission for him in the 95th Foot.

Even in the army, Havelock's diligence and scholarly instincts were evident: he was determined to master the science of war and his laborious study of the campaigns of Marlborough, Frederick the Great and Napoleon so exasperated his fellow subalterns that they used to throw his books out of the window. When his father lost the remnants of his fortune in 1823, Havelock decided to transfer to a regiment bound for India, where hard-up officers had a better standard of living and a better chance of promotion. Typically, before leaving, he enrolled in the Oriental Institute to learn Persian and Hindustani. Once in India he further isolated himself from his fellow officers by his increasingly radical religious beliefs. He had always regarded himself as a 'Christian' soldier and the first troops he commanded in battle, during the First Burma War, were known as 'Havelock's Saints'. In 1829 he married the daughter of Dr Marshman, the famous Baptist missionary, and thereafter devoted much time to the 'spiritual welfare of his men', holding religious meetings, preaching sermons and giving Bible lessons.

Unable to buy promotion, it took Havelock twenty-three years to become a captain. The logjam was broken by his daring exploits in the First Afghan and Gwalior Wars, which won him a CB and promotion without purchase to lieutenant-colonel. Havelock's reputation as a staff officer *par excellence* resulted in successive appointments as quartermaster-general and adjutant-general of the Queen's troops in India. His first operational command, that of a division in Sir James Outram's Persian Expeditionary Force, did not arise until late 1856. But Havelock did well during his brief stint in Persia, and it was he who planned the successful capture of Mohamerah on the Euphrates. The Indian government was particularly fortunate that the war ended when it did, for it not only released much needed European reinforcements but also commanders of the experience and talent of Outram and Havelock to fight the mutineers.

Havelock reached Calcutta on 17 June aboard the same ship that brought Sir Patrick Grant, the acting Commander-in-Chief, from Madras. The coincidence was to Havelock's advantage because Grant, an old comrade-in-arms, at once told Canning: 'Your Excellency, I have brought you the man.' Years earlier Lord Hardinge had remarked: 'If India is ever in danger, the Government have only to put Havelock in command of an army, and it will be saved.' India was in danger, and Havelock was given the Cawnpore relief force. As well as the troops under Renaud and Spurgin, the command included a new column being formed at Allahabad from an artillery battery and two infantry regiments that had served under Havelock in Persia: the 64th Foot and 78th Highlanders. He was instructed, 'after quelling all disturbances at Allahabad, to lose not a moment in supporting Sir Henry Lawrence at Lucknow, and Sir Hugh Wheeler at Cawnpore', and to 'take prompt measures for dispersing and utterly destroying all mutineers and insurgents'. The situation was too fluid for his instructions to be more precise and, in any case, Grant had 'entire confidence in his well-known and often proved high ability, vigour and judgment'.

Some were not so sure. 'An old fossil, dug up and only fit to be turned into pipe-clay,' declared one critic. Havelock's age and appearance did not help. He was sixty-two years old, barely five feet high, with a pinched, leathery face and hair that had long since gone white. He wore an old-fashioned beard and insisted on dining with all his medals 'as if he carried his money tied up in a bunch on his shoulders'. And yet he retained an alertness and vigour that inspired confidence. 'General Havelock is not in fashion,' wrote Lady Canning, 'but all the same we believe he will do well. No doubt he is fussy and tiresome, but his little, old, stiff figure looks as active and fit for use as if he were made of steel.' Havelock was content to put his trust in the Lord. 'May God give me wisdom to fulfil the expectations of Government,' he wrote to his wife, Hannah, 'and to restore tranquillity to the disturbed provinces.' But it was worldly, logistical difficulties that preoccupied him most as he left Calcutta by horse-*dâk* on 25 June: in particular the scarcity of guns, European artillerymen and draught animals.

On 30 June, after a punishing five-day journey, Havelock reached Allahabad and relieved Neill of his command. He intended to advance with the new column as soon as it was ready, while Neill remained behind as commander of the Allahabad garrison. But within twenty-four hours came the catastrophic news, in the form of a message from Sir Henry Lawrence, that Cawnpore had already fallen. At first it was not believed, but confirmation arrived in the early hours of 3 July. At dawn Havelock telegraphed the acting Commander-in-Chief: 'The news of the entire destruction of the Cawnpore force confirmed by cossid who, carrying letters from Lucknow to Allahabad, witnessed it.' The response was addressed to Neill. 'If you are satisfied of the truth of the account given by the cossid,' wrote Grant, 'you should halt Renaud's force until Havelock's column can support him.' Neill was not satisfied, but he no longer gave the orders. 'General Havelock has halted Renaud's force,' he informed Grant. 'I would not, as it is strong enough for anything that could be brought against it; and if the report is true, should move on steadily to [Fatehpur], to be there overtaken by the General.' As it happened Renaud, in the face of conflicting orders,* decided to continue his advance. By 10 July he had reached Arrahpur, just ten miles from Fatehpur. There he learned that Havelock's column was within five miles and would join him the following morning. But he was determined to press on and relieve Fatehpur, which, an Indian spy had assured him, was being held by only a few rebel matchlockmen. In truth a powerful rebel army, led by Brigadier Jwala Prasad, was rapidly approaching Fatehpur from Cawnpore.

Nana Sahib's raj had got off to a good start on 27 June, the day of the ghat massacre, with a grand review on the plain near Savada House. He praised his advisers, in particular Azimullah Khan and Jwala Prasad, by saying that 'it was to their wisdom that so easy a conquest was owing'. Bala congratulated the troops and promised them a reward of a lakh of rupees. In response the artillery gave the Nana the twenty-one-gun royal salute that the British had so long denied him.

On 1 July, the Nana returned to Bithur for his coronation. That afternoon

* Sir Patrick Grant, influenced by Neill, had sent orders for Renaud to 'push on' to Cawnpore.

he was seated on the throne of the Peshwas, sacred marks were fixed to his forehead, and salutes were fired. By his order, two proclamations were read out to joyous crowds in the illuminated cities of Bithur and Cawnpore. One declared that 'as . . . the yellow face and narrow-minded people have been sent to hell and Cawnpore has been conquered, it is necessary that all the subjects and landholders would be as obedient to the present Government as they have been to the former one'.

But real power still lay with the rebel troops at Cawnpore who were, according to one loyal Indian's diary, growing increasingly anxious about their lack of financial reward and the approach of European troops. In his memoir Nanuk Chund wrote:

> 4th July – The sepoys complain that the Nana has taken away all their treasure and gone and quartered himself at Bithoor, and they will not suffer such treatment, but will make him feel the consequences . . .
>
> 5th July – The Nana is still at Bithoor. Teeka Singh, subadar, the general of the cavalry regiment, and several sepoys . . . have gone to Bithoor to fetch the Nana.
>
> 7th July – There is a great commotion to-day in the rebel army, and the sepoys . . . declare that if the Nana does not come back to-day, they will release the Nunny Nawab from confinement, and place him on the *guddee*. The rebel force further declares that their enemy (the British) is about to come up, and it is necessary to go up to Bithoor, and bring the Nana away by force.
>
> 8th July – The goinda have come in and reported that Europeans and Seikhs and artillery have left Allahabad, and would come in shortly . . . The rebels are in great alarm. Baba Bhut, Jwala Pershad and Azeemoollah are doing their best to get ready the magazine, carriage, and supplies.
>
> 10th July – My servant came from Cawnpoor and stated . . . that he had *certain* news that the Nana had returned to the city and the camel-sowar had returned and reported that Europeans were coming up . . . and had reached Moorutgunge; also that the Europeans hang people as they come along . . .

If Nanuk Chund's information was impeccable, his recollection of dates was sometimes a little hazy, The rebel army – about 3,500 strong* under Jwala Prasad, with Teeka Singh commanding the cavalry and Tatya Tope the

* Including representatives from the following units: the 1st, 6th, 10th, 12th, 53rd and 56th Native Infantry; the 4th and 5th Oudh Irregular Infantry; two half-regiments of newly raised infantry from Cawnpore; the 2nd Light Cavalry; the 13th and 14th Irregular Cavalry; No. 18 Field Battery; some *zemindars* from the Cawnpore district with their retainers.

Commissariat – actually left Cawnpore on 9 July. The following day it was in striking distance of Fatehpur. Unaware of the danger, Major Renaud was closing in on the city from the opposite direction.

Only General Havelock could avert a catastrophe. His column of 1,185 men and six guns had finally left Allahabad on 7 July in pouring rain. The sun came out the following morning and for the next three days the column proceeded by regular marches, its commander not wanting to overwork his men until they were acclimatized to the heat. But all this changed on 10 July, when Havelock learnt that Renaud was in imminent danger of being overwhelmed by a vastly superior rebel force. He at once ordered his troops to press on, and, after a series of heroic forced marches in blistering heat, they caught up with Renaud on the road to Fatehpur in the early hours of 12 July. 'We drew up in line by the side of the road to receive them,' recalled one of Renaud's officers. 'Up came the brave band, the 78th Highlanders playing on their bagpipes the "Campbells are coming", while all along our line a cheer arose as we welcomed them.' The combined force of 1,403 Europeans, 560 Indians and eight guns then continued on to Betinda, four miles from Fatehpur, where it camped on an open plain. 'Arms were piled on line, ground was taken up for each corps, and the weary, wayworn men, overcome by oppressive heat and brilliant sunshine, lay down in groups.'

Lieutenant-Colonel Fraser-Tytler, the deputy quartermaster-general, and the volunteer cavalry were sent ahead to reconnoitre. Near the bridge on the outskirts of the city they were confronted by the mounted vanguard of the Nana's army. 'We retired slowly along the road,' recalled one officer volunteer, 'the cannon balls flying on each side of us.' As they neared the camp, closely followed by the rebel army, the alarm was sounded. 'The troops all fell out so quickly and steadily,' wrote another volunteer, 'it was quite charming to see them. The camp was beautifully laid out, the guns in the centre of the road, and the troops on both sides, so they had only to move from their tents to come to the front. Out they came eager for the fray, like so many bull dogs, and as jolly as possible, although just off a long march.'

Convinced they only had Renaud's small force to contend with, the rebel commanders hastened to attack without properly deploying their troops. Two guns and some cavalry and infantry were pushed to the front in an attempt to outflank the British position. Havelock made no countermoves beyond posting three hundred men of the 64th, armed with Enfield rifles, in an advanced copse. 'But the enemy maintained his attack,' reported Havelock, 'with the audacity which his first supposition had inspired and my inertness fostered. It would have injured the *morale* of my troops to permit them thus to be bearded, so I determined at once to bring on an action.'

The eight British guns, mostly 9-pounders under Captain Francis Maude, R.A., were deployed in the centre of the line, protected by a hundred riflemen of the 64th. The rest of the infantry was formed slightly to the rear in quarter-distance columns, while the volunteer horse and loyal members of the 13th Irregular Cavalry guarded the flanks. Opening fire at a range of 800 yards, the British artillery soon disabled the forward rebel battery. As the supporting rebel infantry fell back in confusion, the British guns were limbered up and moved forward. This prompted the sepoys to turn and reform, while a large body of rebel cavalry advanced down the road. Again the guns were deployed, and one salvo was enough to scatter the rebel horse and foot.

The sepoys tried to make a stand at their principal battery on the road further back. But Maude, rehitching his guns to their bullocks, was dogged in his pursuit through the increasingly swampy terrain. Once in range he engaged the enemy guns. To their rear was a large body of infantry and in its midst, gesturing frantically, was one of their commanders on a richly caparisoned elephant. Fraser-Tytler urged Maude to knock him over. 'Accordingly, I dismounted,' wrote Maude, 'and laid the guns myself, a nine-pounder, at "line of metal" (700 yards range) and, as luck would have it, my first shot went in under the beast's tail and came out of his chest, of course rolling it over, and giving its rider a bad fall . . . It was said at the time that the man on the elephant was Tatya Tope, who afterwards showed some courage and a great deal of military aptitude, giving us a lot of trouble. But his fall that day certainly completed the panic of the enemy.'

On seeing one of their commanders fall, the rebels abandoned their guns and fell back. 'In succession they were driven by skirmishers and columns from the garden enclosures,' wrote Havelock, 'from a strong barricade on the road, from the town wall, into and through, out of and beyond, the town.' About a mile from Fatehpur they attempted to make a final stand. By now the British troops were in 'such a state of exhaustion' that Havelock 'almost despaired' of being able to drive the enemy further. To keep up the pressure the ninety-five irregular sowars under Lieutenant Palliser were pushed to the front. But they showed their true colours when confronted by just thirty mutineers of the 2nd Cavalry, instantly recognizable in their French-grey tunics. 'On seeing the enemy,' recalled an officer present, 'Palliser called the men to charge, and dashed on; but the scoundrels scarcely altered their speed, and met the enemy at the same speed that they came down upon us.' He added:

[The rebels'] design was evident. They came waving their swords to our men, and riding round our party making signs to them to come over to their side. We could not dash out upon them, as we were only four [Europeans] to their thirty [riders] . . . One or two [rebels] came in at us, and one or two blows were exchanged. Palliser was unseated by his horse swerving suddenly, and then the row commenced. The 2nd Cavalry tried to get at him, and his Native officers closed round him to save him, and they certainly fought like good men and true – the few of them.

By the time the main body of the enemy's cavalry appeared, most of Palliser's rear files had turned tail and the few who had been prepared to fight had no option but to follow.

The damage of this minor reverse was repaired by Maude's guns and the riflemen of the Madras Fusiliers. 'Their fire soon put the enemy to final and irretrievable flight,' recorded Havelock, 'and my force took up its present position in triumph.' But even in victory the British took no prisoners. Maude was passing the elephant he had killed with a roundshot when he saw a fusilier walk up to a badly wounded sepoy and cock his rifle. 'The poor creature joined his hands together, crying piteously "*Amân! Amân!* (Pardon!)"', recalled Maude. 'I added an entreaty that a wounded man should not be shot. But [Captain] Beatson overruled me, saying sternly that there would be "no mercy shown in that campaign". Accordingly the fusilier promptly blew the man's brains out.'

That night Havelock wrote to his wife: 'One of the prayers oft repeated throughout my life since my school days has been answered, and I have lived to command in a successful action. The enemy sallied forth and insulted my camp . . . We fought, and in ten minutes' time the affair was decided. But away with vainglory! Thanks to Almighty God, who gave me victory. I captured in four hours eleven guns, and scattered the whole enemy's force to the winds.'

In fact Havelock had captured ten guns and two mortars, and routed a numerically superior force at a cost of just five dead, four wounded and four missing. It was a stunning victory due in no small part to the fact that two of Havelock's partial regiments – the 1st Madras Fusiliers and the 64th Foot – were equipped with the new Enfield rifle, the weapon whose greased cartridges were supposed to have sparked the mutiny in the first place. Even the columns made up of other units were preceded by skirmishers armed with the Enfield. The rifle was accurate up to 800 yards, four times the effective range of the Brown Bess musket, and the advantage it gave British troops was as much psychological as tactical. The other key factor was the mobility and accuracy of the British artillery, which was able to provide the advancing infantry with constant close support. The combined effect of the disciplined British cannon and rifle fire was to disrupt the enemy formations before they got anywhere near close-quarter fighting. Havelock wrote later: 'In [the first] ten minutes the affair was decided.'

On 14 July, after a day's rest, Havelock's column marched unopposed to Kalyanpur, where his Indian irregular cavalry were disarmed and dismounted. In addition to their disgraceful behaviour at the Battle of Fatehpur, they had created a panic during the march from Fatehpur by trying to drive off the baggage animals. The European troops got their own back by looting the sowars' private property.

The following day the column fought and won two minor engagements en route to the Pandu Nadi River, 22 miles from Cawnpore. During the first, an assault on a strongly entrenched position at the village of Aong, Major Renaud was badly wounded in the thigh and died after his leg was amputated below the knee. The second took place at the stone bridge over the Pandu Nadi with Captain Maude and the riflemen of the Madras Fusiliers again to the fore. Havelock's casualties were one killed, one mortally wounded (Renaud) and twenty-three wounded.

On 16 July a 16-mile march under a blazing sun brought the British column to the village of Maharajpur, within six miles of Cawnpore. There Havelock discovered that the rebels had taken up a strong position two miles ahead at Aherwa, where the Grand Trunk Road forked with the road that led to the cantonment. 'His entrenchments cut and rendered impassable both roads,' noted the British commander, 'and his guns, seven in number, two light and five of siege calibre, were disposed along his position which consists of a series of villages . . . It was evident that an attack in front would expose the British to a murderous fire from [the Nana's] heavy guns sheltered in his entrenchment. I resolved therefore to manoeuvre to turn his left.'

Having paused for a couple of hours' rest at Maharajpur, the column resumed its march up the Grand Trunk Road at one thirty in the afternoon, 'dreadfully tired, and with the sun fearfully bright'. Captain Maude recalled:

> We had not gone five hundred yards before the men began to fall out, lying down on the right and left of the road. Several of them died from sunstroke; others, who were not able to stagger back to the baggage, were cut to pieces by the enemy's cavalry, who had come down between us, when we made our flank movement.

When we came within about a mile of their position, we moved off the road to the right, and though we were a little too near them when we executed this movement, and so lost several men of our column by the fire of their heavy guns, yet we succeeded in turning their left flank, and as soon as we had done so we came into action, at nine hundred yards' range, and commenced to engage the guns upon their left.

Havelock now ordered his troops to attack the rebel left in echelon of regiments, screened by riflemen skirmishers. The 78th Highlanders were the first into action, as Havelock, anxious to test their mettle, gave them the task of capturing three rebel guns that were 'strongly posted' in a village to the left of the cantonment road. 'As they approached the village,' wrote their admiring commander, 'they cheered and charged with the bayonet, the pipes sounding the pibroch; need I add that the enemy fled, the village was taken, and the guns captured?' After a short pause while the Highlanders reformed, the general pointed to the neighbouring village where the bulk of the rebels had rallied and shouted, 'Now, Highlanders, another charge like that wins the day!' They responded with a roar and, supported by the 64th, drove the rebels from their formidable central position. Here the exhausted Scots were halted and it was left to the 64th, 84th and Sikhs to race on and take the village of Aherwa and three guns on the extreme right of the rebel front. In all these assaults the infantry were greatly assisted by accurate counter-battery fire from Maude's guns, one cannonball actually slicing a piece out of a rebel gun muzzle 'like a scoop of cheese'.

With the rebels in full retreat, Havelock ordered Captain Lousada Barrow and his seventeen volunteer horsemen to harry them. As the volunteers moved forward, they were confronted by a far larger body of rebel horse, mainly 2nd Cavalry, who were covering the fleeing sepoys. Undeterred, Barrow and his men made straight for the enemy sowars, causing them to turn and fly. 'Give point, lads,' shouted Barrow, 'damn cuts and guards!' On they galloped in pursuit, emptying a dozen rebel saddles before their own casualties – one killed, one wounded and four horses disabled – forced them to rein in. As they rode back the British infantry greeted them with a cheer and Havelock exclaimed: 'Well done, gentlemen Volunteers, I am proud to command you.'

But the battle was far from over. A large number of rebels had rallied for a second time in a village between the Grand Trunk Road and the Cawnpore road. By now the artillery cattle were so exhausted that Maude's guns were left on the Grand Trunk Road near the centre of the original rebel position while the infantry advanced alone. Leading them was the familiar small but spry figure of Havelock. 'Come, who'll take this village?' he challenged. 'The Highlanders or 64th?' The response was inevitable as the two regiments charged together and cleared the village. On reforming, the infantry columns were amazed to see the whole rebel army drawn up in battle array on either side of a 24-pounder sited on the Cawnpore road. As the enemy drums and horns sounded their defiance, the rebel commander could be seen riding among his troops, exhorting them to one last effort. It was none other than Nana Sahib himself, desperate to do all he could to prevent his ten-day-old raj from coming to a premature end.

Havelock at once ordered his weary troops to lie down as a rider was dispatched to bring forward the artillery. 'Whilst in this position,' wrote Major Bingham of the 64th, 'we were exposed to a dreadful fire from the guns in our front, 24 pounders and some 9 pounders as well as a heavy fire of musketry on our right flank and rear, a 24 pounder shot struck my regiment and killed and wounded seven men. We were therefore ordered to retire nearer to the village which we had just taken and to lie down under shelter of an embankment; which we did. The wounded men's groans were dreadful to hear.' Yet still there was no sign of artillery support. Maude explained why:

Just then there came an order for us to 'advance'. This, with our tired bullocks and men, the fearfully heavy ground in front of us, and also in view of our previously received order, I at first hesitated to do. I turned to Stuart Beatson, who was lying on one of my wagons, and asked him what he advised. He said he 'thought it would be better to wait a little', but at that moment Hargood came up with a pressing order to advance to the succour of the infantry, saying that he thought he could pick out a fairly good bit of road. So we limbered up and plunged into the sodden ground. If the cavalry, who were close to us, had possessed one atom of dash, they could have taken the whole of our eight guns at that moment without losing a dozen men. However, as it was, we most providentially arrived in time to prevent an attack upon our tired handful of infantry by the whole force of the enemy, who, seeing them without artillery, and lying down, were re-forming in beautiful order. On our again coming up with the force, we were loudly cheered by them, and the whole line advanced at that moment.

Havelock's report of the battle paints a slightly different picture. 'My artillery cattle wearied by the length of the march could not bring up the guns to my assistance, and the 1st Madras Fusiliers, 64th, 84th and 78th

Detachments, formed in line, were exposed to a heavy fire from the 24-pounder on the road. I was resolved this state of things should not last, so calling upon my men, who were lying down in line, to leap on their feet, I directed another advance. It was irresistible. The enemy sent round shot into our ranks, until we were within three hundred yards, and then poured in grape with such precision and determination as I have seldom witnessed.' But gallantly led on by Major Stirling and Lieutenant Harry Havelock,* the general's son and aide-de-camp, the 64th charged and captured the 24-pounder. On seeing this the rebels 'lost all heart, and after a hurried fire of musketry gave way in total rout'. Only now did four of Maude's guns appear to hasten the rebels' departure with a 'heavy cannonade'. If Havelock was unimpressed by Maude's tardy arrival, he made no specific criticism in his report. Fortunately his infantry had had the dash and discipline to get him out of a hole, just as Barnard's had done at Badli-ki-Serai. Both battles had been won largely by the bayonet, proof that not all British victories in the Indian mutiny were due to the tactical use of artillery and long-range rifle fire. The close-quarter nature of the fighting at Cawnpore was reflected in the relatively heavy British casualties: six men killed (including Captain Currie, the commanding officer of the 84th) and one hundred and two wounded. The 64th Foot was the worst hit, with three officers and thirty-two men wounded, most of them during the final charge against the 24-pounder.

That night the weary British troops bivouacked without food or tents on the battlefield with the roofless artillery barracks of Wheeler's entrenchment dimly visible in the distance. An elated Havelock slept among his troops, 'my waterproof coat serving me for a couch on the damp ground'. He had good reason to be pleased. In nine days he and his men had marched 126 miles at the hottest time of year, won four pitched battles against superior numbers and captured twenty-four guns and mortars. With Cawnpore in their grasp, all thoughts now turned to the captive women and children.

Shortly before Nana Sahib's return to Cawnpore on 6 July the captives had been moved to an outbuilding in Sir George Parker's wrecked compound known as the Bibigarh. As the name suggests, it had originally been built for an officer's *bibi*, but at the time of the rising it was occupied by the magistrate's *babu*. No doubt Azimullah and his fellow rebel leaders enjoyed the cruel irony

* For this act, General Havelock recommended his son for the Victoria Cross and it was duly conferred. He did not recommend Major Stirling because he felt that he had simply been doing his duty. Instead Stirling was promoted to lieutenant-colonel without purchase.

of incarcerating British women and children in the former house of an Indian mistress. A more practical reason was that it was not far from the Old Cawnpore Hotel, which had been earmarked as the Nana's new headquarters.

Built round a central courtyard, the Bibigarh was a single-storey building that consisted of two main rooms, 10 feet by 24 feet, with square pillars and cusped arches that looked out on to an inner veranda. It also had a number of smaller rooms, including four sleeping rooms off the two main rooms, and a complex of servants' quarters where the sepoy guard lived. The Bibigarh provided ample space for a *babu* and his family, but was hopelessly inadequate to house the ever growing number of Christian women and children. For since 27 June the original number had been swelled by captured fugitives from Vibart's boat and a second flotilla from Fatehgarh to more than two hundred, the majority of them children. The only males in captivity were a handful of boys under the age of thirteen, three senior officials from Fatehgarh who had been kept alive as potential bargaining chips, an indigo planter and his son, and six Christian drummers of the 6th Native Infantry. According to Jonah Shepherd, who was being held in a separate location, the captives received 'only a small quantity of *dhall* and *chuppatties* daily for food for the first few days, after which a little meat and milk for the children was allowed, as also clean clothes were issued from those forcibly taken from the washermen of the station'. They were also allowed a sweeper woman and a *bhisti*. Yet the conditions in which they lived were still pitiful by European standards. Shepherd wrote:

It is not easy to describe, but it may be imagined, the misery of so many helpless persons, some wounded, others sick, and all labouring under the greatest agony of heart for the loss of those, so dear to them, who had so recently been killed (perhaps before their own eyes), cooped up night and day in a small low pukka-roofed house, with but four or six very small rooms, and that in the hottest season of the year, without beds or punkhas, for a whole fortnight, watched most carefully on all sides, by a set of unmannerly, brutish, rebellious sepoys.

Many Britons were convinced that some women were raped. Yet, according to one of the captive drummers, John Fitchett, they were not 'ill-treated or disgraced in any way', though they resented being made to take the air on the veranda because 'people came to look at them'. The only other indignity that Fitchett could recall was two different ladies being taken to the stables of the Old Cawnpore Hotel each day to grind gram. Even this was not particularly objectionable because they often managed to smuggle back some ground gram to give to the children. If the captives suffered physically during their time at Savada House and the Bibigarh, it was mainly through neglect. Wounds were treated with cold water and at least 'two or three women and children died daily'. The situation improved a little after Nana Sahib returned to Cawnpore and appointed an Indian doctor to attend the captives. But he could not prevent cholera and dysentery from claiming at least fourteen lives by 11 July. The daily supervision of the captives was the responsibility of a Muslim woman named Hossaini Khanum, the servant of the Nana's favourite courtesan Adla. One of four slave girls owned by Baji Rao II, she was now about thirty, tall and fair-skinned. Most people called her the 'Begum', on account of her imperious manner, and she is said to have made the prisoners' lives a misery. It was she who selected the women to grind gram; yet she was also responsible for improving the food and serving out 'fresh clothes', presumably on the Nana's orders.

The fate of the prisoners was sealed by Havelock's rapid advance. When news of the first British victory at Fatehpur reached Cawnpore on 13 July, Bala Rao hurried down to the rebel camp with reinforcements. But he was wounded in the shoulder during the reverse at Aong on 15 July and in the afternoon returned to Cawnpore, where he persuaded the Nana to hold an immediate council of war. It was attended by all his senior advisers and those who had lent money to the rebel cause. A great many schemes for checking the advance of the British were proposed: some suggested abandoning Cawnpore and joining forces with the rebel Nawab of Farrukhabad further north; others wanted to make a stand at Bithur; but the majority, 'either more courageous or desperate', wanted to fight it out at Cawnpore. This last option was eventually adopted. On the question of what to do with the prisoners, most of the Nana's advisers – including Bala, Baba Bhutt, Azimullah Khan and Tatya Tope – were in favour of murdering them. Why? Because it was assumed that 'if they were left alive, they would reveal everything, and thus everyone concerned in the rebellion at Cawnpore would be known'. Even the Nana could see the logic of this argument and, reluctantly, he gave the necessary orders.

The first to die were the two colonels and magistrate from Fatehgarh,* who are said to have told the Nana that they would 'have the fort of

* Colonel Andrew Goldie, the Bengal Army's auditor-general; Colonel George Smith, the commanding officer of the 10th Native Infantry that had mutinied at Fatehgarh on 18 June; and Robert Thornhill, the Magistrate of Fatehgarh and son of a director of the East India Company.

Allahabad given up' to him if he spared their lives. It was about four thirty in the afternoon when they, the indigo planter and his son, and the fourteen-year-old grandson of Rose Greenway were led outside the gate of the Bibigarh and shot by a squad of sepoys. Half an hour later, according to John Fitchett, the Begum 'told the ladies they were to be killed by the Nana's orders'. One of them went straight to Jemadar Yusuf Khan of the 6th Native Infantry, the commander of the sepoy guard, and asked him if the Begum were telling the truth. He replied that he had 'not received any orders, that she was not to be afraid'. Soon after one of his sepoys told the Begum that her orders 'would not be obeyed', and who was she to give orders anyway. Outraged, she went straight to the Old Cawnpore Hotel to consult with the Nana. While she was away the sepoys on guard – mainly men of the 1st and 6th Native Infantry – 'took counsel and decided that they would not lift their hands against women, though they would kill every man'. They later told Fitchett that 'they intended to save the ladies, in order that their own lives might be saved'.

The Begum returned with Tatya Tope, and his threat to have the sepoys blown from guns if they did not obey the Nana's orders seemed to do the trick. First Fitchett and the Christian drummers were removed from the house and placed in a nearby shed. Then the sepoys made a half-hearted attempt to drag the hysterical women and children into the yard. When that failed it was decided to shoot them through the shutters. At least one volley was fired into the packed room by a squad of sepoys, though a bugler insisted it was aimed at the ceiling. Sickened by their task, the sepoys would do no more. So the Begum sent word for her lover, Sarvur Khan, to bring his own execution squad. Sarvur, a burly member of the Nana's personal bodyguard, was the half-caste son of a Pathani prostitute and a soldier of the 87th Foot. The identity of his father was unknown because his mother had serviced most of the regiment, including the sergeant-major's cook, and Sarvur never forgave the British for the shame he had to endure as a child. Now was his chance for revenge. The sun was almost setting when Sarvur, wearing his red bodyguard's uniform, arrived at the Bibighar with four companions. Two of them were Muslim butchers wearing white aprons: both tall and about forty years old; one stout with a small beard and a dark, pockmarked face. The other two were Hindus in the Nana's employ, both dressed in white: one was named Souracun, a Brahman from an Ooghoo village, 'about 35 years of age, fair and tall' with 'a beard, a flat face, black eyes'; the other was about ten years older with a sallow complexion. All five were carrying *tulwars*.

John Fitchett saw them enter the Bibighar and, in the doorway, cut down the lady who had spoken to the jemadar (possibly Mrs Moore, the wife of the gallant captain). As they moved into the room and out of sight, 'fearful shrieks' could be heard coming from the building. The scene inside the Bibighar as the executioners went methodically about their work is almost too awful to contemplate. One of the Hindus later boasted that some had tried to save themselves by clinging to his feet and pleading for mercy; but he had shown them 'no pity'. Some may even have offered resistance. Yet, according to Fitchett, none of them tried to escape. At one point during the killings, Sarvur broke his sword and had to replace it with another from the nearby hotel. This too broke in a 'few minutes' and he had to fetch a third. Finally, after more than half an hour of butchery, the blood-spattered murderers left the building and locked the doors.

But not all their one hundred and ninety-seven victims* were dead. Some, despite horrific sword wounds, took a long time to die. Fitchett, who was just 15 yards from the main house, recalled that the 'groans lasted all night'. In the morning the four sweepers who lived in the compound were ordered to throw the bodies into a dry well near the house. They were dragged out one by one, stripped of their clothes and tipped down the well as a huge crowd of city people and villagers looked on from the wall of the compound. Six were found to be still alive: three women and three boys between the ages of five and seven. The women, one of whom was a 'very stout' Eurasian who had been wounded in both arms, 'prayed for the sake of God that an end might be put to their sufferings'. But as no one was prepared to act without the Nana's say-so, the women were propped against a bank near the well while a messenger was sent to the Old Cawnpore Hotel. Eventually word came back that all were to be disposed of. By this time the three little boys, with nowhere to go, were running hysterically round the well. So one of the sweepers walked up, grabbed the youngest and tossed him over the parapet. The other two soon followed, as did the three conscious women. 'No one said a word or tried to save them,' recalled Fitchett, who was watching from a distance of a hundred paces. They simply stared as the six were buried alive in a mountain of naked corpses.

When news of the defeat at Aherwa reached Cawnpore during the evening of 16 July, the 'entire population was so panic-struck that, leaving house

* 73 women and 124 children.

and property, every man that had a hand in the rebellion took to his heels'. Some 'crossed over to Lucknow from Bithoor Ghat, others went towards Delhi, and the most part of the city hid themselves in the neighbouring villages, where they were nicely robbed by the zemindars'. Many sepoys 'paid a rupee a head to the ferry to cross the river, on the banks of which they pitched away their muskets, coats, pantaloons, etc., and dispersed in different directions'. The Nana himself fled with the remnants of his army to Bithur, but not before ordering his rearguard to blow up the Cawnpore magazine. It did so as it abandoned the city during the early hours of 17 July, and so violent was the explosion that John Sherer, the former Magistrate of Fatehpur who was accompanying Havelock's column, 'experienced a slight shock, like a weak electric current, and then the mighty thunder broke in the distance, and seemed to roll towards us and around us'.

Later that morning Havelock and his troops marched the short distance to Cawnpore. At the entrance to the cantonment the vanguard came across a filthy, bearded man stumbling up the road in chains. It was none other than Jonah Shepherd, the sole male Eurasian survivor of the siege, who had been abandoned by his gaolers during the night. He provided the first authentic account of the garrison's treacherous demise, prompting an officer of the Madras Fusiliers to write home: 'The frightful massacre that was reported to have taken place, I am grieved to say, is too true.' Before long the column was looking aghast at the ruins of Wheeler's entrenchment. 'It is a couple of oblong buildings,' wrote Lieutenant Grant of the volunteer cavalry, 'in one of them the roof is completely fallen in and both are battered with round shot . . . The ground inside and out is strewed with broken bottles, old shoes, pieces of chairs, and quantities of paper, books, letters, and other documents. It was a melancholy sight and the suffering must have been more than humanity could bear.'

But it was not long before the locals revealed the location of a far greater crime: the Bibighar. Major Bingham of the 64th, one of the first officers to visit the charnel-house, noted in his diary:

> The place was literally running ankle deep in blood, ladies' hair torn from their heads was lying about the floor, in scores, torn from them in their exertions to save their lives no doubt; poor little children's shoes lying here and there, gowns and frocks and bonnets belonging to these *poor, poor* creatures scattered everywhere. But to crown all horrors, after they had been killed, and even some alive, were all thrown down a *deep* well in the compound. I looked down and saw them lying in heaps. I very much fear there are some of my friends included in this most *atrocious*

fiendish of murders. A Mrs Lindsay, her daughter and son who was in the 1st Regt Bengal N.I. . . . This is a sight I wish I had never seen.

Bingham's worst fears were realized when a scrap of paper written by one of the Misses Lindsay was found in the Bibighar. It read:

Mamma died, July 12th.
Alice died, July 9th.
George died, June 27th.
Entered the barracks, May 21st.
Cavalry left, June 5th.
First shot fired, June 6th.
Uncle Willy died, June 18th.
Aunt Lilly died, June 17th.
Left barracks, June 27th.

With emotions running high among Havelock's troops, few were able to retain a sense of perspective. A notable exception was John Sherer, the new Magistrate of Cawnpore, who later insisted that most British descriptions of the Bibighar 'were exaggerated'. He explained:

The whole of the pavement was thickly caked with blood. Surely this is enough, without saying 'the clotted gore lay ankle deep', which, besides being most distressing, was absolutely incorrect. Then, as to what was lying about, most of us thought it wonderful that the small litter we saw could be the traces of the numbers who had been shut up there. There is no question in my mind that when the bodies were taken away the place had been tidied a little, and painful objects had been removed. There were certainly a few odds and ends of clothing, some lumps of hair, some little shoes, straw hats, and so on. Of mutilation, in that house at least, there were no signs, nor at that time was there any writing on the walls . . . From this dreadful place we passed down the garden to the narrow well into which so many of the bodies . . . had been thrown. I say many, because the receptacle was far too small for all, and there can be no doubt that bodies were dragged across the open space to the river, which was at no great distance. Indeed we were told as much at the time. When we got to the coping of the well and looked over, we saw, at no great depth, a ghastly tangle of naked limbs. I heard a low cry of pain, and saw Bews almost crouching with a sickening anguish. There is no object in saying more.

Sherer was also anxious to dispel the rape rumours. There was, he wrote in his official report, no clear evidence of 'dishonour'. Major G. W. Williams, the commissioner of military police who took numerous witness statements, was also convinced that none of the Bibigarh inmates was violated before being killed. The question of rape was very much on Canning's mind during the summer of 1857, and he asked William Muir, John Colvin's intelligence chief, to investigate. After exhaustive inquiries, Muir reported in December that there was no definite proof that any Europeans had been raped. Various reasons were put forward by the officials whom Muir consulted. Edward Reade, a member of the Sudder Board at Agra, argued: 'The natives of India, both Hindoos and Mahomedans . . . have a repugnance to sexual connection with European females. During 30 years of Indian experience, the only instances that have come to my knowledge have been a few cases of voluptuaries sated with oriental beauty seeking for variety. If it were otherwise would not Indian gold easily procure from England and France any number of fallen creatures . . . Indian lust is almost always the lust of bloodshed and plunder only.' C. B. Thornhill, the Inspector-General of Prisons of the North-Western Provinces, pointed out that 'Hindoos would regard connexion with a Christian as involving loss of caste and that the feelings of the Mahomedans would lead them to veil such an act with the closest secrecy.'

Muir was not convinced by these arguments. While he agreed with Thornhill that Hindus risked becoming outcastes if they slept with European women, and that Muslims would never have 'done so in the unconcealed manner which has been supposed at home', he added that there was 'nothing in the habits or tenets of the Mussulman population which would prevent them from taking females seized at the general outbreak to their homes with sinister designs'. Nor did he accept Reade's point that European females were 'repugnant to the oriental taste':

> I do not myself allow the natives of this country credit for dislike or insensibility towards the European complexion; and, even if admitted, it might not prove a conclusive argument in the present question; because it is apparently one of the current theories that dishonour was done not to gratify passion, but to inflict shame and degradation upon the English name. But the object of the mutineers was, I believe, not so much to disgrace our name, as to wipe out all trace of Europeans, and of everything connected with foreign rule . . . There was cold and heartless blood thirstiness at the farthest remove from the lust of desire.

But as far as the retained honour of the Bibighar captives was concerned, Lieutenant Mowbray Thomson* had an even simpler explanation. 'Such was the loathsome condition into which, from long destitution and exposure, the fairest and youngest of our women had sunk,' he wrote, 'that not a sepoy would have polluted himself with their touch.'

At the time Havelock's troops were only too willing to believe that European females had been raped. But even if they had been disabused of that notion, the brutal murder of women and children was more than enough to fill them with a fierce desire for vengeance. None was more zealous in this regard than the recently promoted Brigadier-General James Neill. Ordered up to Cawnpore by General Grant, he arrived with two hundred European reinforcements on 20 July to a less than cordial reception. Havelock was aware that Neill had been criticizing his generalship in letters to the Commander-in-Chief and, on first meeting him at Cawnpore, said sternly: 'Now General Neill, let us understand each other; you have no power or authority whilst I am here, and you are not to issue a single order.'

Fortunately the two were not together at Cawnpore for long, because Havelock, having secured Bithur, was anxious to push on to Lucknow. Nana Sahib, wrote Sherer, had 'found it impossible to get any of the soldiers to rally round him'. Instead they had 'abused him and Baba Bhutt in open terms, clamouring with threatening gestures for money, and so off, helter-skelter, for [Fatehgarh]'. During the evening of 17 July the Nana had escaped with his family across the Ganges. When Major Stephenson reached Bithur with a detachment two days later, he found it deserted. So he set fire to part of the Nana's palace and blew up his powder magazine before returning to Cawnpore with sixteen captured guns. 'We looted a good deal,' wrote one British officer. 'One man of mine (my own servant) got six hundred rupees; I have a chair and a silver plate, which I hope I shall be able to keep.'

On 20 July Havelock began the laborious task of ferrying the bulk of his small force over to the Oudh bank. By 25 July the operation was complete and Havelock had also crossed over, leaving a furious Neill and three hundred troops in a new entrenchment sited to the north of the Ganges Canal. Neill took his anger out on captured rebels, as he wrote:

* He, Lieutenant Delafosse and the two privates had returned to Cawnpore shortly after its recapture. Thomson was appointed assistant field engineer to the force left to protect the recaptured city; Delafosse advanced with Havelock and the main body of troops into Oudh.

> Whenever a rebel is caught he is immediately tried, and unless he can prove a defence he is sentenced to be hanged at once; but the chief rebels or ringleaders I first make clean up a certain portion of the pool of blood, still two inches deep, in the shed where the fearful murder and mutilation of women and children took place. To touch blood is most abhorrent to high-caste natives, they think that by doing so they doom their souls to perdition. Let them think so . . .
>
> The first I caught was a subadhar, a native officer, a high-caste Brahmin, who tried to resist my order to clean up the very blood he had helped to shed; but I made the Provost-Marshal do his duty, and a few lashes soon made the miscreant accomplish his task. Which done, he was taken out and immediately hanged, and after death buried in a ditch at the roadside.

But for some officers this gruesome ordeal was not degrading enough. 'We made the Nana Sahib's Collector prisoner,' wrote Major Bingham. 'We broke his caste. We stuffed pork, beef and everything which could possibly break his caste down his throat, tied him as tight as we could by the arms and told the guard to be *gentle* with him . . . The guard treated him *gently*. I only wonder he lived to be hung which I had the sincere pleasure of witnessing.' Liberal administrators in India, including Lord Canning himself, thought this humiliation of high-caste prisoners was going too far. But their counterparts in Britain, replete with exaggerated accounts of rebel atrocities, were not so sensitive. 'It is rumoured,' wrote Robert Vernon Smith to Canning, 'that your Government has disapproved of Neill's defilement of the Brahmin mutineers, by making them wash up the blood of their victims, before they were hung. It seems to me a proper characteristic punishment without being brutal or offensive.'

Most Britons in India were of a similar opinion, particularly those troops who passed through Cawnpore and saw the Bibighar in person. Second-Lieutenant Arthur Lang of the Bengal Engineers was typical. 'I felt as if my heart was stone and my brain fire, and that the spot was enough to drive one mad,' he wrote in his journal in late October. 'All these fiends will never be repaid one-tenth of what they deserve . . . Every man across the river whom I meet shall suffer for my visit to Cawnpore. I will never again, as I used to at Delhi, let off men, whom I catch in houses or elsewhere.' After viewing the remnants of the entrenchment, with the 'blood, brains and hair' of Wheeler's son still smeared on a barrack wall, Lang was more furious still. 'I felt that I could vow my life to revenge,' he wrote, 'to take blood from that race every day, to tear all pity from one's heart.'

Queen Victoria's chief emotion, on learning of the atrocities, was one of compassion for the victims. 'We are in sad anxiety about India, which engrosses all our attention,' she wrote to her uncle Leopold from Balmoral in early September. 'Troops cannot be raised fast or largely enough. And the horrors committed on the poor ladies – women and children – are unknown in these ages . . . There is not a family hardly who is not in sorrow and anxiety about their children, and in all ranks – India being *the* place where every one was anxious to place a son!'

16. Enter Sir Colin Campbell

By mid June 1857 Delhi and large swathes of northern and central India were under rebel control and the revolt was spreading by the day.* In an attempt to suppress it, every European soldier that arrived at Calcutta was immediately dispatched up-country, leaving the Christian inhabitants of the capital understandably nervous.

'We are very weak here where we ought to be . . . as strong as possible,' wrote J. P. Grant, a member of the Supreme Council, to Lord Canning. 'We have as enemies three Native Infantry regiments and a half . . . one, two, three (for no one knows) thousand armed men at Garden Reach; some hundred armed men of the Sind Amirs at Damdamah; half the Muhammadan population; and all the blackguards of all sorts of a town of six hundred thousand people. Against these we have one and a half weak regiments, most of whom dare not leave the Fort.' Grant's solution was to accept the Christian community's offer to form a Volunteer Defence Corps, and on 12 June Canning grudgingly gave his assent. 'About 180 horsemen and 600 foot have been enrolled,' he informed Vernon Smith. 'After a little training they will make a very useful patrol guard when needed, but I was not long in finding out that any duty which should take them away from their homes for any length of time, such for instance as garrisoning the Fort in place of European troops, would be strongly objected to by more than three-fourths of them.'

The following day Canning forfeited any goodwill this measure had engendered by introducing a bill to control the press. Popularly known as the 'Gagging Act', it was mainly aimed at the 'incendiary tone' of the Indian press but in practice restricted the content of Indian and English-language publications alike by making them apply for licences that could be withdrawn at any moment. 'The English Press has been very bad,' noted Lady Canning in her journal. 'Civil enough to C. himself, but running down others – but that is not the mischief – it points out all sorts of imaginary reasons and

* During the week of 3–10 June 1857 there were outbreaks in twenty-six regiments of infantry, seven regiments of cavalry, seven companies of foot artillery, one troop of horse artillery and one princely contingent.

grievances as causes for Mutiny, it spreads alarms, and shews up weakness, and gives information, which, translated, may do untold mischief among the natives.' Many in Calcutta had lost faith in the government and believed that it had gagged the press to prevent reports of its errors reaching London. As such, the measure was universally condemned. In England, on the other hand, the reaction was positive. 'Your, or rather Lady Canning's, fears of unpopularity for bullying the press have proved utterly groundless,' Lord Granville informed Canning. 'Everybody is enchanted, and even the newspapers themselves seem to approve, although *si va di loro decoro* to give a subdued grunt.'

The general mood in Calcutta at this time was one of suppressed panic. When Elizabeth Sneyd finally reached the city on 11 June, with her daughter Louisa and newly born grandson, she was told by the proprietor of Mountain's Hotel that 'a terrible conspiracy had only on that day been discovered, to blow up the shipping on the river, & murder all the Europeans in Calcutta, and that many of the ladies and children had gone on board the ships'. So many fugitives had arrived from up-country, he explained, that 'every hotel, private house, & even public offices, were *crammed* with them!', including his own. Mrs Sneyd and her family were eventually taken in by friends of Cecil Beadon, the secretary to the Home Department, who had a house in nearby Alipore. There Louisa was overjoyed to receive a letter from her husband, Dr Hutchinson, who had escaped the outbreak at Fatehpur, though Mrs Sneyd 'got *none* from my precious ones at Shahjehanpore which caused me the greatest grief & alarm'. Of particular irritation to Mrs Sneyd during this time of uncertainty was the insolence of the Indian servants. 'My Ayah would often stand before the looking-glass,' she recalled, 'throwing herself into a variety of attitudes while admiring herself & dancing with a shawl fantastically thrown over her shoulders, like the nautch girls, instead of dressing me when I wanted her, & this she did in my presence with the taunt . . . "Ah! Your rule will soon come to an end, & we shall have our *own* King!"'

The fears of the jumpy Calcutta residents were not entirely without foundation. In the early hours of Sunday, 14 June, Canning received a letter from General Hearsey 'saying that he had received evidence he could not resist that the regiments at Barrackpore were going to rise' the following day and asking for permission to disarm them. 'General Hearsey had shown such firmness and nerve hitherto,' recorded Canning, 'that I could not resist his appeal.' Anticipating the Governor-General's support, Hearsey had already instructed the 78th Highlanders at Chinsurah to march on Barrackpore. They arrived on the morning of 14 June and helped to disarm the three and a half regiments of native infantry* at four in the afternoon. The troops at Calcutta were disarmed simultaneously. But Canning soon regretted his decision. 'I am not now satisfied that there was any sufficient ground for a general disarming,' he wrote to Vernon Smith on 19 June, '& although all in Calcutta is delighted at it, I look forward with some apprehension to the effect which the measure will have at the several stations in lower Bengal . . . The 43rd, the best behaved regiment in Bengal against which there has never been a breath of reproach, is completely panic-stricken, the men desert one day & come back the next not knowing what to do with themselves, but confident that some further disgrace is intended to them.'

In the same letter to Vernon Smith, Canning mentioned a 'return of the panic more severe than ever' among the European inhabitants of Calcutta. He was referring to 'Panic Sunday'. For on 14 June, the day the disarmaments took place, rumours spread through the European quarter that the regiments at Barrackpore had mutinied and were marching towards the city, that the inhabitants of the suburbs had risen, and that the King of Oudh and his followers were plundering Garden Reach. The resultant hysteria was, Canning's private secretary told the Governor of Ceylon, 'beyond all belief'. He added:

My table was heaped with notes from all quarters, stating what was coming – imploring, threatening, urging, all sorts of schemes. Merchants, officials, men of all ranks came pouring in to know the state of the case and what we meant to do. I never did and hope I never shall go through such a scene again! People deserted their houses and went on board the ships in the River. Some drove into the Fort and finding no room, obstinately remained in their carriages. The clergy preached to empty benches, in short every man expected some awful calamity, and all prepared for it in their various ways.

According to Kaye, those 'highest in office were the first to give the alarm', with 'Secretaries to Government running over to Members of Council, loading their pistols, barricading their doors', while the latter 'abandoned their houses with their families' and took refuge on board ships. Virtually every Christian house in the city had been abandoned and a 'score of London thieves would have made their fortunes by plundering' houses in the fashionable neighbourhood of Chowringee.

That same day a sepoy guarding one of the gates of Fort William was

* Three whole regiments – the 2nd, 43rd and 70th – and the three companies of the 34th that had not disbanded on 6 May.

asked by a Muslim man 'when the Europeans were most off their guards – and other questions'. As the sepoy seemed eager to help, the man told him he was an emissary of the King of Oudh. The sepoy's quick response was that he had no time to talk, but would be on guard again at a certain hour when they could speak more freely. Meanwhile he informed his superiors and when the agent returned he was promptly arrested. 'On examination he gave such evidence as justified the Governor-General in arresting the King of Oude,' wrote Canning's private secretary, 'which . . . was quietly done at 4 o'clock on Monday morning. The emissary was to have been hung forthwith, but he was most culpably allowed to escape. Fortunately what he did say was recorded, and His Majesty is now comfortably in Fort William with his Minister and four other State Prisoners. I believe this to be very wise. The rebellion is now pretty well understood to be a Mahomedan one – and the Cartridge question to have been only a pretext to unite the Hindoos with them, and the King was a puppet ready at hand for any intrigues – even if he did nothing himself (which is very probable). The King of Delhi is another and I hope the last of these??!'

The senior adviser arrested with the King of Oudh was Ali Naki Khan, his former chief minister. Colonel Sleeman, who knew him well during his time as Resident, described Ali Naki as 'one of the cleverest, most intriguing, and most unscrupulous villains in India; who had obtained influence over his master by entire subservience to his vices and follies, and by praising all he did, however degrading to him as a man and a sovereign'. If any member of the King's entourage was behind this and other attempts to tamper with the sepoys at Calcutta and Barrackpore, Ali Naki was. But the evidence was never more than circumstantial. 'Although no complicity has been fixed upon the King or his courtiers,' Canning told Vernon Smith, 'I deem it necessary for the safety of the state that it should be put out of the power of any one to seduce the state's soldiers by speaking in the name of the King of Oude & that his name should not be made a rallying point for disaffected soldiers.'

Another major problem facing the Indian government was a lack of money: increased military expenses and a massive loss of revenue from the rebellious districts had put a severe strain on public finances. All public works had ceased and only the 'real necessities of the Military and Civil Establishments' were being provided for. One saving made as a result of the mutiny was the 35 lakhs of rupees owed in pensions to suspected rebels: 12 'for the Delhi family', 22 ('10 due for last year and 12 for this') for the King of Oude and 1 'for the Jhansi family'. But that still left Canning's administration short of at least three crores (roughly £3 million). Its solution was to borrow public money in India by offering a government loan at 6 per cent. The British Cabinet agreed.

On Monday, 29 June, three days after the first official reports of the outbreaks had reached England, an emergency debate was held in the House of Commons. The main speaker was Benjamin Disraeli, the Leader of the Opposition, who demanded to know how 'insurrectionary and rebellious troops' had been able to take possession of the 'ancient capital of Hindostan'. He also asked what measures Lord Palmerston's government was taking to combat the rebellion and whether the Governor-General was about to resign. Replying for the government, Vernon Smith said that 10,000 European troops – mainly reliefs and recruits – were already due to sail for India in the middle of July. A further 4,000 troops requested by the East India Company's Court of Directors would accompany them. Yet Vernon Smith was keen to underplay the danger. 'Our Indian empire is not "emperilled",' he declared, 'and I hope that in a short time the disaster, dismal as it undoubtedly is, will be effectually suppressed by the force already in the country.' As for Canning's resignation, it was unthinkable. 'He has behaved in this emergency with the vigour and judgment which I should always have anticipated,' said Vernon Smith. 'His letters [show] no want of calmness, no lack of confidence. He says that he is certain that he shall be able to put this revolt down, and he adds, that when he has done so he shall turn his mind to ascertaining the causes which have led to it, and the best means of remedying them . . .'

This was not mere rhetoric. On 26 June, the day he received the news from India, Lord Palmerston told the Queen that he had 'no fear' of the mutiny's 'results'. He added: 'The bulk of the European force is stationed on the North-West Frontier, and is, therefore, within comparatively easy reach of Delhi, and about six thousand European troops will have returned to Bombay from Persia. It will, however, seem to be advisable to send off at once the force amounting to nearly eight thousand men, now under orders for embarkation for India.' Queen Victoria agreed, informing Lord Panmure, the Secretary of State for War, that 'she had long been of opinion that reinforcements waiting to go to India ought not to be delayed'.

In the event, not a single infantry regiment reached the Bengal Presidency from England until October 1857.* Part of the reason for this tardy arrival of reinforcements was the government's insistence on sending the majority,

* The 34th Foot and 3rd/60th Rifles arrived at Calcutta in October 1857. A further nine British regiments arrived in November.

including the first batch, in sailing ships rather than steamers. When criticized in Parliament, Lord Panmure gave the excuse that steamers had to visit several ports to restock their coal supply, whereas sailing ships 'were able to shorten the course by keeping further from shore'. As a result, they would arrive at their destination 'as soon, if not sooner, than steam vessels'. This was nonsense and Vernon Smith admitted as much to Canning when he wrote: 'I think it most advisable you should send steamers to tow the sailing vessels from Point de Galle on Madras if you stand in greater need of their accelerated arrival.'

By early August, with no news of Delhi's recapture, the Queen was convinced the government had not done enough. She wrote to Palmerston:

> The last accounts from India show so formidable a state of things that the military measures hitherto taken by the Home Government, on whom the salvation of India must depend, appear to the Queen as by no means adequate to the emergency. We have nearly gone to the full extent of our available means, just as we did in the Crimean War, and may be able to obtain successes; but we have not laid in store of troops, nor formed Reserves which could carry us over a long struggle, or meet unforeseen new calls. Herein we are always most shortsighted, and have finally to suffer either in power or reputation, or to pay enormous sums for small advantages in the end – generally both.

The Queen was right. The government was not displaying the urgency the situation in India demanded because it had underestimated its seriousness. This was partly wishful thinking: in the wake of the Crimean War the government was anxious to avoid the expense of another full-blown conflict. But it was also partly the fault of Canning's overly optimistic dispatches. On 5 June, for example, in the same letter informing Vernon Smith of Anson's death, Canning gave it as his opinion that once Delhi had been cleared of mutineers 'the neck of the insurrection will be broken'. Events would prove him wrong. That said, even in early June Canning was anxious to stress the need for reinforcements to guarantee India's long-term security. 'Be the issue what it may,' he wrote, 'whither with the speedy fall of Delhi, the rebellion at once collapses or whither before this happens, ravages extend & the Europeans are driven from the Central Provinces, Oude or elsewhere, & these parts have to be recovered, I reckon we shall require an additional European force of 12 regiments of infantry & one of dragoons. We must not conceal from ourselves that our Government must henceforth rest much more openly upon military strength.' It was not a question of *if* but *when* the rebellion was suppressed.

This is exactly what Palmerston's government wanted to hear and, in return, it gave the Governor-General its full support. 'The Cabinet . . . have full confidence in you,' wrote Lord Granville to Canning on 10 July, 'and I believe will thoroughly support you both as regards your administrative acts and in Parliament.' What the government was not prepared to do, however, was endorse Canning's choice of Sir Patrick Grant as the new Commander-in-Chief. In his letter to Vernon Smith of 5 June, Canning had given his reasons for choosing Grant: 'If you wish to give the Government of India the most effective aid & support in the difficulties which will rise up after calm has been restored [i.e. during the reform of the Bengal Army] . . . you cannot do more effectually than by the appointment of Sir Patrick Grant as C.-in-C. . . . There is no Queen's officer in India who will be the slightest service in this work. I know of none at home . . . Experience, temper, no rashness & the confidence of the Army officers & men, ought to unite in the person chosen. They are all combined in Sir Patrick Grant.'

But the government – with advice from the Horse Guards* – had other ideas. 'You have done excellently I think in naming P. Grant,' wrote Vernon Smith on 10 August. 'We could not do otherwise than send Colin Campbell.' Lieutenant-General Sir Colin Campbell was one of the most experienced officers in the British Army. Born in Glasgow in 1792, the son of a carpenter named Macliver, he had mistakenly been given the name of his uncle, Colonel John Campbell, by the Duke of York† when he was commissioned. But lacking money and social standing, his promotion had been slow: he took thirty years to rise from captain to colonel and forty to clear his debts. In that time, however, he had seen action in numerous campaigns, including the ill-fated Walcheren expedition, the Peninsular War, the War of 1812 with the United States, the Opium War of 1842, the Second Sikh War (for which he was knighted) and, most recently, the Crimean War. In the last conflict he had commanded the Highland Brigade at the Battle of the Alma and won everlasting fame for his repulse of the Russian cavalry attack on Balaklava, the so-called 'Thin Red Line'. Yet he was a cautious, methodical commander, rather than a dashing one – more Montgomery than Rommel – and was known from a previous stint in India as 'Old Khabardar (Old Careful)'. One officer opined: 'His whole thoughts were centred on a peerage and he'd risk nothing for fear of losing it, nay more he'd sacrifice

* The headquarters of the British Army at Whitehall in London.

† Born Prince Frederick, the second son of George III, the Duke of York was Commander-in-Chief of the British Army from 1798 to 1809, and from 1811 to 1827.

all and anybody for its attainment . . . A brave man undoubtedly, but too cautious for India, and too selfish for any place.'

In fact, like Montgomery, he was popular with his men because they knew he would not sacrifice their lives needlessly. He was interested in the welfare of ordinary soldiers, promoting healthy living, opposing drunkenness, providing shelters in the Crimea and sun helmets in India. He looked like a concerned grandfather, with his shock of grey curly hair, furrowed brow and small goatee beard. But there were many in India who did not approve of his appointment. He had left the subcontinent in 1853 under something of a cloud, after a difficult time as commander of the Peshawar Brigade, and those in the know were not happy to see him return. Canning said as much in a private letter to the President of the Board of Control. The reply was dismissive. 'I trust he may prove different when at the head,' wrote Vernon Smith, 'than what he was when previously known in India.'

Campbell left England by mail packet on 12 July and – travelling via Marseilles and the Suez isthmus – reached Calcutta just over a month later. 'Our voyage . . . was a very trying one,' wrote a fellow passenger. 'The heat in the Red Sea was overpowering, and all hands were in a state of feverish anxiety which was not allayed in any wise by the rumours we picked up at Aden of fresh mutinies and further atrocities.' The bad news was confirmed when they reached India. Mutinies and rebellions in Bundelkhand, Nowgong and Gwalior in June, Mhow, Sagar and Indore in July, and Bhopal in early August had left much of central India in flames.* Other recent mutinies had taken place in the Punjab, in the Benares Division and in Bihar province.

The most serious took place at Dinapore in Bihar. Despite intelligence that a disgruntled raja, Kunwar Singh of Jagdispur, was 'carrying on an intimate correspondence with the sepoys at Dinapoor', the station commander, Major-General George Lloyd, did not order the garrison's disarmament until 25 July. Even then it was hopelessly mismanaged and more than 2,000 sepoys managed to escape to the nearby town of Arrah where they linked up with Kunwar Singh's retainers. When Lloyd heard that the civil station at Arrah was under siege,† he sent a force of four hundred men to

* Gwalior and Indore were independent Maratha principalities. Both Maharaja Scindia of Gwalior and Maharaja Holkar of Indore were suspected of sympathizing with the mutineers, but neither openly rebelled. See Appendix Three.

† The 'loyal' garrison at Arrah was made up of sixteen male civilians – Europeans, Eurasians and the Indian deputy collector – and forty-five Sikhs of the newly raised Bengal Police Battalion.

relieve it. But the force was ambushed on the outskirts of Arrah and only half its number returned to Dinapore.* Arrah was finally relieved on 3 August by an even smaller expedition led by Major Vincent Eyre, an aged artillery officer. A week later, reinforced by three hundred men from Dinapore, Eyre again defeated the rebels near Jagdispur before capturing Kunwar Singh's stronghold. The district, however, was far from pacified.

The initial reverse at Arrah had been preceded by an even more serious British defeat near Agra. On 4 July the Kotah Contingent had risen and joined up with mutineers from Nimach in central India. The following day, as this combined force of around 4,000 rebels approached to within four miles of the fort, Brigadier Polwhele marched out to meet it with seven companies of the 3rd Europeans, a battery of European artillery and a few volunteer cavalry. Polwhele was loath to risk his infantry and tried to win the battle with his guns alone. But they were eventually disabled by counter-fire and he was forced to order a humiliating retreat.† In the wake of this defeat, Agra's entire Christian community‡ was confined to the fort in a virtual state of siege. It was kept there not by the Nimach and Kotah mutineers, who had made for Delhi the day after their victory, but by civilian rebels who had risen in the city and surrounding districts.

Even Havelock's first advance into Oudh had been a failure. He had begun his march on 29 July from Mangalwar, six miles beyond the Ganges, with just 1,500 men and twelve field guns. But the rebels put up a stiff resistance in two battles that day at the villages of Unao and Bashiratganj, and, despite prevailing, Havelock did not feel strong enough to continue. He had already lost a sixth of his force to battle casualties and disease. He was also low on ammunition and had barely enough transport to carry the sick and wounded. The final straw was a message from Neill on 31 July announcing that Bihar had risen in the wake of the mutiny at Dinapore and the two regiments he was daily expecting to reinforce him – the 5th Fusiliers and 90th Light Infantry§ – would not be available for at least two months. That day Havelock retired to Mangalwar, informing Sir Patrick Grant by telegram that he 'could not . . . move against Lucknow with any prospect of success'. On 6 August, having fought a second successful action at

* The casualties were 7 officers and 184 men killed and 3 officers and 63 men wounded.

† British casualties at the so-called Battle of Sasia were 140 killed and wounded.

‡ A total of 5,844 souls, including 1,989 Europeans, 1,541 Eurasians, 858 Indian Christians and 1,456 Hindus and Muslims (mostly servants).

§ The first regiments from the China expedition to reach India.

Bashiratganj a day earlier, he told Grant that he had 'with great grief and reluctance' abandoned his 'hope of relieving Lucknow'. He explained:

The only three staff officers in my force whom I ever consult confidentially . . . are unanimously of the opinion that an advance to the walls of Lucknow involves the loss of this force. In this I concur. The only military question that remains, therefore, is whether that, or the unaided destruction of the British garrison at Lucknow, would be the greatest calamity to the State in this crisis. The loss of this force in a fruitless attempt to relieve Colonel Inglis would, of course, involve his fall. I will remain, however, till the latest moment in this position strengthening it, and hourly improving my bridge-communication with Cawnpore, in the hope that some error of the enemy may enable me to strike a blow at them, and give the garrison an opportunity of blowing up their works and cutting their way out.

Despite a third victory at Bashiratganj on the 11th, against a rebel force estimated at 4,000, Havelock and his rapidly dwindling column were back in Cawnpore by 13 August. Many of the general's subordinates were unimpressed by his toing and froing. 'He is a brave old man,' wrote Lieutenant John Grant after the first two battles, 'but awfully wanting in Generalship.' After returning to Cawnpore, Grant told his brother that had Havelock continued to advance after his second victory at Bashiratganj, on the 5th, he could have relieved Lucknow. He added: 'Our unsuccessful attempt will certainly counterbalance all the good effects of beating the enemy four times. Our Force was certainly very very small, but it is wonderful what a few determined Englishmen can do.' Grant ended the letter by mentioning that there had been 'a great deal of cholera here but it is going off now'. Within days he himself had succumbed to the deadly water-borne disease.

Havelock returned from Oudh to the unwelcome news that some of Nana Sahib's forces, reinforced by mutineers from Sagar, had regrouped at Bithur.* Having given his exhausted troops two days' rest, he set off for Bithur on 16 August and found the rebels well entrenched to the front of the Nana's ruined palace. Fortunately for Havelock, the rebels had only two guns and he was able to pound them with his superior artillery for more than twenty minutes. Yet still they held their ground and, as at Cawnpore, it required a succession of bayonet charges to dislodge them. Victory came

* They numbered about 2,000 men, including elements of the 6th, 17th, 31st, 41st and 42nd Native Infantry and the 3rd Irregular Cavalry. Nana Sahib himself was still at large in Oudh.

at a price: sixty killed and wounded, including twelve deaths from sunstroke. Moreover, a body of two hundred rebel sowars had attacked the British rear, killed thirty camp followers and made off with the volunteer cavalry's baggage.

The worst news to greet the newly arrived Commander-in-Chief was the continued stalemate at Delhi. Soon after General Barnard's decision in mid June to delay an assault, the mutineers had taken the initiative with almost daily attacks on the Ridge. They all failed, but the position of the British rapidly became weaker not stronger. By early June Barnard's force had been swelled by more than 3,000 reinforcements* from the Punjab – including the newly promoted Brigadier-General Neville Chamberlain, who had been appointed adjutant-general – to around 6,600. During the same period, however, the rebel army at Delhi was joined by elements of no less than fourteen infantry regiments, five cavalry regiments and two artillery batteries from stations in Rajputana, the Punjab and Rohilkhand. A further 2,000 troops had been raised near Delhi in the King's name. This brought the total strength of the rebel army to at least 15,000, most of them regulars.

A fascinating insight into the early days of rebel rule in Delhi was provided by Devi Deen, a trooper in the 3rd Light Cavalry, in conversation with a British officer after the mutiny. Devi's recollections confirm that for a time the mutinous regiments retained their discipline and organization:

> When we first came all was quiet, and the regiments did exactly as if they were in cantonments. We heard the British had all been killed. The regiment mounted guards in the Palace and at the Kashmir Gate . . . Our Resaldar-Major was very strict, and made us turn out as we did in Meerut . . . After about ten days the King was proclaimed as the Great Mogul. And the day after I arrived I saw him come on an elephant and open the main bazaar . . . We had our regimental *bunnias*, and the country people brought in supplies after the King had opened the bazaars.

Before long, the rebels' preoccupation with money began to undermine their discipline. On 28 May the cavalry and infantry had a 'violent, abusive altercation over pay'. The cavalry wanted 30 rupees a month, whereas the sepoys were prepared to accept their old pay of 7 rupees. The sowars

* The British reinforcements included 600 of the 8th Foot, 450 of the 61st Foot, 200 European artillerymen, 800 of the 1st Punjab Rifles, 800 of the 4th Sikh Infantry and 400 Punjab Cavalry – a total of 3,250.

eventually settled for 20. According to Mainodin Hassan Khan, the mutineers 'thought more of plunder than of fighting'. He added: 'The rebels were becoming clamorous for pay. They were really laden with money, but they wished to extort as much more as they could. They threatened to leave the King's service unless paid, and they proposed that the wealthy men of the city should be ordered to subscribe for their mainenance . . . Gangs of armed men were collected to stop Sepoys from plundering.'

Such infighting was rife by the time the Rohilkhand mutineers,* commanded by Subedar Bakht Khan, reached Delhi on 2 July. Bakht Khan himself had been prevented from reaching Delhi earlier by the sort of Commissariat difficulties that were inevitable in times of civil disorder: notably the unwillingness of Bareilly bankers to lend funds and the tendency of *mahajuns* to close their shops. At his first public audience with the King on 2 July, Bakht Khan 'solicited orders for the employment of his force'. Bahadur Shah replied that his 'orders were that the inhabitants of the city must not be plundered', yet up till now they had not been obeyed by the rebel soldiers because he had 'no one to enforce them'. Hearing this, Bakht 'offered his services as Commander-in-Chief of the forces, with a view to enforce general discipline'. The King's response was to grasp his hands 'in token of friendship'.

Within hours of his arrival at Delhi, Bakht had replaced four ineffectual royal princes – Mirza Mogul, Mirza Kizr Sultan, Mirza Abu Bakr and Mirza Abdulla – at the head of the rebel army, though Mirza Mogul, the King's eldest surviving son, stayed on as his adjutant-general. One of Bakht's first acts was to inform the King that if any of the royal princes attempted to plunder the city he would cut off their noses and ears. 'You have full authority,' replied the King. 'Do whatever seems good unto you.' Bakht also told the King that he had come to Delhi with 400,000 rupees and his men had been given six months' pay in advance. As such he did not require any financial assistance and would pay the balance of his money into the King's treasury if the rebels were victorious. Delighted that the Rohilkhand troops would not be a financial burden, the King ordered 4,000 rupees to be distributed among them 'for festivities'.

The British force in Delhi too was about to have a new commander. On 5 July, two days after yet another assault was postponed, General Barnard died of cholera. His successor was, unfortunately, the ineffectual General

* The 8th Irregular Cavalry, the 18th, 28th, 29th and 68th Native Infantry and a battery of field artillery.

Reed, whom Wilson thought more 'fit for an invalid couch' than to command an army. By now the British troops on the Ridge were 'more besieged than besiegers'. As if heat, disease, battle casualties and a lack of supplies were not enough, they also had to contend with the 'enemy within'. On 2 July some sowars of the 2nd Punjab and 9th Irregular Cavalry were disarmed for inciting the Sikh regiments to mutiny. A company of the 4th Sikh Infantry was also deprived of its weapons. 'This Company were not Seikhs,' noted Wilson, 'but enlisted in the Plains. Some 4 or 5 of them – two of them native officers – were hung. They ought all of them to have been shot, but it is very dreadful having such wretches in our Camp, to do all sorts of mischief while we are repelling attacks from Delhi. I believe our Seikhs and Goorkhas to be as true as steel, but not another Native soldier is to be trusted.'

The truth of this was demonstrated on 9 July when, during the heaviest rebel attack yet, the faithlessness of a picket of 9th Irregulars and the pusillanimity of a troop of Carabiniers enabled a body of the mutinous 8th Irregulars to penetrate to the heart of the European camp. Harriet Tytler, the only European woman still on the Ridge, recalled:

> They tore in as if they were mad and passed my bell of arms. Immediately there was a cry from all our men, 'Treachery, treason.' The alarm was sounded and in a minute every man was standing, musket in hand, waiting for the word of command, some with their shirt-sleeves tucked up, others without their shoes or socks on, just as they had turned out of bed when off duty. Next moment the word of command came and they were off to meet the enemy, which they did in front of the cantonment cemetery. This was the only battle I ever saw fought with my own eyes. I shall never forget the sight, the glistening of the bayonets even through the smoke as both sides fired. Almost in the twinkling of an eye, all was over. Leaving some fifty of their own men dead, they dashed off.

For not abandoning his outpost when the Carabiniers fled, Lieutenant Hills of the Bengal Horse Artillery was awarded the Victoria Cross. His commander, Major Tombs, was similarly honoured for coming to Hills's rescue. But everyone knew the real cause of the incursion was the duplicity of the 9th Irregulars. 'The mistake of leaving an inlet into camp to be guarded by Hindustanis,' wrote Hervey Greathed, 'will not again be committed. Brigadier Wilson had in vain protested against it.'

The other rebel attacks on the Ridge that day were also repulsed, but at an overall cost to the British of 40 men killed, 168 wounded and 11 missing.

Rebel losses were estimated at more than 500 killed. They could afford such a rate of attrition; the British could not. Second-Lieutenant Chichester summed up the reality of the situation in a letter home on 11 July. 'Here we are still before the walls of Delhi, fighting hand to hand with the rebels every other day nearly, and they are joined by fresh regiments that have mutinied in different parts of the country every day. I suppose they muster now at Delhi about 30,000 fighting men* very near, but whenever they come out to attack us we kill a frightful number of them while our loss compared to theirs is comparatively small. Yet we cannot afford at the present moment to lose a single man, our strength being 6,000 men.'

On 14 July an even heavier rebel attack was made on the pickets under Hindu Rao's House and at the Sabzi Mundi. The British remained on the defensive until the afternoon, when a column was formed under Brigadier Showers to dislodge the rebels. Brigadier-General Chamberlain accompanied the column, which had great difficulty in driving the enemy out of the many serais and walled gardens that covered the ground between the Ridge and the city walls. Yet position after position was carried, until the British column found itself in sight of the Lahore Gate. In its eagerness it had gone too far. Musket and artillery fire from the walls inflicted many casualties, and the column was forced to retire, pressed all the way by the emboldened rebels.

Chamberlain was wounded in the advance, hit in the shoulder as he tried to rally the wavering British troops by jumping his horse over a wall lined with sepoys. 'There is not a braver heart or cooler head in camp,' commented Hodson, who had also distinguished himself in the fight. 'His fault is too great hardihood and exposure in the field, and a sometimes too injudicious indifference to his own life or that of his men.' Archdale Wilson's assessment was blunter: 'He ought never to have been there at all.'

Wilson would soon have even more reason to rue Chamberlain's incapacity because, on 17 July, he became the fourth commander of the Delhi Field Force in three months. Reed had tacitly acknowledged that the task at Delhi was beyond him by agreeing to return to the Punjab to regain his health. Though Wilson was not the next senior officer on the Ridge, Reed nominated him because of his victory at Ghazi-ud-din-Nagar and because he was known to be an active officer who 'knew his work'. Most of the force approved of the decision. Wilson himself, now a brigadier-general, was not so sure. He described the promotion to his wife as a 'fearful

* In fact it was closer to 20,000.

responsibility' and 'knowing as I do my own weakness and incapacity I feel as if I should faint under the burden, but the Lord God . . . will surely give me strength'.

The pressure to retake Delhi was still immense. Unaware of Barnard's death, Sir Patrick Grant addressed the following letter to him on 13 July:

> The latest tidings from Delhi are dated the 16th June and we learn that it had then been determined to defer the assault until the reinforcements should reach you. I cannot doubt that you had good and sufficient reasons for this delay, but I must tell you that it has already produced incalculable mischief, increasing with every day the capture of Delhi and the destruction of its vile defenders is postponed.
>
> We learn from a letter from Sir John Lawrence, received here today and dated 17th June, that a strong reinforcement of 3,250 men of all arms despatched from the Punjab was expected to be with you on or before the 6th Instant, and a letter of prior date mentions that you had already received abundant supply of ammunition of every description. I most earnestly trust therefore that you will have found yourself in sufficient strength to make your attack, and I can hardly doubt that Delhi has been for some days in your possession.

Six days later, having seen Barnard's letter of 18 June explaining the reasons for postponing the assault, Grant struck a more conciliatory tone. He assured the long-dead Barnard that he had been wise not to go ahead with the attack. Yet reinforcements since then, wrote Grant, had surely made victory certain and 'we are in hourly expectation of hearing that you are master of the Imperial City'. He was to be disappointed. The rapidly increasing strength of the rebels had resulted in yet another postponement and Wilson, the latest commander, was thinking more in terms of survival than conquest. Soon after taking command, he wrote to warn Sir John Lawrence that 'unless speedily reinforced' by at least two regiments the Delhi Field Force 'will soon be so reduced by casualties and sickness that nothing will be left but a retreat to Karnal'. Lawrence wired back on the 21st that 'we can send you off at once seventeen hundred men'* to be followed up by 'two thousand more'. But the most cheering news was that John Nicholson was on his way.

With the disarmament of the Peshawar garrison and the dispersal of the mutinous 55th in May, Nicholson and Edwardes had felt the frontier to be

* 600 of HM 52nd Light Infantry; 400 Military Police; 400 of the Kumaon Battalion; 200 Multani Horse; and a 9-pounder battery of 100 men.

reasonably secure. The most obvious threat was from Dost Mohammed, the Amir of Afghanistan, who had fought against the British during the Second Sikh War in an effort to recover the Vale of Peshawar. But Dost had recently signed an alliance with the British* that both Edwardes and Nicholson were confident would be honoured. Edwardes was shocked, therefore, to receive a letter from Sir John Lawrence on 11 June that advocated a withdrawal from Peshawar and the Trans-Indus frontier region. This was necessary, said Lawrence, to release British troops and loyal levies for the recapture of Delhi. His proposal was to 'make a merit of necessity' by inviting Dost Mohammed to hold the Vale and the Trans-Indus as an ally, with the promise of a permanent occupation once the crisis was over.

Horrified by this show of weakness, Edwardes was moved to remark that had the letter not been in Lawrence's own handwriting, he 'would not have credited it'. Having consulted Nicholson and Cotton, he drafted a no-nonsense protest signed by all three: 'We are unanimously of the opinion that with God's help we can and will hold Peshawar, let the worst come to the worst, and it would be a fatal policy to abandon it and retire across the Indus. It is the anchor of the Punjab, and if you take it up the whole ship will drift to the sea . . . As to a friendly transfer of Peshawar to the Afghans, Dost Mohammed would not be a mortal Afghan – he would be an angel – if he did not assume our day to be gone in India, and follow after us as an enemy. Europeans cannot retreat – Kabul would come again!' Ignoring these objections, Lawrence asked the Governor-General for permission to withdraw from the frontier. Canning's response in early July was emphatic: 'Hold on to Peshawar to the last.' To relinquish it would, he believed, cause the rebellion to spread to southern India: 'If we were now to abandon territory, no matter how distant, it would be impossible that faith in the permanency of our Rule should not be shaken. The encouragement to join the league against us would be irresistible and immediate; its effect would be felt long before we should secure any material benefit from the force which would be set free by the abandonment.' Accompanying this letter was a private note of condolence. 'I cannot put into a letter on public matters,' wrote Canning, 'the expression of the deep grief which I feel at the death of your noble-hearted

* The first peace treaty, initiated by Edwardes and signed in March 1855, bound the Afghans to be 'friends of our friends and enemies of our enemies' and in return the East India Company promised not to expand its borders westward. Dost Mohammed signed a supplementary treaty in January 1857, declaring that he had made an irrevocable alliance with the British and that, 'happen what may, I will keep it faithfully till death'.

brother [Sir Henry Lawrence]* . . . There is not a man in India who could have been less well spared at the present moment.'

Nicholson, meanwhile, had replaced Neville Chamberlain as commander of the Movable Column. With this appointment went the temporary rank of brigadier-general, a considerable achievement for a 34-year-old who held only the permanent rank of captain. He left Peshawar on 14 June and caught up with the Movable Column at Jullundur six days later. With him was his personal bodyguard of Indian frontier horsemen. 'They came out of a personal devotion to Nicholson,' wrote Ensign Reginald Wilberforce† of the 52nd Light Infantry. 'They took no pay from the Government, they recognised no head but Nicholson, and him they obeyed with a blind devotion and faithfulness that won the admiration of all who saw them. These men, some 250 in number, mounted on their wiry ponies, surrounded the Column like a web.' Chief among them was 'a huge Pathan, black-whiskered and moustachioed; this man never left his [Nicholson's] side, he slept across the doorway of Nicholson's tent, so that none could come in save over his body. When Nicholson dined at mess this Pathan stood behind his chair with a cocked revolver in one hand, and allowed none to pass a dish to his master save himself.' His name was Muhammad Hayat Khan, the son of a man who had saved Nicholson's life many years earlier. Nicholson had shown his gratitude by appointing the younger Khan as *darogah* of police in Peshawar and they had been close friends ever since.

Nicholson's ruthlessness was soon in evidence. On 26 June, near Phillour, he disarmed the two Bengal regiments with the column – the 33rd and 35th Native Infantry – on the grounds that they could not be trusted. The reaction of the two colonels on hearing the fate of their regiments was very different. Sandeman of the 33rd burst into tears, exclaiming that he would answer for the loyalty of his regiment with his life. The 35th's Younghusband said simply: 'Thank God!' Just over a fortnight later the 59th Native Infantry was also disarmed by Nicholson at Amritsar as a precaution. Colonel Boyd, the commanding officer, wrote: 'Subsequent to being disarmed, two men were found guilty of secreting ammunition, and were executed. The regiment, as a body, have remained passive and obedient throughout.' That same day, 9 July, Nicholson's precipitate action seemed justified when the 46th Native Infantry and a wing of the 9th Light Cavalry rose at nearby

* On 22 July, unaware of his death, the Court of Directors appointed Sir Henry Lawrence as the Governor-General-in-waiting in case anything should happen to Lord Canning.

† Son of the well-known Samuel Wilberforce, Bishop of Oxford.

Sialkot and murdered a number of officers and civilians, including Brigadier Frederick Brind, the station commander, and Dr James Graham, the superintending surgeon.* Having plundered the station as the surviving Europeans huddled in the fort, the mutineers headed for Delhi.

Nicholson heard about the mutiny the following day. His first act was to arrange for the disarming of the other wing of the 9th Light Cavalry that formed part of his column. This took place at nine in the evening, shortly before he set off for Gardaspur to intercept the mutineers with a portion of the 52nd Light Infantry, a battery of horse artillery and his Pathan horsemen. To give his column extra mobility, Nicholson had arranged for the 52nd to be transported in *ekkas*, small pony-carts capable of carrying four men and a driver. These enabled him to reach Gardaspur, 40 miles north of Amritsar, in eighteen hours. Early next morning, having learnt that the mutineers were in the act of crossing the Ravi River at a ford known as Trimmu Ghat, about nine miles distant, he moved off to confront them. The two forces met about a mile from the river. Warned about Nicholson's approach by cavalry scouts, the sepoys were drawn up in a line, their right resting on a disused mud fort and their left on a small village, with groups of sowars on either flank.

Nicholson advanced his nine field guns to within 600 yards, but as they prepared for battle the sepoy line fired a volley and then raced forward with fixed bayonets. At the same time the mutinous sowars charged the right of the British line. These twin threats caused the Pathan levies who had advanced with the guns to bolt to the rear, and for a brief moment it seemed as if the British force was about to be overwhelmed. But the men of the 52nd quickly formed squares to receive the enemy horse and the guns managed to open up with grape before the sepoys could reach them. 'For about ten minutes [the rebels] stood up very well indeed,' reported Nicholson, 'many of them advancing boldly up to the very guns. Meanwhile the cavalry had made several rushes in detached parties on our flanks and rear, but had always been repulsed by the file-firing of our infantry.' The mutineers' muskets and single cannon could not match the firepower of the British battery and Enfield rifles. Within twenty minutes the rebels were falling back towards the river.

They retreated on to a large island, but could go no further because the water on the other side was too deep. Realizing the mutineers were trapped,

* Incredibly, two popular British officers were invited to command the Sialkot mutineers with offers of high pay and furlough to the hills every hot season. They declined and were allowed to escape.

Nicholson left a guard at the ford and took the rest of his men back to Gardaspur to await the arrival of enough boats to enable him to assault the island. By the 15th all was ready. The following morning Nicholson and the British infantry crossed over to a point a mile from the rebel position. Screened by thick brushwood, they were upon the mutineers before they could be detected. 'The real business was over in a few minutes without any check,' recalled Nicholson, 'and with a loss to us of only six wounded. A few resolute men among the mutineers died manfully at the gun; the rest fled, and were either slain on the bank or driven into the river.'

Sir John Lawrence was impressed, telling his aides that had other commanders acted with the same vigour as Nicholson, Delhi would long since have fallen. Nicholson was clearly the man for the job, and on 21 July, at a meeting in Lahore, Lawrence ordered him to march the Movable Column to Delhi as quickly as possible. Nicholson left Amritsar on 25 July, and nine days later, somewhere north of Ambala, he received an urgent message from Wilson to hasten his advance because the rebels had rebuilt the bridge over the Najafgarh Canal and were threatening to cut communications to the north. So he left the column at Ambala on 6 August and, travelling by mail-cart, arrived at the Ridge a day later. Having consulted Wilson, he rejoined his column,* which finally reached Delhi on 14 August.

Nicholson's reinforcements increased the British strength on the Ridge to almost 9,500 men, but 1,500 of them were *hors de combat* from sickness and wounds. The rebels had more than twice that number. According to one official estimate, compiled from the reports of Indian spies, the number of mutineers inside Delhi at this time was no more than 4,000 horse and 12,000 foot. A further one hundred cavalry and 3,000 infantry were 'undisciplined levies' and, in the opinion of the Commissioner of Ambala, 'of no account whatever'. Contrary to expectations, however, Nicholson's appearance was not the prelude to a grand assault. For Lawrence had promised yet more troops and a heavy siege train from Ferozepore, and the cautious Wilson was not going to act until they had arrived. He explained his safety-first policy in a letter to his wife of 14 August:

> Nicholson joined me with his Force this morning. I have a little more than 5000 Infantry, but I can do nothing towards battering the Town and making a breach

* It comprised a field battery of European artillery, HM 52nd Light Infantry, a wing of HM 61st Foot, the 2nd Punjab Infantry, a wing of the 1st Baluch Regiment, 200 Multani Horse and 400 Military Police.

until my siege train comes up, which will not be until the beginning of next month. The Mutineers are too much on the alert, for any hope of being able to surprise them and blow open their gates, and even if I could do I do not think it would be good policy as yet, as they would escape out of the city with their light guns, and overrun and harass the whole country. We could spare only a small Brigade to go after them, and they would bolt in every direction. If we can hold them in check until Grant or Havelock come up, they will be unable to escape except as an unarmed rabble.

Sir Colin Campbell's arrival at Calcutta in mid August coincided with the high-water mark of the rebellion. The outbreaks were still not over, but already more than 60,000 trained troops, two thirds of them regulars of the Bengal Army, had mutinied. While some had lain down their arms and returned to their villages, many more had returned from furlough or disbanded regiments to join the revolt. The rebel ranks had been further swelled by tens of thousands of armed civilians.

British commanders had had their successes: notably Wilson at Ghazi-ud-din-Nagar, Barnard at Badli-ki-Serai, Havelock en route to Cawnpore, and Eyre at Gujraganj and Jagdispur. But these were tactical victories. In a wider, strategic sense, the rebels still held the whip hand. British troops at Delhi, Agra and Lucknow were in a virtual state of siege. Havelock was stalled at Cawnpore, and the revolt in Bihar meant that communications between Calcutta and the crucial North-Western Provinces were intermittent at best. Set-piece battles, moreover, had not always gone the way of the British. At Chinhut, Sasia and Arrah the rebels had humiliated European troops – albeit with a numerical advantage. However, with more British reinforcements on the way, and loyal Indian units of the Bombay and Madras Armies advancing into the disaffected areas of central India, time was running out for the mutineers. The only way they could end British rule for good was by spreading the rebellion across the subcontinent. No ruling Indian princes had yet joined the rebels, though some were wavering. They feared the power of the British and were waiting on events. But if the revolt had spread deep into western and southern India, great princes like the Nizam of Hyderabad and the Maharajas of Indore and Gwalior would have been tempted to join it.

Many of the Company-recruited and European-officered forces that served these princes had already mutinied.* So too had some of the princes'

* The Bharatpur Legion mutinied in May, the Gwalior and United Malwa Contingents in June, the Kotah Contingent in July, the Bhopal Contingent and the Jodhpur Legion in August.

personal, Indian-officered troops: notably the Raja of Ulwar's army in May and two of the Maharaja of Indore's infantry regiments in June. Even the Hyderabad Contingent, nominally part of the Bombay Army, had experienced unrest in June when the Muslim sowars of the 1st Cavalry, based at Aurungabad in the Deccan, refused to 'fight against their King [of Delhi]'. Major-General Woodburn was sent with a column from Poona to put an end to the disaffection; but his hesitation at a punishment parade enabled one hundred and sixty mutineers to escape, of whom sixty-four were recaptured. Of the three ringleaders sentenced to death, two were shot and the other one blown away from a gun. A British eyewitness described the death of the last: 'Fire! and in an instant he was blown to atoms. His head flew up into the air some thirty or forty feet – an arm yonder, another yonder, while the gory, reeking trunk fell in a heap beneath the gun. Scarcely had the head and arms fallen to the ground before the carrion birds were glutting themselves upon the warm and mangled flesh, and the whole air was tainted with a most sickening effluvium.'

The danger of a general rising in the Deccan, the heartland of the Marathas, was very real. At Poona there were nightly patrols, and both the post office and treasury were guarded by cavalry. 'We always go to bed with fear of having our throats cut,' wrote the wife of a Bombay officer who was with Woodburn's column. 'If the Nizam's Army rise we shall all be obliged to go to Bombay. The mutineers have threatened to burn down Poona and the whole of the Deccan and to murder every European man, woman and child.' At around the same time as the mutiny at Aurungabad, a plot by sowars of the Nagpur irregular cavalry to rise and murder all the Europeans at Sitabuldi was foiled by loyal Madras troops. The regiment, six hundred strong, was disarmed on 23 June, and three Indian officers were hanged a week later. The only other serious mutiny below the Nerbudda was that of the 27th Bombay Native Infantry at Kolhapur, south of Poona, on 31 July. Raised in 1846, following the conquest of Sind, the regiment had an unusually high proportion of *purbias* and 'no record of past warfare to keep it steady'. The mutiny, which was eventually quelled by Lieutenant Kerr's detachment of Southern Maratha Horse, was thought to be part of an attempt to restore the ancient House of Satara. Of the one hundred and sixty-five mutineers captured by Kerr's men, more than two thirds were *purbias*.

By the end of August there had been mutinies at Jhansi, Nowgong, Banda, Gwalior, Indore, Mhow, Sagar and Sehore in central India. Large areas of Bundelkhand, Bhopal and the Sagar and Nerbudda Territories were in rebel hands. On 25 August Prince Firoz Shah, the nephew of the King of Delhi, had been placed on the *musnud* at Mandsaur in Rajputana; a day later the Green Flag of Muslim revolt was raised and men flocked to join Firoz Shah's cause. September would see further mutinies at Nagode and Jabalpur, the latter outbreak sparked by the execution of Raja Shankar Shah, a descendant of the Gond Kings of Garha-Mandla, for plotting rebellion with the sepoys of the 52nd Native Infantry.

What prevented the outbreak of rebellion in western and southern India, and enabled the British to regain the upper hand in the central belt, was the departure of trained rebel troops. In far too many cases the mutineers abandoned their stations and headed for the rebel centres of Delhi and Cawnpore, leaving civilian insurgents to oppose a British return. When the sepoys did remain, or entered the region after suffering reverses further north, they showed what redoubtable opponents they could be.

But even regular troops were deficient in three key areas: they lacked a unified command, their officers had no experience of handling large bodies of troops in battle, and their weapons were generally inferior to those used by the British. Under the circumstances, it is surprising that they won any set-piece battles at all. Yet if they had avoided direct confrontation and waged a guerrilla war from the start, severing lines of communication and appearing when least expected, they might well have prevailed. In particular they should have spread the flame of rebellion by marching south. Instead, as if preoccupied by the concept of safety in numbers, they concentrated on a few urban centres – Delhi, Cawnpore and Lucknow – and gave the British time to regroup.

Looking back, few observers realize how close the British came to losing India. They assume that British reinforcements were bound to reconquer the country sooner or later. Yet it is almost impossible to rule any foreign country without the tacit acceptance of a sizeable proportion of its population. Once the majority want you out, as occurred in America during the War of Independence, no amount of military force can save you. This critical mass was almost reached during the Indian mutiny. If the rebellion had spread into western and southern India, some of the ruling princes and significant elements of the Bombay and Madras Armies would have turned against the British, and the game might well have been up. This was still a possibility in August 1857. Yet the aims of most rebels were too localized and disparate; they lacked a George Washington, a leader with the vision to see the wider strategic picture and the military genius to take advantage of it.

17. The Fall of Delhi

Nicholson's arrival at Delhi raised British spirits immeasurably. 'As we stood by the roadside and cheered each regiment,' recalled Lieutenant 'Butcher' Vibart, 'the predominant feeling in our minds was one of supreme elation at the thought that with the arrival of this additional reinforcement and its masterful leader, a victorious issue of the long protracted struggle was at length assured . . . !'

Vibart had only been back at Delhi a matter of weeks, having volunteered to serve with the 1st Bengal Fusiliers on hearing of the murder of his family. Harriet Tytler, on the other hand, had endured the privations of the siege since the beginning. When the other women in camp were escorted to Meerut in mid June, she was given permission by General Barnard to remain on account of her advanced pregnancy. Two days later, in the back of a cart, she gave birth to a baby boy and named him Stanley Delhiforce. He was born with dysentery and not expected to live; incredibly he survived. Harriet recorded:

A week after the birth of my baby the monsoon broke with great force. Up to that time we thought the thatched roof would have kept the water out, instead of which it leaked like a sieve and in a few minutes we were drenched, baby and all, to the skin. My husband on observing this said, 'My Harrie, this will never do. I must see if I cannot get some place to protect you and the children from the rain.' Fortunately he found an empty bell of arms close by, which he was allowed to take possession of, and then took our only manservant to Captain Scott's battery to bring away some fresh straw to place on the ground for us to lie on. I walked bare-footed with a wet sheet wrapped around my baby and went into that bell of arms, and there we remained.

So short of clothes were the Tytlers that Harriet spent most of her time darning; when her clothes were being washed, she had nothing but a sheet to wrap herself in. Her husband was slightly better off thanks to the generosity of some British recruits he had travelled to India with in 1854: on hearing that he had lost everything on 11 May, they placed a bundle of clothes on his chair with the words, 'You will excuse us, sir, but some of us thought they might be acceptable!'

The battered Ridge was no place for civilians: the constant threat of sudden death was brought home to Harriet when a huge piece of shell landed next to the cart in which her baby lay. But after a time she became immune to the danger. One evening, as a recently arrived friend of Captain Tytler was paying her a visit, a shell exploded near by. 'My God, what was that?' said the friend, jumping up. 'Oh!' replied Harriet calmly. 'It is only a shell.' Astounded by her *sang froid*, the friend repeated Harriet's response in his mess that night and it quickly became a byword for coolness under fire.

Even the high temperatures – rising to one hundred and ten degrees in the soldiers' tents – could be coped with. Harriet's young son Frank used to spend his days 'running about in the sun, with no hat on for he did not possess one, playing with one soldier and then another'. Her daughter Edith, on the other hand, had to be kept in because she had just recovered from a life-threatening abscess on the liver. 'Never did a day go by without her fainting,' recalled Harriet, 'and to keep her in the cart was so difficult that I was at my wits' end what to do.' She eventually came up with the idea of scratching holes in her feet and telling Edith she had to tend to them like a doctor. No sooner did the wounds heal than Edith would make them bleed again 'for the simple pleasure of stopping the blood' with Harriet's handkerchief. It kept her amused for hours.

From late June the soaring temperatures were interspersed with torrential downpours. 'The rains are something frightful,' wrote Hugh Chichester in a letter to his mother, 'everything gets so damp and horrid, it is nearly impossible to keep the waters out of the tent, and as for one's boots they are never perfectly dry . . . My pistol I have to clean every day to keep from rust and so procure it going off in case of emergency.' But nothing was more of a torment than the flies. Delhi had always been noted for its summer plague of flies, but during the siege they multiplied on the 'putrid corpses of dead men and animals which lay rotting and unburied in every direction'. Those prone in hospital were the worst affected. 'For the short time I was laid up,' wrote Lieutenant Frederick Roberts,* 'I fully realized the suffering which our sick and wounded soldiers had to endure. At night the inside of my tent was black with flies. At the first ray of light or the smallest shake to the ropes, they were all astir, and for the rest of the day there was no peace; it was even difficult to eat without swallowing one or more of the loathsome insects. I had to brush them away with one hand while I put the food into my mouth with the other.' One British surgeon, having tried in vain to

* Roberts had arrived at Delhi from the Punjab on 28 June 1857.

poison the flies, 'applied glue mixed with sugar to sheets of paper and hung them on the beds of the patients . . . and the sweepers after sweeping them off the paper in heaps destroyed them'. Bored officers used to amuse themselves by laying a train of gunpowder to a table covered with sugar; when enough flies had congregated they blew it up.

With an unbroken line of communication to the Punjab, supplies were never in danger of running out, though the price of luxury items was high. Hugh Chichester wrote home:

> A pair [of field glasses] exactly the same as mine, belonging to poor Lt Jones of the Engineers who was killed a few days ago, sold for 160 rupees, double what they cost, his revolver a Colt sold for 280 rupees, 4 times its value in London, this shows you what demand there are for these things . . .
>
> I went yesterday to Peake and Allen's shop. They have just arrived from Umballa and set up a shop here, selling paper, pen ink, pocket books, Tobacco, Soap, Tooth Powder, Brushes, Pencil etc. They are the largest chemists we have in India and do a wonderful quantity of business, make soda water for all the Messes in the North West and Punjaub. The first night they arrived there was a great deal of fighting going on, and I hear they had serious intention of hooking it back to Umballa, but they have been persuaded to stay, and no doubt will make a very good thing of it as all kinds of things are wanted by the officers, many of whom have lost everything.

Ammunition was not so plentiful, and the thousands of Indian servants who daily risked their lives to take food and water to the troops in the pickets and batteries were paid 2 annas for every used cannonball they collected. The unseemly scramble for shot was often comical. On one occasion, according to Lieutenant Griffiths of the 61st Foot, a party of servants carrying cooked provisions up the slope from the camp were distracted by two roundshots that had hit the top of the Ridge and were rolling past them. They immediately put the dishes on the ground and ran towards the shot. 'I watched the race with interest,' recalled Griffiths, 'and anticipated some fun, knowing that in their eagerness they would forget that the shots had not had time to cool. Two men in advance of the rest picked up the balls and, uttering a cry, dropped them quickly, rubbing and blowing their hands. The remainder stood patiently and then . . . two men placed the shot on their heads, and all in a body moved off towards the Commissariat quarters to receive and divide the reward.'

One event in August did much to lift the air of despondency that had hung over the British camp for most of the summer: the arrival of a Eurasian woman who had been hiding in the city since the May massacres. Her name was Mrs Leeson, the daughter of the postmaster of Delhi, and she was brought into the camp by two Afghans who refused Hodson's reward of 1,000 rupees, saying they had 'not saved her life for money, but for humanity's sake'. She was immediately taken to Harriet Tytler, the only other woman in camp. Harriet recalled: 'She was dressed like a native Afghan boy, in khaki, and as soon as she arrived she asked me for a Bible. Fortunately I had one and gave it to her. From that time she never said a word but she pored over that Holy book till about three o'clock, when she asked me for some water. I then ventured to ask of her . . . how she had been saved.' Mrs Leeson explained that she had been trying to escape Delhi on 12 May with her three young children and some other Christians when they were captured by a party of the King's servants who promised to take them to their master. Instead, having relieved them of their valuables, their captors opened fire. Mrs Leeson was shot in the waist, the same bullet hitting her baby boy and throwing him out of her arms. One by one the other Christians were shot and stabbed to death. Mrs Leeson, lying helpless but conscious, was forced to witness the pitiless murder of her children.

Before [they] had killed all the others [recorded Harriet], Mrs Leeson's little boy of about six drew close to his mother and, raising her head, put it on his lap and began caressing her face. The little girl of three, running up to her wounded mother, laid herself down by her side . . . After those soldiers of the King had butchered the rest of the family they came up to her little boy and cut his throat . . . They then took the poor little girl and cut her from ear to ear through her mouth . . . That poor child was some six hours before she died, all the time writhing away, in her agony, further and further from her mother till she heard one piercing shriek and then no more, so the mother supposed somebody must have killed her outright. There the poor baby lay on the ground, picking the grass and moaning pitifully, till he died too.

That evening she was rescued by the two Afghans who hid her and tended her wounds until she was well enough to attempt the hazardous journey to the British camp. But her ordeal did not end with her safe arrival on the Ridge. Brigadier-General Nicholson mistook one of her two saviours for a '*very bad* character' he knew from Peshawar and promptly clapped him in irons. Mrs Leeson, by association, was suspected of being a spy and told to leave the camp. Her tears and Harriet Tytler's remonstrations were to no avail: Nicholson was adamant and she was forced to take the next *dâk-gharry* to Ambala, where she had an aunt. Nicholson later realized his error and released the Afghan. But it was too late to right the wrong done to Mrs Leeson, a woman who had cheated death at the hands of the rebels only to be cast out by her own people. Harriet's one consolation during this tragic affair was the news that Mrs Leeson had reached Ambala safely.

The road north of Delhi was far from secure. On 16 August, having discovered that a body of mutineers had left the city and were heading north-west towards Rohtak, Archdale Wilson sent Hodson to keep an eye on them. He took with him 100 of the Guides Cavalry, 25 Jhind horsemen and 230 of his own newly raised corps of irregular horse. Smartly dressed in their khaki tunics offset by scarlet sashes and turbans, the Sikhs and Punjabi Muslims of Hodson's Horse certainly looked the part. But Henry Daly, the commander of the Guides who was recovering from a serious wound, was not fooled. He wrote: 'Many of the men, hastily collected, caught at the plough's tail, cut a ludicrous figure mounted on the big, obstinate stud horses with English saddles, bumbling through the Delhi camp.' Even Hodson was prepared to admit their deficiencies, telling one correspondent that the corps 'is merely an aggregation of untutored horsemen, ill-equipped, half-clothed, badly provided with everything, quite unfit for service in the usual sense of the term, and only forced into the field because I have willed that it shall be so'. In battle, however, they would prove their worth.

By the end of the first day, defying muddy roads and swollen rivers, Hodson's column had routed a couple of small bodies of rebel horse and reached the outskirts of Rohtak. But the rebels were holding the town in far larger numbers than Hodson had expected, and, with a direct attack out of the question, he decided to draw the enemy into the open. Next morning, having repulsed one attack by rebel foot and horse, he gave the order to retire. The stratagem worked perfectly:

The enemy moved out the instant we withdrew [he recalled], following us in great numbers, yelling and shouting and keeping up a heavy fire of matchlocks. Their horsemen were principally on their right, and a party galloping up the main road threatened our left flank. I continued to retire until we got into open and comparatively dry ground, and then turned and charged the mass who had come to within from one hundred and fifty to two hundred yards of us. The Guides, who were nearest to them, were upon them in an instant, closely followed by and soon intermixed with my own men.

The enemy stood for a few seconds, turned, and then were driven back in utter confusion to the very walls of the town, it being with some difficulty that the officers could prevent their men entering the town with the fugitives. Fifty of the enemy, all horsemen, were killed on the ground, and many must have been wounded.

With just thirteen casualties, Hodson returned to camp a hero. But his victory was slightly tarnished when word leaked out that, en route to Rohtak, he had executed a ressaldar named Bisharat Ali who had absconded from the 1st Punjab Cavalry. As Ali was caught leading a party of deserters from his regiment, Hodson had a good excuse to kill him. Nicholson and others would have done the same. Unfortunately for Hodson, Neville Chamberlain was an old friend of Ali and not convinced of his guilt. It quickly became camp gossip that Hodson had shot Ali for reasons of personal animosity, rather than summary justice. Nothing came of it, but the mud stuck, leaving Hodson open to more serious allegations of impropriety.

A week after Hodson's return, Nicholson left camp with a much larger column of 1,600 infantry, 450 cavalry and 16 horse artillery guns. His orders were to pursue and bring to action a superior force of 6,000 mutineers* and 15 guns which, led by the rebel Commander-in-Chief Bakht Khan, was attempting to intercept the siege-train as it crawled down the Grand Trunk Road towards Delhi. The rebel force had departed a day earlier and, acting on intelligence that it was heading for the canal bridge at Najafgarh, 20 miles west of Delhi, Nicholson moved in the same direction. It was a torturous march: heavy rain had turned the road into a quagmire; in places it was lost in swamps and floods through which the guns had to be dragged by hand. The sun was beginning to set when the advance guard reached a swollen branch of the Najafgarh Canal and got its first sight of the enemy position. It extended from the bridge over the canal proper to the town of Najafgarh, a distance of almost two miles. Expecting an attack across the bridge, the rebels had concentrated their batteries between the bridge on the right of their line and an old serai, a stone enclosure, on their left centre: three guns were on the bridge, four in the serai and three each in two villages in between; all the batteries were protected by entrenchments, parapets and embrasures.

As the strongest point in the enemy position was the serai, Nicholson chose to attack it first before rolling up the line of rebel guns to the bridge. But first his men had to struggle across the flooded tributary, waist deep in water, under heavy fire from the serai's battery. Once over, Nicholson led

* Composed mainly of the Nimach and Bareilly Brigades.

his assault troops – the 61st Foot, the 1st Bengal Fusiliers and the 2nd Punjab Infantry – to a point 300 yards from the serai, where they were ordered to lie down. Then, rising in his stirrups, he reminded them of the words Sir Colin Campbell had spoken at the battles of Chilianwala and Alma: 'Hold your fire till you are within twenty or thirty yards of the enemy, then pour your volleys into them, give them a bayonet-charge, and the serai is yours.' Soon after, the battery of horse artillery galloped up, unlimbered and opened fire with roundshot on the serai. 'The order was then given to the attacking column to stand up,' recalled 'Butcher' Vibart, who was with the 1st Bengals, 'and having fixed bayonets, the three regiments, led by General Nicholson in person, steadily advanced in an almost unbroken line to within one hundred yards of the enclosure, when the word of command rang out from . . . Major Jacob, "Prepare to charge!" "Charge!"'

On they ran through a storm of musket-balls and grape. Nicholson's horse was hit, forcing him to continue on foot; Vibart had a narrow escape when a bullet deflected off the blade of his sword. 'Thank you, sir,' cried a soldier in the ranks behind him, 'that saved me.' The first officer to cross the stone wall was Lieutenant Gabbett of the 61st. As he made for the nearest gun he slipped on the wet ground and was bayoneted by a 'gigantic pandy'; but Captain Trench, Nicholson's ADC, 'quickly avenged his death by bringing down the rebel with his revolver'. Within minutes the assault troops had 'scaled the walls, carried the serai, and captured all the guns'. Vibart recalled: 'Only a few of the rebels fought with any pluck, and these were seen standing on the walls, loading and firing with the greatest deliberation until we were close upon them. But few of these escaped, as they were nearly all bayoneted within the enclosure.'

Now, changing front, the British column swept along the entrenchment to the bridge, capturing thirteen guns and driving the enemy before it. Lieutenant Griffiths of the 61st Foot recalled:

Our Horse Artillery, under Major Tombs, mowed down the fugitives in hundreds, and continued following and firing on them till darkness set in. The cavalry also – a squadron of the gallant 9th Lancers, with the Guides and Punjabees – did their share of work, while the European infantry were nobly supported by the corps of the Punjab Rifles, who cleared the town of the sepoys. The battle had lasted a very short time, and after dark we bivouacked in the pouring rain, completely exhausted from our long march and subsequent fighting, and faint from want of food, none of which passed our lips for more than sixteen hours.

But one village to the rear still held out. 'I immediately sent orders to Lieutenant Lumsden [of the 1st Punjab Rifles] . . . to drive them out,' wrote Nicholson, 'but though few in number, they had remained so long that our troops were on all sides of them, and seeing no line of retreat they fought with extreme desperation.' The initial assault was repulsed and Lumsden killed. So the 61st joined in, but they 'met with only partial success . . . the enemy evacuating the place during the night'. That apart, the action had been the most decisive since Badli-ki-Serai: all but two of the rebel guns had been captured; the vaunted Nimach Brigade, the victor of Sasia, had been comprehensively defeated; and the only bridge by which the mutineers could get to the British rear had been captured and destroyed. But Nicholson had been lucky: he had caught the Nimach Brigade alone because its commander had refused to cooperate with the Rohilkhand Brigade of Bakht Khan, his nominal superior, which was four miles further on and 'unable or unwilling to come up'. The rebel casualties, according to Munshi Jiwan Lal, were 'a thousand killed and wounded'.

On hearing of the Nimach Brigade's defeat, Bakht Khan made straight for Delhi, where the King accused him of being 'false to his salt' for 'turning away from the field of battle'. The King did not relieve him of the Supreme Command because there was no obvious alternative. Yet Bakht Khan's failure to engage the British at Najafgarh had destroyed his credibility in the eyes of many mutineers. They were, in any case, still unhappy about their pay.* On 1 September five hundred officers and nobles attended a royal durbar to discuss the issue. According to Munshi Jiwan Lal, a number of those present 'were loud in their complaints that Mirza Mogul and Mirza Kizr had taken several lakhs of rupees from the people in the city, and had given nothing to the Army, and prayed the King to insist on them disgorging some of the money, threatening to arrest and imprison them'. The upshot of this stormy meeting was that the rebel officers were promised the first instalment of their pay in a day's time and the balance within two weeks. This seemed to satisfy them and they rejoined their regiments.

Nicholson, meanwhile, had returned to Delhi a hero. In under two days his men had marched 40 miles, won a battle against a superior force, captured thirteen guns and demolished a key bridge. 'Considering that the country was nearly impassable from swamps,' wrote an admiring Wilson to his wife, 'I look upon it as one of the most heroic instances of pluck and endurance on record, and [it] does credit as well to Nicholson as the gallant fellows under him.' Sir

* See Appendix Three, pp. 394–5.

John Lawrence was just as impressed. 'I wish I had the power of knighting you on the spot,' he wrote to Nicholson from Lahore. 'It should be done.'

Wilson's thoughts now returned to his chief objective: the capture of Delhi. But even after the arrival of the siege-train* on 4 September he was loath to order an assault. By 6 September reinforcements had increased the number of effectives to more than 11,000 men† (though 2,200 of them were the Maharaja of Jammu's troops and of doubtful quality); a further 3,000 men were in hospital and the number was rising daily. Wilson had been told by Sir John Lawrence that he could expect no more troops and that an assault was imperative. 'Every day disaffection and mutiny spread,'‡ wrote Lawrence on 29 August. 'Every day adds to the danger of the European Princes taking part against us.' Wilson knew that the number of sick was steadily rising. Yet still he procrastinated. Fred Roberts, then on Nicholson's staff, wrote later:

Everyone felt that the time had come for the assault to be made, and Wilson's hesitation caused considerable anxiety. For some unaccountable reason he kept hoping that assistance would come from the South. I say unaccountable because we all knew: –

1. That Cawnpore had fallen into the enemy's hands.
2. That Henry Lawrence was dead and that Lucknow was still being besieged.
3. That Havelock had written on the 25th July that he had found it impossible to force his way through to Lucknow and had been obliged to fall back upon Cawnpore.
4. That all the British troops and residents at Agra were shut up in the fort.

In the early days at Delhi we had hoped that troops would arrive from England in time to help us, but by September it was clear that this was impossible . . . There was no place to retreat to and on the slightest sign of our giving in the Punjab would have risen – in more places than one disturbances had already broken out.

* Thirty-two howitzers and heavy mortars and more than a hundred bullock-carts of ammunition.

† But only 3,317 were European troops: 580 artillery, 443 cavalry and 2,294 infantry. The infantry regiments were shadows of their former selves, the strongest numbering 409 effectives. The 52nd, which had arrived 600 strong, had already dwindled to 242 fit for duty.

‡ Particularly in the Punjab. There had already been an attempted conspiracy of Muslim tribes in the Murree Hills and an insurrection in Gogaira; moreover, many Sikhs were unconvinced about the durability of British rule and were refusing to enlist. Late August also saw three mutinies by disarmed corps in the Punjab: the 10th Light Cavalry at Ferozepore, the 51st Native Infantry at Peshawar, and the 62nd and 69th Native Infantry at Multan.

When Wilson first took over the command he did very well – far better than either of his two predecessors. We artillerymen especially were proud of having an officer of our own regiment at the head of the Delhi Field Force. But six weeks of responsibility told heavily upon him. The strain was tremendous, and there is no doubt he was quite broken down by the beginning of September.

Wilson confirmed as much in a letter to his wife of 5 September: 'We are busy preparing for the final struggle, and my work is almost more than I can carry through. I get so exhausted and my head so confused that I at times almost despair. It is made worse by my not sleeping well at night.' The consequences of a failed assault were clearly uppermost in his mind; at the same time the pressure on him to act was becoming irresistible. No one was more voluble in this respect than his chief engineer, Lieutenant-Colonel Richard Baird-Smith, who 'fully appreciated the tremendous risks which an assault involved', but who felt 'they were less than those of delay'. Baird-Smith was strongly supported by his executive engineer, Lieutenant Alex Taylor, and most of the senior officers on the Ridge, including Nicholson, Chamberlain, Daly and Norman, the acting adjutant-general. At last Wilson bowed to the pressure and agreed to let the engineers prepare a plan of attack. But his objections continued. Baird-Smith recalled: 'I believe his mind to have been a little off its usual balance all the time we were at work, and he was literally more difficult to deal with than the enemy. It was only by constantly reminding him that if he interfered with my plans, I would throw the whole responsibility for the consequences on him, that I could get on at all.'

The question of an assault finally came to a head at a council of war in Wilson's tent on 7 September. Fred Roberts recalled:

I was sitting in [Nicholson's] tent before he set out to attend the council. He had been talking to me in confidential terms . . . and ended by telling me of his intention to take a very unusual step should the council fail to arrive at any fixed determination regarding the assault. 'Delhi must be taken,' he said, 'and it is absolutely essential that this should be done at once; and if Wilson hesitates longer, I intend to propose at today's meeting that he should be superseded.' I was greatly startled, and ventured to remark that, as Chamberlain was *hors de combat* from his wound, Wilson's removal would leave him, Nicholson, the senior officer with the force. He smiled as he answered: 'I have not overlooked that fact. I shall make it perfectly clear that, under the circumstances, I could not possibly accept the command myself, and I shall propose that it be given to Campbell of the 52nd; I am prepared to serve under him for the time being, so no one can ever accuse me of being influenced by personal motives.

As it happened, Nicholson's resolve to overthrow his commander was not put to the test because, at the council of war, Wilson bowed to the inevitable. He accepted Baird-Smith's plan of assault in its entirety, but with the proviso that the chief engineer would take the blame if it failed. In a letter to Sir John Lawrence, an elated Nicholson could not hide his contempt for Wilson: 'I have seen lots of useless generals in my day; but such an ignorant, croaking obstructive as he is, I have hitherto never met with . . . The purport of his last message in reply to the Engineers ran thus: 'I disagree with the Engineers entirely. I foresee great, if not insuperable difficulties in the plan they propose. But as I have no other plan myself, I yield to the urgent remonstrances of the chief engineer.'

The engineers' plan was to build batteries close enough to the city walls for the new siege guns to be effective. The site chosen was the area between Ludlow Castle, the commissioner's residence that the rebels had left unoccupied, and the Kashmir and Water Bastions at the north of the city. A ravine here, running east to west, offered the sappers a modicum of cover as they worked. The intention was first to establish a heavy battery on the western side of the ravine to suppress the fire from the Mori and Kashmir Bastions. Then three siege batteries could be constructed in front of Ludlow Castle, the closest only 180 yards from the walls. These would make the breaches. It is unclear who was chiefly responsible for the plan: Baird-Smith has generally been given the credit because he was the senior engineer; but Taylor was the one who, with Nicholson, undertook the hazardous task of reconnoitring the sites and who personally supervised their construction.

Work began on the first battery, known as No. 1, during the night of 7 September. By sunrise its four 24-pounders, five 18-pounders and one 18-inch mortar were ready to open fire. The adjutant of the 75th Foot recalled:

The Moree proceeded to administer its usual dose to the piquets, but the smoke had scarcely spurted from its embrasures when the leafy screen was torn from our battery and we could see the iron hail strike the wall, sending up clouds of dust and bringing the masonry down into the ditch. It must have been an astonisher to the fellows in the bastion, but they quickly recovered from their surprise and turning the guns on the battery commenced a regular duel with it; our fellows continued to fire salvos, that is, all the guns fired together like an infantry volley, and the effect of such a weight of metal striking the walls at once soon became apparent, for the Moree began to look like a large heap of earth, and gun after gun was disabled in the front of it till at length not one was fit for service.

That evening, Ludlow Castle was occupied and work began on No. 2 Battery, just 500 yards from the Kashmir Bastion. The rebels had assumed that the focal point of any British attack would be against the Kabul and Lahore Gates on the west side of the city. Now, disabused of that notion, they did everything they could to prevent the siege batteries from being constructed. But the engineers would not be deterred. No. 2 Battery* was ready on 11 September, the remaining two† a day later. No. 3 Battery, the closest to the walls, had been built under 'a constant fire of musketry' that inevitably cost the Indian workmen‡ many casualties: thirty-nine during the first night of work. Fred Roberts, who was in charge of two guns in No. 2 Battery, had nothing but admiration for the bravery of these unarmed pioneers. 'As man after man was knocked over,' he wrote, 'they would stop a moment, weep a little over a fallen friend, place his body in a row with the rest, and then work on as before.'

The morning of 12 September saw the combined fire of all four batteries – a total of fifty guns and mortars – unleashed upon Delhi's walls. The rebels, unable to fire from their ruined bastions, brought their guns out into the open and enfiladed the siege batteries. They also sited a gun in the curtain wall near the Kashmir Bastion, fired rockets from one of their towers and 'maintained a perfect storm of musketry from their advanced trench and from the city walls'. British casualties alone were more than three hundred during the six days prior to the assault.

At dusk on 13 September two pairs of engineer officers – Lieutenants Lang,§ Medley, Greathed and Home – went to reconnoitre the breaches near the Kashmir and Water Bastions. Lieutenants Lang and Medley made

* Seven heavy howitzers, two 18-pounders and nine 24-pounders.

† No. 3 Battery comprised six 18-pounders and twelve 5½-inch mortars; No. 4 Battery, sited between 2 and 3, ten heavy mortars.

‡ The British camp on the Ridge was a magnet for thousands of Indian camp-followers who were prepared to risk their lives for a few annas a day.

§ Lieutenant Arthur Lang, who arrived at Delhi from Lahore on 27 July, had already carried out a daring daytime reconnaissance on the breach near the Kashmir Bastion, but was sent back in company with Medley to ascertain whether ladders would be required to scale the ditch.

it across the ditch and were about to ascend the rubble in the breach when the appearance of two sepoy sentries forced them to retire. Both pairs reported to Baird-Smith that the breaches were 'practicable'. He, in turn, convinced Wilson that to delay any longer would be fatal. Finally Wilson gave orders for the attack to take place the following morning.

The infantry assigned to the assault was divided into five columns:* the first, commanded by Brigadier-General Nicholson, was given the task of storming the broken face of the Kashmir Bastion and the nearby breach in the wall, before clearing the ramparts and bastions as far as the Ajmir Gate; the second, under Brigadier Jones of the 61st Foot, was to storm the breach in the Water Bastion and follow Nicholson as far as the Kabul Gate; the third, led by Colonel Campbell of the 52nd Light Infantry, was to enter through the shattered Kashmir Gate and head through the heart of the city towards the Jama Masjid mosque; the fourth, under Major Reid of the Sirmur Battalion, was to attack the suburbs of Kisenganj and Paharipur, and support 'the main attack by effecting an entrance at the Cabul Gate after it should be taken'; the fifth, under Brigadier Longfield, was to cover Nicholson's column and form a reserve. In addition the Cavalry Brigade, under Brigadier Hope Grant, was to take up a position on the right of No. 1 Battery to oppose any attempt at taking the storming columns in the flank. With so many soldiers devoted to the attack, only a thin covering screen of cavalry, artillery and convalescents was available to protect the camp. 'A very insufficient guard,' wrote one officer, 'when it is considered that the enemy might well, out of their vast numbers, have detached part of their horsemen and infantry to harass, if not imperil, its safety and that of the many sick and wounded.'

The plan was to attack at dawn. But many of the men assigned to the storming columns had been on picket duty and it took some time for them to rejoin their corps. A further delay was caused by the need to destroy the partial repairs to the breaches that the rebels had effected during the night. It was, therefore, daylight when the breaching guns ceased fire and the order to advance was given. 'No sooner were the front ranks seen by the rebels,' recalled Fred Roberts, who was watching with Wilson from Ludlow Castle,

* The 1st column (1,000 men) was made up of HM 75th Foot, 1st Bengal Fusiliers and 2nd Punjab Infantry; the 2nd column (850 men) of HM 8th Foot, 2nd Bengal Fusiliers and 4th Sikhs; the 3rd column (950 men) of HM 52nd Light Infantry, Kumaon Battalion and 1st Punjab Infantry; the 4th column (860 men) of the Sirmur Battalion, Guides Infantry and various other units, as well as 1,200 men of the Jammu Contingent; the reserve column (1,000 men) of HM 61st Foot, 4th Punjab Infantry and the Baluch Battalion, as well as 300 of the Jhind Contingent.

than a storm of bullets met them from every side, and officers and men fell thick on the crest of the glacis. Then, for a few seconds, amidst a blaze of musketry, the soldiers stood at the edge of the ditch, for only one or two of the ladders had come up, the rest having been dropped by their killed or wounded carriers. Dark figures crowded on the breach, hurling stones upon our men, and daring them to come on. More ladders were brought up, they were thrown into the ditch, and our men, leaping into it, raised them against the escarp on the other side. Nicholson, at the head of a part of his column, was the first to ascend the breach in the curtain. The remainder of his troops diverged a little to the right to escalade the breach in the Kashmir bastion.

The engineer officer leading this party was Lieutenant Arthur Lang, who recorded:

Up went our ladder, but once on the berm we instantly saw that there was no place for placing our long ladders, so we scrambled just a steep, crumbling wall of masonry. I have seen it since in cold blood, and wondered how we got up at all. I was just falling backwards on our own bayonets when a Gurkha pushed me up luckily, and presently over we were, and, with the 75th and men from the Water Bastion breach, were tearing down the ramp into the Main Guard behind the Kashmere Gate.

While the 1st and 2nd Columns were storming the breaches, the 3rd Column was attacking the Kashmir Gate. On reaching the ditch in front of the gate, the infantry were ordered to lie down while Lieutenants Home and Salkeld of the Bengal Engineers, eight sappers and a bugler from the 52nd Light Infantry went forward to blow the gate. The bridge in front of the gate had been destroyed, and it was no easy task for Home and the men carrying the powder-bags to cross the single beam that remained. All the while the rebels kept up a stream of fire from the top of the gate, the city walls and through the open wicket, killing Sergeant Carmichael and wounding Havildar Mad-hoo. But their comrades managed to nail the bags to the gate before dropping down into the ditch to make way for Salkeld and the firing party. Salkeld was about to fire the charge when he was hit in the leg and arm. He handed the slow-match to Corporal Burgess, who, though mortally wounded, managed to complete the task.* As the noise of the explosion died away,

* Four of the eleven-strong party received the Victoria Cross: Lieutenants Duncan Home and Philip Salkeld (Bengal Engineers), Sergeant John Smith (Bengal Sappers and Miners) and Bugler Robert Hawthorne (HM 52nd Light Infantry). Both officers were dead within a month: Home was killed at Malagarh; Salkeld died of his wounds.

Bugler Hawthorne sounded the advance. Ensign Wilberforce, part of the storming party of the 52nd that was sheltering in the ditch, remembered:

Away we went. Inside that sheltering glacis was security from the murderous fire to which we had been exposed . . . I saw my Captain, Crosse, go in through the Gate. It was only large enough to admit one at a time. I was going next when Corporal Taylor pushed me on one side and got second. I came next – third man in. Through the gateway we saw an open square, the sunlight pouring into it – empty. Under the arch of the gateway stood a nine-pounder gun . . . Near to and around the gun lay some dead bodies, the defenders of the Gate, the men who had shot the devoted Salkeld . . . The Gate was soon thrown open, and our men, Coke's Rifles, and the Kumaon battalion, which formed our assaulting column, poured in after us.

As the 3rd Column entered the open space between the Main Guard and the charred ruins of St James's Church, its men met and mingled with soldiers from the first two columns. Gradually the columns sorted themselves out and set off towards their various objectives: the 1st and 2nd Columns up the narrow road that followed the ramparts; the 3rd Column towards the Jama Masjid and the *kotwali*. For a time, however, the 1st Column was without Nicholson because he and Alex Taylor had taken a wrong turn towards Skinner's House. Instead it was left to Lieutenant Lang to lead the way. He recalled:

On we rushed, shouting and cheering, while the grape and musketry from each bend, and from every street leading from our left, and from rampart and housetop, knocked down men and officers. It was exciting to madness and I felt no feeling except to rush on and hit: I only wondered how much longer I could possibly go on unhit, when the whole air seemed full of bullets . . .

We poured past the Kabul Gate and we went swimmingly along until we nearly reached the Lahore; then a short check was given by a barricade with a gun firing grape from behind it. Brig. Jones came up and called for the Engineer officer and asked where the Kabul Gate was . . . 'Far behind,' I said. 'We shall have the Lahore presently.' Alas, he declared that his orders were to stop at the Kabul.

Lang and others in the vanguard were all for continuing. But the opposition had stiffened and it was as much as they could do to hold the ground already gained. 'As long as we rushed on cheering and never stopping, all went well,' recalled Lang. 'But the check was sad: the men, crouching behind corners, and in the archways which support the ramparts, gradually nursed a panic.' Assailed by a storm of rebel musket and cannon fire, the advance troops began to retire in ones and twos. The officers did their best to stem the flow. But, within half an hour, the trickle had became a flood, and the officers were swept along in the headlong retreat back to the Kabul Gate.

It was now that Nicholson rejoined his column and resumed command. Minutes earlier he had been spotted on the walls of the Mori Bastion by Brigadier Hope Grant, commander of the cavalry brigade supporting the 4th Column. Nicholson had shouted down to Grant that all was going to plan, and that he was about to attack the Lahore Gate. Grant had less encouraging news: the 4th Column's attack, led by Major Reid of the Sirmur Battalion, had been repulsed from the suburbs outside the Kabul Gate. A rebel counter-attack was now driving the entire column back to its starting point in the gardens of Sabzi Mundi. 'We saw the repulse of Reid's column,' wrote the recuperating Neville Chamberlain, who was watching from his stretcher on the roof of Hindu Rao's house, 'and could not fail to admire the conduct of the mutineer native officers as they rode along in front of their regiments endeavouring to incite their men to press home their advantage against the Cashmere Contingent . . . The Jummoo troops bolted,* lost the whole or a portion of their guns, came back on our men, created a panic, and we were driven back in confusion . . . So critical did affairs then look that it seemed possible the enemy might succeed in passing through, or might turn our right defences and attack them from the rear.' Chamberlain's response was to order his bearers to carry him down to the gardens, where he rallied the beaten troops and organized a defensive position from his stretcher.

All this time Grant's cavalry brigade had been watching helplessly, unable to ride to the assistance of Reid's column because of the broken and built-up nature of the ground. Instead they had moved round to a position on the far right, less than 500 yards from the Lahore Gate. But the failure of Reid's column to take the ground in front of the Kabul Gate, and Nicholson's inability to progress beyond the same point within the city, meant that Grant's men were subjected to a galling fire from the untouched heavy guns of the Burn Bastion and Lahore Gate. Grant and four of his staff had their horses killed under them; two of them were wounded, and Grant himself

* Wilson also blamed the failure of the attack on 'the cowardice of the Jummoo contingent, who ran away leaving their guns to the enemy' (Wilson to his wife, 15 September 1857, Wilson Letters, NAM, 6807-483).

was hit by a spent musket-ball. Tombs's troop of horse artillery lost half its 50 men and a further 17 horses; the 9th Lancers had 38 casualties and 71 horses wounded. 'Nothing daunted,' wrote Grant, 'those gallant fellows held their trying position with patient endurance; and on my praising them for their good behaviour, they declared their readiness to stand the fire as long as I chose.'

It may well have been the plight of the cavalry that made Nicholson so determined to achieve his last objective by capturing the Lahore Gate. But to do so he first had to take the Burn Bastion, which lay at the end of a narrow lane, 200 yards long, flanked on one side by the city wall and on the other by flat-roofed houses swarming with rebel snipers. Twice men from the 1st Bengal Fusiliers had tried to advance down the lane and twice they had been driven back with heavy losses, including their commander, Major Jacob, who was mortally wounded. Now Nicholson himself took charge. Calling on the demoralized fusiliers to follow him, he ran forward into the lane. But halfway down he realized that only a handful of men were still with him. He was in the act of calling the rest to come on, his sword above his head, when he was shot below his exposed right armpit by a sepoy firing down from one of the flat roofs. As he fell, a sergeant of the 1st Fusiliers caught him and dragged him into a small recess below the city wall. For some time he refused to be moved, saying he would stay until Delhi had been taken. Eventually he relented and was carried back to the Kabul Gate and placed in a doolie. The bearers were told to take him to the field hospital beyond the Ridge, but they preferred to plunder and left him on the side of the road a short way beyond the Kashmir Gate.

General Wilson had watched the start of the assault from the roof of Ludlow Castle. When it became clear that the first three columns had gained a foothold in the city, he rode with his staff through the Kashmir Gate and set up his advanced headquarters in the ruins of St Thomas's Church. There he remained for the rest of the day, becoming 'more anxious and depressed' as report after discouraging report came in. 'He heard of Reid's failure,' recalled Fred Roberts, 'and of Reid himself having been severely wounded; then came the disastrous news that Nicholson had fallen, and a report (happily false) that Hope Grant and Tombs were both killed. All this greatly agitated and depressed the General, until at last he began seriously to consider the advisability of leaving the city and falling back on the Ridge. I was ordered to go and find out the truth of these reports, and to ascertain exactly what had happened to No. 4 column and the Cavalry on our right.'

Roberts had just ridden through the Kashmir Gate when he came upon an abandoned doolie. Dismounting to see if he could be of any assistance to the occupant, he discovered to his 'grief and consternation, that it was John Nicholson, with death written on his face'. Nicholson told him that he was in great pain and wished to be taken to hospital. Roberts, observing no visible sign of injury, expressed the hope that he was not seriously wounded. 'I am dying,' replied Nicholson, 'there is no chance for me.' Roberts was shocked. He had seen many men die, but to lose Nicholson at that moment was to 'lose everything'. Only with difficulty did he gather four doolie-bearers from the multitude of camp-followers who were looting property in the vicinity and place them under the orders of a sergeant of the 61st Foot. He never saw Nicholson again.

Continuing his mission, Roberts eventually came across the Cavalry Brigade. Delighted to discover that both Tombs and Hope Grant were still alive, and that there was 'no need for further anxiety about Reid's column', he galloped back to the church to report to Wilson. The news cheered Wilson without entirely dispelling his forebodings – and these increased when word arrived soon after that Campbell's column had been forced to retire from the Jama Masjid, its furthest point of advance, to the area around the church. This failure, coupled with the 'hopelessness of Nicholson's condition, and, above all, the heavy list of casualties which he received later,* appeared to crush all spirit and energy' out of Wilson. He became more convinced than ever of the need to withdraw from the city and would, in Roberts's opinion, have 'carried out this fatal measure' had it not been for the presence of his chief engineer, Richard Baird-Smith, who had insisted on remaining at headquarters despite suffering from dysentery and a painful leg wound. When asked for his opinion, Baird-Smith's reply was emphatic: 'We *must* hold on.'

Chamberlain gave the same response to a letter from Wilson, written at four in the afternoon, stating that 'if the Hindu Rao's picquet cannot be moved, I do not think we shall be strong enough to take the city'. It was, said Chamberlain, imperative to hold on to the last, not least because the ground already gained would have severely demoralized the enemy. The dying Nicholson was just as determined. When told of Wilson's suggestion to retire, he rose up in bed and roared: 'Thank God I have strength yet to shoot him, if necessary.'

* During the first day of the assault, 14 September 1857, the Delhi Field Force's casualties were sixty-six officers and 1,104 men killed and wounded, or two men in nine.

Faced with this consensus of opinion, Wilson gave up all idea of retreating. But he could not dispel his fear of failure for some days yet, as his letters to his wife demonstrate. 'We are now holding what we have taken, but nothing more,' he wrote on the 15th. 'Our position is from the Cabul Gate to the College, and I cannot say we have complete possession of that. I am in Skinner's house . . . The Europeans with the Column with me got hold of lots of beer in the Shops, and made themselves helpless. I have not a Queen's officer under me worth a pin, or who can preserve any sort of discipline except Jones of the 60th Rifles, in fact the men are so badly officered that they will and can do nothing tomorrow . . . All we can now expect to do, is to get on gradually, but this street fighting is frightful work. Pandy is as good a soldier at that as our men.'

The fighting technique employed by Lieutenant Lang and soldiers of the 1st Column in the vicinity of the Kabul Gate was to climb on to the roof of a house and fire down into the next yard while sappers picked a hole through the wall into the adjoining house. They would then storm through the hole, turn out any non-combatants* and secure the house. And so on. But on the 15th they were forced to concede some ground and spent the day erecting parapets on the rooftops out of 'gaily painted doors and sandbags'.

The following day the 61st Foot took the magazine and Lang was given the task of setting up a battery to play on the Selimgarh Fort and neighbouring Royal Palace. Yet Wilson's spirits were lower than ever. 'Our force is too weak for this street fighting, where we have to gain our way inch by inch,' he informed his wife on the 16th. As Wilson's letter of the 15th mentioned, part of the problem was drunkenness, particularly among his European and Sikh troops who had got hold of an 'immense quantity of wines, spirits and beer' and were 'incapable of doing their duty'.

On 17 September the 52nd Light Infantry occupied the Bank of Delhi on the Chandni Chauk ('Silver Bazaar'), the famous main street of jewellers and cloth merchants that ran from the Red Fort to the Lahore Gate. Also

* In his 'General Order' of 6 September 1857, Wilson had told his men to give 'no quarter' to the mutineers. But for the 'sake of humanity, and the honour of the country they belong to', he asked them 'to spare all women and children that may come in their way'. On the whole this request was adhered to. Able-bodied men, on the other hand, were invariably 'taken for rebels and shot'. Mainodin Hassan Khan, the rebel *kotwal* of Delhi, recorded: 'The green as well as the dry trees were consumed; the guiltless shared the same fate as the guilty. As innocent Christians fell victims on the 11th of May, so the same evil fate befel the Mahommedans on the 20th September, 1857. The gallows slew those who had escaped the sword.' (*Two Native Narratives*, 72.)

that day Hodson's spies reported that most of the mutineers had already fled the city in the direction of Mathura, and that those remaining were about to follow. This news reinvigorated Wilson, who told his wife that the rebels appeared to be 'very disheartened' and that he would not be surprised 'to find the whole City with exception to the Palace evacuated in two or three days'.

Unknown to Wilson until the following day, the King of Delhi and his family had left the Red Fort during the afternoon of the 18th and taken refuge in Humayun's tomb,* six miles south of the city. Bakht Khan is said to have begged the King to accompany him and a large force to Lucknow. But the King refused and Bakht Khan departed without him, taking as many men as he could muster. With the rebel garrison greatly reduced, Wilson's men made significant gains on the 19th, notably the Burn Bastion, which was captured by Lang, Roberts and fewer than fifty men. Even now Wilson's letters to his wife were only cautiously optimistic. 'We are . . . progressing favourably through bombarding the City and gradually seizing strong posts,' he wrote.

The following day it was all over. First Lang and Roberts repeated their feat of the previous day by taking the Lahore Gate from the rear with a small force; then they advanced up the deserted Chandni Chouk, 'finding none but dead and wounded Pandies, and wondering at our finding our way all clear before us'. Meanwhile a separate column had occupied the Jama Masjid and Ensign McQueen of the 4th Punjab Infantry had ascertained that the Red Fort was all but denuded of defenders. So Lang and Roberts pushed on to the Lahore Gate of the fort. Powder was brought by another engineer officer, Lieutenant Home, and the outer gate was blown in. 'As soon as the smoke of the explosion died away,' recalled Roberts, 'the 60th [Rifles], supported by the 4th Punjab Infantry, sprang through the gateway; but we did not get far, for there was a second door beyond, chained and barred, which was with difficulty forced open, when the whole party rushed in. The recesses in the long passage which led to the palace buildings were crowded with wounded men, but there was very little opposition, for only a few fanatics still held out.'

According to Lang, the race to 'sit first in the crystal throne of the Moghuls in the Diwan-i-Khas' was between an officer named Murray and a private of the 60th. He does not mention the victor, but adds:

* Humayun (1530–56) was the second of the six great Mogul Emperors.

British soldiers and Sikhs rummaged all the swell private rooms and marble baths of the Zenana. All the valuables seemed to have been taken away, and what was left the troops seized and tossed about. I took a little book which I *say* was a present from the Prince of Bokhara to the Delhi family! It was in an elegant private room in the Zenana; there I took too five pachisi* markers of glass which young princesses had been playing with just before their flight: but no real valuable plunder are we allowed to take.

Wilson's 'General Order' of 6 September had prohibited 'indiscriminate plunder' and instead appointed prize agents to collect and sell 'all captured property' with the proceeds divided 'fairly among all men engaged'. It was widely ignored as both officers and men 'appropriated to their own use much treasure that ought to have gone towards swelling the general fund'. Nevertheless, goods worth more than £350,000 were handed in. And honesty did not pay because, shortly after the fall of Delhi, Canning countermanded Wilson's order by forbidding the payment of prize money for goods stolen from British subjects, which the Indians technically were. The official reward for the victors of Delhi was restricted to the standard campaign batta of 36 rupees and 10 annas for privates and 450 rupees for lieutenants. The soldiers were incensed and took care not to surrender plunder during subsequent operations. Eventually the Indian government gave in to public pressure in Britain and agreed to distribute the prize money for Delhi in two instalments: the first in 1862, the second in 1865. The basic share for privates was £17 (almost a year's pay); ensigns received five shares, captains eleven and a half and Wilson, the Commander-in-Chief, a sixteenth of the total, 'an immense sum'.

That evening, 20 September, Lang and others celebrated the taking of Delhi by riding their horses up the steps of the Jama Masjid, dancing jigs and drinking toasts of beer and brandy. Sikh soldiers celebrated by lighting fires in the sacred mosque.

The following morning Wilson established his headquarters in the Diwan-i-Khas. One of his first visitors was Hodson, who had discovered that Bahadur Shah and the principal members of his family were sheltering in Humayun's tomb. Hodson volunteered to arrest them, pointing out that 'victory would be incomplete if the King and his male relatives were allowed to remain at large'. Wilson replied that the enterprise was too dangerous.

* An Indian game similar to ludo.

Even when Hodson enlisted the support of Neville Chamberlain, Wilson 'would not consent to any force being sent after them, and it was with considerable reluctance that he agreed to Hodson going on this hazardous duty with some of his men only'. Hodson set off at once with a hundred horsemen and soon reached the tomb, a magnificent structure of red sandstone inlaid with white marble whose grounds were thronged with thousands of armed retainers. Halting at the gateway, he sent in two emissaries to negotiate with Bahadur Shah. In return for surrendering, his life and that of his favourite wife, Begum Zinat Mahal, and her son, Mirza Jawan Bakht, would be guaranteed. After two hours of tense negotiations, Bahadur Shah and the Begum appeared in a *gharry* and Hodson escorted them back to Delhi, where they were placed under an armed guard in the Begum's house in Chandi Chauk.

Bahadur Shah remained in Delhi until his trial in January 1858,* a figure of curiosity for the many Europeans who found it hard to believe that this was the man in whose name the rebellion had begun. Among his visitors was 'Butcher' Vibart, who had more reason to resent him than most, but who actually felt more pity than anger. Vibart recorded:

> At the door stood a European sentry, but I had no difficulty in gaining admittance, and there I saw, sitting cross-legged on a native bedstead, on which he was rocking himself to and fro, a small and attenuated old man apparently between eighty and ninety years of age, with a long white beard, and almost totally blind. He was repeating to himself, in a low but audible murmur, some verses of the Koran, or it may be of some of his own poetical compositions – for he aspired to be a poet – and he certainly looked an object of pity and compassion . . . and not feeling inclined to disturb them by making any remarks, I merely stood and gazed for a while in silence on this woe-begone picture of fallen greatness, and then left the poor old man still mumbling to himself in the solitude of his dreary apartment.

On 24 September, having convinced Wilson of the need to arrest the King's sons, Hodson returned to Humayun's tomb. Lieutenant Macdowell, Hodson's second-in-command, takes up the story:

* Bahadur Shah was arraigned before a military commission at Delhi on 27 January 1858 on charges of rebellion, treason and murder. After a trial lasting forty days, he was found guilty on all counts, but no sentence was passed because Hodson had guaranteed his life. Instead the government exiled him, Begum Zinat Mahal and the surviving members of his family to Rangoon. He died there in 1862.

We started at eight o'clock, and halted half a mile from the tomb where the Princes were. Close by were about 3,000 of their Mussalmen followers, so it was rather a ticklish bit of work. We sent in to say the Princes must give themselves up unconditionally, or take the consequences. A long half hour elapsed, when a messenger came out to say the Princes wished to know if their lives would be promised them if they came out. 'Unconditional surrender,' was the answer. Again we waited. It was a most anxious time . . . We heard the shouts of the fanatics . . . begging the Princes to lead them on against us. And we had only one hundred men and were six miles from Delhi. At length . . . they resolved to give themselves up . . . Soon the Princes [two of the King's sons, Mirza Mogul and Mirza Kizr Sultan, and his grandson, Mirza Abu Bakr] appeared in a cart. Behind them thronged about 2,000 or 3,000 Mussulmans (I am not exaggerating).

Hodson told ten sowars to hurry the princes into the city while he and the rest of his men kept back the mob. The best way to do this, Hodson reasoned, would be to disarm the crowd. So accompanied by just four men he entered the garden in front of the tomb and ordered the men there to lay down their arms. Macdowell recorded: 'There was a murmur. He reiterated the command and (God knows why, I never can understand it) they commenced doing so.'

When all the weapons had been thrown into a cart, Hodson and his men set off for Delhi, overtaking the princes and their small escort about a mile from the city walls. 'I came up *just in time*,' wrote Hodson, 'as a large crowd had collected and were turning on the guard. I rode in among them at a gallop, and in a few words appealed to the crowd, saying that these were the butchers who had murdered and brutally used helpless women and children, and that the Government had now sent their punishment: seizing a carbine from one of my men, I deliberately shot them one after another.' Hodson's version of events is open to question. According to Macdowell, there was no overt threat from the crowd when Hodson caught up with the princes and declared: 'I think we had better shoot them here. We shall never get them in.' He did not help his cause by stripping the princes of some signet rings, a turquoise armlet and their swords. Forced to relinquish the jewellery, he was determined to hang on to at least one sword. 'If I ever part with it,' he wrote, 'it shall be to . . . our Good Queen . . . Tombs declares I shall get a CB . . . and, between ourselves, I *ought* to have anything they can give me, for it was a fearful risk.' Reaction to Hodson's summary executions was mixed. Most British officers at Delhi thought the princes had got their just deserts. Even Wilson was supportive, telling his wife that two of the princes 'have been most virulent against us' and that 'Hodson, as a Partizan Officer, has not his equal'. But others, further afield, were not convinced the shootings were necessary, and Hodson's battered reputation suffered still further.

On 23 September, the day after Hodson shot the princes, Nicholson at last succumbed to the wound he had received on the 14th. He had spent most of the intervening period high on morphine, though in his more lucid moments he dictated a number of messages, including one to Sir John Lawrence, begging him to replace Wilson with Chamberlain. Other – more personal – notes were to his mother and Herbert Edwardes. Many officers, including Roberts, tried to visit Nicholson on his deathbed, but were turned away by the faithful Muhammad Hayat Khan, who did not want his master disturbed. Told on the 20th that Delhi had fallen, Nicholson replied that his last wish had 'been granted'. Two days later he was too weak to say more than a few words to Chamberlain. The following day, at one in the afternoon, he died.

Much of British India was grief-stricken – but no one was hit harder than Herbert Edwardes in Peshawar. 'I feel as if all happiness has gone out of my public career,' he telegraphed to Chamberlain. 'It was a pleasure even to behold him. And then his nature was so fully equal to his frame! So undaunted, so noble, so tender, so good, so stern to evil, so single-minded, so generous, so heroic, yet so modest. I never saw another like him, and never expect to do so. And to have had him for a brother, and now to lose him in the prime of life. It is an inexpressible and irreparable grief.' Of the old Punjab hands only Sir John Lawrence, with whom he had crossed swords in the past, was less than fulsome in his praise, though even Lawrence was prepared to acknowledge that he had played the major role in the victory at Delhi. As for Wilson, he mourned the passing of that 'fine fellow Nicholson' with the words: 'What an assistance he would have been to me.'

Nicholson's funeral took place on 24 September in the newly prepared cemetery between the Kashmir Gate and Ludlow Castle. It was a sombre occasion: no 'Dead March', no volleys over the grave. Just a large, respectful crowd of Europeans, Gurkhas, Pathans and Afghans, led by the chief mourner, Neville Chamberlain. Only after the grave had been filled in did Nicholson's frontier horsemen give vent to their grief by throwing themselves on the ground and weeping. Ensign Wilberforce, who was present, recorded:

Probably not one of these men had ever shed a tear; but for them Nicholson was everything. For him they left their frontier homes, for him they had forsaken their beloved hills to come down to the detested plains; they acknowledged none but him, they served none but him. They believed, as others, that the bullet was not cast, the sword not ground, that could hurt him; over and over again in the frontier skirmishes they had seen Nicholson pass unharmed where others must have been killed; and now that the earth was placed on his coffin, they threw their tradition to the wind.

Fred Roberts was among those who missed the funeral. As it took place, he was marching out of Delhi with a mobile column of 2,650 men* and sixteen guns, under Lieutenant-Colonel Edward Greathed of the 8th Foot, sent in pursuit of the 'flying Rebels'. Roberts later described their route along the Chandni Chauk as a 'veritable city of the dead'. He added: 'Dead bodies were strewn about in all directions, in every attitude that the death-struggle had caused them to assume, and in every stage of decomposition . . . Here a dog gnawed at an uncovered limb, there a vulture, disturbed by our approach from its loathsome meal, but too completely gorged to fly, fluttered away to a safer distance . . . Our horses seemed to feel the horror of it as much as we did, for they shook and snorted in evident terror.'

General Wilson remained at Delhi until 4 October, when he was relieved by General Penny and given two months' sick leave with his wife in the hills. For his services at Delhi he was successively awarded a CB, a knighthood, a baronetcy – Sir Archdale Wilson of Delhi – and finally a pension of £1,000 a year. No mention was made in public of his hesitant – almost defeatist – conduct at Delhi until much later. And yet if men of the calibre of Chamberlain, Baird-Smith and, above all, Nicholson, had not stood up to him, he might well have withdrawn his troops from Delhi – an act whose consequences could have been fatal for British India. As it was, the success of the assault was in the balance for at least four days, a fact not lost on Wilson himself. 'Had the fellows had any pluck,' wrote Wilson to his brother on 27 September, 'our small Force must have been annihilated, after getting into the City, which is built of brick houses each a fortification with few exceptions, narrow winding streets, and large masses of shops and buildings. It is only by God's Providence in putting dismay into the Rebels' hearts,

* 750 British and 1,900 Indian troops, including detachments from the 9th Lancers, 8th and 75th Foot, 1st, 2nd and 5th Punjab Cavalry, 2nd and 4th Punjab Infantry, Bengal Sappers and Miners.

that we have succeeded . . . I trust my success will have the effect of cutting the neck of the Rebellion, but there is much to be done yet.'

No sooner had news of Delhi's capture reached Agra than the authorities there* were urging Wilson to move to their assistance 'with a large moveable Column'. But it was as much as Wilson could do to scrape together the troops that he did. The retaking of Delhi had cost the British 992 killed and 2,845 wounded,† out of an effective force that was never more than 10,000 men. Many hundreds more had died of disease and exposure. Most of the seven European regiments were down to barely two hundred effectives. All were 'sadly disorganized', ill-disciplined and, according to Wilson, 'badly commanded from the loss of most of their old Officers'. Yet Wilson was not disheartened. 'If Havelock could only relieve Lucknow and move up this way,' he wrote on 22 September, 'the whole rebellion could be put down.'

* John Colvin, the Lieutenant-Governor of the North-Western Provinces, had died of a mysterious illness on 9 September. E. A. Reade, the next senior civilian, assumed charge of the Agra administration until Calcutta appointed a military officer, Colonel Hugh Fraser of the Bengal Engineers, as Colvin's replacement with the inferior rank of chief commissioner. Colonel Cotton continued as military chief.

† The casualties of the three corps that bore the brunt of the fighting at Delhi were as follows: 60th Rifles, 389 out of 640 men; Sirmur Battalion, 319 out of 540; Corps of Guides, 303 out of 550.

18. The Relief of Lucknow

Wilson could not know it, but the relief of Lucknow was no longer the responsibility of Brigadier-General Havelock alone. On his return to Cawnpore from Bithur in mid August, Havelock learnt from a copy of the *Calcutta Gazette*, dated the 5th, that he had been superseded by Major-General James Outram of the Bombay Army. As the commander of the combined Dinapore and Cawnpore Divisions and Lawrence's successor as chief commissioner of Oudh, Outram was Havelock's military *and* political superior.

Fortunately Outram was a man of great experience and tact. Born in 1803, the younger son of a Derbyshire civil engineer, he had arrived in India four years after Waterloo as an ensign in the Bombay infantry. But his zeal and aptitude for languages were quickly noticed, and at the age of twenty-three, after just six years' service, he was given command of a corps of Bhils, the wild, rapacious tribes who inhabited the Bombay province of Khandesh. Having subdued the more unruly tribes, he quickly gained their trust by his acceptance of their rough sense of justice and honour. It helped that he was powerfully built and afraid of nothing. On one occasion, having shot a tiger that had sprung on him, he is said to have declared: 'What do I care for the clawing of a cat!'

He acted as both soldier and 'political' during the First Afghan War, protecting Nott's line of march through the Bolan Pass in 1842. Sir Charles Napier, on succeeding him as the senior military and political officer in Sind that year, declared: 'Gentlemen, I give you the "Bayard of India", *sans peur et sans reproche*.' The epithet stuck. A year later Outram returned to Sind to act as Napier's right-hand man, and his brilliant defence of the Residency at Hyderabad earned him a CB and a lieutenant-colonelcy. From then until the outbreak of war with Persia in 1856 he was given a succession of important political appointments, including Resident and later Chief Commissioner of Oudh. His successful handling of the Persian campaign, however, had reminded the authorities of his military talents, and Canning toyed with various appointments before putting him in charge of the vast swathe of country between the Presidency Division and Lucknow. 'Outram's arrival was a godsend,' wrote Canning in a private letter. 'There was not a man to whom I could with any approach of confidence entrust the command in Bengal and the Central Provinces.' Lady Canning was not so impressed by the unprepossessing figure who stayed at Government House for five days in early August. 'He is a very common looking little dark Jewish bearded man,' she recorded, 'with a desponding slow hesitating manner, very unlike descriptions – or rather the idea raised in one's mind by the old Bombay name the "Bayard of the East" . . . He is not the least my idea of a hero.'

Outram finally reached Cawnpore on 15 September. In a gesture of extraordinary generosity, he immediately announced his intention to waive his right to military command so that Havelock could complete the task for which he and his brave troops 'have so long and gloriously fought'. He would accompany the relieving force in a purely civil capacity and, if Havelock wished to make use of his military talents, he was prepared to serve under him as a volunteer. Only when Lucknow had been relieved would Outram 'resume his position at the head of the forces'. Havelock was quick to acknowledge Outram's generosity, expressing the hope that his men would strive to 'justify the confidence thus reposed in them'. But his gratitude soon gave way to anger when it became clear that Outram was not content to take a back seat. According to Havelock's son and aide-de-camp, Outram continued to issue orders as 'though he had never resigned in the first place', which meant that 'no one in the force knew who actually was commanding'. The result was 'a hesitancy, tardiness and inexactness of execution [of orders] which put everything into confusion'. When Havelock senior raised the issue, Outram insisted that he had no intention of interfering; yet, after a pause of a couple of hours, he continued to issue directions 'on all sides'. Havelock never regained his self-confidence:

> His false position preyed upon him night and day [wrote his son] . . . In place of being prompt, deciding and unhesitating he appeared to vacillate and falter, often when asked for orders saying 'You had better go to Sir James first' . . . He sacrificed his fame as a soldier to his desire to avoid the appearance of returning Sir James's professed generosity (which I will not undertake to say was not *bona fide* in *intention*, at the same time as it was fatally mischievous in practice) with coldness and ingratitude.

Nevertheless Havelock's force, which had shrunk to less than seven hundred effectives by the middle of August, now stood at almost 3,200 men, most of them European.* It was divided into three brigades – two of infantry and one of artillery – with the 1st Brigade commanded by Brigadier-General

* European Infantry, 2,388; European Volunteer Cavalry, 109; European Artillery, 282; Sikh Infantry, 341; Native Irregular Cavalry, 59. Total: 3,179.

Neill, the 2nd by Colonel Hamilton of the 78th Highlanders and the 3rd by a Major Cooper. The headquarters of the 64th Regiment was detailed to protect Cawnpore.

On 19 September the main body of troops began to cross into Oudh by the newly completed bridge-of-boats. That same day, a Company pensioner called Ungud arrived in camp with a message from Brigadier Inglis at Lucknow, dated 16 September. Sealed in a tiny piece of quill and written in Greek, it read: 'The enemy have continued to persevere unceasingly in their efforts against this position, and the firing has never ceased night and day . . . [We] have been living on reduced rations, so I hope to be able to get on pretty well until the 18th proximo. If you have not relieved us by that time, we shall have no meat left, as I must keep some bullocks to move my guns about the position . . . I am most anxious to hear of your advance to reassure the native soldiers.' The previous message, also delivered by Ungud, had been more pessimistic still. 'I hope to be able to hold on to the 20th–25th [September],' wrote Inglis. 'I must be frank and tell you that my force is daily diminishing from the enemy's musketry fire and our defences are daily weaker. Should the enemy make any really determined effort to storm this place I shall find it difficult to repulse him.'

This was no exaggeration. Since the death of Sir Henry Lawrence in early July, the Residency compound had been under constant attack. A number of sorties were made – notably one on 7 July, when twenty rebel snipers were killed in a house opposite the Cawnpore Battery – but this did little to lessen the intensity of the enemy fire. All rebel attempts to storm the compound, however, had been beaten off with heavy casualties.* British hopes were first raised in late July, when Ungud brought news that Havelock had retaken Cawnpore from Nana Sahib and was preparing to march on Lucknow. But they were dashed a couple of weeks later when word arrived that Havelock had withdrawn across the Ganges. The garrison's spirits were then at their lowest: snipers, shellfire, disease and hunger were carrying off more than twenty people a day. 'The heart aches while watching for relief,' wrote one tormented soul, 'but none comes. Will Cawnpore be repeated at Lucknow? Alas, it seems so! Our number is visibly decreasing.' Many of those dying – inevitably – were children. 'Mrs Clark's infant died today,' noted Kate Bartrum in her diary on 3 August. 'Her other little child was taken care of by Mrs Pitt, but notwithstanding the tender care which was

* The biggest general assault took place on 10 August, when more than four hundred and fifty rebels are said to have been killed.

taken of him, he sank from exhaustion and died about a fortnight after.' Five days later she recorded that 'poor Mrs Kaye has lost her child, such a sweet little thing it was petted and loved by all in the room'. Mrs Bartrum's own baby son had also been taken ill, but he gradually recovered. 'If I could only get him good food and fresh air,' she wrote on the 12th, 'I think he would get quite well again.'

On 16 August, replying to Havelock's suggestion that the garrison should try to cut its way out, Inglis wrote:

I have upwards of 120 sick and wounded, and at least 220 women, and about 230 children, and no carriage of any description, besides sacrificing twenty-three lacs of treasure, and about thirty guns of sorts . . . I shall soon put the force on half rations, unless I hear again from you. Our provisions will last us then till about the 10th of September. If you hope to save this force, no time must be lost in pushing forward. We are daily being attacked by the enemy, who are within a few yards of our defences. Their mines have already weakened our post, and I have every reason to believe they are carrying on others; their 18-pounders are within 150 yards off . . . My strength now in Europeans is 350 and about 300 natives, and the men dreadfully harrassed [sic] . . . Our native force, having been assured on Colonel Tytler's authority, of your near approach some twenty days ago, are naturally losing confidence; and if they leave us, I do not see how the defences are to be manned.

Havelock's response of 29 August was hardly encouraging: 'I can only say do not *negotiate*, but rather perish sword in hand. Sir Colin Campbell, who came out at a day's notice, . . . promises me *fresh troops* and you will be my first care. The *reinforcements* may reach me in from *twenty to twenty-five days*, and I will prepare everything for a march on Lucknow.'

Meanwhile the garrison continued to lose men and three deaths were particularly grievous: Major Banks, acting chief commissioner, shot by a sniper at Gubbins's post on 21 July;* Major Bruère, commanding the loyal detachment of 13th Native Infantry, mortally wounded by a musket-ball on 4 September; and Captain Fulton, the intrepid engineer, decapitated by a roundshot on 14 September.† Bruère's death was much lamented by his

* He was succeeded as acting chief commissioner by Brigadier-General Inglis, who, like Lawrence before him, became the senior military and civil officer.

† Like Captain Moore at Cawnpore, Fulton had led by example, particularly during his gallant counter-mining operations. His admiring comrades dubbed him 'The Defender of Lucknow'.

17. The interior of the Bibigarh at Cawnpore after the massacre of 15 July 1857

18. Kunwar Singh (*centre with white beard*), the rebel Raja of Jagdispur

19. The battered Kashmir Gate at Delhi after it was successfully stormed by Wilson's troops on 14 September 1857

20. The storming of Delhi

21. The Baillie Guard Gate of the Residency compound at Lucknow. Havelock, Outram and the relieving army entered through the opening on the extreme right

22. The battered Residency at Lucknow after its recapture by Sir Colin Campbell in March 1858

23. General Sir Colin Campbell (*right*)
and his chief of staff,
Major-General William Mansfield

24. T. H. Kavanagh VC

25. The 93rd Highlanders entering the breach in the Sikandarbagh at Lucknow
on 16 November 1857

26. The interor of the Sikandarbagh and the skeletons of the rebels slaughtered by the 93rd Highlanders and the 4th Punjab Infantry

27. Havelock and Sir James Outram greet their deliverer, Campbell (*group standing centre, shaking hands*) near the mess house at Lucknow on 17 November 1857

28. Captain Charles Gough saving the life of his brother, Lieutenant Hugh Gough, at Khurkowdah on 15 August 1857. Captain William Hodson (*left*) is firing the pistol

29. British and Indian officers of Hodson's Horse, photographed shortly after Hodson's death at Lucknow on 11 March 1858. Lieutenant Clifford Mecham is standing. Assistant Surgeon Thomas Anderson, who comforted Hodson in his last hours, is sitting

30. Lakshmi Bai, the Rani of Jhansi. 'The Ranee was remarkable for her beauty, cleverness and perseverance,' wrote her opponent General Rose. 'These qualities, combined with her rank, rendered her the most dangerous of all the rebel leaders.'

31. Lord Canning receiving the Maharaja of Kashmir after the mutiny

32. One of Nana Sahib's many impostors.
The real Nana almost certainly died of
fever in the Nepal *terai* in 1859

sepoys, who, in contravention of their caste rules, insisted on carrying his remains to the grave.

Good news finally reached the garrison late on 22 September in the form of a reply to Inglis's letter of the 16th. Written by Outram on the 20th, it stated: 'The army crossed the river yesterday, and all the material being over now, marches towards you to-morrow, and with the blessing of God will now relieve you . . . I beg to warn you against being enticed far from your works. When you see us engaged in the vicinity, such diversion as you could make without in any way risking your position should only be attempted.' When word leaked out, the garrison was in a fever of anticipation. 'Such joyful news!' wrote Kate Bartrum, whose doctor husband was with Havelock's force. 'A letter is come from Sir J. Outram, in which he says we shall be relieved in a few days: everyone is wild with excitement and joy. Can it really be true? And shall we meet once more after these weary months of separation? Distant firing has been heard all day.'

It was Havelock's men nearing the city. On the 19th his advance guard had driven a strong rebel force out of some sand-hills close to the bridgehead. Two days later – 20 September having been taken up with ferrying Major Eyre's battery of heavy guns across the river – the advance began. Once again the rebels were massed at the village of Mangalwar; but this time Havelock chose to outflank them on the left, marching his infantry through a swamp and on to hard ground to the rear. The ploy was successful and successive bayonet charges by the 90th Light Infantry and 78th Highlanders drove the rebels out of Mangalwar. A charge by the volunteer cavalry, headed by Outram, completed the rout. 'We followed across country,' wrote one officer, 'and the rain now commenced again and came down in torrents . . . The whole country off the road appeared under water and we knew the enemy were in front of us and in full retreat. Shoes, camels with ammunition, hackeries (country carts) loaded with grain strewed the road and showed unmistakeably the hurry Pandy was in.'

Havelock's aide-de-camp, Lieutenant William Hargood, had delivered a message to the volunteer cavalry shortly before their charge and decided to accompany them. 'It was most exciting,' Hargood informed his parents,

> 80 horsemen going at full gallop amongst the scoundrels, cutting right and left. We killed about 150, but the ground was so bad that hundreds escaped by hiding themselves in the grass, which was 6ft high. Sergeant Mahoney of my Company, who is acting Sergeant Major of the Cavalry, particularly distinguished himself. He cut down three of the mutineers who were carrying the Regimental Colours of the

1st B.N.I. and, notwithstanding he had two fingers cut off, persisted in riding another charge, and would not get off his horse, [but] fell from it in a fainting fit. He is to have the Victoria Cross.

So close was the pursuit by Outram and the volunteer cavalry that the rebels fled through the nearby villages of Unao and Bashiratganj without making any effort to defend them. That night, Havelock bivouacked his men in a large stone serai at Bashiratganj, having reached in a day the furthest point of his two previous incursions.

On 22 September, after an uneventful march of 16 miles in pouring rain, the column reached the village of Banni on the River Sai. Once again the rebels made no attempt to hold this naturally strong position, neglecting even to destroy the large stone bridge. Their intention became clear the following morning, when Havelock's troops found them occupying a strong position five miles from Lucknow, their left resting on a walled enclosure known as the Alambagh ('Garden of the World') and their centre and right behind a chain of hillocks. As Havelock's leading brigade, the 2nd, advanced along the Grand Trunk Road between two swamps, it sustained a number of casualties from accurate cannon fire, one of the first balls knocking over three officers of the 90th Light Infantry. But once into the open ground beyond, the brigade was able to deploy, while Neill's 1st Brigade made a flanking movement through ditches, swamps and heavy ground to the left of the rebel line. Having driven the enemy from a succession of villages, Neill's men attacked and took the Alambagh, the key to the rebel position, at the point of the bayonet. Then Outram and the cavalry pursued the fleeing rebels to within sight of Lucknow's minarets and domes. Their advanced position, however, had to be abandoned when it was heavily shelled with guns brought out from the city.

Most of Havelock's men were anxious to press on and finish the job. Not their commander. 'The troops had been marching for three days under a perfect deluge of rain, irregularly fed, and badly housed in villages,' he wrote later. 'It was thought necessary to pitch tents and permit them to halt on the 24th.' The only threat that day – other than rebel artillery fire – was from a large force of rebel cavalry that used the long grass as cover to make a surprise attack on the baggage-train to the rear. The sowars were eventually driven off by the baggage-guard from the 90th Light Infantry, but not before inflicting a number of casualties and causing considerable alarm. That night all the baggage and wounded were placed in the Alambagh under a guard of two hundred and fifty men.

The final assault began on the morning of the 25th. With Outram leading from the front, the 1st Brigade drove the rebels from a succession of gardens and walled enclosures until it reached the Charbagh Bridge over the canal. Protected by an earthen parapet and six guns, the bridge appeared all but impregnable. But Harry Havelock was convinced it could be taken and, without consulting his father, he gave the necessary order. He, Fraser-Tytler and twenty-six men of the 1st Madras Fusiliers dashed on to the bridge; all but Havelock and a private were disabled by a hail of grapeshot and musket-balls. Fortunately the supports were close behind and the bridge was captured. One officer, who crossed the bridge minutes later with the 2nd Brigade, recalled that the 'dead and dying lay so thick it was impossible to avoid treading on them'.

Havelock and Outram had already discussed what to do next. 'From this point the direct road to the Residency was less than two miles,' recalled Havelock, 'but it was known to have been cut by trenches, and crossed by palisades at short intervals, the houses, also, being all loopholed. Progress in this direction was impossible, so the united column pushed on, detouring along the narrow road which skirts the left bank of the canal.' A little way beyond the bridge to La Martinière, the column turned left towards the Residency, passing between the European barracks and the Sikandarbagh. No serious opposition was encountered until the lead troops reached a narrow bridge over a nullah, commanded by two guns and a large force of rebels in the adjacent Kaisarbagh.* Scores of men fell as they attempted to cross over, but those who made it were able to cover their comrades from the relative safety of the buildings opposite the Farhatbaksh Palace. It was here, just half a mile from the Residency, that Havelock and Outram held a council of war. The light was failing, and Outram, weak with loss of blood from a flesh wound to the arm, suggested occupying the nearby Moti Mahal for a few hours so the rearguard could close up. But Havelock would not have it. He explained later:

> I esteemed it to be of such importance to let the beleaguered garrison know that succour was at hand, that with [Outram's] ultimate sanction I directed the main body of the 78th Highlanders and the regiment of Ferozepore to advance. This column rushed on with a desperate gallantry led by Sir James Outram and myself and Lieutenants Hudson and Hargood of my staff, through streets of flat-roofed loopholed houses, from which a perpetual fire was kept up, and overcoming every obstacle, established itself within the enclosure of the Residency.

* Literally 'King's Palace', the principal residence of the ex-King of Oudh.

Hargood was the first to reach the Baillie Guard Gate. 'How I escaped,' he wrote, 'I cannot tell, as I was a conspicuous mark being on horse-back.' Brigadier-General Neill, the scourge of Allahabad and Cawnpore, was not so lucky. Just beyond the archway that led to the Khas Bazaar, he reined in his horse and sent his aide-de-camp after a half-battery that had gone down the wrong road. As he waited he was shot in the head by a sepoy on top of the arch.

Meanwhile, the garrison was busy clearing the earth barricade from behind the Baillie Guard Gate so that the relieving force could gain entry. Mrs Harris, who was in Dr Fayrer's compound near by, recalled:

We had no idea they were so near, and were breathing the air in the portico as usual at that hour, at five p.m., speculating where they might be now, when suddenly, just at dusk, we heard a very sharp fire of musketry close by, and then a tremendous cheering; an instant after, the sound of the bagpipes, then of soldiers running up the road. Our compound and verandah filled with our deliverers, and all of us shaking hands frantically and exchanging fervent 'God bless yous!' with the gallant men and officers of the 78th Highlanders. Sir J. Outram and staff were next to come in, and the state of joyful confusion was beyond description. The big, rough, bearded soldiers were seizing the little children out of our arms, kissing them with tears running down their cheeks, and thanking God they had come in time to save them from the fate of those at Cawnpore.

Among the excited crowd that gathered near the Baillie Guard Gate was Mrs Bartrum. 'The noise, confusion, and cheering, were almost overwhelming,' she wrote later. 'My first thought was of my husband, whether he had accompanied the reinforcement, and I was not long left in suspense, for the first officer I spoke to told me he was come up with them . . . I ran out with baby amongst the crowd to see if I could find him, and walked up and down the road to the Baillie guard gate, watching the face of every one that came in; but I looked in vain . . . I was told that my husband was with the heavy artillery and would not be in till next morning.'

In fact, the majority of Havelock's troops were still out in the streets of Lucknow. Some spent the night on the ground between the Baillie Guard Gate and the Farhatbaksh Palace and rejoined their comrades the following morning. But by noon there was still no sign of the rearguard – the heavy guns and some of the wounded – so Outram, who had resumed command, sent a detachment of four hundred and fifty men to find them. They were discovered safe and well in the walled passage fronting the Moti Mahal and moved that night to the Residency compound and the Farhatbaksh Palace. Many casualties did not make it. Abandoned by their doolie-bearers in the last desperate dash down the Khas Bazaar, they were murdered where they lay. Only a handful survived, thanks to the gallantry of three surgeons: Anthony Home and William Bradshaw of the 90th Light Infantry, and Robert Bartrum of the 3rd Oudh Irregular Cavalry.* These three, helped by some bearers and a small escort of soldiers, managed to move at least twenty wounded men to the safety of a nearby house that they defended until it was set on fire. They then moved the wounded to a shed and remained there, under fire, for a further twenty-two hours until rescued.

All the while, Kate Bartrum waited anxiously for her husband's arrival. Of 26 September she wrote: 'Was up with the daylight, and dressed myself and baby in the one clean dress which I had kept for him throughout the siege until his papa should come. I took him out and met Mr Freeling who told me that dear Robert was just coming in, that they had been sharing the same tent on the march, and that he was in high spirits at the thought of meeting his wife and child again. I waited, expecting to see him, but he did not come . . . In the evening I took baby up to the top of the Residency, to look down the road, but I could not see him coming and returned back to my room disappointed.' By 27 September Kate was sick with worry. 'This afternoon,' she recalled, 'Dr Darby came to me: he looked so kindly and so sadly in my face, and I said to him, "How strange it is my husband is not come in!" "Yes," he said, "it *is* strange!" and turned round and went out of the room. Then the thought struck me: something has happened which they do not like to tell me!'

Her worst fears were realized on 28 September when two of her husband's servants arrived with the 'sad news that their master was killed'. Next day Dr Bradshaw visited her and explained that her husband had died trying to save the wounded. 'It made me almost forget my own sorrow to hear him spoken of in such high terms of praise,' she remembered. 'His was a glorious death: coming to the rescue of his wife and child, he fell at his post doing his duty. Dr B. told me that as he was going across the courtyard with my husband, he said to him, "Bartrum, you are exposing yourself too much!" "Oh," he answered, "there is no danger;" when he was suddenly struck in the temple and fell across his companion, saying, "It is all up with me," and died instantly.' Kate Bartrum gained some temporary comfort in the

* Home and Bradshaw were later awarded the Victoria Cross for this feat. Bartrum would have been if he had survived.

knowledge that her husband would live on in her infant son of the same name. Tragically he fell ill and died in Calcutta in February 1858, a few days short of his second birthday and the day before he and his mother were due to leave India for ever.

In just two days of fighting – 25 and 26 September – the relieving force had suffered 535 casualties, of whom 11 officers and 185 men were killed, including two brigade commanders, Neill and Cooper. These heavy losses, Outram informed Sir Colin Campbell on 30 September, made it impossible to return to Cawnpore with the 1,500 sick, wounded and non-combatants. 'Want of carriage alone,' he wrote, 'rendered the transport through five miles of disputed suburb an impossibility.' Earlier that month Canning had told Outram that his main objective was to rescue the garrison. If that could best be achieved by retiring to Cawnpore, then he was at liberty to do so; alternatively he could stay at Lucknow if he could 'hold it securely'. Either way he should not expect 'early reinforcements' because the China regiments were yet to arrive in any strength. With these considerations in mind, Outram decided to stay at Lucknow and reinforce the original garrison so that it was in a position to 'make an active defence', 'repel attacks by sorties' and 'prevent the enemy occupying the whole of their old positions'. To this end, his men had occupied a chain of palaces from the Residency to near the Kaisarbagh – including the Tehri Kottee ('Crooked House'), Chattar Manzil and Farhatbaksh – and had carried out a series of successful raids. The small garrison at the Alambagh, he added, was strong enough to hold out until relieved.

For the non-combatants, the news was bitterly disappointing. 'Everyone is depressed,' noted Colonel Case's widow, 'and all feel that we are in fact *not relieved*. The fighting men we have are too few for our emergency, and too many for the provisions we have in the garrison.' Many of the defenders, on the other hand, thought they owed their lives to Havelock and Outram. 'But for their timely arrival,' wrote L. E. R. Rees, 'our native troops, who had up to that time behaved nobly and adhered to us with exemplary fidelity, would certainly have abandoned us . . . Our houses had already been perforated with cannon balls. The Cawnpore battery was one mass of ruins, the outpost at Innes's house was partly roofless, and the other garrisons were as badly off. From one alone, the brigade mess, 435 cannon balls that had fallen within it were actually counted.'

If the relieving troops were disappointed to find themselves besieged, they did not show it. The discovery of a network of deep mines under the Residency compound, ready to be blown, convinced many that they had arrived in the nick of time. All, in any case, had confidence in their commanders, particularly Outram. 'A more gallant fellow never trod this earth,' wrote one officer. 'Rash perhaps & a little uncertain, but brave & generous & never so happy as when under fire. He is a man of first rate ability & I should say the best General we have.'

Colonel Greathed's mobile column, meanwhile, had crossed the Hindan at the site of Wilson's first victory at Ghazi-ud-din-Nagar on 24 September. Two days later it sacked the Gujar village of Dadri as retribution for its inhabitants' attacks on loyal Indians. Already Fred Roberts had formed a low opinion of his commander, describing him in a letter to his father as a 'muff of a fellow' who 'knows nothing'. He added: 'I am very jolly. In my appointment, 150 Cavalry are attached to me, and with these I go ahead of the Column scouring the whole country. Our present destination is Agra, but we have one or two small Rajahs and Forts to walk into on the road.' The first local chief to be dealt with was Walidad Khan, a partisan of the King of Delhi, whose forces were defeated at Bulandshahr on 28 September. A couple of days later Lieutenant Home, VC,* of the Bengal Engineers was accidentally killed as he supervised the destruction of Khan's fort at nearby Malagarh.

Greathed was at Bryjgarh on 8 October when he received an 'urgent call for assistance' from Agra, where 'a combined attack by insurgents from Gwalior, Mhow and Delhi was imminent'. Orders were issued for the column to march that night, with the cavalry and horse artillery setting the pace. But having covered three quarters of the 48 miles, the mounted portion learnt that the column's presence was no longer urgently required at Agra because the rebels, on hearing of the column's approach, had retired. So the horsemen waited for the infantry to come up and together they entered Agra during the morning of 10 October. Fred Roberts recalled:

> The European residents who had been prisoners within the walls of the fort for so long streamed out to meet and welcome us, overjoyed at being free at last. We presented, I am afraid, but a sorry appearance, as compared to the neatly-dressed ladies and the spick-and-span troops who greeted us, for one of the fair sex was overheard to remark, 'Was ever such a dirty-looking lot seen?' Our clothes were, indeed, worn and soiled, and our faces so bronzed that the white soldiers were hardly to be distinguished from their Native comrades.

* Home was the sole survivor of the gallant band of engineers and sappers who blew in the Kashmir Gate at Delhi on 14 September.

Not all the inhabitants of the fort were disappointed with the column's appearance. 'The spectacle was imposing from the impression it gave of strength and power,' remembered Mark Thornhill, 'but it had nothing of the show and glitter of a review . . . In short, it was the reality of war – not its dress rehearsal.'

When Greathed asked the authorities at Agra what had become of the rebels, he was told they had withdrawn across the Kari Naddi, a river 13 miles to the south, and were heading towards Gwalior. And yet, according to Mark Thornhill, the senior military and civil officers had ignored reports from many 'reliable' natives that the rebel army of 2,000 men 'was still on our side of the Kari Naddi, and much nearer to us than the authorities had any idea of'. They had also ignored the warnings of the militia commander, an officer of the 'highest character', who had 'expressed his opinion that the enemy were near, and that his position was unsafe'. Fred Roberts wrote later:

> We were then not aware of what soon became painfully apparent, that neither the information nor the opinions of the heads of the civil and military administration at Agra were to be relied upon. That administration had, indeed, completely collapsed; there was no controlling authority; the crisis had produced no one in any responsible position who understood the nature of the convulsion through which we were passing; and endless discussion had resulted (as must always be the case) in fatal indecision and timidity.

The consequences were soon apparent. Greathed had chosen the abandoned brigade parade-ground, about a mile from the fort, as the column's campsite. But trusting Agra's intelligence, he decided to wait until nightfall to post pickets. It was a mistake because for three days the rebel army had 'bivouacked within a mile and a half of the fort, concealed in the gardens and among the high crops that enclosed the parade-ground'. At nine in the morning, as the column's cooks were preparing breakfast, four Muslim 'fanatics' entered the camp and began beating drums. A cavalry sergeant confronted one, and was immediately cut down with a *tulwar.* Two more British NCOs were seriously wounded before the four rebels were cornered and killed. 'At this moment,' recorded a British trooper, 'the enemy who were lying in ambush in the high standing corn, called bugra, opened a cannonade from three batteries on to the camp.' This caused a great crowd of onlookers – fort inhabitants and townspeople – to flee from the parade-ground in terror. They met the column's heavy baggage moving in the opposite direction. 'Instantly,' wrote Fred Roberts, who was on his way from the fort to the scene of the action, 'elephants, camels, led horses, doolie-bearers carrying the sick and wounded, bullocks yoked to heavily-laden carts, all becoming panic-stricken, turned round and joined in the stampede.' Having struggled through this seething mass – 'by dint of blows, threats and shouts' – Roberts could scarcely believe his eyes.

Independent fights were going on all over the parade-ground. Here, a couple of Cavalry soldiers were charging each other. There, the game of bayonet *versus* sword was being carried on in real earnest. Further on, a party of the enemy's Cavalry were attacking one of Blunt's guns (which they succeeded in carrying off a short distance). Just in front, the 75th Foot (many of the men in their shirt-sleeves) were forming square to receive a body of the rebel horse. A little to the left of the 75th, Remmingon's troops of Horse Artillery and Bourchier's battery had opened fire from the park without waiting to put on their accoutrements . . . Still further to the left, the 9th Lancers and Gough's squadron of Hodson's Horse were rapidly saddling and falling in. On the right the 8th Foot and 2nd and 4th Punjab Infantry were busy getting under arms, while beyond, the three squadrons of Punjab Cavalry, under Probyn and Younghusband, were hurrying to get on the enemy's flank.

The rebel cavalry, three hundred in number, had hoped to make a surprise flank attack but they were met by the 9th Lancers and, after a brief fight, fled. By now the 3rd Europeans and a battery of guns had arrived from the fort. The latter 'opened fire on the rebel guns in the gardens and silenced them, while the Sikhs and English infantry charged the battery at the [nearby Wrestler's] Tomb' where the main body of rebels was drawn up. 'As our men charged and our cannon shot began to fall,' recalled Mark Thornhill, 'the rebel infantry lost heart, as had previously their cavalry. When their guns were taken they turned and fled . . . back through the village and across the fields beyond, till they reached the Gwalior road; along it they continued their flight, carrying one or two of their guns with them.' Fred Roberts was with the pursuing cavalry:

It was a most exciting chase. Property of all sorts and descriptions fell into our hands, and before we reached the Kari Naddi we had captured thirteen guns, some of them of large calibre, and a great quantity of ammunition. The enemy's loss on this occasion was not very great, owing to the extraordinary facility with which Native troops can break up and disappear, particularly when crops are on the ground . . .

There is no doubt that the enemy were almost as much taken by surprise as we were . . . Their astonishment first became known when they were repulsed by the 75th Foot, and were heard to say to one another, '*Arrah bhai! Ye Diliwhale hain!* (I say, brother! These are the fellows from Delhi!)'

Greathed's column remained at Agra for four days. Colonel Fraser, Colvin's successor, was anxious for it to follow the routed rebels at least as far as Dholpur in case they tried to regroup. But Greathed refused: his orders were to pacify the Doab and, if possible, assist the relief of Lucknow. He left Agra on 14 October and four days later, at Mainpuri, was superseded by Brigadier Hope Grant, who had arrived from Delhi to take command of the column. Having destroyed the fort of the rebel Raja of Mainpuri, Hope Grant pushed on to Bewar, where, on 21 October, he was handed a letter from Sir James Outram at Lucknow, written in Greek, 'begging that aid might be sent as soon as possible, as provisions were running short'. The column set off at once for Cawnpore, arriving on 26 October. Next day Hope Grant received an order from Sir Colin Campbell, the new Commander-in-Chief, to advance into Oudh and make contact with the small garrison in the Alambagh. Campbell would join him there.

Since arriving in India on 13 August, Sir Colin had been kicking his heels at Government House while reinforcements slowly appeared. This gave Canning the opportunity to compare his strengths with those of his predecessor, General Grant.

I think [wrote Canning on 23 August] that Sir Patrick Grant was a better man for the work actually in hand, and for any that will have to be done up to the time when the Commander in Chief will take the field. When that day comes I shall be glad that Sir Colin is here. Grant is admirable in the way of preparation and organisation. He knows the army and all its machinery thoroughly, what to look for, and what to guard against. The two months which I have had of him have been invaluable, and I should have liked to keep him for a month or two more, but as a leader in the field Sir Colin inspires me with more confidence.

Lady Canning, expecting a dour Scot, was pleasantly surprised. 'We find him very amiable and cheerful,' she wrote in August, 'an endless talker and *raconteur*. He will be sure to fight well, but when will he have the opportunity? The 14,000 men from England will not arrive for long & there is no sufficient force for him to take the field. Only detachments & reinforcements go up now.' Yet Campbell's enforced stay at Calcutta was not entirely fruitless.

He helped to speed up supplies for the expected troops – including Enfield ammunition, remounts, tents and transport – and was chiefly responsible for the establishment of a bullock train between Raniganj and Allahabad. He also formed movable columns of six hundred men – infantry and artillery – to provide security along the Grand Trunk Road.

By the first week in October, the gloom at Calcutta had been partially dispelled by the news from Delhi and Lucknow and the arrival of troops from the China expedition: the 23rd Fusiliers, the 93rd Highlanders, the 82nd Foot, two companies of Royal Artillery and one company of sappers. Around the same time a company of Royal Artillery and five hundred men of the 13th Light Infantry sailed in from the Cape. But the danger was far from over: Kunwar Singh and the Dinapore mutineers were still at large; recent mutinies had occurred at Jabalpur and Nagode in central India; and much of Bundelkhand, Oudh and the North-Western Provinces was still in rebel hands. Campbell's priority, however, was the relief of Lucknow, and with this in mind he sent all new troops up the Grand Trunk Road by bullock-train. They followed in the wake of the Naval Brigade – formed from, and using the guns of, the China force's warships (HMSs *Shannon* and *Pearl*) – which had set off from Calcutta under the command of Captain William Peel, VC,* the late Prime Minister's son, in August. Campbell himself did not leave for Cawnpore until 27 October, by which time elements of eight more infantry regiments† had arrived from England.

Having narrowly avoided capture near Shergati in Bihar, by sepoys of the 32nd Native Infantry who had mutinied in mid October, Campbell and his chief of staff, Major-General William Mansfield, reached Cawnpore on 3 November. There they received the alarming intelligence that Tatya Tope and the 5,000-strong Gwalior Contingent, which the pro-British Maharaja Scindia had kept quiet at Gwalior city until early September, were marching towards Kalpi, just 45 miles to the south-west. Even Outram was of the opinion that Campbell should consider Lucknow of secondary importance since it was 'so obviously to the advantage of the state that the Gwalior rebels should be first effectually destroyed'. But the Commander-in-Chief did not agree. For him the relief of Lucknow was of vital strategic and symbolic importance: it would strike a blow at the new epicentre of the

* Peel had won the VC with the Naval Brigade in the Crimea. He was knighted for his service during the mutiny but died of smallpox in April 1858.

† The 34th, 38th, 54th and 88th Foot, 42nd Highlanders, 3rd/60th Rifles, and 1st and 2nd Battalions Rifle Brigade.

rebellion and it would prevent another Satichaura Ghat. According to Fred Roberts, Havelock himself had warned that his food 'will only last till the *10th November*, by which date unless we relieve them, they will either starve or give themselves up'.

On 9 November, leaving Major-General Charles Windham, a Queen's officer of Crimean fame, and five hundred soldiers to guard Cawnpore, Campbell set off to join the force that Hope Grant had led into Oudh at the end of October. He found it camped on a sandy plain four miles beyond Banni. The following morning, as he was making arrangements for the relief of the wounded at the Alambagh, Campbell was surprised by the arrival of a European gentleman from Lucknow, disguised as an Indian. His name was T. Henry Kavanagh and he was carrying a vital message from Sir James Outram.

A tall, well-built, garrulous Irishman of thirty-six, Kavanagh had become Sir Henry Lawrence's chief clerk in March 1857. Yet his spendthrift ways had almost cost him his job, and he saw the siege as an ideal opportunity to redeem his reputation. He had, for example, taken an active role in the dangerous counter-mining operations that were orchestrated by the late Captain Fulton. When word reached the Residency on 9 October that a force under Sir Colin Campbell was on its way to Lucknow, Kavanagh leapt at the chance to win fresh laurels. 'I had,' he wrote, 'some days previously witnessed the drawing of plans . . . to assist the Commander-in-Chief in his advance upon the Residency. It then occurred to me that some one of intelligence, with the requisite local knowledge, ought to attempt to reach His Excellency's force beyond, or at the Alam Bagh, because the plans would be of little use without some one to explain them.' That someone was him. Having persuaded Outram's spy, Kanauji Lal, to incur the additional risk of taking along a second courier, and a European at that, Kavanagh went to speak to Sir James himself. At first Outram tried to talk him out of it, emphasizing the 'impossibility of any European being able to escape through the city unmolested'. But Kavanagh was so 'earnest' in his 'entreaties to be allowed to go' that Outram 'yielded' on condition that he was satisfied with his disguise. That evening, dressed in Indian clothes and with his exposed skin dyed black, he walked into Outram's quarters and sat down without permission. 'Questions and answers were exchanged without detecting the disguise,' recalled Kavanagh, 'although my plain features were known to every one of the outraged officers.' Even Outram, when he entered the room, 'took some time' to recognize Kavanagh.

I regarded this first step in the adventure as presaging success [wrote Kavanagh], and was glad to lay hold on any little thing to keep up my confidence. I was daubed once more by the General himself, and, considering where I was going to, there was extraordinary hilarity in the whole proceeding, which was most beneficial to my nerves. My turban was readjusted; my habiliments subjected to close inspection; and my waistband adorned by a loaded double-barrelled pistol . . . which was intended for myself should there be no possibility of escaping death at the hands of the mutineers.

But those in the know were not sanguine about the Irishman's chances. 'Noble fellow!' said Captain Hardinge as he passed Kavanagh out of the picket on the River Gumti, 'you will never be forgotten!'

Putting on a bold front by keeping to the main streets, and telling all who inquired that they were on their way to their homes in the city, Kavanagh and Kanauji Lal made it to the outskirts of Lucknow without incident. Five miles on, however, they realized they had taken a wrong turn and were in Dilkusha Park, which was crawling with armed rebels. They eventually found their way out and began walking in the direction of the Charbagh Bridge. But when they ordered an old peasant they came across to show them the way, he 'ran off screaming, and alarmed the dogs of the village, which made us run quickly into the canal'. After the alarm had subsided, they continued on to another village, where Kavanagh, now desperate, 'entered a wretched hut, and groping in the dark for an occupant, pressed the soft thigh of a woman, who started, but heeded my earnest whisper to be quiet'. She woke her mother, who put Kavanagh on the right road.

By now Kavanagh was 'tired and in pain' from his swollen feet, but Kanauji Lal persuaded him not to make for the Alambagh because it was surrounded by rebels. Instead they headed straight for Campbell's camp on the Bunni road. En route, in a mango grove, they were stopped by a squad of sepoys. 'It was an anxious moment,' recalled Kavanagh. '[Kanauji Lal] lost heart for the first time, and threw away the despatch entrusted to him for Sir Colin Campbell. I drew their attention to his fright, and begged they would not terrify poor travellers, unaccustomed to being questioned by so many valorous soldiers.' Kavanagh explained that they were on their way to a nearby village to inform a friend of the death of his brother. The sepoys believed the story and even gave them directions. A couple of hours later, having crossed a muddy swamp by moonlight, Kavanagh and Kanauji Lal were startled by an abrupt, 'Who comes there?' They had reached the British lines – and safety.

Kavanagh was escorted to the Commander-in-Chief's tent. At the entrance he asked 'an elderly gentleman with a stern face' for Sir Colin Campbell. 'I am Sir Colin Campbell!' came the abrupt reply. 'And who are you?'

By way of response, Kavanagh took off his turban and produced a note of introduction from Sir James Outram. 'This, sir, will explain who I am, and from where I came.'

As Campbell read it, he kept raising his eyes to look at his bizarrely attired visitor. 'It is true?' he asked.

'I hope, sir,' replied Kavanagh, 'you do not doubt the authenticity of the note?'

'No! I do not!' said Campbell sharply. 'But it is surprising. How did you do it?'

Kavanagh pleaded exhaustion and said that he would be only too happy to tell his story after he had rested. Once alone, Kavanagh knelt and thanked God for his deliverance. The worst was over and he could now look forward to the fruits of his enterprise.* 'The most delicious visions of the future lingered in my mind,' he wrote. 'For less than this, names have descended from age to age as if never to be obliterated.'

Kavanagh's intelligence allowed Campbell to put the finishing touches to his plan of attack. Outram had advised him not to enter the city by the Charbagh Bridge, as he and Havelock had done, but to march south-east of Lucknow to the Dilkusha, cross the canal north of the Dilkusha near the Martinière, and then advance through the palace area to the Residency. Campbell issued his orders accordingly.

On 12 November Campbell marched his army to the Alambagh, where he deposited his heavy baggage. Two days later, armed with Outram's map and with Kavanagh at his side, he began his advance on Lucknow with a force that now numbered 4,700 men and forty-nine guns and mortars. The rebel defenders were thought to number 30,000, though only a fraction were professional troops. Light opposition was encountered in the Dilkusha, and it was swiftly brushed aside. The Martinière too was taken with barely a fight. That evening the rebels attempted a counter-attack across the Dilkusha Bridge but were beaten back with heavy losses.

Most of the 15th was taken up with preparing the final advance. The heavy baggage and stores were brought up, and the Dilkusha was turned

* Kavanagh's incredible feat was rewarded with the Victoria Cross. Of the five VCs won by civilians, four were awarded for gallantry during the Indian mutiny.

into a general depot with five field guns, three cavalry squadrons and an infantry regiment to protect it. Next morning, having feinted an attack over the canal from the left of his position, Campbell's advance guard crossed on the right and headed straight for the Sikandarbagh, a large fortified garden, about a mile in front. But as it moved down a lane that ran parallel to the Sikandarbagh's east wall, it was checked by fire from three directions: on the right from the garden itself; on the left and left front from a serai and some barracks; and in front from the mess house, Kaisarbagh and other buildings.

The threat from the left was removed when the 93rd Highlanders took the serai and the barracks. But the position of the force was still critical, and Campbell decided that the Sikandarbagh – 130 yards square with loopholed walls 20 feet high and flanked at the corners by circular bastions – had to be taken before the advance could continue. It was while reconnoitring the garden that the Commander-in-Chief called out, 'I am hit.' Luckily for him it was a spent bullet that had just passed through and killed a British gunner before striking Campbell on the thigh, causing a severe bruise. Soon after two heavy guns opened fire on the south-east corner of the wall – the point selected by Campbell – and within half an hour a breach 3 feet square and 3 feet from the ground had been made in the masonry. The order was then given to storm the breach, and men from three regiments – the 93rd Highlanders, 4th Punjab Infantry and 53rd Foot – vied to be first through it.

A Highlander was the first to reach the goal [wrote Fred Roberts], and was shot dead as he jumped into the enclosure; a man of the 4th Punjab Infantry came next, and met the same fate. Then followed Captain Burroughs and Lieutenant Cooper of the 93rd, and immediately behind them their Colonel (Ewart), Captain Lumsden of the 30th Bengal Infantry, and a number of Sikhs and Highlanders as fast as they could scramble through the opening. A drummer-boy must have been one of the first to pass that grim boundary between life and death, for when I got in I found him just inside the breech, lying on his back quite dead – a pretty, innocent-looking, fair-headed lad, not more than fourteen years of age.

Arthur Lang was with a party that leapt over a loopholed mud wall, cheering and shouting, 'Remember Cawnpore!', and smashed a way through the gateway on the south side with axes. 'Such a sight of slaughter I never saw,' he recalled. 'In the open rooms right and left of the archway Pandies were shot down and bayoneted in heaps . . . It was a glorious sight to see.' Roberts estimated that there were 2,000 rebels in the Sikandarbagh, adding:

They were now completely caught in a trap, the only outlets being by the gateway and the breach, through which our troops continued to pour. There could therefore be no thought of escape, and they fought with the desperation of men without hope of mercy . . . Inch by inch they were forced back to the pavilion, and into the space between it and the north wall, where they were all shot or bayoneted. There they lay in a heap as high as my head, a heaving, surging mass of dead and dying inextricably entangled. It was a sickening sight . . . The wretched wounded men could not get clear of their dead comrades, however great their struggles, and those near the top of this ghastly pile of writhing humanity vented their rage and disappointment on every British officer who approached.

Eventually the mass of bodies was set on fire, 'and to hear the living . . . calling out in agony to be shot was horrible even in that scene where all men's worst passions were excited'. In each corner tower 'a few desperate men' continued to hold out 'and lives were being thrown away in attempting to force little narrow winding staircases where men were determined to hold out as long as possible'. Lang was almost killed when the muzzle of a musket was pressed against his chest, but he sprang back before it could be fired. He wrote:

The same man held out for two hours up his staircase, and when his ammunition was done, appeared on the roof at top, and with fury, hurled his tulwar down amongst us, and fell amongst a volley of bullets. Sixty or more were taken alive and put up in a line, and they got no mercy, being caught when our fellows' blood was so much up; they got kicked and spat at and pricked with swords, and always with 'Cawnpore, you scoundrels', and then they were all shot: a great many were 1st N.I., *the* bad regiment at Cawnpore.

Not all the victims were men. 'I saw the body of a woman lying with a cross-belt upon her and by her a dead baby also shot with two bullet wounds in it,' wrote Lieutenant Fairweather of the 4th Punjab Infantry. 'The poor mother had tied the wounds round with a rag . . . [Ensign] McQueen told me he had seen a Highlander bayonet another woman and on his upbraiding him for such a brutal act, the man turned upon him like a madman and for a minute he almost expected to be run through with his bayonet himself.'

That afternoon, with the Sikandarbagh in British hands, the advance on the Residency continued. For a time it appeared as if the Shah Najaf – with support from rebel guns at the Kaisarbagh, the mess house and across the river – would not be taken before nightfall. Scores of men were killed and wounded as they tried to move up the narrow lane to the large enclosure, including Sir Archibald Alison, Campbell's aide-de-camp, who lost an arm. Eventually the order was given for the 93rd Highlanders to withdraw. But before it could be obeyed, Brigadier Adrian Hope found a gap in the Shah Najaf's walls and discovered that its defenders were on the point of leaving. The order was rescinded, and Campbell and his staff ate their 'scratch dinner' within the enclosure's walls. Most of the troops bivouacked on the ground.

After a night of little sleep, the assault was resumed and the mess house and Moti Mahal were taken after more hard fighting. Outram's men, meanwhile, had occupied the buildings between the Moti Mahal and the Chatter Manzil. A junction was imminent. Roberts was looking over the western wall of the Moti Mahal with Norman, the acting adjutant-general, when he spotted Outram and Havelock. He wrote:

> I had never before met either of them . . . [Outram] was then fifty-four years of age, strong and broad-shouldered, in no way broken down by the heavy load of responsibility and anxiety he had had to bear, or the hardships he had gone through. Havelock, the hero of a hundred fights, on the contrary, looked ill, worn and depressed, but brightened up a little when Norman told him he had been [knighted].

Campbell received the two heroes of Lucknow on sloping ground near the mess house. But their discussion did not last long because the guns from the Kaisarbagh were tearing up the ground around them. Campbell confined himself to saying that the troops would be withdrawn from Lucknow as soon as the women and children had been escorted out, and he expressed his 'thankfulness that the relief of the garrison had been accomplished'. Then Outram and the weary Havelock returned to the Residency compound, accompanied by Roberts and Norman. As they passed through the shot-battered Bailie Guard Gate, the two young officers 'could not resist stopping to speak to some of the Native officers and sepoys, whose magnificent loyalty throughout the siege was one of the most gratifying features of the Mutiny'.

Outram and Havelock tried to persuade Campbell to attack the Kaisarbagh and take the whole city. But mindful of the small force he had left at Cawnpore and the casualties he had already incurred – 45 officers and 496 men – Campbell decided to confine his operations to the rescue of the garrison. Roberts approved. 'Every man was on duty day and night,' he wrote, 'and had he listened to these proposals, and allowed himself to be drawn into complications in the city, it is more than probable that those he had come to succour would have been sacrificed.' The first step was to evacuate the women and children and, during the afternoon of 19 November, they were led under fire to the blood-streaked Sikandarbagh, where they were 'regaled with tea and bread and butter, a luxury indeed, after siege fare'. After dark they set off again towards the Dilkusha. The journey was not without its alarms for the recently widowed Kate Bartrum, who was travelling in a doolie with her infant son.

We had been going on for a long time, when I thought it was remarkably quiet, for I could not hear the tramp of the doolie bearers behind, and I looked out and found I was quite alone in an open plain. I asked the bearers whither they were taking me, when they said they had lost their way. It immediately occurred to me that they were taking me to the sepoys: I sprang out of the doolie, and ran with my child in my arms, screaming across the plain until I heard voices answering. I knew not whether they were friends or foes: but still I ran on and met a party of our own men.

They too had lost their way and only knew that enemy pickets were close by. So together they retraced their steps and eventually found their way to the British camp in the Dilkusha, where, 'wearied and exhausted with fatigue and terror', Mrs Bartrum sat on the ground and burst into tears. 'I had been on my feet with my baby in my arms for upwards of three hours,' she remembered, 'walking through deep sand and wet grass, and my dress had become so coated with mud, that it was with difficulty I could get on.' A friendly officer took her to a large tent, where she was given 'some milk for baby, and a delicious cup of tea, and then we lay down upon the ground and slept till morning'.

During the next three days 'everything that was worth removing and for which carriage could be provided was brought away' from the Residency compound. The booty included 'jewels and other valuables belonging to the ex-royal family, twenty-five lakhs of treasure, stores of all kinds, including grain' and a large quantity of obsolete guns. The troops were finally withdrawn from the Residency and the buildings nearby at midnight on the 22nd. 'Not a sound was heard,' wrote Lieutenant Montagu Hall, 'not a bayonet clashed, and we filed out of the Hirun Kanah without a word spoken. We found the rest of our force (Outram's) covering the rear, and marched along in the dark. We passed the [Sikandarbagh] as we knew by the smell, which was something fearful, and then past the 9th Lancers. There they sat like statues. It is impossible to believe horses could be so still, not a sound to be heard, not a movement to be seen. I never was more struck with the perfection to which drill, discipline and training can be carried, than I was on that night. At last we find ourselves in a large park, the Martinière grounds, and here we were halted till morning.'

Sir Henry Havelock did not enjoy his knighthood for long. Suffering from dysentery, he had been carried to the Dilkusha in a doolie and placed in a small tent. There his son Harry, his wounded arm in a sling, tended him and read him passages and verses from his hymn book. Havelock knew the end was near and kept muttering, 'I die happy and contented.' At dawn on 24 November he called for his son. 'Harry,' he said, smiling, 'see how a Christian can die.' He died in his son's arms.

On 27 November, leaving Outram and 4,000 troops to garrison the Alambagh until enough reinforcements had arrived to retake Lucknow, Campbell set off for Cawnpore with the balance of his force: 3,000 fit men encumbered by half that number of women, children, sick and wounded. A day later he received an alarming message from General Windham in Cawnpore, dated the 26th, stating that he was being attacked by a large rebel force and required immediate assistance. Two more letters followed, the last with the disheartening news that Windham had withdrawn with most of his men into the entrenchment, leaving the city and the cantonment in the possession of the rebels. Campbell hastened his men forward and crossed the bridge-of-boats, which was still intact, on 29 and 30 November, taking up a position to the south-east of the city between the river and the Grand Trunk Road. For the next few days, while arrangements were being made to send the women, children and wounded to Allahabad,* Campbell remained on the defensive. Then, on Sunday, 6 December, he struck.

The rebels numbered about 13,000 men and were divided into two distinct bodies: on the right, covering the line of retreat to Kalpi, were the Gwalior Contingent and the mutinous regiments that had been stationed in Bundelkhand, central India and Rajputana; on the left, holding the city and the ground between it and the Ganges, were the troops loyal to Nana Sahib, both regular and irregular. Tatya Tope was in overall command, with Bala Rao leading the Nana's troops. The Nana himself was keeping his distance to the north-west of Bithur.

* One lady, who met the survivors from Lucknow during their brief stay at Allahabad Fort, was surprised by their demeanour. 'They were all a most cheerful party,' she wrote, 'and with few exceptions you would hardly find out the widows and childless. We must not blame the poor creatures for their apparent heartlessness, for perhaps continued exposure to such fearful scenes caused their feelings to be blunted.' (Spry Letters, OIOC, MSS Eur/B219.)

As the centre and left of the rebel position was protected by the city and broken ground, Campbell feinted an attack there before advancing on the right. The ruse worked. The 4th Punjab Infantry and 53rd Foot won a bridgehead across the canal near the brick-kilns, south-east of the city, enabling two fresh brigades to march down the Kalpi road towards the rebel camp. A few shots were fired and then the British charged. 'We were evidently unexpected visitors,' wrote Fred Roberts, 'wounded men were lying about in all directions, and many sepoys were surprised calmly cooking their frugal meal of unleavened bread. The tents were found to be full of property plundered from the city and cantonment of Cawnpore – soldiers' kits, bedding, clothing.' The fleeing rebels were pursued by cavalry and horse artillery for 14 miles down the Kalpi road. Roberts, who rode with them, remembered: 'The sepoys scattered over the country, throwing away their arms and divesting themselves of their uniform, that they might pass for harmless peasants. Nineteen guns, some of them of large calibre, were left in our hands.' Bala Rao, meanwhile, had withdrawn the Nana's troops in the direction of Bithur. On 8 December, after a brief skirmish with Hope Grant's flying column, many escaped across the Ganges to Oudh. The Nana and his entourage went with them. For one British officer, the defeat of the Gwalior Contingent was a turning point. 'Our star was in the ascendant,' he wrote, 'and the attitude of the country people showed that they understood which was the winning side.'

Having narrowly failed to capture the self-styled Peshwa, Grant proceeded to Bithur, where he promised his men a share in whatever treasure they could dredge from the Nana's wells. For two weeks they laboured in the freezing waters, bringing out two million rupees in ammunition boxes, the Peshwa's silver howdah and a never-ending stream of precious objects. Yet they never received a penny for their efforts because Calcutta decided that most of the treasure was loot and had to revert to the state. 'We even had to pay from our own pockets for the replacement of our kits,' wrote one bitter soldier, 'which were taken by the Gwalior Contingent when they captured [Windham's] camp.'

Fred Roberts took the opportunity to visit the Nana's palace, finding it in 'good order', and in one of the rooms discovered a bundle of Azimullah's letters from Lucie Duff Gordon and his Brighton fiancée. 'Such rubbish I never read,' he wrote. 'How English ladies can be so infatuated. Miss — was going to marry Azimula, and I have no doubt would like to still, altho' he was the chief instigator in the Cawnpore massacres. You would not believe them if I sent home the letters.'

19. The Reconquest of Oudh

Sir Colin Campbell now turned his attention to Fatehgarh, the last rebel-held city in the Doab and the scene of an infamous massacre of Christians in July 1857. The man held responsible for the atrocity was the rebel Nawab of Farrukhabad. But real power at Fatehgarh lay in the hands of the mutinous officers, and there is evidence to suggest that they forced the nawab both to join the rebellion in June and to execute the prisoners a month later. Since then the area around Fatehgarh had been ruled in the nawab's name, with ex-subedars from Sitapur regiments occupying senior government posts.

By capturing Fatehgarh, Campbell hoped to restore order throughout the Doab and open land communications between the Punjab and Bengal. He was prevented from leaving Cawnpore until 23 December, however, because he had to wait for the return of his transport from Allahabad. On New Year's Day, 1858, he halted his troops at Gursahaiganj where the road forked to Fatehgarh. His original plan had been to link up with two other columns: Brigadier Walpole's, which he had sent to clear the country along the left bank of the Jumna as far as Mainpuri; and Brigadier Seaton's, which was advancing from Delhi. But with no sign of either column, and intelligence that the Nawab of Farrukhabad and 5,000 troops* were approaching the bridge over the Kali Naddi, five miles ahead, Campbell decided to act alone. The following morning, having crossed the river under heavy fire, his men drove the rebels from the nearby village of Khudaganj and captured seven guns. The mopping up was left to the cavalry.

On the line thundered [recalled Fred Roberts, who charged with the 5th Punjab Cavalry], overtaking groups of the enemy, who every now and then turned and fired into us before they could be cut down, or knelt to receive us on their bayonets before discharging their muskets. The chase continued for nearly five miles, until daylight began to fail and we . . . overtook a batch of mutineers, who faced about and fired into the squadron at close quarters. I saw Younghusband fall, but I could not go to his assistance, as at that moment one of his *sowars* was in dire peril from a

* Part of the nawab's forces were under the command of General Bakht Khan, the former rebel Commander-in-Chief, who had arrived in Fatehgarh after the fall of Delhi.

sepoy who was attacking him with his fixed bayonet, and had I not helped the man and disposed of his opponent, he must have been killed.

Moments later Roberts noticed two sepoys making off with a standard. Determined to capture it, he rode after them and 'while wrenching the staff out of the hands of one of them, whom I cut down, the other put his musket close to my body and fired; fortunately for me it missed fire, and I carried off the standard'. For these two acts of gallantry, Roberts was awarded the Victoria Cross.*

That night the nawab's beaten forces evacuated the city and station of Fatehgarh in such a hurry that they left the bridge over the Ganges and the valuable gun-carriage factory intact. Campbell's army entered in triumph the following morning and found 'what must have been a pretty station . . . now a heap of ruins'. In the evening Campbell and his staff were invited to dinner by a leading citizen, Najir Khan, a relative of the rebel nawab. However, within twenty-four hours Khan had been arrested on the authority of Mr Power, the new magistrate, for complicity in the nawab's crimes.

No wild beast could have attracted more attention [wrote Major Anson of the 9th Lancers]. He was for ever being surrounded with soldiers, who were stuffing him with pork and covering him with insults. He was well flogged and his person exposed, which he fought against manfully, and then hung, but as usual the rope was too weak and down he fell and broke his nose; before he recovered his senses he was strung up again and made an end of. He died game, menacing a soldier who rubbed up his nose with, 'If I had a tulwar in my hand you wouldn't dare do so.' He it was who wouldn't spare our women, and treated them with every possible indignity.

More retribution was to follow. 'There were fourteen men hung, or rather tortured to death (some of them), in the town here yesterday afternoon,' wrote Anson. 'Only fancy, fourteen hanging at the same time close to one another, some dead, and some living, and it being very difficult to distinguish between the two.'

It had been Campbell's intention to follow up victory at Fatehgarh by crossing over into rebel-held Rohilkhand. He wanted to postpone the reconquest of Oudh until the autumn when it was cooler. But Lord Canning would not agree, pointing out that the 'political effect of leaving Lucknow in

* Roberts, like many other ambitious young officers, had set his heart on winning a VC because he thought it would help his career.

the hands of the rebels would be so mischievous that the city should be taken ere Rohilkhand was invaded'. He wrote to Campbell: 'Every eye in India is upon Oude, as it was upon Delhi: Oude is not only the rallying place of the sepoys, the place to which they all look, and by the doings in which their own hopes and prospects rise or fall; but it represents a dynasty; there is a king of Oudh "seeking his own" . . . Oude, and our dealings with it, have been in every native's mind for the last two years.' Campbell acquiesced, as he was bound to, but to keep the rebels guessing he remained at Fatehgarh for a month while more troops and guns were brought up to Cawnpore.

In late January, in response to criticisms from England that he should be nearer the scene of action, Canning moved his seat of government to the fort at Allahabad. Campbell met him there a week later to discuss the forthcoming campaign. A vivid description of the Governor-General's camp inside the fort has been left by William Howard Russell, the celebrated war correspondent, who visited Allahabad a few days later. He recorded:

> After a short delay, I was told his Excellency would receive me, and I was introduced to one of those grand tents which would be a palace in the eyes of any field-marshal in Europe. A few servants, in the red and gold of the Viceroy's livery, were sitting under one of the spacious canvas eaves . . . There were purdahs of fine matting, and doors, and flaps to pass, ere one could get inside. There soft Persian carpets received the feet in beds of flowers; the partitions of the tent, which was as large as a London saloon, were fitted with glass doors; but I was told afterwards, that Lord Canning had by no means carried tent-luxury to its fullest extent, and that, in fact, as governor-general, he had rather curtailed the usual establishment . . . I passed in through a partition into a tent where Lord Canning was sitting, surrounded by maps, and boxes, and papers, at a table covered with documents – just as I had first seen him.

During his conference with Campbell, Canning emphasized the importance of according Jung Bahadur's Gurkhas a prominent role in the capture of Lucknow. Jung Bahadur, the Prime Minister and effective ruler of Nepal, had first offered troops in June 1857. That offer was not taken up by the government until late July, when Nepalese soldiers crossed into the Gorakhpur district and did much to pacify the area around Jaunpur and Azimgarh. Jung Bahadur's subsequent offer of 8,000 troops and twenty guns to take part in the subjugation of Oudh had been accepted, Canning told Campbell, because there was 'no immediate hope' of more soldiers from England and 'things are not clearing in your part of the world'.

On his return to Cawnpore on 10 February, Campbell named his senior commanders for the forthcoming campaign. The cavalry division went to Hope Grant, the three infantry divisions to Outram, Major-General Sir Edward Lugard and Brigadier-General Robert Walpole, the artillery to Archdale Wilson (recently returned from leave) and the engineers to Colonel Robert Napier* – all men with considerable experience of India. These appointments caused much disquiet among senior officers recently arrived from England. But, as Campbell explained to the Duke of Cambridge, it was impossible for an officer not used to India to 'weigh the value of intelligence . . . he cannot judge what are the resources of the country, and he is totally unable to make an estimate for himself of the resistance the enemy opposed to him is likely to offer'.

On 12 February Campbell informed Canning that he had 10,000 men under his immediate command and would be ready to begin operations in Oudh in six days. But he doubted whether Jung Bahadur's 8,000 men and a separate column of 4,000 British troops, operating under Major-General Franks in the districts south of Oudh, would be able 'to take part in the fray' until the 27th. His preference was to delay his own advance on the ground that a combined force would incur fewer casualties; it would also give him time to make Cawnpore more secure. Canning agreed. 'I am sure that, as matters stand,' he wrote, 'we do better to accept the necessity and wait for Jung Bahadoor. It would drive him wild to find himself jockeyed out of all share in the great work of the campaign.'

Campbell began his preliminary operations at Lucknow on 2 March. The rebels, now numbering more than 100,000 armed men,† had greatly strengthened their defences by throwing up a triple line of earthworks from the canal to the Kaisarbagh, anticipating a third assault from the south-east of the city. But Campbell got wind of this and, on the advice of Colonel Napier, decided on a two-pronged attack: the main force would advance across the canal near La Martinière and head straight for the Kaisarbagh, while Outram's division crossed the Gumti and outflanked the rebel positions to the east. The Alambagh and Nepalese forces were expected to hem in the western side of the city and, with luck, would link up with Outram's troops to prevent any rebels escaping to the north.

The Dilkusha was occupied on the 3rd. Two days later Major-General

* Later Lord Napier of Magdala.

† On 27 January 1858 Outram estimated that there were 96,000 soldiers in Lucknow, including 27,500 trained sepoys. His total figure did not include artillerymen, nor the armed followers of *taluqdars* who were at least 20,000 in number.

Franks arrived with his combined Euro-Nepalese force and, that night, Outram's column* crossed two pontoon bridges over the Gumti near Bibiapur. After marching north for about two miles, Outram's men engaged a force of rebel cavalry and drove them back with artillery fire. A regiment of British horse – the Bays† – was sent in pursuit, but the broken nature of the ground impeded its progress. It eventually became a target for a battery of heavy rebel guns and was forced to beat a hasty retreat without its commander, Major Percy Smith, who was killed. That afternoon, Outram set up his camp on the Faizabad road, about half a mile from the village of Chinhut. The next two days were spent reconnoitring the rebel position across the river. On 8 March Campbell and Mansfield arrived to discuss a combined assault the following day.

Outram's task was to capture the Chakar Kothi, the racecourse bandstand, just across the river from the palace area of the city, so that his heavy guns could be sited on high ground to the north. This was accomplished on 9 March by the 1st Bengal Fusiliers and a regiment of Sikhs, but at a cost of one officer and twenty men. Most of the casualties were inflicted by a small group of desperate sepoys who were holding out in one of the downstairs rooms. Lieutenant Majendie, a British gunner, recalled:

At last, General Outram, seeing that it was death to any one to attempt to enter, and thinking that enough lives had been sacrificed in the attempt, ordered some guns to be brought to bear on to the house; five accordingly came into action, and fired about twenty shells, in quick succession, at the windows and doorways of the building, and as the smoke of the last round cleared away, the Sikhs, who had been held in readiness for the purpose, received the signal, and dashing forward entered the house *en masse*. It was most exciting to see them racing up to the place, where, when they reached it, there was for a moment a confused scrambling at the doorways, then a sharp report or two, then a sort of shout and scuffling, then bang! bang! bang! sharp and distinct, and finally there burst from the building, with loud yells, a crowd of Sikhs bearing among them the sole survivor of this garrison.

The Sikhs were angry at losing a popular officer, Lieutenant Anderson, but nothing can excuse the barbarity of their revenge on this lone sepoy. 'Seizing him by the two legs,' wrote Majendie, '*they attempted to tear him in two!* Failing in this, they dragged him along by the legs, stabbing him in the face with their bayonets as they went. I could see the poor wretch writhing as the blows fell

* Most of the cavalry and horse artillery and a division of infantry.

† 2nd Dragoon Guards

upon him, and could hear his moans as his captors dug the sharp bayonets into his lacerated and trampled body, while his blood, trickling down, dyed the white sand over which he was being dragged.' He added:

> But the worst was yet to come: while still alive, though faint and feeble from his many wounds, he was deliberately placed upon a small fire of dry sticks, which had been improvised for the purpose, and there held down, in spite of his dying struggles, which, becoming weaker and more feeble every moment, were, from their very faintness and futile desperation, cruel to behold. Once during this frightful operation, the wretched victim, maddened by pain, managed to break away from his tormentors, and, already horribly burnt, fled a short distance, but he was immediately brought back and placed upon the fire, and there held till his life was extinct.

Writing later, Majendie was appalled that 'in this nineteenth century, with its boasted civilization and humanity, a human being should lie roasting and consuming to death, while Englishmen and Sikhs, gathered in little knots around, looked calmly on'. Yet so infuriated were the Sikhs by Anderson's death that neither he nor any other officer dared to intervene.

Lieutenant Montagu Hall was also present and his account barely mentions the incident. 'For some reason,' he wrote, 'the Sikhs were particularly enraged against [the sepoys] and catching one of them they roasted him alive.' He added:

> While this was going on on our side of the river the Commander-in-Chief had advanced on his side and taken the Martinière and opened a heavy artillery fire on the enemy's entrenchments. The position we had taken completely enfiladed these works and we could see right into them and [Lieutenant] Butler, observing that the enemy had vacated their position and that the Chief was pounding away at empty entrenchments, swam across the river and by himself entered the entrenchments and mounting the parapet waved a handkerchief to intimate that the works were in our possession. It was a good day's work and practically decided the fate of Lucknow, for our advance had turned the flanks of the enemy position and rendered utterly useless all the defensive works which they had during the last three months erected to withstand our advance.

Two days later, as Outram's troops attacked positions covering the iron and stone bridges and his batteries pounded the rebels' second line of defence, Hope Grant and Roberts rode across the river to see how Lugard's assault on the Begum Kothi* was progressing. Their arrival at Campbell's headquarters coincided with a 'visit of ceremony' by Jung Bahadur. In honour of the occasion, Campbell had changed from his 'usual workmanlike costume' to full dress-uniform. But he was outdone by the Gurkha prince, who was 'most gorgeously attired, with magnificent jewels in his turban, round his neck, and on his coat'. Not long after Jung's arrival, word came that the assault on the Begum Kothi had been successful.

No fewer than six hundred rebels were killed in the brutal hand-to-hand fighting at the Begum Kothi. British casualties were 'nothing in proportion to those of the enemy', but they did include William Hodson, who had been visiting Campbell's headquarters when the signal-gun announced the attack. He immediately mounted his horse and rode off with his orderly, a powerful Sikh by the name of Nihal Singh, in the direction of Banks's House. They arrived as the storming party was about to set off, and so fell in with it. Once the breach had been gained, the troops fanned out to search for sepoys. Hodson did likewise, kicking open a door with the words, 'I wonder if there is anyone in this house.' As he entered the dark room he was shot by a musket-ball that passed through his liver and out of his back. He staggered backwards for a few paces, and then fell, at which point some Highlanders rushed into the room and bayoneted the lone sepoy. Hodson was carried by his orderly to a doolie and then taken back to Banks's House, where his wound was dressed. Dr Anderson, his regimental surgeon, finally reached him at ten that night, four and a half hours after he had been hit. Anderson recorded:

> I lay beside him on the ground all night, holding his hand, on account of the great pain he suffered. He was very weak when I came, but by means of brandy and other stimulants he rallied wonderfully and slept for an hour or two during the night. At daybreak he was much better, his hands were warm and his pulse was good . . . He drank two cups of tea and said he felt very well . . . About 9 o'clock I had the doolie lifted into a room which I had got cleared out, where he was much quieter. About 10 o'clock however the bleeding came on profusely again, and he rapidly became worse. I then told him that recovery was hopeless. He sent for Col. [Robert] Napier to whom he gave directions about his property and business matters and a message to Mrs Hodson. He rapidly sank and died at 1.25 p.m. on the 12th March.

Hodson's death was much regretted by his fellow soldiers. Sir Colin Campbell wrote to Mrs Hodson: 'I followed your noble husband to the grave myself, to

* Literally: 'Queen Mother's Palace'.

mark in the most public manner my respect and esteem for the most brilliant soldier under my command, and one whom I was proud to call my friend.' 'A more daring, fearless, brave man never existed,' commented Montagu Hall. 'Danger was to him a source of perfect delight.' Arthur Lang lamented the death of 'the finest Cavalry and "Intelligence" officer in the army', but added: 'He had no right to be at the Begum Kothi.' Archdale Wilson made the same comment in a letter to his wife: 'He should have been 5 miles off with his Horse.' From such comments arose the rumour, avidly circulated by his enemies, that Hodson had been killed in the act of looting. Roberts, who was not a particular friend of Hodson, rejected this charge. 'Hodson could not have been looting,' he wrote, 'as he was wounded almost as soon as he reached the palace.' But even if Hodson had been looking for loot, and there is no evidence that he was, it was hardly the 'crime' that some implied. Looting, by both officers and men, was commonplace during the the capture of Lucknow, not least because of the government's failure to honour Wilson's promise to distribute prize money for the booty taken at Delhi.

On 13 March Lugard's division was relieved by Franks's, while Jung Bahadur's Gurkhas were put into the line between Banks's House and the Charbagh Bridge. The following morning one of Franks's brigades captured the Imambara, a large mosque between the Begum Kothi and the Kaisarbagh. It was not Campbell's intention to advance beyond the Imambara that day, but so close was the pursuit of the fleeing rebels that the storming party soon found themselves in a building overlooking the Kaisarbagh. Franks wisely decided to follow up his success by ordering the troops occupying the Sikandarbagh and Shah Najaf to advance and, by nightfall, the Kaisarbagh, the mess house and numerous other buildings in between were in his possession. 'In camp they would not for some time believe that we had the Kaisar Bagh,' wrote Arthur Lang, who, with Brayser and twenty of his Sikhs, reached the furthest point of the advance.

Our carrying it all so fast was a glorious piece of pluck and luck. It was a splendid palace: magnificent and gorgeous, yet much more tasteful than most native buildings. Such jolly gardens, with marble honeycombed arbours, marble canals and high bridges, and *such* loot – jewellery and shawls, gold and silks! I was *knee* deep in valuables . . . A man held up a bag of jewels – a bag as big as his head – and said: 'Take a share, sir. Take this.' Like a fool I came up magnanimous and rejected everything! I took some handsome tulwars which I stuck in my belt. One officer in the tent next to mine has upwards of 500,000 rupees worth of diamonds, pearls and rubies! I never saw such precious stones as I have here.

William Russell, the first civilian into the Kaisarbagh, was appalled by the indiscipline of the British soldiers:

At every door [he noted in his diary] there is an eager crowd, smashing the panels with the stocks of their firelocks, or breaking the fastenings by discharges of their weapons . . . Here and there the invaders have forced their way into the long corridors, and you hear the musketry rattling inside; the crash of glass, the shouts and yells of the combatants, and little jets of smoke curl out of the closed lattices. Lying amid the orange-groves are dead and dying sepoys; and the white statues are reddened with blood. Leaning against a smiling venus is a British soldier shot through the neck, gasping, and at every gasp bleeding to death! Here and there officers are running to and fro after their men, persuading or threatening in vain. From the broken portals issue soldiers laden with loot or plunder. Shawls, rich tapestry, gold and silver brocade, caskets of jewels, arms, splendid dresses. The men are wild with fury and lust for gold – literally drunk with plunder. Some come out with china vases or mirrors, dash them to pieces on the ground, and return to seek more valuable booty.

Despite all the successes that day, a great opportunity was missed. Outram, who had been kept informed of Franks's progress by field telegraph, offered to assist him by advancing across the Gumti with his three brigades. Mansfield's extraordinary response was that he might cross the iron bridge, but he was not to do so if he thought he would lose 'a single man'. Outram took this injunction literally and stayed where he was – with disastrous consequences. Fred Roberts wrote:

The bridge, no doubt, was strongly held, but with the numerous guns which Outram could have brought to bear upon its defenders its passage could have been forced without serious loss; the enemy's retreat would have been cut off, and Franks's victory would have been rendered complete, which it certainly was not, owing to Outram's hands having been so effectually tied.

Lucknow was practically in our hands on the evening of the 14th March, but the rebels escaped with comparatively slight punishment . . . Sir Colin saw his mistake . . . too late. The next day orders were issued for the Cavalry to follow up the mutineers, who were understood to have fled in a northerly direction. One brigade under Campbell (the Colonel of the Bays) was directed to proceed to Sandila, and another, under Hope Grant, towards Sitapur. But the enemy was not seen by either.

Vibart could not understand why the stone bridge, which had been in Outram's possession, was abandoned.

We had the intense mortification of seeing, from our position at their iron bridge, several thousands of mutineers quietly defiling over it . . . thus making good their escape to Fyzabad and the heart of Oudh with scarcely any molestation on our part. A few shells, it is true, were occasionally fired at them from a couple of field guns posted at the iron bridge, but these mostly burst over their heads without inflicting any damage. I think I am not wrong in saying that it was generally considered that the wholesale escape of the rebels on this occasion, when they might have been so easily circumvented and destroyed, had Sir Colin Campbell willed it, was the one blot on his otherwise masterly tactics by which the capture of the fortified city of Lucknow . . . was effected.

Not quite. As late as 19 March the Commander-in-Chief threw away another chance to intercept a large body of rebels by misusing his cavalry. 'For instead of both brigades being collected on the Lucknow bank of the river,' wrote Roberts, 'which was now the sole line of retreat open to the enemy (the bridges being in our possession), only one (Campbell's) was sent there.' The other brigade, under Hope Grant, was ordered to take up its old position on the opposite side of the Gumti. Only Colonel William Campbell's brigade, therefore, was in a position to intervene when Outram's division drove 9,000 rebels – under Begum Hazrat Mahal, her lover Mammu Khan and the boy-King Birjis Qadr – from the Musabagh, a large palace four miles north of the city, on 19 March. Even then Colonel Campbell failed to act. The official explanation was that he lost his way. One of his officers explained why: 'He moved his force in utter disregard of the statement of his guides, in opposition to the protestations and explanations of all to whose information and advice he was bound to listen.' Yet his commander, Sir Colin Campbell, must take the major share of the blame: not only for dividing his cavalry but for giving such a critical task to a Queen's officer who was new to India and could not understand his guides. What might have been achieved was demonstrated by two squadrons of 9th Lancers with Outram's force: they chased the rebels for four miles, killing a hundred and capturing four guns.

The final action at Lucknow took place on 21 March when a large rebel force, under the Maulvi of Faizabad, was driven from a fortified house in the centre of the city by the 93rd Highlanders and 4th Punjab Rifles. This time Campbell's brigade of cavalry was ready, and a great many rebels were killed during the six-mile chase that ensued. The Maulvi, however, was not among them.

Sir Colin Campbell's general unwillingness to cut off the rebels' line of retreat, or to pursue them with any vigour, was probably deliberate. General Mansfield said as much when he asked: 'What is the use of intercepting a desperate soldiery whose only wish was to escape?' Certainly Campbell, who had seen more than enough butchery in the Crimea, was determined to keep his casualties to a minimum. And in many ways he succeeded: in twenty days' fighting at Lucknow he lost 127 men killed and 595 wounded; by contrast, British casualties at Delhi, where the attacking force was a third as large, were 1,674 killed and wounded over thirteen days (8–20 September 1857). Yet Campbell's parsimony was to reap a bitter harvest: the escape of so many mutineers from Lucknow meant that the flames of rebellion in Oudh and neighbouring Rohilkhand were not finally extinguished for a further twelve months, and many thousands of British lives were lost as a result.*

Shortly before the final assault on Lucknow, a five-year-old English girl was smuggled into the British camp at the Alumbagh by an Indian horseman. Her name was Louisa Orr and her mother, Annie, was still being held with another English woman, Madeline Jackson, in a house on the outskirts of the city. Every effort was made to secure the release of these captives but without success, until a letter stating their location was handed to two British officers, Captain Carstairs McNeill and Lieutenant Bogle. Accompanied by a detachment of Gurkhas, the pair went straight to the house in question and, having driven off the rebel guard, carried them to safety.

Madeline Jackson later wrote an account of their tragic experiences. She and her fellow fugitives from Sitapur – her brother Mountstuart, Lieutenant Barnes, Quartermaster-Sergeant Morton and little Sophie Christian, the daughter of the commissioner – had remained with the Orrs in the jungle near Kutchiani until the autumn of 1857. During that time their protector Loni Singh, the Raja of Mithauli, twice defied the rebel government's demand to send them into Lucknow. But on 20 October, when the demand was made for a third time, he agreed because Havelock's failure to retake Lucknow had convinced him that the 'English would not conquer'. The fugitives were handed over to a party of mutineers and taken into Lucknow in the back of two bullock-carts, the men in chains. A large, hostile crowd impeded their progress, and they were forced to walk the last few hundred yards to the Kaisarbagh through a gauntlet of insults and blows.

For almost a month they were kept in a small apartment in the Kaisarbagh,

* In May 1858 alone more than a thousand British soldiers died of sunstroke, fatigue and disease, while about a hundred were killed in action.

expecting every day to be their last. Finally, on 14 November, as Sir Colin Campbell's relieving force fought its way into the Dilkusha, Mammu Khan received Raja Jai Lal Singh's permission to execute the male prisoners. Mammu also wanted to kill the women, but the Maulvi of Faizabad stopped him, 'saying no success attended them because women were killed, and that we were the only ones left and must be kept as hostages'. The task of killing the men was given to a squad of sepoys from the 71st Native Infantry. They entered the prisoners' room and told the men to prepare to leave. 'My dear brother kissed me and we all said goodbye,' remembered Madeline. 'The last I saw they were tying their hands, and Mountstuart was resisting. I rushed to him, but the Sepoys pushed me back and drew a curtain, and I don't know what happened. I suppose I fainted, for I woke up and found myself on a sofa and Mrs Orr pouring water over me.' She never saw her brother again. He, Orr, Barnes and Morton were taken into the courtyard outside and shot.

All this time little Sophie Christian was suffering from dysentery. A few days after the men were executed, her condition worsened. 'I did not understand,' wrote Madeline, 'but Mrs Orr at once saw she was going and laid her on a *rezai* in the open air. The natives brought one of their priests to say prayers over her, and bless a cup of water which they gave her, and said she would be well; – but she only breathed hard a little and went to sleep, poor little darling. I had no idea she was so ill and was heart broken. Mrs Orr sent word by Wajid Ali, the headman who took care of us and all the native ladies in the Kaiser Bagh. He came and ordered people to bury her, and at night they took her away.' Madeline was the hardest hit by Sophie's death. Only by spending so much time caring for the child had she been able to blank out the horror of her predicament. Now, with 'no-one to do anything for', she became apathetic and depressed. But worse was to come when one of the guards laughingly told her that she looked like a girl who had been dragged by her hair into a large square at Lucknow before being butchered with a sword. Her worst fears were soon confirmed: the victim was her sister Georgina, executed with a number of other Christians at the time of Havelock's first relief. With Mrs Orr's support, however, Madeline gradually regained the will to live.

In the New Year, Wajid Ali moved the three remaining prisoners 'to another house and gave us native clothes to wear, as it was safer'. He told Madeline that it was the house her sister had been held in before she was killed. She looked everywhere to see if Georgina had left a message on the walls, 'but there was nothing'. She wrote:

Now we began to hear rumours that the English troops were close and would soon storm the place, – letters were sent and received, and Wajid Ali knew the rewards offered for us, but seemed very hopeless of saving us. Then he arranged to send little Loui Orr to the camp. She was dressed like a native, her face, feet and hands stained, and was carried out of the house like a bundle of clothes on the ayah's back. She was a very slight child, could speak the language perfectly, and knew she was to pretend she was the Ayah's sick child. Then the Ayah made her over to a sowar who was to say she had smallpox, and he rode off with her to the English camp. He was stopped by natives several times, but at the word 'smallpox' they left him, and she was got safely in – and Mrs Orr got a letter from her brother-in-law; but those two or three days were dreadful for the poor mother.

As the British assault progressed, and shells began to fall uncomfortably close to where they were being held, Madeline and Mrs Orr were moved to 'a big house on the outskirts where the Court Ladies and Wajid Ali's wives had been taken'. There they remained until Wajid managed to get a letter through to the British. The first Madeline knew about a rescue attempt was the sound of gunshots outside, followed by footsteps on the stairs.

I flew out to see what was happening, and there was a tall Englishman! 'We are saved,' I called out to Mrs Orr. He came in and another Englishman ran up, – Captain McNeill and Mr Bogle. They said, 'Are you Miss Jackson and Mrs Orr?' – 'Come at once' . . . Mr Bogle was left to take care of Wajid Ali and the Court ladies and the rest. Capt. McNeill came with us and a lot of little ghoorkas, and carried us off, up and down ravines like cats, and we were in the English Camp – saved! It seemed such an impossible thing! English soldiers rushed up to greet us. Sir Colin Campbell and the Ghoorka Chief and a lot of officers came and shook hands with us. Telegrams were sent to England at once and to Calcutta. They asked me who I wanted sent to in India, and I burst into tears, and said all mine were killed.

In fact she had one relation left. Her cousin, Elphinstone Jackson, was a High Court judge in Calcutta. They later married.

'The capture of Lucknow,' wrote Fred Roberts, 'though not of such supreme importance in its consequences as the taking of Delhi, must have convinced the rebels that their cause was now hopeless. It is true that Jhansi had not yet fallen, and that the rest of Oudh, Rohilkhand, and the greater part of Central India remained to be conquered, but there was no very important city in the hands of the enemy, and the subjugation of the country was felt to be merely a matter of time.' He knew, of course, that the balance of trained troops had tipped decisively in the British favour. By April 1858 reinforcements had increased the number of European soldiers in India to 96,000, supported by a similar number of 'loyal' Indian troops, including many new levies from the Punjab. The total number of mutineers (as opposed to armed civilians), even at the outset of the rebellion, was never more than about 60,000.

But the task of completing the pacification of India would take much longer than many people expected, particularly in Oudh. Sir Colin Campbell must bear some responsibility for his failure to prevent the bulk of the rebels at Lucknow from escaping into the countryside. An even more important factor, however, was Lord Canning's 'Oudh Proclamation', which was made public by Sir James Outram, chief commissioner, on 14 March 1857. The proclamation's main provision was the confiscation of all 'proprietory right in the soil of the Province' to the British government 'which will dispose of that right in such manner as it may seem fitting'. Only six minor landholders* – those who had been 'steadfast in their allegiance' – would be re-established in the possessions they held prior to annexation. All the rest – including the most powerful *taluqdars* like Man Singh, Lal Madho Singh and Beni Madho – would be dispossessed. Their lives and those of their followers were to be spared if they made 'immediate submission' to the chief commissioner, but only if their hands were 'not stained with English blood'. Any 'further indulgence' would be at the discretion of the British government.

Sir James Outram's initial reaction, on receiving the draft text in early March, was that the proclamation was far too severe. It was his 'firm conviction', he told Canning, 'that as soon as the chiefs and talookdars become acquainted with the determination of Government to confiscate their rights, they will betake themselves at once to their domains, and prepare for a desperate and prolonged resistance'. He urged instead that 'not only should complete pardon be offered to all (except those concerned in murders) but that it should be declared that upon their coming in they should be secure in all their old possessions, i.e. not only those which they held when the mutinies broke out, but those which they held under the old Oude Government, and some of which they were compelled to disgorge when we took the country'. Canning, however, 'flatly refused' Outram's proposal on the grounds that it would make the *taluqdars* 'so much the better for having rebelled, and this without waiting for any sign of submission on

* Among the six was Dirigibijah Singh, Raja of Bulrampur, who had given refuge to the four male survivors of the massacre at Satichaura Ghat.

their part'. His only concession was to add a further sentence to the original text, stating that he would 'be ready to view liberally the claims' of those who were quick to submit to British authority.

Outram's was not the only influential voice urging leniency in Oudh. Sir John Lawrence had gone even further, Canning told Lord Granville, by 'advocating an amnesty to the *mutineers* in Oude (*not* the rebels only), literally before a dozen of them had been brought to justice'. Once again Canning had stood his ground. 'I do not want more of general hanging and shooting,' he wrote, 'but I do intend that large numbers of those men shall be transported . . . and that those who remain shall understand that mutiny is not a game in which, if they get safely through the first hot scurry, they may reckon upon escaping scot-free.'

By refusing to moderate his proclamation, Canning was at odds with most opinion on the ground. 'I have not heard one voice raised in its defence,' wrote Russell from Campbell's headquarters on 22 March, 'and even those who are habitually silent, now open their mouths to condemn a policy which must perpetuate the rebellion in Oudh. In fact, unless there be some modification of the general terms of the Proclamation, it will be but *irritamenta malorum* to issue it.' Outram was in complete agreement. 'The Proclamation,' he wrote to Canning on 20 March, 'has not been attended hitherto with the slightest effect, although the city itself is beginning to be populated, not however I fear from the inducements held out by your Lordship, but in consequence of the Proclamation issued by the Commander-in-Chief, that the town would be bombarded if the inhabitants did not open their shops.' Under the circumstances, Outram was anxious to take up his new appointment as military member of the Governor-General's Council as soon as possible. Canning gave his consent, and Outram was replaced by Robert Montgomery, the man who had saved Lahore, on 3 April. Within three weeks Montgomery was able to report that twenty-six principal *taluqdars* had come in or sent their agents on their behalf. A month later he wrote: 'Every hour appearances improve, & a very large proportion of the landholders have tendered their allegiance by letter; and many personally.'

But much of this initial momentum was halted by a military setback in Rohilkhand. With Lucknow in his hands, Campbell wanted to concentrate on bringing the rest of Oudh to heel. He also preferred to wait until the hot season was over before embarking on any fresh campaigns. But he was overruled by Canning on the political grounds that Rohilkhand contained a significant number of pro-British Hindus who were anxious to be released from Muslim rule, particularly that of Khan Bahadur Khan at Bareilly. So on 7 April Campbell sent a sizeable British column, including three Highland regiments, into Rohilkhand from the west of Oudh. It was commanded by Major-General Walpole, whose orders were to link up with two separate columns entering the province from Bulandshahr and Rurki respectively. Unfortunately Walpole was not a popular choice as commander. 'We are surprised that Sir Colin trusts his Highlanders to Walpole,' wrote Russell the day before the column departed. Dr Hadow was more explicit in his criticism, describing Walpole as a 'great dolt' and noting that the whole army was 'horribly disgusted' by his appointment. And with good reason. On the ninth day of his leisurely march into Rohilkhand, Walpole came upon the rebel-held fort of Ruiya. He had been told by a trooper of Hodson's Horse who had escaped from the fort that the local chief, Nirput Singh, had only about five hundred men and would certainly retire after making a show of resistance. But Walpole refused to believe him and decided, instead, to take the fort by a frontal assault without making any preliminary reconnaissance. He failed to discover, therefore, that the western and southern walls of the fort were weak and incapable of sustained defence. Ensign Glascock of the 79th Highlanders wrote later:

> We were kept under the walls of the fort under heavy fire, on the strongest side of the place, nearly the whole day. At last, being tired himself, I presume, with doing nothing, the General ordered two companies of the 42nd Highlanders to storm the place alone, while we looked on. Also two companies of a Sikh regiment were sent up but these poor fellows were unable to scale the steep sides of the mud fort, though many tried to fall back into the muddy ditch pursued by many a bullet. At length, seeing that the efforts of these fellows were useless, Walpole sent Brigadier Adrian Hope to recall them. Endeavouring to do so, he received his death wound . . . Towards evening the whole force was withdrawn – to give, I suppose, the rebels a chance of escape which of course they availed themselves of, as the fort was evacuated by them during the night, and was found quite empty and deserted the next morning. We halted there three days, to bury the dead. The whole force followed Hope's body to the grave.

Six officers and one hundred and twelve men were killed and wounded in the action. The reaction of one sapper officer to the news was typical. Walpole 'is a poor incompetent wretch,' he noted in his diary, 'and I hope Sir Colin's strong arm will give him the chastisement he so rightly deserves'.

In the event, Walpole retained his command and made a better fist of subsequent engagements; as did the Commander-in-Chief when he took control of all British troops in Rohilkhand in late April, liberating Shahjahanpur and then defeating Khan Bahadur Khan outside Bareilly on 5 May 1858. But, as Montgomery told Canning in late May, Walpole's defeat at Ruiya, in conjunction with Hope Grant's 'retrograde movement' in the Doab and the arrival in Oudh of armed fugitives from Rohilkhand, meant that the pacification of Oudh was not going as well as he had hoped. There were almost seven hundred *taluqdars* of varying importance in Oudh and it was undoubtedly the severity of Canning's proclamation, as well as the military situation, that prevented many of them from submitting sooner. On the other hand, only eight had had their estates confiscated by the time Montgomery left Oudh in 1861: the rental value of these estates ranged from 10,000 to 180,000 rupees a year. One other case was pending, and smaller estates to a total value of 30,000 rupees had also been seized. In most other cases, the *taluqdars* were given back the property they had held prior to annexation. Montgomery had followed the spirit, rather than the letter, of the proclamation.

The criticism of Canning's proclamation was, if anything, even harsher in England. This was partly because Palmerston was no longer in power. He had been forced to resign in February when an anti-terrorist measure – inspired by the attempted assassination of Napoleon III – was defeated by eighty-four members of his own party. He was succeeded by the Earl of Derby's minority Tory government, with Benjamin Disraeli as Chancellor of the Exchequer and Leader of the Commons and Lord Ellenborough, the former Governor-General, replacing Robert Vernon Smith as President of the Board of Control. Both Disraeli and Ellenborough criticized Canning in Parliament, but it was the latter's coruscating attack on Dalhousie and Canning's recent policy with regard to Oudh, in the form of a secret dispatch of 19 April, that brought matters to a head. Ellenborough had failed to discuss the dispatch with his Cabinet colleagues and, once that fact became public, he was left with no option but to resign. The day he did so, 10 May 1858, *The Times* left its readers in no doubt as to where its sympathy lay:

No statesman is entitled to more generous consideration from the Government, the Parliament, and the people of England than LORD CANNING. He met the catastrophe of the Sepoy revolt with unshrinking firmness. Feebly supported by his Council, bitterly thwarted and calumniated by the English community of Calcutta, he neither allowed himself to be goaded into acts of severity by the frantic urgency of the European community, nor terrified by massacres and reverses into overtures of undignified concession.

20. The Rani of Jhansi

The death throes of rebellion were played out in central India by a cast of colourful characters that included Lakshmi Bai, the beautiful Rani of Jhansi.* Born in the holy city of Benares in 1828, the daughter of a senior Maratha official,† the Rani had grown up with Nana Sahib and Bala Rao at the Peshwa's exiled court in Bithur. She attended their Sanskrit and (occasional) English lessons and – more unusual still for a well-born Indian lady – became skilled in the martial arts of riding, shooting and fencing. The Rani, it seems, was never in any doubt that she was destined to rule. On one occasion, when the Nana and Bala refused to let her ride on their elephant, she shouted: 'I'll show you! For your one elephant, I will have ten!' And so she did, by marrying the elderly Maharaja of Jhansi in 1842.

Unfortunately the marriage was childless, and in 1854, soon after her husband's death, the British annexed Jhansi as a 'lapsed' state. On hearing the heart-breaking news that Lord Dalhousie would not allow her five-year-old adopted son, Damodar Rao, to succeed his father, she vowed: '*Mera Jhansi nahin denge!* ["I will not give up my Jhansi!"]' But all her efforts to persuade the Company to reverse its decision were in vain. She was forced to relinquish both the government and Jhansi Fort to a British superintendent, Captain Skene. In return she was granted a pension of 5,000 rupees a month (the equivalent of £6,000 a year) and allowed to remain in the modest, two-storey royal palace. Henceforth, by leading a simple life devoted to religious worship and charity, she gave the impression of being resigned to

* One Briton, who met her in 1854, wrote: 'Her face must have been very handsome when she was younger, and even now it had many charms . . . The eyes were particularly fine, and the nose very delicately shaped . . . Her dress was a plain white muslin, so fine in texture, and drawn about her in such a way, and so tightly, that the outline of her figure was plainly discernible – and a remarkably fine figure she had. What spoilt her was her voice, which was something between a whine and a croak.' (Lang, *Wanderings in India*, 93–4.)

† The Rani's father was Moropant Tambe, a Maratha Brahman, who served for many years as chief adviser to Baji Rao II's younger brother, Chimnaji. On Chimnaji's death in 1832, Moropant joined the Peshwa's court at Bithur. His only daughter was named Manakarnika, or 'Manu'. She assumed the name of Lakshmi Bai – in honour of the Hindu goddess of wealth and victory – at the time of her marriage to the Maharaja of Jhansi.

her lot. She was anything but, and there is good reason to suspect that she was in contact with other disgruntled princes prior to the rebellion of 1857. According to one authority, when Nana Sahib arrived in nearby Kalpi in early 1857, 'he was met by the Ranee's men, though the British officials at Jhansi knew nothing of his visit'.

A week after the mutinies at Meerut and Delhi, Captain Skene told his superiors that he did 'not think there is any cause for alarm about this neighbourhood'. During the latter part of May, however, Skene's deputy is said to have received 'private information . . . that the Ranee and the troops were one and that some treachery was intended'. The mutiny of the Jhansi garrison – a wing of the 12th Native Infantry and a squadron of the 14th Irregular Cavalry – took place on 5/6 June. According to a sepoy of the 12th, the rising was sparked by the 'receipt' of a letter from mutineers at Delhi stating that the Jhansi troops would be regarded as 'outcastes' unless they joined the rebellion. The same sepoy insisted that, prior to the mutiny, the plotters 'did not consult the Ranee'.

At the first sign of trouble, Skene ordered all Christians in Jhansi to take refuge in the town fort. There they remained, under siege, until 8 June when the rebel leaders offered to guarantee their lives in return for the fort. Skene eventually agreed: his tiny garrison was low on ammunition and food, and he considered the fall of the fort to be only a matter of time. But first he wrote to the Rani, asking her 'to tell the sepoys to take their oath and to sign her name on the letter'. This was apparently done, with the Hindu rebels swearing to eat beef and the Muslims pork if they broke their word, and the Rani's name appearing 'on the top of the letter'. But as at Cawnpore, the rebels had no intention of honouring their promise. Once in possession of the fort, they led the fifty-six Christian inhabitants* to the Jokhan Bagh, a large orchard beyond the city walls, and hacked them to death with swords. The only survivors were Mrs Mutlow, a pregnant Eurasian, and her young son, who were mistaken for Indians and allowed to escape.

The Rani's personal responsibility for the massacre is still hotly debated. Thornton, the deputy collector of nearby Samthar, was not in any doubt, stating in a letter of 21 August 1857 that the 'Ranee's people' carried out the brutal killings. But neither F. W. Pinkney, in his official narrative of the Jhansi rebellion, nor Sir John Kaye were able to come to a definite conclusion. 'I have been informed on good authority,' wrote Kaye, 'that none of the Rani's servants were present on the occasion of the massacre.'

* 18 men, 19 women and 19 children.

The Rani's own denial was contained in a letter of 12 June to Major Erskine, Commissioner for the Sagar and Nerbudda Territories, at Jabalpur. In it she expressed her regret at not being able to prevent the massacre because she 'had only 100 or 50 people engaged in guarding her house' and was not therefore in a position to intervene. She too had been at the mercy of the mutineers and was 'in continual dread of her own life and that of the inhabitants'. Indian historians have tended to take this document at face value, arguing with some justification that the Rani was not in control of events. They have also been quick to devalue any evidence that seems to implicate the Rani in a plot to overthrow the British. Yet it cannot be denied that an end to British rule is exactly what the Rani must have hoped for. Given her forceful nature, it would have been quixotic in the extreme for her not to have at least sounded out the possibility of a rising. In true Maratha fashion, however, she would have been unwilling to commit herself publicly until the success of any rebellion had been guaranteed. For this reason – and this alone – she was probably not responsible for the massacre.

On 14 June, three days after the mutineers had left Jhansi for Delhi, the Rani wrote a second letter to Erskine. She told him that she had enlisted troops to protect Jhansi and its major towns, but Company troops and funds were urgently required to prevent the spread of anarchy. She therefore awaited the government's orders 'which she will see carried out'. Erskine's response was to entrust the district to her keeping. He told her that if she collected the revenue, raised police and did everything in her power to restore order, she would be 'liberally' dealt with when the British returned. Erskine had been persuaded by her protestations of innocence, telling his superiors that her version of events – that 'she in no way lent assistance to the mutineers' and was herself 'plundered and forced to take charge of the district' – was corroborated by other reports. Lord Canning was not convinced. On 23 July one of his senior officials informed Erskine that the Governor-General did not blame him for accepting the Rani's 'account of her own proceedings' and putting the district in her care, 'yet this circumstance will not protect her if her account should turn out to be false'. Canning's suspicions had been raised by a separate political officer's account that insisted 'the Ranee did lend assistance to the mutineers and rebels'.

Unaware of these misgivings, the Rani was delighted to receive Erskine's endorsement of her rule. Mutinies had left all the British districts in Bundelkhand in a state of rebellion and she was anxious to join the scramble for territory. But in doing so she clashed with the female rulers of Orchha and Datia, two neighbouring princely states that had stayed loyal to the British.

By early September, with Jhansi besieged by Orchha troops, the Rani appealed to Major Erskine for assistance. He replied on 19 October that Jhansi was not a priority for the British and loyal Indian troops that were beginning to concentrate in the Jabalpur and Sagar areas. When the British did return to Jhansi, he added ominously, they would examine the conduct of all, high or low, and deal with them accordingly.

This letter was a major blow. It must have caused the Rani to suspect that she would be made to pay for the Jhansi massacre; there was also the possibility that she would be implicated – unfairly or otherwise – in the pre-mutiny plotting. Either way she would be forced to relinquish control of Jhansi if the British were victorious. She was not yet ready, however, to cast in her lot with the rebels. In late October, having helped to raise the siege of her capital, the Raja of Banpur* tried to persuade the Rani to join a confederation of rebel chiefs. She refused to commit herself and, in January 1858, Banpur left Jhansi for his own state to prepare to meet the advancing Central India Field Force under Major-General Sir Hugh Rose. The Rani, meanwhile, had made another attempt to sound out British opinion. On 1 January 1858, in a letter to Sir Robert Hamilton, the Governor-General's Agent for Central India who had recently returned from leave, she accused the chiefs of Datia and Orchha of 'taking advantage of the disturbed state of the country' to attack her. As such 'short-sighted individuals' seemed 'unmindful of the British supremacy' and were doing their best to ruin her and the whole country, she begged for his support. Hamilton did not reply, possibly because the Rani's collusion with the Raja of Banpur, and her conflict with the 'loyalist' Ranis of Datia and Orchha, had already marked her down as a rebel.

Still the Rani hesitated. A British intelligence report of 8 January 1858, compiled by a spy in Jhansi, noted that 'Bukshish Ali, the Duroga of the Jhansee Jail asking the Ranee whether she would fight or not with the English forces, was informed by the Ranee that she would not', and instead would 'return all the districts under her to the British officers when they come to Jhansee'. On hearing this Bukshish Ali 'did not take service with the Ranee', preferring to join the Raja of Banpur. A second report of 26 January stated that she had resumed her fight with the Orchha troops in Mauranipur. She had also sent an envoy to Erskine and had let it be known

* A leading Bundela Rajput, Banpur had taken advantage of the mutiny at Lalitpur to force the deputy commissioner to sign the subdivision over to him. He and his Bundela neighbour, the Raja of Shahgarh, had since wrested control of north-west Sagar district.

that if she was treated 'kindly' she would 'in no way oppose the British force'; if not she would 'fight to the last'. In the meantime her warlike preparations – in the form of arms and ammunition manufacture – went on unabated.

As the Rani procrastinated, it was her particular misfortune that Sir Hugh Rose, the British general fast approaching Jhansi, was one of the most able of the conflict. Born in Berlin in 1801, the son of a Scottish diplomat, Rose had entered the British Army at the age of nineteen, though he did not see action until 1840 when he fought for the Turks against their Egyptian rebels in Syria. Despite being badly wounded in a hand-to-hand fight with Egyptian cavalry, Rose personally captured the enemy commander and was rewarded by the Sultan with a sword of honour and the Order of the Nishan Iftihar. Since then he had occupied a succession of diplomatic posts, including consul-general in Syria, first secretary (and later acting ambassador) at the embassy in Constantinople, and finally British liaison officer at French headquarters during the Crimean War.

But his relative lack of command experience and apparently frail constitution caused many observers in India to question his appointment. According to Dr Lowe, who accompanied his force, Rose was 'laughed at and called a griff [ignorant newcomer] by a good many'. To another doctor he appeared 'very effeminate, weak and I should think unable to rough it much'. For a time, Rose did nothing to dispel these doubts. Having left Sehore in central India with one of his two brigades on 16 January, he took eight days to cover the 120 or so miles of jungle and river that lay between it and the rebel hilltop fortress of Rathgarh. No sooner had he taken the town and laid siege to the fort than a large rebel force under the Raja of Banpur arrived to relieve it. This new threat was eventually repulsed, but few casualties were inflicted. That night, to add insult to injury, the garrison of the fort retired without hindrance. It was, noted one British officer, 'a very badly managed affair'.

Sagar was relieved on 3 February, but a lack of supplies and carriage forced Rose to postpone his march north to Jhansi until early March. The alternative was to bypass Jhansi and continue his advance north-east to Kalpi on the River Jumna, where the remnants of the Gwalior Contingent, under Rao Sahib and Tatya Tope, had regrouped after the defeat at Cawnpore. Rose knew that Jhansi was bristling with rebels and that any assault on the walled town would incur heavy casualties; on the other hand, to leave such a sizeable rebel force astride his lines of communication was asking for trouble. Sir Robert Hamilton, Rose's political adviser, was of the same opinion. Jhansi would have to be taken first and if its Rani chose to fight – then so be it.

Either way she was going to be the subject of an investigation. In his dispatch of 11 February the Governor-General had instructed Hamilton that if the Rani were captured 'she must be tried, not by a Court Martial, but by a Commissioner appointed for that purpose'. Though the Rani was not aware of Hamilton's instructions, she had been left in no doubt as to British intentions by the tone of Erskine's letter in October. Even if she had been prepared to take her chance with British justice, she could not have carried the inhabitants of Jhansi with her, determined as they were to oppose the British. Far better to die fighting the accursed *feringhis* than to betray her people for the likely reward of a hangman's noose. Her chief advisers were far from unanimous as to the best course of action. At a council meeting in early March, some advisers 'proposed to make terms with the English', while others (including the Rani's father, Moropant Tambe) 'were of the opinion that it was not proper to give up the state which was recovered after much difficulty without fighting'. The balance was tipped by the Rani's troops, who threatened to leave her service and demand their arrears of pay if she did not agree to fight the British.

With the decision made, the Rani threw herself into preparing for the British assault with her customary vigour and determination. 'She enlisted in her army as many men as volunteered to join and placed them in position,' wrote a visitor to the town. 'The bastions and turrets were now manned day and night . . . Hundreds of tons of rice and grain were roasted and stored for ready distribution to the poor. Large quantities of flour, *ghee* and sugar and other eatables were stocked for the troops and the citizens. The priests and holy men offered prayers and invoked victory for the Rani's armies; special messengers were sent to Rao Sahib and Tatya Tope asking them for their help. In this way the brave woman, undaunted by the coming storm and with great calmness and forethought, went about organising the defence of the city.'

Meanwhile Rose's army was drawing ever nearer. On 4 March, in another hard and some said poorly managed battle, he defeated the Raja of Shahgarh at Madanpur Pass and annexed his state. Banpur's capital was also sacked, though the Raja had wisely withdrawn his troops to fight another day. Just a few miles from Jhansi, Rose received the news that Tatya Tope and the main rebel army had appeared before Chirkari, the capital of a small independent Bundela state that had hitherto remained loyal. Should he go to the raja's relief or reduce Jhansi first? He decided upon the latter because there was a danger that Chirkari would fall before he could reach it, whereas an attack on Jhansi might cause Tatya to abandon Chirkari and come to its aid.

In the early morning of 21 March Rose's troops appeared to the south of Jhansi. To their immediate front were the ruined buildings of the military cantonment: officers' bungalows, the gaol, the Star Fort, even the sepoys' huts. Nearer the granite walls of the town – 25 feet high, loopholed and bastioned – could be seen several large temples and small clusters of tamarind trees. Overlooking the town to the north, perched atop a high granite rock, was Jhansi Fort, the Rani's standard fluttering from its highest tower. As his troops piled their arms on the right of the road, about a mile and a half from the fort, Rose and his staff rode off to reconnoitre the town and surrounding countryside, not returning until six that evening. They discovered that the Rani's scorched earth policy had removed all possible cover and forage for miles around: trees had been cut down and walls dismantled. The rebel defences, on the other hand, were formidable. 'They had built up the old bastions of the fort and mounted large guns upon them,' noted Dr Thomas Lowe of the Bombay Engineers, 'thrown up batteries in other commanding positions outside the fort, and mounted guns upon other works erected upon the town wall, so as to command every possible approach, and admirably to enfilade each other.' Garrisoning the town and fort were about 10,000 Bundelas and *vilayatis*, and a further 1,500 sepoys. Rose, by contrast, had just 3,000 men at his disposal.

The siege began on 22 March as Rose's cavalry surrounded the town and his engineers constructed artillery sites. But mindful of the cost of storming such a formidable position, Rose allowed Hamilton to open secret negotiations for a surrender. A letter addressed to the Rani was delivered to one of the town gates by a rider under a flag of truce. It invited her and six of her ministers to a secret rendezvous with Hamilton. Suspecting treachery, the Rani refused to attend, though she did agree to send her Prime Minister with an armed escort. There is no record of such a meeting. If it actually took place, its outcome was unsatisfactory because the siege continued.

On 23 March the British camp was cheered by the appearance of a five-year-old boy named Francis Double who had been brought in from Datia. A refugee from the mutiny at Orai in Bundelkhand on 11 June 1857, Double had been saved by the faithfulness of his Indian ayah. At first she took him to Jhansi, realizing her error only after she had arrived. But while there she and Double were given assistance by Dowlah Ram, the Sagar banker who was also protecting Mrs Mutlow and her two boys of ten years and four months. Eventually another sympathetic Indian, Ganishi Lal, arranged for Double and his ayah to be taken in safety to Datia. Double's family were not so lucky. 'I regret to say,' wrote Captain Pinckney, the newly appointed Superintendent of Jhansi, to the Indian government on 26 March, 'that the child's parents, his grandmother, and his sister were all killed or died of exhaustion, it is not clear which, at Oosergaon near Kalpee.' Pinkney added that Mrs Mutlow and her two children were still in Jhansi and that Sir Robert Hamilton was doing everything in his power to rescue them.

Meanwhile, on 25 March, the first of Rose's batteries had opened fire on the 'mamelon', a raised bastion whose five guns protected the centre of the town's southern wall. A day later more batteries began to cannonade the ramparts of the fort. But, inspired by their Rani, who made regular tours of inspection, the rebels put up a fierce resistance. Rose would later remark: 'The manner in which the Rebels served their guns, repaired their defences, and reopened fire from batteries and Guns repeatedly shot up, was remarkable. From some batteries they returned shot for shot. Even women could be seen working in the batteries and carrying ammunition.'

With their heads wrapped in cold towels, the British gunners kept up a constant bombardment through even the hottest hours of the day. Gradually their fire began to tell. 'Every ten minutes in the twenty-four hours shell and shot fell in various parts of this doomed place,' recorded Dr Lowe, 'and fresh fires burst out among the different buildings – each fire greeted with loud hurrahs by the men in our batteries.' By 29 March the parapets of the fort bastions had been torn down and their guns rendered useless. At the same time a breach was made in the town wall near the fort, but it was promptly stockaded. Then on 31 March, as Rose was making his final preparations for an assault, word reached him that Tatya Tope had crossed the Betwa River to the south-east of Jhansi with 22,000 men and twenty-eight guns, among them 'the redoubtable Gwalior Contingent, who had recently destroyed the British camp at Cawnpore under General Wyndham'.

Having taken up a position to the right of the main British position, Tatya's men lit an immense bonfire on a nearby hill to signal their arrival. Jhansi's defenders welcomed it with raucous cheering and salutes from all their guns. Rose was now in a quandary: if he confronted Tatya with the whole of his 3,000-strong force, the Jhansi garrison might take him in the rear; but if he detached too small a force, Tatya might defeat it. He eventually decided that the siege was his main priority and took just 1,200 troops (only five hundred of whom were British) to oppose Tatya.

The Battle of Betwa began in the morning of 1 April. Tatya Tope had divided his army into two lines, sending the first one against the small British position and keeping the second one in reserve. So much broader was the rebel front that it seemed only a matter of time before the British line was enveloped. But Rose countered with accurate fire from his howitzers and field guns. He also sent two bodies of cavalry with light guns to take the rebels in the flank. This tactic worked, and the rebel attack began to founder. Tatya 'was not in the first line', noted Rose, 'where he ought to have been, to remedy mistakes'. Furthermore his reserve, three miles further back and protected by a belt of jungle, was too far away to prevent 'a retreat from becoming a flight'. The end result was that Tatya, in typical Maratha fashion, decided to cut his losses by ordering his second line to withdraw. To facilitate this the jungle was set on fire, but the pursuing British cavalry and horse artillery simply galloped through it. Little quarter was given to the fugitives, who were cut down in their hundreds. In total the rebels lost 1,500 men and eighteen guns. British casualties were fewer than a hundred.

The defeat at the Betwa sounded the death knell for Jhansi. On 2 April 1858, with the breach in the town wall big enough to justify an assault, General Rose gave orders for it to take place early the following morning: the right column would scale the walls while the left stormed the breach. In the event the right assault was detected on its approach to the wall and subjected to a ferocious bombardment. 'For a time,' recalled Lowe, 'it appeared like a sheet of fire, out of which burst a storm of bullets, round-shot, and rockets, destined for our annihilation. We had upwards of 200 yards to march through this fiendish fire, and we did it, and the sappers planted the ladders against the wall in three places for the stormers to ascend.' Inspired by the example of three officers of the Bombay Engineers – two of whom were killed* – the attackers scrambled up the ladders and gained a foothold on the walls. Almost at the same time men from the left column appeared, driving the enemy before them.

Hearing that the British had forced an entry at the south wall, the Rani led a counter-attack by her 1,500 Afghan troops in person. Its ferocity took the British by surprise, forcing many to take cover before returning fire. But the British were being steadily reinforced and ultimate victory was only a matter of time. Eventually a 75-year-old Bundela chief advised the Rani to save herself before it was too late. 'Maharaj,' he said, 'all the city gates are

* Lieutenants Dick and Meiklejohn. The other officer, Lieutenant Bonus, was knocked senseless but survived.

thrown open and hundreds of whites are inside. They are shooting from behind the houses. To be killed by their bullets is as useless as dying an ignoble death . . . Take my advice and return to the fort and do whatever God wills you to do.' She saw the sense of this advice and withdrew into the fort with a number of her men.

Before long the British had reached the Rani's palace. 'In the first moments of excitement,' recalled Lowe, 'our troops smashed and destroyed everything before them. Doors inlaid with plate-glass, mirrors, chandeliers, chairs and other native furniture . . . Every room was ransacked and covered with heaps of things broken and torn to atoms.'

Fifty of the Rani's bodyguard were killed in the palace stables, though not before they had cut down some dozen Europeans. No mercy was expected or given. Lowe wrote: 'Every house, almost, had its inmates of rebels, who fought to the death like tigers, so the bayoneting went on till after sunset.' By nightfall most of the town was in British hands, though the north-east quarter and the fort were still held by the Rani. Possibly the only inhabitant of Jhansi who was actually pleased to see the British was Mrs Mutlow, the sole adult survivor of the June massacre, who had spent the previous ten months in daily fear of discovery. But for the courageous intervention of Dowlah Ram, she and her two boys would surely have perished. Dowlah's reward from Sir Robert Hamilton: 'a miserly 400 rupees'.

Rose's thoughts now turned to the Rani. At dinner that evening he asked his aide-de-camp, Lieutenant Lyster, if he could suggest any means of capturing her without the huge loss of life that storming the fort would inevitably entail. When Lyster failed to come up with anything feasible, Rose himself made a proposal: 'Suppose I withdrew a picket from the cordon of troops surrounding the town and fort, she could then escape in the night, as, if I carried out my plan in the day, she will hear of it at once, and will escape with her women and followers in the night.' The plan was agreed on and the following morning one of the pickets was duly removed, leaving a 400-yard gap in the perimeter. As Rose waited for the Rani to take the bait, the mopping-up operation continued. 'No quarter was awarded them as a word of warning to others,' wrote Lowe. 'I exaggerate not when I say I saw the streets stained with blood . . . It was an awful sight to see [women and children] follow out of their houses some rebel husband, brother, or son, who was at once shot, and then to see them huddled together, pale and trembling, beneath the walls . . . But the soldier was as compassionate to these poor wretches as he was unrelenting to all male inhabitants found in arms. Many I saw dividing the contents of their haversacs among these half-starved women and children, and every woman was treated with kindness and respect.' Lowe does not tell the whole story – for many non-combatants were deliberately killed. A Brahman by the name of Vishnu Godse saw temples filled with the dead bodies of priests and worshippers. He also claimed that women were killed, particularly in the weavers' locality, where the death toll was at its highest.

Up in the fort, the Rani was so appalled by the suffering of her people that she threatened to commit a form of delayed suttee by blowing herself up with gunpowder. She was dissuaded by the old Bundela chief, who exhorted her to escape to Kalpi from whence she could continue the fight with Rao Sahib. To help her make up her mind, the Rani visited the small temple she had had built in one of the fort's outer courtyards. After a moment of quiet contemplation, the Rani came to a decision: she would fight on. That night, having learnt of the gap in the perimeter, she made her bid for freedom. Wearing a breastplate, a sword and two revolvers, she rode out of the Bhanderi Gate of the fort, accompanied by her ailing father (who had been wounded in the leg during the siege), some armed retainers and an elephant with her baggage. Tied to her waist with a silken shawl was her adopted son, Damodar Rao, now eight years old.

According to Lieutenant Lyster, the Rani and her followers made straight for the gap between the pickets, where they were detected and fired upon. But it was a dark night and no one was hit. When Rose heard about the escape in the morning, he immediately sent a squadron of the 14th Light Dragoons in pursuit. The cavalry finally caught up with the Rani and her escort at a small village, about 20 miles from Jhansi, where they had stopped for food. Lieutenant Dowker 'saw her on her famous chestnut horse, her little brother [*sic*] in her lap', and was in the act of grabbing her petticoat 'when he was knocked off his horse by a matchlock ball'. As Dowker's men went to his assistance, the Rani and her bodyguard made their escape. Knocked up by their swift pursuit, the British horses were in no condition to follow; but the dragoons did manage to capture the Rani's breakfast, her elephant and her baggage, including a 'batterie de cuisine de voyage' and a 'beautiful parasol'. Rose's mistake had been to assume that the Rani and her female attendants were not used to riding on horseback and could therefore be captured by his cavalry at their leisure.

After this narrow escape, the Rani pushed on with her remaining attendants and reached Rao Sahib's headquarters at Kalpi before midnight on 5 April. She had covered more than a hundred miles of difficult country in just under twenty-four hours – an incredible feat of horsemanship and endurance. Her father, hampered by his leg wound, was not so lucky. He and Lalu Bukshi, the Rani's paymaster, became separated from the main group, lost their way and were eventually captured by a pro-British *zemindar* 12 miles from Jhansi. Returned to Rose's camp in a 'miserable condition', they were hanged from a tree in the Jokhan Bagh on 19 June.

Four days earlier the British had held a Christian burial service over the pit in which the massacre victims had been buried. The anger felt by individual soldiers towards this brutal murder of women and children had fuelled their vengeful actions during the taking of Jhansi. Lowe estimated that the British 'burnt and buried upwards of a thousand bodies' in Jhansi, and that the total number of rebels killed since the siege began was nearly 3,000. The British troops had good reason to suspect the Rani of complicity in the massacre. 'Some relic or other of the unfortunate officers who perished', wrote Lowe, was found in 'most of the rooms' of the Rani's palace. Among them were 'copies of Longfellow and Byron, and other books, and clothing and plate', which 'showed that the Ranee had not only participated in their murder, but had positively shared in the plunder of their property'.

Of course the presence of European property in the Rani's palace is only evidence that she was willing to profit from the massacre, rather than absolute proof of her complicity. On the other hand, it would have been reckless – not to say immoral – for a wholly innocent party to have accepted such tainted booty. Rose, for one, was not in any doubt as to the Rani's involvement. 'Everything proves the Ranee's guilt as to the massacre,' he informed the Governor of Bombay on 10 April. 'She gave the sepoys & irregular cavalry money not to leave Jhansee, but to attack the English. She lent two cannon with which the mutineers attacked them. Her own people and the Irregulars began the massacre. I am afraid she is very bad, & what makes her inexcusable is that she is very ugly.' How Rose came to impugn the Rani's looks is a mystery, given that he had never met her.* He was wrong in this assessment, and may have been in his belief that she was responsible for the massacre. How genuine her pro-British sentiments were during the early stages of the rebellion, however, is another matter.

In the early hours of 6 April 1858, shortly after her arrival in the rebel camp at Kalpi, the Rani of Jhansi strode into the tent of Rao Sahib, the 24-year-old son of Nana Sahib's elder brother, Baba Bhutt. As the nephew and representative of the Peshwa – who was still fighting the British in Oudh – Rao

* He later reversed his low opinion of the Rani's physical appearance. See p. 367.

Sahib was the titular head of the rebellion in Bundelkhand. He began by expressing regret that his field commander, Tatya Tope, had failed to relieve Jhansi – but the Rani would not be mollified. Unsheathing the sword that had been presented to her ancestor by a previous Peshwa, she placed it in front of the Rao with the words: 'Now that we cannot have your support I beg to return it to you!' The Rao's reply was suitably disarming: 'Our ideal of independence can only be attained by leaders who are brave soldiers of genius like yourself. I beg you to take back this sword and give me all your support in my struggle.'

Keen to continue the fight, the Rani picked up her sword and reaffirmed her allegiance. 'Nothing will give me greater happiness than to die on the battlefield, serving the Maratha standard,' she told him. 'Give me men and I will go and fight the enemy!' Whereupon Rao Sahib made her one of his generals under the overall command of the beaten but unbowed Tatya Tope, whom she had known since childhood. The Rani's greatest contribution to the rebel cause at this stage was to attempt to instil some courage and discipline into the Peshwa's rag-tag army. However, her suggestions for putting the men through daily drill and exercise were only partially put into practice by Tatya, who probably resented her interference.

Meanwhile the British continued to gain ground in Bundelkhand with General Whitlock's defeat of the rebel Nawab of Banda at Bhowragarh on 19 April. Banda arrived in Kalpi with his remaining 4,000 troops a couple of days later. But the chief threat was still posed by Rose's army, which left Jhansi on the 26th. To block its advance, Tatya Tope and the Rani took an advance guard of 10,000 soldiers and twelve guns to the town of Kunch, 23 miles south-west of Kalpi. According to one source, the Rani urged Tatya to protect his flanks. It was just such neglect that had cost him the Betwa battle. Yet Tatya would not listen: he put his faith in the strong western defences of the town and was convinced that the woods, gardens and temples that skirted the city would prevent any flanking manoeuvre. He was wrong. Informed by scouts that the north-western side of the town was unfortified, Rose ordered a long night march in that direction. The following morning – 7 May – he attacked the rebels from the rear and was soon in possession of the fort. With their position turned, the rebels began to retreat across the immense plain that led to Kalpi, pursued by British cavalry and horse artillery, until the effects of the fierce sun caused the latter to halt. Rose was particularly impressed with the sepoy skirmishers who covered the retreat by 'facing about, kneeling and firing with great coolness'. The rebels still lost 600 men and 15 guns.

Once safely back at Kalpi, the rebel recriminations began. The infantry accused the cavalry of abandoning them – with some justice – and the Rani's Afghans came in for particular criticism. But the rebel cause was not yet hopeless. Situated on a high rocky plateau on the banks of the Jumna River, surrounded by ravines, Kalpi was a natural stronghold that had been made even more formidable by the construction of elaborate defence works on the roads that led to Kunch. Moreover its fort had an underground magazine full of stores and ammunition, as well as four foundries for making cannon, and it was defended by a rebel army that Rose described later as 'unusually strong'. He added:

They were under three leaders of considerable influence, Rao Sahib, a nephew of Nana Sahib, the Nawab of Banda, and the Ranee of Jhansie. The high descent of the Ranee, her unbounded liberality to her Troops and retainers, and her fortitude which no reverses could shake, rendered her an influential and dangerous adversary. The Rebel Army was composed of the Gwalior Contingent, the finest men, best drilled and organized Native Troops of all arms in India; other mutinous Bengal Infantry Regiments . . . All the Sepoy Regiments kept up, carefully, their English equipment and organization; the words of command for drill, grand rounds etc., were given, as we could hear, in English.

Faced with such a formidable task, Rose decided to sidestep the main rebel defences by linking up with Brigadier Maxwell at Gulauli, six miles to the east of Kalpi, on 19 May. His plan was for Maxwell to bombard the fort from the northern bank while he fought his way through the ravines that protected the east of the city. But the rebels struck first. Having sworn on the sacred waters of the Jumna that they would either drive the British into the river or die, they attacked Rose's camp at Gulauli on the morning of 22 May.

At an earlier council of war the Rani had warned Rao Sahib not to send his men through ground that would make it difficult for them to reply to the British guns. Yet that is exactly what happened on the 22nd and before long the attack on the centre and left of Rose's line was being driven back by accurate British artillery fire. 'We had been upwards of two hours pounding at the enemy,' recalled Dr Lowe, 'then the general saw the moment for advance, and with the horse artillery, field batteries and cavalry dashed off towards them; they then turned round quickly and fled, vast masses of their infantry making for the villages and the ravines towards Calpee, others flying south.'

At this point Rao Sahib lost his nerve and was about to leave the field when the Rani convinced him that all was not yet lost. As if to emphasize the point, she mounted her horse and galloped off with a force of cavalry to reinforce the infantry attack on the right of the British line. Led by the Rani, the troops fought with such desperation and fury that the defenders began to give ground. She and her men were within 20 feet of a light field battery when Rose himself appeared on the scene with reinforcements. 'As we mounted the crest of the hill,' he recalled, 'the sepoys were sending out skirmishers towards our two guns, and the Brigadier so hard pressed that he was ordering the Artillerymen to draw their swords and defend the guns. The sepoys were in great numbers and running forward & at the same time keeping up a very hot fire. Three of my staff . . . had their horses killed or wounded at the same time. I ordered the Rifles to charge the sepoys with the bayonet, which they did most gallantly, driving them back into the ravines, and bayoneting numbers of them.' Thus did the two opposing commanders come within a few yards of each other during the battle, though Rose was not aware of – or had never acknowledged – the Rani's presence. Nevertheless his arrival turned the course of the battle and the rebel retreat soon became general.

That night, convinced that Kalpi could not be saved, the Rani and Rao Sahib left for Gopalpur, where they met up with Tatya Tope, the Nawab of Banda and the remnants of their army on 26 May. At a council of war on the 27th it was decided to march west towards Gwalior in the hope of persuading the pro-British Maharaja Scindia, the most powerful Maratha ruler in central India, to join the rebellion. Exactly how that decision was reached is not known. Colonel Malleson was convinced that the Rani was responsible. Of the four rebel leaders, wrote Malleson, only she 'possessed the genius, the daring, the despair necessary for the conception of great deeds'. But most circumstantial evidence points to Tatya Tope as the architect of the scheme. He had travelled in secret to Gwalior before the fall of Kalpi to assess the mood of Scindia's armed forces. There he probably received assurances from senior officers that Gwalior troops would not oppose a rebel invasion.

On 28 May the 4,500-strong rebel army crossed the Sind River and entered the maharaja's territory. Unaware of the level of anti-British feeling within his army, Scindia instructed the rebels to leave 'on pain of immediate attack by his troops'. When Rao Sahib refused, adding that his men required 'supplies, clothing and a little money', Scindia appealed to the British for assistance. He also prepared his 8,000 troops for action. The collision occurred on 31 May at Baragaon, eight miles from Gwalior, when Scindia's artillery opened fire on the advancing rebels. This alarmed the rebel troops, who were not expecting any opposition, and some began to withdraw. They were rallied by the Rani, who led two hundred of her cavalrymen in a skirmish with the Gwalior cavalry. But it was a half-hearted affair, and the Gwalior troops soon revealed their true colours by repeating the rebels' loud cry of '*Deen!*' As the two sides began to fraternize, Scindia fled to Agra with the loyal remnants of his Maratha bodyguard. His Prime Minister and his wives joined him on the road.

That same day the rebels entered Gwalior in triumph. Rao Sahib occupied Scindia's palace and on 3 June, at a grand durbar, was formally recognized as the Peshwa's viceroy. Hundreds of guests gathered under a huge canopy decorated with Maratha flags, festoons and green mango branches. The Rao entered wearing his family's royal robes, pearl earrings and necklaces of diamonds and pearls. As he ascended the makeshift throne, Brahman priests chanted Vedic prayers and a royal salute of one hundred and one guns was fired from the fort to herald the restoration of the Maratha Confederacy. The Rani refused to attend the durbar. In her opinion the Rao was indulging in hollow ceremony when he should have been preparing his army for battle. She confronted him two days later, pointing out that the capture of Scindia's army and treasury was a 'golden opportunity' for him 'to prepare for the coming struggle by putting in order the defences of the city', paying the soldiers and 'putting them under capable commanders who will maintain discipline'. Suitably chastened, the Rao agreed to attend to these matters: pay arrears were cleared, new levies were raised, and troops were posted on all the main routes into Gwalior.

Meanwhile Sir Hugh Rose, having resigned his command after the capture of Kalpi on the grounds of ill health,* had been induced by the news from Gwalior to undertake one last campaign. He left Kalpi on 6 June and 'after a rapid march of unparalleled hardships' came within sight of the Morar cantonment, four miles east of Gwalior city, on the 16th. That same day, as his troops were driving the rebel covering force out of the cantonment and into the heights beyond, two other columns under Brigadier Smith and Major Orr joined forces to the south of the city.

* The real reason for Rose's resignation was that he resented the Commander-in-Chief's decision to dissolve the Central India Field Force and put him in command of a mere division at Gwalior. Campbell later censured Rose for reassuming the command of the field force without his permission.

The rebel battle plans, according to *The Times* war correspondent, 'were effected mainly under the direction and personal supervision of the Ranee, who, clad in military attire and attended by a picked and well-armed escort, was constantly in the saddle, ubiquitous and untiring'. Her main position was a line of entrenchments along the base of the hills that separated the Kotah-ki-Serai plain from that of Gwalior, about four miles south-east of the city. During the morning of 17 June these field works were approached by a cavalry troop from Brigadier Smith's column. It went rather too close, and Smith, who had accompanied it, had a horse shot from under him. So he ordered his infantry to advance and, after a hard fight, they managed to drive the rebels out of their trenches and into the hills beyond. But, owing to a false report that rebel cavalry were attacking their baggage party about a mile and a half to the rear, Smith ordered his men to retreat. By the time the error was discovered, the Rani's men had reoccupied their old positions. 'So there was a second advance of Infantry and guns which sent them back again,' wrote Major Robert Poore of the 8th Hussars. As the 95th Foot struggled up the heights, a squadron of Poore's regiment burst through the narrow pass that led to the Gwalior plain. 'When we got clear,' he recalled, 'we front formed and went at them, the Brigadier leading for a short way. The enemy cut when we came up and we pursued for a mile or perhaps half, and then turned, and came back and got in among a lot of very deep nullahs during which time it was precious lucky the enemy did not come down on us. We got back with few casualties.'

The Rani was on horseback, watching the bombardment from a nearby battery, when the British cavalry made their surprise appearance, causing her escort to scatter in all directions. According to one eyewitness account, she boldy 'attacked one of the 8th in their advance, was unhorsed and wounded', possibly by a sabre cut. A short while later, as the British retired with the captured guns, she recognized her former assailant as she sat bleeding by the roadside and fired at him with her pistol. Unfortunately she missed and he 'dispatched the young lady with his carbine'. But because she was 'dressed as a sowar', the trooper never realized 'that he had cut off one of the mainstays of the mutiny, that there was a reward of a lac [lakh] on his victim's head, or that at that moment she was wearing jewels worth a crore of rupees'.

At the time of her death, so General Rose told the Duke of Cambridge, the Rani was 'dressed in a red jacket, red trousers and white puggary'. She was also wearing 'the celebrated pearl necklace of Scindia, which she had taken from his Treasury, and heavy gold anklets'. Rose added: 'As she lay mortally wounded in her Tent she ordered these ornaments to be distributed amongst her Troops; it is said that Tantia Topee intercepted the necklace. The whole rebel army mourned for her; her body was burned with great ceremony under a tamarind tree under the Rock of Gwalior, where I saw her bones and ashes.'

The British reaction to news of the Rani's death ranged from quiet satisfaction to fierce exultation. 'The Ranee of Jhansee is killed,' stated the brief telegram sent by Sir Robert Hamilton to the Governor-General on 18 June. Lieutenant-Colonel Bingham of the 64th Foot, who had taken part in Havelock's epic relief of Lucknow the previous year, was almost disappointed. 'The Ranee was the *beast* who ordered all our people at Jhansie to be *cruelly* murdered after they placed their faith in her,' he noted in his diary on 20 June. 'She has had too easy a death.' Other Britons, while pleased to hear of the Rani's demise, could not hide their regard for a worthy opponent. 'The Ranee was remarkable for her beauty, cleverness and perseverance,' wrote General Rose, 'her generosity to her subordinates was unbounded. These qualities, combined with her rank, rendered her the most dangerous of all the rebel leaders.' Dr Lowe, normally one of the Rani's fiercest critics, noted that she was the rebels' 'most determined, spirited, and influential head'. She and her 'sister',* who died with her on the 17th, had 'fought like bricks', recorded Major Poore. 'But now that she is dead the whole thing seems disorganised.'

There were even some who were prepared to acquit the Rani of her alleged crimes. 'The cruelties attributed to her at Jhansie have since been officially contradicted,' wrote John Latimer of the Central India Field Force on 9 July.

Our unhappy countrymen and countrywomen may have been, it is true, killed with her sanction, but it is generally believed that she could not have saved them had she wished it . . . She seems to have animated and encouraged her men in every stand they made, and it was mainly through her exhortations and promises of reward that the rebels made their determined assault on our little army before Calpee on the 22nd of May. Seeing her army broken and defeated, with rage in her heart and tears in her eyes, she mounted her horse and made her course towards Gwalior. Here the last stand was made, she disdained further flight, and died, with a heroism worthy of a better cause. Her courage shines pre-eminent and can only be equalled but not eclipsed by that of Joan of Arc.

* As she did not have a sister, Poore is probably referring to one of her female attendants who was killed at the same time.

Latimer's assessment of the Rani is uncannily accurate. She had every reason to resent the British – both for the confiscation of her realm and their insensitive treatment of her thereafter – and may well have been involved in the pre-mutiny plotting at Jhansi. Her responsibility for the actual massacre, however, is unproven, and Latimer is surely right to point out that she could not have prevented it even if she had wanted to. The most likely scenario is that events at Jhansi in June 1857 were beyond her control, though their end result – the expulsion of the British – was exactly what she had been praying for (and possibly working towards) for years. She may even have believed at that time, as many others did, that the British Raj in India was at an end. This might explain why some of the possessions of the murdered British officers were found in her palace. She was, nevertheless, far too canny a diplomatist not to cover herself by making contact with the British and professing her allegiance. Only when it became clear that the British intended to hold her personally responsible for the atrocities at Jhansi did she consider casting in her lot with the rebels. And only as the British approached the very walls of her town did she actually do so.

The Rani of Jhansi's death, wrote Sir Robert Hamilton, 'quite upset the chiefs, and caused the greatest consternation' among the rebel troops. Certainly it weakened the spirit of resistance at Gwalior and on 19 June, 'after a general action which lasted for 5 and a half hours', Rose entered the city in triumph and restored the maharaja to his throne. Rao Sahib and Tatya Tope, meanwhile, had fled across the Chambal River into Rajputana with 5,000 troops and ten guns. For almost seven months, Tatya Tope remained at large in central India, living off the land and using guerrilla tactics to evade the clutches of countless British columns sent to destroy him. When he did stand and fight, as he did at Rajgarh in September 1858, he was badly defeated and lost all his guns. But he managed to escape with a hard core of adherents and, the following month, met up again with Rao Sahib. Together they decided to march south to Nagpur, the recently annexed Maratha state, in the hope that its people would rise up and join them. At the end of October, having lost half their men en route, they crossed the Nerbudda into Nagpur territory. 'Thus in the dying agony of the mutiny,' wrote a contemporary historian, 'was accomplished a movement which, carried out twelve months earlier, would have produced an effect fatal for the time to British supremacy; a movement which would have roused the whole of the western Presidency, have kindled revolt in the dominions of the Nizam, and have, in its working, penetrated to southern India.'

But it was too late: the fate of British rule was no longer in the balance and, unlike their counterparts further north, the Nagpur peasantry were not sympathetic to the rebel cause. Harried by British columns, the pair recrossed the Nerbudda and, in January 1859, linked up with Prince Firoz Shah* at Indragarh in Rajputana. But British troops were closing in and, after yet another defeat at Sikar on the 21st, the three rebel leaders parted company. Accompanied by just two cooks and a groom, Tatya Tope made his way to the jungles of Narwar, where he was betrayed to the authorities by Raja Man Singh, a Gwalior rebel, who received an amnesty in return. Seized on 7 April, Tatya was taken to Sipri and charged with rebellion. His defence has modern echoes. 'I only obeyed, in all things that I did, my master's orders, i.e., the Nana's orders, up to the capture of Kalpi, and, afterwards, those of Rao Sahib. I have nothing to state, except that I have had nothing to do with the murder of any European men, women, or children.' The court did not believe him and he was hanged on 18 April.

Rao Sahib evaded capture until 1862 when he too was betrayed. At his trial the Indian jury was unconvinced by the evidence and would find him guilty only of 'modified rebellion'. But the judge overruled them and sentenced him to death. He was hanged at Satichaura Ghat on 20 August 1862. Even Damadar Rao, the Rani of Jhansi's ten-year-old adopted son, could not escape British retribution. On account of his mother's rebellion, the private possessions of the Jhansi Raj were confiscated and he was deprived of the 600,000 rupees that the government of India had held in trust for him since the death of his father. A monthly allowance of 150 rupees, later raised to 200, was considered more than adequate.

Firoz Shah escaped from India and died in poverty in Mecca in 1877.

What of the other leading rebels? Kunwar Singh, after his defeat near Arrah in August 1857, had led the Dinapore mutineers west to Kalpi, where, for a time, he joined forces with Tatya Tope and the Gwalior Contingent. But he eventually returned east and, in March 1858, took Azimgarh and repulsed two British attempts to recapture it. Only when a strong British force was sent from Allahabad, under Lord Mark Kerr, did Kunwar Singh withdraw to his homeland. On 21 April, while crossing the Ganges at Sheopur Ghat, he was badly wounded by British artillery fire. He lived long enough to oversee one last victory: over Captain Le Grand's pursuing column at Jagdispur on the 23rd. Three days later he died of his wounds.

* Firoz Shah led an earlier rebellion at Mandesar and had recently been expelled from Rohilkhand by Campbell.

He was succeeded by his brother, Amar Singh, who kept up a dogged resistance in the hills around Shahabad until November.

The Maulvi of Faizabad, having escaped from Lucknow, was defeated by Hope Grant at Bari in April. Undeterred he led the remnants of his force to Rohilkhand, where, in concert with the rebel Raja of Mithauli, he took advantage of Campbell's advance on Bareilly to capture the town of Shahjahanpur on 3 May. Despite being reinforced by troops under Firoz Shah and Begum Hazrat Mahal, he could not reduce the British entrenchment and was eventually driven back into Oudh by Campbell. In early June he re-entered Rohilkhand with the intention of persuading a border chieftain, the Raja of Powayun,* to join the rebel cause. He approached the raja's fort on an elephant and asked for the gates to be opened. When the raja refused, he told his mahout to break them down. Before he could do so, the Maulvi was shot and killed by the raja's brother. The following day his severed head was delivered to the British magistrate at Shahjahanpur in exchange for a reward of 50,000 rupees.

An opportunity to heal some of the wounds of the previous twelve months was provided in early August by the passing of an Act that transferred the government of India from the East India Company to the Crown. The Court of Directors and the Board of Control were abolished and replaced by a Secretary of State and an advisory council of fifteen members: eight to be nominated by the Crown and seven by the outgoing Court. The Governor-General was henceforth known as the Viceroy, the Queen's representative in India, though he would continue to be assisted by a Supreme Council. On 1 September the Court of Directors held its last meeting in Leadenhall Street. The East India Company retained a shadowy legal existence until 1874 as it wound up its financial commitments.

The formal announcement of the transfer of authority from Company to Crown was made on 1 November 1858, when Queen Victoria's 'Proclamation' was read out across India. It confirmed all offices held under the East India Company and guaranteed all existing treaties with the princes of India. It also denied any further territorial ambitions and promised religious freedom. 'We declare it our Royal will and pleasure that none be in anywise favoured, none molested or disquieted, by reason of their religious faith or observances, but that all shall alike enjoy the equal and impartial protection of the law . . . And it is our further will that, so far as may be, our subjects,

* The same raja who, on 31 May 1857, told the fugitives from Shahjahanpur that they could stay only one night. A few days later they were murdered near Aurungabad.

of whatever race or creed, be freely and impartially admitted to offices in our service, the duties of which they may be qualified, by their education, ability, and integrity, duly to discharge.' But, most importantly, it offered an unconditional pardon to all rebels who were prepared to return peacefully to their homes. The only exceptions were those who had 'taken part in the murder of British subjects' and those who had knowingly harboured murderers or 'acted as leaders or instigators in revolt'. Those in the final category were guaranteed their lives but not immunity from lesser punishment.

The amnesty, which lasted until 1 January 1859, was designed to separate the more notorious rebels from their foot-soldiers. Aware of this, Begum Hazrat Mahal issued a counter-proclamation in the name of her son, urging the rebels not to place their faith in the offer of pardon, 'for it is the unvarying custom of the English never to forgive a fault be it great or small'. The document then proceeded to attack the various promises made by the Queen's Proclamation by pointing out that treaties in the past had been ignored, territory stolen and religion interfered with. 'The rebellion began with religion,' it stated, 'and for it millions of men have been killed. Let not our subjects be deceived.'

Many minor rebels were tired of fighting and gladly accepted the amnesty. Those who did not, the hard core, were targeted by Sir Colin Campbell, now Lord Clyde,* in his final Oudh campaign, which began in early November. His plan was to herd the rebels towards the Nepal border, where they could either be destroyed *in toto* or, if they crossed over, left to die of starvation and disease in the fever-infested forests of the Nepal Terai. By the turn of the year most of the leading rebels had entered the Terai. They included Hazrat Mahal, her son Birjis Qadr, Mammu Khan, Khan Bahadur Khan, Nana Sahib, Bala Rao and Jwala Prasad. Hazrat Mahal, in particular, was hopeful that Jung Bahadur would give the rebels refuge. But on 15 January 1859 he formally notified her that she could expect no help from the state of Nepal. He also gave permission for British troops to enter Nepal in pursuit.

In the event, pursuit was unnecessary because the privations of the Terai quickly reduced the rebels to a beleaguered rabble. Some died of disease; others were captured by Jung Bahadur's troops and handed over to the British. Among the latter were Amar Singh, Khan Bahadur Khan and Jwala Prasad, all seized in December 1859. Amar Singh died in Gorakhpur Gaol,

* Sir Colin Campbell was ennobled as Lord Clyde of Clydebank on 16 August 1858.

awaiting trial; Khan Bahadur Khan and Jwala Prasad were both hanged in the spring of 1860 at Bareilly and Cawnpore respectively. Mammu Khan, having been dismissed by the Begum for want of 'courage and devotion', gave himself up to the British and was also hanged in 1860. The Begum refused to surrender and Jung Bahadur eventually gave her permission to remain in Nepal with her son. She died there in 1879.

Nana Sahib's fate is unclear. He was still alive in April 1859 when he and his brother Bala sent letters to the nearest British camp, petitioning the Indian government for clemency. Bala blamed his brother for their predicament and insisted he was not guilty of murder. The Nana also protested his innocence. 'You have forgiven the crimes of all Hindoostan,' he wrote, 'and murderers have been pardoned . . . It is surprising that I who have joined the rebels from helplessness have not been forgiven. I have committed no murder.' The people responsible for the massacres at Cawnpore, he added, were sepoys and hooligans. He ended on a note of defiance: 'You have drawn all to your side, and I alone am left but you will see what the soldiers I have been preserving for two years can do. *We will meet, and then I will shed your blood and it will flow knee deep. I am prepared to die.*'

The reply, from a major named Richardson, referred him to the Queen's amnesty that had been extended beyond 1 January 1859. 'Those terms are open to you and all those who may wish to surrender,' wrote Richardson. 'In writing as you do that you have not murdered women and children, it becomes you to come in without fear.' Nana Sahib's response was that he would surrender only if the Queen herself wrote to him. When Canning learnt about this exchange, he censured Richardson for even suggesting that Nana Sahib might escape the hangman's noose. Public opinion would not stand for it. 'Whether he surrenders or be taken,' Richardson was told, 'he will be tried for the crimes of which he stands charged.' Nothing more was heard from the 'arch fiend' of the rebellion.

Later that year Bala is said to have died from fever. Nana Sahib's death was reported soon after. 'There can be no doubt that Nana is dead,' insisted a mutineer who gave himself up in October 1859. 'His death was communicated to me by Sirdar Allie, a Naick of the 68th Regiment N.I. who not only saw the dead body, but was present when it was burned.' Confirmation was provided by Jwala Prasad, the Nana's brigadier, as he awaited his execution in Cawnpore Gaol. 'He knew his sentence did not depend on me,' wrote the Magistrate of Cawnpore, 'so he was not afraid, and answered readily when I spoke to him. He told me, if I remember his words rightly, that he was not present when the Nana died, but that he attended when the body was burned. He spoke apparently without intention to deceive, and I fully believed him.' According to a mutineer of the 22nd Native Infantry, Jwala Prasad 'assumed the command of the Nana's forces on the death of the latter'. But others were not so sure, including a spy who reported that 'Nana Rao was ill, but not dead'. Over the years countless 'sightings' were made of Nana Sahib. The last was in 1895, at a rural station in Gujerat, when an old *sadhu* told a young British officer that he was the notorious rebel. 'Have arrested the Nana Sahib,' the officer excitedly informed Calcutta. 'Wire instructions.' The reply was dismissive: 'Release at once.'

Baba Bhutt, Nana Sahib's older brother, was last seen travelling in secret towards Calcutta with an ailing Azimullah Khan. One account has Azimullah dying of smallpox en route; another says he managed to escape the country with a 'Miss Clayton' and eventually settled in Constantinople as an emissary of the Sherif of Mecca. He was murdered, so the story goes, after Miss Clayton died of old age.

Two other notorious rebels were caught in bizarre circumstances. In February 1859 Sergeant William Forbes-Mitchell of the 93rd Highlanders was sitting in his tent at Cawnpore when a 'very good looking, light-coloured native in the prime of his life' appeared selling cakes. He said that his name was Green and that he had been mess *khansaman* for a regiment of native infantry. Forbes-Mitchell admired his front, though not the look of his assistant, a 'villainous-looking' Eurasian named Mickey. The pair left but were arrested the following day: Green for spying and 'Mickey' for having been recognized as Sarvur Khan, leader of the Bibighar murder squad. As they awaited execution, Forbes-Mitchell prevented his Scottish comrades from stuffing pork down the throats of the condemned men; he also provided them with a last meal and a hookah. In gratitude, Green told him that he was none other than Mohamed Ali Khan, the Rohilkhand nobleman who had accompanied Azimullah to London and Constantinople where they had 'formed the resolution of attempting to overthrow the Company's Government'. Mohamed Ali added: 'Thank God we have succeeded in doing that, for from the newspapers which you lent me, I see that the Company's rule has gone, and that their charter for robbery and confiscation will not be renewed.' He and Sarvur Khan were hanged the following morning.

One of the few rebel leaders to avoid a judicial execution was the Nawab of Farrukhabad. He gave himself up in early 1859 after Major Barrow, a special commissioner, guaranteed his life. The court ignored this unauthorized offer and sentenced him to death. But, on reflection, the authorities decided to give him the option of exile to Mecca and he took it. In the event he was put ashore at the Red Sea port of Aden and died within a few years.

Liaqat Ali, the Maulvi of Allahabad, was the last rebel to be brought to justice. He remained on the run for fourteen years, visiting Baroda, Bombay and even Baghdad, it was said, in the guise of a respectable Muslim gentleman. He was finally captured at Byculla railway station, clutching a hollow cane filled with 2,000 rupees worth of gold ingots, and sent to Allahabad for trial. He pleaded guilty but said, in mitigation, that he had saved the life of Amy Horne at Cawnpore. This plea may have saved his neck because his sentence was transportation for life to the penal colony of Port Blair in the Andaman Islands.

21. 'War is at an end'

On 8 July 1859 a 'State of Peace' was officially declared throughout India. A day later, as a symbolic gesture, ex-King Wajid Ali of Oudh and his advisers were released from Fort William. Canning had wanted to mark the declaration of peace with a day of thanksgiving and prayer; but he agreed to postpone it until all operations in Oudh had ceased. It eventually took place on 28 July, with the Viceroy proclaiming: 'War is at an end. Rebellion is put down. The Noise of Arms is no longer heard where the enemies of the State have persisted in their last struggle. The Presence of large Forces in the Field has ceased to be necessary. Order is re-established; and peaceful pursuits everywhere have been resumed.'

Canning's reward for 'saving' India was a GCB and an earldom. Neither honour gave him much pleasure: the former because Sir John Lawrence, his subordinate, had received his a full eighteen months earlier; the latter because he had always looked upon viscounts as 'a more select caste' than earls. He had, in any case, no heir to leave the title to.

Lawrence had also received a promotion at the beginning of the year when his post was upgraded from Chief Commissioner to Lieutenant-Governor of the Punjab. Soon after he returned home to England to take up a seat on the new Council of India. Before he left, however, he sent Canning a list of Indian princes who deserved recognition for their support during the mutiny. Chief among them were the three great Sikh rulers of the Cis-Sutlej States – the Maharaja of Patiala and the Rajas of Jhind and Nabha – who had safeguarded the lines of communication to the Punjab and made the reconquest of Delhi possible. Patiala, the most influential of the three, was given land with a rental value of 2 lakhs a year, a mansion in Delhi that had belonged to a rebel and the dubious honour of calling himself 'Choicest son of the British Government'. Jhind, the only prince to lead his troops in person to Delhi, was allotted land worth a lakh of rupees, a house in Delhi, an increase in his royal salute from nine to eleven guns and the even more dubious title of 'Most cherished son of the true Faith'. Nabha received similar rewards. As a further concession, all three were given the right to resolve disputed successions or failures of line among themselves.

The great princes were also rewarded. Maharaja Scindia of Gwalior got land worth 3 lakhs a year and the authority to increase his personal army from 3,000 to 5,000. Maharaja Holkar of Indore, whose conduct was not so clear cut, gained no territory but, his two sons having died, was granted the right of adoption with undisputed succession. The Nizam of Hyderabad received back a parcel of land that Dalhousie had confiscated from his father; he was also given the vacant state of Shorapur and his debts, estimated at half a million pounds, were cancelled. Nepal was thanked for its military assistance by the return of territory that had been annexed in 1815. In addition, Jung Bahadur was awarded the GCB. And all Indian princes benefited from the reinstatement of the right of adoption.

Canning continued as Viceroy of India until March 1862, presiding over a series of government measures designed to make the British Raj more inclusive. In 1861, for example, he enlarged the legislative council to make room for Indian non-official members. He also encouraged education: Calcutta, Bombay and Madras universities were founded during the mutiny and grants were given to private colleges. This was a deliberate attempt to create a 'westernized' Indian middle class that would cooperate rather than confront. In one respect it succeeded: by the mid 1880s there were 8,000 Indians with degrees and a further half a million had graduated from secondary schools. Yet it was this English-speaking elite – Gandhi *et al.* – that would ultimately spearhead the campaign for independence.

Canning's other post-mutiny initiatives included the introduction of a penal code, the acceleration of railway building and a Bengal Rent Act to protect tenants against eviction or gratuitous rent increases. But the most important reform of his viceregal administration was that of the army.* Prompted by the recommendations of the Peel Commission† – set up in London in July 1858 to advise on the reorganization of the Indian Army – Canning's government introduced a number of changes to prevent a large-scale mutiny from ever happening again. They succeeded. From 1858 to independence in 1947, the Indian Army had just twenty minor mutinies, half of them during the First and Second World Wars. The smallest involved twenty men, the largest a single regiment. Only one – the mutiny of four companies of the 5th Light Infantry at Singapore in 1915 – resulted in sepoy violence against their officers. Most of the mutinies – including the seven that occurred between 1886 and 1914 – were little more than peaceful

* See Appendix Four.

† Named after its chairman Major-General Jonathan Peel, Secretary of State for War and brother of the late Prime Minister.

collective protests over professional issues such as pay, allowances, promotions and conditions of service.

That the mutinies did not develop into anything more significant can be put down to the post-1857 military reforms: the increased ratio of European to Indian troops (which remained at around 1:2 until 1914), the concentration of artillery in European hands and the brigading of one European regiment with every two Indian corps so that no major station was left without a European presence. Just as significant were the improvements made to the service conditions of all three presidency armies, and the Bengal Army in particular: the creation of a Staff Corps and the selection of European officers for more lucrative regimental duties that came to be regarded as an honour rather than a chore; the increase in the power of commanding officers to punish and reward, including the replacement of seniority with merit as the dominant principle of promotion; the switch to irregular regiments with fewer Europeans, which gave Indian officers more responsibility and greater job satisfaction; the increase in pay for Indian infantry officers and all native cavalrymen; the switch from tight and uncomfortable European-style uniforms to those more suited to the Indian climate; and, crucially, the Bengal Army's shift in recruitment from the high-caste Hindus of Oudh and the North-Western Provinces to the Sikhs and Muslims of the Punjab, the Gurkhas of Nepal and the lower castes of Hindustan.

No one was more central to the creation of the new 'irregular' system than Brigadier-General John Jacob, who had been urging similar reforms since the 1840s. If Jacob had been listened to earlier, the Indian mutiny might not have occurred. He died in December 1858; but he would have been gratified to hear the judgement passed on the 'irregular' system by Lord Napier, the Commander-in-Chief of India, in 1875: 'No impartial observer, who knows what the old army was, and what the present one is, can hesitate for a moment to pronounce the regiments of the present day greatly superior to those of the old army; better drill [*sic*] and disciplined, more obedient, less fettered by assumptions of religious restraint, more moveable, more ready for every service.' A greater contrast with the indisciplined, caste-ridden, disaffected Bengal Army of 1857 is hard to imagine.

In November 1861, just four months before her husband was due to return home, Lady Canning died of jungle fever. A heartbroken Earl Canning handed over the viceroyalty to Lord Elgin in March 1862 and arrived back in London a month later. But the burden of six years as head of the Indian government had taken its toll and he died on 17 June at the age of fifty. 'I was assured by a great doctor on his return that he was perfectly sound,' wrote Lord Granville. 'He died, and nearly all his organs were found to be destroyed by the heavy strain, possibly by that of the last additional year, which a sense of duty made him go through.'

Within a year Lord Elgin had followed Canning to the grave. He was succeeded by Sir John Lawrence, who had been created a baronet and given a life pension of £2,000. As in the Punjab, Lawrence sought to centralize authority by keeping financial control in the Viceroy's hands and blocking the creation of executive councils for his lieutenant-governors. He was also successful in resisting the Indianization of the higher civil service. It had been open to Indians since 1853, when public competition was introduced, but only one Indian actually entered the service before 1871. Lawrence's rule was typically paternalistic: he tried to lighten the fiscal burden on the peasantry by limiting government expenditure, lowering the salt tax and taxing the middle classes; he also set in motion an ambitious programme of railway and canal building, and did much to promote public health, prison reform and primary education. He had become increasingly convinced that British rule in India was part of God's purpose. 'We have not been elected or placed in power by the people,' he wrote, 'but we are here through our moral superiority, by the force of circumstances and by the will of Providence.' Lawrence's views were representative of the shift in the British perception of Empire from trading opportunity to civilizing mission (or 'white man's burden'). He was made Baron Lawrence of the Punjab on his return to England in 1869 and died ten years later.

Lawrence's senior advisers in the Punjab in 1857 also did well. Robert Montgomery was made GCB and Lieutenant-Governor of the Punjab. Herbert Edwardes was also knighted, but had to turn down Lawrence's offer of the Punjab because of ill health. He died of pleurisy in 1868. Of the Punjab soldiers who survived the mutiny, Neville Chamberlain was the most successful. After a six-year spell as Commander-in-Chief of the Madras Army in the 1870s, he joined the Viceroy's Supreme Council and eventually retired to England in 1881. He lived long enough to criticize the conduct of the Boer War and finally died, as Field-Marshal Sir Neville Chamberlain, in 1902 at the age of eighty-two.

As well as the Barony of Clyde, Sir Colin Campbell received the thanks of Parliament and a pension of £2,000 a year. He did not enjoy it for long. Having left India in June 1860, he died at Chatham in Kent three years later. He was succeeded as Commander-in-Chief of India by the most successful British general of the mutiny: Sir Hugh Rose (later Baron Stathnairn). Rose himself was replaced, in 1866, by Campbell's chief of staff, Sir William Mansfield (later Baron Sandhurst). But all these illustrious careers were eclipsed by that of young Fred Roberts, who rose to become Field-Marshal Earl Roberts, VC, the sole Company officer to command both the Indian and British Armies. The only other junior officer to achieve a similar prominence was Captain Garnet Wolseley of the 90th Foot, who served under Campbell at Lucknow in 1858. Wolseley became one of the great reforming generals of the British Army and was Roberts's predecessor as Commander-in-Chief.

Few of the senior Bengal officers had been able to cope with the emergency of May 1857. Fred Roberts put this down to their age and inefficiency and blamed the Bengal Army's seniority system of promotion. He added:

> Nearly every military officer who held a command or high position on the staff in Bengal when the Mutiny broke out, disappeared from the scene within the first few weeks, and was never heard of officially again. Some were killed, some died of disease, but the great majority failed completely to fulfil the duties of the positions they held, and were consequently considered unfit for further employment. Two Generals of divisions were removed from their commands, seven Brigadiers were found wanting in the hour of need,* and out of the seventy-three regiments of Regular Cavalry and Infantry which mutinied, only four Commanding Officers were given other commands, younger officers being selected to raise and command the new regiments.

Even Major-General John Hearsey, the one divisional commander who responded energetically to the outbreak of mutiny, was not re-employed. He was knighted, however, and died of bronchitis at Boulogne in 1865.

What of the lesser lights? 'Butcher' Vibart, the sole survivor of his family, retired as a colonel and later published an account of the mutiny. He died in 1923 at the age of eighty-six. Lieutenant Hugh Gough of the 3rd Light Cavalry won a Victoria Cross for two outstanding acts of bravery at the Alambagh in November 1857 and Jelalabad three months later. He retired as General Sir Hugh Gough, VC, and also published his memoirs.† Ensign

* Among the few exceptions were Brigadiers Stuart Corbett and George Campbell, of the Lahore and Rawalpindi stations respectively, who both went on to command divisions.

† His elder brother, Major Charles Gough, also received the VC during the Indian mutiny. Among the deeds mentioned in the citation was saving Hugh Gough's life at Khurkowdah in August 1857. Charles's son, Major John Gough, was awarded the same medal in Somaliland in 1903, making the Goughs the only family to win three VCs.

Everard Phillipps, who had joined the 60th Rifles after the mutiny of his regiment at Meerut, was killed at Delhi on 18 September 1857. Fifty years later, his gallantry at Delhi was rewarded when his family was presented with his posthumous VC.*

Elizabeth Sneyd and her daughter Louisa were eventually reunited with Louisa's husband, Dr Robert Hutchinson, who had survived the outbreak at Fatehpur. But Louisa's baby son died in Calcutta at the age of two and a half months. Stanley Delhiforce Tytler, another child born during the mutiny, lived through the hazards of the Ridge and accompanied his parents to England in 1860. Before leaving, Robert Tytler had bought the King of Delhi's crown – a sort of cap set with diamonds, emeralds, rubies and pearls – and two of his gilt throne chairs at an auction of the Delhi prizes. He was offered £1,000 for the crown by a Bond Steet jeweller but was persuaded to sell it to Queen Victoria by Sir Charles Wood, then Secretary of State for India. The most the Queen was prepared to pay, however, was £500. Tytler accepted it because Wood assured him that he would be given a plum appointment on his return to India. Wood added that the Queen was interested in buying the throne chairs and so Tytler sent them to Buckingham Palace. But he was never paid for them. When he made inquiries, Wood told him that Her Majesty was under the impression that the chairs were included in the original price. Afraid of losing his appointment, he let the matter drop. 'But he was very loyal,' wrote Harriet, 'which made it very difficult for him to understand how Her Majesty could lend herself, for the sake of filthy lucre, to deprive one of her subjects, a poor military man who, she should have known, had lost his all in the mutiny.' The crown and chairs are still in the Royal Collection at Windsor Castle. To add insult to injury, Tytler never got his plum appointment. Instead, in 1862, he was given the superintendency of the Andaman Islands' penal colony, a post that Harriet thought was 'worth having as a major, but not as a colonel'. He accepted it anyway, 'hoping that by doing so it might lead to something better'. It did not. Robert fell ill in 1870 and died a year later. Harriet outlived him by thirty-six years.

But the most poignant and tragic denouement of the mutiny involved a

* In 1859 it was announced in the *London Gazette* that had Phillipps lived he would have been awarded the Victoria Cross for leading the storming party that took the Water Bastion on 14 September. This unusual practice – known as the 'Memorandum Procedure' – was repeated only five more times during the nineteenth century (and only once during the mutiny itself). In 1907 King Edward VII ordered VCs to be given to the families of the six men.

loyal Indian soldier: Jemadar Sitaram Pandy of the 63rd Bengal Native Infantry. In June 1857 Sitaram was on leave at his village in the Rai Bareilly district of Oudh when a band of mutineers appeared. 'I explained to them the folly of going against the English Government,' he recalled, 'but these men were so intoxicated with the plunder they had taken, and by their hope of reward from the Emperor of Delhi, that they turned on me and were about to shoot me on the spot for having dared to speak out in favour of the English Government. They called me a traitor, and ended by taking me prisoner.' But as the mutineers neared Cawnpore they were attacked by a troop of volunteer cavalry under Captain Lousada Barrow – part of Havelock's relief column – and Sitaram was released. As he was not a horseman, but could read and write Persian, Barrow made him the troop interpreter.

I went about with this *rissalah* for about six weeks [he remembered], during which time it destroyed several bands of mutineers and one day had a hand-to-hand fight with a party of regular cavalry. They fired off their pistols and made off as hard as they could although they were three times the size of our party. Nineteen *sowars* were killed and twenty-one of the best of the Government's horses were taken. We lost five men killed and seven wounded. After this our Troop returned to Cawnpore, which had been re-taken twice by the English.

At Cawnpore Sitaram was transferred to the 12th Punjab Infantry as a supernumerary jemadar. Thereafter he fought in several actions, culminating in the pursuit of the rebels to the Nepal border. But it was during the capture of Lucknow, in March 1858, that Sitaram faced his greatest test of loyalty. A number of mutineers had been captured in one of the enclosed buildings near Lucknow and Sitaram was told to execute them. To his horror he discovered that one of them was his long-lost son, Ananti Ram, whom he had not seen for twenty-five years. He wrote later:

The prisoners were to be shot at four o'clock in the afternoon and I must be my son's executioner! Such is fate! I went to see the Major *sahib* and requested that I might be relieved of this duty as a very great favour. He was very angry and said he would bring me before a court-martial for trying to shirk my duty . . . I burst into floods of tears. I told him that I would shoot every one of the prisoners with my own hands if he ordered me but I confessed that one of them was my own son . . . He ordered my unfortunate son to be brought before him and questioned him very strictly.

I shall never forget this terrible scene. Not for one moment did I consider requesting that his life should be spared – that he did not deserve. Eventually the Major came to believe in the truth of my statement and ordered me to be relieved from this duty. I went to my tent bowed down with grief which was made worse by the gibes and taunts of the Sikhs who declared I was a renegade. In a short time I heard a volley. My son had received the reward for mutiny! . . . Through the kindness of the Major I was allowed to perform the funeral rites over my misguided son. He was the only one of the prisoners over whom it was performed, for the remainder were all thrown to the jackals and the vultures.

Two years later Sitaram was promoted to the rank of subedar. But at sixty-five he was too old to perform his duties. 'I was expected to be as active as ever,' he wrote, 'and no allowance was made for my forty-eight years' service. No one bothered to remember that I had carried a musket for thirty years and had been present in as many battles as most of the officers had lived years. I was shouted at by the Adjutant as if I was a bullock, and he a mere boy, young enough to be my grandson. I was abused by the Commanding Officer, and called a fool, a donkey, and an old woman!' It was a relief when, later that year, he was pensioned off by an invaliding committee. 'The Company *Bahadur* and its officers were much kinder to the people of India than the present Government,' he reminisced. 'If it were not for the old servants of the Company, it would be even worse than it is.'

Among those 'old servants' was J. T. Norgate, Sitaram's former commandant, who persuaded Sitaram to write his memoirs. Sitaram completed the manuscript in 1861, shortly after his retirement, and sent a copy to Norgate. He translated it into English and it was finally published in 1873. It remains the only printed account of the mutiny period by an Indian soldier.

Sitaram had seen much, but his regrets were few. He signed off:

Thanks be to God the Creator! I lack nothing thanks to the bounty of the *Sirkar*, and I have a son left to perform my funeral ceremonies. If your Lordship, when you return to your own country, will always remember that the old Subedar Sita Ram was a true and faithful servant of the English Government, it will be enough for me.

Appendix One

Was 31 May 1857 the Date Fixed for a General Mutiny of the Bengal Army?

After the suppression of the mutiny, James Cracroft Wilson, the former Judge of Moradabad, was appointed a Special Commissioner to punish guilty and reward deserving Indians. The evidence he collected, he said, was proof that 'Sunday, 31st of May, 1857, was the day fixed for mutiny to commence throughout the Bengal Army; that there were committees of about three members in each regiment, which conducted the duties of the mutiny; that the sepoys, as a body, knew nothing of the plans arranged; and that the only compact entered into by regiments, as a body, was, that their particular regiments would do as the other regiments did'.

However, Major G. W. Williams, Cracroft Wilson's fellow Special Commissioner, did not agree. It was only after the outbreak at Meerut, he wrote, that 'corps after corps caught the infection, excited and encouraged by the uncontradicted boast of the extermination of all Europeans, and the overthrow of the British rule' by the Indian troops at Meerut and Delhi. Even when the boast proved hollow, they were 'still lured on by the glowing accounts of unbounded wealth obtained from the plunder of Europeans and Government treasuries, and the honors and promotions expected from a rebel King'. Many also believed the rumours, 'kept alive by evil and designing men', that their religion was in danger. If any such plot for a general mutiny had existed, Williams concluded, the Meerut troops 'were indeed rash and insane to mar the whole'.

The truth probably lies somewhere in between. Cracroft Wilson omitted to specify the evidence from which he drew his conclusion. But his point about secret committees coordinating the uprising is supported by a wealth of documentation in this book. For security reasons alone, those made party to such a plot would necessarily have been few in number. Williams, on the other hand, is surely right in his assessment of the motives that drove many sepoys to mutiny. If the two theories are combined, we are left with a loose network of conspirators who were prepared to incite mutiny as and when the occasion presented itself. Their success would depend upon a number of variables: the closeness of the relationship between Indian troops and their European officers (particularly the commanding officer); the presence of other European troops; the proximity to unguarded treasure and other regiments that had already mutinied; and, of course, the number of sepoys prepared to believe (or appear to believe) that their religion and caste were in danger. Given that most soldiers were in the dark, however, the conspirators would not have been foolish enough to imagine that they could coordinate a general mutiny on a single day.

But to understand why the cartridge question was manipulated to provide a pretext for mutiny, it is necessary to identify the aspirations of the army ringleaders themselves. They were, by definition, ambitious men. They were drawn from a complete cross-section of army ranks – including Indian officers who were close to receiving their pensions and therefore had the most to lose – and were probably united by a shared exasperation with the limitations of Company service. Their pre-mutiny links to the courts of disaffected princes like the ex-King of Oudh and the King of Delhi are surely indicative of an aim that was both political and professional: the replacement of their British employers with an indigenous government that would provide greater career opportunities and increased pay.

Appendix Two

The Civilian Conspiracy and Rebel Chiefs

Nana Sahib's involvement in the Cawnpore outbreak is significant for a number of reasons. In the first place, his pre-mutiny machinations indicate the existence of a plot for a rebellion by both civilians and sepoys that pre-dated the cartridge question by almost a year. Sitaram Bawa's claim that the conspiracy got off the ground only after the annexation of Oudh is entirely consistent with the fact that two of the regiments then stationed at Lucknow – the 19th and 34th Native Infantry – were at the forefront of the disaffection in 1857. In this context, the cartridge controversy was a heaven-sent opportunity for the conspirators to unite Hindu and Muslim sepoys against their European masters. It may be no coincidence that the rumour about bone dust being added to flour originated at Cawnpore. Then there is Sitaram Bawa's point that the 'military classes' were enticed by the promise that the old days of licence would be restored. This is important because it identifies plunder as a motive for mutiny. By 1856, with most of India under the heel of the British, the opportunity for Indian soldiers to supplement their relatively meagre pay with plunder had all but vanished. Only the replacement of the British with Indian rulers would bring back this cycle of war and rapine. Lastly the mutineers' offer of a kingdom or death to Nana Sahib confirms that they were the real power behind the rebel movement (just as they were at Delhi and elsewhere). Yet only a handful of mutineers tried to set themselves up as rulers in their own right: possibly because they realized that only legitimate princes had a chance of gaining enough grass-roots support to defeat the British; and possibly because their chief aim had always been to attach themselves to a viable employer.

Of the six ruling princes named by Sitaram Bawa as party to the Nana's conspiracy – the Nizam of Hyderabad, Maharaja Holkar of Indore, Maharaja Scindia of Gwalior and the Maharajas of Jaipur, Jodhpur and Jammu – not one openly rebelled during the Indian mutiny. But that was probably because they had the most to lose. The British certainly suspected more than one of them of disloyalty and came to the conclusion that they were waiting to see how events unfolded before they committed themselves. These suspicions were partly founded upon the inability or unwillingness of these princes to prevent their own troops from mutinying. Most of the European-officered Gwalior Contingent mutinied in the first two weeks of June 1857, as did a cavalry regiment of the Hyderabad Contingent. Two of Holkar's Indian-controlled regiments rose and attacked the British Residency at Indore on 1 July, and the whole of the Jodhpur Legion turned against its officers in late August. Referring to the first three of these mutinies in a letter of 23 July, the Governor of Madras wrote: 'Holkar's and Scindiah's conduct appears questionable, at all events they appear to have been shaken for a short time but subsequently to have recovered themselves & remained staunch . . . The Nizam [of Hyderabad] appears true at present but from all I can learn he is a wretched weak creature who will certainly go wrong if his present Minister, Salar Gang, should not be got rid of.'

The mutinies at Gwalior and Scindia's reaction are particularly revealing. In late May Scindia told the British political agent, Major Macpherson, that the worst affected of his contingent (most of whom were *purbias* from Bengal) had been holding 'nightly meetings for administering pledges' and had been 'boasting of the destruction of the English power and of all Christians' since the arrival of news from Meerut. Furthermore 'emissaries and letters from Delhi, Calcutta, and other centres of the revolt' had been circulating in Gwalior. Six of these emissaries had been arrested and discharged as deserters from Bengal regiments, said Macpherson, but nothing more serious could be proved against them. Scindia's own inquiries as to the cause of the revolt had revealed a 'general hostility to our rule' with the 'cartridge question being declared to be merely its pretext'. Macpherson added:

> Scindia and the *Dewan* [chief minister] . . . said most confidently that, as no reigning prince of influence had joined the revolt, and as its leaders at Delhi were plainly unequal to their great enterprise, but especially as Benares, Gya [Gaya], and the other centres of Hindu opinion, to which all had looked, had abstained from sanctioning any religious pretext alleged for it, when Delhi should be crushed, the belief in our ascendancy would at once return, and the revolt be arrested.

This may explain why Scindia never sided with his mutinous troops, despite severe pressure for him to do so after Macpherson and the other European survivors left Gwalior for Agra on 17 June. 'I may observe,' wrote Macpherson, 'that had Scindia, in this the dark hour of the storm, supported by the Dewan alone with the two chiefs of his troops, yielded to the pressure of the opinions and temptations which impelled him to strike against us, the character of the revolt had been entirely changed . . . But he believed in our final triumph, and that it was his true policy to strain his power to contribute to it.' For four months the troops 'menaced, beseeched, dictated, wheedled, and insulted Scindia by turns'. He, in turn, used every stratagem available to keep them at Gwalior until the British had concentrated enough forces to retake Delhi. Then, said Macpherson, he 'despatched them to rout by our arms'.

According to Ahsanullah Khan, the mutinous troops at Delhi persuaded the King to send *shukkas* (messages) to a number of princes – including the Maharajas of Gwalior, Jodhpur, Jaipur and Jammu – 'calling upon them to come over with their troops and munitions of war'. But none of the above four replied because they had 'no inclination to side with the King'. However, Scindia might have been hedging his bets. In a letter attributed to him of 18 November 1857, he congratulated the rebel Nawab of Banda for having reclaimed his former domain. 'You have beaten and driven out the English,' he wrote. 'This is good news to me. Tell me of whoever comes to fight with you and I will give you assistance with my army . . . I hear that the Rewa Raja has allowed the English to stay with him. At this I am much displeased . . . I have published your name from this to Delhi.' Such behaviour was certainly in line with Maratha diplomatic tradition: during the Second Maratha War the Peshwa, Baji Rao, was an official ally of the Company but kept in regular contact with its enemies, the Maharajas of Gwalior and Nagpur.

Former rulers – such as the Nawabs of Farrukhabad and Banda, the Raja of Assam, and the families of the late Rajas of Kolhapur, Satara and Jhansi – had less to lose and were more willing to risk rebellion. The young Raja of Assam, for example, was arrested and sent out of his province in September 1857 after being implicated in a plot to incite the 1st Assam Light Infantry to mutiny. The extent to which the Rani was complicit in the outbreak at Jhansi, on the other hand, is much disputed. As for the other former rulers, it is surely no coincidence that by far the most serious mutiny in the Bombay Army was perpetrated by sepoys of the 27th Native Infantry at Kolhapur. The Nawab of Farrukhabad, on the other hand, appears to have taken no part in any pre-mutiny plotting and agreed to set himself up as subordinate ruler to the King of Delhi only when mutineers threatened to kill him if he did not.

Other influential rebels included large landholders who had had their estates broken up by revenue settlements of the Company. The most notable was Raja Kunwar Singh of Jagdispur in Bihar, the recruiting heartland of the Bengal Native Infantry. S. B. Chaudhuri is not entirely convinced that Kunwar Singh incited the three regiments at Dinapore – the 7th, 8th and 40th Native Infantry – to mutiny on 25 July 1857. Yet the circumstantial evidence is compelling: the three regiments made straight for Jagdispur and put themselves under the raja's command; they were joined, three weeks later, by the mutinous 5th Irregular Cavalry from Bhagalpur. Another disgruntled landholder was the Raja of Mainpuri, who had forfeited one hundred and forty-nine of his two hundred villages as a result of the British land settlement. He was indirectly implicated in the rising of the 10th Native Infantry at Fatehgarh on 18 June by the interception, two weeks earlier, of a letter from his uncle, exhorting the sepoys of the 10th to mutiny. The raja himself later petitioned the King of Delhi for troops, but the mutinous officers insisted that none could be sent until the British had been driven from the Ridge.

Appendix Three

The Motive for Mutiny

The fact that the mutinies began in May and peaked in June, the height of the hot season, was almost certainly deliberate. European troops were at a disadvantage in hot weather and many were stationed in the hills. In the majority of cases – as if in confirmation of Ahsanullah Khan's claim that it was agreed by the conspirators beforehand – the mutinous regiments headed for Delhi. By mid August – according to one British spy – the rebel army at Delhi was composed of twenty and a half regiments of infantry and three and a half regiments of cavalry, giving a grand total of 17,975 mutineers and 33 guns. But not all the rebel troops made it to Delhi. Some, notably in the Punjab, were intercepted and destroyed en route. Others coalesced around alternative rebel authorities, such as: Nana Sahib who was proclaimed the new Peshwa at Bithur on 1 July; Birjis Qadr, the younger son of Wajid Ali, who was crowned King of Oudh at Lucknow on 5 July; Raja Kunwar Singh of Jagdispur in Bihar; and the Nawabs of Banda and Farrukhabad. In each case, however, the mutinous troops were anxious to set up some form of alternative government to the British.

This determination to transfer their allegiance to an Indian employer was motivated by considerations that were both political and professional in nature: political in the sense that they were seeking to replace their colonial overlords with traditional Indian rulers; professional in that many of them, particularly the conspirators, hoped that service under these new employers would be more rewarding than it had become under the British. They were, as Dirk Kolff has put it, simply exercising their rights under the terms of the traditional military labour market. 'To take leave of a master, whose "salt one had eaten",' writes Kolff, 'did neither amount to a breach of faith nor to the end of a relationship.' He gives the example of a battalion of Bombay sepoys that, having arrived in Poona in July 1805 one thousand strong, had less than four hundred men six months later. By 1857, however, the East India Company had so successfully dominated the military labour market that it was no longer possible for sepoys to pick and choose their employer with impunity. The only way to create an alternative was to destroy British power. In this sense it was all or nothing, which may explain why, according to Ahsanullah, the mutineers decided in advance 'to kill all Europeans including women and children, in every cantonment'. Such atrocities would tar whole regiments with the same mutinous brush and help to ensure that the less enthusiastic sepoys joined the rebellion because they no longer had anything to lose. 'There were some who remained faithful,' wrote Sitaram Pandy, 'and there were still more whose fate it was to be in a regiment that mutinied. These had no desire to rebel against the *Sirkar*, but feared that no allowance would be made for them when so many others had gone wrong. This was well understood by those who instigated the mutiny. Their first object was to implicate an entire regiment so that everyone had to throw in their lot with them.'

The argument that the ringleaders were seeking to replace one employer with another is supported by the way in which many mutinous corps retained their command structure and cohesiveness. Stokes observed that the 'problem of re-establishing discipline and internal order within a unit' could be 'formidable', partly because the mutinous faction was usually 'composed of men from the ranks'. This was true in a number of cases. But in many more instances, Indian officers took an active part in the plotting and perpetration of mutiny.

Many of these Indian officers were working hand-in-glove with other non-commissioned and sepoy conspirators. But no sooner had a regiment mutinied than its remaining Indian officers tended to take, or to be given, control. Lal Khan, a Muslim subedar of the 3rd Light Cavalry, is said to have been elected generalissimo of the Meerut Brigade with Bulcho Singh, a Hindu subedar from the 20th Native Infantry, as his second-in-command. They might have been the same two subedars who, according to the courtier Munshi Jiwan Lal, 'formally tendered the services of the [mutinous] troops to the King' on 11 May. A day later the 'whole body of native officers' of the Meerut regiments presented *nazirs* to the King and 'described themselves as faithful soldiers awaiting his orders'. But they were the real power in Delhi, as was proven by the King's acquiescence in their demand that he should proceed through the streets on an elephant to 'allay the fears of the citizens and order the people to resume their ordinary occupations'. The political influence of Indian officers was also evident in Lucknow, where they agreed to the coronation of Birjis Qadr as King of Oudh only on the following conditions: orders from Delhi were to override any other authority; the King's *wazir* (chief minister) was to be selected by the army; officers were not to be appointed to the mutinous regiments without the consent of the army; double pay was to be issued from the date of their leaving the English service; and no one was to interfere with the 'treatment and disposal of those who were friends to the English'. The Indian officers were demanding not just financial reward but professional autonomy *and* a say in the political process as well.

Some Indian officers even set themselves up as *de facto* rulers. Shortly after the mutiny of two companies of the 56th Native Infantry at Hamirpur on 14 June, their senior subedar, Ali Bux, proclaimed the rule of the Mogul dynasty with himself as the King of Delhi's agent. Three days later, Bux ordered the execution of the magistrate, Lloyd, and another European official. In the Fatehgarh district, Subedar Thakur Pandy of the 41st Native Infantry assumed administrative control of the eastern division, while two other subedars 'formed a kind of Appellate Court and appear to have been invested with the same powers as the Lieutenant-Governor of the N.W.P. had under the British rule'. All three were under the nominal authority of the reluctant Nawab of Farrukhabad.

But most Indian officers were content to monopolize the command structure of mutinous regiments, brigades and even armies. Following the mutiny at Nimach, for example, Subedar Shaikh Riadut Ali of the 1st Light Cavalry was appointed brigadier. He 'issued orders in the name of the King of Delhi', wrote Colonel G. H. D. Gimlette, 'and promoted subedars and jemadars to be colonels and majors'. Subedar Gurres Ram of the 72nd Native Infantry was given command of his regiment, and a jemadar in the 1st Light Cavalry was made the brigade major. Even after the defeat of the Nimach Brigade at Najafgarh in late August, a portion of the 72nd Native Infantry kept together under the command of another subedar, Hira Singh, who was promoted to the rank of colonel. At Cawnpore, Subedar Teeka Singh of the 2nd Light Cavalry, the senior conspirator, was given the rank of general and command of the rebel cavalry, while the subedar-major of the 1st Native Infantry controlled the infantry. The 56th Native Infantry was initially led by its havildar-major; but he was replaced by a subedar after the 1st Native Infantry had 'established it as a rule that men who joined from Furlough should get their places and promotion'. A jemadar commanded the 53rd Native Infantry, probably because no subedar was available. Colonel Lennox of the 22nd Native Infantry named Subedar Dulip Singh of his own regiment and the ressaldar of the troop of 15th Irregular Cavalry as the chief instigators of the mutiny at Faizabad. Gimlette added: 'The Subedar Major of the 22nd . . . assumed command of the station . . . and ordinary routine was carried on. Subedars became Majors and Captains. Jemadars became

Lieutenants, and all with these ranks annexed the horse, carriages and property of their predecessors.' Even at Jhansi, where the chief conspirators were identified as four sepoys, the rebel leaders were Indian officers: Ressaldar Faiz Ali of the 14th Irregular Cavalry and Subedar Lal Bahadur of the 12th Native Infantry. Ali was allegedly responsible for the infamous massacre of fifty-six Christian men, women and children on 8 June.

The Indian officer to achieve the greatest prominence during the mutiny was Subedar Bakht Khan of the 6/8th Foot Artillery, which mutinied at Bareilly on 31 May. One of the chief conspirators, Bakht Khan was in command when the Bareilly mutineers – augmented by the 28th and 29th Native Infantry from Shahjahanpur and Moradabad respectively – arrived in Delhi on 2 July. At his request the King of Delhi made him Commander-in-Chief of the rebel army. After the fall of Delhi, Bakht Khan fled with part of his force to Fatehgarh, where he joined up with the Nawab of Farrukhabad. He was commanding a wing of the nawab's army when it was defeated by Campbell at Khudaganj in January 1858. He later joined the Begum Hazrat Mahal in Oudh and probably accompanied her into Nepal the following January.

Indian officers did not always dominate in rebel regiments. According to Major Macpherson, Subedar-Major Amanut Ali of the 1st Infantry, Gwalior Contingent, was promoted to 'general' by the rebels at Gwalior, 'but the most violent sepoys in fact commanded'. This power-sharing arrangement was similar to the *panchayat* system that had held sway in the Khalsa (Sikh Army) prior to the First Sikh War (not to mention the military committees that had dominated the parliamentary army after the English Civil War), and probably explains why Scindia found it so easy to play one faction of the Gwalior Contingent off against another. Occasionally other ranks assumed positions of authority. When Jemadar Sitaram Pandy, on leave from the 63rd Native Infantry, was taken prisoner in Oudh by a band of mutineers, he noted that the 'leader of this party was a *sepoy*, although there were two *subedars* with it'.

In general, however, former Indian officers dominated the military hierarchy of rebel regiments: partly because so many of them had taken an active part in the pre-mutiny plotting; but mainly because most mutineers realized that adherence to military rank was the best and fairest way to maintain regimental cohesion and discipline. The willingness with which many sepoy conspirators were prepared to submit to the post-mutiny authority of their military superiors is surely proof that professional considerations were paramount. The sensitivity of the rank and file towards service issues like seniority, for example, was much in evidence. In late August the Indian officers of the 3rd Native Infantry petitioned the King of Delhi on behalf of the regiment's other ranks who objected to the fact that latecomers to the royal service had recently been placed on the same general list of seniority that applied to those who had been fighting all summer. Formerly, said the petition, these late arrivals had been 'kept on as supernumeraries, in the grades in which they had formerly served'.

A rough estimate of the number of Bengal sepoys who mutinied, were disarmed and disbanded, or remained loyal indicates that Indian officers were over-represented in the last category.* This is not surprising, given their age and proximity to a Company pension. More remarkable is the significant proportion of Indian officers involved in the planning and execution of mutiny, and the conduct of military operations thereafter. Prior to the mutiny, Napier and Lawrence highlighted the inadequacy of career prospects for Indian officers and the danger of thwarting legitimate ambition. Both were ignored, but the accuracy of their predictions seems to have been confirmed by the significant role played by Indian officers during the mutiny. According to Major O'Brien of the 6th Oudh Irregular Infantry, a 'large body' of the Indian officers of his regiment, the 22nd Native Infantry and the 15th Irregular Cavalry were 'active instigators of the mutiny' at Faizabad on 8 June. He added: 'The prizes they hope to gain by being put in the position the European officers formerly held, & having perhaps from one to four hundred rupees pay per mensum, being in my opinion one of their chief inducements to side with the rebels.'

Long-term financial reward and regimental cohesion went hand in hand. The mutineers could hardly expect to be employed as a body by the restored Indian rulers unless they retained their discipline. Their political influence was also dependent upon an outward display of unity – as were their lives in that only disciplined troops had a hope of defeating European regiments in the field. A host of accounts confirm this retention of regimental organization. When the 11th and 20th Native Infantry arrived at Delhi on the morning of 11 May, one European officer described them as 'coming up in military formation . . . in subdivisions of companies with fixed bayonets and sloped arms'. As the Nimach mutineers marched towards Delhi, via Agra, the infantry were in front, followed by the artillery and cavalry, with advance and rear guards 'told off, and Cavalry flanking parties thrown out'. At Faizabad the 'band played at mess every night', guards 'were posted, and

* Approximately 150 Indian officers and 5,600 other ranks remained loyal.

parades ordered as usual'. Even the internal disciplinary system of mutinous regiments was similar to that which had operated under the British. When a sepoy of the 11th Native Infantry was found asleep on sentry duty at Delhi in July, he was tried and found guilty by a court martial of all the regiment's officers. The only deviation from the British system was that the Commander-in-Chief, Bakht Khan, was asked to award a punishment instead of confirming the court's.

Tapti Roy commented on a similar degree of organization among the rebel troops in Bundelkhand (the majority of whom were from the splendidly disciplined Gwalior Contingent):

> A series of orders issued practically every day from Kalpi in the name of Tantia Topey strikingly illustrates the meticulous planning and organization that went into the soldiers' actions. A strict hierarchy of ranks was specified for each regiment with a brigadier-major in command, followed by a subahdar-major, havildar-major, jamadar, naik and the soldiers . . . Regular inspection, muster rolls and daily drill were compulsory . . . For hearing representations or dispensing justice, periodic courts represented by one soldier, one sardar and jamadars of infantry and artillery together with moulavies [Muslim scholars] and pandits [learned Brahmans] were summoned . . . Every offence would call for an appropriate punishment . . . Provisions were made for the families of those injured or killed. Strict orders were given for enlistment, recruitment and discipline.

Even during the defeat of the rebels at Kunch in May 1858, Sir Hugh Rose, the British commander, was moved to praise the professionalism and courage of the skirmishers of the 52nd Native Infantry who 'covered the retreat very well . . . facing about kneeling and firing with great coolness'.

The importance of military discipline and financial incentives was recognized by all rebel governments. On 6 July Nana Sahib issued a series of proclamations detailing the internal organization of regiments and their officers' monthly rates of pay. But as pay was being distributed in early July, after the destruction of the Europeans at Cawnpore, the rebel troops began 'quarrelling about the rewards' and 'General Teeka Singh' and his men went to see the Nana at Bithur to insist on their share of the treasure. Their demands must have been met because the Nana returned to Cawnpore and – according to a sowar in the 2nd Light Cavalry – distributed two months' pay.

The Delhi Proclamation, issued in the name of the King in mid May, promised to pay Company sepoys 10 rupees a month and sowars 30 if they switched their allegiance to him. *Ishtihars* (administrative notes) specifying the organization and pay of troops were regularly issued at Delhi. One such, published on 6 July, stated that there would be one colonel as commanding officer, one major as second-in-command and one adjutant for every regiment of infantry and cavalry. 'Duties and emoluments commensurate with each rank were also spelled out.' According to Mainodin, *perwanahs* (warrants) were extorted daily from the King and addressed to Bengal regiments, promising monthly salaries of 30 rupees to sepoys and 50 to sowars if they joined the King's army. 'In every instance,' recalled Mainodin, 'the King's *perwanah* had the effect of causing the soldiers to mutiny and make their way to Delhi. At the sight of the King's *perwanah* the men who had fought for the English forgot the past, in the desire to be re-established under a native sovereign.'

Such generous rates of pay, however, were not realistic. The King had no treasury in May 1857, and the new government's fund-raising efforts could not keep pace with its expenses. In an undated letter the King instructed his son, Mirza Moghul, not to accept any more applications for enlistment in the royal army by non-Company troops because there was no money to pay them. The regular forces in Delhi had not even brought enough treasure for their own expenses, he explained, and it was impossible to collect the land revenue until the country had been pacified. Therefore only those irregulars who were financially self-sufficient for at least two months were to be given permission to come to Delhi. They would be compensated when order had been re-established, but only after the pay arrears of regular troops had been dealt with. These latter had become so acute by early September that the army was threatening to plunder the city unless its pay demands – said to be 573,000 rupees a month – were met. A partial payment was made on 2 September, but only enough to give each sepoy 1 rupee and each sowar 2.

At Lucknow too the rebel government was unable to redeem its promises of pay. The official salaries ranged from 1,000 rupees for colonels and 165 for subedars to 30 for troopers and 12 for sepoys. But according to the *Bengal Hurkaru*, these figures were 'purely nominal' as no man had 'yet received full salary for any month'. Firoz Shah, the cousin of the King of Delhi, who took charge of the insurrection at Mandesur in the state of Gwalior in August, promised to pay his sepoys 15 rupees a month. By late September, however, money was scarce and pay had been reduced to the pre-mutiny level of 7 rupees.

But the inability of rebel governments to make good their pledges over pay does not undermine the importance of financial incentives as a motive to mutiny. 'I consider that the native troops mutinied in the hope of worldly gain,' stated Ahsanullah Khan, who was in a good position to judge. 'The admixture of religion was only intended to disguise their real object. If they were really fighting for religion, they would not have plundered the houses and property of the people, nor would they have oppressed and injured them . . .' Some regiments (as we have seen) handed the Company treasure they had been guarding over to the rebel authorities, others kept it to pay their men, and a few – like the 17th Native Infantry – simply divided it among themselves. But most sepoys were able to benefit by plunder or extortion during the anarchy that ensued. At Gwalior the mutineers offered their services to Scindia in return for the 4½ lakhs of treasure the British had made over to him; but if he refused to 'lead them against Agra, which they would make over to him, with such provinces as he desired', he would have to pay '12 or 15 lacs more', and provide supplies and carriage for them 'to move whither they pleased'. They were eventually placated by a 'donation of three months' pay, and the promise of service'. According to Sir Hugh Rose, every sepoy killed by his Central India Field Force had 'generally from 90 to 100 rupees about him'.

Some mutinous sepoys used promises of higher pay to induce those still loyal to rise. At Jhansi, for example, the fifty-two NCOs and sepoys of the 12th Native Infantry who mutinied on 5 June 'invited all men of the *deen* [faith] to flock to their standard, offering to remunerate each man for his services at the rate of twelve rupees per month'. They were joined by the remaining troops in the station the following day. In January 1858 the Indian officers of the mutinous Gwalior Contingent offered the sepoys in the service of the pro-British Raja of Chirkari 10 rupees a month to come over to them. Many did, while others refused to fight, giving the raja no option but to surrender. He was forced to pay an indemnity of 3 lakhs of rupees, part of which was sent to the Nana while the rest was used to settle the soldiers' wage arrears. The Nana had promised his troops a gratuity of one month's pay, pensions for those who fell in action and licence to plunder goods up to the value of 1,001 rupees if the attack was successful.

There is no statistical proof that mutineers from one branch of the Bengal Army were any more motivated by the lure of financial gain than those from another. But given that most irregular cavalrymen were Muslims – and therefore had neither caste nor religion in common with the majority of military conspirators – it is probably fair to conclude that they reacted to, rather than initiated, the disorder, regarding it as an opportunity both to restore the Moguls and to enrich themselves. No irregular cavalrymen appear to have been involved in the plotting prior to the Meerut outbreak, and only two regiments had mutinied by the end of May. They were, moreover, the most debt-ridden Indian troops in the Bengal Army, and debt was an obvious incentive to mutiny. Captain Dennys of the Kotah Contingent blamed penury for the mutiny of his Muslim horse on 4 July. 'I always felt that our cavalry could not be relied upon,' he wrote later. 'They were well dressed and fairly well mounted but their general state of hopeless indebtedness was sufficient to prevent their remaining loyal, if anything like absolute anarchy should ever come.' The Bengal irregular cavalrymen were in a similar position. So when, for example, the sowars of the 12th Irregular Cavalry mutinied at Sigauli on 23 July, killing their commandant and his wife in the process, their first act was to raid the regimental bank of 50,000 rupees and to plunder the local *banias*. Having divided the proceeds, they headed for the Opium Agency at Gobind Ganj, which they also pillaged.

The mutinies – planned as well as actual – that succeeded the Delhi and Meerut outbreak were not all the result of a knock-on effect. If they had been, they would have spread outwards in roughly concentric circles. Instead, some of the earliest mutinies took place in stations as far apart as Nasirabad in Rajputana and Nowshera in northern Punjab. They were undoubtedly prompted by the initial outbreak; but their timing tended to depend upon the level of disaffection in particular regiments. The 15th Native Infantry at Nasirabad, for example, had only recently moved from Meerut, where it probably became tainted by association. In general, the ringleaders would have considered a regiment ripe for mutiny when they had succeeded in convincing a sizeable proportion of their fellow sepoys that the British really did intend to take away their caste and religion. Then they either planned a mutiny in advance with conspirators in other regiments – as at Lahore, Peshawar, Hansi, Lucknow, Bareilly and Cawnpore – or they simply took advantage of a suitable opportunity to encourage their comrades to rise, such as the execution of the Brahman *zemindar* at Aligarh, the movement of treasure at Mathura and Azimgarh, or the disarmament of Indian corps at Benares and Dinapore.

Most of the joint mutinies were planned in conjunction with civilian conspirators. This is entirely consistent with the prime aim of most active mutineers: to be re-employed by a restored Indian ruler. 'All regiments took their Colours with them,' observed Sitaram Pandy of the 63rd Native Infantry. 'They did not break their oath by deserting them. They left the service of the English and were supposed to have entered the service of another government.' Tapti Roy has interpreted the soldiers' actions in a purely political light. 'The decision of every rebel unit to move towards the centre [Delhi and Cawnpore] was . . . part of an implicit strategy, to build, uphold and strengthen an alternative supra-local political order.' In fact this strategy had been predetermined by the sepoy plotters whose original incentive was probably more professional than political in that they hoped their new employers would provide more pay and greater career opportunites than the British had. Their political involvement, therefore, was simply a means to a professional end, though it became for some an end in itself.

Roy herself noted that the mutinous sepoys 'maintained not only the military organizations of their regiments but also the hierarchy of rank and order within each regiment'. Yet she failed to draw the obvious conclusion: that the mutinies were more about professional than religious, or even political, grievances. Some activists were undoubtedly 'politicized' in that they sought the overthrow of British rule. But they would not have been able to hoodwink enough of their fellow soldiers unless the Bengal Army generally had been unhappy with the terms of its employment. Set in the historical context of the Indian military labour market, where there was a long tradition of mercenary soldiers from eastern Hindustan who were liable to switch employers if the occasion demanded, the Indian mutiny makes perfect sense.

A key factor in the gradual alienation of the sepoys from their employer was their deteriorating relationship with their European officers. The link between a commanding officer's length of service and the relative disaffection of his regiment in 1857 indicates that a familiar and popular commanding officer could slow down the process of alienation. In some cases the presence of such an officer was enough to deter a regiment from mutinying; in others it helped to save European lives. But even a popular officer was not always able to prevent his men from succumbing to peer pressure and the material lure of higher wages and plunder.

Appendix Four

The Post-mutiny Reform of the Indian Army

In November 1857, with Delhi recaptured but the rebellion far from over, the Court of Directors instructed Lord Canning to assemble a mixed commission of officers and civil servants to report on the future organization of the Indian Army. Canning was unwilling to devote his key personnel to such an onerous task, and, in May 1858, he appointed a single officer, Lieutenant-Colonel Henry Durand,* to conduct the inquiry. Durand sent a detailed questionnaire to eighty-five military and civil officers. They were required to provide written responses to a series of questions on recruiting, discipline, promotion and various other aspects of army life. In August Durand began drafting summaries of the replies for Lord Canning.

Meanwhile, on 15 July 1858, a Royal Commission had been set up in London 'to inquire into the organisation of the Indian Army'. Known as the Peel Commission – after its chairman Major-General Jonathan Peel, Secretary of State for War and brother of the late Prime Minister – it was asked to respond to eleven questions regarding the army's future organization. By December 1858 the Commission had examined forty-seven witnesses and collected a vast amount of written evidence (including the responses to Durand's questionnaire and Durand's own summaries). Its report, which was submitted on 7 March 1859, made a number of important recommendations:

The number of European troops necessary for the security of India 'should . . . be about 80,000'; the ratio of Indian to European troops should never be greater than 2:1 in Bengal and 3:1 in Madras and Bombay; all brigades should have both Indian and European troops; all Bengal native cavalry should be on the 'irregular system' (with a commandant, an adjutant, a medical officer and one European officer per squadron, and the sowars receiving an increase in pay to enable them 'to purchase

* An experienced 'political', Durand was acting Governor-General's Agent for Central India at the outbreak of the mutiny. Forced to leave Indore when Holkar's troops mutinied in July 1857, he joined Brigadier Stuart's column of Bombay troops and helped to crush the rebellion in Malwa. In December, shortly after returning to Indore, he relinquished the agency to Sir Robert Hamilton, who was back from leave.

and maintain horses and arms of a superior description'), and the other presidencies following suit if it was thought necessary; the native infantry, on the other hand, should be 'mainly regular'; Artillery 'should be mainly a European force'; European cadets for native corps should 'be thoroughly drilled and instructed in their military duty' in Britain before they were sent out to India.

Only a couple of the recommendations, however, were an attempt to redress the type of professional grievances that many believed were responsible for the mutiny. This was mainly because the questions themselves had not been drafted with any such intention in mind: they were more concerned with the deterrent value of an enlarged European force, and therefore concentrated on its size and organization vis-à-vis its Indian counterpart. But during their examination of the evidence, the Commissioners had had their attention drawn to a number of 'important points', many of which *were* about issues of recruitment and conditions of service. The Commissioners therefore made nine additional recommendations:

1. That the Native Army should be composed of different nationalities and castes, and as a general rule, mixed promiscuously through each regiment. 2. That all men of the regular Native Army . . . should be enlisted for general service. 3. That a modification should be made in the uniform of the Native troops, assimilating it more to the dress of the country, and making it more suitable to the climate. 4. That Europeans should, as far as possible, be employed in the scientific branches of the service . . . 5. That . . . the power of commanding officers be increased. 6. That the promotion of Native commissioned and non-commissioned officers, be regulated on the principle of efficiency, rather than of seniority . . . 7. That . . . the attention of H.M. Government be drawn to the expediency . . . of adopting, if practicable, fixed scales of allowances for the troops in garrison or cantonments, and the field. 8. That the Commander-in-Chief in Bengal be styled the Commander-in-Chief in India . . . 9. [That] the efficiency of the Indian Army has hitherto been injuriously affected by the small number of officers usually doing duty with the regiments to which they belong.

Of all the recommendations made by the Peel Commission, the most contentious was the one that advocated irregular cavalry (at least in Bengal) but 'mainly' regular infantry. In his evidence Lieutenant-General Sir Henry Somerset, the Commander-in-Chief of Bombay, had come out against irregular corps because they were less disciplined and gave too much power to Indian officers. But in a minute of 4 June 1858 J. P. Grant, the President of the Governor-General's Council, approved of irregulars on the basis that they were the most effective soldiers and could be recruited from untainted areas. Canning's opinion was a compromise. In a memorandum of August 1858 he suggested that all cavalry and thirty regiments of Bengal Native Infantry should be on the irregular system, with a further twenty of the latter as regulars. But others like Sir Bartle Frere, Commissioner of Sind, and Brigadier-General John Jacob, Commandant of the Sind Irregular Horse, believed that the system should be wholly irregular. Frere and Jacob were supported by the members of the influential Punjab Committee – Sir John Lawrence, Brigadier-General Neville Chamberlain and Lieutenant-Colonel Herbert Edwardes – who recommended extending the system that operated within the Punjab Irregular Force to the rest of the Bengal Army, including promotion by merit and substantial powers for commanding officers. But to ensure its success, they added, the European officers would have to be carefully selected: a 'bad European officer cannot work a system of merit, he would soon spoil the best native officer in the world'.

In June 1859, having considered the Peel Commission's report, the Military and Political Committee of the Council of India concurred with the view that all Bengal native cavalry regiments should be organized on the irregular system. They could not, however, agree about native infantry. Three members (J. P. Willoughby, John Lawrence and J. Eastwick) wanted all infantry regiments on the irregular system; the other two (R. J. H. Vivian and H. M. Durand) were, like Canning, in favour of twenty regular and thirty irregular corps. Sir Charles Wood, Secretary of State for India from 1859 to 1866, sided with the majority on grounds of economy and politics: the irregular system was cheaper and would encourage Indians of a higher rank to enter the army. European officers, he added, could be appointed to the irregular regiments by selection from a Staff Corps.

The idea for a Staff Corps – whereby unattached officers on a general list would be appointed to staff, civil and regimental duty – had been suggested first by Sir John Malcolm, the Governor of Bombay, in 1830. Other officers and senior officials – including Lieutenant-General Sir Willoughby Cotton, Commander-in-Chief of Bombay, and Lord Dalhousie, the Governor-General – had urged the creation of such a corps prior to the mutiny. But it had always been rejected on the ground of expense. However, once the Peel Commission had accepted that the 'efficiency of the Indian Army' had been 'injuriously affected by the small number of officers usually doing duty with [their] regiments', not least because those left behind resented such duty, reform became a priority.

Supported by the majority of Canning's Council and most other senior figures in India bar the Governor-General and the Commander-in-Chief, Wood's preference for irregular regiments and a Staff Corps prevailed. Drafts of the warrant for the formation of a separate Staff Corps in each presidency were laid before the Council on 8 January 1861. All Company and Queen's officers under the rank of field officer were eligible for admittance (as were all officers then in staff employ under the substantive rank of colonel). Henceforth staff employ would include appointments to civil and political posts, to the general and personal staff, and to regimental duty. Ten days after the formation of the Staff Corps, Wood instructed that all Indian regiments were to be organized on the irregular system with six European officers (not including a medical officer). The Bengal Army complied later that year; the Bombay and Madras Armies in 1863 and 1866 respectively.

The chief importance of the irregular system was that it did away with the tendency of European officers to regard regimental duty as a sign of professional failure: henceforth officers were selected for regimental appointments from the Staff Corps. The financial incentive to avoid regimental duty was also removed by the equalization of military allowances with 'those obtainable in the early stages of civil . . . or quasi-military employ'. Regimental positions were now regarded as staff appointments with allowances as well as pay. The irregular system also provided Indian troops with the incentives of greater responsibility and higher pay. In a cavalry regiment, for example, the six senior Indian officers were in command of troops (or ressalahs) and received from 120 to 300 rupees per month, depending upon seniority. Even the sowars were paid 27 rupees a month, with the maximum good conduct pay increasing it to 30. Only in infantry regiments did the pay of NCOs and sepoys remain at its former monthly rate.

Another crucial area of military reform was an increase in the power of commanding officers to punish and reward. The vast majority of witnesses who gave evidence to the Peel Commission were of the opinion that Bengal officers, in particular, needed more authority over their men. But some, like John Jacob and the Punjab Committee, accepted that the quality of commanding officers had to be improved if they were to be entrusted with enhanced powers. This was achieved by the switch to the irregular system and the institution of the Staff Corps in 1861: henceforth regimental officers were selected. Later that year the revised Articles of War went a long way to satisfying the reformers' other demands by giving commanding officers the summary power to reduce NCOs to the ranks and to discharge NCOs and ordinary soldiers (a punishment that carried with it a mandatory loss of pension). They were also given the authority to hold summary trials of NCOs and soldiers and, on conviction, to carry out sentences without confirmation from higher authorities, as long as the sentences were not more severe than could be awarded by district courts martial. By 1873 commanding officers could also deprive soldiers of good conduct pay.

In an effort to bolster further the authority of Bengal commanding officers, the Peel Commission recommended that efficiency should replace seniority as the dominant factor in the promotion of Indian troops. The reforms of the 1860s acted on this advice. No sepoy was to be promoted to NCO unless he possessed 'a competent knowledge of reading and writing in at least one character, except when commanding officers may deem it desirable or expedient to make exceptions in the case of men who have displayed conspicuous courage, or who possess [other useful] qualifications'. In general, seniority was to be taken into account, but commanding officers had the discretion to override it. 'The vicious system of promotion by seniority, in itself sufficient to destroy the discipline of any army, has been abolished,' wrote Chesney in 1868, 'and by the new Articles of War commanding officers are vested with considerable powers, both for reward and punishment.'

Another recommendation of the Peel Commission was that the uniform of Indian troops should be assimilated 'more to the dress of the country' and made 'more suitable to the climate'. The hated leather stock had already been discontinued by a 'General Order' of 15 February 1859. So too had the bulky shako headdress, as the loyal sepoys of the Bengal Native Infantry took to wearing their undress Kilmarnock caps (first introduced in 1847) instead. From March 1860 commanding officers of native infantry regiments were given the option to issue *pugris* (turbans). Another major alteration took place in 1863 when the tight coatee was replaced by a long, red single-breasted tunic with cut-away skirts and no collar, not that dissimilar to the coat worn by the British Army. It was not particularly 'Indian' in style, but it was certainly more comfortable and durable than the old coatee.

Lastly, the Peel Commission recommended that 'the Native Army should be composed of different nationalities and castes, and as a general rule, mixed promiscuously through each regiment' and that 'all men of the regular Native Army . . . should be enlisted for general service'. Both suggestions were aimed at dismantling the high-caste Hindu brotherhood in the Bengal Native Infantry that had made a general mutiny possible. Even before the appointment of the Commission, Indian levies had been raised in Bengal from mainly low-caste recruits. 'The low castes and the untouchables sided with the British,' wrote a leading Indian military historian, 'probably because in the Hindu hierarchy they occupied a peripheral position and also because in the princely armies of pre-British India, they had no place. Military service with the British provided them with economic security and a channel for upward mobility.' However, no decision had been taken on their long-term future by 1860 when Sir Hugh Rose, the new Commander-in-Chief of India, came down in favour of mixed recruitment. 'The homogeneous composition of the old Native Army, fostering caste, combination and indiscipline,' he remarked to Lord Canning, 'was one of the springs of the mutiny, and has been proved to be an element of danger in a Native army.' He therefore suggested limiting the proportion of any one sect or caste in each regiment to a quarter, with Sikh and Gurkha corps the only exceptions.

Sir Charles Wood disagreed. He was in favour of a general mixture system (different races and castes throughout the companies of regiments) in conjunction with a district system whereby each regiment was recruited from a particular locality. 'The difference,' he informed Rose on 25 April 1862, 'will be greater in some regiments than in others, some regiments will be more, others less homogeneous and here another sort of variety will be created.' His intention was divide and rule. He never wanted to 'see again a great Army, very much the same in its feelings and prejudices and connections, confident in its strength, and so disposed to unite in rebellion together. If one regiment mutinies, I should like to have the next so alien that it would be ready to fire into it.'

A compromise was finally reached in November 1862 when the Government of India authorized three different systems of enlistment for regiments of Bengal Native Infantry: single class (the same type of recruits throughout), general mixture and class company (whereby each company was composed of a different race or caste). These systems remained unchanged for two decades. But during that time more and more commanding officers of the general mixture regiments began to report that long association removed any class or race differences between their men, thereby fostering a general *esprit de corps*. This trend was seen as increasing the threat of a mutinous combination, and the general mixture system was abolished in 1883. In general terms, the chief recruitment ground for the Bengal Army had moved from Oudh and its adjacent provinces to Nepal, the Punjab and the North-West Frontier. In 1893, for example, only nine of the sixty-four regiments of Bengal infantry were composed of high-caste men: seven of Rajputs and two of Brahmans.

Sequence of Events

1857

22|01 'Cartridge Question' sparked when a labourer tells a high-caste sepoy at the Dum-Dum musketry depot, near Calcutta, that the British had deliberately greased the new Enfield cartridges with cow and pig fat.

LATE|01 First recorded sighting of the mysterious chapatties that spread across central and northern India in the first few months of 1857.

26|02 Armed disobedience by sepoys of the 19th Native Infantry at Berhampore in Bengal after their CO orders blank firing exercise with ungreased cartridges.

29|03 Sepoy Mungul Pandy of the 34th Native Infantry wounds two Europeans – his adjutant and sergeant-major – in a failed attempt to incite his regiment to mutiny at Barrackpore in Bengal.

31|03 19th Native Infantry disbanded at Barrackpore for 'open and defiant mutiny' on 26 February.

08|04 Mungul Pandy hanged at Barrackpore.

24|04 Eighty-five skirmishers of the 3rd Light Cavalry at Meerut, northern India, refuse orders to fire ungreased blank carbine cartridges.

06|05 Seven companies of the 34th Native Infantry disbanded at Barrackpore for 'passive' mutiny on 29 March.

08|05 3rd Light Cavalry skirmishers found guilty of collective disobedience by a native court martial and given sentences ranging from five to ten years' hard labour.

09|05 Convicted skirmishers are shackled at a punishment parade and marched to Meerut's civil gaol.

10|05 Indian troops rise at Meerut and head for Delhi.

11|05 Meerut mutineers arrive at Delhi and are joined by the local garrison. Wholesale murder of Christians.

13|05 Bahadur Shah proclaimed as the new Mogul Emperor. Brigadier Stuart Corbett disarms the garrison at Lahore in the Punjab.

13/14|05 Partial mutiny at Ferozepore in the Punjab.

16|05 Lord Canning, Governor-General, issues a proclamation denying that the Indian government wanted to 'interfere' with its subjects' religion or caste. Bengal sappers mutiny at Meerut.

20–23|05 Detachments of 9th Native Infantry mutiny near Agra.

22|05 Peshawar garrison disarmed.

25|05 55th Native Infantry mutinies at Hoti Mardan on the North-West Frontier.

27|05 General the Hon. George Anson, Commander-in-Chief of India, dies of cholera at Karnal. Lieutenant-General Sir Patrick Grant appointed his temporary successor in early June.

28|05 Mutiny at Nasirabad in Rajputana.

30|05 Lucknow garrison mutinies and kills Brigadier Handscomb. Brigadier Archdale Wilson defeats the Delhi rebels at the first battle of Ghazi-ud-din-Nagar on the Hindan River.

31|05 Wilson wins a second, smaller battle on the Hindan River. Mutinies at Shahjahanpur and Bareilly in Rohilkhand.

3–14|06 Mutinies and massacres at stations across Oudh, the North-Western Provinces, central India, Rajputana and the Punjab: in particular at Sitapur (3 June), Nimach (3 June), Benares (4 June), Cawnpore (5 June), Jhansi (5–6 June), Allahabad (6 June), Jullundur (7 June), Nowgong (10 June) and Gwalior (14 June).

06|06 Major-General Sir Hugh Wheeler besieged in his entrenchment at Cawnpore by local garrison.

08|06 Major-General Sir Henry Barnard, commanding the Delhi Field Force, defeats the rebels at Badli-ki-Serai and establishes a British camp on the Ridge north of Delhi.

17|06 General Grant arrives at Calcutta as temporary Commander-in-Chief.

27|06 Massacre of Europeans at the Satichaura Ghat in Cawnpore after Wheeler had agreed terms with Nana Sahib to vacate the entrenchment in return for safe passage down the Ganges.

30|06 Oudh rebels defeat Sir Henry Lawrence at Chinhut. Siege of the Lucknow Residency begins.

01|07 Nana Sahib proclaimed the new Peshwa at Bithur. Mutinies at Indore, Mhow and Sagar in central India.

05|07 General Barnard dies of cholera. Major-General Thomas Reed takes command of the Delhi Field Force. Nimach and Kotah rebels defeat Brigadier Pole at Sasia, near Agra. Lucknow rebels crown Birjis Qadr as King of Oudh.

12|07 Brigadier-General Henry Havelock defeats Cawnpore rebels at Fatehpur.

15|07 Two more victories by Havelock over the Cawnpore rebels at Aong and Pandu Nadi. Defeats prompt Nana Sahib to order the execution of nearly two hundred women and children in the Bibighar at Cawnpore.

16|07 Havelock defeats Nana Sahib in person near Cawnpore. Brigadier-General John Nicholson destroys the Sialkot mutineers at Trimmu Ghat.

17|07 Havelock retakes Cawnpore. Wilson replaces the sick Reed as commander of the Delhi Field Force, the fourth in two months.

25|07 Dinapore garrison mutinies and joins up with Raja Kunwar Singh to besiege Arrah House.

30|07 Dinapore rebels annihilate small British force sent to relieve Arrah House.

31|07 Canning issues his infamous 'Clemency' Resolution (which advises the civil authorities not to execute mutineers innocent of murder), provoking a storm in the Indian and British newspapers.

02 | 08 Major Eyre defeats Dinapore rebels and relieves Arrah House.

13 | 08 Havelock abandons his first invasion of Oudh and returns to Cawnpore. General Sir Colin Campbell, Anson's permanent successor as Commander-in-Chief of India, arrives at Calcutta.

14 | 08 Nicholson arrives at the British camp at Delhi with his mobile column.

17 | 08 Major William Hodson defeats a large body of rebel Horse near Rohtak.

24 | 08 Nicholson defeats the Nimach Brigade at Najafgarh.

04 | 09 Siege-train reaches the British camp at Delhi from the Punjab.

09 | 09 John Colvin, Lieutenant-Governor of the N. W. Provinces, dies in Agra Fort.

14 | 09 Wilson's assault on Delhi begins.

20 | 09 Delhi finally cleared of rebel troops.

23 | 09 Nicholson, shot during the assault on the 14th, dies of his wounds.

25 | 09 First relief of the Lucknow Residency by Havelock and Sir James Outram. Brigadier James Neill killed by a sniper during the final advance.

10 | 10 Colonel Greathed's column defeats the Mhow and Indore Brigades at Agra.

17 | 11 Second relief of the Lucknow Residency by Campbell.

24 | 11 Havelock, recently knighted, dies of dysentery at Lucknow before the evacuation of the Residency is complete.

26/27 | 11 Tatya Tope and the Gwalior Contingent defeat General Windham at Cawnpore and force him to withdraw into the new entrenchment near the bridge-of-boats.

06 | 12 Campbell defeats Tatya Tope and recaptures Cawnpore.

15 | 12 Brigadier Stuart's Bombay column occupies Indore in central India.

1858

02 | 01 Campbell defeats the Nawab of Farrukhabad and Bakht Khan at Khudaganj.

03 | 02 Central India Field Force under Major-General Sir Hugh Rose relieves Sagar after a seven-month siege.

20 | 02 Lord Palmerston resigns as British Prime Minister after his Liberal government is defeated over a new terrorism bill.

21 | 02 Lord Derby succeeds Palmerston. Lord Ellenborough replaces Robert Vernon Smith at the Board of Control.

02 | 03 Campbell begins operations to recapture Lucknow.

09 | 03 Bahadur Shah is found guilty of rebellion, treason and murder by a military tribunal at Delhi and exiled to Rangoon in Burma.

14 | 03 Premature announcement of Canning's 'Oudh Proclamation' by Sir James Outram, the chief commissioner. The controversial proclamation – which deprived all Oudh rebels of their land – provoked widespread criticism in India and Britain and was later blamed for prolonging the pacification of Oudh.

21|03 Lucknow cleared of rebels.

22|03 Rose invests Jhansi.

01|04 Rose splits his force and defeats a vastly superior rebel army under Tatya Tope on the Betwa.

03|04 Rose captures Jhansi but fails to prevent the Rani from escaping to Kalpi.

15|04 Nirput Singh repulses an attack on his fort at Ruiya by a British column under Major-General Walpole. Brigadier Adrian Hope killed during the ill-conceived assault.

19|04 Major-General Whitlock of the Madras Army defeats the Nawab of Banda at Bhowragarh.

21|04 Kunwar Singh mortally wounded by British artillery fire while crossing the Ganges at Sheopur Ghat.

23|04 A dying Kunwar Singh destroys a British force under Captain Le Grand at Jagdishpur.

05|05 Campbell defeats Khan Bahadur Khan at Bareilly.

07|05 Rose defeats a large rebel force under Tatya Tope and the Rani of Jhansi at Kunch.

11|05 Lord Stanley replaces Lord Ellenborough at the Board of Control.

22|05 Rose defeats the rebels under Rao Sahib and the Rani of Jhansi at Kalpi.

28|05 The defeated rebel leaders – Rao Sahib, Tatya Tope, the Rani of Jhansi and the Nawab of Banda – enter Gwalior territory with the remnants of their force.

31|05 Gwalior army defects to the rebels at Baragaon. Maharaja Scindia flees to Agra.

12|06 Major-General Hope Grant defeats Beni Madho and 16,000 rebels at Nawabganj in the final decisive battle in Oudh.

15|06 Maulvi of Faizabad killed by the brother of the loyal Raja of Powayun.

17|06 Rani of Jhansi killed during a skirmish with British cavalry at Kotah-ki-Serai near Gwalior city.

19|06 Rose defeats the rebels at Gwalior and reoccupies the city.

02|08 India Bill – transferring the administration of the subcontinent from the East India Company to the Crown – receives the Royal Assent.

01|11 Queen Victoria's 'Proclamation' – the formal announcement of the transfer of authority from Company to Crown – is read out across India. Offers an unconditional pardon to all rebels who had neither committed murder nor harboured murderers.

1859

04|01 Bala Rao and the remaining Oudh rebels are driven into the Nepal Terai by Hope Grant. There Bala joins a host of other rebel leaders, including his brother Nana Sahib, Jwala Prasad, Hazrat Mahal, Birjis Qadr and Khan Bahadur Khan.

07|01 Oudh rebellion is officially over, though minor operations continue.

21|01 Tatya Tope and Prince Firoz Shah defeated at Sikar by Colonel Holmes.

18|04 Tatya Tope hanged at Sipri after Raja Man Singh of Narwar betrays him to the British.

08|07 Canning declares a 'State of Peace' throughout India.

Glossary

ADC aide-de-camp, a general's personal staff officer
alkalah long, loose tunic worn by irregular cavalry
anna one sixteenth of a rupee
Aryan belonging to, or descended from, the ancient people who spoke the parent Aryan language (often called Indo-European) from which Sanskrit, Greek, Latin, Teutonic and Persian (and their modern representatives) are derived; one of those who invaded and conquered India *c.* 1500 BC
assami a payment made, or debt incurred, by a silladar trooper upon receiving his uniform, weapons and horse
atta flour
ayah Indian nanny or maidservant
baba-logs affectionate term for children
babu title of respect; derogatory term for Indian clerks who wrote English
badmash bandit, bad character
bagheelog mutineers (literally runaways)
bahādur champion, hero
bania (banya) a Hindu trader in grain, merchant or shopkeeper, often a money-lender
batta a soldier's allowance for war service or for being posted outside British India
bell-of-arms conical bell-shaped building used for storing weapons
bhainchute sister-violator
bhang infusion of hemp
bhisti water-carrier
bibi a European's Indian mistress or a Muslim wife
Brahman member of the first *varna*, traditionally priests and scholars; the highest Hindu caste
brigade a military formation commanded by a brigadier and containing a mixture of infantry, cavalry and artillery units
burkandaze a matchlockman, watchman, guard or escort
Burra Sahib big or most important European
caste ascribed ritual status in the Hindu social hierarchy
CB Companion of the Order of the Bath
chapatti small, thin cake of coarse unleavened bread
chaprassi police constable; government messenger
charpoy simple bedstead
chaukidar watchman
chobdar mace-bearer
company a body of infantry, usually between eighty and a hundred men, led by a captain, lieutenant or subedar, and forming part of a battalion or regiment
cossid hand-delivered message
crore 100 lakhs, or 10,000,000, usually rupees (equivalent to £1 million)

cutcherry court of justice; office of a magistrate or other civil official

DAAG Deputy Assistant Adjutant-General. Staff officer with responsibility for discipline

dacoit armed bandit

dâk the postal system provided by relays of men or horses

dal split pulses like peas and lentils

darogah superintendent or overseer

dhoti loin cloth worn tucked between the legs and fastened at the waist

dhurrie mattress

Din (Deen) Muslim faith or religion

division (1) A military formation commanded by a major-general and containing a number of subunits such as field forces, brigades and regiments. The Bengal Army was geographically divided into seven military divisions (from south-east to north-west): Presidency, Dinapore, Cawnpore, Meerut, Sirhind, Lahore, Peshawar. (2) A civil administrative unit containing a number of districts. The civil divisions (Agra, Benares, Meerut, etc.) do not correspond to the military divisions.

Diwan (Dewan) chief minister of a royal court

doab tract of land between two converging rivers; from Persian *do* (two) and *ab* (water)

doolie covered litter or stretcher

durbar royal court; synonym for government

fakir religious mendicant

feringhi literally 'Frank', or 'foreigner'; derogatory term for a European

firman imperial edict or order

GCB Knight Grand Cross of the Order of the Bath

gharry a slow horse-drawn, box-like carriage

ghee clarified butter

godown warehouse or store for goods

gora-logs Indian term for European men

guddi literally cushion, but taken to mean the throne of a prince or noble

Gujar a semi-nomadic caste of northern India

hackery a bullock cart; a carriage

hakim physician

havildar Indian NCO, equivalent to sergeant

havildar-major senior Indian NCO, equivalent to sergeant-major

Hindi major Aryan vernacular of northern India, spoken (with many dialects) from the frontiers of Bengal to those of the Punjab and Sind

Hindustan originally the region of the River Indus; in the colonial period it denoted upper India (the plain of the Ganges, except Bengal)

Hindustani a simplified form of Urdu using Hindi script and Sanskritized words

Id Muslim festival that marks the end of Ramadan

jagir assignment of government revenue from a district, often in return for military service

jemadar junior Indian officer in regular infantry or cavalry regiment

jezail long-barrelled musket favoured by Pathan tribesmen

jhil a marsh, lake or pond

jihad holy war waged by Muslims against non-believers

jullad executioner

KCB Knight Commander of the order of the Bath
khalasi labourer
khansaman cook, house steward, table servant
khidmatgar senior household servant, equivalent to a butler
kotwal chief police officer of a town or city
kotwali police headquarters
Kshatriya member of the second, or warrior, *varna*
kurta loose frock coat worn by irregular cavalry
lakh 100,000 units, usually rupees (equivalent to £10,000)
lathi thick iron-bound club
limber carriage used for towing artillery
lota brass drinking vessel used by high-caste Indians
mahajun money-lender or banker
mahout elephant-driver
maulvi Muslim holy man
mirza Mogul prince
mohur gold coin introduced by the Moguls
mulligatawny curried soup
munshi a scribe or clerk, or, more particularly, a language teacher or translator
musnud a cushioned throne used by Indian princes
naik Indian NCO, equivalent to corporal
nautch erotic entertainment by professional Indian dancers
nazir ceremonial gift
NCO non-commissioned officer
nullah a deep ditch or dry river bed
palanquin one-man covered litter carried on poles by men or beasts
paltan a regiment of Indian infantry from the French 'peloton' and later English 'platoon'
Pandit learned Hindu Brahman
pargana a revenue subdivision; a group of mutually connected villages
Parsi adherent of the Zoroastrian faith
Pathan a member of the Pushtu-speaking Muslim people inhabiting south-east Afghanistan and the North-West Frontier
perwanah order or warrant
Peshwa hereditary leader of the Maratha Confederacy; originally the minister of the Raja of Satara
pice a quarter of an anna
pugri light turban or thin scarf worn round hat
pukka proper, as in pukka roof, tiled rather than thatched
pulao spiced rice
punchayet informal native court; council of village elders
punkah rudimentary fan in the form of a piece of cloth attached to the ceiling
punkah-wallah servant who kept the punkah in motion by pulling on a string
purbia (purbiya) inhabitant of the north Indian region that included Oudh, Bihar and Benares
purdah seclusion or isolation, especially of Muslim women. From Urdu and Persian *pardah* (veil)
pyjamas loose Indian trousers
quarter-guard a regiment's armed guard; building that housed the guard and was used to detain prisoners
raj kingdom or principality; rule; often used loosely to denote British rule in India

raja Indian prince or ruler; title of nobility

Rajput member of the most prominent military and landholding caste in northern India; Kshatriya class

Ramadan (Ramazan) ninth month of the Muslim year, observed as a thirty-day fast during the hours of daylight

regiment a body of soldiers, composed of around ten infantry companies or six cavalry troops, and usually led by a colonel

ressalah (rissala) troop or squadron of irregular horse

ressaldar (rissaldar) senior Indian officer in irregular cavalry regiment

rezai quilt stuffed with raw cotton

rupee Indian silver coin, valued at one tenth (2 shillings) of a pound sterling (gold) until about 1870

ryot cultivator or farmer, distinct from labourer

sadhu ascetic holy man

Sadr Amin (Sudder Ameen) Indian judge

sahib master or lord, most frequently applied to European officers and officials

sahib-log Europeans (literally 'Master race')

sepoy an Indian infantry private, from the Persian for soldier

serai a stopping-place for travellers, usually in the form of a square courtyard with animals inside and small rooms to sleep in

Shahzadah son of a shah

shako a cylindrical military hat with a peak

Shudra member of the fourth *varna*, of serfs or labourers

Sikh member of a monotheistic religion founded in the Punjab in the fifteenth century by disillusioned Hindus

silladar irregular cavalryman who provides, or pays for, his own weapons, horse and accoutrements

sirdar Indian military chief or leader

sirkar (sircar) state or government

sowar cavalry trooper

subedar (subadar) senior Indian officer of an infantry company or cavalry troop

subedar-major senior Indian officer in regular cavalry or infantry regiment

suttee Hindu custom requiring the self-immolation of a widow on her husband's funeral pyre

syce groom

tahsil administrative subdivision of a district

tahsildar Indian civil servant in charge of a *tahsil*

taluq (1) Fiscal lordship or estate, in which the holder is responsible for the revenue collection from a number of dependent villages (N. India). (2) A group of villages held in mutual dependence by lineage ties among the proprietary bodies

taluqdar Holder of a ***taluq***. Under British revenue law in N.W. Provinces, a superior proprietor drawing a fixed percentage on revenue payments made by village sub-proprietors. In Oudh a full proprietor of a number of villages

tank freshwater pond

thakur Rajput landholder

thana a police station, or area under the jurisdiction of a local police station

thanadar chief police officer of a ***thana***

tope grove of trees

tulwar curved Indian sword introduced by the Muslims

tykhana an underground room

Urdu language of the Muslim conquerors of Hindustan, derived from Hindi, but written in Arabic script; also known as Hindustani

Vaishya member of the third *varna*, of farmers and merchants

vakil an agent, particularly of a ruler; sometimes a lawyer

varna one of the four preordained classes – Brahmans, Kshatriyas, Vaishyas and Shudras – into which all Hindu society is divided

vilayati foreign mercenary (often Afghan)

zemindar landholder; a person recognized by British law as the proprietor of land

Bibliography

Primary Sources, Unpublished

Official Documents

ORIENTAL AND INDIA OFFICE COLLECTION (OIOC), BRITISH LIBRARY, LONDON

Bengal Military Consultations
India Military Consultations
Military Department Records

NATIONAL ARCHIVES OF INDIA (NAI), NEW DELHI

Foreign Department Political Consultations
Foreign Department Political Proceedings
Foreign Department Secret Consultations
Military Department Papers

Private Papers

ORIENTAL AND INDIA OFFICE COLLECTION (OIOC), BRITISH LIBRARY, LONDON

Chamberlain Correspondence: correspondence of Field Marshal Sir Neville Chamberlain

Chichester Letters: typescript copy of letters home, dated 1856–1864, by Major-General Hugh Chichester (1836–1895), Bengal (later Royal) Artillery, 1856–1886

Dalhousie Letters: typescript of letters from the Marquess of Dalhousie to General Sir William Gomm concerning military administration and operations 1849–1856

Elphinstone Papers: papers of John, 13th Baron Elphinstone

Elphinstone (Mountstuart) Papers: papers of Hon. Mountstuart Elphinstone

Ewart Letters: letters from Emma Ewart, wife of Colonel John Ewart (1st Bengal NI), to her sister

Glascock Journal: typescript copy of the journal of Ensign (later Major-General) Talbot Glascock (1839–1900), Bengal Army, 1857–1887

Goldney Papers: memoirs of Mrs Louisa Goldney

Grant Letters: two letters from Lieutenant-General Sir Patrick Grant, Commander-in-Chief India May–August 1857, to Major-General Sir Henry Barnard, in command of siege of Delhi

Grant Papers: copies of letters, dated June 1857–April 1858, between Lieutenant John A. Grant, Madras Army, and his brothers, Lieutenant-Colonel Francis Grant, Bengal Army, and Surgeon-Major Alexander Grant, BMS

Hickman Papers: papers of Major George Hickman, late 70th Bengal NI

Jacob Papers: papers of Brigadier John Jacob

Johnson Diaries: diaries of General Sir Allen B. Johnson, Bengal Army, while serving as an ensign in the 5th NI, 1849–1850

Kantzow Papers: record of the services of Colonel Charles Adolphus de Kantzow in India, 1853–1888

Kaye Mutiny Papers: the mutiny papers of Sir John Kaye

Latimer Letters: letters of John Latimer, serving as a volunteer or ordinary soldier with the Central India Field Force

Lawrence Correspondence: correspondence of Lord Lawrence to Brigadier-General Neville Chamberlain

Lawrence Letters: the letters of Sir Henry Lawrence

Littledale Letters: letters from Arthur Littledale, collector and deputy judge, Saran District, to his mother-in-law, Mrs Law

Lyveden Papers: the papers of Robert Vernon Smith, 1st Baron Lyveden

McGuiness Letters: letters of Sergeant Christopher McGuiness

Martineau Letters: letters from Lieutenant Edward Martineau to Captain Septimus Becher, AAG of the Army

Mawe Letters: letters from Dr Thomas Mawe, BMS, to his sister, describing the early stages of the mutiny

Nicholl Letters: letters of Lieutenant Thomas Nicholl, BA

Sandhurst Papers: memoranda, correspondence and telegrams of Major-General Sir William Rose Mansfield, 1st Baron Sandhurst

Scot Papers: personal narrative of the escape from Nowgong by Captain P. G. Scot, 12th Bengal NI

Sitwell Letters: letters from Captain Francis Sitwell, describing his experiences during the Indian mutiny

Sneyd Papers: 'Reminiscences of the Dreadful Mutiny in India in 1857' by Mrs Elizabeth Sneyd

Spry Letters: letters, dated 1841–1867, from the Revd Arthur Browne Spry, Chaplain at Allahabad, and his wife, Matilda, to relatives in Norfolk

Talbot Papers: private diary and letter-book of the Hon. Gerald Talbot, PS to Lord Canning, 1856–1858

Timbrell Narrative: narrative of her family's escape from Nasirabad in 1857 by Mrs Agnes Timbrell, wife of Captain Charles Timbrell (1823–1860), Bengal Artillery

Vansittart papers: Diaries and memorabilia of Mary Amelia Vansittart, wife of Henry Vansittart (1818–1896) BCS
Walcot Papers: letters from Lieutenant William Walcot, 47th Bengal NI, to his wife
Warner Letters: letters from Ensign Wynyard Warner, 40th Bengal NI, and Lieutenant Ashton Warner, 7th Bengal LC, to members of their family
Wood Papers: papers of Sir Charles Wood, President of the Board of Control, 1853–1855, and Secretary of State for India, 1859–1860

NATIONAL ARCHIVES OF INDIA (NAI), NEW DELHI

Mutiny Papers

NATIONAL ARCHIVES OF SCOTLAND (NAS), EDINBURGH

Dalhousie Papers: papers of the 10th Earl and 1st Marquess of Dalhousie

DEPARTMENT OF MANUSCRIPTS, NATIONAL LIBRARY OF SCOTLAND (NLS), EDINBURGH

Grey Diaries: diaries of Veterinary Surgeon Edward Simpson Grey, 8th Hussars

DEPARTMENT OF MANUSCRIPTS, BRITISH LIBRARY (BL), LONDON

Horne Narrative: Miss Amy Horne's [Haine's] narrative
Mutiny Papers: letters and papers relating to the Indian mutiny
Napier Papers: papers of Sir Charles J. Napier
Peel Papers: correspondence of Sir Robert Peel
Pierce Letters: the letters of Thomas Pierce
Service Record of the 31st Bengal NI: services of the late 31st now 2nd LI during the mutiny and rebellion in 1857

DEPARTMENT OF DOCUMENTS, NATIONAL ARMY MUSEUM (NAM), LONDON

Bingham Diary: diary of General G. W. P. Bingham during and after the Indian mutiny
Chamier Letters: letters from Lieutenant Edward Chamier (34th Bengal NI), ADC and Persian interpreter to General Sir James Outram, GCB
Coghill Papers: papers of Lieutenant and Adjutant Kendal Coghill, 2nd Bengal EF
Dennys Memoirs: memoirs of General J. B. Dennys
Edwards Papers: R. M. Edwards, 'Diary of Events in the Districts of Saharunpore and Mozuffurnugger from 11th May 1857 to April 27th 1858'
Ewart Letters: letters of Ensign Charles H. Ewart, 2nd Bengal EF
Gambier Letters: letters of Lieutenant Charles ('Harry') F. Gambier, 38th Bengal NI
Hall Papers: Colonel Montagu Hall, 'Reminiscences of the Indian Mutiny'
Hargood Letters: 'Extract from the Letters Received from My Son, Lieutenant William Hargood, First Madras Fusiliers – Aide-de-Camp to Generals Sir Henry Havelock and Sir James Outram 1857–1858'

Intercepted Letter: an intercepted letter from Peshawar
Jackson Narrative: 'A Personal Narrative of the Indian Mutiny' by Madeline Jackson
Lawrence Letters: letters of the Lawrence family
Lind Papers: the diary and correspondence of Francis M. Lind, Collector of Benares
Lindsay Letters: letters of Major William Lindsay, AAG Cawnpore
Lowry Letters: letters of Captain Edward Lowry of the 25th Bombay NI and his wife
Lyster Papers: the papers of Lieutenant-General Harry H. Lyster, VC
Nicholson Diary: diary of Brevet Lieutenant-Colonel Lothian Nicholson, RE
Poore Letters: letters of Major Robert Poore, 8th Hussars, 1854–1858
Potiphar Papers: documents of Private Frederick Potiphar, 9th Lancers, 1845–1860
Prichard Papers: account of the mutiny at Nuseerabad by Lieutenant Illitudus Prichard, 15th Bengal NI
Richardson Papers: Major-General J. F. Richardson (8th Bengal IC), memoirs of service in India, 1841–1858
Rogers Papers: reminiscences of foreign service by Henry Rogers, MD, late surgeon, HM 70th Regiment
Shebbeare Letters: letters of Major Robert H. Shebbeare, VC, 60th Bengal NI
Sneyd Letters: letters of Captain Henry Sneyd, 28th Bengal NI
Spy Letters: copies of letters from spies in the city of Delhi
Stansfeld Letters: letters of Ensign H. H. Stansfeld of the 8th Bengal NI
Wilkie Correspondence: correspondence of Colonel David Wilkie, 4th Bengal NI
Wilson Letters: letters of Sir Archdale Wilson to his wife
Wilson Correspondence: correspondence of Sir Archdale Wilson

Primary Sources, Published

Parliamentary Papers

PP, House of Commons, 1852–1853, XXVII: First Report from the Select Committee on Indian Territories (2 May 1853)
PP, House of Commons, 1852–1853, XXVIII: Fourth Report from the Select Committee on Indian Territories
PP, House of Lords, 1852–1853, XXXI: First Report from the Select Committee of the House of Lords appointed to inquire into the operation of the Act 3 & 4, Will. IV, c. 85, for the better Government of Her Majesty's Indian Territories
PP, House of Commons, 1857, XXX: Papers relative to the mutinies in the East Indies
PP, House of Commons, 1857–1858, XLIV: Accounts and papers, mutinies in the East Indies
PP, House of Commons, 1859, V: Report of the Commissioners appointed to inquire into the organization of the Indian Army

PP, House of Commons, 1859, VIII: Papers connected with the reorganization of the Army in India, supplementary to the Report of the Army Commission

PP, House of Commons, 1859, XVIII, pp. 1–64: A return 'of the Name or Number of each Regiment and Regular and Irregular Corps in India which has mutinied, or manifested a disposition to mutiny, since the 1st day of January 1857 . . .'

PP, House of Commons, 1859, XVIII, pp. 111ff.: A copy of the evidence taken before the Court appointed for the trial of the King of Delhi

Other Contemporary Publications

Carey, W. H., *The Mahomedan Rebellion* (Rurki, 1857)

Carmichael-Smyth, Lieutenant-Colonel C., *A Rough Sketch of the Rise and Progress of the Irregular Horse of the Bengal Army* (privately printed, 1847)

Chesney, George, *Indian Polity: A View of the System of Administration in India* (London, 1868)

Edwardes, Sir H. B., and Merivale, Herman, *The Life of Sir Henry Lawrence* (3rd edition, 1887)

Hansard's Parliamentary Debates, 3rd Series, 1830–1891

Hodgson, Colonel J. S., *Opinions on the Indian Army: Originally Published at Meerut in 1850, under the Title of Musings on Military Matters* (London, 1857)

Hunter, W. W., *Imperial Gazetteer of India* (London, 1881)

—*Notes on Sir C. Napier's Posthumous Work* (London, 1854)

Kaye, Sir John, *History of the Sepoy War*, 3 vols. (London, 1864–7)

—*Lives of Indian Officers*, 2 vols. (London, 1867)

Khan, Sir Syed Ahmad, *An Essay on the Causes of the Indian Revolt* (Calcutta, 1860), Captain W. N. Lees (trans.)

—*Rissalah Asbab-e-bhagawat-i-hind* (Benares, 1873), G. F. Graham and A. Colvin (trans.)

Lawrence, Sir Henry, *Essays, Military and Political, Written in India* (London, 1859)

Malcolm, Sir John, *The Government of India* (London, 1833)

—*Political History of India*, 2 vols. (London, 1826)

Malleson, Colonel G. B. (ed.), *Kaye and Malleson's History of the Indian Mutiny of 1857–1858*, 6 vols. (London, 1888)

Napier, Sir Charles, *Defects, Civil and Military, of the Indian Government* (London, 1853)

Narrative of Events Attending the Outbreak of Disturbances and the Restoration of Authority in India in 1857–1858 (Calcutta, 1881)

Nolan, Captain L. E., *Cavalry: Its History and Tactics* (London, 1853)

O'Conor, J. E., *Prices and Wages in India* (Calcutta, 1886)

Pelly, Lewis (ed.), *The Views and Opinions of Brigadier-General John Jacob, CB* (London, 1858)

Raikes, Charles, *Notes on the Revolt of the North-Western Provinces of India* (London, 1858)

Skene, W. F., *Memorials of the Family of Skene of Skene* (Aberdeen, 1887)

Published Documents, Diaries, Letters and Memoirs

Anderson, G., and Subedar, M. (eds.), *The Last Days of the Company: A Source Book of Indian History 1818–1858*, 2 vols. (London, 1918)

Anderson, Captain R. P., *A Personal Journal of the Siege of Lucknow* (London, 1858), Carnegy Anderson (ed.)

Anson, Major O. H. S. G., *With HM 9th Lancers during the Indian Mutiny* (London, 1896)

Baird, J. G. A. (ed.), *Private Letters of the Marquess of Dalhousie* (London, 1910)

Bandopadhyay, Durgadas, *Amar Jivancharit* (in Bengali) (1925, reprint, Calcutta: Ananya Prakashan, [n.d.])

Bartrum, Katherine Mary, *A Widow's Reminiscences of the Siege of Lucknow* (London, 1858)

Benson, A. C., and Esher, Viscount (eds.), *The Letters of Queen Victoria: A Selection from Her Majesty's Correspondence between the Years 1837 and 1861*, 3 vols. (London, 1907)

Bhatnagar, O. P. (ed.), *Private Correspondence of J. W. Sherer, Collector of Fatehpur* (Allahabad, 1968)

Blomfield, David (ed.), *Lahore to Lucknow: The Indian Mutiny Journal of Arthur Moffat Lang* (London, 1992)

Bonham, Colonel John, *Oude in 1857: Some Memories of the Indian Mutiny* (London, 1928)

Bute, Marchioness of (ed.), *The Private Journals of the Marquess of Hastings: Governor-General and Commander-in-Chief in India*, 2 vols. (London, 1858)

Duberly, Mrs Frances, *Campaigning in Rajputana and Central India during the Suppression of the Mutiny* (London, 1859)

Forbes-Mitchell, William, *The Relief of Lucknow* (London, 1962, first published in 1893 as *Reminiscences of the Great Mutiny*), Michael Edwardes (ed.)

Forrest, G. W. (ed.), *Selections from the Letters, Dispatches and Other State Papers Preserved in the Military Department of the Government of India 1857–1858*, 4 vols. (Calcutta, 1893–1912)

Germon, Maria, *Journal of the Siege of Lucknow: An Episode of the Indian Mutiny* (London, 1958)

Godse, Vishnu Bhatta, *Maujhar Pravas* (Poona, 1948)

Gough, General Sir Hugh, *Old Memories* (London, 1897)

Greathed, H. H., *Letters Written during the Siege of Delhi* (London, 1858)

Griffiths, Charles, *A Narrative of the Siege of Delhi* (London, 1910)

Gubbins, M. R., *An Account of the Mutinies in Oudh* (London, 1858)

Harris, Mrs G., *A Lady's Diary of the Siege of Lucknow* (London, 1858)

Harrison, A. T. (ed.), *The Graham Indian Mutiny Papers* (Belfast, 1980)

Hervey, Captain Albert, *A Soldier of the Company: Life of an Indian Ensign 1833–1843* (London, 1988), Charles Allen (ed.)

Hewitt, James (ed.), *Eyewitnesses to the Indian Mutiny* (Reading, 1972)

Hodson, G. H., *Twelve Years of a Soldier's Life in India: Being Extracts from the Letters of the Late Major W. S. R. Hodson* (London, 1859)

Humbly, W. W. W., *Journal of a Cavalry Officer* (London, 1854)

Hutchinson, Major-General George, *Narrative of the Mutinies in Oude* (London, 1859)

Inglis, Lady, Hon. Julia Selina, *The Siege of Lucknow. A Diary* (London, 1892)

Jacquemont, Victor, *Letters from India 1829–1832* (London, 1936), C. A. Philips (trans.)

Kavanagh, T. Henry, *How I Won the Victoria Cross* (London, 1860)

Lang, John, *Wanderings in India: And Other Sketches of Life in Hindostan* (London, 1859)

Lowe, Thomas, *Central India: During the Rebellion of 1857 and 1858* (London, 1860)

Loy Smith, George, *A Victorian RSM* (London, 1987)

Majendie, Sir Vivian Dering, *Up Among the Pandies; or, A Year's Service in India* (London, 1859)

Metcalfe, Charles T. (trans.), *Two Native Narratives of the Mutiny in Delhi* (London, 1898)

Metcalfe, Henry, *The Chronicle of Private Henry Metcalfe, HM 32nd Regiment of Foot* (London, 1953), Lieutenant-General Sir Francis Tuker (ed.)

O'Callaghan, Daniel, *Scattered Chapters of the Indian Mutiny: The Fatal Falter at Meerut* (London, 1897)

Pandy, Sitaram, *From Sepoy to Subedar: Being the Life and Adventures of Subedar Sita Ram, a Native Officer of the Bengal Army, Written and Related by Himself* (London, 1970, first translated and published by Lieutenant-Colonel J. T. Norgate in 1873), James Lunt (ed.)

Philips, C. H. (ed.), *The Correspondence of Lord William Cavendish Bentinck: Governor-General of India 1828–1835*, 2 vols. (Oxford, 1977)

Rees, L. E. R., *A Personal Narrative of the Siege of Lucknow* (London, 1858)

Rizvi, S. A. A., and Bhargava, M. L. (eds.), *Freedom Struggle in Uttar Pradesh: Source Material*, 6 vols. (Lucknow, 1957)

Roberts, Field Marshal Lord, *Forty-one Years in India: From Subaltern to Commander-in-Chief* (London, 1898)

—[Fred Roberts], *Letters Written during the Indian Mutiny* (London, 1924)

Robson, Brian (ed.), *Sir Hugh Rose and the Central India Campaign* (Stroud, 2000)

Russell, W. H., *My Diary in India*, 2 vols. (London, 1859)

—*My Indian Mutiny Diary* (London, 1957, abridged), Michael Edwardes (ed.)

Shepherd, W. J., *A Personal Narrative of the Outbreak and Massacre at Cawnpore during the Sepoy Revolt of 1857* (Lucknow, 1879)

Sherer, J. W., *Daily Life during the Indian Mutiny: Personal Experiences of 1857* (London, 1898)

—*Havelock's March on Cawnpore: A Civilian's Notes* (London, 1910)

Sleeman, Major-General Sir William, *Rambles and Recollections of an Indian Official* (London, 1843, revised edition, 1915)
—*A Journey through the Kingdom of Oude in 1849–1850*, 2 vols. (London, 1858)
Thackwell, E. J., *Narrative of the Second Sikh War* (London, 1851, 2nd edition)
Thomson, Captain Mowbray, *The Story of Cawnpore* (London, 1859)
Thornhill, Mark, *The Personal Adventures and Experiences of a Magistrate during the Rise, Progress, and Suppression of the Indian Mutiny* (London, 1884)
Tytler, Harriet, *An Englishwoman in India: The Memoirs of Harriet Tytler 1828–1858* (Oxford, 1986), Anthony Sattin (ed.)
Vibart, Colonel Edward, *The Sepoy Mutiny* (London, 1898)
Wilson, Major T. F., *The Defence of Lucknow* (London, 1858)
Young, Colonel Keith, *Delhi – 1857: The Siege, Assault and Capture as Given in the Diary and Correspondence of the Late Colonel Keith Young, CB* (London, 1902), General Sir Henry Norman and Mrs Keith Young (eds.)

Newspapers and Journals

Bengal Hurkaru and India Gazette
Calcutta Review
Delhi Gazette
Friend of India
Hindoo Patriot
The Mofussilite
The Times
United Service Gazette
United Service Magazine

Secondary Sources

Articles and Chapters

Anderson, Olive, 'The Growth of Christian Militarism in Mid Victorian Britain', *English Historical Review (EHR)*, vol. 86, 1971, pp. 46–72
Baker, David, 'Colonial Beginnings and the Indian Response: The Revolt of 1857–1858 in Madhya Pradesh', *Modern Asian Studies*, vol. 25, no. 3, 1991, pp. 511–43
Bhadra, Gautam, 'Four Rebels of Eighteen Fifty-seven' in Ranajit Guha and Gayatri Chakravorty Spivak (eds.), *Selected Subaltern Studies* (Oxford, 1988), pp. 129–75
Brodkin, E. I., 'The Struggle for Succession: Rebels and Loyalists in the Indian Mutiny of 1857', *Modern Asian Studies*, vol. 6, no. 3, 1972, pp. 277–90
Cadell, Sir Patrick, 'The Outbreak of the Indian Mutiny', *Journal of the Society of Army Historical Research (JSAHR)*, vol. 33, 1955, pp. 118–22

Cohn, Bernard S., 'The Command of Language and the Language of Command' in Ranajit Guha (ed.), *Subaltern Studies IV* (Delhi, 1985), pp. 276–329

Crowell, Lorenzo M., 'Military Professionalism in a Colonial Context: The Madras Army circa 1832', *Modern Asian Studies*, vol. 24, no. 2, 1990, pp. 249–74

Harding, David, 'Arming the East India Company's Forces' in Alan J. Guy and Peter B. Boyden (eds.), *Soldiers of the Raj: The Indian Army 1600–1947* (London, 1997), pp. 138–47

Kolff, Dirk H. A., 'The End of an *Ancien Régime*: Colonial War in India 1798–1818' in J. A. de Moor and H. L. Wesseling (eds.), *Imperialism and War: Essays on Colonial Wars in Asia and Africa* (Leiden, 1889), pp. 22–49

Luke, P. V., 'How the Electric Telegraph Saved India' in Colonel E. Vibart, *The Sepoy Mutiny* (London, 1898), pp. 250–67

Mackenzie, Colonel A. R. D., 'The Outbreak at Meerut' in Colonel E. Vibart, *The Sepoy Mutiny* (London, 1898), pp. 213–44

Menezes, S. L., 'Race, Caste, Mutiny and Discipline in the Indian Army, from Its Origins to 1947' in Alan J. Guy and Peter B. Boyden (eds.), *Soldiers of the Raj: The Indian Army 1600–1947* (London, 1997), pp. 100–117

Mukherjee, Rudrangshu, '"Satan Let Loose upon the Earth": The Kanpur Massacres in India in the Revolt of 1857', *Past & Present*, no. 128, 1990, pp. 92–116

Peers, Douglas M., 'Between Mars and Mammon: The East India Company and Efforts to Reform Its Army 1796–1832', *Historical Journal*, vol. 33, no. 2, 1990, pp. 385–401

—'The Habitual Nobility of Being: British Officers and the Social Construction of the Bengal Army in the Early Nineteenth Century', *Modern Asian Studies*, vol. 25, no. 3, 1991, pp. 545–69

—'Imperial Vice: Sex, Drink and the Health of British Troops in North Indian Cantonments 1800–1858' in David Killingray and David Omissi (eds.), *Guardians of the Empire: The Armed Forces of the Colonial Powers* c. *1700–1964* (Manchester, 1999), pp. 25–52

—'Sepoys, Soldiers and the Lash: Race, Caste and Army Discipline in India 1820–50', *Journal of Imperial and Commonwealth History (JICH)*, vol. 23, no. 2, 1995, pp. 211–47

Ray, Rajat Kanta, 'Race, Religion and Realm' in M. Hasan and N. Gupta (eds.), *India's Colonial Encounter: Essays in Memory of Eric Stokes* (1993), pp. 135–6

Robson, Brian, 'The British Cavalry Trooper's Sword 1796–1853', *Journal of the Society of Army Historical Research (JSAHR)*, vol. 46, 1968, pp. 106–9

—'The Organization and Command Structure of the Indian Army' in Alan J. Guy and Peter B. Boyden (eds.), *Soldiers of the Raj: The Indian Army 1600–1947* (London, 1997), pp. 9–19

Roy, Kaushik, 'The Historiography of the Colonial Indian Army', *Studies in History*, vol. 12, no. 2, 1996, pp. 255–73

—'Recruitment Doctrines of the Colonial Indian Army: 1859–1913', *Indian Economic and Social History Review (IESHR)*, vol. 34, no. 3, 1997, pp. 321–54
—'Company Bahadur against the Pandies: The Military Dimension of the 1857 Mutiny Revisited', *Jadavpur University Journal of History (JUJH)*, vols. 19–20, 2001–2
Ryder, Brigadier Stuart, 'Everard Lisle Phillipps, VC', *Royal United Services Institute Journal (RUSI)*, June 1998, p. 70–75
Scurfield, R., 'British Military Smoothbore Firearms', *Journal of the Society of Army Historical Research (JSAHR)*, vol. 33, 1955, pp. 62–9, 111–61
Steele, Captain Russell V., 'Uniforms Worn by Sir Colin Campbell's Force in the Rohilkhand Campaign 1858', *Journal of the Society of Army Historical Research (JSAHR)*, vol. 33, 1955, pp. 115–17
Strachan, H. F. A., 'The British Army and Society', *Historical Journal*, vol. 22, no. 1, 1979, pp. 247–54
—'The Origins of the 1855 Uniform Changes: An Example of Pre-Crimean Reform', *Journal of the Society of Army Historical Research (JSAHR)*, vol. 55, 1977, pp. 85–117
Tylden, Major G., 'The Principal Small Arms Carried by British Regular Infantry', *Journal of the Society of Army Historical Research (JSAHR)*, vol. 45, 1967, pp. 244–5

Books

Alavi, Seema, *The Sepoys and the Company: Tradition and Transition in Northern India 1770–1830* (Delhi, 1995)
Allen, Charles, *Soldier Sahibs: The Men Who Made the North-West Frontier* (London, 2000)
Anglesey, The Marquess of, *A History of the British Cavalry 1816–1919. Vol. II: 1851–1871* (London, 1975)
Barat, Amiya, *The Bengal Native Infantry: Its Organization and Discipline 1796–1852* (Calcutta, 1962)
Barthorp, Michael, *The British Troops in the Indian Mutiny 1857–59* (Oxford, 1994)
Bayly, C. A., *Empire and Information: Intelligence Gathering and Social Communication in India 1780–1870* (Cambridge, 1996)
—*Rulers, Townsmen and Bazaars: North Indian Society in the Age of British Expansion 1770–1870* (Cambridge, 1983)
Bayly, Susan, *The New Cambridge History of India. Vol. IV: 3 – Caste, Society and Politics in India from the Eighteenth Century to the Modern Age* (Cambridge, 1999)
Bence-Jones, Mark, *Clive of India* (London, 1974)
Bernstein, Jeremy, *Dawning of the Raj: The Life and Trials of Warren Hastings* (Chicago, 2000)
Cadell, Sir Patrick, *History of the Bombay Army* (London, 1938)

Carman, W. Y., *Indian Army Uniforms under the British: From the Eighteenth Century to 1947*, 3 vols. (1861–9)
Chaudhuri, S. B., *Civil Rebellion in the Indian Mutinies 1857–1859* (Calcutta, 1957)
Cohen, Stephen P., *The Indian Army: Its Contribution to the Development of a Nation* (Delhi, 1971)
Dutt, Nripendra Kumar, *Origin and Growth of Caste in India*, 3 vols. (London, 1931)
Fitzmaurice, Lord Edmond, *The Life of Granville George Leveson Gower, Second Earl Granville*, 2 vols. (London, 1905)
Forrest, Sir George, *The Life of Lord Clive*, 2 vols. (London, 1918)
Gimlette, Lieutenant-Colonel G. H. D., *A Postscript to the Records of the Indian Mutiny: An Attempt to Trace the Subsequent Careers and Fate of the Rebel Bengal Regiments 1857–1858* (London, 1927)
Guha, Ranajit, *Elementary Aspects of Peasant Insurgency in Colonial India* (Delhi, 1983)
Guy, Alan J., and Boyden, Peter B. (eds.), *Soldiers of the Raj: The Indian Army 1600–1947* (London, 1997)
Harding, D. F., *Smallarms of the East India Company 1660–1856*, 4 vols. (London, 1997–9)
Heathcote, T. A., *The Indian Army: The Garrison of British Imperial India 1822–1922* (London, 1974)
—*The Military in British India: The Development of British Land Forces in South Asia 1600–1947* (Manchester, 1995)
Hibbert, Christopher, *The Great Mutiny: India 1857* (London, 1980)
Holmes, T. R. E., *A History of the Indian Mutiny* (London, 1883)
Ingram, Edward, *Empire-building and Empire-builders: Twelve Studies* (London, 1995)
—*In Defence of British India: Great Britain in the Middle East 1775–1842* (London, 1984)
James, Lawrence, *Raj: The Making and Unmaking of British India* (London, 1997)
—*Warrior Race: A History of the British at War* (London, 2001)
Jocelyn, Colonel Julian R. J., *The History of the Royal and Indian Artillery in the Mutiny of 1857* (London, 1915)
Jones, Kenneth W., *The New Cambridge History of India. Vol. III: 1 – Socio-religious Reform Movements in British India* (Cambridge, 1989)
Kolff, Dirk H. A., *Naukar, Rajput and Sepoy: The Ethnology of the Military Labour Market in Hindustan 1450–1850* (Cambridge, 1990)
Lambrick, H. T., *John Jacob of Jacobabad* (London, 1960)
Lawrence, John, *Lawrence of Lucknow* (London, 1990)
Lumsden, P. S., and Elsmie, G. R., *Lumsden of the Guides* (London, 1899)
Maclagan, Michael, *'Clemency' Canning* (London, 1962)
Majumdar, R. C., *The Sepoy Mutiny and the Revolt of 1857* (Calcutta, 1957)
Mason, Philip, *A Matter of Honour: An Account of the Indian Army, Its Officers and Men* (London, 1974)
Metcalf, Thomas R., *The Aftermath of Revolt: India 1857–1870* (Princeton, 1965)

Mollo, Boris, *The Indian Army* (Poole, 1981)
Mukherjee, Rudrangshu, *Awadh in Revolt 1857–1858: A Study of Popular Resistance* (Delhi, 1984)
Omissi, David, *The Sepoy and the Raj: The Indian Army 1860–1940* (London, 1994)
Palmer, J. A. B., *The Mutiny Outbreak at Meerut in 1857* (Cambridge, 1966)
Porter, Andrew, *The Oxford History of the British Empire. Vol. III: The Nineteenth Century* (Oxford, 1999)
The Register of the Victoria Cross (Cheltenham, 1997)
Robinson, Jane, *Angels of Albion: Women of the Indian Mutiny* (London, 1996)
Roselli, John, *Lord William Bentinck: The Making of a Liberal Imperialist* (London, 1974)
Roy, Tapti, *The Politics of a Popular Uprising: Bundelkhand in 1857* (Delhi, 1994)
Savarkar, V. D., *The Indian War of Independence of 1857* (London, 1909)
Sen, S. N., *Eighteen Fifty-seven* (Delhi, 1957)
Sinha, S. N., *The Revolt of 1857 in Bundelkhand* (Lucknow, 1982)
Smith, C. B. W., *Florence Nightingale* (London, 1950)
Smyth, Sir John, *The Rebellious Rani* (London, 1966)
Stanley, Peter, *White Mutiny: British Military Culture in India 1825–1875* (London, 1998)
Stokes, Eric, *The English Utilitarians and India* (1959)
— *The Peasant and the Raj: Studies in Agrarian Society and Peasant Rebellion in Colonial India* (Cambridge, 1978)
— *The Peasant Armed: The Indian Revolt of 1857* (Oxford, 1986)
Strachan, Hew, *Wellington's Legacy: The Reform of the British Army 1830–1854* (Manchester, 1984)
Tahmankar, D. V., *The Ranee of Jhansi* (London, 1958)
Taylor, P. J. O., *A Companion to the 'Indian Mutiny' of 1857* (New Delhi, 1996)
— *What Really Happened During the Mutiny: A Day-by-Day Account of the Major Events of 1857–1859 in India* (New Delhi, 1997)
Temple, Sir Richard, *Lord Lawrence* (London, 1889)
Trotter, Lionel J., *The Life of Hodson of Hodson's Horse* (London, 1901)
Vibart, Colonel E., *The Sepoy Mutiny* (London, 1898)
Ward, Andrew, *Our Bones are Scattered: The Cawnpore Massacres and the Indian Mutiny of 1857* (London, 1996)
Watson, Bruce, *The Great Indian Mutiny: Colin Campbell and the Campaign at Lucknow* (New York, 1991)
Winant, Lewis, *Early Percussion Firearms: A History of the Early Percussion Firearms Ignition* (New York, 1959)
Woodward, Llewellyn, *The Age of Reform: England 1815–1870* (Oxford, 1962, this edition, 1992)
Yapp, M. E., *Strategies of British India: Britain, Iran and Afghanistan 1798–1850* (Oxford, 1980)

Unpublished Theses

Bourne, J. M., 'The Civil and Military Patronage of the East India Company 1784–1858', Ph.D. thesis, University of Leicester, 1977

David, Saul, 'The Bengal Army and the Outbreak of the Indian Mutiny', Ph.D. thesis, University of Glasgow, 2001

Shibly, A. H., 'The Reorganization of the Indian Armies 1858–1879', Ph. D. thesis, SOAS, University of London, 1969

Notes

Full bibliographical references for the sources cited can be found in the Bibliography.

Abbreviations

Alavi Seema Alavi, *The Sepoys and the Company: Tradition and Transition in Northern India 1770–1830* (Delhi, 1995)

Allen Charles Allen, *Soldier Sahibs: The Men Who Made the North-West Frontier* (London, 2000)

Barat Amiya Barat, *The Bengal Native Infantry: Its Organization and Discipline 1796–1852* (Calcutta, 1962)

BL Department of Manuscripts, British Library, London

David Saul David, 'The Bengal Army and the Outbreak of the Indian Mutiny', Ph.D. thesis, Glasgow University, 2001

FC Foreign Consultations

Fitzmaurice Lord Edmond Fitzmaurice, *The Life of Granville George Leveson Gower, Second Earl Granville*, 2 vols. (London, 1905)

Freedom Struggle S. A. A. Rizvi and M. L. Bhargava (eds.), *Freedom Struggle in Uttar Pradesh: Source Material*, 6 vols. (Lucknow, 1957)

Gimlette Lieutenant-Colonel G. H. D. Gimlette, *A Postscript to the Records of the Indian Mutiny: An Attempt to Trace the Subsequent Careers and Fate of the Rebel Bengal Regiments 1857–1858* (London, 1927)

GOGG General Order of the Governor-General

HC House of Commons

Hibbert Christopher Hibbert, *The Great Mutiny: India 1857* (London, 1980)

HL House of Lords

JICH *Journal of Imperial and Commonwealth History*

JSAHR *Journal of the Society of Army Historical Research*

JUJH *Jadavpur University Journal of History*

Kaye and Malleson Colonel G. B. Malleson (ed.), *Kaye and Malleson's History of the Indian Mutiny of 1857–1858*, 6 vols. (London, 1888)

Kolff Dirk Kolff, *Naukar, Rajput and Sepoy: The Ethnology of the Military Labour Market in Hindustan 1450–1850* (Cambridge, 1990)

Lang David Blomfield (ed.), *Lahore to Lucknow: The Indian Mutiny Journal of Arthur Moffatt Lang* (London, 1992)

Maclagan Michael Maclagan, *'Clemency' Canning: Charles John, 1st Earl Canning* (London, 1962)

Mukherjee Rudrangshu Mukherjee, *Awadh in Revolt 1857–1858: A Study of Popular Resistance* (Delhi, 1984)

NAI National Archives of India, New Delhi

NAM National Army Museum, London

Napier Sir Charles Napier, *Defects, Civil and Military, of the Indian Government* (London, 1853)

NAS National Archives of Scotland, Edinburgh

NLS National Library of Scotland, Edinburgh

OIOC Oriental and India Office Collection, British Library, London

PP Parliamentary Papers

Roberts Field Marshal Lord Roberts of Kandahar, *Forty-one Years in India: From Subaltern to Commander-in-Chief* (London, 1898)

Roy Tapti Roy, *The Politics of a Popular Uprising: Bundelkhand in 1857* (Delhi, 1994)

RUSI *Royal United Services Institute Journal*

SC Secret Consultations

Sen S. N. Sen, *Eighteen Fifty-seven* (Delhi, 1957)

Sitaram James Lunt (ed.), *From Sepoy to Subedar: Being the Life and Adventures of Subedar Sita Ram, a Native Officer of the Bengal Army, Written and Related by Himself* (1873, this edition, 1970)

SSS Ranajit Guha and Gayatri Chakravorty Spivak (eds.), *Selected Subaltern Studies* (Oxford, 1988)

State Papers G. W. Forrest (ed.), *Selections from the Letters, Dispatches and Other State Papers Preserved in the Military Department of the Government of India 1857–1858*, 4 vols. (Calcutta, 1893–1912)

Two Native Narratives Charles T. Metcalfe (trans.), *Two Native Narratives of the Mutiny in Delhi* (London, 1898)

Tytler Anthony Sattin (ed.), *An Englishwoman in India: The Memoirs of Harriet Tytler 1828–1858* (Oxford, 1986)

Vibart Colonel Edward Vibart, *The Sepoy Mutiny* (London, 1898)

Ward Andrew Ward, *Our Bones are Scattered: The Cawnpore Massacres and the Indian Mutiny of 1857* (London, 1996)

Young General Sir Henry Norman and Mrs Keith Young (eds.), *Delhi – 1857: The Siege, Assault and Capture as Given in the Diary and Correspondence of the Late Colonel Keith Young, CB* (London, 1902)

PROLOGUE

xv *It was the start . . . 'cool'*: Loy Smith, *A Victorian RSM*, 38.

xv *It was an unofficial . . . guns*: Luke, 'How the Electric Telegraph Saved India', in Vibart, 253–5.

xvi *At eight the following . . . 'killed'*: ibid., 257–62.

xvi *'Black Hole in'*: Mr Wagentreiber's narrative, quoted in Kaye and Malleson, II, 70.

xvi–xvii *Despite his withered . . . murdered*: Luke, op. cit., 262–5.

xvii *From Ambala . . . ammunition*: Kaye and Malleson, II, 319–22.

xvii *'none of that incapacity'*: ibid., 322.

xvii–xviii *When Montgomery arrived . . . stations*: statement by Brigadier S. Corbett, PP, HC, 1859, XVIII, 48.

xviii *'The evening has'*: Lang, 31.

xviii *'The Brigadier soft-sawdered'*: ibid.

xviii–xix *Then came the critical . . . parade-ground*: ibid., 31–2.

xix *Montgomery and Corbett's*: statement by Brigadier S. Corbett, PP, HC, 1859, XVIII, 48.

xix *The previous evening . . . fled*: return of the 45th NI at the outbreak of the mutiny, 3 March 1858, ibid., 49.

xix *'disarm the native'*: Sir Herbert Edwardes, quoted in Luke, op. cit., 265–6.

xix *'The Electric Telegraph'*: D. F. MacLeod to Bartle Frere, 15 May 1857, Elphinstone Papers, OIOC, MSS Eur/F87/Box 6B/8/1.

CHAPTER ONE

1 *Its yearly sales*: James, *Raj*, 15–16.

2 *To protect its . . . European model*: Alavi, 35.

5 *'from a few scattered'*: Chesney, *Indian Polity*, 28.

6 *The Company had . . . subjects*: The East India Company waged successful campaigns against the princely states of Bharatpur in 1825–6 and Gwalior in 1843. It also put down rebellions by the Bundelas in 1841–2, Pathan tribesmen in 1850–55 and the Sonthals in 1855.

6 *But Dalhousie refused . . . 'midst of them'*: Kaye and Malleson, I, 53.

6 *'too good a "plum"'*: Dalhousie to Sir George Couper, 8 January 1854, Baird (ed.), *Dalhousie Letters*, 284.

7 *'the system of annexing'*: Kaye and Malleson, I, 98.

7 *The confiscation of Satara . . . the body*: ibid., 58–9.

7–8 *'Sunk in the uttermost'*: ibid., 95–6.

8 *Sir John Kaye*: Sir John Kaye (1814–76) served in the Bengal Artillery for nine years before joining the staff of the *Bengal Hurkaru* in 1841. Three years later he established the *Calcutta Review*. In 1856 he joined the Home Service of the East India Company, rising to Secretary of the Political and Secret Department. He had completed only three volumes of his magisterial history of the mutiny by the time of his death. The remaining three were written by Colonel G. B. Malleson.

8 *The pressure for intervention . . . 'and extreme'*: Kaye and Malleson, I, 99 and 103.

8 *'vest all power'*: ibid., 105.

8 *Sir John Kaye . . . 'the empire'*: ibid.

8 *as many as three quarters of all sepoys*: Sleeman, *Rambles and Recollections*, 624.

9 *In 1857 the total strength*: PP, HC, 1859, V, app. 17, 379.

9 *a ratio of 1:5*: The Madras Army had 10,730 European and 51,244 Indian troops; the Bombay Army 10,430 Europeans and 45,213 Indians. The breakdown for all the European troops is as follows: 6,170 officers and 38,562 other ranks (24,263 of whom were Queen's troops).

9 *The Bengal Army . . . 1:7 for Bengal*: Lawrence, *Essays, Military and Political*, 370–71; PP, HC, 1859, VIII, 13.

9 *1:7 for Bengal*: The total number of Indian troops commanded by European officers was 275,304 in India as a whole and 176,834 in Bengal.

9 *It has often been stated*: see Hibbert, 19.

9 *In fact the ratio . . . proportionately*: Philips (ed.), *Bentinck Correspondence*, II, 1450–52.

10 *British government*: In 1852 the Indian garrison contained 29 Queen's regiments. This total was reduced by three during the Crimean War, with only one added by the outbreak of the mutiny. There were, therefore, 27 Queen's regiments (4 cavalry and 23 infantry) assigned to India in May 1857: 18 to Bengal, 5 to Bombay and 4 to Madras. Each presidency had, in addition, three regiments of Company European infantry. But three of Bombay's European regiments were serving in Persia, while two of Bengal's and one of Madras's were stationed in Burma. As a result, the Bengal presidency had only 19 European regiments (2 of HM's cavalry, 14 of HM's infantry and 3 of Company infantry) located within its territory: 12 of whom were in the Punjab and the neighbouring Cis-Sutlej region.

10 'any *European infantry' . . . 'now before us'*: Dalhousie to Couper, 24 February 1858 and 6 August 1855, Baird (ed.), *Dalhousie Letters*, 405 and 351.

CHAPTER TWO

11 *the Governor-General received . . . the Queen's birthday*: Maclagan, 38–9.

11 *Dalhousie considered . . . 'savings in hand'*: Lord Canning's Diary, 2 March 1856, quoted in Maclagan, 44.

11–12 *'I wish for a peaceful term'*: Fitzmaurice, I, 125.

12 *'He was handsome'*: ibid., 409–10.

12–13 *'More cocoa and palm trees'*: Majendie, *Up Among the Pandies*, 21–2.

13 *'long, low river steamers' . . . 'silks or indigo'*: ibid., 23, 28 and 31–2.

13–14 *'Dalhousie was on'*: Lord Canning's Diary, 29 February 1856, quoted in Maclagan, 43–4.

14 *Canning admired . . . in Calcutta*: Hibbert, 25; Maclagan, 44.

14 *'little better than a galley slave' . . . 'impracticable'*: Canning to Granville, 2 April 1856, quoted in Fitzmaurice, I, 151.

14 *'Any attempt to go out'*: Hibbert, 26.

14–15 *'as all day'*: Dunkellin to Lady Clanricarde, 3 July 1856, quoted in Maclagan, 57.

15 *'assumed the appearance'*: Hibbert, 27.

15 *'The free and easy'*: Dunkellin to Lord Clanricarde, 17 June 1856, quoted in Maclagan, 57.

15 *'creaking footmen' . . . 'very underbred'*: Hibbert, 28.

15–16 *'Aunt C.'*: Dunkellin to Lady Clanricarde, 3 July 1856, quoted in Maclagan, 57.

16 *'rather pasty' . . . with his meals*: Dunkellin to Lord and Lady Clanricarde, 17 June and 3 July 1856, ibid., 56–7.

16 *'a civilian from the North-West Provinces'*: Kaye and Malleson, I, 292.

16 *'Noble and peasant'*: W. Crooke, 'Songs about the King of Oudh', *Indian Antiquary*, XL, 62, quoted in Mukherjee, 36.

16–17 *As most Indian revenue . . . respectively*: Mukherjee, 40, 43 and 54.

17 *'a tough, no-nonsense'*: Allen, 47.

17 *'When anything mean' . . . 'half-naked'*: Lawrence, *Lawrence of Lucknow*, 19–20.

18 *'a summary and equitable'*: *State Papers*, II, intro., 11–12.

18 *'Above the middle height'*: Kaye and Malleson, I, 7.

CHAPTER THREE

19 *'Na Iran ne'*: Taylor, *Companion*, 33.

19 *Historians have tended*: Many scholars believe the mutiny was simply a reflection of tensions within Indian society. The sepoys were an integral part of peasant society, they argue, and were therefore susceptible to the same social, economic and religious preoccupations that affected civilians. Seen in this light, the mutiny was little more than a precursor to a general revolt by disaffected elements of the native population. Yet such a viewpoint loses sight of the fact that the mutiny was, first and foremost, a military uprising and that, without it, the civil rebellion would not have taken place. See: Chaudhuri, *Civil Rebellion in the Indian Mutinies*; Stokes, *The Peasant and the Raj* and *The Peasant Armed*; Bayly, *Rulers, Townsmen and Bazaars*; Mukherjee, *Awadh in Revolt* and 'Satan Let Loose upon the Earth', 92–116.

19 *composed of Gurkhas*: The 21st, 31st and 66th (Gurkhas) regiments of Bengal Native Infantry.

19 *native infantry regiments*: The 12th, 21st and 27th regiments of Bombay Native Infantry.

19 *the Madras Army*: Lord Harris to Robert Vernon Smith, 27 August 1857, Lyveden Papers, OIOC, MSS Eur/F231/5.

20 *'drilled and disciplined' . . . find employers*: Kolff, 177–8 and 87.

20 *Most of these new recruits . . . 'rule'*: Alavi, 45.

20 *marriage*: According to N. K. Dutt, there are now more than 3,000 castes in India, some 'confined to a few score men', while others claim 'millions of members'. See Dutt, *Origin and Growth of Caste in India*, I, 3–4.

21 *'not scrupulous in admitting'*: Kolff, 185.

21 *'The boundaries between'*: Susan Bayly, *The New Cambridge History of India*, IV:3, 188.

21 *As the nineteenth century . . . appeared*: ibid., 190, 197, 201.

21 *The same could be said . . . Bengal Army*: Kolff, 185.

21–2 *As Seema Alavi . . . 'sanskritization of the military'*: Alavi, 45 and 76.

22 *'acted as the guarantor'*: ibid., 48.

22 *'My uncle'*: Sitaram, 4–5.

22 *In 1815*: Barat, 122.

22 *newly raised battalion*: The breakdown was as follows: Brahmans, 392 (43.9 per cent); Rajputs, 304 (34.1 per cent); Hindus of inferior caste, 108 (12.1 per cent); Muslims, 92 (10.3 per cent).

22 *Yet by 1842*: Barat, 123.

22 *around two thirds*: The breakdown was as follows: Rajputs, 27,993 (34.9 per cent); Brahmans, 24,480 (31.0 per cent); Hindus of inferior caste, 13,920 (17.3 per cent); Muslims, 12,411 (15.4 per cent); Christians, 1,076 (1.3 per cent).

22–3 *'men belonging'*: GOGG, 31 December 1834, Abstract of General Orders from 1817 to 1840, OIOC, L/MIL/17/2/435.

23 *Sir Charles Napier . . . 'mutinous spirit'*: Napier, 38.

23 *'I resolved to show'*: ibid., 130.

23 *'never to exceed 200'*: Bengal Army Regulations 1855, OIOC, L/MIL/17/2/442, 215.

23 *The high-caste monopoly . . . general service*: GOGG, 25 July 1856, quoted in PP, HC, 1859, V, app. 14, 376.

24 *recruited for general service*: The six regiments of Bengal Native Infantry were the 27th, 47th and 65th, which were then at Pegu, and the 40th, 67th and 68th, which had all served there as recently as 1854.

24 *The General Service . . . mutiny*: See Hibbert, 54, and Kaye and Malleson, I, 344.

24 *'Not a murmur'*: Canning to Vernon Smith, 23 March 1857, Lyveden Papers, OIOC, MSS Eur/F231/4.

24 *'The General Service Enlistment'*: Anderson (ed.), *The Last Days of the Company*, I, 109–10.

24 *'the old race of [sepoys]'*: Kaye and Malleson, I, 345.

24 *On 21 April . . . 52.6 per cent*: *State Papers*, I, 177.

24 *just 52.6 per cent*: The breakdown was as follows: Brahmans, 335 (30.8 per cent); Rajputs, 237 (21.8 per cent); Muslims, 237 (21.8 per cent); Hindus of inferior caste, 231 (21.2 per cent); Sikhs, 74 (6.8 per cent); Christians, 12 (1.1 per cent).

24 *There are no figures . . . high caste*: evidence of Lieutenant-Colonel Durand, PP, HC, 1859, V, app. 71.

24 *57 per cent were high caste*: The breakdown was as follows: Rajputs, 6,635 (28.6 per cent); Brahmans, 6,549 (28.2 per cent); Hindus of

inferior caste (18.8 per cent); Muslims, 4,214 (18.2 per cent); Gurkhas, 590 (2.5 per cent); Christians, 511 (2.2 per cent); Sikhs and Punjabis, 327 (1.4 per cent).

24 *'He was a Hindu'*: Barat, 125–6.

25 *'was composed of Mahommedans'*: PP, HC, 1859, V, app. 71, 536–7.

25 *reversing this trend*: In summing up the apprehensions of the 19th and 34th regiments of native infantry at Lucknow during the annexation of Oudh in early 1856, Pandit Kanhyalal, a nineteenth-century scholar, wrote: 'They were discontented because they thought their rights had been taken away from them, and were angry over the introduction of Punjabi and Sikh soldiers in the army.' See Pandit Kanhyalal, *Tarikh-i-baghawat-i-hind, 1857* (Kanpur, 6th edition, 1916), quoted in Alavi, 295–6. Eric Stokes reached the same conclusion. 'The "closed shop" of the *Purbias* (easterners) of the middle Ganges was under obvious threat,' he wrote, 'and with it all those privileges of "home service" and a certain independent negotiating power characteristic of mercenary armies. Hence solid material fears underlay the apprehension over any infringement of caste rules by British authority.' Stokes also believed, unlike Barat, that the main reason the high-caste sepoys were so determined to 'retain their monopolistic grip on the Bengal regiments' was because 'military service was often the only honourable escape for men from families whose "ownership" of the land had failed to keep pace with growing numbers, and who were steadily being forced down into the position of the humbler tillers of the soil' (Stokes, *The Peasant Armed*, 50–51).

25 *'lived in cantonments'*: Roy, 49–50.

25 *Lord Elphinstone . . . 'rest followed'*: Lord Elphinstone's minute of 21 September 1857, PP, HC, 1859, V, app. 67, 501.

25 *By 1857*: evidence of Lieutenant-Colonel Harington, 24 August 1858, PP, HC, 1859, V, 48. Lieutenant-Colonel Harington told the Peel Commission that his regiment – the 5th Bengal Light Cavalry – was composed of roughly 'one-fourth Mussulmans and two thirds Brahmins, of the fighting class, and the others a lower class'.

25 *The members of . . . (and always had been)*: PP, HC, 1859, V, app. 65, 490.

25 *Their proportion . . . 57 per cent*: PP, HC, 1859, V, app. 22, 382.

26 *helped them to escape*: The only murders that appear to have been carried out by artillerymen were those of a European staff sergeant's wife and three children by the Golundaz of the 4th Troop, 1st Brigade, Bengal Horse Artillery, at Nimach on 3 June 1857. Source: 'List of Regiments and Detachments of the Native Army which have taken part in the Mutinies', 11 August 1858, FC, NAI, Nos. 1753–4 of 30 December 1859.

26 *Bengal counterpart*: The Madras Army was dominated by Muslims

and Telingas from the Madras provinces of northern Circars, and the central and southern Carnatics. Fewer than one in twenty Madras soldiers were high-caste Hindus, with around the same proportion recruited from the Bengal Presidency. This absence of a common link with the Bengal soldiers is reflected in the fact that only two Madras units – the 8th Light Cavalry and 36th Native Infantry – showed any signs of a mutinous disposition in 1857.

26 *supplied the Bengal Army*: Of the Bombay Army's 29,000 regular troops, a quarter were high-caste Hindus and almost one in two were from the traditional recruiting grounds of the Bengal Presidency. Given the close ties of country and caste that bound many Bombay and Bengal sepoys, the fact that the Bombay cavalry was dominated by Hindustani Muslims to whom the re-establishment of the Mogul Emperor at Delhi was expected to appeal, and the likelihood that the Maratha element – the biggest single group in the native infantry – might well have sympathized with rebel Maratha princes like Nana Sahib (who declared himself Peshwa) and the former ruling families of Satara, Baroda, Kolhapur, it is surprising that more mutinies did not take place in the Bombay Army. Instead a large number of Bombay units played a key role in suppressing mutiny.

26 *'a heavy unwieldy* thing': Allen (ed.), *A Soldier of the Company*, 148.

26 *'At first I found'*: Sitaram, 23.

26–7 *'On his back' . . . black leather stock*: Allen (ed.), *A Soldier of the Company*, 148–9.

27 *Sitaram found his musket 'very heavy'*: Sitaram, 23.

27 *The Madras officer noted*: Allen (ed.), *A Soldier of the Company*, 148.

27 *There were many calls*: See *Delhi Gazette*, 24 April 1852; *The Times*, 12 January 1853; Pelly (ed.), *Views and Opinions*, 129.

27–8 *'campaigns were waged'*: Barat, 155.

28 *'relics of barbarism' . . . 'decimated by disease'*: Smith, *Florence Nightingale*, 48.

28 *Given that the cost of living*: Barat, 313.

29 *By contrast . . . 20 rupees*: ibid., 138–9.

29 *A private . . . capital*: Pay and Audit Regulations 1849, OIOC, L/MIL/17/2/459, 147.

29 *while a private . . . good conduct*: Strachan, *Wellington's Legacy*, 69–70.

29 *'of some serious offence'*: GOGG, 17 April 1837, Abstract of General Orders from 1817 to 1840, OIOC, L/MIL/17/2/435; GOGG, 5 May 1837, ibid.

29 *New pension regulations . . . than done*: GOGG, 17 April 1837, ibid.

29 *'There is no chance'*: Colonel K. Young to Colonel H. B. Henderson, 2 May 1857, in Young, 10.

29–30 *They were charged . . . a month*: Barat, 136–7, 177.

30 *Above all . . . 'social obligations'*: Barat, 173–4, 177.

30 *In an essay published in 1844 . . . own horse*: Lawrence, *Essays, Military and Political*, 32–3.

30–31 *Other experienced officers*: ibid., 412; Pelly (ed.), *Views and Opinions*, 155–6; evidence of Lord Gough, 14 March 1853, PP, HC, 1852–3, XXVII, 123.

31 *'owed nearly £10,000'*: evidence of Lieutenant-Colonel Harington, 24 August 1858, PP, HC, 1859, V, 47.

31 *Writing in the* Calcutta Review ... *third generations*: Lawrence, *Essays, Military and Political*, 27–8, 57.

31–2 *To allow a veteran ... 'military'*: Napier, 255–7.

32 *'until we treat'*: *State Papers*, II, 6.

32 *'hard wear and tear' ... 'years earlier'*: Sitaram, 172.

32 *The subedar-major*: evidence of Lieutenant-Colonel Robert Master, 24 August 1858, PP, HC, 1859, V, 59.

32 *unavoidable outcome*: Pelly (ed.), *Views and Opinions*, 211.

32–3 *'dangerously discontented'*: Lawrence, *Essays, Military and Political*, 395.

33 *'preferring inefficiency'*: Hardinge to Sir Charles Napier, 31 October 1844, Napier Papers, BL, Add. MSS 54517, f. 104.

CHAPTER FOUR

34 *'well-educated, hardy'*: Allen, 10–11.

34 *'People do not come here'*: Jacquemont, *Letters from India*, 23.

34 *'from the "pseudo-gentry"'*: Bourne, 'Civil and Military Patronage', Ph.D. thesis, 172.

35 *'offered an accessible'*: ibid., 194 and 200.

35 *A newly commissioned ... normal pay*: Pay and Audit Regulations, 1849, OIOC, L/MIL/17/2/459, 124c, 222a and 273.

35 *'Financial considerations'*: Bourne, op. cit., 210–11.

35 *'trifles of more use' ... 'perfunctory'*: ibid., 254, 258–9.

35 *'My education consisted in kicks'*: Edwardes and Merivale, *The Life of Sir Henry Lawrence*, 20.

35 *'slavish devotion'*: Bourne, op. cit., 236 and 250.

36 *In 1835 the total ... three and a half*: evidence of Philip Melvill, 14 December 1852, PP, HC, 1852–3, XXVII, 9–10.

36 *At the outset of the mutiny*: Colonel Holland's memo, PP, HC, 1859, V, app. 7, 371.

36 *If officers on sick leave ... 'company duty'*: memo by Lieutenant-General Sir Patrick Grant to the Governor-General, 29 June 1857, PP, HC, 1859, V, app. 66, 497.

36 *'any clever officer'*: Sitaram, 77.

36 *One of the reasons ... 'painful task'*: Napier, 195 and 197.

36 *'I was awfully disappointed'*: Hall Papers, NAM, '1857' (54)/11919, 4.

36–7 *'The "REFUSE" only remain' ... to each regiment*: Pelly (ed.), *Views and Opinions*, 124, 126 and 130–32.

37 *'want of officers' ... 'don't bother me!'*: memo by Lieutenant-General Sir Patrick Grant to the Governor-General, 29 June 1857, PP, HC, 1859, V, app. 66, 496.

37 *'did credit to [his master's]'*: quoted in Hibbert, 30.

38 *'Smoking, drinking'*: Allen (ed.), *A Soldier of the Company*, 30.

38 *'Ladies' society there is none'*: Trotter, *Hodson of Hodson's Horse*, 39.

38 *'My disgraceful laziness'*: Johnson Diaries, OIOC, MSS Eur/A101.

38 *'The* sahibs*'* . . . *'his children'*: Sitaram, 24.

39 *'The root of the problem'* . . . *'natives'*: Robinson, *Angels of Albion*, 13.

39 *'I have lived'*: Sitaram, 24–5.

39 *It is surely no coincidence*: Service Records, Hodson Index, NAM.

39 *'small by degrees'* . . . *'to the devil'*: *United Service Magazine*, August 1853.

40 *'now more numerous'* . . . *'Indian renown'*: Napier, 239–40, 248 and 250.

40 *'The sepoy is esteemed'*: quoted in Sen, 23.

40 *leading up to the mutiny*: It was not a problem confined to Bengal. According to one Madras officer, many young cadets arrived in India with scant respect for the natives, referring to their men as '*those horrible black nigger sepoys*', and cursing them on parade. That said, he also gave many examples of the close bond that existed between the officers and men of his second regiment: of cricket matches, hunting expeditions and picnics enjoyed by both, and of one incident when a sepoy saved his adjutant's life by tackling a cheetah armed only with a knife (Allen, ed., *A Soldier of the Company*, 38, 103–4). This cordiality was partly due to the fact that English was much more commonly spoken in Madras than in other parts of India, making communication between sepoys and officers easier. In Bombay too the pre-mutiny relationship between officers and men was not always harmonious. In a letter to the governor of 22 January 1854, the Commander-in-Chief contrasted the ignorance with which his officers went about their duty with the 'intelligence and knowledge of the sepoy' and concluded that such a state of affairs was '*dangerous* to the Empire'. His solution was to extend the examination for extra-regimental military appointments – which tested officers on the duty of more senior ranks – to civil appointments as well. He had already instituted examinations for adjutants, for company commanders and even for newly joined officers (Elphinstone Papers, OIOC, MSS Eur/F87/Box 7A/26). These reforms undoubtedly improved the efficiency and knowledge of his officers and, by extension, their relationship with their men.

40 *'Seldom is anything'*: Lawrence, *Essays, Military and Political*, 398–9.

41 *In 1857 the average age* . . . *seniority*: David, 115–16.

41 *fifty years respectively*: In May 1857 the average age of the Bengal major-generals was 66.4 years: the youngest was 64 (John Hearsey) and the eldest 68 (George Gowan). The average age of the Bengal brigadiers was 55.6: the youngest was 51 (Alexander Jack) and the eldest was 66 (Hugh Sibbald). The average age of the 74 officers commanding regiments of Bengal

Native Infantry was 50.5 years, though this figure includes 23 officers in temporary command: the eldest was 61 (Lieutenant-Colonel John Liptrap of the 45th NI) and the youngest 35 (Major John Shakespear of the 24th NI). The average age of the 10 officers commanding regiments of Bengal Light Cavalry was 49.7 years: the eldest was 53 (Brevet Lieutenant-Colonel Barton of the 6th LC) and the youngest 42 (Major Alfred Harris of the 1st LC).

41 *rather than seniority*: The average age of the 18 officers commanding regiments of Bengal Irregular Cavalry was 39.7 years: the eldest was 52 (Brevet Major Verner of the 10th IC) and the youngest 23 (Lieutenant James Campbell of the 14th IC).

41 *strangers to their men*: In May 1857, 31 of the 74 regiments of Bengal Native Infantry were commanded by men who had been present for less than five of the previous twenty years. Statistically, a regiment was more prone to mutiny if it was commanded by an unfamiliar face. If, on the other hand, it had a commander who had been with it for more than ten of the previous twenty years, it was more likely to stay loyal or allow itself to be disarmed. See David, 112–13.

41 *new commanding officers . . . 'next'*: Sitaram, 77.

41 *An even more important . . . 'Governor-General'*: Stokes, *The English Utilitarians*, 55, 51.

42 *By 1845 . . . accoutrements*: Articles of War, Act No. XX of 6 September 1845, OIOC, V/8/32.

42 *'I saw very great laxity'*: Lieutenant-Colonel R. Drought to Major Ewart, 23 March 1858, PP, HC, 1859, XVIII, 63.

43 *'young men' . . . 'whole service'*: Philips (ed.), *Bentinck Correspondence*, II, 1430–31.

43 *'We might as well pretend'*: Strachan, *Wellington's Legacy*, 81.

43 *After much lobbying . . . 'the army'*: resolution of the Supreme Council of India, 30 August 1845, replies by Major-General R. J. H. Birch, 28 August 1858, PP, HC, 1859, V, app. 61, 436.

43 *particularly Bengal*: During the period 1850 to 1854 the lash was inflicted upon an average of just 24 Bengal, 20 Madras and 12 Bombay sepoys per annum. Given the relative size of the regular Bengal Army – two and a half times that of Madras and three times that of Bombay – it had by far the lowest annual incidence of corporal punishment: an average of one in 5,000, compared with one in 2,500 in Madras and one in 3,300 in Bombay. By contrast, the average annual incidence of flogging in the pre-abolition period of 1829 to 1833 was about one in 100 in the Bengal Army (50 times greater), one in 33 in the Madras Army (75 times greater) and one in 20 in the Bombay Army (150 times greater). The frequency of corporal punishment after reintroduction, therefore, was much, much lower. See India Military Consultations,

OIOC, P/43/37, P/44/18 and P/45/59, No. 5 of 30 April 1852, No. 333 of 4 April 1853 and No. 41 of 13 April 1855. See also David, 132–3.

43 *'As long as [the lash]'*: evidence of Lieutenant-Colonel R. Master, PP, HC, 1859, V, 61.

43 *According to Brigadier Coke . . . 'the mutiny'*: replies of Lieutenant-Colonel H. M. Durand, 4 September 1858, PP, HC, 1859, V, app. 71, 557.

43–4 *'lackadaisical, discontented'*: *United Service Gazette*, 21 February 1857.

44 *'fake and hollow' . . . 'proper authority'*: Francis Lind to his mother, 31 May 1857, Lind Papers, NAM, 5108–4.

44 *Giving evidence . . . 'large army'*: evidence of Major-General Sir S. Cotton, PP, HC, 1859, V, app. 72, 557.

44 *white officers*: Rudrangshu Mukherjee wrote: 'Throughout the previous century of colonial rule the sepoys had seen how harshly their masters dealt with the sepoys' own crimes and misdemeanours. Their movement, like other movements of the "lower orders" of society, could hardly fail to learn from the example set by social superiors' (Mukherjee, 72).

44 *'The principal cause'*: Sitaram, 174.

CHAPTER FIVE

45 *'In all mutinies'*: Napier, 61–2.

45 *'thorough system of espionage'*: Lieutenant-Colonel Burroughs to Captain I. H. Chamberlain, January 1860, *Freedom Struggle*, I, 347.

46 *'twenty-five chiming clocks'*: Ward, 34.

46 *Baji Rao died . . . public securities*: ibid., 38–9.

46–7 *Lang's recollection . . . skullcap*: Lang, *Wanderings in India*, 104–8.

47 *'an excessively uninteresting person'*: quoted in Ward, 54.

47 *Nana began . . . 'not a grievance'*: Lang, *Wanderings in India*, 113–18.

47–8 *'He was not a servant' . . . 'to some advantage'*: ibid., 410–11.

48 *But Azimullah would not submit . . . trusted advisers*: Ward, 23–6.

48–9 *As such he was sent to London . . . 'get burned'*: ibid., 40–45.

49 *'handsome, slim young man' . . . 'that of the French'*: Russell, *My Diary in India*, I, 165–8.

49 *'[The] news was always fabricated'*: Sitaram, 73.

50 *Mahomed Ali later claimed . . . 'Company's Government'*: Forbes-Mitchell, *The Relief of Lucknow*, 110–11.

50 *the 'worthy couple'*: Russell, *My Diary in India*, I, 170.

50 *Corroboration of Nana's scheming . . . 'of Government'*: statement of Sitaram Bawa to H. B. Devereux, 28 January 1858, *Freedom Struggle*, I, 372–6.

50–51 *Kaye . . . was convinced*: Kaye and Malleson, I, 425.

51 *Kaye believed that the Nana*: ibid., 423.

51 *He began by requesting . . . 'the north'*: Nana Sahib to Azimullah Khan, 30 December 1856, Miscellaneous Papers, OIOC, MSS Eur/B147.

51 *The answer was soon . . . 'the Ex King'*: Captain E. M. Martineau to Sir John Kaye, 20 October 1864, Kaye Mutiny Papers, OIOC, H725, 469–70.

CHAPTER SIX

52 *Over the next decade or so*: Harding, *Smallarms of the East India Company*, I, 232–3, 239.

52 *'unserviceable and should be replaced'*: ibid., 123–44; Colonel A. Abbott to Colonel R. J. H. Birch, 7 April 1856, and Birch to Abbott, 25 April 1856, India Military Consultations, OIOC, P/43/36, Nos. 194 and 195 of 25 April 1856.

52 *A total of 12,000 Enfields*: Birch to Abbott, 29 April 1857, ibid., OIOC, P/47/18, No. 81 of 19 June 1857.

52 *musketry depots*: The distribution of Enfield rifles in the Bengal Presidency as of 29 April 1857 was as follows: HM 60th Rifles, 1,040; Fort William, 4,395; Allahabad, 3,000; Ferozepore, 3,000; School of Musketry, 525; Delhi, 41.

53 *Enfield rifle*: The two-grooved Brunswick rifle had been used by the 60th Rifles and rifle companies in some Indian infantry regiments since the early 1840s. Its ammunition consisted of a powder cartridge and a separate ball covered with a 'patch' of fine cloth smeared with beeswax and coconut oil. This grease was inoffensive to both Hindus and Muslims.

53 *In 1853 . . . to report on them*: Kaye and Malleson, I, 379–80.

53 *Instead the same combination*: evidence of Lieutenant M. E. Currie, commissary of ordnance, 23 March 1857, PP, HC, 1857, XXX, 261; memorandum by J. G. Bonner, inspector-general of stores, 23 March 1857, ibid., 4.

53–4 *The origin of the rumour . . . 'caste be?'*: Major-General J. B. Hearsey to Colonel R. J. H. Birch, 11 February 1857, *State Papers*, I, 25.

54 *A report of the incident . . . north of Calcutta*: Major J. Bontein to the station staff officer, 23 January 1857, ibid., 2–3.

54 *'There could hardly'*: Kaye and Malleson, I, 385.

54 *'totally groundless'*: Hearsey to Major W. A. J. Mayhew, 24 January 1857, *State Papers*, I, 1–2.

54 *'to apply, with their own hands'*: Colonel R. J. H. Birch to Mayhew, 27 January 1857, Birch to Colonel C. Chester, PP, HC, 1857, XXX, 37–9.

54 *'a mixture of tallow' . . . tallow was necessary*: evidence of Lieutenant Currie and Colonel A. Abbott, 23 March 1857, PP, HC, 1857, 261.

54 *'turned out to be'*: Lyveden Papers, OIOC, MSS Eur/F231/4.

54–5 *In March the officer . . . 'other animals'*: evidence of Lieutenant Currie and Colonel A. Abbott, 23 March 1857, PP, HC, 1857, XXX, 261.

55 *Moreover, no greased cartridges*: evidence of Major J. Bontein, 18 March 1857, PP, HC, 1857, XXX, 259.

55 *At a subsequent court*: proceedings of a Special Court of Inquiry, 6

February 1857, *State Papers*, I, 7–13.

55 *Suspicions had arisen*: evidence of Major J. Bontein and Lieutenant M. E. Currie, 18 March 1857, PP, HC, 1857, XXX, 259–60.

55 *Canning suspected*: Canning to Vernon Smith, 22 February 1857, Lyveden papers, OIOC, MSS Eur/F231/4.

55 *The first definite signs . . . refused to cooperate*: evidence of Jemadar Darriow Sing, 17 April 1857, *State Papers*, I, 156–60.

56 *General Hearsey reported*: Hearsey to Major W. A. J. Mayhew, 28 January 1857, *State Papers*, I, 4–5.

56 *'Both these regiments'*: *Two Native Narratives*, 37–9.

56 *'would enable the applicant'*: Colonel Sleeman to C. Allen, 14 October 1852, India Military Consultations, OIOC, P/43/61, No. 375 of 5 November 1852; GOGG, 16 February 1853, Abstract of General Orders from 1848 to 1853, OIOC, L/MIL/17/2/437.

56–7 *'present bad feeling' . . . 'pipes in my face'*: Anderson (ed.), *The Last Days of the Company*, I, 110.

57 *Sitaram Pandy later admitted*: Sitaram, 161.

57 *The commanding officer of the 17th*: Burroughs to Chamberlain, January 1860, *Freedom Struggle*, I, 342.

57 *'Brahmins or agents'*: Hearsey to Major W. A. J. Mayhew, 28 January 1857, *State Papers*, I, 4–5.

57 *'I cannot say' . . . 'Oude herd'*: Canning to Vernon Smith, 7 February and 23 March 1857, Lyveden Papers, OIOC, MSS Eur/F231/4.

57–8 *'Rajah Maun Sing'*: Hearsey to Colonel R. J. H. Birch, 5 April 1857, Mutiny Papers, BL, Add. MSS 41489, f. 78.

58 *In a letter to government*: Hearsey to Birch, 11 February 1857, *State Papers*, I, 24.

58 *'informing them that ten'*: statement by Major H. W. Matthews, 12 February 1857, ibid., 29–30.

58 *less than eighteen months*: Service Records, Hodson Index, NAM.

58–9 *Matters came to a head . . . to their lines*: Lieutenant-Colonel W. Mitchell to Major Ross, 27 February 1857, *State Papers*, I, 41.

59 *During the subsequent . . . and the guns*: *State Papers*, I, 45–7.

59–60 *The reference . . . Dickinson & Co*: Harding, 'Arming the East India Company's Forces', in Guy and Boyden (eds.), *Soldiers of the Raj*, 145.

60 *'seduced from without'*: Canning to Vernon Smith, 11 March 1857, Lyveden Papers, OIOC, MSS Eur/F231/4.

60 *In two petitions . . . cause of the mutiny*: *State Papers*, I, 103–4.

60 *In May, for example . . . the 17th mutinied soon after*: return by Major F. W. Burroughs, 4 June 1857, PP, HC, 1859, XVIII, 25.

61 *'had threatened them'*: Hearsey to Colonel R. J. H. Birch, 4 April 1857, Mutiny Papers, BL, Add. MSS 41489, f. 73.

61 *On the morning of 16 March . . . 22nd regiments*: Captain E. M. Martineau to Sir John Kaye, 20 October 1864, Kaye Mutiny Papers, OIOC, H725, 1023–4.

62 *'good sense and tact' . . . 'excellent judge of character'*: Elphinstone to Sir Charles Wood, 14 November 1854, Wood Papers, OIOC, MSS Eur/F78/82B; Roberts, 50.

62 *Canning found him a disappointment*: Canning to Lord Granville, 3 June 1856, quoted in Fitzmaurice, I, 150.

62 *'His temper is charming'*: Canning to Vernon Smith, 17 June 1856, quoted in Maclagan, 55.

62 *Martineau conducted . . . anything but sound*: Lieutenant E. M. Martineau to Captain S. H. Becher, AAG, 20 March 1857, Martineau Letters, OIOC, MSS Eur/C571.

63 *'utterly groundless'*: Becher to Colonel R. J. H. Birch, 25 March 1857, India Military Consultations, OIOC, P/47/11, No. 335 of 3 April 1857.

63 *'universally credited' . . . 'to our Rule'*: Lieutenant E. M. Martineau to Captain S. H. Becher, 23 March 1857, Martineau Letters, OIOC, MSS Eur/C571.

63 *'laughed at it'*: examination of Captain E. M. Martineau, 23 February 1858, PP, HC, 1859, XVIII, 210.

63 *'The "Cartridge" question'*: Anson to Elphinstone, 29 March 1857, Elphinstone Papers, OIOC, MSS Eur/F87/Box 11B/18.

63 *Yet he accepted*: Captain S. H. Becher to Colonel R. J. H. Birch, 25 March 1857, India Military Consultations, OIOC, P/47/11, No. 335 of 3 April 1857.

63 *'unvarying rule of the Government'*: *State Papers*, I, 94–7.

63 *In mid March*: Lieutenant E. M. Martineau to Captain S. H. Becher, 20 March 1857, Martineau Letters, OIOC, MSS Eur/C571.

64 *'I was excessively startled'*: Martineau to Sir John Kaye, 20 October 1864, Kaye Mutiny Papers, OIOC, H725, 1023.

64 *According to W. H. Carey . . . at Cawnpore*: Carey, *The Mahomedan Rebellion*, 27–8.

64 *The fact that the mills*: *Freedom Struggle*, I, 396.

64 *It was taken so seriously*: ibid., II, 22.

64–5 *'dirty little cakes' . . . 'for the time forgotten'*: Thornhill, *Personal Adventures*, 2–3.

65 *said to have originated*: Kaye and Malleson, I, 420–21.

65 *One official estimated*: Harvey, *Narrative of Events*, 4.

65 *Sir Syed Ahmed Khan pointed out*: Khan, *An Essay on the Causes of the Indian Revolt*, 3.

65 *'an invitation to the whole country'*: examination of Chuni, 9 February 1858, PP, HC, 1859, XVIII, 195.

65 *'significant of some greater disturbance'*: *Two Native Narratives*, 39–41.

65 *one food and one faith*: examination of Jat Mall, 3 February 1858, PP, HC, 1859, XVIII, 184.

65 *'the sepoys of every regiment'*: examination of Captain E. M. Martineau, 23 February 1858, ibid., 210.

65 *'They all think'*: quoted in Maclagan, 67.

65 *'various speculations'*: Thomson, *The Story of Cawnpore*, 24.

65–6 *'few who remembered'*: Thornhill, *Personal Adventures*, 2.

66 *'firm conviction'*: Sneyd Papers,

OIOC, MSS Eur/Photo.Eur.44, 25.

66 *'in some way a signal'*: Mackenzie, 'The Outbreak at Meerut', quoted in Vibart, 216–17.

66 *'some bearing upon'*: Harvey, *Narrative of Events*, 4.

CHAPTER SEVEN

67 *Eliza Sneyd . . . civil surgeon*: Sneyd Papers, OIOC, MSS Eur/Photo. Eur.44, 1–11.

67 *civil surgeon*: Only four of the many guests who attended the Hutchinsons' wedding at the picturesque church in Shahjahanpur would survive the mutiny.

67–8 *In the spring . . . reached her destination*: Sneyd Papers, OIOC, MSS, Eur/Photo.Eur.44, 21–2, 25–6, 36–7.

68–9 *'night after night' . . . family to Cawnpore*: Horne Narrative, BL, Add. MSS 41488 ff. 53–6.

69 *In the late afternoon . . . collapsed under him*: testimony of Sergeant-Major J. Hewson, 6 April 1857, *State Papers*, I, 117–18.

69 *Having extricated himself . . . 'engaged the prisoner'*: testimonies of Lieutenant B. H. Baugh and Havildar (late Sepoy) Shaik Pultoo, 6 and 9 April 1857, ibid., 121 and 130.

70 *'Mungul Pandy made a cut'*: testimony of Sergeant-Major J. T. Hewson, 6 April 1857, ibid., 118–19.

70 *He and Hewson were saved . . . if he did not*: testimony of Havildar Shaik Pultoo, 6 and 9 April, ibid.

70 *Colonel Steven Wheler . . . 'to the Brigadier'*: testimony of Colonel S. G. Wheler, 30 March 1857, ibid., 147–8.

70–71 *By now word . . . 'to the hospital'*: Major-General J. B. Hearsey to Colonel R. J. H. Birch, 8 April 1857, ibid., 109–12.

72 *'Come out, you* bhainchutes*'*: testimony of Havildar Shaik Pultoo, 6 April 1857, ibid., 124.

72 *the 'guns and Europeans'*: ibid., 9 April 1857, ibid., 129–30.

72 *'Nikul ao, pultun'*: testimony of Sergeant-Major J. T. Hewson, 6 April 1857, ibid., 119.

72 *Mungul himself admitted*: interrogation of Mungul Pandy, 4 April 1857, ibid., 108.

72 *one sepoy told Colonel Wheler*: testimony of Colonel S. G. Wheler, 30 March 1857, ibid., 147–8.

72 *bad 'opinion of their comrades'*: evidence of Captain Drury, ibid., 150.

72 *'natives of all classes'*: Wheler to the Officiating Brigade-Major, 4 April 1857, PP, HC, 1857, XXX, 202.

72 *'not fit to command'*: Canning to Vernon Smith, 9 April 1857, Lyveden Papers, OIOC, MSS Eur/F231/5.

73 *'by what law'*: *Friend of India*, 13 April 1857.

73 *the 'least likely way'*: *Bengal Hurkaru*, 19 April 1857.

73 *did not think 'they cared'*: examination of Captain E. M. Martineau, 23 February 1858, PP, HC, 1859, XVIII, 210.

73 *could be 'traced'*: Anson to Lord Elphinstone, 10 May 1857, Elphinstone Papers, OIOC, MSS Eur/F87/Box 6A/No. 4.

73 *'no reason to suppose' . . . 'from Government'*: *Bengal Hurkaru*, 28 and 29 May 1857.

73 *In 1813 . . . should be funded*: Jones, *The New Cambridge History of India*, III:1, 27.

73 *'who may be interpreters'*: quoted in Stokes, *English Utilitarians in India*, 46.

73–4 *Already a new Anglicized . . . age of twenty-two*: Jones, *The New Cambridge History of India*, III:1, 28–9.

74 *'positively ordered'*: Hearsey to Birch, 8 April 1857, Mutiny Papers, BL, Add. MSS 41489, f. 85.

74 *'The Prisoner shouted out'*: Hearsey to Birch, 21 April 1857, ibid., ff. 113–14.

74 *disbanded on 6 May*: There were ten exceptions to the disbandment order: three Indian officers (including Shaik Pultoo who had been promoted to jemadar), three NCOs and four sepoys.

75 *'admitted the justice'*: Birch to Colonel C. Chester, 3 April 1857, India Military Consultations, OIOC, P/47/11, No. 346 of 3 April 1857.

75 *'I have had a very mauvais'*: Canning to Lord Granville, 9 April 1857, quoted in Fitzmaurice, I, 245.

75–6 *'not later than June' . . . Company infantry*: Canning to Vernon Smith, 9 and 22 April 1857, Lyveden Papers, OIOC, MSS Eur/F231/5.

76 *The Indian troops*: examination of Captain E. M. Martineau, 23 February 1858, PP, HC, 1859, XVIII, 210.

76 *continued on into May*: The targets included the depot hospital, a barrack in the European lines, an empty bungalow, a European officer's stables and huts belonging to two high-caste Indian officers and a havildar from the 5th Native Infantry, who, according to their colonel, had 'fired the new cartridges without demur' because there was 'nothing objectionable in them'. See Captain E. W. E. Howard to G. C. Barnes, 4 May 1857, PP, HC, 1857, XXX, 443; return by Major F. Maitland, 5th NI, 24 February 1858, PP, HC, 1859, XVIII, 44.

76 *'a certain sign'*: ibid.

76 *Live Enfield cartridges*: Major J. Bontein to Major Ross, 23 April 1857, India Military Consultations, OIOC, P/47/15, No. 334 of 15 May 1857.

76 *'highly pleased'*: Lawrence to Canning, 4 May 1857, quoted in Kaye and Malleson, I, 427–8.

76 *At Dum-Dum . . . but would say no more*: statement by Lieutenant-Colonel F. W. Burroughs, 3 June 1857, *Freedom Struggle*, I, 344–5; Burroughs to Captain I. H. Chamberlain, 23 January 1860, ibid., 348.

77 *'Feeling . . . is as bad'*: Lieutenant E. M. Martineau to Captain S. H. Becher, 5 May 1857, quoted in Palmer, *Meerut*, 32.

CHAPTER EIGHT

78 *not as 'pleasant'*: Loy Smith, *A Victorian RSM*, 42.

78 *The station . . . its original gates*: Palmer, *Meerut*, 48–53.

78 *1:1¼*: The breakdown of officers and men, as of 10 May 1857, was as follows. European: 6th Dragoon Guards, 652; 60th Rifles, 901; Bengal Artillery, 225. Total: 1,778. Indian: 3rd Light Cavalry, 504; 11th Native Infantry, 780; 20th Native Infantry, 950. Total: 2,234. (See Palmer, *Meerut*, 53 and 35; O'Callaghan, *Scattered Chapters*, 4.)

78 *The European garrison . . . gunners*: O'Callaghan, *Scattered Chapters*, 34–5; Major-General A. Wilson to Captain S. H. Becher, AAG of the Army, 18 October 1857, *State Papers*, I, 260.

79 *'He was not wanting in intelligence'*: Kaye and Malleson, II, 32.

79 *'I have been 36 years'*: Palmer, *Meerut*, 58.

80 *'The weather'*: 2nd Lieutenant Hugh Chichester to his father, 8 April 1857, Chichester Letters, OIOC, MSS Eur/Photo.Eur.271.

80–81 *Among the absentees . . . Norfolk*: Service Records, Hodson Index, NAM; Wilson Letters, NAM, 6807-483, 117; Kaye and Malleson, II, 48; Hibbert, 75.

81 *'more or less picked men'*: Cadell, 'The Outbreak of the Indian Mutiny', *JSAHR*, vol. 33, 1955, 119.

81 *Among their senior ranks*: Major G. W. Williams's memo of 15 November 1857, *Freedom Struggle*, V, 10–11; Palmer, *Meerut*, 60.

81 *'if they fire'*: Captain H. C. Craigie to Lieutenant Melville-Clarke, 23 April 1857, *State Papers*, I, 228–9.

81 *'beyond that they would get a bad name'*: evidence of Colonel G. M. Carmichael-Smyth, 25 April 1857, ibid., 230–32.

82 *'Our Colonel Smyth'*: Cornet John MacNabb to his mother, 10 May 1857, quoted in Cadell, *JSAHR*, vol. 33, 1955, 120–21.

82 *The former quartermaster-havildar*: evidence of Quartermaster-Havildar Thakoor Sing and Havildar Pursaud Sing, *State Papers*, I, 232–3.

82 *'no adequate cause'*: ibid., 237.

83 *'They could not have hit upon' . . . 'for the officers' lives'*: Cornet John MacNabb to his mother, 10 May 1857, quoted in op. cit., 121.

83 *'In sullen silence'*: Mackenzie, 'The Outbreak at Meerut', a chapter in Vibart, 218–19.

83 *'we would have been grilled'*: Cornet John MacNabb to his mother, 10 May 1857, op. cit., 121.

84 *'They say it was heart-rending'*: ibid., 122.

84 *'We have no kisses'*: Robinson, *Angels of Albion*, 30, 32.

84 *Soon after dark . . . European troops*: Gough, *Old Memories*, 21–3.

84 *'calling upon all true Mussulmans'*: Elisa Greathed's intro., Greathed, *Letters*, xiv.

84–5 *Lieutenant Gough remembered . . . his wife Elisa*: Gough, *Old Memories*, 23–4.

85 *'the tall, commanding presence'*: Mutiny papers, BL, Add. MSS 41996, f. 95.

85 *Gough played . . . artillery lines*: Gough, *Old Memories*, 24–5; Mackenzie, 'The Outbreak at Meerut',

a chapter in Vibart, 220; Cadell, *JSAHR*, vol. 33, 1955, 118.

85 *The gentleman . . . 'made of defence'*: Mutiny Papers, BL, Add. MSS 41996, f. 95.

85 *Just after five . . . from the bazaar*: Palmer, *Meerut*, 72–7.

86 *'We were suddenly called'*: Phillips to his mother, 15 May 1857, in Ryder, 'Everard Lisle Phillipps, VC', *RUSI*, June 1998, 70–75.

86–7 *Phillipps and the rest . . . Dragoon Bridge*: Palmer, *Meerut*, 77–8.

87 *Colonel Carmichael-Smyth . . . edge of the city*: ibid., 80–81.

87 *Mr and Mrs Greathed*: Greathed, *Letters*, xv–xvi.

87 *When Carmichael-Smyth arrived . . . did likewise*: Palmer, *Meerut*, 81; Brigadier A. Wilson to his wife, 11 May 1857, Wilson Letters, NAM, 6807-483; Wilson to Captain S. Becher, AAG of the Army, 18 October 1857, *State Papers*, I, 261.

87–8 *He had been woken . . . 'to the European barracks'*: Mutiny Papers, BL, Add. MSS 41996, f. 95.

88 *At a quarter to six . . . comrades*: Palmer, *Meerut*, 82.

88–9 *'Most of the men'*: Mackenzie, 'The Outbreak at Meerut', in Vibart, 222–5.

89 *'Fortunately I was not hurt'*: ibid., 224–6.

89–90 *On the way . . . their new refuge*: ibid., 227–34.

90 *The mob threatening . . . and later hanged*: Palmer, *Meerut*, 88; Robinson, *Angels of Albion*, 39.

91 *Another to perish . . . Her parents survived*: Palmer, *Meerut*, 89; Mackenzie, 'The Outbreak at Meerut', in Vibart, 235–6.

91–2 *Of the officers killed*: Cadell, *JSAHR*, vol. 33, 1955, 118.

92 *Another fatality . . . and the city*: Palmer, *Meerut*, 103 and 95.

92 *Though news . . . circuitous route*: ibid., 97–102.

92 *'The whole had made off'*: Wilson to his wife, 11 May 1857, Wilson Letters, NAM, 6807-483.

92 *In his official report*: Hewitt to Adjutant-General, 11 May 1857, *State Papers*, I, 249–50.

92–3 *The only offensive action . . . compound*: Palmer, *Meerut*, 102–3.

93 *It was midnight*: Mackenzie, 'The Outbreak at Meerut', in Vibart, 238–40.

93 *The Greatheds hid until morning*: Greathed, *Letters*, xvi–xix.

93 *The official body count*: 'List of Fatalities in the Bengal Presidency as of 15 December 1857', OIOC, L/MIL/17/2/504, 13.

93 *A later estimate*: Palmer, *Meerut*, 105.

93 *The bulk of mutineers . . . with a warning*: Palmer, *Meerut*, 113–14, 120–21.

93 *mutineers left Meerut*: Of the 2,234 Indian troops of the Meerut garrison, 1,949 mutinied and 285 remained loyal or returned to their duty the following day. The loyal troops numbered 85 members of the 3rd Light Cavalry and 200 of the 11th Native Infantry (including the two treasury guards). There is no record of any members of the 20th Native Infantry remaining loyal. (See Palmer, *Meerut*, 79 and

87; Phillipps to his mother, 15 May 1857, in Ryder, *RUSI*, June 1998, 71.)

94 *But the government believed*: memo by Major-General Mansfield, 20 August 1858, Sandhurst Papers, OIOC, MSS Eur/D174, 1285.

94 *Hewitt was relieved*: Colonel R. J. H. Birch to the Lieutenant-Governor of the NW, 2 June 1857, PP, HC, 1857, XXX, 396.

94 *'more harm than 5000 Pandees'*: Lawrence to Chamberlain, 1 and 11 July 1857, Lawrence Correspondence, OIOC, MSS Eur/C203/1.

94 *'pusillanimous behaviour'*: Vernon Smith to Canning, 10 August 1857, Lyveden Papers, OIOC, MSS Eur/F231/4.

94 *'[Wilson's] recommendation' . . . 'become a reality'*: memo by Major-General Mansfield, 20 August 1858, Sandhurst Papers, OIOC, MSS Eur/D174, 1285–6.

94 *'The European troops'*: Mackenzie, 'The Outbreak at Meerut', in Vibart, 242–3.

94–5 *'The Major-General's'*: DAG to Colonel R. J. H. Birch, 6 July 1857, *State Papers*, I, 259.

95 *India's official historian*: Surendra Sen concluded that the rising at Meerut 'was not pre-meditated'. See Sen, 402.

95 *The rumour was believed*: *State Papers*, I, 250.

95 *But this account . . . other regiments*: Palmer, *Meerut*, 72–6.

95 *The 20th's leading role . . . 'suspicious facts'*: *Freedom Struggle*, V, 397–9; Major G. W. Williams's memorandum, 15 November 1857, ibid., 10.

95 *Two other events . . . 10 May*: Vibart, 255–6.

95 *There is also evidence*: deposition of Gulab Jan, *Freedom Struggle*, I, 404.

95 *The conclusion drawn . . . exactly what happened*: address by Major F. J. Harriott, 9 March 1858, PP, HC, 1859, XVIII, 246.

96 *'It is very possible'*: Sir John Lawrence's minute of 19 April 1858, Anderson (ed.), *The Last Days of the Company*, I, 111–12.

CHAPTER NINE

97 *'in this guise'*: Sir Syed Ahmad Khan, *Rissalah Asbab-e-bhagawat-i-hind*, 4.

97 *'There is no cause for shame'*: Hibbert, 91–2.

97–8 *'built of white marble' . . . 'it is this!'*: *Two Native Narratives*, 11.

98 *'Inside . . . was a maze' . . . 'any conspiracy was possible'*: ibid., 12–13.

98–9 *Bahadur Shah ruled . . . 15,000 rupees a month*: Kaye and Malleson, II, 10–25; supplementary evidence of Ahsanullah Khan, PP, HC, 1859, XVIII, 264.

99 *According to his personal physician*: ibid., 265–6.

99 *An itinerant mendicant*: petition from Muhammad Darwash to the Lieutenant-Governor of the NWP, 24 March 1857, ibid., 179.

99 *'that the splendour'*: examination of Chuni, 9 February 1857, ibid., 194–5.

99 *The anticipation . . . contents to the*

King: examination of Ahsanullah Khan, 11 February 1858, ibid., 201.

99 *Ahsanullah was not aware*: supplementary evidence of Ahsanullah Khan, ibid., 266.

99 *According to the King's secretary*: examination of Mukund Lal, 12 and 13 February 1857, ibid., 207.

99–100 *The key evidence . . . 'Delhi troops'*: examination of Jat Mall, 3 February 1858, ibid., 182.

100 *An officer of the 38th*: examination of Captain Tytler, 13 February 1858, ibid., 208–9.

100 *His wife concluded*: Tytler, 114.

100 *Jat Mall confirmed . . . to Delhi*: examination of Jat Mall, 5 February 1858, PP, HC, 1859, XVIII, 185.

100 *The first mutineers*: Palmer, *Meerut*, 123.

100–101 *The lone rider . . . guard could act*: examination of Makhan, Captain Douglas's mace-bearer, 6 February 1858, PP, HC, 1859, XVIII, 188.

101 *Meanwhile . . . to fetch Captain Douglas*: examination of Ahsanullah Khan, 12 February 1858, ibid., 198–9.

101 *Douglas leant over*: examination of Ghulam Abbas, 29 January 1858, ibid., 136–7.

101–2 *Douglas went first*: *Two Native Narratives*, 79–80.

102 *Douglas and the others . . . too late*: examination of Makhan, 6 February 1858, PP, HC, 1859, XVIII, 188–9; examination of Jat Mall, 3 February 1858, ibid., 182; examination of Ahsanullah Khan, 12 February 1858, ibid., 199.

102–3 *Fraser, armed only with a sword . . . Ali Khan*: examination of Jat Mall, 3 February 1858, ibid., 182.

103 *The crowd . . . 'on a bed'*: examination of Makhan, 6 February 1858, ibid., 189.

103–4 *When Bahadur Shah . . . 'loudly together'*: examination of Ghulam Abbas, 29 January 1858, ibid., 137.

104–5 *'angel of the regiment'*: Tytler, 69.

105 *That morning . . . 'the fanj [army] has come'*: ibid., 115.

105 *Tytler buckled on his sword*: Captain Tytler's statement in Tytler, 186.

105 *'creating disturbances'*: Vibart, 12–13.

106 *Within the Kashmir Gate . . . managed to escape*: ibid., 18, 22–3; Hibbert, 98; Kaye and Malleson, II, 64.

106–7 *The two guns . . . to attack them*: Lieutenant Harry Gambier to Mrs Knyvett, 29 May 1857, Gambier Letters, NAM, 6211/67, 4; Vibart, 16–19.

107 *Vibart later marvelled . . . could not be trusted*: Vibart, 20–26; Kaye and Malleson, II, 65.

107 *Major Herbert Abbott*: Abbott was born in Calcutta in November 1814 and joined the 74th as an ensign at the age of seventeen. Apart from two brief absences, he had served all his career with the same regiment, including stints as adjutant and interpreter. He assumed command of the 74th in 1856 and his familiarity with his men probably saved his life. See Service Records, Hodson Index, NAM.

107–8 *Back at the cantonment . . . 'absent since the morning'*: Vibart, 34–7.

109 *'He was a very blue-eyed, fair child'*: Tytler, 118.

109 *'You can never save her'*: ibid., 118–19.

109 *'forced to remain'*: Vibart, 26–7.

109 *When the Delhi Bank . . . on her spear*: Kaye and Malleson, II, 62.

109 *'dense pillars of smoke'*: Vibart, 28.

110 *Most galling of all . . . blown up*: Forrest to Colonel A. Abbott, 27 May 1857, *State Papers*, I, 272–3.

110 *showing signs of insubordination*: In retrospect, Lieutenant Forrest was convinced that the magazine's Indian employees were expecting an uprising. For several days prior to the outbreak, he later testified, they had been 'insolent and overbearing', particularly the Muslims. It was only after reaching the safety of Meerut, however, that he heard a second-hand account that someone in the magazine at Delhi had been sending circulars to all the native regiments to the effect that the cartridges prepared in the magazine had been smeared with an objectionable fat, and that they were not to believe their European officers when they denied it. Forrest suspected Karim Baksh, the head of the Indian establishment, 'an intelligent man and also a good scholar, capable of writing Persian well'. So suspicious was Baksh's conduct during the attack on the magazine that Willoughby ordered Forrest to remove him from the gate and shoot him if he returned to it. He was later hanged 'for his treacherous conduct on that occasion' (see examination of Captain Forrest, 5 February 1858, PP, HC, 1859, XVIII, 186).

110 *'the subadar of the guard'*: Forrest to Abbott, 27 May 1857, *State Papers*, I, 273–4.

110 *'a son and grandson of the King's'*: examination of Captain Forrest, 5 February 1858, PP, HC, 1859, XVIII, 187.

110–11 *Conductor Buckley . . . 'blown into the air'*: Forrest to Abbott, 27 May 1857, *State Papers*, I, 274.

111 *'blown far into the city'*: *Two Native Narratives*, 52.

111–13 *About this time . . . food and beer*: Vibart, 45–57.

113 *'When I went into'*: Tytler, 186.

113–14 *The two officers . . . European community*: ibid., 124, 187; Lieutenant Harry Gambier to Mrs Knyvett, 29 May 1857, Gambier Letters, NAM, 6211/67, 4.

115 *'It was a terrible crush'*: Tytler, 125.

115–17 *The carriages . . . 'three days to live'*: ibid., 190–95.

117 *The last Europeans . . . 'native attire' for the men*: Lieutenant Harry Gambier to Mrs Knyvett, 29 May 1857, op. cit., 5–14.

117 *Francis Cohen*: Cohen was later punished for assisting the fugitives when Gujars and the followers of the rebel *zemindar* Shah Mal 'plundered him of 7 or 8000 rupees worth of property' and took him prisoner, 'releasing him on a ransom of 600 rupees'. See Bhadra, 'Four Rebels of Eighteen Fifty-seven' in SSS, 137.

117–18 *That afternoon . . . 'these two officers'*: Vibart, 112–15.

118 *The seventeen fugitives . . . 'like*

convicts': Lieutenant Harry Gambier to Mrs Knyvett, 29 May 1857, op. cit., 13–14.

119–20 *The Indians . . . when it was dark*: *Two Native Narratives*, 40–51.

120 *'We were very much crowded together'*: examination of Mrs Aldwell, 11 February 1858, PP, HC, 1859, XVIII, 202.

121 *'Ahsanullah looked much perplexed'*: *Two Native Narratives*, 83.

121 *'inability to take any measures'*: supplementary evidence of Ahsanullah Khan, PP, HC, 1859, XVIII, 266.

121–2 *The following day . . . 'to mock and humiliate him'*: *Two Native Narratives*, 84–7.

122 *'to march at once upon Delhi'*: ibid., 85.

122 *'promising monthly salaries'*: ibid., 60.

122 *Mainodin . . . '30 to a sowar'*: *Freedom Struggle*, III, 438–9.

122 *A chilling example . . . Eurasian prisoners*: *Two Native Narratives*, 59 and 93.

122 *'treacherously' handed over*: ibid., 59.

122 *Bahadur Shah tried to intervene*: Munshi Jiwan Lal in ibid., 94.

123 *'The women and children began crying'*: examination of Mrs Aldwell, 11 February 1858, PP, HC, 1859, XVIII, 203.

123 *'A sowar first fired a carbine'*: *Two Native Narratives*, 59.

CHAPTER TEN

124 *Charles Raikes . . . 'more or less, absent'*: Raikes, *Notes*, 1–2.

124 *Raikes was a senior member . . . 'will upon others'*: ibid., 4–6; Kaye and Malleson, III, 97.

125 *'One officer rushed in'*: Raikes, *Notes*, 10.

125–6 *The following morning . . . 'devilish scowl'*: Raikes, *Notes*, 11–12.

126 *'I am doing everything possible'*: telegraph messages from Colvin to Canning, 15 and 16 May 1857, in *State Papers*, I, 251–2.

126–7 *News of the Meerut rising . . . towards Ferozepore*: Maclagan, 82–3; Canning to Vernon Smith, 19 May 1857, Lyveden Papers, OIOC, MSS Eur/F231/5; Canning to Colvin, 16 May 1857, *State Papers*, I, 25.

127 *Also on 16 May . . . 'danger and disgrace'*: Governor-General's Proclamation of 16 May 1857 (published in the *Calcutta Gazette*), PP, HC, 1857, XXX, 19.

127 *Canning regretted . . . Order of Merit*: Maclagan, 83.

128 *'I have asked for'*: Canning to Vernon Smith, 19 May 1857, Lyveden Papers, OIOC, MSS Eur/F231/5.

128 *'Our hold of Bengal'*: Canning to Elgin, 19 May 1857, quoted in Maclagan, 84–5.

129 *'Delhi is in the hands'*: Canning to Vernon Smith, 19 May 1857, Lyveden Papers, OIOC, MSS Eur/F231/5,

129 *A similar appeal*: Maclagan, 85–6; Governor–General in Council's dispatch to the Court of Directors, PP, HC, 1857, XXX, 10.

129 *There was little more . . . loaded revolvers*: Kaye and Malleson, II, 88–9; *Friend of India*, 28 May 1857.

129–30 *'I never came across'*: Canning to

Vernon Smith, 20 May 1857, Lyveden Papers, OIOC, MSS Eur/F231/5.

130 *Canning's disgust . . . Special Constables*: Kaye and Malleson, II, 87.

130 *'If this disaffection should spread'*: Canning to Granville, 19 May 1857, in Fitzmaurice, I, 248.

130 *'regiments there had mutinied'*: Mrs Keith Young to her sister, 14 May 1857, in Young, 16.

130 *A fuller account*: General Anson's précis of events in *State Papers*, I, 277.

130 *'He appears to rather pooh-pooh'*: Colonel K. Young's Diary in Young, 11.

130–31 *'When he first received the bad news'*: Mrs Keith Young to her sister, 15 May 1857, ibid., 16.

131 *'I have sent express'*: Kaye and Malleson, II, 104–5.

131 *'They are still doing'*: General Anson's précis of events in *State Papers*, I, 278.

131–2 *The uncertain loyalty . . . 'quite quietly'*: Mrs Keith Young to her sister, 15 May 1857, in Young, 18.

132 *'I haven't the least fear'*: Colonel K. Young to Colonel H. B. Henderson, 17 May 1857, ibid., 12.

132 *professional grievances*: The Gurkhas are said to have objected to the fact that no arrangements had been made for the protection of their families during their absence. They were also in arrears of pay. See Kaye and Malleson, II, 109.

132 *'totally unprepared'*: General Anson's précis of events, in *State Papers*, I, 278.

133 *'It becomes' . . . 'be maintained'*: Kaye and Malleson, II, 112, 116.

133 *'I venture to say'*: Anson to Canning, 23 May 1857, ibid., 118.

133 *'advisable or immediately necessary'*: General Anson's précis of events in *State Papers*, I, 279.

134 *'They had survived'*: Kaye and Malleson, II, 121.

134 *Soon after . . . British would prevail*: Roberts, 57.

134 *For that reason it contained*: PP, HC, 1859, V, app. 34, 411.

135 *Robert Montgomery . . . for the British*: Kaye and Malleson, II, 324–7.

135 *'all the four disarmed corps' . . . Ferozepore itself*: statement by Brigadier S. Corbett, PP, HC, 1859, XVIII, 48.

135 *The existence . . . a day later*: Kaye and Malleson, II, 329–30.

135–6 *That evening . . . their attackers*: return of the 45th NI, 3 March 1858, PP, HC, 1859, XVIII, 49; Gimlette, 156–7.

136 *'Such cowards'*: Roberts, *Letters*, 9.

136 *'vigorously pursued' . . . late June*: D. F. MacLeod to Bartle Frere, 15 May 1857, Elphinstone Papers, OIOC, MSS Eur/F87/Box 6B/8/1; PP, HC, 1857–8, XLIV, 307.

136 *'Our military rulers'*: 'Secret Letters Received 14 July 1857 from the Govenor-General', 6 June, No. 29, Lyveden Papers, OIOC, MSS Eur/F231/31.

136–7 *'Even you, who foresaw all this' . . . 'much vigour'*: Jacob Papers, OIOC, MSS Eur/F75/7.

137 *The leading civil authorities . . . misfired*: Allen, 107 and 126.

137–8 *Edwardes's deputy . . . 'escape noticing'*: ibid., 217–18, 304.

138 *'Nicholson impressed me'*: Roberts, 32–3.

138–9 *Nicholson was dining . . . 'rebel movement'*: Roberts to his father, 22 May 1857, in Roberts, *Letters*, 7; Roberts, 34–5.

139 *It 'should take the field'*: Kaye and Malleson, II, 342.

139 *'He was in the prime'*: ibid., 343.

139 *a man of 'unusual energy'*: Roberts, 25n.

139 *'greatly impressed'*: ibid., 36.

139 *'Neither greased cartridges'*: Allen, 266.

140 *'Edwardes and Nicholson' . . . Attock Ferry*: Roberts, 37–8.

140 *'The old General'*: Allen, 267.

140 *'Old Reed'*: Roberts to his mother, 14 May 1857, in Roberts, *Letters*, 1.

140–41 *'It was a position' . . . 'Peshawar again'*: Roberts, 38, 40.

141–2 *Reed he found . . . evening of 19 May*: quoted in Allen, 68–9.

142 *'immersed in cares'*: ibid., 274.

142 *'O brother!'*: an intercepted letter from Peshawar (translation by H. Edwardes, 30 May 1857), NAM, 5504-63.

142 *The bearer . . . 'moved by the cartridges'*: *Freedom Struggle*, I, 353–4.

143 *That night . . . 'them obeyed'*: Allen, 274–5; Kaye and Malleson, II, 358–60.

143 *'It was a painful and affecting'*: Allen, 276.

143–4 *'As we rode down'*: Kaye and Malleson, II, 361.

144–5 *Cotton's thoughts . . . rebelled to protect*: ibid., 363–6; Gimlette, 171–3.

145 *'The officers . . . all concur'*: Kaye and Malleson, II, 367–8.

145 *Edwardes . . . same punishment*: Brigadier S. Cotton to Captain H. R. James, officiating secretary to the chief commissioner, 3 June 1857, SC, NAI, No. 1 of 26 February 1858.

146 *'I fancy you will ere long'*: Dr James Graham to Lieutenant James Graham, 7 June 1857, in Harrison (ed.), *The Graham Indian Mutiny Papers*, 25.

CHAPTER ELEVEN

147 *'[The order] could only tend' . . . on 2 July 1857*: R. M. Edwards to H. Williams, Commissioner of Meerut, 1 December 1857, *Freedom Struggle*, V, 75, 79–89.

147 *'We ran straight into'*: Lieutenant Chapman to Captain Chamberlain, 21 June 1860, ibid., 100–102.

147–8 *'We were at first led astray'*: Wilson to his wife, 17 May 1857, Wilson Letters, NAM, 6807-483.

148 *During the night of 16 May*: narrative by Allan Hume, Magistrate of Etawah, 18 November 1858, *Freedom Struggle*, V, 630–34.

148 *'Behold, a martyr to our faith'*: Gimlette, 92–3.

148 *Only in Etawah . . . Raja of Mainpuri*: John Power, Magistrate of Mainpuri, to C. B. Thornhill, 25 May 1857, PP, HC, 1857, XXX, 475–7.

148 *'Mr V. [ansittart] called on [Colvin] today'*: Vansittart Papers, OIOC, MSS Eur/B167.

148–9 *General Anson . . . if necessary*:

General Anson's précis of events, 20–25 May 1857, *State Papers*, I, 280–82; Anson to Major-General Hewitt, 23 May 1857, ibid., 275–6.

149 *'a constitutional tendency'*: Hodson, *Twelve Years of a Soldier's Life in India*, 318.

149–50 *'It was a fearful crisis'*: Allen, 68.

150 *'the finest regiment in India'*: Trotter, *The Life of Hodson of Hodson's Horse*, 31.

150–51 *He was not with them long . . . 'good news to send you'*: Allen, 104–5, 229 and 235, 258–60.

151 *'very imperfect' information*: General Anson's précis of events, 17 May 1857, *State Papers*, I, 280.

151 *'He had left Karnal'*: Allen, 261.

152 *'A tallish man'*: Sherer, *Daily Life during the Indian Mutiny*, 139.

152 *'As a cavalry soldier'*: Gough, *Old Memories*, 220–21.

152 *'Barnard, I leave you the command'*: Barnard to Sir Charles Yorke, 27 May 1857, in Kaye and Malleson, II, 123.

152 *'Poor General Anson!'*: Young, 26–7.

152 *'He ought to have been'*: Dr Thomas Mawe to his sister, 29 May 1857, Mawe Letters, OIOC, MSS Eur/C324.

152 *Even Canning . . . unnecessarily*: Canning to Vernon Smith, 19 June, in Maclagan, 90–91.

153 *Born in Oxfordshire . . . 'with Meerut'*: Service Records, Hodson Index, NAM; Young, 33; Kaye and Malleson, II, 127.

153 *'We burnt every village'*: Hibbert, 122.

153 *'There were eleven more'*: Anson, *With HM 9th Lancers*, 6.

154 *'News was gained today'*: Potiphar Papers, NAM, 7201-45, 9.

154 *'From what we could gather'*: Tytler, 144.

155 *'I hope Barnard's force'*: Wilson to his wife, 30 May 1857, Wilson Letters, NAM, 6807-483.

155 *'perpetual sand storms'*: 2nd Lieutenant Chichester to his mother, 3 June 1857, Chichester Letters, OIOC, MSS Eur/Photo.Eur.271, 23.

155 *'On reaching the bridge'*: Ensign Phillipps to his mother, 1 June 1857, in Ryder, 'Everard Lisle Phillipps, VC', *RUSI*, June 1998, 72.

155–6 *'From time to time'*: *Two Native Narratives*, 52.

156 *'nearly the same position'*: 2nd Lieutenant Chichester to his mother, 3 June 1857, op. cit., 23.

156 *'so knocked up'*: Brigadier Wilson to his wife, 1 June 1857, Wilson Letters, NAM, 6807-483.

156 *'Our object is Delhi'*: Young, 39–40.

156–7 *'While we are before Delhi'*: Brigadier Wilson to his wife, 3 and 4 June 1857, Wilson Letters, NAM, 6807-483.

157 *'I can't tell you'*: Young, 43.

157 *Barnard's force*: The European troops were as follows: 60th Rifles (six companies); 75th Foot (nine companies); 1st Bengal European Fusiliers; 2nd Bengal European Fusiliers (six companies); 6th Dragoon Guards (two squadrons); 9th Lancers; 2nd/1st (four guns), 2nd/3rd and 3rd/3rd Troops of Bengal Horse Artillery; 3rd/3rd and 4th/

6th Companies of Bengal Foot Artillery (with No. 14 Field Battery); detachment of artillery recruits.

157 *twenty-four siege guns*: The siege guns comprised eight 18-pounders, four 8-inch and twelve 5½-inch mortars. One officer wrote: 'The guns, if not exactly obsolete, were quite unsuited for the work that had to be done, but they were the best procurable' (Roberts, 50).

157 *'with a view' . . . 'sickness and fatigue'*: Major-General Barnard to the Adjutant-General of the Army, 12 June 1857, *State Papers*, I, 290–91.

158 *'I have never seen'*: Lieutenant Coghill to 'Cid', June 1857, Coghill Papers, NAM, 7207-4-1.

158 *'never under a hotter fire'*: Ensign Charles Ewart to his mother, 9 June 1857, Ewart Letters, NAM, 7310-48.

158 *'We had marched'*: 2nd Lieutenant Chichester to his mother, 10 June 1857, Chichester Letters, OIOC, MSS Eur/Photo.Eur.271, 29.

158 *'It seems he lived'*: Colonel K. Young to his wife, 9 June 1857, in Young, 50.

158 *'When [the 1st Brigade were]'*: Lieutenant Coghill to 'Cid', June 1857, op. cit.

159 *'hurrying back'*: *Two Native Narratives*, 63.

159 *'I soon found'*: Major-General Barnard to the Adjutant-General of the Army, 12 June 1857, op. cit., 291.

159 *'At the foot of the hill'*: Lieutenant Coghill to 'Cid', June 1857, op. cit.

159 *These two English rebels*: Ensign Charles Ewart to his mother, 9 June 1857, Ewart Letters, NAM, 7310-48.

159 *Barnard 'had the satisfaction' . . . 'imagined'*: Major-General Barnard to the Adjutant-General of the Army, op. cit., 290–91; Wilson to his wife, 8 June 1857, Wilson Letters, NAM, 6807-483.

159 *'No, no'*: Tytler, 145.

159–60 *'If they had instantly'*: *Two Native Narratives*, 63–4.

160 *'Had just made ourselves'*: Kaye and Malleson, II, 145.

160 *Thirteen rebel guns*: *State Papers*, I, 292.

160 *The rebel deaths*: Potiphar Papers, NAM, 7201-45, 12.

160 *'only the walls standing'*: Colonel K. Young to his wife, 9 June 1857, in Young, 50.

160 *'I saw some'*: Tytler, 145.

160–61 *'It would have done'*: Allen, 273.

161 *'The Guides Corps'*: Anson, *With HM 9th Lancers*, 10.

161 *'The men hotly engaged' . . . 'patria mori'*: Allen, 274; Roberts, 90.

161 *'not only a coign'*: Roberts, 86.

162 *Barnard approved . . . cancelled*: Kaye and Malleson, II, 397–8n; Wilson to his wife, 13 June 1857, Wilson Letters, NAM, 6807-483.

162 *'Most fortunate'*: Young, 59.

162 *'few who did not feel'*: Kaye and Malleson, II, 398n.

162–3 *'I have nothing left'*: ibid., 399.

163 *'disappoint expectations'*: ibid., 400.

163 *'his talk was too fiery'*: Young, 63.

163 *'perfectly safe'*: ibid.

163 *'It would be impossible'*: Kaye and Malleson, II, 401–2.

163 *'It has been decided'*: Wilson to his wife, 16 June 1857, Wilson Letters, NAM, 6807-483.

163 *'I confess'*: Kaye and Malleson, II, 404.

164 *They had been joined . . . 7,000 troops in all*: 'Statement showing the Number of Troops and the Places from which they revolted, and arrived at Delhi', 14 August 1857, PP, HC, 1857–8, XLIV, 307; David, 243–4.

CHAPTER TWELVE

165 *The province of Oudh . . . 7,000 native soldiers*: Bonham, *Oude in 1857*, 11–12, 24–7.

165 *20,000 Indian troops*: The regular Bengal native troops stationed in Oudh in May 1857 were one regiment of cavalry, five of infantry and two batteries of foot artillery. The irregulars were mostly from the Oudh Irregular Force, raised by the British in early 1856 for local service, and included three regiments of cavalry, ten of infantry, two of military police (equipped as infantry) and four batteries of artillery. There was also a single regiment of Bengal Irregular Cavalry.

166 *'a vision of palaces'*: Russell, *My Indian Mutiny Diary*, 57–8.

166 *'as bad as bad can be'*: Hibbert, 219.

166 *'plenary military power'*: *State Papers*, II, 19–21.

167 *'When we drove up'*: Germon, *Journal*, 27–8.

167 *'I never witnessed'*: ibid., 28.

167 *'Sir Henry Lawrence'*: Hewitt (ed.), *Eyewitnesses to the Indian Mutiny*, 129–30.

167–8 *'His face bore'*: Holmes, *A History of the Indian Mutiny*, 246.

168 *'with all speed' . . . 'the best I can do for you'*: *State Papers*, II, 22–3.

168 *'strongly' advised . . . 'Spare no expense'*: ibid., 24.

168 *'safe against all'*: Kaye and Malleson, III, 247.

168–9 *'All quiet'*: *State Papers*, II, 24.

169 *'Seditious placards' . . . 'and even less!'*: Anderson, *A Personal Journal*, 9–11.

169 *During the early evening . . . Muriaon*: *State Papers*, II, intro., 23; Wilson, *The Defence of Lucknow*, 1–2.

169–70 *But Lawrence refused . . . 'enter the house'*: *State Papers*, II, intro., 24.

170 *'His men remained'*: Wilson, *The Defence of Lucknow*, 4.

170 *Of the Indian troops . . . Muriaon*: Gimlette, 63 and 100; *State Papers*, II, intro., 24; list of Corps that have mutinied, FC, NAI, Nos. 1753–4 of 30 December 1859.

170–71 *Shortly after . . . sixty mutineers between them*: Gimlette, 63–4; *State Papers*, II, intro., 25.

171 *In total . . . 7 June*: Sir H. Lawrence to Canning, 1 June 1857, *State Papers*, II, 25; list of Corps that have mutinied, FC, NAI, Nos. 1753–4 of 30 December 1859.

171 *The loyalty . . . forty-nine*: Service Records, Hodson Index, NAM.

171 *The mutiny . . . court martial*: Hutchinson, *Narrative*, 71–5; Wilson, *The Defence of Lucknow*, 18.

172 *'We are in a much better position'*: *State Papers*, II, 25.
172 *'to confer with [General] Wheeler'*: Bonham, *Oude in 1857*, 30.
172 *a 'splendid library'*: Rees, *A Personal Narrative*, 115.
172 *'Owing to the intense heat'*: Bonham, *Oude in 1857*, 30.
172 *After a few days . . . to consult the magistrate*: letter from William Martin, head clerk at Mainpuri, 21 May 1858, *Freedom Struggle*, V, 636–40.
173 *'They were on one road'*: *State Papers*, II, intro., 28–9.
173 *'The poor lad'*: ibid., 29–30; eyewitness account of the outbreak at Mainpuri by H. J. McGlow, magistrate clerk, *Freedom Struggle*, V, 645.
174 *'a nice little bungalow'*: Jackson Narrative, NAM, 6409-67-1, 1–4.
174 *the men 'went off in good spirits'*: 'Brief Narrative of the Emeute at Sitapur', *Freedom Struggle*, II, 21–2.
174 *'If the [41st] go over'*: Bonham, *Oude in 1857*, 49–51.
175 *At around ten . . . towards Lucknow*: ibid., 51–2; 'Brief Narrative of the Emeute at Sitapur', op. cit., 24–5; 'Account of the Outbreak at Sitapur' in Anderson, *Siege of Lucknow*, 19–21.
175–6 *The rest . . . 'abandoning his post'*: 'Brief Narrative of the Emeute at Sitapur', op. cit., 24–5.
176 *'The confusion was dreadful'*: Jackson Narrative, NAM, 6409-67-1, 4–5.
176–8 *The 'bridge' in question . . . outskirts of Mithauli*: ibid., 5–8; *State Papers*, II, intro., 31.
178–9 *They were taken in . . . Then nothing*: Jackson Narrative, NAM, 6409-67-1, 10–13.
179 *'If anything happens to me'*: *State Papers*, II, 26n.
180 *'prime of his life'*: ibid., intro., 66–7; Kaye and Malleson, III, 277.
180 *Before Canning's . . . almost eight hundred*: *State Papers*, II, intro., 38; Kaye and Malleson, III, 278–9.
180 *'Fancy if the enemy had got them'*: *State papers*, II, intro., 38–9n.
181 *'An attack may be expected'*: A. Couper to the authorities at Benares, 15 June 1857, *State Papers*, II, intro., 26–7.
181 *'I would risk'*: Sir H. Lawrence to H. Tucker, 16 June 1857, ibid., 27.

CHAPTER THIRTEEN

182 *he 'had no Friends'*: Ward, 77.
182 *'promiscuous, uncultivated'*: ibid., 14–15.
182 *'My service has been extraordinary'*: ibid., 77.
183 *'short, of a spare habit'*: Thomson, *The Story of Cawnpore*, 141.
183 *'the most anxious position'*: Lady Canning's diary entry of 21 June 1857, *State Papers*, II, intro., 144n.
183 *'too much reliance'*: Thomson, *The Story of Cawnpore*, 141.
183 *News of the outbreak . . . 190 feet*: *State Papers*, II, intro., 145–6.
184 *He 'ought to have gone there'*: ibid.
184 *'probable signal for revolt'*: Thomson, *The Story of Cawnpore*, 28–9.
184 *That same night . . . to destroy them*: statement of Jemadar Shaikh Salamut Ali, 25 June 1857, Kaye Mutiny Papers, OIOC, H725, 569.

184 *'confidence in them'*: Mrs Ewart to her sister, 27 May 1857, Ewart Letters, OIOC, MSS Eur/B267.

185 *'confusion, fright'*: Ward, 123.

185 *'kindly' received ... 'not to be depended on'*: Gubbins, *An Account of the Mutinies in Oudh*, 30–31.

186 *'lamented the outbreak'*: Ward, 97.

186 *On 20 May ... 'coalesce with others'*: ibid., 68, 117–18; *State Papers*, II, intro., 147–8.

186 *On 1 June ... did not get his way*: memorandum by Lieutenant-Colonel Williams, 29 March 1859, *State Papers*, III, app., xliv–xlv.

186–7 *With the formal greetings ... time was right*: Ward, 147.

187 *'firm and loyal'*: memorandum by Lieutenant-Colonel Williams, op. cit., xlv.

187 *'on the part of the government'*: Ward, 147.

187 *'Our weak position'*: Ewart Letters, OIOC, MSS Eur/B267.

187 *'This leaves me weak'*: *State Papers*, II, 112–15.

187 *'almost acknowledgeable state of Mutiny'*: Wheeler to Sir H. Lawrence, 4 June 1857, BL, Add. MSS 39922, f. 10.

188 *'only obey and serve Government'*: Ward, 158–60.

188 *'My children!'*: ibid., 161–2.

188–9 *Meanwhile the 53rd and 56th ... return to the entrenchment*: deposition of Khoda Bux, late Subedar 56th NI, *State Papers*, III, app., cxvii–cxviii.

189 *'We told him'*: Kaye Mutiny Papers, OIOC, H725, 570.

189 *No sooner had ... not yet mutinied*: deposition of Sepoy Bhola Khan, 53rd NI, *State Papers*, III, app., cvi–cviii.

189–90 *As Wheeler scanned ... had been misplaced*: Ward, 164–5; deposition of Sepoy Bhola Khan, 53rd NI, *State Papers*, III, app., cvi–cvii.

190 *three guns burst into life*: Major Hillersdon and his officers were furious with Wheeler for giving the order to fire at their regiment. 'The men were peacefully occupied in their lines, cooking,' wrote Lieutenant Thomson, not entirely accurately. 'No signs of mutiny had appeared amidst their ranks, they had refused all the solicitations of the deserters to accompany them, and seemed quite steadfast, when Ashe's battery opened upon them by Sir Hugh Wheeler's command, and they were literally driven from us by nine-pounders.' (See Thomson, *The Story of Cawnpore*, 39.) Even allowing for Thomson's exaggeration, it does appear that the majority of the regiment had little appetite for rebellion until fired upon. After exhaustive inquiries, Lieutenant-Colonel Williams noted that the 53rd was the 'least tainted' regiment at Cawnpore, and that many of those who deserted and joined their mutinous comrades 'did so from fear of being implicated in the consequences of revolt' (see memorandum by Lieutenant-Colonel G. W. Williams, 29 March 1859, *State Papers*, III, app., xlv). At Cawnpore, like many earlier mutinies, there seems to be some correlation between

a regiment's level of disaffection and the relative familiarity of its commanding officer. Lieutenant-Colonel Ewart of the 1st Infantry, for example, had known his men for only two years. Much of his previous service had been in the judge advocate's department. That he was considered to be something of a martinet is proved by the way his former sepoys carried out a mock parade before murdering him as he was being carried from the shattered entrenchment on 27 June. Colonel Stephen Williams had spent even less time with the 56th Infantry, the next most disaffected infantry regiment, though he was more regimentally experienced and had seen more active service than Ewart. Major Hillersdon, however, had served all his twenty-year career with the 53rd Infantry (the least disaffected regiment at Cawnpore). The cavalry regiment – the 2nd – is the exception to the rule, just as it was at Meerut. It was being temporarily commanded by Major Vibart, who, like Hillersdon, had begun his service with the same regiment. However, the original corps had been disbanded for cowardice in the face of the enemy in 1840 during the First Afghan War. The regiment that mutinied in 1857, therefore, had only been in existence for fifteen years. Originally designated the 11th Light Cavalry, it was accorded the honour of being renamed the 2nd Light Cavalry after illustrious service at the Battle of Multan in 1848. Vibart's cousin had gained particular renown during this action by cutting down a Sikh standard-bearer and capturing a regimental standard. The fact that Vibart's former sowars helped to carry his possessions during the ill-fated march to the boats at Satichaura Ghat on 27 June indicates that he was not personally unpopular.

190 *into the entrenchment*: A total of 76 loyal Indian soldiers garrisoned the artillery hospital: 10 Indian officers and 37 men of the 53rd; and 16 men of the 56th.

190 *'plundered the treasury'*: Mowbray Thomson wrote: 'The detachment of the 53rd posted at the treasury held their ground against the rebels about four hours. We could hear their musketry in the distance, but were not allowed to attempt their relief.' See Thomson, *The Story of Cawnpore*, 40.

190–91 *That morning . . . 'Native army'*: memorandum by Lieutenant-Colonel Williams, 29 March 1859, *State Papers*, III, app., xlv.

191 *Nana could see . . . birth-mark*: Ward, 170–2.

192 *'Some Christians'*: deposition of Futteh Sing, *State Papers*, III, app., ccxviii–ccxix.

192 *'With such expedition'*: Thomson, *The Story of Cawnpore*, 61–4.

192–3 *'they caught sight of the enemy' . . . 'to the spot'*: ibid., 64–6.

193 *'The site of our entrenchment'*: Hewitt (ed.), *Eyewitnesses to the Indian Mutiny*, 88.

194 *'Creeping up by hundreds' . . . 'four*

and twenty hours': Thomson, *The Story of Cawnpore*, 70–71.

195 *'The 'agony' of the parents*: Horne Narrative, BL, Add. MSS 41488, f. 64.

195 *Sometime during the second day . . . bodies*: Ward, 186, 190–92; Thomson, *The Story of Cawnpore*, 89.

195–6 *'I write this'*: Emma Larkins to Mrs Henrietta Coffin, 9 June 1857, OIOC, MSS Eur/Photo.Eur.233.

196 *'never showed himself outside'*: Thomson, *The Story of Cawnpore*, 90.

196–7 *'His never-say-die disposition'*: ibid., 141–2.

197 *'go out with about a dozen Europeans'*: *State Papers*, II, intro., 165.

197 *'We knew that the number of sick'*: Horne Narrative, BL, Add. MSS 41488, f. 61.

197–8 *Nana Sahib . . . Allahabad*: Ward, 194–5.

198 *'a most cowardly set of men'*: Mr Shepherd's narrative, *State Papers*, II, intro., 123.

198 *'The Major then told us'*: deposition of Pay Havildar Ram Buksh, 53rd NI, *State Papers*, III, app., cx.

198 *'Next morning'*: deposition of Sepoy Bhola Khan, 53rd NI, ibid., cviii.

199 *'brought back to Cawnpore'*: statement of Jemadar Shaikh Salamut Ali, 25 June 1857, Kaye Mutiny Papers, OIOC, H725, 572.

199 *'in a most distressed' . . . 'to our strength'*: Thomson, *The Story of Cawnpore*, 120–21.

199 *'It took us a long time'*: deposition of Hingun, *State Papers*, III, app., ccxiii–ccxiv.

200 *On reaching . . . necessary arrangements*: Ward, 225–6; deposition of Futteh Sing, *State Papers*, III, app., ccxx.

200 *It was mid afternoon . . . the wounded*: ibid.; deposition of Bukkee Singh, ibid., ccxxxii–ccxxxiii; deposition of Hingun, ibid., ccxiv.

CHAPTER FOURTEEN

201 *'Not a few'*: Thomson, *The Story of Cawnpore*, 91–2.

201 *'The women and children' . . . 'dreadful sufferings'*: Horne Narrative, BL, Add. MSS 41488, f. 62.

201 *'a little girl of five'*: Ward, 238.

201–202 *'without regard to sex' . . . 'in the open'*: Thomson, *The Story of Cawnpore*, 93–4.

202 *'Every drop of medicine'*: Horne Narrative, BL, Add. MSS 41488, ff. 62–3.

202 *As the siege wore on . . . 'on that head'*: Thomson, *The Story of Cawnpore*, 82–3.

203 *'He jocosely said' . . . 'promised it'*: ibid., 86–7.

203 *'mixed with human blood'*: Horne Narrative, BL, Add. MSS 41488, f. 66.

203 *'sucking the pieces' . . . 'poor little babes'*: Thomson, *The Story of Cawnpore*, 87.

203 *'We have been besieged'*: *State Papers*, II, intro., 170.

203 *'I am very sorry'*: ibid.

203–4 *At Wheeler's request . . . 'to the last'*: ibid., 170–71.

204 *Moore had provided . . . beaten off*: Ward, 244–5; *State Papers*, II, intro., 171–2.

204 *'displace him if he did'*: Nunne

Nawab's diary, 17 June 1857, *State Papers*, III, app., xiv.

205 *'This evening'*: *State Papers*, II, intro., 173.

205 *Nana Sahib . . . the assault*: Ward, 274–5; Nunne Nawab's diary, op. cit., xvi; Mr Shepherd's narrative, *State Papers*, II, 130.

205 *'Some few had on'*: Shepherd, *A Personal Narrative*, 49–50.

205–6 *The first move . . . 'and retired'*: Thomson, *The Story of Cawnpore*, 126–7.

206 *But Vibart . . . 'general dispersion'*: Shepherd, *A Personal Narrative*, 50.

206 *Simultaneously . . . twenty-five volunteers*: Thomson, *The Story of Cawnpore*, 126; Shepherd, *A Personal Narrative*, 50.

207 'favourite . . . darling son': State Papers, II, intro., 40–41.

207 *'British spirit alone remains'*: ibid.

207 *Lawrence's reply*: ibid., 41.

207 *'Tattered in clothing'*: Thomson, *The Story of Cawnpore*, 88.

207 *stench 'from the dead bodies'*: Mr Shepherd's narrative, *State Papers*, II, 132.

207–8 *On 24 May . . . release was imminent*: Shepherd, *A Personal Narrative*, 59–70.

208 *his own release*: On 12 July 1857 Jonah was tried by Baba Bhutt's court for running away from the English entrenchment and sentenced to three years' hard labour. He was released from captivity when the British retook Cawnpore on 17 July. All his family had perished.

208–9 *That evening . . . offered terms*: Thomson, *The Story of Cawnpore*, 148–50; Ward, 297–8.

209 *The following morning . . . 'not go back'*: ibid., 299; deposition of Futteh Sing, *State Papers*, III, app., ccxxi.

209 *Wheeler now appeared . . . while they still could*: Thomson, *The Story of Cawnpore*, 150; Ward, 299–300; *State Papers*, II, intro., 176–7.

209–10 *Whiting agreed . . . 'never breathed'*: Thomson, *The Story of Cawnpore*, 150–51; Ward, 300.

210 *The meeting . . . report to his master*: Thomson, *The Story of Cawnpore*, 152–3.

210 *An hour later . . . without hesitation*: ibid., 153–6; Ward, 301–2.

210 *'The soldiers were singing'*: Horne Narrative, Mutiny Papers, BL, Add, MSS 41488, f. 67.

210 *'draught after draught' . . . 'in safety'*: Thomson, *The Story of Cawnpore*, 157–8.

210–11 *Shortly after midday . . . 'river's bank'*: ibid., 156–7.

211 *The garrison's forebodings . . . 'all that [they] could'*: ibid., 155–6; Ward, 309–10.

211–12 *'loading themselves' . . . 'for the wounded'*: Thomson, *The Story of Cawnpore*, 160–62.

212 *An hour or two . . . Amy Horne's ears tingle*: ibid., 162–3; Horne Narrative, BL, Add. MSS 41488, ff. 68–70.

212 *But not all . . . 'firm belief'*: Thomson, *The Story of Cawnpore*, 163–4.

213 *'The sowars and sepoys'*: *State Papers*, III, app., lxxxviii.

213 *The loyal sepoys . . . similar fate*: depositions of Ewuz Khan, Gob-

ind Singh, Sheik Elahee Buksh and Ghouse Mahomed, and Khoda Bux, ibid., cii, cxiii and cxx–cxxi.

213–14 *Towards the back . . . cut her down as well*: depositions of Ayodhya Prasad, Ewuz Khan and Perma Nund, quoted in Ward, 316.

214 *Unaware of the murders*: Ward, 319–20.

214 *'The boats were not very close'*: Horne Narrative, BL, Add. MSS 41488, f. 70.

214 *'Mr McMullen'*: *State Papers*, III, app., lxxxviii.

214 *'Every boat was crowded'*: Horne Narrative, Mutiny Papers, BL, Add. MSS 41488, f. 70.

215 *'They were flat down'*: Thomson, *The Story of Cawnpore*, 165–6.

215 *'Now, from ambush'*: ibid., 166–7.

215 *Oudh bank of the river*: Nana Sahib's letter to Bhondu Sing, 26 June 1857, read: 'Arrangements for the destruction of these English will not be made here, but as these people will keep near the bank on the other side of the river, it is necessary that you should be prepared, and make a place to kill and destroy them on that side of the river, and having obtained a victory come here' (PP, HC, 1857–8, XLIV 112.) Confirmation that Nana wrote to Bhondu Sing, asking him to 'take care that no European of this party escaped', is provided by the statement of John Saunders, a drummer of the 17th NI (see FC, NAI, Nos. 525–30 of 30 December 1859, 23).

215–16 *'Those of us'*: Thomson, *The Story of Cawnpore*, 167–8.

216 *With most of the boats . . . 'women and children'*: *State Papers*, III, app., lxxxviii–lxxxix, xc–xci.

216 *'After the consultation' . . . 'being destroyed'*: ibid.

216 *Nana did not actually witness*: One writer has suggested that Nana Sahib was opposed to the massacre at the ghat. 'Nana could not see what would be gained by such treachery. The garrison was half dead already, and under the blistering sun, bumbling through the shallows of the receding Ganges, how many would ever reach Allahabad anyway? . . . But no one listened to him' (Ward, 344). In fact, as Nana's letter to Subedar Bhondu Sing of the 17th NI makes clear (see note above, p. 215), he wanted to escape responsibility for the massacre by arranging for non-Cawnpore troops to carry it out. On 27 June, the day of the massacre, Nana wrote the following to the Indian officers of the 41st NI and 1st Oudh Irregular Cavalry: 'Here . . . the white faces have fought with us. The whole of them, by the grace of God, and the destroying fortune of the King, have entered hell. A salute in honour of this event has been fired as usual. It behoves you also to celebrate this victory with rejoicings and peals of artillery' (*Freedom Struggle*, IV, 601).

216 *Nana's response*: *State Papers*, III, app., ccxxxviii; memorandum by Lieutenant-Colonel Williams, op. cit., xlvii.

216 *The shocked and bedraggled survivors*:

State Papers, III, app., lxxxix, ccxxiv.

217 *'Now the crowded state'*: Thomson, *The Story of Cawnpore*, 169–71.

217–18 *Among those tragically killed . . . but no food*: ibid., 91 and 171–3, 175–7.

218–19 *That night a storm blew . . . 'Company's raj would cease'*: ibid., 177–93.

220 *an unnamed European lady*: deposition of Futteh Sing, *State Papers*, III, ibid., ccxxiv.

220–21 *'The Cavalry surrounded us' . . . brought to justice*: Horne Narrative, BL, Add. MSS 41488, ff. 71–93.

221 *'rare and exceptional cases'*: C. B. Saunders to W. Muir, 17 December 1857, *Freedom Struggle*, V, 23–4.

221 *It was widely reported*: Ward, 504.

221 *'age 22 or 23 years'*: deposition of Ewuz Khan, *State Papers*, III, app., ciii.

221 *'during the outbreak'*: deposition of Manuck, ibid., cclxxx–cclxxxi.

221 *Two other spies*: Deposition of Narain and Bhow Raie, ibid., cclxxxi–cclxxxii.

221–2 *Nothing more was heard . . . long-lost daughter*: Ward, 505–6.

222 *'had entered into a treaty' . . . 'no treaties'*: *State Papers*, II, intro., 42.

222 *'We must try and blood them'*: ibid., 42–3.

222–3 *manned by Europeans*: The exact composition of the force was as follows. Infantry: 300 of 32nd Foot; 150 of 13th NI; 60 of 48th NI; 29 of 71st NI (Sikhs). Cavalry: 35 of Volunteer Cavalry; 120 of 1st, 2nd and 3rd Oudh Irregular Cavalry. Artillery: Four guns of No. 9 Field Battery (Europeans); two guns of the No. 2 Oudh Field Battery; four guns of No. 3 Oudh Field Battery; one 8-inch howitzer.

223 *'as fine an officer'*: 'Account of Chinhut' by Lieutenant Birch, in Hon. Julia Inglis, *The Siege of Lucknow*, 49.

223 *'very close and suffocating'*: Hewitt (ed.), *Eyewitnesses to the Indian Mutiny*, 132.

223 *'Neither Brigadier Inglis'*: 'Account of Chinhut' by Lieutenant Birch, op. cit., 51.

224 *'its shells being seen'*: Gubbins, *An Account of the Mutinies in Oudh*, 186.

224 *'That is it'*: *State Papers*, II, intro., 45.

224 *'It was one moving mass'*: Hewitt (ed.), *Eyewitnesses to the Indian Mutiny*, 132.

224 *'The Oudh Artillerymen and drivers were traitors'*: Brigadier Inglis to Colonel Birch, 26 September 1857, *Freedom Struggle*, II, 61.

225 *'noble fellows' . . . 'cowardice of the enemy'*: Tuker (ed.), *The Chronicle of Private Henry Metcalfe*, 29.

225 *'The notes of our trumpet'*: Hewitt (ed.), *Eyewitnesses to the Indian Mutiny*, 133.

225–6 *'I shan't last long' . . . 'soon put to rest'*: Tuker (ed.), *The Chronicle of Private Henry Metcalfe*, 30.

226 *'behaved with much steadiness' . . . 'had become foul'*: Gubbins, *An Account of the Mutinies in Oudh*, 188.

226 *'covered with foam'*: ibid., 182.

226 *in no condition to resist*: Tuker (ed.), *The Chronicle of Private Henry Metcalfe*, 30.

227 *'It is all right'*: Germon, *Journal*, 57.
227 *The Residency . . . Indian servants*: *State Papers*, II, intro., 60, 69.
227 *The British . . . 'forty-eight hours'*: ibid., 61–3n.
227–8 *'While we clustered round'*: Gubbins, *An Account of the Mutinies in Oudh*, 198.
228 *'precious health of Europeans' . . . 'MERCY ON HIM'*: Hewitt (ed.), *Eyewitnesses to the Indian Mutiny*, 137.
228 *'his expression was so happy'*: *State Papers*, II, intro., 64.
228 *'Dear Inglis'*: Tuker (ed.), *The Chronicle of Private Henry Metcalfe*, 34.
228 *Gubbins wrote later . . . 'the crisis'*: Kaye, *History of the Sepoy War*, III, app., 669–71.
229 *'cast a sad gloom'*: Anderson, *Siege of Lucknow*, 67.
229 *'He was buried'*: Germon, *Journal*, 59.
229 *'treatment and disposal'*: statement of Mir Wajid Ali, 8 July 1859, *Freedom Struggle*, II, 85.

CHAPTER FIFTEEN

230 *'The ground is covered'*: Humbly, *Journal*, 354.
230 *'ruffian population'*: Lind Papers, NAM, 5106-1-36, 1–4.
231 *'could not be trusted'*: Francis Lind's diary entry for 19 May 1857, Lind Papers, NAM, 5105-70-2, 62.
231 *'fully equal'*: Kaye and Malleson, II, 96.
231 *'He was the finest-looking'*: Hibbert, 200.
231–2 *Neill had arranged . . . eventually agreed*: Lieutenant-Colonel J. G. Neill to the Adjutant General, 6 June 1857, PP, HC, 1857, XXX, 479.
232 *'Our officers are deceiving us'*: Lieutenant-Colonel A. C. Spottiswoode to Brigadier J. Christie, 11 March 1858, PP, HC, 1859, xviii, 29.
232–3 *Once in possession . . . the news*: ibid., 29–30; Lieutenant R. W. Glasse to Captain F. J. Nelson, 16 March 1858, ibid., 32.
233 *'It was done hurriedly'*: Canning to Vernon Smith, 19 June 1857, Lyveden Papers, OIOC, MSS Eur/F231/5.
233 *'some young boys'*: Kaye and Malleson, II, 177.
233 *'exciting mutiny' . . . 'artistic manner'*: ibid., 207–8n, 177.
234 *'a few brick buildings'*: Humbly, *Journal*, 304.
234 *'to man the fort'*: *State Papers*, II, intro., 121.
234 *'European cheers'*: ibid., 122.
234 *'the Europeans were coming'*: deposition of Drummer John Fitchett of the 6th NI, ibid., III, app., l–li.
234–5 *Five officers . . . 'neglect of his wounds'*: *State Papers*, II, intro., 122–3; Kaye and Malleson, II, 188–90.
235 *The fort had been saved . . . 'diabolical nature'*: Kaye and Malleson, II, 190–93; *Red Pamphlet*, 92–8, quoted in *Freedom Struggle*, IV, 544.
235 *Liaqat Ali*: One official source describes the Maulvi as a 'weaver by caste, and by trade a schoolmaster' who 'had gained some respect in his village by his

excessive sanctity' (Kaye and Malleson, II, 197). A Indian witness at his trial, on the other hand, stated that 'he became a Maulvi and began to lead prayers at the Mahagaon Mosque' after his dismissal from the army 'as a result of mischief and violence' (*Freedom Struggle*, IV, 550).

235 *'I saw one or two'*: deposition of Drummer John Fitchett, op. cit., liii.

236 *'began to make appointments' . . . 'religious war'*: depositions in the criminal case against Maulvi Liaqat Ali, *Freedom Struggle*, IV, 550–51.

236 *'Thank God, sir'*: Kaye and Malleson, II, 197.

236 *'I was quite done up'*: ibid., 198n.

236 *'little or nothing'*: *State Papers*, II, intro., 126.

236 *'some on slight proofs'*: Hibbert, 202.

236–7 *'God grant'*: Kaye and Malleson, II, 202n.

237 *'inhuman insurrection'*: Part of the reason why Neill and his subordinates treated suspected rebels with such harshness was because they believed the exaggerated accounts of atrocities up-country. In the same journal entry for 17 June, Neill wrote: 'Miss Jennings and her father, a clergyman at Delhi, are both brutally murdered in the palace before the king, she, poor creature, subjected to the most unheard-of indignities and torture beforehand.' In fact, as we have seen, she was neither killed in front of the king nor raped.

237 *'arrest all suspected'*: C. Chester to W. Glynn, 20 June 1857, PP, HC, 1857–8, XLIV, 14.

237 *'a policy of burning villages' . . . 'tried and hanged'*: extract of an unofficial letter from Allahabad, 36.

237 *When Canning learnt . . . outrage took place*: resolution of the Government of India, 31 July 1857, PP, HC, 1857–8, XLIV, 8.

237–8 *'Lenity towards'*: Maclagan, 136.

238 *'It really is a most amiable'*: *The Times*, 17 October 1857.

238 *'As long as I have breath'*: Canning to Granville, 11 December 1857, in Fitzmaurice, I, 274.

238 *'I never liked'*: Granville to Canning, 24 October 1857, ibid., 261.

238 *'From nobody but yourself'*: Canning to Granville, 11 December 1857, ibid., 276.

238–9 *'Lord Canning'*: Queen Victoria to Canning, 9 November 1857, in Maclagan, 141.

239 *Colonel Neill . . . 'chastising Englishmen'*: *State Papers*, II, intro., 126; Kaye and Malleson, II, 202.

240 *'Attack and destroy'*: ibid., 207.

240 *'In the first two days'*: Hewitt (ed.), *Eyewitnesses to the Indian Mutiny*, 111.

240–42 *Born in Sunderland . . . draught animals*: Hibbert, 198–9; *State Papers*, II, intro., 106–16; Kaye and Malleson, II, 209–14.

242 *'The news' . . . 'overtaken by the General'*: *State Papers*, II, intro., 127.

242 *Nana Sahib's raj . . . so long denied him*: Ward, 341–2.

243 *two proclamations*: *State Papers*, II, 119.

243 *'4th July'*: *State Papers*, III, app., cccxxx–cccxxxii.

244 *actually left . . . on 9 July*: deposition of Futteh Sing, ibid., ccxxv.

244 *1,185 men*: Havelock's column was composed as follows: European troops: 3rd Coy, 8th Bn, Royal Artillery – 76; Bengal Artillery – 22; 1st Madras Fusiliers – 376; 64th Foot – 435; 78th Highlanders – 284; 84th Foot – 190; Volunteer Cavalry – 20. Indian troops: Ferozepore Sikhs – 448; 13th Irregular and 3rd Oudh Irregular Cavalry – 95; Golundaze – 18.

244 *'We drew up in line' . . . 'lay down in groups'*: *State Papers*, II, intro., 129–30.

244 *'We retired slowly'*: Lieutenant John A. Grant to his brother, 8 July 1857, Grant Papers OIOC, MSS Eur/C323.

244 *'The troops all fell out'*: Major North, 'Journal of an English Officer in India', *State Papers*, II, intro., 130n.

244–5 *'But the enemy maintained'*: Brigadier-General Havelock to the Deputy Adjutant-General, 12 July 1857, ibid., 86.

245 *'Accordingly, I dismounted'*: Hewitt (ed.), *Eyewitnesses to the Indian Mutiny*, 113.

245 *'In succession they were driven'*: Havelock to the Deputy Adjutant-General, 12 July 1857, op. cit., 87–8.

245–6 *'On seeing the enemy'*: quoted in *State Papers*, II, intro., 132.

246 *'Their fire'*: Brigadier-General Havelock to the Deputy Adjutant-General, 12 July 1857, op. cit., 87.

246 *'The poor creature'*: Hewitt (ed.), *Eyewitnesses to the Indian Mutiny*, 113–14.

246 *'One of the prayers'*: Havelock to his wife, 12 July 1857, *State Papers*, II, intro., 133.

246 *ten guns and two mortars*: Two light brass 6-pounders, five light brass 9-pounders, one iron 12-pounder garrison gun, one iron 24-pounder garrison gun, one brass 24-pounder howitzer, one iron 10-inch mortar, one brass 5½-inch mortar.

247 *'In [the first] ten minutes'*: quoted in Stokes, *The Peasant Armed*, 59.

247 *Havelock's casualties*: Brigadier-General Havelock to the Deputy Adjutant-General, 15 July 1857, op. cit., 92–3.

247 *'His entrenchments cut'*: 20 July 1857, ibid., 99.

247–8 *'dreadfully tired' . . . 'upon their left'*: Hewitt (ed.), *Eyewitnesses to the Indian Mutiny*, 115.

248 *'strongly posted' . . . 'guns captured?'*: Brigadier-General Havelock to the Deputy Adjutant-General, 20 July 1857, *State Papers*, II, 100.

248 *'Now, Highlanders'*: *State Papers*, II, intro., 138.

248 *'like a scoop of cheese'*: Hewitt (ed.), *Eyewitnesses to the Indian Mutiny*, 116.

248 *'Give point, lads'*: *State Papers*, II, intro., 138.

249 *'Come, who'll take this village?'*: ibid., 139.

249 *'Whilst in this position'*: Bingham Diary, NAM, 5903-105.

249 *'Just then there came'*: Hewitt (ed.), *Eyewitnesses to the Indian Mutiny*, 116–17.

249–50 *'My artillery cattle' . . . in his report*: Brigadier-General Havelock to the Deputy Adjutant-General, 20 July 1857, op. cit., 100–101.

250 *heavy British casualties*: *State Papers*, II, 102.
250 *'my waterproof coat'*: ibid., intro., 141.
251 *'only a small quantity' . . . 'rebellious sepoys'*: Mr Shepherd's narrative, ibid., 138.
251 *not 'ill-treated'*: deposition of John Fitchett, *State Papers*, III, app., lviii and lxii.
252 *'two or three women'*: deposition of Futteh Sing, ibid., ccxxvii.
252 *'fresh clothes'*: deposition of John Fitchett, ibid., lxii.
252 *council of war*: memorandum of Lieutenant-Colonel G. W. Williams, 29 March 1859, ibid., xlvii–xlviii.
252 *most . . . were in favour of murdering them*: deposition of Hulas Sing, ibid., clxi.
252 *'if they were left alive'*: deposition of Futteh Sing, ibid., ccxxvi.
252–3 *'the fort of Allahabad'*: ibid., ccxxi.
253 *the Begum 'told the ladies' . . . 'might be saved'*: deposition of John Fitchett, ibid., lxiv.
253 *So the Begum*: memorandum of Lieutenant-Colonel G. W. Williams, 29 March 1859, ibid., xlviii–xlix.
253 *Two of them*: ibid., lxv.
253 *'about 35 years of age'*: deposition of Gunga Bishen, ibid., cclxxii.
253 *with a sallow complexion*: deposition of Punchum, ibid., cclxxi.
254 *'fearful shrieks'*: deposition of John Fitchett, ibid., lxiv.
254 *'no pity'*: deposition of Punchum, ibid., cclxx.
254 *'few minutes'*: deposition of John Fitchett, ibid., lxiv–lxv.
254 *'groans lasted all night' . . . a hundred paces*: ibid., lxv–lxvi.
254–5 *When news . . . 'different directions'*: Mr Shepherd's narrative, *State Papers*, II, 139–40.
255 *'experienced a slight shock'*: report of J. W. Sherer, 13 January 1859, ibid., III, app., xxxv.
255 *'The frightful massacre'*: Lieutenant William Hargood to his parents, 18 July 1857, Hargood Letters, NAM, 5206-10.
255 *'It is a couple of oblong buildings'*: Lieutenant J. A. Grant to his brother, 17 July 1857, Grant Papers, OIOC, MSS Eur/C323.
255–6 *'The place was literally running'*: Bingham Diary, NAM, 5903-105.
256 *'Mamma died'*: Thomson, *The Story of Cawnpore*, 217.
256 *'The whole of the pavement'*: Hewitt (ed.), *Eyewitnesses to the Indian Mutiny*, 119–20.
257 *no clear evidence of 'dishonour'*: report of J. W. Sherer, 13 January 1859, *State Papers*, III, app., xxxi.
257 *Major G. W. Williams*: quoted in William Muir's 'Memorandum containing the result of enquiries made by the desire of the Governor-General into the rumours of European females having been dishonoured during the late Mutinies', 30 December 1857, Kaye Mutiny Papers, OIOC, H725, 642.
257 *'The natives of India'*: memorandum by E. A. Reade, 2 December 1857, ibid., 641–2.
257 *'Hindoos would regard'*: letter from C. B. Thornhill to W. Muir, 26 December 1857, ibid., 646–7.

257 *Muslims would never have 'done so' . . . 'lust of desire'*: William Muir's memorandum, op. cit., 30 December 1857, ibid., 637 and 634.

258 *'Such was the loathsome'*: Thomson, *The Story of Cawnpore*, 212.

258 *'Now General Neill'*: Hewitt (ed.), *Eyewitnesses to the Indian Mutiny*, 121.

258 *Nana Sahib . . . had 'found it impossible'*: report of J. W. Sherer, 13 January 1859, *State Papers*, III, app., xxxvi–xxxvii.

258 *'We looted a good deal'*: Hewitt (ed.), *Eyewitnesses to the Indian Mutiny*, 121.

259 *'Whenever a rebel is caught'*: ibid., 122.

259 *'We made the Nana Sahib's Collector'*: Bingham Diary, NAM, 5903-105.

259 *'It is rumoured'*: Vernon Smith to Canning, 9 October 1857, Lyveden Papers, OIOC, MSS Eur/F231/5.

259 *'I felt as if my heart was stone'*: Lang, 121–3.

260 *'We are in sad anxiety'*: Benson and Esher (eds.), *The Letters of Queen Victoria*, III, 313.

CHAPTER SIXTEEN

261 *'We are very weak'*: Kaye and Malleson, III, 9–10.

261 *'About 180 horsemen'*: Canning to Vernon Smith, 19 June 1857, in Maclagan, 102.

261–2 *'The English Press'*: quoted in ibid., 103–4.

262 *'Your, or rather Lady Canning's'*: Granville to Canning, 10 August 1857, in Fitzmaurice, I, 256.

262 *'a terrible conspiracy' . . . '"our own King"'*: Sneyd Papers, OIOC, MSS Eur/Photo.Eur.44, 97–111.

262–3 *The fears . . . 'intended to them'*: Canning to Vernon Smith, 19 June 1857, Lyveden Papers, OIOC, MSS Eur/F231/5.

263 *a 'return of the panic'*: ibid.

263 *'beyond all belief'*: Hon. G. Talbot to Sir H. G. Ward, 19 June 1857, Talbot Papers, OIOC, MSS Eur/F271/1.

263 *'highest in office'*: Kaye and Malleson, III, 16–17.

263–4 *That same day . . . 'the last of these??!'*: Talbot to Ward, 19 June 1857, Talbot Papers, op. cit.

264 *'one of the cleverest'*: Sleeman, *A Journey through the Kingdom of Oudh*, II, 58.

264 *'Although no complicity'*: Canning to Vernon Smith, 19 June 1857, Lyveden Papers, OIOC, MSS Eur/F231/5.

264–5 *Another major problem . . . Cabinet agreed*: Maclagan, 110–11.

265 *On Monday, 29 June . . . 'remedying them'*: *Hansard's*, 3rd Series, CXLVI, June–July 1857, 537–44.

265 *'The bulk of the European force'*: Palmerston to Queen Victoria, 26 June 1857, Benson and Esher (eds.), *The Letters of Queen Victoria*, III, 297–8.

265 *'she had long been'*: Queen Victoria to Lord Panmure, 29 June 1857, ibid., 298–9.

266 *'were able to shorten the course'*: *Hansard's*, 3rd Series, CXLVI, June–July 1857, 949.

266 *'I think it most advisable'*: Vernon Smith to Canning, 27 July 1857, Lyveden Papers, OIOC, MSS Eur/F231/4.

266 *'The last accounts'*: Queen Victoria to Lord Palmerston, 2 August 1857, Benson and Esher (eds.), *The Letters of Queen Victoria*, III, 306.

266 *'the neck of the insurrection'*: Canning to Vernon Smith, 5 June 1857, Lyveden Papers, OIOC, MSS Eur/F231/5.

267 *'The Cabinet'*: Lord Granville to Canning, 10 July 1857, in Fitzmaurice, I, 251.

267 *'If you wish'*: Canning to Vernon Smith, 5 June 1857, op. cit.

267 *'You have done excellently'*: Vernon Smith to Canning, 10 August 1857, ibid., MSS Eur/F231/4.

267–8 *'His whole thoughts'*: Captain Barter, quoted in Hibbert, 334.

268 *'I trust he may prove different'*: Vernon Smith to Canning, 10 August 1857, op. cit.

268 *'Our voyage'*: Richardson Papers, NAM, 8207-94, 92.

268 *'intimate correspondence'*: narrative of events by Robert Taylor, Officiating Joint Magistrate of Jaunpur, 6 November 1858, *Freedom Struggle*, IV, 116.

269 *'could not . . . move'*: Havelock to Grant, 31 July 1857, *State Papers*, II, intro., 199.

270 *'with great grief' . . . 'their way out'*: 6 August 1857, ibid., II, 172.

270 *'a brave old man'*: Grant to his sister-in-law, 31 July 1857, Grant Letters, OIOC, MSS Eur/C323.

270 *'Our unsuccessful attempt'*: Grant to his brother Alexander, 14 August 1857, ibid.

270–71 *Havelock returned . . . baggage*: Stokes, *The Peasant Armed*, 64–5; Kaye and Malleson, III, 343–4.

271 *During the same period . . . most of them regulars*: PP, HC, 1857–8, XLIV, 307.

271 *'When we first came'*: Devi Deen in conversation with Lieutenant-General Sir George MacMunn, quoted in Hewitt (ed.), *Eyewitnesses to the Indian Mutiny*, 27.

271 *'violent, abusive altercation'*: *Two Native Narratives*, 104–5.

272 *'The rebels were becoming'*: ibid., 65.

272 *Such infighting . . . shops*: Bandopadhyay, 87–9, 97–8.

272 *close their shops*: Kaushik Roy wrote: 'All these commissariat difficulties delayed Bakht Khan's plan of marching to Delhi quickly and this ruined the Rebels' prospect of a quick victory over the emaciated Delhi Field Force' (Roy, 'Company Bahadur against the Pandies: The Military Dimension of the 1857 Mutiny Revisited', *JUJH*, vols. 19–20, 2001–2).

272 *At his first . . . 'for festivities'*: *Two Native Narratives*, 133–5.

273 *'fit for an invalid couch'*: Brigadier Wilson to his wife, 6 July 1857, Wilson Letters, NAM, 6807-483.

273 *'more besieged than besiegers'*: ibid., 17 July 1857.

273 *'This Company were not Seikhs'*: ibid., 3 July 1857.

273 *'They tore in'*: Tytler, 153.

273 *'The mistake of leaving'*: Greathed, *The Siege of Delhi*, 104–5.

273–4 *The other rebel attacks . . . 500 killed*: *State Papers*, I, intro., 64.

274 *'Here we are'*: 2nd Lieutenant Chichester to his mother, Chichester Letters, OIOC, MSS Eur/Photo. Eur.271, 31–2.

274 *'There is not a braver heart'*: quoted in *State Papers*, I, intro., 65.

274 *'He ought never to have been there'*: Wilson to his wife, 15 July 1857, Wilson Letters, NAM, 6807-483.

274 *'knew his work'*: Brigadier Sir J. Hope Grant, quoted in *State Papers*, I, intro., 65.

274–5 *'fearful responsibility'*: Brigadier Wilson to his wife, 17 July 1857, Wilson Letters, NAM, 6807-483.

275 *'The latest tidings'*: Grant to Major-General Barnard, 13 July 1857, Grant Letters, OIOC, MSS Eur/C569.

275 *'in hourly expectation'*: ibid., 19 July 1857.

275 *'unless speedily reinforced'*: Wilson to Sir J. Lawrence, 18 July 1857, Wilson Correspondence, NAM, 5710-38.

275 *'we can send you'*: Lawrence to Wilson, 21 July 1857, ibid.

276 *'make a merit of necessity' . . . 'We are unanimously'*: quoted in Allen, 283.

276–7 *'Hold on to Peshawar' . . . 'present moment'*: quoted in Maclagan, 113.

277 *'They came out of a personal devotion*: Allen, 288.

277 *Nicholson's ruthlessness . . . 'Thank God'*: Gimlette, 138 and 142.

277 *'Subsequent to being disarmed'*: return of the 59th Regiment by Lieutenant-Colonel Hugh Boyd, 11 March 1858, PP, HC, 1859, XVIII, 64.

278 *'For about ten minutes'*: quoted in Allen, 292.

279 *'The real business'*: ibid., 293.

279 *Nicholson's reinforcements*: Roberts, 114.

279 *one official estimate*: PP, HC, 1857–8, XLIV, 307.

279 *'no account whatever'*: A separate source put the rebel strength in Delhi at 17,975 troops and 33 guns (a letter of news from Futteh Mahomed Khan, 13 August 1857, copies of letters from spies in the city of Delhi, 6807-138, NAM). Most of the spies were of the opinion that no more than 20,000 armed rebels were at Delhi by mid August. Their reports tended to emphasize the low morale of the mutineers. The following is typical: 'General Bukht Khan wishes to leave the City with his Division. It is said he intends to go to Nepaul. The officers of the Nusseerabad Brigade represented to the King that 5,000 fresh troops had reached the British camp and that more are coming, and that a great number of their own men had fallen & that the rest were discomfited, that they had neither ammunition or food & that it was useless to fight. The King replied that he had neither ammunition nor treasure & told them to take what they could find. On this the officers went away in dejection' (intelligence from the city, 15 August 1857, copies of letters from spies in the city of Delhi, 6807-138, NAM).

279–80 *Nicholson joined me*: Wilson Letters, NAM, 6807-483.

280 *60,000 trained troops . . . had mutinied*: David, 257.

281 *'fight against their King'*: Captain H. D. Abbott, commanding 1st Cavalry, Hyderabad Contingent, to Mr C. Davidson, Resident at Hyderabad, 13 June 1857, PP, HC, 1857, XXX, 579.

281 *'Fire!'*: Lowe, *Central India*, 30–33.

281 *'We always go to bed'*: Mrs Lowry to her sister-in-law, 28 June 1857, Lowry Letters, NAM, 6711-24.

281 *At around the same time . . . a week later*: Lowe, *Central India*, 24–5; Governor-General to the Court of Directors, 30 June 1857 (No. 193), PP, HC, 1857, XXX, 500.

281 *'no record of past warfare'*: Cadell, *History of the Bombay Army*, 202.

281 *The mutiny . . . purbias*: return by the military secretary to the Government of Bombay, 29 January 1858, PP, HC, 1859, XVIII.

282 *for plotting rebellion*: Baker, 'Colonial Beginnings and the Indian Response', 528.

282 *losing India*: One of the few exceptions is Dr Kaushik Roy, a leading Indian military historian. In a recent article he concluded that the defeat of the rebels was not 'inevitable'. He added:

> The reinforcements from England reached India in substantial quantity only in November. So, the Rebels had five precious months to destroy the British presence in India . . . The Rebels could have achieved decisive battlefield success by following [what Liddell Hart termed as indirect] strategy. Simultaneous attacks at the enemy's weak points like the depots and hospitals, which the Rebels could have done easily given their superiority in cavalry, would have generated a synergy and this would have destabilized the British position. The Company would have been forced to dissipate its troops in manning its ever-lengthy lines of communications. And this could have weakened their main field army, thus setting the stage for the decisive phase. Such a stage might have been reached when, due to continuous dissipation, the Company's field army would have been too weak to meet the Rebels' field army. However, the Rebels finally resorted to mobile guerrilla warfare in 1858, when the military balance had already swung against them . . .

Roy also believes that the rebels of central India should have advanced into the Bombay Presidency where – thanks to the social and regional composition of the Bombay Army – 'there was a high chance of Bombay Army personnel sympathizing with their brethren in the Bengal Army'. He adds: 'Unlike the Bengal Army, in the Bombay Army, young Indian soldiers were promoted on the basis of their military performance and not on the basis of seniority. So, if the Bombay Army rebelled, then the Rebels would have acquired an excellent crop of young Indian officers full of determination and capable of seizing the initiative even under adverse conditions.' Mobile warfare, Roy concluded, 'would have resulted in an attritional campaign and the fate of 1857 India might have turned out like Vietnam of the 1970s' (Roy, 'Company Bahadur against the Pandies', *JUJH*, vols. 19–20, 2001–2).

CHAPTER SEVENTEEN

283 *'As we stood'*: Vibart, 136.

283–4 *'A week after' . . . amused for hours*: Tytler, 147–51.

284 *'The rains are something frightful'*: 2nd Lieutenant H. Chichester to his mother, 3 August 1857, Chichester Letters, OIOC, MSS Eur/Photo.Eur.271.

284 *'putrid corpses'*: Lieutenant C. J. Griffiths, quoted in Hewitt (ed.), *Eyewitnesses to the Indian Mutiny*, 29.

284 *'For the short time'*: Roberts, 107.

284–5 *'applied glue mixed with sugar'*: Surgeon E. Hare, quoted in Hewitt (ed.), *Eyewitnesses to the Indian Mutiny*, 30.

285 *Bored officers*: Tytler, 152.

285 *'A pair [of field glasses]'*: 2nd Lieutenant H. Chichester to his mother, 3 August 1857, Chichester Letters, OIOC, MSS Eur/Photo.Eur.271.

285 *'I watched the race'*: Griffiths, *Narrative*, 84.

285–7 *One event in August . . . Ambala safely*: Tytler, 155–8.

286 *'till he died too'*: Lieutenant-Colonel Gambier, in a letter to Miss Annie Forrest of 20 August 1857, wrote: 'A Mrs Leeson was brought in to our pickets yesterday by two Peshawar men. She has been all this time under the protection of a Moulvie by the Lahore gate. She is a half caste and dark enough to pass muster in native clothes. She is related to Collins and her husband was in some office. The day of the row her baby was shot at her breast, the shot passing through into her body; the wound is healed. Two other little children had their throats cut before her eyes' (Gambier Letters, NAM, 6211-67).

287 *'Many of the men'*: quoted in Allen, 306.

287 *'an aggregation of untutored horsemen'*: *State Papers*, I, intro., 72.

287–8 *'The enemy moved out'*: ibid., 72–3.

289 *'Hold your fire' . . . "Charge!"*: Vibart, 138.

289 *'Thank you, sir'*: ibid., 139.

289 *'gigantic pandy'*: Kaye and Malleson, II, 492n.

289 *'Only a few'*: Vibart, 138–9.

289 *'Our Horse Artillery'*: quoted in Hewitt (ed.), *Eyewitnesses to the Indian Mutiny*, 41–2.

290 *'I immediately sent orders'*: *State Papers*, II, intro., 74.

290 *'only partial success'*: Lieutenant C. J. Griffiths, quoted in Hewitt (ed.), *Eyewitnesses to the Indian Mutiny*, 41–2.

290 *'unable or unwilling'*: Gimlette, 18.

290 *'a thousand killed'*: *Two Native Narratives*, 208.

290 *'false to his salt' . . . 'loud in their complaints'*: ibid., 209–12, 215–16.

290 *'Considering that the country'*:

Wilson to his wife, 27 August 1857, Wilson Letters, NAM, 6807-483.

291 *'I wish I had the power'*: Kaye and Malleson, II, 494.

291 *'Every day'*: Roberts, 116–17.

291–2 *'Everyone felt'*: Field Marshal Earl Roberts to Sir William Lee Warner, 3 December 1911, Wilson Correspondence, NAM, 5710-38.

292 *'We are busy preparing'*: Wilson Letters, NAM, 6807-483.

292 *'fully appreciated'*: Roberts, 117.

292 *'I believe his mind'*: quoted in Allen, 313.

292–3 *'I was sitting'*: Roberts, 118.

293 *'I have seen lots'*: quoted in Allen, 314.

293–4 *'The Moree proceeded'*: General R. Barter, quoted in Allen, 315.

294 *'a constant fire' . . . 'on as before'*: Roberts, 120.

294 *'maintained a perfect storm'*: *State Papers*, II, 79.

295 *breaches were 'practicable'*: Roberts, 121–3.

295 *The infantry . . . form a reserve*: ibid., 123–4; *State Papers*, II, 80–81.

295 *'A very insufficient guard'*: Lieutenant C. J. Griffiths, quoted in Hewitt (ed.), *Eyewitnesses to the Indian Mutiny*, 50.

295–6 *'No sooner were the front ranks'*: Roberts, 125–6.

296 *'Up went our ladder'*: Lang, 90.

297 *'Away we went'*: quoted in Hewitt (ed.), *Eyewitnesses to the Indian Mutiny*, 60.

297–8 *'On we rushed' . . . to the Kabul Gate*: Lang, 92.

298 *'We saw the repulse'*: Allen, 321–2.

299 *'Nothing daunted'*: Roberts, 127–8.

299–300 *'more anxious' . . . 'shoot him, if necessary'*: ibid., 129–32.

301 *'We are now holding'*: Wilson to his wife, 15 September 1857, Wilson Letters, NAM, 6807-483.

301 *'gaily painted doors'*: Lang, 93.

301 *'Our force is too weak' . . . 'doing their duty'*: Wilson to his wife, 16 September 1857, Wilson Letters, NAM, 6807-483.

302 *Hodson's spies*: Colonel K. Young to his wife, 17 September 1857, in Young, 290.

302 *'very disheartened'*: Wilson to his wife, 17 September 1857, Wilson Letters, NAM, 6807-483.

302 *Unbeknown to Wilson . . . as he could muster*: *Two Native Narratives*, 70.

302 *'We are . . . progressing favourably'*: Wilson to his wife, 19 September 1857, Wilson Letters, NAM, 6807-483.

302 *'finding none but dead'*: Lang, 96.

302 *'As soon as the smoke'*: Roberts, 136.

302–3 *the race to 'sit first' . . . 'allowed to take'*: Lang, 97.

303 *'indiscriminate plunder'*: general order of 6 September 1857, Wilson Letters, NAM, 6807-483.

303 *'appropriated . . . much treasure'*: Ensign Wilberforce, quoted in Hewitt (ed.), *Eyewitnesses to the Indian Mutiny*, 71–2.

303 *honesty did not pay*: Stanley, *White Mutiny*, 91–2; James, *Warrior Race*, 331–2.

303 *'an immense sum'*: Ensign Wilberforce, quoted in Hewitt (ed.), *Eyewitnesses to the Indian Mutiny*, 72.

303 *Lang and others celebrated*: Lang, 97.

303–4 *'victory would be incomplete' . . . 'his men only'*: Roberts, 137.

304 *'At the door stood'*: Vibart, 146–7.
305 *'We started at eight o'clock'*: Hibbert, 315.
305 *'There was a murmur'*: ibid., 315–16.
305 *'I came up* just in time': Allen, 333.
305 *'I think we had better shoot them' . . . 'a fearful risk'*: Hibbert, 316.
306 *'most virulent against us'*: Wilson to his wife, 22 September 1857, Wilson Letters, NAM, 6807-483.
306 *'I feel as if all happiness'*: Allen, 326–7.
306 *that 'fine fellow Nicholson'*: Wilson to his wife, 23 September 1857, Wilson Letters, NAM, 6807-483.
307 *'Probably not one of these men'*: Hewitt (ed.), *Eyewitnesses to the Indian Mutiny*, 73–4.
307 *'flying Rebels'*: Wilson to his wife, 22 September 1857, Wilson Letters, NAM, 6807-483.
307 *'city of the dead'*: Roberts, 142.
307–8 *'Had the fellows any pluck'*: Wilson Letters, NAM, 6807-483.
308 *No sooner had news . . . 10,000 men*: Roberts, 139.
308 *'sadly disorganized' . . . 'put down'*: Wilson to his wife, 21, 22 and 23 September 1857, Wilson Letters, NAM, 6807-483.

CHAPTER EIGHTEEN

309 *Fortunately Outram . . . 'clawing of a cat!'*: *State Papers*, II, intro., 1–2n.
309 *He acted . . . Commissioner of Oudh*: ibid., 2–4.
309 *'Outram's arrival'*: Maclagan, 118–19.
310 *'very common looking'*: ibid., 122.
310 *'gloriously fought' . . . 'reposed in them'*: Kaye and Malleson, III, 352–3.
310 *According to Havelock's son . . . 'coldness and ingratitude'*: Hibbert, 259–60.
311 *'The enemy have continued'*: *State Papers*, II, intro., 95 and 100.
311 *'The heart aches'*: ibid., 186.
311–12 *'Mrs Clark's infant died' . . . 'quite well again'*: Bartrum, *Reminiscences*, 35–7.
312 *'I have upwards'*: Brigadier Inglis to Brigadier-General Havelock, 25 August 1857, *State Papers*, II, 34–5.
312 *'I can only say'*: Hewitt (ed.), *Eyewitnesses to the Indian Mutiny*, 146.
312–13 *'Bruère's death'*: Inglis, *The Siege of Lucknow*, 142.
313 *'The army crossed the river'*: *State Papers*, II, intro., 102.
313 *'Such joyful news!'*: Bartrum, *Reminiscences*, 43.
313 *'We followed across country'*: Hall Papers, NAM, '1857' (54)/11919, 6–7.
313–14 *'It was most exciting'*: Lieutenant Hargood to his parents, 18 November 1857, Hargood Letters, NAM, 5206-10.
314 *'The troops had been marching'*: Havelock to Captain Norman, assistant adjutant-general, 30 September 1857, *State Papers*, II, 221.
315 *'dead and dying'*: Hall Papers, NAM, '1857' (54)/11919, 11.
315 *'From this point' . . . 'the enclosure of the Residency'*: Havelock to Norman, 30 September 1857, op. cit., 221–2.
316 *'How I escaped'*: Lieutenant Hargood to his parents, 18 November

1857, Hargood Letters, NAM, 5206-10.

316 *shot in the head*: Hall Papers, NAM, '1857' (54)/11919, 12; Kaye and Malleson, III, 364.

316 *'We had no idea'*: Harris, *A Lady's Diary*, 120.

316 *'The noise, confusion'*: Bartrum, *Reminiscences*, 43–4.

317–18 *'Was up with the daylight' . . . leave India for ever'*: ibid., 44–7, 70–72.

318 *In just two days*: *State Papers*, II, 223.

318 *'Want of carriage'*: Outram to Campbell, 30 September 1857, ibid., 228.

318 *Earlier that month . . . in any strength*: Coming to Outram, 18 September 1857, PP, HC, 1857–8, XLIV.

318 *Outram decided to stay*: Outram to Campbell, 30 September 1857, *State Papers*, II, 227–8.

318 *'Everyone is depressed'*: Hewitt (ed.), *Eyewitnesses to the Indian Mutiny*, 150–51.

318 *'But for their timely arrival'*: ibid., 151.

319 *'A more gallant fellow'*: Captain F. Sitwell to his parents, 1 December 1857, Sitwell Letters, OIOC, MSS Eur/Photo./Eur.357.

319 *a 'muff of a fellow' . . . 'on the road'*: Roberts, *Letters*, 69.

319 *'urgent call for assistance' . . . 'Native comrades'*: Roberts, 148–9.

320 *'The spectacle was imposing'*: Thornhill, *Personal Adventures*, 295.

320 *When Greathed asked*: Roberts, 149.

320 *many 'reliable' natives . . . 'position was unsafe'*: Thornhill, *Personal Adventures*, 291.

320 *2,000 men*: Made up largely of mutineers from Mhow and Indore in central India, including the 23rd NI.

320 *'We were then not aware'*: Roberts, 149.

320 *'bivouacked within a mile'*: Thornhill, *Personal Adventures*, 298–9.

320 *'At this moment'*: Potiphar Papers, NAM, 7201-45, 97.

321 *'Instantly' . . . 'enemy's flank'*: Roberts, 151.

321 *'As our men charged'*: Thornhill, *Personal Adventures*, 302–3.

321 *'a most exciting chase'*: Roberts, 153.

322 *'begging that aid might be sent'*: ibid., 158–60.

322 *'I think that Sir Patrick Grant'*: Maclagan, 125.

322 *'We find him very amiable'*: ibid., 123.

323 *'so obviously to the advantage'*: Hibbert, 336.

324 *food 'will only last till the* 10th *November'*: Roberts, *Letters*, 88.

324 *'I had,' he wrote . . . 'never to be obliterated'*: Kavanagh, *How I Won the Victoria Cross*, 75–93.

326 *The rebel defenders*: Roberts, 184.

326 *Most of the 15th . . . 'fourteen years of age'*: ibid., 174–82.

327 *'Remember Cawnpore!'*: Lang, 139.

328 *'They were now completely caught'*: Roberts, 182.

328 *Eventually the mass . . .* 'the *bad regiment at Cawnpore'*: Lang, 139.

328 *'I saw the body of a woman'*: Hibbert, 341.

329 *'I had never before met either' . . . 'of the Mutiny'*: Roberts, 188–9.

329 *'Every man was on duty'*: ibid., 190.

330 *'regaled with tea' . . . 'slept till morning'*: Bartrum, *Reminiscences*, 54–6.

330 *'including grain'*: One Indian historian has written:

One of the principal factors behind the successful British defence of Lucknow Residency was the construction of a superior commissariat system, a feature which was absent in General Wheeler's entrenchment at Kanpur. From 24 October 1856 onwards, the Deputy Commissioner with the aid of civilian officials started buying up grain from the local sources. A far-sighted policy indeed. Those European grain traders cooperated with the British bureaucracy. The Chief Commissioner was assigned the task of preparing an inventory of all the supplies including rum, port and fodder for the baggage animals. Further, he was ordered to prepare an average of daily expenditure. Daily expenditure of grain was calculated to about 8,000 lb. The total strength of the garrison under siege was 3,420 soldiers. The scale of daily ration was fixed. Each British combatant received 1 lb of meat and 1 lb of flour with some salt. Along with the soldiers, many civilians were also cooped up within the Residency . . . A child over 12 years of age received 12 oz of meat and those below that age received about 8 oz of meat. Every day, a woman was served 6 oz meat, 12 oz *atta*, 1.5 oz rice, 1 lb grain and .5 oz salt. Each Indian follower received 1 lb of *atta*, 2 oz of grain and .25 oz of salt. Initially mutton and sheep were provided. But, when they were finished, the dead gun bullocks were used for meat. The siege lasted from 1 July 1857 till 17 November 1857. On 2 October 1857, the Residency had 280,000 lb of grain. When the garrison marched out, it still had 160,000 lb of grain. (Roy, 'Company Bahadur against the Pandies', 2001–2.)

330–31 *'Not a sound was heard'*: Hall Papers, NAM, '1857' (54)/11919, 25.

331 *'I die happy'*: Hibbert, 350.

331 *On 27 November . . . he struck*: Roberts, 200–204.

331 *The rebels . . . north-west of Bithur*: Ward, 488.

332 *'We were evidently unexpected' . . . 'left in our hands'*: Roberts, 205–6.

332 *'Our star was in the ascendant'*: Forbes-Mitchell, *The Relief of Lucknow*, 93.

332 *'We even had to pay'*: Ward, 492.

332 *'Such rubbish I never read'*: Roberts, 210; Roberts, *Letters*, 120–21.

CHAPTER NINETEEN

333 *But real power*: *Freedom Struggle*, V, 730–33; Ward, 463.

333 *Since then . . . posts*: list of notable rebels, FC, NAI, Nos. 1354–5 of 30 December 1859, Nos. 118–20.

333–4 *'On the line thundered'*: Roberts, 214–15.

334 *'while wrenching the staff'*: Roberts, *Letters*, 124–5.

334 *'a pretty station'*: Anson, *With HM 9th Lancers*, 225–6.

334 *'No wild beast' . . . 'between the two'*: ibid., 229–30.

334–5 *the 'political effect'*: Russell, *My Indian Mutiny Diary*, 32.

335 *'Every eye in India'*: Maclagan, 151.

335 *'After a short delay'*: Russell, *My Indian Mutiny Diary*, 23–4.

335 *'no immediate hope'*: Maclagan, 155.

336 *to 'weigh the value of intelligence'*: Roberts, 217n.

336 *'take part in the fray' . . . 'great work of the campaign'*: Maclagan, 173.

336 *a two-pronged attack*: Kaye and Malleson, IV, 256–8.

337–8 *'At last, General Outram' . . . dared to intervene*: Majendie, *Up Among the Pandies*, 185–7.

338 *'For some reason' . . . 'withstand our advance'*: Hall Papers, NAM, '1857' (54)/11919, 42–3.

339 *'visit of ceremony' . . . announced the attack*: Roberts, 224–5.

339 *'I wonder' . . . 'on the 12th March'*: letter from Dr Anderson, Surgeon of Hodson's Horse, March 1858, Hodson Letters, NAM, 5903-146.

339–40 *'I followed your noble husband'*: Sir Colin Campbell to Mrs Hodson [n.d.], ibid.

340 *'A more daring'*: Hall Papers, NAM, '1857' (54)/11919, 44.

340 *'the finest Cavalry and "Intelligence" officer'*: Lang, 163.

340 *'He should have been 5 miles off'*: Wilson to his wife, 12 March 1858, Wilson Letters, NAM, 6807-483.

340 *'Hodson could not have been looting'*: Roberts, 225.

340 *'In camp'*: Lang, 165–6.

341 *'At every door'*: Russell, *My Indian Mutiny Diary*, 100-101.

341 *'a single man' . . . 'not seen by either'*: Roberts, 226–7.

342 *'We had the intense mortification'*: Vibart, 187.

342 *'For instead of both brigades'*: Roberts, 227.

342 *'He moved his force'*: Kaye and Malleson, IV, 284–5.

342 *What might have been achieved*: Ibid., IV, 285.

343 *'What is the use'*: Sherer, *Daily Life during the Indian Mutiny*, 143.

343 *in twenty days' fighting*: Kaye and Malleson, IV, 287.

343 *British casualties at Delhi*: Maclagan, 175.

343 *Shortly before the final assault . . . insults and blows*: Jackson Narrative, NAM, 6409-67-1, 24–5, 14.

343–4 *For almost a month . . . 'kept as hostages'*: written statements of Mata Din, Munshi of Raja Jai Lall Singh, 5 July 1857, *Freedom Struggle*, II, 94–5.

344–5 *The task of killing . . . 'all mine were killed'*: Jackson Narrative, NAM, 6409-67-1, 18–25.

345–6 *'The capture of Lucknow' . . . from the Punjab*: Roberts, 229.

346 *The total number of mutineers*: David, 257.

346 *'Oudh Proclamation' . . . 'took the country'*: Maclagan, 183–4.

346 *'flatly refused'*: Canning to Granville, 16 March 1858, Fitzmaurice, I, 207.

347 *His only concession*: Maclagan, 184.

347 *'advocating an amnesty' . . . 'scot-free'*: Canning to Granville, 16 March 1858, op. cit.

347 *'I have not heard'*: Russell, *My Indian Mutiny Diary*, 115.

347 *'The Proclamation'*: Maclagan, 186.

347 *'Every hour appearances improve'*: ibid., 186–7.

347 *With Lucknow in his hands . . . Bareilly*: Maclagan, 213.

348 *'We are surprised'*: Russell, *My Indian Mutiny Diary*, 121.

348 *'great dolt'*: Hibbert, 369.

348 *'We were kept under the walls'*: Glas-

cock Journal, OIOC, MSS Eur/ C603, 1–2.

348 *'incompetent wretch'*: 22 April 1858, Nicholson Diary, NAM, 8211-125-2.

349 *'retrograde movement'*: Maclagan, 186–7.

349 *There were almost . . . the proclamation*: ibid., 188.

CHAPTER TWENTY

350 *'I'll show you!'*: Tahmankar, *The Ranee of Jhansi*, 26–7.

350 *'Mera Jhansi nahin denge!'*: ibid., 48.

350 *religious worship and charity*: The British historian Forrest, writing fifty years after her death, described the Rani as 'an ardent, daring and licentious woman'. This image of a bold, sensual, highly sexed woman is one that still survives in popular literature. In *Flashman and the Great Game*, for example, she encourages the eponymous hero to support her claims for the return of Jhansi by spending a night of drunken debauchery with him. Sadly this sensual image has no basis in fact. The Rani was not only deeply religious but astute enough to realize – as Joan of Arc and Elizabeth I had been before her – that an aura of chastity actually enhanced her popular appeal.

351 *'he was met by the Ranee's men'*: Tahmantar, *The Ranee of Jhansi*, 52.

351 *'any cause for alarm'*: ibid., 55.

351 *'private information'*: list of natives who have been distinguished by their hostility to the Government, FC, NAI, No. 213 of 30 December 1859, Nos. 1354–5.

351 *'receipt' . . . 'did not consult the Ranee'*: statement of Aman Khan, 14 April 1858, *Freedom Struggle*, III, 26–7.

351 *'to tell the sepoys' . . . 'top of the letter'*: statement by Mrs Mutlow, FC, NAI, 16 July 1858, Nos. 38–48.

351 *'Ranee's people'*: Thornton to Erskine, 21 August 1857, *Freedom Struggle*, III, 9.

351 *'I have been informed'*: Kaye and Malleson, III, 369.

352 *The Rani's own denial*: Rani of Jhansi to Major Erskine, 12 June 1857, *Freedom Struggle*, III, 65–6.

352 *'which she will see carried out'*: Rani of Jhansi to Major Erskine, 14 June 1857, ibid., 66–7.

352 *Erskine's response*: Major Erskine to C. Beadon, 2 July 1857, ibid., 64.

352 *On 23 July . . . 'mutineers and rebels'*: G. Edmonstone to Major Erskine, 23 July 1857, ibid., 70–71.

353 *He replied on 19 October*: Sinha, *The Revolt of 1857*, 138.

353 *On 1 January 1858 . . . down as a rebel*: Sen, 282.

353–4 *A British intelligence report . . . unabated*: ibid., 283; Sinha, *The Revolt of 1857*, 139.

354 *Rose was 'laughed at'*: Lowe, *Central India*, 154.

354 *'very effeminate'*: Dr Sylvester, quoted in Hibbert, 380.

354 *'a very badly managed affair'*: Captain J. G. Lightfoot, ibid.

355 *'she must be tried'*: Sinha, *The Revolt of 1857*, 140.

355 *At a council meeting . . . fight the British*: Sen, 283; Roy, 67.

355 *'She enlisted in her army'*: Vishnu Godse, quoted in Sinha, *The Revolt of 1857*, 141.

355 *poorly managed battle*: Captain Lightfoot described the battle as 'one of the most lamentably mismanaged affairs you ever saw', adding: 'The whole force is crying out against [Rose] and his ridiculous proceedings. I imagine there never was a General who so little possessed the confidence of the men under him' (Hibbert, 380–81). Lieutenant Bonus of the Bombay Engineers was only marginally less critical. 'I do not think that our General Sir Hugh Rose is at present much beloved in his force,' he wrote home on 8 March 1858. 'He, however, has certainly one very good point, his pluck is oustanding. He is always to the front in the thick of the fire and cares no more for bullets than peas, but it seems to me that his place is not here' (Robson, ed., *Sir Hugh Rose and the Central India Campaign*, 93).

356 *'They had built up'*: Lowe, *Central India*, 233.

356 *Garrisoning the town*: Roy, 68.

356 *appearance of a five-year-old boy*: Sir R. Hamilton to G. F. Edmonstone, 24 March 1858, FC, NAI, Nos. 38–48 of 16 July 1858.

357 *'I regret to say'*: Pinckney to the Under-Secretary of the Government of India, 26 March 1858, ibid.

357 *'The manner in which the Rebels'*: Sinha, *The Revolt of 1857*, 143.

357 *'Every ten minutes' . . . 'redoubtable Gwalior Contingent'*: Lowe, *Central India*, 245.

358 *Tatya 'was not in the first line' . . . fewer than a hundred*: Rose to Lord Elphinstone, 10 April 1858, Elphinstone Papers, OIOC, MSS Eur/F87/Box 6A/4.

358 *'For a time'*: Lowe, *Central India*, 254–5.

358–9 *'Maharaj'*: Tahmankar, *The Ranee of Jhansi*, 124–5.

359 *'In the first moments' . . . 'till after sunset'*: Lowe, *Central India*, 263, 258–9.

359 *'a miserly 400 rupees'*: Sir R. Hamilton to G. F. Edmonstone, 8 April 1858, FC, NAI, Nos. 38–48 of 16 July 1858.

359 *'Suppose I withdrew'*: Lyster Papers, NAM, 6702-72, 45.

359–60 *'No quarter was awarded'*: Lowe, *Central India*, 262–3.

360 *temples filled with dead bodies*: Vishnu Bhatta Godse, *Maujhar Pravas*.

360 *straight for the gap*: Lyster Papers, NAM, 6702-72, 45–6.

360 *'on her famous chestnut horse' . . . 'beautiful parasol'*: Rose to Elphinstone, 10 April 1858, op. cit.

361 *'miserable condition'*: Lowe, *Central India*, 267–8.

361 *'burnt and buried' . . . 'their property'*: ibid., 261, 264.

361 *'Everything proves the Ranee's guilt'*: Rose to Elphinstone, 10 April 1858, op. cit.

362 *Unsheathing the sword . . . resented her interference*: Tahmankar, *The Ranee of Jhansi*, 141–2.

362 *According to one source . . . flanking manoeuvre*: ibid., 142–3.

362 *'facing about, kneeling'*: Rose to Elphinstone, 28 June 1858, Elphin-

stone Papers, OIOC, MSS Eur/F87/Box 6A/4,

363 *'unusually strong' . . . 'in English'*: Rose to Major-General Mansfield, 22 June 1858, Robson (ed.), *Sir Hugh Rose*, 249–50.

363 *'We had been upwards'*: Lowe, *Central India*, 289.

364 *'As we mounted the crest'*: Rose to Elphinstone, 28 June 1858, op. cit.

364 *only she 'possessed the genius'*: Kaye and Malleson, V, 144.

364–5 *On 28 May . . . joined him on the road*: Sinha, *The Revolt of 1857*, 152–3.

365 *That same day . . . 'maintain discipline'*: Tahmankar, *The Ranee of Jhansi*, 160.

365 *'after a rapid march'*: Lowe, *Central India*, 300.

366 *'personal supervision of the Ranee'*: *The Times*, 3 August 1857.

366 *'So there was a second advance' . . . 'few casualties'*: Major R. Poore to his mother, 21 June 1858, Poore Letters, NAM, 9504-22.

366 *'attacked one of the 8th . . . 'crore of rupees'*: 24 June 1858, Grey Diaries, NLS, MS 15395, 31.

366 *'dressed in a red jacket' . . . 'her bones and ashes'*: Rose to the Duke of Cambridge, 28 June 1858, Robson (ed.), *Sir Hugh Rose*, 268–9.

366–7 *'The Ranee of Jhansee is killed'*: SC, NAI, No. 154 of 27 August 1858.

367 *'The Ranee was the* beast*'*: Bingham Diary, 20 June 1858, NAM, 5903-105.

367 *'The Ranee was remarkable'*: Rose to Cambridge, 28 June 1858, op. cit., 269.

367 *'most determined, spirited'*: Lowe, *Central India*, 301.

367 *'fought like bricks'*: Major R. Poore to his mother, 21 June 1858, Poore Letters, NAM, 9504-22.

367 *'The cruelties attributed to her'*: John Latimer to his uncle, 9 July 1858, Latimer Letters, OIOC, MSS Eur/C596.

368 *'quite upset the chiefs' . . . 'after a general action'*: Sinha, *The Revolt of 1857*, 156.

368 *'the dying agony of the mutiny'*: Kaye and Malleson, V, 239.

369 *'I only obeyed . . . my master's orders'*: ibid., 264.

369 *Rao Sahib . . . 1862*: Ward, 532; Taylor, *What Really Happened*, 224.

369 *Firoz Shah . . . 1877*: Taylor, *What Really Happened*, 225.

369 *What of the other leading rebels? . . . November*: ibid., 186–7.

370 *The Maulvi . . . 50,000 rupees*: Kaye and Malleson, V, 372–80.

370 *the passing of an Act*: Act 21 & 22, Vict., Ca. 106, PP, HC, 1857–8, II, 367–94.

370–71 *Queen Victoria's 'Proclamation'*: Taylor, *What Really Happened*, 213–14.

371 *The amnesty . . . 'subjects be deceived'*: Sen, 382–4.

371 *Many minor rebels . . . in pursuit*: Maclagan, 230.

371–2 *Among the latter . . . Cawnpore respectively*: Taylor, *What Really Happened*, 220, 223–4.

372 *Mammu Khan . . . 1860*: ibid., 223; Taylor, *Companion*, 44.

372 *The Begum . . . 1879*: Taylor, *Companion*, 44.

372 *Nana Sahib's fate . . . 'arch fiend' of the rebellion*: Ward, 524–5.

372 *Bala is said to have died*: ibid., 525.

372 *'There can be no doubt'*: statement of Mir Bahadur Ali, 26 October 1859, 'Deposition of Certain Individuals Regarding the Death of the Nana Sahib', FC, NAI, Nos. 525–30 of 30 December 1859.

372–3 *'He knew his sentence'*: Sherer, *Havelock's March*, 330.

373 *'assumed the command' . . . 'ill, but not dead'*: Commander of Gorakhpur to Secretary to the Government of the NW, 3 November 1859, FC, NAI, Nos. 525–30 of 30 December 1859.

373 *Over the years . . . 'Release at once'*: Ward, 530.

373 *Baba Bhutt . . . died of old age*: ibid., 535.

373 *Two other notorious rebels . . . hanged the following morning*: Forbes-Mitchell, *The Relief of Lucknow*, 104–11.

373–4 *One of the few . . . a few years*: Taylor, *Companion*, 121.

374 *Liaqat Ali . . . Andaman Islands*: ibid., 194.

CHAPTER TWENTY-ONE

375 *'State of Peace' . . . 'have been resumed'*: Maclagan, 232.

375 *'a more select caste'*: ibid., 233–4.

375–6 *Lawrence had also . . . right of adoption*: ibid., 235–6.

376 *From 1858 . . . Second World Wars*: see table of mutinies in Menezes, 'Race, Caste, Mutiny and Discipline', in Guy and Boyden (eds.), *Soldiers of the Raj*, 100–117.

376–7 *The smallest . . . European presence*: ibid., 132; Shibly, 'The Reorganization of the Indian Armies', Ph.D. thesis, 374.

377 *That the mutinies . . . Hindustan*: David, 260–75.

377 *'No impartial observer'*: quoted in Shibly, op. cit., 179.

378 *'I was assured'*: Fitzmaurice, I, 410.

378 *It had been open . . . 1871*: Woodward, *The Age of Reform*, 441n.

378 *'We have not been elected'*: Allen, 339.

379 *'Nearly every military officer'*: Roberts, 244.

380 *Elizabeth Sneyd . . . months*: Sneyd Papers, OIOC, MSS Eur/Photo.Eur.44.

380 *Stanley Delhiforce . . . thirty-six years*: Tytler, 176–82.

380–82 *But the most poignant . . . 'enough for me'*: Sitaram, 164, 168, 172–3, 178.

APPENDIX ONE

383 *'Sunday, 31st of May' . . . 'regiments did'*: Kaye, *History of the Sepoy War*, II, 107–8.

383 *'corps after corps' . . . 'mar the whole'*: Major G. W. Williams's memo of 15 November 1857, *Freedom Struggle*, V, 20–23.

APPENDIX TWO

385 *Sitaram Bawa's claim . . . 'military classes'*: statement of Sitaram Bawa to H. B. Devereux, 28 January 1858, *Freedom Struggle*, I, 372–6.

386 *'Holkar's and Scindiah's conduct'*: Lord Harris to Robert Vernon

Smith, 23 July 1857, Lyveden Papers, OIOC, MSS Eur/F231/5.

386 *'nightly meetings' . . . 'revolt be arrested'*: Major S. C. Macpherson to Sir R. Hamilton, 10 February 1858, *Freedom Struggle*, III, 166–89.

386–7 *'I may observe' . . . 'rout by our arms'*: ibid.

387 *According to Ahsanullah . . . 'with the King'*: supplementary evidence of Hakim Ahsanullah Khan, PP, HC, 1859, XVIII, 274.

387 *'You have beaten'*: *Freedom Struggle*, IV, 626–7.

387 *during the Second Maratha War*: Kolff, 'The End of an *Ancien Régime*', 25–6.

387 *The young Raja of Assam*: Lieutenant-Colonel S. F. Hannay to Major Ross, 13 March 1858, PP, HC, 1859, XVIII, 16–17.

387 *The Nawab of Farrukhabad*: 'Narrative of What Occurred at Farrukhabad', *Freedom Struggle*, V, 730–33.

388 *S. B. Chaudhuri . . . 1857*: Chaudhuri, *Civil Rebellion*, 32.

388 *He was indirectly implicated*: list of notable rebels, FC, NAI, Nos. 1354–5 of 30 December 1859, No. 83.

388 *The Raja himself*: supplementary evidence of Hakim Ahsanullah Khan, PP, HC, 1859, XVIII, 276.

APPENDIX THREE

389 *in the hills*: Three of the four European regiments in the Sirhind Division, for example, were in hill stations.

389 *By mid August . . . 33 guns*: letter from Futteh Mahomed Khan, 13 August 1857, Spy Letters, NAM, 6807-138.

389 *'To take leave'*: Kolff, 'The End of an *Ancien Régime*', in Moor and Wesseling (eds.), *Imperialism and War*, 26–7.

390 *'kill all Europeans'*: supplementary evidence of Hakim Ahsanullah Khan, PP, HC, 1859, XVIII, 268.

390 *'There were some who remained faithful'*: Sitaram, 174.

390 *'problem of re-establishing discipline' . . . 'from the ranks'*: Stokes, *The Peasant Armed*, 55.

390 *number of cases*: Notably the mutinies of the 3rd LC at Meerut, the 6th NI at Allahabad, the 12th NI at Nowgong and Jhansi, the 28th NI at Shahjahanpur, the 32nd NI (two companies) at Deogurh, the 37th NI at Benares, the 53rd and 56th NI at Cawnpore, the 71st NI at Lucknow, and Scindia's Contingent at Gwalior.

390 *perpetration of mutiny*: These ringleaders include: the subedar-majors of the 1st, 34th, 41st, 51st, 69th NI; subedars in the 2nd and 4th LC 5th, 10th, 12th, 15th, 17th, 20th, 22nd, 34th, 42nd, 50th, 52nd and 72nd NI, 5/7th and 6/8th Foot Artillery, 6th, 7th and 10th Oudh Irregular Infantry, 3rd and 7th Gwalior Infantry. Mhairwarrah Battalion and 2nd Punjab Irregular Cavalry; ressaldars in the 4th, 8th, 9th, 10th, 12th, 14th and 15th Irregular Cavalry, 2nd Oudh Irregular Cavalry and Nagpore Irregular Cavalry; and jemadars in the 5th, 32nd, 33rd, 34th, 50th and

70th NI, and 1st Hyderabad Cavalry.

390 *Lal Khan . . . second-in-command*: *United Service Magazine*, August 1857, 475.

390 *'formally tendered' . . . 'ordinary occupations'*: *Two Native Narratives*, 83–6.

391 *'treatment and disposal'*: statement of Mir Wajid Ali, 8 July 1859, *Freedom Struggle*, II, 85.

391 *Shortly after the mutiny . . . official*: list of notable rebels, FC, NAI, Nos. 1354–5 of 30 December 1859, No. 248.

391 *In the Fatehgarh district*: ibid., Nos. 118, 119 and 120.

391 *But most Indian officers . . . rank of colonel*: Gimlette, 36, 187–9.

391 *At Cawnpore*: statement of Sowar Jahangir Khan, *Freedom Struggle*, IV, 501–2; Gimlette, 72.

391 *The 56th Native Infantry . . . available*: *Freedom Struggle*, IV, 669; *State Papers*, II, intro., 159.

391 *Colonel Lennox . . . Faizabad*: statement by Colonel W. G. Lennox, 1 August 1857, NAM, 5204-73.

391 *'The Subedar Major'*: Gimlette, 121.

391–2 *Even at Jhansi . . . 8 June*: *Freedom Struggle*, III, 22–3, 26–7; list of notable rebels, FC, NAI, 1354–5 of 30 December 1859, No. 229.

392 *The Indian officer . . . following January*: *Two Native Narratives*, 63, 89, 96, 133-5, 204–5; Taylor, *Companion*, 35.

392 *'the most violent sepoys . . . commanded'*: Macpherson to Hamilton, 10 February 1858, *Freedom Struggle*, III, 166–89.

392 *'leader of this party was a* sepoy*'*: Sitaram, 165.

393 *'kept on as supernumeraries'*: petition of the commissioned officers of the 3rd NI, 26 August 1857, PP, HC, 1859, XVIII, 170.

393 *A rough estimate*: David, app. 3.

393 *'large body' . . . 'side with the rebels'*: Major Charles O'Brien, 'Account of the Mutiny of the Troops at Fyzabad', Kaye Mutiny Papers, OIOC, H725, 573.

393 *'coming up in military formation'*: examination of Captain Forrest, 5 February 1857, PP, HC, 1859, XVIII, 186.

393 *rear guards 'told off'*: Gimlette, 36.

393 *the 'band played at mess every night'*: ibid., 121.

393–4 *When a sepoy . . . the court's*: petition of the officers of the 11th NI, 16 July 1857, PP, HC, 1859, XVIII, 162.

394 *'A series of orders'*: Roy, 64–5.

394 *'covered the retreat'*: Rose to Lord Elphinstone, 28 June 1858, Elphinstone Papers, OIOC, MSS Eur/F87/Box 6A/4.

394 *a series of proclamations*: SC, NAI, Nos. 86–9 of 31 July 1857.

394 *'quarrelling about the rewards'*: narrative of events by Nanukchund, *State Papers*, III, app., cclxxxiii–ccclvii.

394 *Their demands*: *Freedom Struggle*, IV, 500–501.

394 *The Delhi Proclamation*: ibid., I, 438–9.

395 *'Duties and emoluments'*: Roy, 53–4.

395 *'In every instance'*: *Two Native Narratives*, 60.

395 *In an undated letter . . . dealt with*: King of Delhi to Mirza Mughal [n.d.], PP, HC, 1859, XVIII, 172.

395 *These latter . . . each sowar 2*: *Two Native Narratives*, 215–17.

395 *'purely nominal*: *Bengal Hurkaru and India Gazette*, 15 April 1858.

395 *Firoz Shah . . . 7 rupees*: Lieutenant-Colonel H. M. Durand to G. F. Edmonstone, 28 September 1857, *Freedom Struggle*, III, 140–44.

395–6 *'the native troops mutinied'*: supplementary evidence of Hakim Ahsanullah Khan, PP, HC, 1859, XVIII, 268.

396 *a few . . . simply divided it*: statement of Drummer John Saunders, 17th NI, FC (Su), NAI, Nos. 525–30 of 30 December 1859.

396 *At Gwalior . . . 'promise of service'*: *Freedom Struggle*, III, 187–8.

396 *'90 to 100 rupees'*: Rose to Lord Elphinstone, 10 April 1858, Elphinstone Papers, OIOC, MSS Eur/F87/Box 6A/No. 4.

396 *'invited all men of the* deen*'*: deposition of a native of Bengal, *Freedom Struggle*, III, 43.

396 *In January 1858 . . . successful*: Roy, 62–4.

397 *'I always felt'*: Dennys Memoirs, NAM, 7901-95, 41–2.

397 *So when . . . also pillaged*: memorandum by Captain C. A. Byers regarding the death of Major Holmes, 5 August 1857, Mutiny Papers, BL, Add. MSS 41488, ff. 49–51.

397 *'All regiments took their Colours with them'*: Sitaram, 174.

398 *'The decision of every rebel'*: Roy, 45.

398 *'maintained . . . the military organizations'*: ibid., 44.

APPENDIX FOUR

399 *In November 1857 . . . Lord Canning*: Shibly, 'The Reorganisation of the Indian Armies, 1858–1879', Ph.D thesis, 45; Maclagan, 240–41.

399 *Meanwhile . . . future organization*: PP, HC, 1859, V, i.

399–400 *By December 1858 . . . 'out to India'*: ibid., ix–xiv.

400 *Only a couple of recommendations . . . Indian counterpart*: The pre-mutiny strength of the European force in India was 43,000: 19,000 Company troops and 24,000 Europeans. During the mutiny, three more regiments of infantry and four of cavalry were added to the Company's establishment of nine European infantry regiments; the 27 Queen's regiments (4 cavalry and 23 infantry) were increased to 76 (11 cavalry and 65 infantry). By the final suppression of the mutiny in 1859, the total number of European officers and men in India was 98,000 (21,000 Company and 77,000 Queen's troops) Sources: Return by Col. J. Holland, HC, 1859, V, App. 7, 371; Shibly, op. cit., 47–8; PP, HC, 1859, V, xiv.

400 *nine additional recommendations*: PP, HC, 1859, V, xiv.

400–401 *Of all the recommendations . . . as regulars*: Shibly, op. cit., 128.

401 *But others . . . wholly irregular*: ibid., 733 and 745.

401 *Frere and Jacob . . . 'in the world'*: ibid., 649–89.

401 *In June 1859 . . . Staff Corps*: ibid., 133–5.

401 *The idea for a Staff Corps . . . priority*: ibid., 199–211.

402 *Supported by the majority . . . respectively*: ibid., 144–5, 149–60, 170–76.

402 *The chief importance . . . monthly rate*: ibid., 156–7, 147, 166.

402–3 *Another crucial . . . district courts martial*: Articles of War, Act XXIX of 1861, OIOC, L/MIL/17/11/15.

403 *By 1873 . . . good conduct pay*: Bengal Army Regulations 1873, OIOC, L/MIL/17/2/443, 98.

403 *No sepoy was to be promoted . . . to override it*: ibid., 43 and 96.

403 *'The vicious system'*: Chesney, *Indian Polity*, 290.

403 *Another recommendation . . . instead*: Mollo, *The Indian Army*, 98 and 101.

403 *From March 1860 . . . old coatee*: Carman, *Indian Army Uniforms*, II, 108.

403 *Lastly . . . 'general service'*: PP, HC, 1859, V, xiv.

404 *'The low castes'*: Kaushik Roy, 'Company Bahadur against the Pandies: The Military Dimension of 1857 Mutiny Revisted', *JUJH*, vols. 19–20, 2001–2.

404 *'The homogenous composition' . . . only exceptions*: Adjt-Gen. of the Army to the Sec. to the Govt of India in the Mil. Dept, 1 October 1860, quoted in Shibly, op. cit., 325.

404 *Sir Charles Wood disagreed . . . 'fire into it'*: Wood to Rose, 25 April 1862, and Wood to Denison, 8 April 1861, ibid., 336–7.

404 *A compromise . . . of Brahmans*: Shibly, op. cit., 390–92.

Index

Ranks and titles are generally the highest mentioned in the text